WING TO WING, OAR TO OAR

THE ETHICS OF EVERYDAY LIFE

Wing to Wing, Oar to Oar: Readings on Courting and Marrying, ed. Amy A. Kass and Leon R. Kass

The Eternal Pity: Reflections on Dying, ed. Richard John Neuhaus

Everyone a Teacher, ed. Mark Schwehn

Leading and Leadership, ed. Timothy Fuller

Working: Its Meaning and Its Limits, ed. Gilbert C. Meilaender

WING TO WING, OAR TO OAR

Readings on Courting and Marrying

Edited by

AMY A. KASS

and

LEON R. KASS

UNIVERSITY OF NOTRE DAME PRESS

Notre Dame, Indiana

A record of the Library of Congress Cataloging-in-Publication Data is available
upon request from the Library of Congress.

ISBN 0-268-01959-2 (cloth)
ISBN 0-268-01960-6 (paper)

The paper used in this publication meets the minimum
requirements of the American National Standard for Information
Sciences—Permanence of Paper for Printed Library Materials,
ANSI Z39.48-1984.

In Gratitude,
To Our Parents of Blessed Memory
Kalman and Polly Apfel
Samuel and Chana Kass
who never needed such a book

With Love,
To Our Children
Sarah and Judah
Miriam and Rob
who no longer do

With Hope,
For Our Grandchildren
Polly and Hannah
who someday will

THE ETHICS OF EVERYDAY LIFE
Preface to the Series

This book is one of a series of volumes devoted to the ethics of everyday life. The series has been produced by a group of friends, united by a concern for the basic moral aspects of our common life and by a desire to revive public interest in and attention to these matters, now sadly neglected. We have met together over the past five years, under the auspices of the Institute of Religion and Public Life and supported by a generous grant from the Lilly Endowment. We have been reading and writing, conversing and arguing, always looking for ways to deepen our own understanding of the meaning of human life as ordinarily lived, looking also for ways to enable others to join in the search. These anthologies of selected readings on various aspects of everyday life—courting and marrying, teaching and learning, working, leading, and dying—seem to us very well suited to the task. This preface explains why we think so.

We begin by remembering that every aspect of everyday life is ethically charged. Nearly everything that we do, both as individuals and in relations with others, is colored by sentiments, attitudes, customs, and beliefs concerning "how to live." At work or at play, in word or in deed, with kin or with strangers, we enact, often unthinkingly and albeit imperfectly, our ideas of what it means to live a decent and worthy life. Notions and feelings regarding better and worse, good and bad, right and wrong, noble and base, just and unjust, decent and indecent, honorable and dishonorable, or human and inhuman always influence the way we speak to one another, the way we do our work, the way we control our passions, rear our children, manage our organizations, respond to injustice, treat our neighbors, teach the young, care for the old, court our beloved, and face our deaths.

For many centuries and up through the early part of the twentieth century, there was in the West (as in the East) a large and diverse literature on "living the good life," involving manners, patterns of civility, and the meaning of decency, honor, and virtue as these are manifested in daily life. Moralists, both philosophical and religious, wrote voluminously on the moral dimensions of the life cycle (e.g., growing up and coming of age, courting and marrying, rearing the young, aging and dying); on the virtues of everyday life (e.g., courage, endurance, self-command, generosity, loyalty, forbearance, modesty, industry, neighborliness, patience, hope, forgiveness, repentance); on the moral passions or sentiments (e.g., shame, guilt, sympathy, joy, envy, anger, awe) and their proper expression; on the activities of everyday life (e.g., loving, working, caring, giving, teaching, talking, eating); and on basic moral phenomena (e.g., responsibility, obligation, vocation, conscience, praise, and blame). These topics, which once held the attention of great thinkers like Aristotle, Erasmus, and Adam Smith, are now sorely neglected, with sorry social consequences.

The ethics of everyday life have been left behind despite—or perhaps because of—the burgeoning attention given these past few decades to professional ethics and public ethics. Mention ethics today, and the discussion generally turns to medical ethics, legal ethics, journalistic ethics, or some other code of behavior that is supposed to guide the activities of professionals. Or it turns to the need to establish codes of conduct to address and curtail the mischief and malfeasance of members of Congress, generals, bureaucrats, or other public officials. In both cases, the concern for ethics is largely instrumental and protective. The codes are intended to tell people how to stay out of trouble with their professional colleagues and with the law. The latter is especially important in a world in which it is increasingly likely that a challenge or disagreement will be engaged not by civil conversation but by an uncivil lawsuit.

Today's proliferation of codes of ethics, while an expression of moral concern, is at the same time an expression of moral poverty. We write new rules and regulations because we lack shared customs and understandings. Yet the more we resort to such external and contrived codes, the less we can in fact take for granted. "Ethics" and "morality" have their source in "ethos" and "mores," words that refer to the ways and attitudes, manners and habits, sensibilities and customs that shape and define a community. Communities are built on shared understandings, usually tacitly conveyed, not only of what is right and wrong or good and bad, but also of who we are, how we stand, what things mean. These matters are not well taught by ethics codes.

Neither are they communicated, or even much noticed, by the current fashions in the academic study and teaching of ethics or by the proliferating band of professional ethicists. The dominant modes of contemporary ethical discourse and writing, whether conducted in universities or in independent ethics centers, are, by and large, highly abstract, analytically philosophic, interested only in principles or arguments, often remote from life as lived, divorced from the way most people face and make moral decisions, largely deaf to questions of character and moral feeling or how they are acquired, unduly influenced by the sensational or extreme case, hostile to insights from the religious traditions, friendly to fashionable opinion but deaf to deeper sources of wisdom, heavily tilted toward questions of law and public policy, and all too frequently marked by an unwillingness to take a moral stand. Largely absent is the older—and we think richer—practice of moral reflection, which is concrete, rooted in ordinary experience, engaged yet thoughtful, attuned to human needs and sentiments as well as to "rational principles of justification," and concerned for institutions that cultivate and promote moral understanding and moral education. Absent especially is the devoted search for moral wisdom regarding the conduct of life—philosophy's original meaning and goal, and a central focus of all religious thought and practice—a search that takes help from wherever it may be found and that gives direction to a life seriously lived.

Many academic teachers of ethics, formerly professors of moral wisdom, are today purveyors of moral relativism. In the colleges and universities ethics is often taught cafeteria style, with multiple theories and viewpoints, seemingly equal, offered up for the picking. But this apparently neutral approach often coexists with ideologically intolerant teaching. Students are taught that traditional views must give way to the "enlightened" view that all views—except, of course, the "enlightened" one—are culture-bound, parochial, and absolutely dependent on your *point*-of-viewing. The morally charged "givens" of human life—e.g., that we have bodies or parents and neighbors—tend to be regarded not as gifts but as impositions, obstacles to the one true good, unconstrained personal choice. Moral wisdom cannot be taught or even sought, because we already know that we must not constrain freedom, must not "impose" morality. Thus, we insist that our "values" are good because we value them, not that they are valued because they are good. Abstract theories of individual autonomy and self-creation abound, while insights into real life as lived fall into obscurity or disappear altogether. To be sure, not all academic teachers of ethics share these opinions and approaches. But experience and study of the literature convinces us that these generalizations are all too accurate.

The current fashions of ethical discourse are of more than merely academic interest. When teachings of "autonomy" or "self-creation" are disconnected from attention to mores and the cultural ethos and from the search for moral wisdom, we come to know less and less what we are supposed to do and how we are supposed to be. Neither can we take for granted that others know what they are supposed to do and be. Being morally unfettered and unformed may make us feel liberated albeit insecure or lost; but seeing that others are morally unfettered and unformed is downright threatening. Thus, despite our moral codes of ethics with penalties attached, despite the boom in the demand for ethicists and in ethics courses in our colleges, our everyday life declines into relationships of narrow-eyed suspicion. No one can argue that we are as a nation morally better off than we were before professional and academic ethics made such a big splash. Americans of widely differing views recognize the growing incivility and coarseness of public discourse and behavior, the sorry state of sexual mores, the erosion of family life, the disappearance of neighborliness, and the growing friction among, and lack of respect for, peoples of differing ages, races, religions, and social classes. To be sure, contemporary ethicists are not responsible for our cultural and moral difficulties. But they have failed to provide us proper guidance or understanding, largely because they neglect the ethics of everyday life and because they have given up on the pursuit of wisdom.

How to provide a remedy? How to offer assistance to the great majority of decent people who still care about living the good life? How to answer the ardent desires of parents for a better life for their children or the deep longings of undergraduates for a more meaningful life for themselves? How to supply an intellectual defense for the now beleaguered and emaciated teachings of decency and virtue? Any answer to these questions depends on acquiring—or at least seeking—a richer and more profound understanding of the structure of human life and the prospects for its flourishing and enhancement. This series of readings on the ethics of everyday life offers help to anyone seeking such understanding.

The topics considered in the several volumes are central to everyday life. Most of us marry, nearly all of us work (and play and rest), all of us lose both loved ones and our own lives to death. In daily life, many of us teach and all of us learn. In civic life, some of us lead, many of us follow, and, in democratic societies, all of us are called upon to evaluate those who would lead us. Yet rarely do we reflect on the nature and meaning of these activities. The anthologized readings—collected from poets and prophets, philosophers and preachers, novelists and anthropologists, scholars and statesmen; from authors ancient, modern, and contemporary—provide rich materials for such reflection. They are moral, not moralistic; they can yield insights, not maxims. The reader will find here no rules for catching a husband, but rather explorations of the purposes of courting and marrying; no prescriptions for organizing the workplace, but competing accounts of the meaning of work; no discussions of "when to pull the plug," but examinations of living in the face of death; no formulae for "effective leadership," but critical assessments of governance in democratic times; no advice on how to teach, but various meditations on purposes and forms of instruction. The different volumes reflect the differences in their subject matter, as well as the different tastes and outlooks of their editors. But they share a common moral seriousness and a common belief that proper ethical reflection requires a "thick description" of the phenomena of everyday life, with their inherent anthropological, moral, and religious colorations.

The readings in this series impose no morality. Indeed, they impose nothing; they only propose. They propose different ways of thinking about our common lives, sometimes in the form of stories, sometimes in the form of meditations, sometimes in the form of arguments. Some of these proposals will almost certainly "impose" themselves upon the reader's mind and heart as being more worthy than others. But they will do so not because they offer simple abstractable ethical principles or suggest procedures for solving this or that problem of living. They will do so because they will strike the thoughtful reader as wiser, deeper, and more true. We ourselves have had this experience with our readings, and we hope you will also. For the life you examine in these pages is—or could become—your own.

Timothy Fuller
Amy A. Kass
Leon R. Kass
Gilbert C. Meilaender
Richard John Neuhaus
Mark Schwehn

CONTENTS

INTRODUCTION

The seed for this anthology was planted, unbeknownst to its authors, roughly fifteen years ago. It was the first day of an undergraduate seminar at the University of Chicago—where both of us have been teachers since 1976—on the subject of men and women in literary perspectives. The students were asked what they thought was the most important decision that they would ever have to make in their lives. Nearly all the students answered in terms related to personal self-fulfillment: "Deciding which career to pursue," "Figuring out which graduate or professional school to attend," "Choosing where I should live." Only one fellow answered otherwise: "Deciding who should be the mother of my children." For his eccentric opinion, and especially for this quaint way of putting it, he was promptly attacked by nearly every other member of the class, men and women alike. The men and nearly all the women berated him for wanting to sacrifice his freedom or for foolishly putting such matters ahead of his career; the women and some of the men were offended that he would look upon and judge women for their capacities as prospective mothers, worse yet, as mothers for *his* children. From his classmates' point of view, this man was clearly a dinosaur who had not yet heard that his kind were supposed to be extinct.

Our reaction was quite different. As a long and happily married couple, and as parents of children (now grown and married) whose existence and rearing have been central to our happiness, we could—albeit with hindsight—endorse the young man's view. Indeed, we wondered only how he could have acquired such a mature outlook at his tender age. Far from condemning him as a freak, this opinion revealed an admirable seriousness about life and the life cycle—he had it, and still does—which one would be only too pleased to see in one's sons and daughters, or sons-in-law and daughters-in-law. Why, we wondered, were not more of our young people aware of the importance—to their own future flourishing—of private life, marriage, and family? Why did they not foresee the supreme importance of finding the right person with whom they might make a life?

Since then, we have paid increasing attention to the opinions and, to a lesser extent, the practices of our students regarding matters of love and marriage. Repeatedly, we have heard their skepticism about marriage and family life. We have watched many of them, well beyond their college years, bumble along from one unsatisfactory relationship to the next, and we are often profoundly saddened by the thought that they are in danger of missing out on one of life's greatest adventures and, through it, on many of life's deepest experiences, insights, and joys. Yet, for their failures and fumblings in this area they are not entirely to blame. For we—their parents, teachers, and the larger society—have poorly prepared them to get themselves well married. Strangely, even in the midst of all the current concern about "family values" and the breakup of marriages, very little attention is being paid to what makes for marital success. Still less are we attending to the ways and mores of *entering* into marriage, that is, to wooing or courting.

There is, of course, good reason for this neglect. The very terms—"wooing," "courting," "suitors"—are archaic; and if the words barely exist, it is because the phenomena have all but disappeared. Today there are no socially prescribed forms of conduct that help guide young men and women in the direction of matrimony. This is true not just for the lower or under classes. Even—indeed especially—the élite, those who in previous generations would have defined the conventions in these matters, lack a cultural script whose dénouement is marriage. To be sure, there are still exceptions, to be found, say, in closed religious communities or among new immigrants from parts of the world that still practice arranged marriage. But for most of America's middle- and upper-class youth—the privileged college-educated and graduated—there are no known explicit or even tacit social paths directed at marriage. People still get married—though later, less frequently, more hesitantly, and by and large, less successfully. People still get married in churches and synagogues— though often with ceremonies and vows of their own creation. But for the great majority the way to the altar is uncharted territory. It's every couple on its own bottom, without a compass, often without a goal. Those who reach the altar seem to have stumbled upon it by accident.

This anthology on courtship is offered as a response to this cultural silence. It is, quite frankly and unapologetically, a pro-marriage anthology, intended to help young people of marriageable age, and parents of young people now and soon to be of marriageable age, think about the meaning, purpose, and virtues of marriage and, especially, about how one might go about finding and winning the right one to marry. Despite the numerous obstacles to courting and marrying well (of which, as you will see, we are very well aware), we are unwilling to declare the matter lost. On the contrary, we see everywhere major discontent with the present situation, especially on the part of women. And despite their easily verbalized but, we suspect, only superficial cynicism, we even detect among our students certain (albeit sometimes unarticulated) longings—for friendship, for wholeness, for a life that is serious and deep, and for associations that are trustworthy and lasting—longings that they do not realize could be largely satisfied by marrying well. When it comes to erotic desires and aspirations, nature may be backed into the ropes, but she is hard to knock out.

Part of the current trouble lies in the fact that we come to life and love increasingly burdened by theory, not to say ideology. True, human experience is always mediated experience, colored by our imaginings and opinions. But today, more than ever before, we live in the grip of image and opinion makers, often shallow and thoughtless, who deliberately and massively interpose themselves between us and "real life." Academic theorists redescribe all human relations in terms of economic models or power politics; ideologically driven redefinitions of sex and marriage spill over from the academy into the general culture; psychologists and other experts redescribe life and love in sterile jargon; movies, television, and advertising saturate our senses with titillating or shocking images; and the talk shows, filled with shameless chatter about the most intimate matters, reveal how much of private life has been deformed and dehumanized by all our theorizing and manipulation. But if we look less at what people say in public and more at how they live in private, we can see that the issues of courting and marrying still find regular expression, in some form or other.

Everyday life for most people remains, even today, still connected to life within families. Despite the high divorce and illegitimacy rates, most people are still born into contexts formed by marriages; and for the foreseeable future—*pace* the advocates of cloning—nearly everyone will continue to be born of woman, begotten of man. Young and not-so-young people spend a great deal of time engaged with—and much more time thinking and talking about—members of the opposite sex. And though courtship may be in decline, people are still marrying. Even today, many people are trying to figure out, by hook and by crook and even by horoscope, not only whether but also whom to marry. Surely all this is not going to disappear. Yet surely too, it all could be done much better than it now is being done.

We begin, therefore, not from theory but from practice, not with philosophy or ideology but with the grainy particularities of everyday life. In everyday life, people in love or people contemplating marriage ask themselves very specific, concrete questions. Am I really in love, or is this mere infatuation or just plain lust? How can I tell? Is my love for him (or her) reciprocated? How can I be sure? Do I as a man (woman) love in the same way as she (he) loves as a woman (man)? Do we seek the same things from one another? Is sex lovemaking? What has sex to do with love, or love with sex? Is there a difference between being-in-love and loving? Can my lover also be my friend? Can one be-in-love-with, or can one love, more than one person? Can this love I have (or am in) last? Forever? Regardless of how we change or what happens to us? How? Is there really somebody out there who is my destiny? Is there somebody out there who will love me, as I am and for myself? Is there somebody out there for me to love? If not now, when?

And there are everyday-life questions regarding marriage: Why get married? (Or, Why bother marrying rather than just living together?) Can our love survive marriage? Is this love I feel a good enough reason or guide to marry? How do I know whether this is the right one—or a right enough one—for me to marry? Should I live with him or her first to find out? Will she be faithful? Will he stay the course? Do our differing family, ethnic, or religious backgrounds and commitments matter to our prospects for a good marriage? Can we afford to get married? Does his indifference to having children matter? Does my getting married imply having children? Will I lose my independence or identity in marriage? What name should we have as a married couple, and does it matter? Should we have a religious ceremony? What exactly do we think we are undertaking when we decide to marry?

These questions, although clearly recognizable, are intended to be merely illustrative. They could be multiplied, adjusted, and specified more precisely to suit the limitless particular circumstances in which real people find themselves. True, not everybody asks himself or herself these or any other similar questions; some people still manage to proceed from falling-in-love through courtship to marriage relatively thoughtlessly (or, if you prefer, "naturally" or "spontaneously"). And, as a matter of fact, not many people in the midst of their premarital maneuverings, and not even those who consciously ask themselves such questions, recognize the complexities and profundities of the subject. Perhaps this is for the best. Perhaps if men and women really understood what they were undertaking, they would never marry but would flee in panic. Love and marriage, so the argument runs, are too important to be imperiled by thinking too much; hence, one should act first and perhaps gain understanding later of what one has done. We confess more than a little sympathy for this position. We have, after all, taken the side of everyday life against disconnected theorizing, and very little of what we now think we understand about marriage did we suspect when we ourselves got married. Still, in an age in which inherited cultural forms, smoothly reenacted, are no longer available to provide tacit answers to questions which therefore need not be asked, such trust to spontaneity seems to us misplaced. Moreover, mature people prefer not to wander about in life self-deceived, and marriage is, of all things, quite definitely a matter demanding maturity. Accordingly, we shall not shy away from opening up these larger and deeper questions, which—unlike abstract theorizing—are firmly embedded in the immediate, focused, and personal questions of everyday life. Our personal everyday lives and loves no doubt vary greatly, but there are surely common themes on which our own individualized variations get played out.

Before introducing these common themes, we should make clear what we mean by "courtship," especially for those readers new to the idea. Not all activities by which a man shows erotic or sexual interest in a woman, or a woman in a man, qualify as courtship. We use the term "courting" in more or less its original meaning, which goes back to the sixteenth century: "to pay amorous attention to, to woo, with a view to marriage." ("To woo": "to solicit or sue a woman in love, especially with a view to marriage.") Courtship was and is therefore distinguishable from flirting and seducing, from trysting and having an affair, and, to speak in modern idiom, from "hooking up" or even from having or being in "a relationship": these activities, whatever their merits, do not aim at marriage.

Biologists who study animal behavior, borrowing the term from human affairs, call by the name of courtship all male-female interactions that lead up to, or are at least pointed toward, mating. The analogy is not altogether misleading: in their courtship rituals, male birds display qualities of strength, beauty, and vigor that help, say, a female peacock or pigeon select a most fitting father for her offspring. But human beings are not peacocks or pigeons; we not only mate but marry. We do so in part because we understand, as birds do not, what it means to be creatures in need of mating and, more important, of caring for the peculiarly human offspring we alone produce. As human males are more than studs and human females more than wombs, and as their relationship is much more than the perpetuating of genes or the pleasurable act that produces the genetic mixing, human courtship rightly understood necessarily involves more than its animal counterparts. Properly adhering to our student's formula—"deciding who shall be the mother of my children"—requires considering much more than whether she has beautiful blue eyes and is tireless at dancing the macarena.

Accordingly, by courtship we mean that collection of activities aimed at (1) finding and (2) winning (3) the right one (4) for marriage. Finding means more than hunting out or locating; it also means *finding out* if the located one is really right. Winning means both gaining reciprocation of exclusive amorous interest and affection and securing consent and decision to marry. Discovering whether he or she is the right one—the heart of courtship—depends on taste and judgment, discernment and self-knowledge. But knowing the right one *for marriage* means first knowing something of what marriage means and entails, what it means deliberately and self-consciously to make a life with another human being. The meaning of courting will thus depend on the meaning of marrying, a subject to which we shall more than once return.

This "definition of courtship," however useful, is but a rational description of the phenomenon looked at from the outside. The activity itself, however, is at most only partly rational. Though taste and discernment are centrally involved, the entire venture is animated by desire and affection, need and appreciation, by both *amour* and *amour-prôpre* (or vanity). Only the rarest of human beings will be moved to marry by argument alone. Yet precisely because the passions of human beings are shaped by and tied to their opinions and beliefs, the stirrings of the human heart are heavily influenced by the musings of the human mind. The questions of everyday life, and the answers we give them, really do matter.

To be married or not to be married: that is the question. Absent a positive answer to this first question, in favor of marrying, all the other questions of real courtship pass away, as one opts instead for chance encounters, hookings up, and shorter or longer relationships. But this question in fact implies answers to prior questions about the nature and meaning of marriage itself. One cannot really answer the question, "Why marry?" or even "Whom to marry?" without some sense of what marriage is and means. To be sure, it's a free country, and one might therefore say that each of us is entitled to define the meaning of his or her own marriage as he or (better, "and") she sees fit. To some extent we all do just that. But the truth of the matter may be that marriage has its own meanings, which we are free only to accept or reject.

Having said this, we nonetheless face real and worthy alternatives in the understanding of marriage. It may seriously be regarded as a sacrament bestowed by God, as a covenant based upon the exchange of pledges, or as a contract entered into on the basis of calculation of mutual advantage. Its foundation may be held to be *eros*, friendship, duty, or economic gain. It may be thought to exist primarily to provide the proper habitat for nurturing offspring, for rearing the next generation, and for perpetuating one's tradition and ways; to promote personal fulfillment and private happiness; to render mutual service to one another; or to perform the task of loving the one whom it has been given me to love. Traditionally, fidelity, exclusiveness, and permanence—and for Roman Catholics, indissolubility—are regarded as essential aspects of the marital bond. Even where marriage unites people who first came together through romance or erotic love, these passions are often held to be given moral and even spiritual direction by the decision to marry and, in some traditions, by explicit promises or vows publicly made at the marriage ceremony. Marriage is also given legal sanction and protection by the state, for reasons of its own, even while it leaves people free to marry whom, why, when, and even as often as they please. In our pluralistic society, there can of course be no single and authoritative account of what marriage is and means. But, notwithstanding their differences—and the selections in this volume (in the section "Why Marry?") include and respect these differences—all thoughtful treatments of marriage understand it as a serious, indeed, momentous undertaking.

Serious issues attend not only the meaning of marriage, the end or goal of courtship. They attach also to the beginnings or seeds of courtship, to what we shall call the natural elements of marriage: man and woman, sex and love. These are, needless to say, massive subjects in their own right. Today they are also hotly contested topics, not only in universities (where "gender studies" programs are a leading growth industry) but in the culture at large. One is tempted to say that never before has there been such an effort consciously to redefine and recreate the meaning of being man or woman, nor such a faith that "gender" is almost entirely a "cultural construction" (without which faith the current attempts at social engineering would not be thinkable). It is surely true that the still continuing and rapid changes in cultural attitudes toward sex and beliefs about its meaning are without historical precedent, certainly regarding the pace and scale of change and probably also its cultural significance. Yet again, we should be careful not to allow changing fashion to overwhelm good sense. Not everything about man and woman, sex and love, is culturally constructed and relative. For example, every reader, whatever his or her beliefs, has a navel. Contemplate it: it offers clear proof that each of us is born of woman. Moreover, absent a miracle, each of us owes our living existence to exactly one man and one woman—no more, no less, no other—and thus to one act of heterosexual union. This is no social construction, it is natural fact, a fact older even than the human race. Male and female, whatever else they may mean, are, to begin with, sexually complementary and mutually implicated in generation, which is everywhere a crucial, perhaps even primary, meaning of sexuality. Another fact, nearly as old as the human race, is human self-consciousness regarding sexual difference and the difference it makes—and also the troubles it causes. Difficulties in *being* man and woman, like difficulties in *understanding* man and woman, are a very old story. The reason lies, we suspect, in certain permanent and irreducible truths about man, woman, and sexuality as such.

Among these truths (explored by the readings in the section "What About Sex?"), we suggest the following. All human beings, both men and women, experience needy, private, and self-loving interests in their own personal survival and well-being. Layered over this sexually neutral aspect of our being is a complementary sexual duality without, experienced as needy incompleteness within, issuing in animal-like lust for bodily union. As in all sexual beings, human males and females live out a divided nature, because sexual impulses directed outwardly toward another are in principle in conflict with self-interested impulses directed toward self-preservation. Differentiation into two sexes, with nonidentical desires and interests, creates differences that both incite union and also threaten divorce. Human sexual self-consciousness, and rational consciousness more generally, add yet an additional (reflective) kind of bifurcation to the human soul, part of whose meaning is expressed imaginatively in shame, modesty, refusal, adornment, flirtation, courtship, display, approbation, acceptance, rejection, beautification, illusion, vanity, coquetry, aspiration, flattery, wiliness, seduction, jealousy, the desire to please, and the search for self-esteem—all intrinsic aspects of the humanization of sex, the sublimation of lust, and the emergent possibility of love and sociability. A strange problem of distance and desire results from the inexplicable connection between sexuality and the love of the beautiful, as beauty beheld at the viewing distance drives us towards merging, unbeautifully and sightlessly, at no distance whatsoever. Finally, sexuality means especially generativity and childbirth, followed by domestication and rearing, and all that that implies, including concern for lineage and hope for transcendence—of privacy, duality, and perishability.

All of these elements can, of course, be clothed by culture and altered by customs, rituals, beliefs, and diverse institutional arrangements. But the elements themselves are none of them cultural constructions, nor is there likely to be any conceivable cultural arrangement that can harmonize to anyone's full satisfaction all their discordant tendencies. On the contrary, political and cultural efforts to rationally solve the problem of man and woman—and we are, to be frank, in the midst of such utopian spasms—may very well be harmful, even dehumanizing, to man, to woman, and especially to children—not least because the matters are so delicate and private, and their deeper meanings inexpressible.

No less mysterious and still more problematic than the meaning of sex is the meaning of love. Here even more than in most places, language fails us. English is perhaps especially impoverished, having but one word, "love," for which ancient Greek, for example, had perhaps a dozen. We say "I love Lucy" and "I love chocolate." We may even say "I'm in love with chocolate," but we do not mean by this that chocolate has a lover. We say, I love my beloved, I love my parents and my children, my dog or cat, my friends, my neighbors, my country, or even my enemies. Yet these are, in each case, very different loves. Thus, when someone wants to know whether he really loves Lucy, or whether she loves him back, it is important to know which or what kind of love is meant.

Three distinguishable kinds of love are especially pertinent to our subject of courtship and marriage. First is what the Greeks called *eros,* a powerful passion, often aroused by beauty, that is fixated on and preoccupied with one particular beloved. Without meaning here to beg any questions (explored by the readings in the section "Is This Love?") as to the nature of this love and what it seeks, we can identify it with what is also called romantic love or passionate love. While not identical to sexual desire, *eros* often comes conflated with it (see essay by Lewis), and their relationship is not easily sorted out. Second, there is friendship, or *philia,* a less passionate and less exclusive but equally deep and powerful feeling toward another person whom one admires and respects, whose company one enjoys, and who cares about the same things as one does. Whereas erotic love can continue even if unrequited, and arguably, even burn just as strongly (some think even more so; see De Rougemont on "The Tristan Myth"), friendship must be mutual. In the best cases, it even presupposes equality—of affection, like-mindedness, virtue, and good will. Finally, there is *agape* or love of neighbor—some call it Christian love—that expresses itself in caring for the other as a fellow human being, even—or rather, precisely—in his weakness, neediness, and vulnerability, ever wishing for and acting to secure the other person's good. In contrast to *eros* and *philia,* agapic love, although expressible toward particular individuals, is not exclusive or exclusionary.

Although distinguishable not only in speech but also in fact, these three kinds of love can and do overlap, and they may even sometimes be felt toward the same person. This accounts in part for our puzzlement about the love we feel when we love—or is it when we are *in* love? Do we, as lovers, seek our own good or the beloved's? Is it her (his) presence, her (his) companionship, or her (his) return of love that we most seek? Possession or appreciation? Receiving or giving? Is our love needy or generous? Which sort of love—or which combination of loves—is the best foundation or ingredient for marriage?

Marriage for love is a relatively recent phenomenon in the West (see essay by Stone). Some communities still practice arranged marriage (see the stories by Abraham and Divakaruni), and there has even been a recent revival—in nearly-twenty-first-century America, believe it or not!—of secular professional matchmaking services, not tied to closed religious or ethnic groups. Here, parents or matchmakers seek to make a good or fitting match for their children or clients. They look to match people with others who are in good health and sound mind, who come from good families, have common or compatible beliefs and practices, enjoy solid economic prospects, cherish kinship ties, and of course, who are well-suited for individual compatibility. The goal is a stable and lasting marriage; the guiding principle (in the best case) is practical wisdom; the means used are calculation, deliberation, and discernment. But for most Americans, including the intended audience of this anthology, the very idea of arranged marriage is offensive to their notions of both love and liberty: far better to allow young people the freedom to find and win partners for themselves, to find and choose the one they love. After all, it is they who will have to live with whichever partner they marry. Here, as with arranged marriage, the good sought may still be a stable and lasting marriage; but the governing principles are instead freedom and desire, that is, *my choice* and *my love.* Yet, as everybody knows, freedom and erotic preference can be, by themselves, unreliable guides for marrying well. However much we welcome the American love of liberty and the modern preference for romance (ahead of economic and social calculations), we must acknowledge that leaving matters to free choice and passionate attachments offers no guarantee that freedom and desire will choose or love wisely and well.

How, then, to find and win the right one, to gain by one's own efforts a life partner who is both good and suitable for marrying? What can substitute for and, it is to be hoped, even improve upon the presumed wisdom of marriage arrangers? This is, or once was, the work of courtship (the subject of the section "How Can I Find and Win the Right One?"). Courtship took romantic or erotic love as its starting point, but sought to discipline it in the direction of marriage. Embedded in the earlier forms of courtship were deep understandings of the human life cycle, of the promise and perils of sexual desire and erotic love, and of the way marriage can be a vehicle to the higher possibilities for human life. Courtship provided rituals for growing up, for making clear the meaning of one's own sexual nature, and for entering into the ceremonial and customary world of ritual and sanctification. By holding back the satisfaction of sexual desire, courtship used its energy as romantic attraction to foster salutary illusions that inspired admiration and devotion. At the same time, it provided opportunities for mutual learning about one another's character and, by locating wooer and wooed in their familial settings, taught the intergenerational meaning of erotic activity. The process of courting provided the opportunity to enact the kind of attentiveness, dependability, care, exclusiveness, and fidelity that the couple would subsequently promise each other when they finally wed. For all these reasons, one does not exaggerate much in saying that going through the forms of courtship provided early practice in being married—a very different kind of practice, for a very different view of marriage, than the practice now thought to be provided by premarital cohabitation. Therefore, when it worked well, courtship provided ample opportunity to discover how good a match and a marriage this was likely to be. In addition, as the natural elements of love between man and woman became a path to marriage, these elements were shaped by courtship into its more than natural foundation. Courtship, a wisely instituted practice, was meant to substitute for any lack of personal wisdom. What, in its absence, is available today to do its work? Courtship once pointed the way to the answers to life's biggest questions: Where am I going? Who is going with me? How—in what manner—are we both going to go? How indeed are today's and tomorrow's men and women going to get these questions answered?

Finally, there are questions of how and where to get married and in whose company. For it turns out that finding and winning the right one for marriage is a matter of concern to more than two isolated individuals, as young lovers eventually discover, sometimes to their surprise and consternation, sometimes only when they get around to getting married and face the question of the wedding ceremony itself. Where and how they are going is connected to where they have come from and toward what they have been reared. People come from families, have obligations, employments, and attachments outside of marriage, and belong to communities, both civil and religious. The prospective bride and groom come not like Adam and Eve, unattached to families of origin, but with many entanglements that have a bearing on and a stake in their marriage. Parents of young lovers have an interest in their well-being and that of prospective grandchildren; the church or synagogue, like the older generation, has an interest in the perpetuation of its ways; the polity has an interest in the civic contributions that stable families make to its peace and well-being (see, for example, the article by Tucker or the selections from Tocqueville). The newlyweds, whether they know it or not, step forward into familial and social places partly marked out and, as it were, waiting for them. Under present conditions—with high geographic mobility, weakened ties to extended family, and greater isolation of many individuals from religious or other nurturing communities—it is easy to overlook the communal meanings and importance of marriage. Yet these meanings are precisely what are symbolized and carried by the traditional rituals of the marriage ceremony, with its traditional liturgy and vows—all performed in public and before God (see essay by May and the other readings in the section "Why a Wedding?"). Indeed, there are those who believe (see, for example, the selections from De Rougemont, Capon, and C. S. Lewis) that not romance or even romance disciplined by courtship but a specifically religious faith or practice is necessary for founding and upholding a sound and flourishing marriage. Finding and winning the right one might mean finding the one with whom to live in Christ or under the laws of Moses or by the teachings of the Koran.

By touching upon these large and serious questions about the meaning of marriage, man and woman, sex and love, disciplining romance, and the familial, religious, and communal dimensions of married love, we may seem to have wandered off from the immediate perplexities and concerns of everyday life: to marry or not to marry? Hélène or Natasha? Mr. Collins or Mr. Darcy? But it is the absence of understood cultural forms that embody tacit answers to these big questions that leave our young would-be lovers and marriage partners bewildered and confused, and that therefore force the "big questions" to starkly emerge. Thus, to deal with the concerns of everyday life now requires addressing these larger questions, at the very least in order to provide some support for the higher longings of young people and for the embattled notions of common decency and common sense that can still be found among them.

We do not deceive ourselves into thinking that today's cultural situation can easily be altered for the better, and certainly not by philosophizing about it. Inherited cultural forms, which grow up organically over centuries without anybody's noticing, can be undermined by public policy and social decision, but once fractured they are hard to repair by rational and self-conscious design. The causes of our present state of affairs are multiple, powerful, and very likely irreversible. If courtship is to make a comeback, it must do so under vastly changed social conditions, and it will have many obstacles to overcome, or at least to recognize and deal with.

Some of the obstacles in the way of getting married are of very recent origin; indeed, they have occurred during the adult lifetime of those of us over the age of fifty. For this reason they may seem to some people to be reversible, a spasm connected with the "abnormal" 1960s. But, when they are rightly understood, one can see that they spring from the very heart of liberal democratic society and of modernity itself.

Here is a (partial) list of the recent changes that hamper courtship and marriage: the sexual revolution, made possible especially by effective female contraception ("Why court a woman for marriage when she may be sexually enjoyed, and regularly, without it?" "Why wait for marriage, now that there is no risk of getting myself pregnant?"); the ideology of feminism and the changing educational and occupational status of women ("Why look for a husband, or have children, when I can have a personally more satisfying career?" "Why should I take on the burden of supporting her when she can support herself?"); the destigmatization of bastardy, divorce, infidelity, and abortion ("Do I really need a husband in order to have children?" "Why should she practice chastity or I be sexually responsible when abortion exists to deal with any accidents?"); the general erosion of shame and awe regarding sexual matters, promoted by the commercialization of sex and the sexualization of commerce, and exemplified most vividly in the ubiquitous and voyeuristic presentation of sexual activity in movies and on television ("Why should I dress or act modestly?" "Why should we have any scruples or feel reverence about giving our bodies?"); widespread morally neutral sex education in schools ("Why think about romance and devotion, if the whole story is pleasure and safety?" "Why see sex as positively related to having children, if the whole story is preventing or getting rid of the consequences?"); the explosive increase in the numbers of young people whose parents have been divorced ("Why trust anyone but myself?" "Who can honestly promise lasting love?") or who are born out of wedlock ("Who needs marriage?" "What's wrong with single parenthood?"); great increases in geographic mobility, with a resulting loosening of ties to place and extended family of origin ("Why think of settling down?" "What do I care about what my family thinks about my 'relationships'"?); and, harder to describe precisely, a popular culture that celebrates youth and independence not as a transient stage en route to adulthood but as "the time of our lives," imitable at all ages ("Why take on the burdens of adulthood, when we can continue to enjoy ourselves without responsibilities?"), and an ethos that lacks transcendent aspirations and asks of us no devotion to family, God, or country, encouraging us simply to soak up the pleasures of the present ("If it feels good, why not 'Just do it'?").

That we Americans should now face these new obstacles to courtship is, in fact, not so surprising. Virtually all of the social changes we have so recently experienced are the bittersweet fruits of the success of our modern democratic, liberal, enlightened society—celebrating equality, freedom, and universal secularized education, and featuring prosperity, mobility, and astonishing progress in science and technology (see the selections from Bailey and Bloom). Even brief reflection shows how the dominant features of the American way of life may be finally inhospitable to the stability of marriage and family life and to the mores that lead people self-consciously to marry.

Consider, for example, the implications of our attachment to equality and freedom. Tocqueville already observed the unsettling implications of American individualism, each person seeking only in himself for the reasons for things. The celebration of equality gradually undermines the authority of religion, tradition, and custom, and within families, of husbands over wives and fathers over sons. A nation dedicated to safeguarding individual rights to liberty and the privately defined pursuit of happiness is, willy-nilly, preparing the way for the "liberation" of women; in the absence of powerful nonliberal cultural forces, such as traditional biblical religion, that defend sex-linked social roles, androgyny (or unisexuality) in education and employment is the most likely outcome, threatening also to establish androgyny in *private* life. Further, our liberal approach to important moral issues in terms of the rights of individuals—e.g., contraception as part of a right to privacy, or abortion as belonging to a woman's right over her own body, or procreation as governed by a right to reproduce—flies in the face of the necessarily social character of sexuality and marriage. The courtship and marriage of people who see themselves as self-sufficient rights-bearing individuals will be decisively different from the courtship and marriage of people who understand themselves as, say, unavoidably incomplete and dependent children of the Lord who have been enjoined to be fruitful and multiply.

Or consider the implications of our attachment to, if not worship of, science. The successes of the scientific project have led to the demystification of the world. Falling in love, should it still occur, is for us to be explained not by demonic possession (Eros) born of the soul-smiting sight of the beautiful (Aphrodite) but by a rise in the concentration of some still-to-be-identified polypeptide hormone in the hypothalamus. The power of religious sensibilities and understandings has also faded. Even if it is true that the great majority of

Americans still profess a belief in God, He is for few of us a God before whom one trembles in fear of judgment. Ancient religious teachings regarding marriage have lost their authority even for people who regard themselves as serious Jews or Christians. How many Jews still find abominable the sexual abominations of Leviticus? How many Christians still hold that husbands should govern their wives as Christ governs the church, or that a husband should love his wife as Christ loved the church, and give himself up to death for her (Ephesians 5:24–25)?

Finally, not all the obstacles to courtship and marriage are cultural. At bottom, there is also the deeply ingrained, natural waywardness and unruliness of the human male. Sociobiologists were not the first to discover that males have a penchant for promiscuity and polygyny. Men are, on the whole, naturally more restless and ambitious than women; lacking woman's powerful and immediate link to life's generative answer to mortality, men flee from the fear of death into heroic deed, great quests, or sheer distraction after distraction. One can make a good case that biblical religion is, not least, an attempt to domesticate male sexuality and male erotic longings, and to put them in the service of transmitting a righteous and holy way of life through countless generations.

For as long as American society kept strong its uneasy marriage between modern liberal political principles and Judaeo-Christian moral and social beliefs, marriage and the family could be sustained and could even prosper. But the gender-neutral individualism of our political teaching has, it seems, at last won the day, and the result has been *male* "liberation"—from domestication, from civility, from responsible self-command. Contemporary liberals and conservatives alike are trying to figure out how to get men "to commit" to marriage, or to keep their marital vows, or to stay home with the children, but their own androgynous view of humankind prevents them from seeing how hard it has always been to make a monogamous husband and devoted father out of the human male.

Ogden Nash had it right: "Hogamus higamus, men are polygamous; higamus hogamus, women monogamous." To make naturally polygamous men accept the conventional institution of monogamous marriage has been the work of centuries of Western civilization, with social sanctions, backed by religious teachings and authority, as major instruments of the transformation, and with female modesty as the crucial civilizing device. As these mores and sanctions disappear, courtship gives way to seduction and possession, and men become again the sexually, familially, and civically irresponsible creatures they are naturally always in danger of being.

Given the enormous new social impediments to courtship and marriage, and given also that they are firmly and deeply rooted in the cultural soil of modernity, and in human nature itself, one might simply decide to declare the cause lost. In fact, many people would be only too glad to do so. For they condemn the old ways as repressive, inegalitarian, sexist, patriarchal, boring, artificial, and unnecessary. Some urge us to go with the flow; others hopefully believe that new modes and orders will emerge, better suited to our new conditions of liberation and equality. Just as new cultural meanings are today being "constructed" for sexuality and gender, so too new cultural definitions can be invented for "marriage," "paternity and maternity," and "family." Nothing truly important, so the argument goes, will be lost.

We do not agree. Yes, new arrangements can perhaps be fashioned. As Raskolnikov put it—and he should know—"Man gets used to everything, the beast!" But it is simply wrong that nothing important will be lost; indeed, many things of great importance have already been lost, and at tremendous cost in personal happiness, child welfare, and civic peace. This should come as no surprise. For the new arrangements that constitute the cultural void created by the demise of courtship and dating rest on serious and destructive errors regarding the human condition: errors about the meaning of human sexuality, about the nature of marriage, and about what constitutes a fully human life.

Sexual desire, in human beings as in animals, points to an end that is partly hidden from, and finally at odds with, the self-serving individual: whatever else it means, and whatever else we choose to make of it, sexuality as such means perishability and serves replacement. The salmon swimming upstream to spawn and die tell the universal story: sex is bound up with death, to which it holds a partial answer in procreation. This truth the salmon and the other animals practice blindly; only the human being can understand what it means. According to the story of the Garden of Eden, our humanization is coincident with the recognition of our sexual nakedness and all that it implies: shame at our needy incompleteness, unruly self-division, and finitude; awe before the eternal; hope in the self-transcending possibilities of children and a relationship to the divine. For a human being to treat sex as a desire like hunger—not to mention as sport—is to live a deception.

Thus how shallow an understanding of sexuality is embodied in our current clamoring for "safe sex." Sex is by its nature unsafe. All interpersonal relations are necessarily risky and serious ones especially so. And to give oneself to another, body and soul, is hardly playing it safe. Sexuality is at its core profoundly "unsafe," and it is only thanks to contraception that we are encouraged to forget its inherent "dangers." These go beyond the hazards of venereal disease, which are always a reminder and a symbol of the high stakes involved, and beyond the risks of pregnancy and the pains and dangers of childbirth to the mother. To repeat, sexuality itself means mortality—equally for both man and woman. Whether we know it or not, when we are sexually active we are voting with our genitalia for our own replacement and demise. "Safe sex" is the self-delusion of shallow souls.

This is not to say that the sole meaning of sexuality is procreative; understood as love-making, sexual union is also a means of expressing mutual love and the desire for a union of souls. It can be a mode of self-revelation and self-giving, of communication and care. Moreover, making love need lose none of its tenderness after the child-bearing years are past. Yet the procreative and regenerative possibility embedded in *eros* cannot be expunged without distorting its meaning.

It is for this reason that procreation remains at the core of a proper understanding of marriage, even in this age of concern for overpopulation. Mutual pleasure and mutual service between husband and wife are, of course, part of the story. So too are mutual admiration and esteem, especially where the partners are deserving. A friendship of shared pursuits and pastimes definitely enhances any marriage, all the more so when the joint activities exercise deeper human capacities. But it is precisely the common project of procreation that holds together what sexual differentiation sometimes threatens to drive apart. Through children, a good common to both husband and wife, male and female achieve some genuine unification (beyond the mere sexual "union" that fails to do so): the two become one through sharing generous (not needy) love for this third being as good. Flesh of their flesh, the child is the parents' own commingled being externalized, and given a separate and persisting existence; unification is enhanced also by their commingled work of rearing. Providing an opening to the future beyond the grave, carrying not only our seed but also our names, our ways, and our hopes that they will surpass us in goodness and happiness, children are a testament to the possibility of transcendence. Gender duality and sexual desire, which first draws our love upward and outside of ourselves, finally provide for the partial overcoming of the confinement and limitation of perishable embodiment altogether. It is as the supreme institution devoted to this renewal of human possibility that marriage finds its deepest meaning and highest function.

Friendship, companionship, and mutual love between the married partners are certainly crucial to the meaning of marriage, especially in modern times. Yet there is no substitute for the contribution that the shared work of raising children makes to the singular friendship and love of husband and wife. Precisely because of its central procreative mission, and even more, because children are yours for a lifetime, this is a friendship that cannot be had with any other person. Uniquely, it is a friendship that does not fly from, but rather embraces wholeheartedly the finitude of its members, affirming without resentment the truth of our human condition. Not by mistake did God create a woman—rather than a dialectic partner—to cure Adam's aloneness; not by accident does the same biblical Hebrew verb mean both to know sexually and to know the truth—including the generative truth about the meaning of being man and woman.

We recognize that there are happily monogamous marriages that remain childless, some by choice, others by bad luck, and that some people will feel the pull of and yield to a higher calling, be it art, philosophy, or the celibate priesthood, seeking or serving some other transcendent voice. But the former often feel cheated by their childlessness, frequently going to extraordinary lengths to conceive or adopt a child. A childless and grandchildless old age is a sadness and a deprivation, even where it is a price willingly paid by couples who deliberately do not procreate.

And for those who elect not to marry, they at least face the meaning of the choice forgone. They do not reject but rather affirm the trajectory of a human life, whose boundaries are given by necessity and our animal nature, and whose higher yearnings and aspirations are made possible in large part because we recognize our neediness and insufficiency. But, until very recently, the aging self-proclaimed bachelor was the butt of many jokes, mildly censured for his self-indulgent and carefree, not to say profligate, ways and for his unwillingness to pay back for the gift of life and nurture by giving life and nurturing in return. (The "old maid" was usually the object of pity rather than censure, since custom rendered her incapable of initiating a move to marry.) No matter how successful he was in business or profession, he could not avoid some taint of immaturity. By never facing squarely "To marry or not to marry," he appeared always to live without seriousness, without a living answer to "To be or not to be."

Marriage and procreation are, therefore, at the heart of a serious and flourishing human life, if not for everyone at least for the vast majority. Most of us know from our own experience that life becomes truly serious when we become responsible for the lives of others for whose being in the world we have said, "We do." It is fatherhood and motherhood that teach most of us what it took to bring us into our own adulthood. And it is the desire to give not only life but a *good way of life* to our children that opens us toward a serious concern for the true, the good, and even the holy. Parental love of children leads once wayward sheep back into the fold of church and synagogue. In the best case, it can even be the beginning of the sanctification of life—yes, even in modern times.

As already noted, the earlier forms of courtship, leading men and women to the altar, understood and indirectly conveyed these deeper truths about human sexuality, marriage, and the higher possibilities for human life. By disciplining erotic desire in the direction of marriage, they helped men and women live more in accordance with their higher possibilities. There may be no going back to the earlier forms of courtship, but no one should be rejoicing over this fact. Anyone serious about "designing" new cultural forms to replace the ones now defunct must bear the burden of finding some alternative means of accomplishing the same, still necessary, ends. And anyone serious about his or her life would still do well to pay careful attention to what courtship means to accomplish, and also why and how.

The organization of this anthology reflects the questions of everyday life discussed above. We begin with readings intended to help us better understand where we are now, both by taking stock of our current situation and by locating our present in relation to previous history. Afterwards we proceed in sequence to the questions that emerge in everyday life: Why marry? What about sex? Is this love, and what does it really want? How can I find and win the right one to marry? Why a wedding and the promises of marriage? What can married life be like? The order selected makes sense on logical, experiential, and educational grounds. Logically, it is fitting to begin with the goal sought (Why marry?), and to then follow the path from the elementary beginnings of desire and love, across the bridge built from these elements by courtship, until the end is realized and enjoyed. Experientially, the order is true to the natural trajectory of events, at least for those people who are inclined—or who can discover that they would do well to be inclined—toward marriage. Finally, experiencing the phenomena in this sequence of readings might, we hope, provide an education of the imagination, helping the reader to appreciate and understand these phenomena in their most natural and logical order and their most beneficial interrelationships.

Most of the readings collected in this anthology are taken from "classic texts," written by some of the major thinkers and writers of Western civilization: poets such as Homer, Shakespeare, Rilke, and Frost; philosophers like Plato, Rousseau, Kant, and Kierkegaard; novelists such as Austen and Tolstoy; humanists like Erasmus and Franklin; historians and social theorists like Herodotus and Tocqueville. There are selections from the Hebrew Bible and theological reflections by Aquinas and a number of twentieth-century Christian thinkers, among them C. S. Lewis and Denis De Rougemont. Some explanation for the selections is in order.

Both of us have taught these books for a quarter-century, and we have found them the best companions for thought and the richest materials for enlarging the horizons, stimulating the imaginations, and challenging the intellectual complacencies of our students. As our late colleague Allan Bloom has written in the introduction to his important book, *Love and Friendship:*

The best books not only help us to describe the phenomena, but help us to experience them. They are living expressions of profound experiences, and without such knowledgeable advocates of those experiences we would find it very difficult to gain access to matters that depend so much on educated feeling and for which merely external observation is not sufficient. Books may provide a voice for whatever remains of nature in us.[1]

It should go without saying—but today it must, alas, be said—that we do not offer these "old" or "great" texts as authoritative, or as authorities. We choose them not because they are old or because they are "traditional." The "great books" disagree too much among themselves to constitute a single coherent traditional teaching. Rather, we offer them in the wisdom-seeking—rather than wisdom-delivering—spirit, as writings that make us think, that challenge our unexamined opinions, expand our sympathies, elevate our gaze, and introduce us to possibilities open to human beings in everyday life that may be undreamt of in our philosophizing.

The general value of thinking with "great authors" is, paradoxically, even greater for our subject of courtship and marriage. Given that courtship leading to marriage is an institution in eclipse, and a subject not much discussed nowadays, we must necessarily repair to earlier times to find suitable materials. This backward look runs the serious risk of losing the sympathy of contemporary readers, the majority of whom would probably prefer more current readings to which they might more easily connect. We are aware of this danger, but we know that it must be run if we are to be able to recover our senses regarding courting and marrying. We do not choose these old readings out of nostalgia for some "good old days," or in the hope or expectation of turning back the courtship clock. Rather, we know that it is mainly through the encounter with writings such as those we have collected here that we can have any real hope of understanding our present situation and the alternatives to it that we have, wittingly and unwittingly, rejected. At the very least, by looking into these deeply silvered mirrors bequeathed to us from the past, we can come to see ourselves the way we truly are—and could be. Beyond this, each of us individually can perhaps learn something from these old books useful not only for self-understanding but even for conducting his or her own courtship or for better educating our children toward the promises of marriage.

---

[1] *Love and Friendship* (New York: Simon and Schuster, 1993), p. 30. Bloom's book offers remarkable interpretative essays on a number of the greatest works on love and friendship, including Plato's *Symposium* and Rousseau's *Emile*, as well as several plays of Shakespeare and a handful of the most important novels of the romantic tradition: *The Red and the Black, Pride and Prejudice, Madame Bovary,* and *Anna Karenina.*

In support of this article of faith we can add as evidence our recent experience teaching these materials in a most successful undergraduate and graduate seminar on courtship (attended by an equal number of men and women). We followed the order of topics used in this anthology and employed many of the selections in the present collection (which has since been augmented by new hunting and finding). No student liked all the readings, but neither was any reading disliked by the majority. More important, the discussions that all of the readings provoked—including ones about such delicate subjects as the nature of male and female desire; female modesty; the effect of casual premarital sex on the possibility of finding lasting love; the standing of marital fidelity; and whether or not procreation is the chief purpose of marriage—were serious, thoughtful, honest, searching, and illuminating (not least, for the instructors). This experience especially has encouraged us to believe that many more people might welcome a collection of readings that could make them more thoughtful about their own everyday concerns with love and marriage.[2]

The readings are not only, for the most part, old. Some are also very long (especially, in the section on courtship, the literary selections from *The Tempest, As You Like It,* and *Pride and Prejudice,* and the account of the courtship that climaxes Rousseau's philosophical novel, *Emile*). Though we prefer either short free-standing essays or poems, or else whole books, we felt it necessary to offer concrete illustrations of successful courtships. But a successful courtship necessarily takes time—indeed, much time—hence, the need for lengthy excerpts, often from widely separated parts of the book. Also, our problem of literary selection was further complicated by the (not inconsequential cultural) fact that the romantic novelists much prefer to describe unhappy love rather than love which leads to happy marriages. Thus Tolstoy, at the start of *Anna Karenina:* "Happy families are all alike; every unhappy family is unhappy in its own way." Finding literary examples of successful courtship was therefore no easy matter.

---

[2]We believe that all readers—both women and men—can profit equally from the readings in this anthology, even though most of them were written by men. Most great writings on this subject were written in earlier times, and the vast majority of those bequeathed to us happen to have been written by men. Also, in the past, most arguments offered in favor of marriage were quite properly addressed *to* males, who arguably were (and perhaps still are) more in need of reasons to marry than women, whether owing to natural differences that make men less inclined to be tied down or to a greater number of competing possibilities available previously only to men. We would have liked to have more writings by women, but we do not believe the imbalance to be damaging. Neither we nor our students have found most of our male authors "insensitive" to women, or incapable of seeing the world through women's eyes or presenting fairly their concerns. For example, if we didn't know it in advance, we doubt that we could tell that the creators of Rosalind or Natasha Rostov were male rather than female. As thoughtful human beings both, we are eager to take help from still more thoughtful human beings wherever we can find them and whoever they may be. We promise our readers that, if they read these selections in this spirit, they will surely be rewarded.

On a subject this complicated and this massive, there can be no pretense of representing all the important alternative points of view, or of doing so comprehensively. Given that most lyric poetry which does not deal with death deals with love, every reader will no doubt have poems or stories he or she prefers to those we have included. We in fact would welcome readers' suggestions, especially if they can be accompanied by reasons for the recommendation. In the end, we have chosen readings that we knew or that were recommended to us, that we thought would help address the most important questions, and of course, that we ourselves admire and enjoy.

As any teacher knows, most good books do not teach themselves. We are all frequently lazy readers who pass off what is puzzling or unfamiliar, and even worse, who fail to see the depth in what is, by contrast, familiar and congenial. Moreover, in delicate subjects our prejudices get in the way, and our inexperience blinds us to crucial subtleties and nuances. Accordingly, we have introduced each reading with some observations and questions designed to encourage active and discerning reading. In some cases, where we thought it helpful, we have taken a decidedly didactic tone in these brief introductions, asking the reader to come at the text with certain questions and concerns in mind. We have done this with mixed feelings; we do not wish to get between author and reader, nor do we wish to imperil understanding of texts written by subtler and greater minds by putting their works upon the Procrustean bed made from our limited understandings and specialized concerns. We thus encourage the readers to use the introductions if they find them helpful, but to treat them with the proverbial grain of salt.

One of the virtues of an anthology is that readers are free to pick and choose what they wish to read, skipping around in no particular order. Yet, as already indicated, there is method in our ordering, and we think there is advantage in following the text straight through. The readings are grouped into seven sections, and each section is preceded by a brief substantive introduction to the theme of the section. This allows some meatier thematic reflections to stand close to the readings that illuminate the themes.

Though we mainly wish the various readings to speak for themselves, the overall organization in which we have arranged them is, we freely confess, guided by an overall substantive argument, which we here summarize in the most general terms. First, we hold that marriage is desirable for multiple yet complementary reasons; the goodness of marriage is, as the logicians say, overdetermined. Next, we subscribe to the modern view that *eros* or romantic love is a most proper beginning for marriage, but only a beginning. *Eros* leads a person outside of himself (or herself) and enables him (or her) to invest his (her) heart in, and to learn to care for, another human being. But *eros*, in principle fickle in its objects and unsteady in its devotions, needs help: if properly disciplined, *eros* can become a stable first bond for a joint life together, the sharing of which in turn will provide new and even stronger bonds to preserve and augment erotic love. We subscribe, in other words, to an erotic view of marriage in which the marital constraint on erotic attachment and sexual desire is seen not as a deprivation of freedom but as the true foundation for a superior way of life and happiness. How, then, to discipline *eros?* This anthology explores (mainly) two alternatives, one basically religious, one basically secular. The first recommends bringing *eros* under religious faith and discipline, so as to complete it or perfect it with the aid, or in the service, of a higher love (see, for example, De Rougemont, Kierkegaard, and Lewis). The second recommends courtship as such, hoping to produce lasting marital love out of what is primordially present in sexual difference and desire, erotic longings, and the specifically human kinds of coupling to which they naturally point (see, for example, Rousseau, Austen, Shakespeare, and Tolstoy). We, the editors, feel the force of both alternatives and have not felt the need to choose between them. As a result, our secular readers may find us too friendly to the religious dimensions of our subject; and our religious readers will no doubt be disappointed in our failure simply to endorse the necessity and supremacy of faith. To both sides, we recommend tolerance, openness, and mutual respect. For in truth, despite their differences, those who treasure marriage in fact stand on common ground: whether religious or secular, they take human life in all its seriousness, affirm its goodness, and commit themselves in hope to its indefinite renewal and perpetuation.

A. WHERE ARE WE NOW? ASSESSING OUR SITUATION

With respect to courting and marrying, as in so many other ways, we live in utterly novel and unprecedented times. One suspects that things were never the way they are, not here, not anywhere. Until what seems like only yesterday, young people were groomed for marriage, and the paths leading to it were culturally well set out, at least in rough outline. In polite society, at the beginning of this century, our grandfathers came a-calling and a-wooing at the homes of our grandmothers, under conditions set by the woman, operating from strength on her own turf. A generation later, courting couples began to go out on "dates," in public and increasingly on the man's terms, given that he had the income to pay for dinner and dancing (see Bailey selection, below). To be sure, some people "played the field," and in the years before World War II, dating on college campuses became a matter more of proving popularity than of proving suitability for marriage. But, especially after the war, going-steady was a regular feature of high-school and college life; the age of marriage dropped considerably, and high-school or college sweethearts often married right after, or even before, graduation. Finding a mate, no less than getting an education that would enable him to support her, was at least a tacit goal of many a male undergraduate; many a young woman, so the joke had it, went to college mainly for her MRS. degree, a charge whose truth was proof against libel for legions of college coeds well into the 1960s.

In other respects as well, the young remained culturally attached to the claims of "real life." Though times were good, fresh memory kept alive the poverty of the recent Great Depression and the deaths and dislocations of the war; necessity and the urgencies of life were not out of sight, even for fortunate youth. Opportunity was knocking, the world and adulthood were beckoning, and most of us stepped forward into married life, readily, eagerly, and, truth to tell, without much pondering. We were simply doing—some sooner, some later—what our parents had done, indeed, what all our forebears had done.

Not so today. Now roughly half the nation goes to college, but very few—women or men—seem to go with the hope or even the wish of finding a marriage partner. Many do not even expect to find a path to a career; they often require several years of postgraduate "time off" to figure out what they are going to do with themselves. Sexually active—in many cases, hyperactive—they bounce about from one relationship to another; to the bewildered eyes of these admittedly much-too-old but still romantic observers, they manage to appear all at once casual and carefree and grim and humorless about getting along with the opposite sex (see Bloom selection, below). On the one hand, they practice strict scrutiny of ordinary speech for taints of sexism, and they rein in even innocent flirtation, which they have trouble distinguishing from sexual harassment; sensitivity training is in many places *de rigeur.* In addition, their legitimate fears of sexually transmitted disease, as well as their quasi-religious preoccupations with the condition and uses of their bodies, have taken much of the joy and ease out of the courtship dance (indeed, there is little of light and loveliness in their actual dancing). On the other hand, many people are perfectly content to "hook up" for a night with someone they just met, or with whom they have been drinking too much, at a party. The young men, nervous predators, act as if any woman is equally good; they are given not to falling in love with one, but to scoring in bed with many. And in this sporting attitude, they are now matched by some female trophy hunters.

But many of the young, and more particularly many of the women, strike us as sad, lonely, and confused. They are, to be sure, very pleased with their new educational and professional opportunities, and with their greater freedom and independence. But in private matters, in relations with men, most of them are, we suspect, hoping for something more. They are not enjoying their hard-won sexual liberation as much as liberation theory says they should. Several young women we know, who would prefer to wait for marriage, have told us with regret that they cannot play the game any other way; given current norms, they know they cannot even hold a man's attention unless they are willing to go to bed with him. Some sincerely believe that once they get involved with him they can teach him something different, but it generally proves impossible, and the women are often soon left behind, feeling used. In the absence of any restraints, collegiate socialization now occurs at the lowest common denominator, and practices and sensibilities thus acquired are extremely difficult to unlearn. Never mind wooing, today's collegians do not even make dates or other forward-looking commitments to see one another; in this, as in so many other ways, they reveal their blindness to the meaning of the passing of time. Those very few who couple off seriously and get married upon graduation as we, their parents, once did are looked upon as freaks.

After college, the scene is even more remarkable and bizarre: singles bars, personal "partner wanted" ads (almost never mentioning marriage as a goal), men practicing serial monogamy (or what someone has aptly renamed "rotating polygamy"), women chronically disappointed in the failure of men "to commit." For the first time in human history, mature women by the tens of thousands live the whole decade of their twenties—their most fertile years—entirely on their own: vulnerable and unprotected, lonely, and out of sync with their inborn nature. Some women positively welcome this state of affairs, but most do not, resenting the personal price they pay for their worldly independence. As age thirty comes and goes, they begin to allow themselves to hear their biological clock ticking, and if husbands continue to be lacking, single motherhood by the hand of science is now an option. Meanwhile, the bachelor herd continues its youthful prowl, with real life in suspended animation, living out what has been called a "postmodern postadolescence."

Those women and men who get lucky enter into what the personal ads call LTRs—long-term relationships—sometimes cohabiting, sometimes not, usually to discover how short an LTR can be. When, after a series of such affairs, marriage happens to them, many enter upon it guardedly and suspiciously, with prenuptial agreements, no common surname, and separate bank accounts. Their ambivalence is reflected in the marriage ceremony itself, as vows are spoken with no promise—or even mention—of permanence (see Blankenhorn selection below).

This stark portrait is no doubt open to challenge. Many young people will not recognize themselves in this picture, perhaps because it is inaccurate and overdrawn, perhaps because readers will regard themselves as exceptions to the general rule, perhaps because the portrait depends on knowing how much things have changed. Young people naturally believe that the world into which they were born is *the* world, the way the world not only is but had to be, and they have no idea that they might be living in what is really act four or five of a tragedy (or comedy). This is, in truth, part of youth's charm and a strong reason for its native hopefulness. But it is becoming clear that it is not only the old-timers who are distressed with the present scene. Women in particular are increasingly vocal about their desires for marriage and increasingly unhappy with the consequences of the practices they have been taught to accept. One sign is the remarkable recent success of a book called *The Rules*,[1] which un-

---

[1] Ellen Fein and Sherrie Schneider, *The Rules: Time-Tested Secrets for Capturing the Heart of Mr. Right* (New York: Warner Books, 1995). The book strikes us as crude and shallow, offering more a cosmetic than a real remedy for the ills it addresses. It is utterly silent about what married life ought to be like and about what sort of a person one should be looking to marry; and its main teaching—"playing hard to get"—however welcome as a corrective to the present lack of female self-restraint, has understood neither the true meaning of modesty nor the dangers of false advertising and the difference between genuine attractiveness and cosmetic guile. Precisely because it does not look beyond getting the man to the altar, its main promise (play by the rules and you can have everything: husband and corporate career) may only serve to exacerbate discontent in the long run. Still, that tens of thousands of women are buying and using the book is a sign that there is real discontent with the current situation.

apologetically tries to teach women how to get the man they want to marry them.

Discontent, however, is not enough. We must try to understand our situation. We must try to characterize it accurately, even if we do not like what it shows us in the mirror. We must try to understand how it came to be our situation. We must try to understand its causes. And we must appreciate the obstacles to any restoration of courtship. These are the purposes of the readings in this section. The first two selections are historical: Bailey on twentieth-century changes in courting practices, Stone on historical changes in passionate attachment. The final two selections are "diagnostic": Bloom on the relationships of the young, Blankenhorn on the marriage ceremony.

Bailey, *From Front Porch to Back Seat*

Our current situation is only the most recent stage in a long historical process of changing modes of behavior between the sexes. Our own century has seen drastic changes in these matters, some of which are well documented in Beth L. Bailey's historical study, From Front Porch to Back Seat: Courtship in Twentieth-Century America *(published in 1988). Bailey (born in 1957) concentrates on what is now regarded as America's "traditional" system of courtship, the system of "dating" that flourished between 1920 and 1965. She shows how dating emerged out of, and replaced, the earlier system of "calling," which had been seen as more closely linked to marriage. Understanding the role of democratization, urbanization, and economic change in these earlier transformations may help us discover how and why, under their continuing influence, courtship is today in such an amorphous and chaotic condition. The selection is excerpted from Bailey's first chapter, "Calling Cards and Money."*

One day, the 1920s story goes, a young man asked a city girl if he might call on her. We know nothing else about the man or the girl—only that, when he arrived, she had her hat on. Not much of a story to us, but any American born before 1910 would have gotten the punch line. "She had her hat on": those five words were rich in meaning to early twentieth century Americans. The hat signaled that she expected to leave the house. He came on a "call," expecting to be received in her family's parlor, to talk, to meet her mother, perhaps to have some refreshments or to listen to her play the piano. She expected a "date," to be taken "out" somewhere and entertained. He ended up spending four weeks' savings fulfilling her expectations.

In the early twentieth century this new style of courtship, dating, had begun to supplant the old. Born primarily of the limits and opportunities of urban life, dating had almost completely replaced the old system of calling by the mid-1920s—and, in so doing, had transformed American courtship. Dating moved courtship into the public world, relocating it from family parlors and community events to restaurants, theaters, and dance halls. At the same time, it removed couples from the implied supervision of the private sphere—from the watchful eyes of family and local community—to the anonymity of the public sphere. Courtship among strangers offered couples new freedom. But access to the public world of the city required money. One had to buy entertainment, or even access to a place to sit and talk. Money—men's money—became the basis of the dating system and, thus, of courtship. This new dating system, as it shifted courtship from the private to the public sphere and increasingly centered around money, fundamentally altered the balance of power between men and women in courtship.

The transition from calling to dating was as complete as it was fundamental. By the 1950s and 1960s, social scientists who studied American courtship found it necessary to remind the American public that dating was a "recent American innovation and not a traditional or universal custom." Some of the many commentators who wrote about courtship believed dating was the best thing that had ever happened to relations between the sexes; others blamed the dating system for all the problems of American youth and American marriage. But virtually everyone portrayed the system dating replaced as infinitely simpler, sweeter, more innocent, and more graceful. Hardheaded social scientists waxed sentimental about the "horse-and-buggy days," when a young man's offer of a ride home from church was tantamount to a proposal and when young men came calling in the evenings and courtship took place safely within the warm bosom of the family. "The courtship which grew out of the sturdy social roots [of the nineteenth century]," one author wrote, "comes through to us for what it was—a gracious ritual, with clearly defined roles for man and woman, in which everyone knew the measured music and the steps."

Certainly a less idealized version of this model of courtship had existed in America, but it was not this model that dating was supplanting. Although only abut 45 percent of Americans lived in urban areas by 1910, few of them were so untouched by the sweeping changes of the late nineteenth century that they could live that dream of rural simplicity. Conventions of courtship at that time were not set by simple yeoman farmers and their families but by the rising middle class, often in imitation of the ways of "society."

By the late nineteenth century a new and relatively coherent social group had come to play an important role in the nation's cultural life. This new middle class, born with and through the rise of national systems of economy, transportation, and communication, was actively creating, controlling, and consuming a national system of culture. National magazines with booming subscription rates promulgated middle-class standards to the white, literate population at large. Women's magazines were especially important in the role of cultural evangelist.

These magazines carried clearly didactic messages to their readership. Unlike general-interest (men's) magazines, which were more likely to contain discussions of issues and events, women's magazines were highly prescriptive, giving advice on both the spiritual and the mundane. But while their advice on higher matters was usually vaguely inspirational, advice on how to look and how to act was extremely explicit.

The conventions of courtship, as set forth in these national magazines and in popular books of etiquette, were an important part of the middle-class code of manners. Conventional courtship centered on "calling," a term that could describe a range of activities. The young man from the neighboring farm who spent the evening sitting on the front porch with the farmer's daughter was paying a call, and so was the "society" man who could judge his prospects by whether or not the card he presented at the front door found the lady of his choice "at home." The middle-class arbiters of culture, however, aped and elaborated the society version of the call. And, as it was promulgated by magazines such as the *Ladies' Home Journal*, with a circulation over one million by 1900, the modified society call was the model for an increasing number of young Americans.

Outside of courtship, this sort of calling was primarily a woman's activity, for women largely controlled social life. Women designated a day or days "at home" to receive callers; on other days they paid or returned calls. The caller would present her card to the maid (common even in moderate-income homes until the World War I era) who answered the door, and would be admitted or turned away with some excuse. The caller who regularly was "not received" quickly learned the limits of her family's social status, and the lady "at home" thus, in some measure, protected herself and her family from the social confusion and pressures engendered by the mobility and expansiveness of late nineteenth-century America. In this system, the husband, though generally determining the family's status, was represented by his wife and was thereby excused from this social-status ritual. Unmarried men, however, were subject to this female-controlled system.

The calling system in courtship, though varying by region and the status of the individuals involved, followed certain general outlines. When a girl reached the proper age or had her first "season" (depending on her family's social level), she became eligible to receive male callers. At first her mother or guardian invited young men to call; in subsequent seasons the young lady had more autonomy and could bestow an invitation to call upon any unmarried man to whom she had been properly introduced at a private dance, dinner, or other "entertainment." Any unmarried man invited to an entertainment owed his hostess (and thus her daughter[s]) a duty call of thanks, but other young men not so honored could be brought to call by friends or relatives of the girl's family, subject to her prior permission. Undesired or undesirable callers, on the other hand, were simply given some excuse and turned away.

The call itself was a complicated event. A myriad of rules governed everything: the proper amount of time between invitation and visit (a fortnight or less); whether or not refreshments should be served (not if one belonged to a fashionable or semi-fashionable circle, but outside of "smart" groups in cities like New York and Boston, girls *might* serve iced drinks with little cakes or tiny cups of coffee or hot chocolate and sandwiches); chaperonage (the first call must be made on daughter and mother, but excessive chaperonage would indicate to the man that his attentions were unwelcome); appropriate topics of conversation (the man's interests, but never too personal); how leave should be taken (on no account should the woman "accompany [her caller] to the door nor stand talking while he struggles into his coat").

Each of these "measured steps," as the mid-twentieth century author nostalgically called them, was a test of suitability, breeding, and background. Advice columns and etiquette books emphasized that these were the manners of any "well-bred" person—and conversely implied that deviations revealed a lack of breeding. However, around the turn of the century, many people who did lack this narrow "breeding" aspired to politeness. Advice columns in women's magazines regularly printed questions from "Country Girl" and "Ignoramus" on the fine points of calling etiquette. Young men must have felt the pressure of girls' expectations, for they wrote to the same advisers with questions about calling. In 1907, *Harper's Bazaar* ran a major article titled "Etiquette for Men," explaining the ins and outs of the calling system. In the first decade of the twentieth century, this rigid system of calling was the convention not only of the "respectable" but also of those who aspired to respectability.

At the same time, however, the new system of dating was emerging. By the mid-1910s, the word *date* had entered the vocabulary of the middle-class public. In 1914, the *Ladies' Home Journal,* a bastion of middle-class respectability, used the term (safely enclosed in quotation marks but with no explanation of its meaning) several times. The word was always spoken by that exotica, the college sorority girl—a character marginal in her exoticness but nevertheless a solid product of the middle class. "One beautiful evening of the spring term," one such article begins, "when I was a college girl of eighteen, the boy whom, because of his popularity in every phase of college life, I had been proud gradually to allow the monopoly of my 'dates,' took me unexpectedly into his arms. As he kissed me impetuously I was glad, from the bottom of my heart, for the training of that mother who had taught me to hold myself aloof from all personal familiarities of boys and men."

Sugarcoated with a tribute to motherhood and virtue, the dates—and the kiss—were unmistakably presented for a middle-class audience. By 1924, ten years later, when the story of the unfortunate young man who went to call on the city girl was current, dating had essentially replaced calling in middle-class culture. The knowing smiles of the story's listeners had probably started with the word *call*—and not every hearer would have been sympathetic to the man's plight. By 1924, he really should have known better.

Dating, that great American middle-class institution, was not at all a product of the middle class. Dating came to the middle class through the upper classes—and from the lower. The first recorded uses of the word *date* in its modern meaning are from lower-class slang. George Ade, the Chicago author who wrote a column titled "Stories of the Streets and of the Town" for the *Chicago Record* and published many slang-filled stories of working-class life, probably introduced the term to literature in 1896. Artie, Ade's street-smart protagonist, asks his unfaithful girlfriend, "I s'pose the other boy's fillin' all my dates?" And in 1899 Ade suggested the power of a girl's charms: "Her Date Book had to be kept on the Double Entry System." Other authors whose imaginations were captured by the city and the variety of its inhabitants—Frank Norris, Upton Sinclair, O. Henry—also were using the term by the first decade of the twentieth century.

The practice of dating was a response of the lower classes to the pressures and opportunities of urban-industrial America, just as calling was a response of the upper stratas. The strict conventions of calling enabled the middling and upper classes to protect themselves from some of the intrusions of urban life, to screen out some of the effects of social and geographical mobility in late nineteenth-century America. Those without the money and security to protect themselves from the pressures of urban life or to control the overwhelming opportunities it offered adapted to the new conditions much more directly.

Dating, which to the privileged and protected would seem a system of increased freedom and possibility, stemmed originally from the lack of opportunities. Calling, or even just visiting, was not a practicable system for young people whose families lived crowded into one or two rooms. For even the more established or independent working-class girls, the parlor and the piano often simply didn't exist. Some "factory girls" struggled to find a way to receive callers. The *Ladies' Home Journal* approvingly reported the case of six girls, workers in a box factory, who had formed a club and pooled part of their wages to pay the "janitress of a tenement house" to let them use her front room two evenings a week. It had a piano. One of the girls explained their system: "We ask the boys to come when they like and spend the evening. We haven't any place at home to see them, and I hate seeing them on the street."

Many other working girls, however, couldn't have done this even had they wanted to. They had no extra wages to pool, or they had no notions of middle-class respectability. Some, especially girls of ethnic families, were kept secluded—chaperoned according to the customs of the old country. But many others fled the squalor, drabness, and crowdedness of their homes to seek amusement and intimacy elsewhere. And a "good time" increasingly became identified with public places and commercial amusements, making young women whose wages would not even cover the necessities of life dependent on men's "treats." Still, many poor and working-class couples did not so much escape from the home as they were pushed from it.

These couples courted on the streets, sometimes at cheap dance halls or eventually at the movies. These were not respectable places, and women could enter them only so far as they, themselves, were not considered respectable. Respectable young women did, of course, enter the public world, but their excursions into the public were cushioned. Public courtship of middle-class and upper-class youth was at least *supposed* to be chaperoned; those with money and social position went to private dances with carefully controlled guest lists, to theater parties where they were a private group within the public. As rebels would soon complain, the supervision of society made the private parlor seem almost free by contrast. Women who were not respectable did have relative freedom of action—but the trade-off was not necessarily a happy one for them.

The negative factors were important, but dating rose equally from the possibilities offered by urban life. Privileged youth, as Lewis Erenberg shows in his study of New York nightlife, came to see the possibility of privacy in the anonymous public, in the excitement and freedom the city offered. They looked to lower-class models of freedom—to those beyond the constraints of respectability. As a society girl informed the readers of the *Ladies' Home Journal* in 1914: "Nowadays it is considered 'smart' to go to the low order of dance halls, and not only be a looker-on, but also to dance among all sorts and conditions of men and women. . . . Nowadays when we enter a restaurant and dance place it is hard to know who is who." In 1907, the same magazine had warned unmarried women never to go alone to a "public restaurant" with any man, even a relative. There was no impropriety in the act, the adviser had conceded, but it still "lays [women] open to misunderstanding and to being classed with women of undesirable reputation by the strangers present." Rebellious and adventurous young people sought that confusion, and the gradual loosening of proprieties they engendered helped to change courtship. Young men and women went out into the world *together,* enjoying a new kind of companionship and the intimacy of a new kind of freedom from adult supervision.

The new freedom that led to dating came from other sources as well. Many more serious (and certainly respectable) young women were taking advantage of opportunities to enter the public world—going to college, taking jobs, entering and creating new urban professions. Women who belonged to the public world by day began to demand fuller access to the public world in general. City institutions gradually accommodated them. Though still considered risqué by some, dining out alone with a man or attending the theater with no chaperone did not threaten an unmarried woman's reputation by the start of the twentieth century.

There were still limits, of course, and they persisted for a long while. Between 1904 and 1907, *Ladies' Home Journal* advisers repeatedly insisted that a girl should not "go out" with a young man until he had called at her home. And in the early 1920s, Radcliffe girls were furnished with a list of approved restaurants in which they could dine with a young man. Some were acceptable only before 7:30 P.M.; others, clearly, still posed a threat to reputations. These limits and conditions, however, show that young men and women of courting age were *expected* to go out—the restrictions were not attempts to *stop* dating, only to control it.

Between 1890 and 1925, dating—in practice and in name—had gradually, almost imperceptibly, become a universal custom in America. By the 1930s it had transcended its origins: Middle America associated dating with neither upper-class rebellion nor the urban lower classes. The rise of dating was usually explained, quite simply, by the invention of the automobile. Cars had given youth mobility and privacy, and so had brought about the system. This explanation—perhaps not consciously but definitely not coincidentally—revised history. The automobile certainly contributed to the rise of dating as a *national* practice, especially in rural and suburban areas, but it was simply accelerating and extending a process already well under way. Once its origins were located firmly in Middle America, however, and not in the extremes of urban upper- and lower-class life, dating had become an American institution.

Dating not only transformed the outward modes and conventions of American courtship, it also changed the distribution of control and power in courtship. One change was generational: the dating system lessened parental control and gave young men and women more freedom. The dating system also shifted power from women to men. Calling, either as a simple visit or as the elaborate late nineteenth-century ritual, gave women a large portion of control. First of all, courtship took place within the girl's home—in women's "sphere," as it was called in the nineteenth century—or at entertainments largely devised and presided over by women. Dating moved courtship out of the home and into man's sphere—the world outside the home. Female controls and conventions lost much of their power outside women's sphere. And while many of the conventions of female propriety were restrictive and repressive, they had allowed women (young women and their mothers) a great deal of immediate control over courtship. The transfer of spheres thoroughly undercut that control.

Second, in the calling system, the woman took the initiative. Etiquette books and columns were adamant on that point: it was the "girl's privilege" to ask a young man to call. Furthermore, it was highly improper for the man to take the initiative. In 1909 a young man wrote to the *Ladies' Home Journal* adviser asking, "May I call upon a young woman whom I greatly admire, although she had not given me the permission? Would she be flattered at my eagerness, even to the setting aside of conventions, or would she think me impertinent?" Mrs. Kingsland replied, "I think that you would risk her just displeasure and frustrate your object of finding favor with her." Softening the prohibition, she then suggested an invitation might be secured through a mutual friend. She had been even stricter two years before, insisting that "a man must not go beyond a very evident pleasure in a women's society, by way of suggestions." Another adviser, "The Lady from Philadelphia," put a more positive light on the situation, noting that "nothing forbids a man to show by his manner that her acquaintance is pleasing to him and thus perhaps suggest that the invitation [to call] would be welcome."

Contrast these strictures with advice on dating etiquette from the 1940s and 1950s: an advice book for men and women warns that "girls who [try] to usurp the right of boys to choose their own dates" will "ruin a good dating career. . . . Fair or not, it is the way of life. From the Stone Age, when men chased and captured their women, comes the yen of a boy to do the pursuing. You will control your impatience, therefore, and respect the time-honored custom of boys to take the first step."

One teen advice book from the 1950s told girls never to take the initiative with a boy, even under some pretext such as asking about homework: "Boys are jealous of their masculine prerogative of taking the initiative." Another said simply, "*Don't ask,*" and still another recounted an anecdote about a girl who asked a boy for a date to the Saturday-night dance. He cut her off in mid-sentence and walked away.

Of course, some advisers stressed that women were not without resource. Though barred from taking the initiative, nothing forbade women from using tricks and stratagems, from showing by a friendly manner that they would welcome an invitation for a date.

This absolute reversal of roles almost necessarily accompanied courtship's move from women's sphere to man's sphere. Although the convention-setters commended the custom of woman's initiative because it allowed greater exclusivity (it might be "difficult for a girl to refuse the permission to call, no matter how unwelcome or unsuitable an acquaintance the man might be"), the custom was based on a broader principle of etiquette. The host or hostess issued any invitation; the guest did not invite himself or herself. An invitation to call was an invitation to visit in a woman's home.

An invitation to go out on a date, on the other hand, was an invitation into man's world—not simply because dating took place in the public sphere (commonly defined as belonging to men), though that was part of it, but because dating moved courtship into the world of the economy. Money—men's money—was at the center of the dating system. Thus, on two counts, men became the hosts and assumed the control that came with that position.

There was some confusion caused by this reversal of initiative, especially during the twenty years or so when going out and calling co-existed as systems. (The unfortunate young man in the apocryphal story, for example, had asked the city girl if he might call on her, so perhaps she was conventionally correct to assume he meant to play the host.) Confusions generally were sorted out around the issue of money. One young woman, "Henrietta L.," wrote to the *Ladies' Home Journal* to inquire whether a girl might "suggest to a friend going to any entertainment or place of amusement where there will be any expense to the young man." The reply: "Never, under any circumstances." The adviser explained that the invitation to go out must "always" come from the man, for he was the one "responsible for the expense." This same adviser insisted that the woman must "always" invite the man to call; clearly she realized that money was the central issue.

The centrality of money in dating had serious implications for courtship. Not only did money shift control and initiative to men by making them the "hosts," it led contemporaries to see dating as a system of exchange best understood through economic analogies or as an economic system pure and simple. Of course, people did recognize in marriage a similar economic dimension—the man undertakes to support his wife in exchange for her filling various roles important to him—but marriage was a permanent relationship. Dating was situational, with no long-term commitments implied, and when a man, in a highly visible ritual, spent money on a woman in public, it seemed much more clearly an economic act.

In fact, the term *date* was associated with the direct economic exchange of prostitution at an early time. A prostitute called "Maimie," in letters written to a middle-class benefactor/friend in the nineteenth century, described how men made "dates" with her. And a former waitress turned prostitute described the process to the Illinois Senate Committee on Vice this way: "You wait on a man and he smiles at you. You see a chance to get a tip and you smile back. Next day he returns and you try harder than ever to please him. Then right away he wants to make a date, and offer you money and presents if you'll be a good fellow and go out with him." These men, quite clearly, were buying sexual favors—but the occasion of the exchange was called a "date."

Courtship in America had always turned somewhat on money (or background). A poor clerk or stockyards worker would not have called upon the daughter of a well-off family, and men were expected to be economically secure before they married. But in the dating system money entered directly into the relationship between a man and a woman as the symbolic currency of exchange in even casual dating.

Dating, like prostitution, made access to women directly dependent on money. Quite a few men did not hesitate to complain about the going rate of exchange. In a 1925 *Collier's* article, "Why Men Won't Marry," a twenty-four-year-old university graduate exclaimed: "Get Married! Why, I can't even afford to go with any of the sort of girls with whom I would like to associate." He explained: "When I was in college, getting an allowance from home, I used to know lots of nice girls. . . . Now that I am on my own I can't even afford to see them. . . . If I took a girl to the theatre she would have to sit in the gallery, and if we went to supper afterward, it would be at a soda counter, and if we rode home it would have to be in the street cars." As he presents it, the problem is solely financial. The same girls who were glad to "go with" him when he had money would not "see" him when he lacked their price. And "nice girls" cost a lot.

In dating, though, the exchange was less direct and less clear than in prostitution. One author, in 1924, made sense of it this way. In dating, he reasoned, a man is responsible for all expenses. The woman is responsible for nothing— she contributes only her company. Of course, the man contributes his company, too, but since he must "add money to balance the bargain" his company must be worth less than hers. Thus, according to this economic understanding, she is selling her company to him. In his eyes, dating didn't even involve an exchange; it was a direct purchase. The moral "subtleties" of a woman's position in dating, the author concluded, were complicated even further by the fact that young men, "discovering that she must be bought, [like] to buy her when [they happen] to have the money."

Yet another young man, the same year, publicly called a halt to such "promiscuous buying." Writing anonymously (for good reason) in *American Magazine*, the author declared a "one-man buyer's strike." This man estimated that, as a "buyer of feminine companionship" for the previous five years, he had "invested" about $20 a week—a grand total of over $5,000. Finally, he wrote, he had realized that "there is a point at which any commodity—even such a delightful commodity as feminine companionship—costs more than it is worth." The commodity he had bought with his $5,000 had been priced beyond its "real value" and he had had enough. This man said "enough" not out of principle, not because he rejected the implications of the economic model of courtship, but because he felt he wasn't receiving value for money.

In all three of these economic analyses, the men are complaining about the new dating system, lamenting the passing of the mythic good old days when "a man without a quarter in his pocket could call on a girl and not be embarrassed," the days before a woman had to be "bought." In recognizing so clearly the economic model on which dating operated, they also clearly saw that the model was a bad one—in purely economic terms. The exchange was not equitable; the commodity was overpriced. Men were operating at a loss.

Here, however, they didn't understand their model completely. True, the equation (male companionship plus money equals female companionship) was imbalanced. But what men were buying in the dating system was not just female companionship, not just entertainment—but power. Money purchased obligation; money purchased inequality; money purchased control.

The conventions that grew up to govern dating codified women's inequality and ratified men's power. Men asked women out; women were condemned as "aggressive" if they expressed interest in a man too directly. Men paid for everything, but often with the implication that women "owed" sexual favors in return. The dating system required men always to assume control, and women to act as men's dependents.

Yet women were not without power in the system, and they were willing to contest men with their "feminine" power. Much of the public discourse on courtship in twentieth-century America was concerned with this contestation. Thousands of sources chronicled the struggles of, and between, men and women—struggles mediated by the "experts" and arbiters of convention—to create a balance of power, to gain or retain control of the dating system. These struggles, played out most clearly in the fields of sex, science, and etiquette, made ever more explicit the complicated relations between men and women in a changing society.

Stone, "Passionate Attachments in the West in Historical Perspective"

While Bailey gives us a historical account of recent transformations of courtship practices in America, a longer and different view is provided by the historian Lawrence Stone (1919–1999), author of The Family, Sex and Marriage in England, 1500–1800. *Whereas Bailey focuses on the external forms, Stone concentrates on the passionate heart of the matter. In the short paper excerpted here, prepared for a 1984 conference on "Passionate Attachments," Stone points out the only relatively recent social approval of romantic love and the correlated acceptability of marriage for love, both of which he ties to the rise of the romantic novel in the nineteenth century. He notes also the unprecedented character of our current situation, thanks to the rise of individualism and, more recently, of enormous sexual freedom. Though he does not say so explicitly, his account raises the question of whether "falling in love" might not become a thing of the past, given the current preoccupation with just plain sex.*

. . . [W]e cannot assume that people in the past—even in our own Western Judeo-Christian world—thought about and felt passionate attachments the way we do.

My remarks will be confined to the two most common of passionate attachments—between two adolescents or adults of different sexes, and between mothers and children [not discussed in this excerpt]. I know there are other attachments—between homosexuals, siblings, fathers and children—but they are not of such central importance as the first two. Before we can begin to examine the very complex issue of passionate attachments in the past, we therefore have to make a fundamental distinction between attachment between two sexually mature persons, usually of the opposite gender, and attachment to the child of one's body.

In the former case, the problem is how to distinguish what is generally known as falling in love from two other human conditions. The first of those conditions is an urgent desire for sexual intercourse with a particular individual, a passion for sexual access to the body of the person desired. In this particular instance the libido is for some reason closely focussed upon a specific body, rather than there being a general state of sexual excitement capable of satisfaction by any promiscuous coupling. The second condition is one of settled and well-tried ties which develop between two people who have known each other for a long time and have come to trust each other's judgment and have confidence in each other's loyalty and affection. This condition of caring may or may not be accompanied by exciting sexual bonding, and may or may not have begun with falling in love, a phase of violent and irrational psychological passion, which does not last very long.

Historians and anthropologists are in general agreement that romantic love—this usually brief but very intensely felt and all-consuming attraction towards another person—is culturally conditioned, and therefore common only in certain societies at certain times, or even in certain social groups within those societies—usually the elite, with the leisure to cultivate such feelings. They are, however, less certain whether or not romantic love is merely a culture-induced sublimated psychological overlay on top of the biological drive for sex, or whether it has biochemical roots which operate quite independently from the libido. Would anyone in fact "fall in love" if they had not read about it or heard it talked about? Did poetry invent love, or love poetry?

Some things can be said with certainty about the history of the phenomenon. The first is that cases of romantic love can be found at all times and places and have often been the subject of powerful poetic expression, from the Song of Solomon to Shakespeare. On the other hand, neither social approbation nor the actual experience of romantic love is at all common to all societies, as anthropologists have discovered. Second, historical evidence for romantic love before the age of printing is largely confined to elite groups, which of course does not mean that it may not have occurred lower down the social scale among illiterates. As a socially approved cultural artifact it began in Europe in the southern French aristocratic courts in the twelfth century, made fashionable by a group of poets, the troubadours. In this case the culture dictated that it should occur between an unmarried male and a married woman, and that it should either go sexually unconsummated or should be adulterous. This cultural ideal certainly spread into wider circles in the middle ages—witness the love story of Aucassin and Nicolette—but it should be noted that none of these models end happily.

By the sixteenth and seventeenth centuries, our evidence for the first time becomes quite extensive, thanks to the spread of literacy and the printing press. We now have love poems, like Shakespeare's Sonnets, love letters, and autobiographies by women primarily concerned with their love life. All the courts of Europe were evidently hotbeds of passionate intrigues and liaisons, some romantic, some sexual. The printing press began to spread pornography to a wider public, thus stimulating the libido, while the plays of Shakespeare indicate that romantic love was a familiar concept to society at large, who composed his audience.

Whether this romantic love was approved of, however, is another question. We simply do not know how Shakespearean audiences reacted to Romeo and Juliet. Did they, like us, and as Shakespeare clearly intended, fully identify with the young lovers? Or, when they left the theatre, did they continue to act like the Montague and Capulet parents, who were trying to stop these irresponsible adolescents from allowing an ephemeral and irrational passion to interfere with the serious business of politics and patronage? What is certain is that every advice book, every medical treatise, every sermon and religious homily of the sixteenth and seventeenth centuries firmly rejected both romantic passion and lust as suitable bases for marriage. In the sixteenth century marriage was thought to be best arranged by parents, who could be relied upon to choose socially and economically suitable partners who would enhance the prestige and importance of the kin group as a whole. It was believed that the sexual bond would automatically create the necessary harmony between the two strangers in order to maintain the stability of the new family unit. This, it seems, is not an unreasonable assumption, since recent investigations in Japan have shown that there is no difference in the rate of divorce between couples whose marriages were arranged by their parents and couples whose marriages were made by individual choice based on romantic love. The arranged and the romantic marriage each has an equal chance of turning out well, or breaking up.

Public admiration for marriage-for-love is thus a fairly recent occurrence in Western society, arising out of the romantic movement of the late eighteenth century, and only winning general acceptance in the twentieth. In the eighteenth century orthodox opinion about marriage shifted away from subordinating the individual will to the interests of the group, and away from economic or political considerations towards those of well-tried personal affection. The ideal marriage of the eighteenth century was one preceded by three to six months of intensive courting, between a couple from families roughly equal in social status and economic wealth, a courtship which only took place with the prior consent of parents on both sides. A sudden falling head over heels in love, although a familiar enough psychological phenomenon, was thought of as a mild form of insanity, in which judgment and prudence are cast aside, all the inevitable imperfections of the loved one become invisible, and wholly unrealistic dreams of everlasting happiness possess the mind of the afflicted victim. Fortunately, in most cases the disease is of short duration, and the patient normally makes a full recovery. To the eighteenth century, the main object of society—church, law, government, and parents—was to prevent the victim from taking some irrevocable step, particularly from getting married. This is why most European countries made marriage under the age of 21 or even later illegal and invalid unless carried out with the consent of parents or guardians. In England this became law in 1753. Runaway marriages based on passionate attachments still took place, but they were made as difficult as possible to carry out, and in most countries were virtually impossible.

It was not, therefore, until the romantic movement and the rise of the novel, especially the pulp novel, in the nineteenth century, that society at large accepted a new idea—that it was normal and indeed praiseworthy for young men and women to fall passionately in love, and that there must be something wrong with those who have failed to have such an overwhelming experience some time in late adolescence or early manhood. Once this new idea was publicly accepted, the dictation of marriage by parents came to be regarded as intolerable and immoral.

Today, the role of passionate attachments between adults in our society is obscured by a new development, the saturation of the whole culture—through every medium of communication—with sexuality as the predominant and overriding human drive, a doctrine whose theoretical foundations were provided by Freud. In no past society known to me has sex been given so prominent a role in the culture at large, nor has sexual fulfillment been elevated to such preeminence in the list of human aspirations—in a vain attempt to relieve civilization of its discontents. If Thomas Jefferson today was asked to rewrite the Declaration of Independence he would certainly have to add total sexual fulfillment to "Life, Liberty and Human Happiness" as one of the basic natural rights of every member of society. The traditional restraints upon sexual freedom—religious and social taboos, and the fear of pregnancy and venereal disease—have now been almost entirely removed. We find it scarcely credible today that in most of Western Europe in the seventeenth century, in a society whose marriage age was postponed into the late twenties, a degree of chastity was practiced that kept the illegitimacy rate—without contraceptives—as low as 2 or 3 percent. Only in Southern Ireland does such a situation still exist— according to one hypothesis, due to a lowering of the libido caused by large-scale consumption of Guinness Stout. Under these conditions, it seems to me almost impossible today to distinguish passionate attachment in the psychological sense—meaning love—from passionate attachment in the physical sense—meaning lust. But the enormous success today of pulp fiction concerned almost exclusively with romantic rather than physical love shows that women at least still hanker after the experience of falling in love. Whether the same applies to men is more doubtful, so that there may be a real gender gap on this subject today, which justifies this distinction I am making between love and lust.

To sum up, the historian can see a clear historical trend in the spread of the cultural concept of romantic love in the West, beginning in court circles in the twelfth century, and expanding outward from the sixteenth century on. It received an enormous boost with the rise of the romantic novel, and another boost with the achievement of near-total literacy by the end of the nineteenth century. Today, however, it is so intertwined with sexuality, that it is almost impossible to distinguish between the two. Both, however, remain clearly distinct from caring, that is, well-tried and settled affection based on long-term commitment and familiarity.

It is also possible to say something about the changing relationship of passionate love to marriage. For all classes who possessed property, that is the top two-thirds economically, marriage before the seventeenth century was arranged by the parents, and the motives were the economic and political benefit of the kin group, not the emotional satisfaction of the individuals. As the concept of individualism grew in the seventeenth and eighteenth centuries, it slowly became accepted that the prime object was "holy matrimony," a sanctified state of monogamous married contentment. This was best achieved by allowing the couple to make their own choice, provided that both sets of parents agreed that the social and economic gap was not too wide, and that marriage was preceded by a long period of courtship. By the eighteenth and nineteenth centuries, individualism had so far taken precedence over the group interests of the kin that the couple were left more or less free to make their own decision, except in the highest aristocratic and royal circles. Today individualism is given such absolute priority in most Western societies, that the couple are virtually free to act as they please, to sleep with whom they please, and to marry and divorce when and whom they please to suit their own pleasure. The psychic cost of such behavior, and its self-defeating consequences, are becoming clear, however, and how long this situation will last is anybody's guess. . . .

The most difficult historical problem concerns the role of romantic love among the propertyless poor, who comprised about one-third of the population. Since they were propertyless, their loves and marriages were of little concern to their kin, and they were therefore more or less free to choose their own mates. By the eighteenth century, and probably before, court records make it clear that these groups often married for love, combined with a confused set of motives including lust and the economic necessity to have a strong and healthy assistant to run the farm or the shop. It was generally expected that they would behave "lovingly" towards each other, but this often did not happen. In many a peasant marriage, the husband seems to have valued his cow more than his wife. Passionate attachments among the poor certainly occurred, but how often they took priority over material interests we may never know for certain.

All that we do know is that courting among the poor normally lasted six months or more, and that it often involved all-night sessions alone together in the dark in a room with a bed, usually with the knowledge and consent of the parents or masters. Only relatively rarely, and only at a late stage after engagement, did full sexual intercourse commonly take place during these nights, but it is certain that affectionate conversation, and discussion of the possibilities of marriage, were accompanied by embracing and kissing, and probably also by what today is euphemistically called "heavy petting." This practice of "bundling," as it was called, occurred in what was by our standards an extremely prudish, and indeed sexually innocent, society. When men and women went to bed together they almost invariably kept on a piece of clothing, a smock or a shirt, to conceal their nakedness. Moreover the sexual act itself was almost always carried out in the "missionary" position. The evidence offered in the courts in cases of divorce in the pre-modern period provide little evidence of that polymorphous perversity advocated in the sex manuals available in every bookstore today.

What is certain is that even after this process of intimate physical and verbal courtship had taken place, economic factors still loomed large in the final decision by both parties about whether or not to marry. Thus passion and material interest were in the end inextricably involved, but it is important to stress that, among the poor, material interest only became central at the *end* of the process of courtship instead of at the beginning, as was the case with the rich.

If an early modern peasant said "I love a woman with ten acres of land," just what did he mean? Did he lust after the body of the woman? Did he admire her good health, administrative and intellectual talents and strength of character as a potential housekeeper, income producer, and mother of his children? Was he romantically head over heels in love with her? Or did he above all prize her for her ten acres? Deconstruct the text as we wish, there is no way of getting a clear answer to that question; and in any case, if we could put that peasant on the couch today and interrogate him, it would probably turn out that he merely felt that he liked the woman more because of her ten acres.

Finally, we know that in the eighteenth century at least half of all brides in England and America were pregnant on their wedding day. But this tells us more about sexual customs than about passionate attachments: sex began at the moment of engagement, and marriage in church came later, often triggered by the pregnancy. We also know that if a poor servant girl was impregnated by her master, which often happened, the latter usually had no trouble finding a poor man who would marry her, in return for payment of ten pounds or so. Not much passionate attachment there, among any of the three persons involved. . . .

Passionate attachments between young people can and do happen in any society as a byproduct of biological sexual attraction, but the social acceptability of the emotion has varied enormously over time and class and space, determined primarily by cultural norms and property arrangements. We are in a unique position today . . . in that . . . contraception is normal and efficient; our culture is dominated by romantic notions of passionate love as the only socially admissible reason for marriage; and sexual fulfillment is accepted as the dominant human drive and a natural right for both sexes. Behind all this there lies a frenetic individualism, a restless search for the sexual and emotional ideal in human relationships, and a demand for instant ego gratification which is inevitably self-defeating and ultimately destructive.

Bloom, "Relationships"

Allan Bloom (1930–1992), a professor of political philosophy who taught at Yale, Cornell, Toronto, and the University of Chicago, was for nearly forty years a masterful teacher of undergraduates. He provocatively challenged his students to examine their own opinions and feelings in the light of the alternatives presented by the great authors, literary and philosophical, a practice evident also in his writings. Drawing on his extensive and intensive conversations with the young, as well as his reflections on the march of equality and individualism (the themes treated by Bailey and Stone), Bloom painted an arresting portrait of contemporary college students in the first part of his much debated best-selling book, The Closing of the American Mind *(1987), which Bloom had originally wanted to entitle "Souls without Longing." In this lengthy excerpt from the chapter on "relationships"— with discussions of self-centeredness, sex, separateness, divorce, love, and eros— Bloom offers deep reasons why most students today are, in his opinion, closed to the higher possibilities of liberal learning. The editors offer it here as a possible explanation why many of them may be equally closed to falling in love, to courtship, and to marriage. To what extent do you think Bloom accurately describes our situation? Does he illuminate contemporary obstacles to courtship?*

Self-Centeredness

Students these days are, in general, nice. I choose the word carefully. They are not particularly moral or noble. Such niceness is a facet of democratic character when times are good. Neither war nor tyranny nor want has hardened them or made demands on them. The wounds and rivalries caused by class distinction have disappeared along with any strong sense of class (as it once existed in universities in America and as it still does, poisonously, in England). Students are free of most constraints, and their families make sacrifices for them without asking for much in the way of obedience or respect. Religion and national origin have almost no noticeable effect on their social life or their career prospects. Although few really believe in "the system," they do not have any burning sentiment that injustice is being done to them. The drugs and the sex once thought to be forbidden are available in the quantities required for sensible use. A few radical feminists still feel the old-time religion, but most of the women are comfortably assured that not much stands in the way of their careers. There is an atmosphere of easy familiarity with their elders, and even of the kind of respect of free young people for them that Tocqueville asserted equality encourages. Above all, there are none of the longings, romantic or otherwise, that used to make bourgeois society, or society in general, repugnant to the young. The impossible dreams of the sixties proved to be quite possible within the loosened fabric of American life. Students these days are pleasant, friendly and, if not great-souled, at least not particularly mean-spirited. Their primary preoccupation is themselves, understood in the narrowest sense. . . .

. . . But the great majority of students, although they as much as anyone want to think well of themselves, are aware that they are busy with their own careers and their relationships. There is a certain rhetoric of self-fulfillment that gives a patina of glamor to this life, but they can see that there is nothing particularly noble about it. Survivalism has taken the place of heroism as the admired quality. This turning in on themselves is not, as some would have it, a return to normalcy after the hectic fever of the sixties, nor is it preternatural selfishness. . . . The affairs of daily life rarely involve concern for a larger community in such a way as to make the public and private merge in one's thought. It is not merely that one is free to participate or not to participate, that there is no need to do so, but that everything militates against one's doing so. . . .

The resulting inevitable individualism, endemic to our regime, has been reinforced by another unintended and unexpected development, the decline of the family, which was the intermediary between individual and society, providing quasi-natural attachments beyond the individual, that gave men and women unqualified concern for at least some others and created an entirely different relation to society from that which the isolated individual has. Parents, husbands, wives and children are hostages to the community. They palliate indifference to it and provide a material stake in its future. This is not quite instinctive love of country, but it is love of country for love of one's own. It is the gentle form of patriotism, one that flows most easily out of self-interest, without the demand for much self-denial. The decay of the family means that community would require extreme self-abnegation in an era when there is no good reason for anything but self-indulgence.

Apart from the fact that many students have experienced the divorce of their parents and are informed by statistics that there is a strong possibility of divorce in their futures, they hardly have an expectation that they will have to care for their parents or any other blood relatives, or that they will even see much of them as they grow older. Social security, retirement funds and health insurance for old people free their children from even having to give them financial support, let alone taking them into their own homes to live. When a child goes away to college, it is really the beginning of the end of his vital connection with his family, though he scarcely realizes it at the time. Parents have little authority over their children when they leave home, and the children are forced to look outward and forward. They are not coldhearted; the substance of their interests merely lies elsewhere. Spiritually, the family was pretty empty, anyway, and new objects fill their field of vision as the old ones fade. American geography plays a role in this separation. This is a large country, and people are very mobile, particularly since World War II and the expansion of air travel. Practically no student knows where he is going to live when he has completed his education. Very likely it will be far away from his parents and his birth-place. . . . He can live in the North, South, East or West, in the city, the suburbs, or the country—who knows which? There are arguments for each, and he is absolutely unconstrained in his choice. The accidents of where he finds a job and of variable inclination are likely to take him far away from all he has been connected with, and he is psychically prepared for this. His investments in his past and those who peopled it are necessarily limited.

This indeterminate or open-ended future and the lack of a binding past mean that the souls of young people are in a condition like that of the first men in the state of nature—spiritually unclad, unconnected, isolated, with no inherited or unconditional connection with anything or anyone. They can be anything they want to be, but they have no particular reason to want to be anything in particular. Not only are they free to decide their place, but they are also free to decide whether they will believe in God or be atheists, or leave their options open by being agnostic; whether they will be straight or gay, or, again, keep their options open; whether they will marry and whether they will stay married; whether they will have children—and so on endlessly. There is no necessity, no morality, no social pressure, no sacrifice to be made that mili-tates going in or turning away from any of these directions, and there are de-sires pointing toward each, with mutually contradictory arguments to buttress them. . . .

Sex

Contrary to the popular prejudice that America is the nation of unintel-lectual and anti-intellectual people, where ideas are at best means to ends, America is actually nothing but a great stage on which theories have been played as tragedy and comedy. This is a regime founded by philosophers and their students. All the recalcitrant matter of the historical *is* gave way here be-fore the practical and philosophical *ought to be,* as the raw natural givens of this wild continent meekly submitted to the yoke of theoretical science. . . . Our story is the majestic and triumphant march of the principles of freedom and equality, giving meaning to all that we have done or are doing. There are almost no accidents; everything that happens among us is a consequence of one or both of our principles—a triumph over some opposition to them, a discovery of a fresh meaning in them, a dispute about which of the two has primacy, etc.

Now we have arrived at one of the ultimate acts in our drama, the informing and reforming of our most intimate private lives by our principles. Sex and its consequences—love, marriage and family—have finally become the theme of the national project, and here the problem of nature, always present but always repressed in the reconstruction of man demanded by freedom and equality, becomes insistent. In order to intuit the meaning of equality, we have no need for the wild imaginative genius of Aristophanes, who in *The Assembly of Women* contrives the old hags entitled by law to sexual satisfaction from handsome young males, or of Plato, who in the *Republic* prescribed naked exercises for men and women together. We only have to look around us, if we have eyes to see.

The change in sexual relations, which now provide an unending challenge to human ingenuity, came over us in two successive waves in the last two decades. The first was the sexual revolution; the second, feminism. The sexual revolution marched under the banner of freedom; feminism under that of equality. Although they went arm in arm for a while, their differences eventually put them at odds with each other, as Tocqueville said freedom and equality would always be. This is manifest in the squabble over pornography, which pits liberated sexual desire against feminist resentment about stereotyping. We are presented with the amusing spectacle of pornography clad in armor borrowed from the heroic struggles for freedom of speech, and using Miltonic rhetoric, doing battle with feminism, newly draped in the robes of community morality, using arguments associated with conservatives who defend traditional sex roles, and also defying an authoritative tradition in which it was taboo to suggest any relation between what a person reads and sees and his sexual practices. In the background stand the liberals, wringing their hands in confusion because they wish to favor both sides and cannot.

Sexual liberation presented itself as a bold affirmation of the senses and of undeniable natural impulse against our puritanical heritage, society's conventions and repressions, bolstered by Biblical myths about original sin. From the early sixties on there was a gradual testing of the limits on sexual expression, and they melted away or had already disappeared without anybody's having noticed it. The disapproval of parents and teachers of youngsters' sleeping or living together was easily overcome. The moral inhibitions, the fear of disease, the risk of pregnancy, the family and social consequences of premarital intercourse and the difficulty of finding places in which to have it—everything that stood in its way suddenly was no longer there. Students, particularly the girls, were no longer ashamed to give public evidence of sexual attraction or of its fulfillment. The kind of cohabitations that were dangerous in the twenties, and risqué or bohemian in the thirties and forties, became as normal as membership in the Girl Scouts. I say "particularly" girls because young men were always supposed to be eager for immediate gratification, whereas young women, inspired by modesty, were supposed to resist it. It was a modification or phasing out of female modesty that made the new arrangements possible. Since, however, modesty was supposed to be mere convention or habit, no effort was required to overcome it. This emancipation had in its intention and its effect the accentuation of the difference between the sexes. Making love was to be the primary activity, so men and women were to be more emphatically male and female. Of course, homosexuals were also liberated, but for the great mass of people, being free and natural meant achieving heterosexual satisfactions, opposite sexes made for each other.

The immediate promise of sexual liberation was, simply, happiness understood as the release of energies that had been stored up over millennia during the dark night of repression, in a great continuous Bacchanalia. However, the lion roaring behind the door of the closet turned out, when that door was opened, to be a little, domesticated cat. In fact, seen from a long historical perspective, sexual liberation might be interpreted as the recognition that sexual passion is no longer dangerous in us, and that it is safer to give it free course than to risk rebellion by restraining it. I once asked a class how it could be that not too long ago parents would have said, "Never darken our door again," to wayward daughters, whereas now they rarely protest when boyfriends sleep over in their homes. A very nice, very normal, young woman responded, "Because it's no big deal." That says it all. This passionlessness is the most striking effect, or revelation, of the sexual revolution, and it makes the younger generation more or less incomprehensible to older folks.

In all this, the sexual revolution was precisely what it said it was—a liberation. But some of the harshness of nature asserted itself beneath the shattered conventions: the young were more apt to profit from the revolution than the old, the beautiful more than the ugly. The old veil of discretion had had the effect of making these raw and ill-distributed natural advantages less important in life and marriage. But now there was little attempt to apply egalitarian justice in these matters, as did Aristophanes' older Athenian women who, because of their very repulsiveness, had a right to enjoy handsome young men before beautiful young women did. The undemocratic aspects of free sex were compensated for in our harmless and mildly ridiculous way: "Beauty is in the eye of the beholder" was preached more vigorously than formerly; the cosmetics industry had a big boom; and education and therapy in the style of Masters and Johnson, promising great orgasms to every subscriber, became common. My favorite was a course in sex for the elderly given at a local YMCA and advertised over the radio with the slogan "Use It or Lose It." These were the days when pornography slipped its leash.

Feminism, on the other hand, was, to the extent it presented itself as liberation, much more a liberation from nature than from convention or society. Therefore it was grimmer, unerotic, more of an abstract project, and required not so much the abolition of law but the institution of law and political activism. Instinct did not suffice. The negative sentiment of imprisonment was there, but what was wanted, as Freud suggested, was unclear. The programmatic language shifted from "living naturally" (with reference to very definite bodily functions) to vaguer terms such as "self-definition," "self-fulfillment," "establishing priorities," "fashioning a lifestyle," etc. The women's movement is not founded on nature. Although feminism sees the position of women as a result of nurture and not nature, its crucial contention is that biology should not be destiny, and biology is surely natural. It is not self-evident, although it may be true, that women's roles were always determined by human relations of domination, like those underlying slavery. This thesis requires interpretation and argument, and is not affirmed by the bodily desires of all concerned, as was the sexual revolution. Moreover, it is very often asserted that science's *conquest* of nature—in the form of the pill and labor-saving devices—has made woman's emancipation from the home possible. It is certain that feminism has brought with it an unrelenting process of consciousness-raising and -changing that begins in what is probably a permanent human inclination and is surely a modern one—the longing for the unlimited, the unconstrained. It ends, as do many modern movements that seek abstract justice, in forgetting nature and using force to refashion human beings to secure that justice.

Feminism is in accord with and encourages many elements of the sexual revolution, but uses them to different ends. Libertinism allows for what even Rousseau called the greatest pleasure. But in making sex easy, it can trivialize, de-eroticize and demystify sexual relations. A woman who can easily satisfy her desires and does not invest her emotions in exclusive relationships is liberated from the psychological tyranny of men, to do more important things. Feminism acted as a depressant on the Bacchanalian mood of the sexual revolution, as nakedness in Plato's *Republic* led not to great indulgences but to an unromantic regulation and manipulation of sexual desire for public purposes. Just as smoking and drinking overcame puritanical condemnation only to find themselves, after a brief moment of freedom, under equally moralistic attacks in the name not of God but of the more respectable and powerful names of health and safety, so sex had a short day in the sun before it had to be reined in to accommodate the feminist sensibility. As a people, we are good not at gratifying ourselves but at delaying gratification for the sake of projects which promise future good. In this case the project is overcoming what is variously called male dominance, machismo, phallocracy, patriarchy, etc., to which men and their female collaborators seem very attached, inasmuch as so many machines of war must be mounted against them.

Male sexual passion has become sinful again because it culminates in sexism. Women are made into objects, they are raped by their husbands as well as by strangers, they are sexually harassed by professors and employers at school and at work, and their children, whom they leave in day-care centers in order to pursue their careers, are sexually abused by teachers. All these crimes must be legislated against and punished. What sensitive male can avoid realizing how dangerous his sexual passion is? Is there perhaps really original sin? Men had failed to read the fine print in the Emancipation Proclamation. The new interference with sexual desire is more comprehensive, more intense, more difficult to escape than the older conventions, the grip of which was so recently relaxed. The July 14 of the sexual revolution was really only a day between the overthrow of the Ancien Regime and the onset of the Terror. The new reign of virtue, accompanied by relentless propaganda on radio and television and in the press, has its own catechism, inducing an examination of the conscience and the inmost sentiments for traces of possessiveness, jealousy, protectiveness—all those things men used to feel for women. There are, of course, a multitude of properly indignant censors equipped with loudspeakers and inquisitional tribunals.

Central to the feminist project is the suppression of modesty, in which the sexual revolution played a critical preparatory role, just as capitalism, in the Marxist scheme, prepared the way for socialism by tearing the sacred veils from the charade of feudal chivalry. The sexual revolution, however, wanted men and women to get together bodily, while feminism wanted them to be able easily to get along separately. Modesty in the old dispensation was *the* female virtue, because it governed the powerful desire that related men to women, providing a gratification in harmony with the procreation and rearing of children, the risk and responsibility of which fell naturally—that is, biologically—on women. Although modesty impeded sexual intercourse, its result was to make such gratification central to a serious life and to enhance the delicate interplay between the sexes, which makes acquiescence of the will as important as possession of the body. Diminution or suppression of modesty certainly makes attaining the end of desire easier—which was the intention of the sexual revolution—but it also dismantles the structure of involvement and attachment, reducing sex to the thing-in-itself. This is where feminism enters.

Female modesty extends sexual differentiation from the sexual act to the whole of life. It makes men and women always men and women. The consciousness of directedness toward one another, and its attractions and inhibitions, inform every common deed. As long as modesty operates, men and women together are never just lawyers or pilots together. They have something else, always potentially very important, in common—ultimate ends, or as they say, "life goals." Is winning this case or landing this plane what is most important, or is it love and family? As lawyers or pilots, men and women are the same, subservient to the one goal. As lovers or parents they are very different, but inwardly related by sharing the naturally given end of continuing the species. Yet their working together immediately poses the questions of "roles" and, hence, "priorities," in a way that men working together or women working together does not. Modesty is a constant reminder of their peculiar relatedness and its outer forms and inner sentiments, which impede the self's free creation or capitalism's technical division of labor. It is a voice constantly repeating that a man and a woman have a work to do together that is far different from that found in the marketplace, and of a far greater importance.

This is why modesty is the first sacrifice demanded by Socrates in Plato's *Republic* for the establishment of a city where women have the same education, live the same lives and do the same jobs as men. If the difference between men and women is not to determine their ends, if it is not to be more significant than the difference between bald men and men with hair, then they must strip and exercise naked together just as Greek men did. With some qualifications, feminists praise this passage in Plato and look upon it as prescient, for it culminates in an absolute liberation of women from the subjection of marriage and childbearing and -rearing, which become no more important than any other necessary and momentary biological event. Socrates provides birth control, abortion and day-care centers, as well as marriages that last a day or a night and have as their only end the production of sound new citizens to replenish the city's stock, cared for by the city. He even adds infanticide to the list of conveniences available. A woman will probably have to spend no more time and effort on children's business than a man would in curing a case of the measles. Only then can women be thought to be naturally fit to do the same things as men. Socrates' radicalism extends to the relation of parent and child. The citizens are not to know their own children, for, if they were to love them above others, then the means that brought them into being, the intercourse of this man and this woman, would be judged to be of special significance. Then we would be back to the private family and the kinds of relatedness peculiar to it.

Socrates' proposal especially refers to one of the most problematic cases for those who seek equal treatment for women—the military. These citizens are warriors, and he argues that just as women can be liberated from subjection to men and take their places alongside them, men must be liberated from their special concern for women. A man must have no more compunction about killing the advancing female enemy than the male, and he must be no more protective of the heroine fighting on his right side than of the hero on his left. Equal opportunity and equal risk. The only concern is the common good, and the only relationship is to the community, bypassing the intermediate relationships that tend to take on a life of their own and were formerly thought to have natural roots in sexual attraction and love of one's own children. Socrates consciously rips asunder the delicate web of relations among human beings woven out of their sexual nature. Without it, the isolation of individuals is inevitable. He makes explicit how equal treatment of women necessitates the removal of meaning from the old kind of sexual relations—whether they were founded on nature or convention—and a consequent loss of the human connections that resulted from them which he replaces with the common good of the city.

In this light we can discern the outlines of what has been going on recently among us. Conservatives who have been heartened by the latest developments within the women's movement are mistaken if they think that they and the movement are on common ground. Certainly both sides are against pornography. But the feminists are against it because it is a reminiscence of the old love relationship, which involved differentiated sexual roles—roles now interpreted as bondage and domination. Pornography demystifies that relationship, leaving the merely sexual component of male-female relationships without their erotic, romantic, moral and ideal accompaniments. It caters to and encourages the longing men have for women and its unrestrained if impoverished satisfaction. This is what feminist anti-pornographers are against—not the debasement of sentiment or the threat to the family. That is why they exempt homosexual pornography from censorship. It is by definition not an accomplice to the domination of females by males and even helps to undermine it. Actually, feminists favor the demystifying role of pornography. It unmasks the true nature of the old relationships. Their purpose is not to remystify the worn-out systems but to push on toward the realm of freedom. They are not for a return to the old romances, *Brief Encounter,* for example, which gave charm to love in the old way. They know that is dead, and they are now wiping up the last desperate, untutored, semicriminal traces of a kind of desire that no longer has a place in the world.

It is one thing, however, to want to prevent women from being ravished and brutalized because modesty and purity should be respected and their weakness protected by responsible males, and quite another to protect them from male desire altogether so that they can live as they please. Feminism makes use of conservative moralism to further its own ends. This is akin to, and actually part of, the fatal old alliance between traditional conservatives and radicals, which has had such far-reaching effects for more than a century. They had nothing in common but their hatred of capitalism, the conservatives looking back to the revival of throne and altar in the various European nations, and to piety, the radicals looking forward to the universal, homogeneous society and to freedom—reactionaries and progressives united against the present. They feed off the inner contradictions of the bourgeoisie. Of course fundamentalists and feminists can collaborate to pass local ordinances banning smut, but the feminists do so to demonstrate their political clout in furthering their campaign against "bourgeois rights," which are, sad to say, enjoyed by people who want to see dirty movies or buy equipment to act out comically distorted fantasies. It is doubtful whether the fundamentalists gain much from this deal, because it guarantees the victory of a surging moral force that is "antifamily and antilife." See how they do together on the abortion issue! People who watch pornography, on the other hand, are always at least a little ashamed and unwilling to defend it as such. At best, they sound a weak and uncertain trumpet for the sanctity of the Constitution and the First Amendment, of which they hope to be perceived as defenders. They pose no threat in principle to anything.

Similarly, some conservatives are heartened by recent feminist discussion about the differences between men and women and about the special fulfillment of "parenting," forbidden subjects at earlier stages of the movement, when equal rights was the primary theme. However, this discussion has really only been made possible by the success of those earlier stages. There may indeed be a feminine nature or self, but it has been definitively shaken loose from its teleological moorings. The feminine nature is not in any reciprocal relation to the male nature, and they do not define one another. The male and female sexual organs themselves now have no more evident purposiveness than do white and black skin, are no more naturally pointed toward one another than white master and black slave, or so the legend goes. Women do have different physical structures, but they can make of them what they will—without paying a price. The feminine nature is a mystery to be worked out on its own, which can now be done because the male claim to it has been overcome. The fact that there is today a more affirmative disposition toward childbearing does not imply that there is any natural impulse or compulsion to establish anything like a traditional fatherhood to complement motherhood. The children are to be had on the female's terms, with or without fathers, who are not to get in the way of the mother's free development. Children have always been, and still are, more the mother's anyway. Ninety per cent or more of children of divorced parents stay with their mothers, whose preeminent stake in children has been enhanced by feminist demands and by a consequent easy rationalization of male irresponsibility. So we have reproduction without family—if family includes the presence of a male who has any kind of a definite function. The return to motherhood as a feminist ideal is only possible because feminism has triumphed over the family as it was once known, and women's freedom will not be limited by it. None of this means returning to family values or even bodes particularly well for the family as an institution, although it does mean that women have become freer to come to terms with the complexity of their situation.

The uneasy bedfellowship of the sexual revolution and feminism produced an odd tension in which all the moral restraints governing nature disappeared, but so did nature. The exhilaration of liberation has evaporated, however, for it is unclear what exactly was liberated or whether new and more onerous responsibilities have not been placed on us. And this is where we return to the students, for whom everything is new. They are not sure what they feel for one another and are without guidance about what to do with whatever they may feel.

The students of whom I am speaking are aware of all the sexual alternatives, and have been from very early on in their lives, and they feel that all sexual acts which do not involve real harm to others are licit. They do not think they should feel guilt or shame about sex. They have had sex education in school, of "the biological facts, let them decide the values for themselves" variety, if not "the options and orientations" variety. They have lived in a world where the most explicit discussions and depictions of sex are all around them. They have had little fear of venereal disease.[1] Birth-control devices and ready abortion have been available to them since puberty. For the great majority, sexual intercourse was a normal part of their lives prior to college, and there was no fear of social stigma or even much parental opposition. Girls have had less supervision in their relations with boys than at any time in history. They are not precisely pagan, but there is an easy familiarity with others' bodies and less inhibition about using their own for a broad range of erotic purposes. There is no special value placed on virginity in oneself or in one's partners. It is expected that there were others before and, incredibly to older folks, this does not seem to bother them, even though it provides a ground for predictions about the future. They are not promiscuous or given to orgies or casual sex, as it used to be understood. In general, they have one connection at a time, but most have had several serially. They are used to coed dormitories. Many live together, almost always without expectation of marriage. It is just a convenient arrangement. They are not couples in the sense of having simulacra of marriage or a way of life different from that of other students not presently so attached. They are roommates, which is what they call themselves, with sex and utilities included in the rent. Every single obstacle to sexual relationships between young

[1]It remains to be seen what effect AIDS will have. The wave of publicity about herpes a couple of years ago had almost no discernible psychological fallout.

unmarried persons has disappeared, and these relationships are routine. To strangers from another planet, what would be the most striking thing is that sexual passion no longer includes the illusion of eternity.

Men and women are now used to living in exactly the same way and studying exactly the same things and having exactly the same career expectations. No man would think of ridiculing a female premed or prelaw student, or believe that these are fields not proper for women, or assert that a woman should put family before career. The law schools and medical schools are full of women, and their numbers are beginning to approach their proportion in the general population. There is very little ideology or militant feminism in most of the women, because they do not need it. The strident voices are present, and they get attention in the university newspapers and in student governments. But, again, the battle here has been won. Women students do not generally feel discriminated against or despised for their professional aspirations. The economy will absorb them, and they have rising expectations. . . . Academically, students are comfortably unisexual; they revert to dual sexuality only for the sex act. Sex no longer has any political agenda in universities except among homosexuals, who are not yet quite satisfied with their situation. But the fact that there is an open homosexual presence, with rights at least formally recognized by university authorities and almost all students, tells us much about current university life.

Students today understandably believe that they are the beneficiaries of progress. They have a certain benign contempt for their parents, particularly for their poor mothers, who were sexually inexperienced and had no profession to be taken as seriously as their fathers'. Superior sexual experience was always one of the palpable advantages that parents and teachers had over youngsters who were eager to penetrate the mysteries of life. But this is no longer the case, nor do students believe it to be so. They quietly smile at professors who try to shock them or talk explicitly about the facts of life in the way once so effective in enticing more innocent generations of students to pay attention to the words of their elders. Freud and D. H. Lawrence are very old hat. Better not to try.

Even less do students expect to learn anything about their situation from old literature, which from the Garden of Eden on made coupling a very dark and complicated business. On reflection, today's students wonder what all the fuss was about. Many think their older brothers and sisters discovered sex, as we now know it to be, in the sixties. I was impressed by students who, in a course on Rousseau's *Confessions,* were astounded to learn that he had lived with a woman out of wedlock in the eighteenth century. Where could he have gotten the idea?

There is, of course, literature that affects a generation profoundly but has no interest at all for the next generation because its central theme proved ephemeral, whereas the greatest literature addresses the permanent problems of man. Ibsen's *Ghosts,* for example, lost all its force for young people when syphilis ceased to be a threat. Aristotle teaches that pity for the plight of others requires that the same thing could happen to us. Now, however, the same things that used to happen to people, at least in the relations between the sexes, do not happen to students anymore. And one must begin to wonder whether there is any permanent literature for them, because there do not seem to them to be permanent problems for them. As I have suggested earlier, this is the first fully historical or historicized generation, not only in theory but also in practice, and the result is not the cultivation of the vastest sympathies for long ago and far away, but rather an exclusive interest in themselves. Anna Karenina and Madame Bovary are adulteresses, but the cosmos no longer rebels at their deed. Anna's son today would probably have been awarded to her in the amicable divorce arrangements of the Kareninas. All the romantic novels with their depictions of highly differentiated men and women, their steamy, sublimated sensuality and their insistence on the sacredness of the marriage bond just do not speak to any reality that concerns today's young people. Neither do Romeo and Juliet, who must struggle against parental opposition, Othello and his jealousy, or Miranda's carefully guarded innocence. Saint Augustine, as a seminarian told me, had sexual hang-ups. And let us not speak of the Bible, every *no* in which is now a *yes.* With the possible exception of Oedipus, they are all gone, and they departed in the company of modesty.

When young people today have crushing problems in what used to be called sexual relationships, they cannot trace them back to any moral ambiguity in man's sexual nature. That was, of course, what was erroneously done in the past.

Separateness

Civilization has seemingly led us around full circle, back to the state of nature taught to us by the founding fathers of modern thought. But now it is present not in rhetoric but in reality. Those who first taught the state of nature proposed it as a hypothesis. Liberated from all the conventional attachments to religion, country and family that men actually did have, how would they live and how would they freely reconstruct those attachments? It was an experiment designed to make people recognize what they really care about and engage their loyalties on the basis of this caring. But a young person today, to exaggerate only a little, actually begins *de novo,* without the givens or imperatives that he would have had only yesterday. His country demands little of him and provides well for him, his religion is a matter of absolutely free choice and—this is what is really fresh—so are his sexual involvements. He can now choose, but he finds he no longer has a sufficient motive for choice that is more than whim, that is binding. Reconstruction is proving impossible. . . .

. . . The nation as a community of families is a formula that until recently worked very well in the United States. However, it is very questionable whether this solution is viable over the very long run, because there are two contrary views of nature present here. And, as the political philosophers have always taught, the one that is authoritative in the political regime will ultimately inform its parts. In the social contract view, nature has nothing to say about relationships and rank order; in the older view, which is part and parcel of ancient political philosophy, nature is prescriptive. Are the relations between men and women and parents and children determined by natural impulse or are they the product of choice and consent? In Aristotle's *Politics*, the subpolitical or prepolitical family relations point to the necessity of political rule and are perfected by it, whereas in the state-of-nature teachings, political rule is derived entirely from the need for protection of individuals, bypassing their social relations completely. Are we dealing with political actors or with men and women? In the former case, persons are free to construct whatever relations they please with one another; in the latter, prior to any choice, a preexisting frame largely determines the relations of men and women.

There are three classic images of the polity that clarify this issue. The first is the ship of state, which is one thing if it is to be forever at sea, and quite another if it is to reach port and the passengers go their separate ways. They think about one another and their relationships on the ship very differently in the two cases. The former case is the ancient city; the latter, the modern state. The other two images are the herd and the hive, which oppose each other. The herd may need a shepherd, but each of the animals is grazing for itself and can easily be separated from the herd. In the hive, by contrast, there are workers, drones and a queen; there is a division of labor and a product toward which they all work in common; separation from the hive is extinction. The herd is modern, the hive ancient. Of course, neither image is an accurate description of human society. Men are neither atoms nor parts of a body. But this is why there have to be such images, since for the brutes these things are not a matter for discussion or deliberation. Man is ambiguous. In the tightest communities, at least since the days of Odysseus, there is something in man that wants out and senses that his development is stunted by being just a part of a whole, rather than a whole itself. And in the freest and most independent situations men long for unconditional attachments. The tension between freedom and attachment, and attempts to achieve the impossible union of the two, are the permanent condition of man. But in modern political regimes, where rights precede duties, freedom definitely has primacy over community, family and even nature.

The spirit of this choice must inevitably penetrate into all the details of life. The ambiguity of man is well illustrated in the sexual passion and the sentiments that accompany it. Sex may be treated as a pleasure out of which men and women may make what they will, its promptings followed or rejected, its forms matters of taste, its importance or unimportance in life decided freely by individuals. . . . Or sex can be immediately constitutive of a whole law of life, to which self-preservation is subordinated and in which love, marriage and the rearing of infants is the most important business. It cannot be both. The direction in which we have been going is obvious.

Now, it is not entirely correct to say that mankind at large is able to treat sex as a matter of free choice, one which initially does not obligate us to others. In a world where the natural basis of sexual differentiation has crumbled, this choice is readily available to men, but less so to women. Man in the state of nature, either in the first one or the one we have now, can walk away from a sexual encounter and never give it another thought. But a woman may have a child, and in fact, as becomes ever clearer, may want to have a child. Sex can be an indifferent thing for men, but it really cannot quite be so for women. This is what might be called the female drama. Modernity promised that all human beings would be treated equally. Women took that promise seriously and rebelled against the old order. But as they have succeeded, men have also been liberated from their old constraints. And women, now liberated and with equal careers, nevertheless find they still desire to have children, but have no basis for claiming that men should share their desire for children or assume a responsibility for them. So nature weighs more heavily on women. In the old order they were subordinated and dependent on men; in the new order they are isolated, needing men, but not able to count on them, and hampered in the free development of their individuality. The promise of modernity is not really fulfilled for women.

The decay of the natural ground for the family relationships was largely unanticipated and unprepared for in the early modern thinkers. But they did suggest a certain reform of the family, reflecting the movement away from the constraints of duty, toward reliance on those elements of the family that could be understood to flow out of free expressions of personal sentiment. In Locke, paternal authority is turned into parental authority, a rejection of a father's divine or natural right to rule and to rule permanently, in favor of a father's and a mother's right to care for their children as long as they need care, for the sake of the children's freedom—which the child will immediately recognize, when he reaches majority, to have been for his own benefit. There is nothing left of the reverence toward the father as the symbol of the divine on earth, the unquestioned bearer of authority. Rather, sons and daughters will calculate that they have benefited from their parents' care, which prepared them for the freedom they enjoy, and they will be grateful, although they have no reciprocal duty, except insofar as they wish to leave behind a plausible model for the conduct of their own children toward them. They may, if they please, obey their father in order to inherit his estate, if he has one, which he can dispose of as he pleases. From the point of view of the children, the family retains its validity on the basis of modern principles, and Locke prepares the way for the democratic family, so movingly described by Tocqueville in *Democracy in America*.

So far, so good. The children are reconciled to the family. But the problem, it seems to me, is in the motive of the parents to care for their children. The children can say to their parents: "You are strong, and we are weak. Use your strength to help us. You are rich, and we are poor. Spend your money on us. You are wise, and we are ignorant. Teach us." But why should mother and father want to do so much, involving so much sacrifice without any reward? Perhaps parental care is a duty, or family life has great joys. But neither of these is a conclusive reason when rights and individual autonomy hold sway. The children have unconditional need for and receive unquestionable benefits from the parents; the same cannot be asserted about parents.

Locke believed, and the events of our time seem to confirm his belief, that women have an instinctive attachment to children that cannot be explained as self-interest or calculation. The attachment of mother and child is perhaps the only undeniable natural social bond. It is not always effective, and it can, with effort, be suppressed, but it is always a force. And this is what we see today. But what about the father? Maybe he loves imagining his own eternity through the generations stemming from him. But this is only an act of imagination, one that can be attenuated by other concerns and calculations, as well as by his losing faith in the continuation of his name for very long in the shifting conditions of democracy. Of necessity, therefore, it was understood to be the woman's job to get and hold the man by her charms and wiles because, by nature, nothing else would induce him to give up his freedom in favor of the heavy duties of family. But women no longer wish to do this, and they, with justice, consider it unfair according to the principles governing us. So the cement that bound the family together crumbled. It is not the children who break away; it is the parents who abandon them. Women are no longer willing to make unconditional and perpetual commitments on unequal terms, and, no matter what they hope, nothing can effectively make most men share equally the responsibilities of childbearing and child-rearing. The divorce rate is only the most striking symptom of this breakdown.

None of this results from the sixties, or from the appeal to masculine vanity begun by advertisers in the fifties, or from any other superficial, pop-culture events. More than two hundred years ago Rousseau saw with alarm the seeds of the breakdown of the family in liberal society, and he dedicated much of his genius to trying to correct it. He found that the critical connection between man and woman was being broken by individualism, and focused his efforts, theoretical and practical, on encouraging passionate romantic love in them. He wanted to rebuild and reinforce that connection, previously encumbered by now discredited religious and civil regulation, on modern grounds of desire and consent. He retraced the picture of nature that had become a palimpsest under the abrasion of modern criticism, and he enticed men and women into admiring its teleological ordering, specifically the complementarity between the two sexes, which mesh and set the machine of life in motion, each differing from and needing the other, from the depths of the body to the heights of the soul. He set utter abandon to the sentiments and imaginations of idealized love against calculation of individual interest. Rousseau inspired a whole genre of novelistic and poetic literature that lived feverishly for over a century, coexisting with the writings of the Benthams and the Mills who were earnestly at work homogenizing the sexes. His undertaking had the heaviest significance because human community was at risk. In essence he was persuading women freely to be different from men and to take on the burden of entering a positive contract with the family, as opposed to a negative, individual, self-protective contract with the state. Tocqueville picked up this theme, described the absolute differentiation of husband's and wife's functions and ways of life in the American family, and attributed the success of American democracy to its women, who freely choose their lot. . . .

This whole effort failed and now arouses either women's anger, as an attempt to take from them rights guaranteed to all human beings, or their indifference, as irrelevant in a time when women do exactly the same things as men and face the same difficulties in ensuring their independence. Rousseau, Tocqueville and all the others now have only historical significance and at most provide us with a serious alternative perspective for analyzing our situation. Romantic love is now as alien to us as knight-errantry, and young men are no more likely to court a woman than to wear a suit of armor, not only because it is not fitting, but because it would be offensive to women. As a student exclaimed to me, with approval of his fellows, "What do you expect me to do? Play a guitar under some girl's window?" Such a thing seemed as absurd to him as swallowing goldfish.

But the parents of this same young man, it turned out, were divorced. He strongly, if incoherently, expressed his distress and performed the now ritualistic incantation for roots. Here Rousseau is most helpful, for he honestly exposed the nerve of that incantation, whereas the discussion of roots is an evasion. There is a passage in *Emile*, his educational novel, which keeps coming back to me as I look at my students. It occurs in the context of the teacher's arrangements with the parents of the pupil whose total education he is undertaking, and in the absence of any organic relation between husbands and wives and parents and children after having passed through the solvent of modern theory and practice:

> I would even want the pupil and the governor to regard themselves as so insepa-
> rable that the lot of each in life is always a common object for them. As soon as
> they envisage from afar their separation, as soon as they foresee the moment which
> is going to make them strangers to one another, they are already strangers. Each
> sets up his own little separate system; and both engrossed by the time they will
> no longer be together, stay only reluctantly. *(Emile, p.* 53, ed. Bloom, Basic Books,
> 1979)

That is it. Everyone has "his own little separate system." The aptest description I can find for the state of students' souls is the psychology of separateness.

The possibility of separation is already the fact of separation, inasmuch as people today must plan to be whole and self-sufficient, and cannot risk interdependence. Imagination compels everyone to look forward to the day of separation in order to see how he will do. The energies people should use in the common enterprise are exhausted in preparation for independence. What would, in the case of union, be a building stone becomes a stumbling block on the path to secession. The goals of those who are together naturally and necessarily must become a common good; what one must live with can be accepted. But there is no common good for those who are to separate. The presence of choice already changes the character of relatedness. And the more separation there is, the more there will be. Death of a parent, child, husband, wife or friend is always a possibility and sometimes a fact, but separation is something very different because it is an intentional rebuff to the demand for reciprocity of attachment which is the heart of these relations. People can continue to live while related to the dead beloved; they cannot continue to be related to a living beloved who no longer loves or wishes to be loved. This continual shifting of the sands in our desert—separation from places, persons, beliefs—produces the psychic state of nature where reserve and timidity are the prevailing dispositions. We are social solitaries.

Divorce

The most visible sign of our increasing separateness and, in its turn, the cause of ever greater separateness is divorce. It has a deep influence on our universities because more and more of the students are products of it, and they not only have problems themselves but also affect other students and the general atmosphere. Divorce in America is the most palpable indication that people are not made to live together, and that, although they want and need to create a general will out of the particular wills, those particular wills constantly reassert themselves. There is a quest, but ever more hopeless, for arrangements and ways of putting the broken pieces back together. The task is equivalent to squaring the circle, because everyone loves himself most but wants others to love him more than they love themselves. Such is particularly the demand of children, against which parents are now rebelling. In the absence of a common good or common object, as Rousseau puts it, the disintegration of society into particular wills is inevitable. Selfishness in this case is not a moral vice or a sin but a natural necessity. The "Me generation" and "narcissism" are merely descriptions, not causes. The solitary savage in the state of nature cannot be blamed for thinking primarily of himself, nor can a person who lives in a world where the primacy of self-concern is only too evident in the most fundamental institutions, where the original selfishness of the state of nature remains, where concern for the common good is hypocritical, and where morality seems to be squarely on the side of selfishness. Or, to put it otherwise, the concern with self-development, self-expression, or growth, which flourished as a result of the optimistic faith in a preestablished harmony between such a concern and society or community, has gradually revealed itself to be inimical to community. A young person's qualified or conditional attachment to divorced parents merely reciprocates what he necessarily sees as their conditional attachment to him, and is entirely different from the classic problem of loyalty to families, or other institutions, which were clearly dedicated to their members. In the past, such breaking away was sometimes necessary but always morally problematic. Today it is normal, and this is another reason why the classic literature is alien to so many of our young, for it is largely concerned with liberation from real claims—like family, faith, or country—whereas now the movement is in the opposite direction, a search for claims on oneself that have some validity. Children who have gone to the school of conditional relationships should be expected to view the world in the light of what they learned there.

Children may be told over and over again that their parents have a right to their own lives, that they will enjoy quality time instead of quantity time, that they are really loved by their parents even after divorce, but children do not believe any of this. They think they have a right to total attention and believe their parents must live for them. There is no explaining otherwise to them, and anything less inevitably produces indignation and an inextirpable sense of injustice. To children, the voluntary separation of parents seems worse than their death precisely because it is voluntary. The capriciousness of wills, their lack of directedness to the common good, the fact that they could be otherwise but are not—these are the real source of the war of all against all. Children learn a fear of enslavement to the wills of others, along with a need to dominate those wills, in the context of the family, the one place where they are supposed to learn the opposite. Of course, many families are unhappy. But that is irrelevant. The important lesson that the family taught was the existence of the only unbreakable bond, for better or for worse, between human beings. . . .

A university teacher of liberal arts cannot help confronting special handicaps, a slight deformity of the spirit, in the students, ever more numerous, whose parents are divorced. I do not have the slightest doubt that they do as well as others in all kinds of specialized subjects, but I find they are not as open to the serious study of philosophy and literature as some other students are. I would guess this is because they are less eager to look into the meaning of their lives, or to risk shaking their received opinions. In order to live with the chaos of their experience, they tend to have rigid frameworks about what is right and wrong and how they ought to live. They are full of desperate platitudes about self-determination, respect for other people's rights and decisions, the need to work out one's individual values and commitments, etc. All this is a thin veneer over boundless seas of rage, doubt and fear.

Young people habitually are able to jettison their habits of belief for an exciting idea. They have little to lose. Although this is not really philosophy, because they are not aware of how high the stakes are, in this period of their lives they can experiment with the unconventional and acquire deeper habits of belief and some learning to go along with them. But children of divorced parents often lack this intellectual daring because they lack the natural youthful confidence in the future. Fear of both isolation and attachment clouds their prospects. A large measure of their enthusiasm has been extinguished and replaced by self-protectiveness. Similarly, their open confidence in friendship as part of the newly discovered search for the good is somewhat stunted. The . . . *eros* for the discovery of nature has suffered more damage in them than in most. Such students can make their disarray in the cosmos the theme of their reflection and study. But it is a grim and dangerous business, and more than any students I have known, they evoke pity. They are indeed victims.

An additional factor in the state of these students' souls is the fact that they have undergone therapy. They have been told how to feel and what to think about themselves by psychologists who are paid by their parents to make everything work out as painlessly as possible for the parents, as part of no-fault divorce. . . . [P]sychologists provide much of the ideology justifying divorce— e.g., that it is worse for kids to stay in stressful homes (thus motivating the potential escapees—that is, the parents—to make it as unpleasant as possible there). Psychologists are the sworn enemies of guilt. And they have an artificial language for the artificial feelings with which they equip children. But it unfortunately does not permit such children to get a firm grip on anything. Of course, not every psychologist who deals with these matters simply plays the tune called by those who pay the piper, but the givens of the market and the capacity for self-deception, called creativity, surely influence such therapy. After all, parents can shop around for a psychologist just as some Catholics used to shop for a confessor. When these students arrive at the university, they are not only reeling from the destructive effects of the overturning of faith and the ambiguity of loyalty that result from divorce, but deafened by self-serving lies and hypocrisies expressed in a pseudoscientific jargon. . . . They do not have confidence in what they feel or what they see, and they have an ideology that provides not a reason but a rationalization for their timidity.

These students are the symbols of the intellectual-political problems of our time. They represent in extreme form the spiritual vortex set in motion by loss of contact with other human beings and with the natural order. But all students are affected, in the most practical everyday way, unaware that their situation is peculiar, because their education does not give them perspective on it.

Love

The best point of entry into the very special world inhabited by today's students is the astonishing fact that they usually do not, in what were once called love affairs, say, "I love you," and never, "I'll always love you." One student told me that, of course, he says "I love you," to girlfriends, "when we are breaking up." It is the clean and easy break—no damage, no fault—at which they are adept. This is understood to be morality, respect for other persons' freedom.

Perhaps young people do not say "I love you" because they are honest. They do not experience love—too familiar with sex to confuse it with love, too preoccupied with their own fates to be victimized by love's mad self-forgetting, the last of the genuine fanaticisms. Then there is distaste for love's fatal historical baggage—sex roles, making women into possessions and objects without respect for their self-determination. Young people today are afraid of making commitments, and the point is that love *is* commitment, and much more. Commitment is a word invented in our abstract modernity to signify the absence of any real motives in the soul for moral dedication. Commitment is gratuitous, motiveless, because the real passions are all low and selfish. One may be sexually attracted, but that does not, so people think, provide any sufficient motive for real and lasting concern for another. Young people, and not only young people, have studied and practiced a crippled *eros* that can no longer take wing, and does not contain within it the longing for eternity and the divination of one's relatedness to being. They are practical Kantians: whatever is tainted with lust or pleasure cannot be moral. However, they have not discovered the pure morality. It remains an empty category used to discredit all substantial inclinations that were once moralizing. Too much emphasis on authenticity has made it impossible to trust one's instincts, and too much seriousness about sex has made it impossible to take sex seriously. Young men and women distrust eroticism too much to think it a sufficient pointer toward a way of life. The burdens implied in and blessed by eros are only burdens without it. It is not cowardice to avoid taking on responsibilities that have no charm even in anticipation.

When marriage occurs it does not usually seem to result from a decision and a conscious will to take on its responsibilities. The couple have lived together for a long time, and by an almost imperceptible process, they find themselves married, as much out of convenience as passion, as much negatively as positively (not really expecting to do much better, since they have looked around and seen how imperfect all fits seem to be). Among the educated, marriage these days seems to be best acquired, as Macaulay said about the British Empire, in a fit of absence of mind.

Part of the inability to make sexual commitments results from an ideology of the feelings. Young people are always telling me such reasonable things about jealousy and possessiveness and even their dreams about the future. But as to dreams about the future with a partner, they have none. That would be to impose a rigid, authoritarian pattern on the future, which should emerge spontaneously. This means they can foresee no future, or that the one they would naturally foresee is forbidden them by current piety, as sexist. Similarly, why should a man or a woman be jealous if his or her partner has sexual relations with someone else? A serious person today does not want to force the feelings of others. The same goes for possessiveness. When I hear such things, all so sensible and in harmony with a liberal society, I feel that I am in the presence of robots. This ideology only works for people who have had no experience of the feelings, have never loved, have abstracted from the texture of life. These prodigies of reason need never fear Othello's fate. Kill for love! What can that mean? It may very well be that their *apatheia is* a suppression of feeling, anxiety about getting hurt. But it might also be the real thing. People may, having digested the incompatibility of ends, have developed a new kind of soul. None of the sexual possibilities students have actualized was unknown to me. But their lack of passion, of hope, of despair, of a sense of the twinship of love and death, is incomprehensible to me. When I see a young couple who have lived together throughout their college years leave each other with a handshake and move out into life, I am struck dumb.

Students do not date anymore. Dating was the petrified skeleton of courtship. They live in herds or packs with no more sexual differentiation than any herds have when not in heat. Human beings can, of course, engage in sexual intercourse at any time. But today there are none of the conventions invented by civilization to take the place of heat, to guide mating, and perhaps to channel it. Nobody is sure who is to make the advances, whether there are to be a pursuer and a pursued, what the event is to mean. They have to improvise, for roles are banned, and a man pays a high price for misjudging his partner's attitude. The act takes place but it does not separate the couple from the flock, to which they immediately return as they were before, undifferentiated.

It is easier for men to get gratification than it used to be, and many men have the advantage of being pursued. Certainly they do not have to make all kinds of efforts and pay all kinds of attention, as men once did. There is an easy familiarity. But at least some of these advantages for men are offset by nervousness about their sexual performance. In the past a man could think he was doing a wonderful thing for a woman, and expect to be admired for what he brought. But that was before he could be pretty sure that he was being compared and judged, which is daunting. And certain aspects of the undeniably male biology sometimes make it difficult for him to perform and cause him to prefer being the one to express the desire.

Women are still pleased by their freedom and their capacity to chart an independent course for themselves. But they frequently suspect that they are being used, that in the long run they may need men more than men need them, and that they cannot expect much from the feckless contemporary male. They despise what men used to think women had to offer (that is partly why it is now offered so freely), but they are dogged by doubt whether men are very impressed by what they are now offering instead. Distrust suffuses the apparently easy commerce between the sexes. There is an awful lot of breaking up, surely disagreeable, though nothing earthshaking. Exam time is a great moment for students to separate. They are under too much stress and too busy to put up with much trouble from a relationship.

"Relationships," not love affairs, are what they have. Love suggests something wonderful, exciting, positive and firmly seated in the passions. A relationship is gray, amorphous, suggestive of a project, without a given content, and tentative. You work at a relationship, whereas love takes care of itself. In a relationship the difficulties come first, and there is a search for common grounds. Love presents illusions of perfection to the imagination and is forgetful of all the natural fissures in human connection. About relationships there is ceaseless anxious talk, the kind one cannot help overhearing in student hangouts or restaurants frequented by men and women who are "involved" with one another, the kind of obsessive prattle so marvelously captured in old Nichols and May routines or Woody Allen films. In one Nichols and May bit, a couple who have just slept together for the first time, assert with all the emptiness of doubt, "We are going to have a *Relationship*." This insight was typical of the University of Chicago in the fifties, of *The Lonely Crowd*. The only mistake was to encourage the belief that by becoming more "inner-directed," going farther down the path of the isolated self, people will be less lonely. The problem, however, is not that people are not authentic enough, but that they have no common object, no common good, no natural complementarity. Selves, of course, have no relation to anything but themselves, and this is why "communication" is their problem. Gregariousness, like that of the animals in the herd, is admitted by all. Grazing together side by side and rubbing against one another are the given, but there is a desire and a necessity to have something more, to make the transition from the herd to the hive, where there is real interconnection. Hence, the hive—community, roots, extended family—is much praised, but no one is willing to transform his indeterminate self into an all too determinate worker, drone or queen, to submit to the rank-ordering and division of labor necessary to any whole that is more than just a heap of discrete parts. Selves want to be wholes, but have lately also taken to longing to be parts. This is the reason why conversation about relationships remains so vacuous, abstract and unprogrammatic, with its whole content stored in a bottle labeled "commitment." It is also why there is so much talk about phenomena like "bonding." In the absence of any connectedness in their souls, human beings seek reassurance in fruitless analogy to mechanisms found in brutes. But this will not work because human attachment always has an element of deliberate choice, denied by such analogy. One need only compare the countless novels and movies about male bonding with Aristotle's discussion of friendship in the *Ethics*. Friendship, like its related phenomenon, love, is no longer within our ken because both require notions of soul and nature that, for a mixture of theoretical and political reasons, we cannot even consider.

The reliance on relationships is a self-delusion because it is founded on an inner contradiction. Relations between the sexes have always been difficult, and that is why so much of our literature is about men and women quarreling. There is certainly legitimate ground to doubt their suitability for each other given the spectrum—from the harem to Plato's *Republic*—of imaginable and actually existing relations between them, whether nature acted the stepmother or God botched the creation by an afterthought, as some Romantics believed. That man is not made to be alone is all very well, but who is made to live with him? This is why men and women hesitated before marriage, and courtship was thought necessary to find out whether the couple was compatible, and perhaps to give them basic training in compatibility. No one wanted to be stuck forever with an impossible partner. But, for all that, they knew pretty much what they wanted from one another. The question was whether they could get it (whereas our question today is much more what is wanted). A man was to make a living and protect his wife and children, and a woman was to provide for the domestic economy, particularly in caring for husband and children. Frequently this did not work out very well for one or both of the partners, because they either were not good at their functions or were not eager to perform them. In order to assure the proper ordering of things, the transvestite women in Shakespeare, like Portia and Rosalind, are forced to masquerade as men because the real men are inadequate and need to be corrected. This happens only in comedies; when there are no such intrepid women, the situation turns into tragedy. But the assumption of male garb observes the proprieties or conventions. Men should be doing what the impersonating women are doing; and when the women have set things right, they become women again and submit to the men, albeit with a tactful, ironical consciousness that they are at least partially playacting in order to preserve a viable order. The arrangement implicit in marriage, even if it is only conventional, tells those who enter into it what to expect and what the satisfactions are supposed to be. Very simply, the family is a sort of miniature body politic in which the husband's will is the will of the whole. The woman can influence her husband's will, and it is supposed to be informed by love of wife and children.

Now all of this has simply disintegrated. It does not exist, nor is it considered good that it should. But nothing certain has taken its place. Neither men nor women have any idea what they are getting into anymore, or, rather, they have reason to fear the worst. There are two equal wills, and no mediating principle to link them and no tribunal of last resort. What is more, neither of the wills is certain of itself. This is where the "ordering of priorities" comes in, particularly with women, who have not yet decided which comes first, career or children. People are no longer raised to think they ought to regard marriage as the primary goal and responsibility, and their uncertainty is mightily reinforced by the divorce statistics, which imply that putting all of one's psychological eggs in the marriage basket is a poor risk. The goals and wills of men and women have become like parallel lines, and it requires a Lobachevskyan imagination to hope they may meet.

The inharmoniousness of final ends finds its most concrete expression in the female career, which is now precisely the same as the male career. There are two equal careers in almost every household composed of educated persons under thirty-five. And those careers are not mere means to family ends. They are personal fulfillments. In this nomadic country it is more than likely that one of the partners will be forced, or have the opportunity, to take a job in a city other than the one where his or her spouse works. What to do? They can stay together with one partner sacrificing his career to the other, they can commute, or they can separate. None of these solutions is satisfactory. More important, what is going to happen is unpredictable. Is it the marriage or the career that will count most? Women's careers today are qualitatively different from what they were up to twenty years ago, and such conflict is now inevitable. The result is that both marriage and career are devalued.

For a long time middle-class women, with the encouragement of their husbands, had been pursuing careers. It was thought they had a right to cultivate their higher talents instead of being household drudges. Implicit in this was, of course, the view that the bourgeois professions indeed offered an opportunity to fulfill the human potential, while family and particularly the woman's work involved in it were merely in the realm of necessity, limited and limiting. Serious men of good conscience believed that they must allow their wives to develop themselves. But, with rare exceptions, both parties still took it for granted that the family was the woman's responsibility and that, in the case of potential conflict, she would subordinate or give up her career. It was not quite serious, and she usually knew it. This arrangement was ultimately untenable, and it was clear in which way the balance would tip. Couples agreed that the household was not spiritually fulfilling for women and that women have equal rights. The notion of a domestic life appropriate to women had become incredible. Why should not women take their careers as seriously as men take theirs, and have them be taken as seriously by men? Terrific resentment at the injustice done to women under the prevailing understanding of justice found its expression in demands seen as perfectly legitimate by both men and women, that men weaken the attachment to their careers, that they share equally in the household and the care of the children. Women's abandonment of the female persona was reinforced by the persona's abandoning them. Economic changes made it desirable and necessary that women work; lowering of infant mortality rates meant that women had to have fewer pregnancies; greater longevity and better health meant that women devoted a much smaller portion of their lives to having and rearing children; and the altered relationships within the family meant that they were less likely to find continuing occupation with their children and their children's children. At forty-five they were finding themselves with nothing to do, and forty more years to do it in. Their formative career years had been lost, and they were, hence, unable to compete with men. A woman who now wanted to be a woman in the old sense would find it very difficult to do so, even if she were to brave the hostile public opinion. In all of these ways the feminist case is very strong indeed. But, though the terms of marriage had been radically altered, no new ones were defined.

The feminist response that justice requires equal sharing of all domestic responsibility by men and women is not a solution, but only a compromise, an attenuation of men's dedication to their careers and of women's to family, with arguably an enrichment in diversity of both parties but just as arguably a fragmentation of their lives. The question of who goes with whom in the case of jobs in different cities is unresolved and is, whatever may be said about it, a festering sore, a source of suspicion and resentment, and the potential for war. Moreover, this compromise does not decide anything about the care of the children. Are both parents going to care more about their careers than about the children? Previously children at least had the unqualified dedication of one person, the woman, for whom their care was the most important thing in life. Is half the attention of two the same as the whole attention of one? Is this not a formula for neglecting children? Under such arrangements the family is not a unity, and marriage is an unattractive struggle that is easy to get out of, especially for men.

And here is where the whole business turns nasty. The souls of men—their ambitious, warlike, protective, possessive character—must be dismantled in order to liberate women from their domination. Machismo—the polemical description of maleness or spiritedness, which was the central *natural* passion in men's souls in the psychology of the ancients, the passion of attachment and loyalty—was the villain, the source of the difference between the sexes. The feminists were only completing a job begun by Hobbes in his project of taming the harsh elements in the soul. With machismo discredited, the positive task is to make men caring, sensitive, even nurturing, to fit the restructured family. Thus once again men must be re-educated according to an abstract project. They must accept the "feminine elements" in their nature. A host of Dustin Hoffman and Meryl Streep types invade the schools, popular psychology, TV and the movies, making the project respectable. Men tend to undergo this re-education somewhat sullenly but studiously, in order to avoid the opprobrium of the sexist label and to keep peace with their wives and girlfriends. And it is indeed possible to soften men. But to make them "care" is another thing, and the project must inevitably fail.

It must fail because in an age of individualism, persons of either sex cannot be forced to be public-spirited, particularly by those who are becoming less so. Further, caring is either a passion or a virtue, not a description like "sensitive." A virtue governs a passion, as moderation governs lust, or courage governs fear. But what passion does caring govern? One might say possessiveness, but possessiveness is not to be governed these days—it is to be rooted out. What is wanted is an antidote to natural selfishness, but wishes do not give birth to horses, however much abstract moralism may demand them. The old moral order, however imperfect it may have been, at least moved toward the virtues by way of the passions. If men were self-concerned, that order tried to expand the scope of self-concern to include others, rather than commanding men to cease being concerned with themselves. . . . In family questions, inasmuch as men were understood to be so strongly motivated by property, an older wisdom tried to attach concern for the family to that motive: the man was allowed and encouraged to regard his family as his property, so he would care for the former as he would instinctively care for the latter. This was effective, although it obviously had disadvantages from the point of view of justice. When wives and children come to the husband and father and say, "We are not your property; we are ends in ourselves and demand to be treated as such," the anonymous observer cannot help being impressed. But the difficulty comes when wives and children further demand that the man continue to care for them as before, just when they are giving an example of caring for themselves. They object to the father's flawed motive and ask that it be miraculously replaced by a pure one, of which they wish to make use for their own ends. The father will almost inevitably constrict his quest for property, cease being a father and become a mere man again, rather than turning into a providential God, as others ask him to be. What is so intolerable about the *Republic*, as Plato shows, is the demand that men give up their land, their money, their wives, their children, for the sake of the public good, their concern for which had previously been buttressed by these lower attachments. The hope is to have a happy city made up entirely of unhappy men. Similar demands are made today in an age of slack morality and self-indulgence. Plato taught that, however laudable justice may be, one cannot expect prodigies of virtue from ordinary people. Better a real city tainted by selfish motives than one that cannot exist, except in speech, and that promotes real tyranny.

I am not arguing here that the old family arrangements were good or that we should or could go back to them. I am only insisting that we not cloud our vision to such an extent that we believe that there are viable substitutes for them just because we want or need them. The peculiar attachment of mothers for their children existed, and in some degree still exists, whether it was the product of nature or nurture. That fathers should have exactly the same kind of attachment is much less evident. We can insist on it, but if nature does not cooperate, all our efforts will have been in vain. Biology forces women to take maternity leaves. Law can enjoin men to take paternity leaves, but it cannot make them have the desired sentiments. Only the rankest ideologue could fail to see the difference between the two kinds of leave, and the contrived and somewhat ridiculous character of the latter. Law may prescribe that the male nipples be made equal to the female ones, but they still will not give milk. Female attachment to children is to be at least partly replaced with promissory notes on male attachment. Will they be redeemed? Or won't everyone set up his own little separate psychological banking system?

Similarly, women, due to the unreliability of men, have had to provide the means for their own independence. This has simply given men the excuse for being even less concerned with women's well-being. A dependent, weak woman is indeed vulnerable and puts herself at men's mercy. But that appeal did influence a lot of men a lot of the time. The cure now prescribed for male irresponsibility is to make them more irresponsible. And a woman who can be independent of men has much less motive to entice a man into taking care of her and her children. In the same vein, I heard a female lieutenant-colonel on the radio explaining that the only thing standing in the way of woman's full equality in the military is male protectiveness. So, do away with it! Yet male protectiveness, based on masculine pride, and desire to gain the glory for defending a blushing woman's honor and life, was a form of relatedness, as well as a way of sublimating selfishness. These days, why should a man risk his life protecting a karate champion who knows just what part of the male anatomy to go after in defending herself? What substitute is there for the forms of relatedness that are dismantled in the name of the new justice?

All our reforms have helped strip the teeth of our gears, which can therefore no longer mesh. They spin idly, side by side, unable to set the social machine in motion. It is at this exercise in futility that young people must look when thinking about their future. Women are pleased by their successes, their new opportunities, their agenda, their moral superiority. But underneath everything lies the more or less conscious awareness that they are still dual beings by nature, capable of doing most things men do and also wanting to have children. They may hope otherwise, but they fully expect to pursue careers, to have to pursue careers, while caring for children alone. And what they expect and plan for is likely to happen. The men have none of the current ideological advantages of the women, but they can opt out without too much cost. In their relations with women they have little to say; convinced of the injustice of the old order, for which they were responsible, and practically incapable of changing the direction of the juggernaut, they wait to hear what is wanted, try to adjust but are ready to take off in an instant. They want relationships, but the situation is so unclear. They anticipate a huge investment of emotional energy that is just as likely as not to end in bankruptcy, to a sacrifice of their career goals without any clarity about what reward they will reap, other than a vague togetherness. Meanwhile, one of the strongest, oldest motives for marriage is no longer operative. Men can now easily enjoy the sex that previously could only be had in marriage. It is strange that the tiredest and stupidest bromide mothers and fathers preached to their daughters—"He won't respect you or marry you if you give him what he wants too easily"—turns out to be the truest and most probing analysis of the current situation. Women can say they do not care, that they want men to have the right motives or none at all, but everyone, and they best of all, knows that they are being, at most, only half truthful with themselves.

Eros

This is the campus sexual scene. Relativism in theory and lack of related-ness in practice make students unable to think about or look into their futures, and they shrivel up within the confines of the present and material *I*. They are willing to mutter the prescribed catechism, the substitute for thought, which promises them salvation, but there is little faith. As a very intelligent student said to me, "We are all obsessively going to the well, but we always come up dry." The rhetoric of the campus gays only confirms this. After all the demands and the complaints against the existing order—"Don't discriminate against us; don't legislate morality; don't put a policeman in every bedroom; respect our orientation"—they fall back into the empty talk about finding life-styles. There is not, and cannot be, anything more specific. All relationships have been ho-mogenized in their indeterminacy.

The eroticism of our students is lame. It is not the divine madness Socrates praised; or the enticing awareness of incompleteness and the quest to overcome it; or nature's grace, which permits a partial being to recover his wholeness in the embrace of another, or a temporal being to long for eternity in the perpe-tuity of his seed; or the hope that all men will remember his deeds; or his con-templation of perfection. Eroticism is a discomfort, but one that in itself prom-ises relief and affirms the goodness of things. It is the proof, subjective but incontrovertible, of man's relatedness, imperfect though it may be, to others and to the whole of nature. Wonder, the source of both poetry and philosophy, is its characteristic expression. Eros demands daring from its votaries and pro-vides a good reason for it. This longing for completeness is the longing for edu-cation, and the study of it is education. Socrates' knowledge of ignorance is identical with his perfect knowledge of erotics. The longing for his conversa-tions with which he infected his companions, and which was intensified after his death and has endured throughout the centuries, proved him to have been both the neediest and most grasping of lovers, and the richest and most giving of beloveds. The sex lives of our students and their reflection on them disarm such longing and make it incomprehensible to them. Reduction has robbed eros of its divinatory powers. Because they do not trust it, students have no reverence for themselves. There is almost no remaining link visible to them between what they learn in sex education and Plato's *Symposium*.

Yet only from such dangerous heights can our situation be seen in proper perspective. The fact that this perspective is no longer credible is the measure of our crisis. When we recognize the *Phaedrus* and the *Symposium* as inter-preting our experiences, we can be sure that we are having those experiences in their fullness, and that we have the minimum of education. Rousseau, the founder of the most potent of reductionist teachings about eros, said that the

Symposium is always the book of lovers. Are we lovers anymore? This is my way of putting the educational question of our times.

In all species other than man, when an animal reaches puberty, it is all that it will ever be. This stage is the clear end toward which all of its growth and learning is directed. The animal's activity is reproduction. It lives on this plateau until it starts downhill. Only in man is puberty just the beginning. The greater and more interesting part of his learning, moral and intellectual, comes afterward, and in civilized man is incorporated into his erotic desire. His taste and hence his choices are determined during this "sentimental education." It is as though his learning were for the sake of his sexuality. Reciprocally, much of the energy for that learning obviously comes from his sexuality. Nobody takes human children who have reached puberty to be adults. We properly sense that there is a long road to adulthood, the condition in which they are able to govern themselves and be true mothers and fathers. This road is the serious part of education, where animal sexuality becomes human sexuality, where instinct gives way in man to choice with regard to the true, the good and the beautiful. Puberty does not provide man, as it does other animals, with all that he needs to leave behind others of his kind. This means that the animal part of his sexuality is intertwined in the most complex way with the higher reaches of his soul, which must inform the desires with its insight, and that the most delicate part of education is to keep the two in harmony.

I cannot pretend that I understand very much of this mystery, but knowing that I do not know keeps me attentive to, and far from the current simplifications of, the phenomena of this aspect of our nature that links the highest and the lowest in us. I believe that the most interesting students are those who have not settled the sexual problem, who are still young, even look young for their age, who think there is much to look forward to and much they must yet grow up to, fresh and naive, excited by the mysteries to which they have not yet been fully initiated. There are some who are men and women at the age of sixteen, who have nothing more to learn about the erotic. They are adult in the sense that they will no longer change very much. They may become competent specialists, but they are flat-souled. The world is for them what it presents itself to the senses to be; it is unadorned by imagination and devoid of ideals. This flat soul is what the sexual wisdom of our time conspires to make universal.

The easy sex of teen-agers snips the golden thread linking eros to education. And popularized Freud finishes it for good by putting the seal of science on an unerotic understanding of sex. A youngster whose sexual longings consciously or unconsciously inform his studies has a very different set of experiences from one in whom such motives are not active. A trip to Florence or to Athens is one thing for a young man who hopes to meet his Beatrice on the

Ponte Santa Trinita or his Socrates in the Agora, and quite another for one who goes without such aching need. The latter is only a tourist, the former is looking for completion. . . .

The student who made fun of playing the guitar under a girl's window will never read or write poetry under her influence. His defective eros cannot provide his soul with images of the beautiful, and it will remain coarse and slack. It is not that he will fail to adorn or idealize the world; it is that he will not see what is there. . . .

Blankenhorn, "I Do?"

David Blankenhorn (born in 1955) is President of the Institute for American Values, an institute he founded in response to his concern for the condition of marriage and family life in America, and author of Fatherless America. *In this column of opinion, written in 1997, Blankenhorn describes two recent changes in marriage ceremonies which he regards as both symptoms and causes of the current weakness in the institution of marriage. Later in this anthology (in the section "Why a Wedding? The Promises of Marriage") readers will find some examples of traditional and contemporary vows and will be able to decide for themselves whether Blankenhorn's diagnoses are sound.*

To understand why the United States has the highest divorce rate in the world, go to some weddings and listen to what the brides and grooms say. In particular, listen to the vows: the words of mutual promise exchanged by couples during the marriage ceremony. To a remarkable degree, marriage in America today is exactly what these newlyweds increasingly say that it is: a loving relationship of undetermined duration created of the couple, by the couple, and for the couple.

Our tendency may be to shrug off the significance of formal marriage vows, viewing them as purely ceremonial, without much impact on the "real" marriage. Yet believing that the vow is only some words is similar to believing that the marriage certificate is only a piece of paper. Both views are technically true, but profoundly false. Either, when believed by the marrying couple, is probably a sign of a marriage off to a bad start.

In fact, the marriage vow is deeply connected to the marriage relationship. The vow helps the couple to name and fashion their marriage's innermost meaning. The vow is foundational: the couple's first and most formal effort to define, and therefore understand, exactly what their marriage is.

. . . As much as shared interests, or good communications skills, or even erotic attraction or feelings of true love, it is the content and the integrity of the dedicating promise itself—what we say and mean when we say "I do"—that shapes the nature and destiny of the marriage.

In recent years, two basic innovations have transformed the marriage vow in the United States. Both innovations are particularly widespread in both mainline and evangelical Protestant churches, in which about half of all U.S. marriages occur.

First, as Barbara Dafoe Whitehead points out in *The Divorce Culture*, marriage vows today commonly downplay or avoid altogether any pledge of marital permanence. The old vow was "till death us do part" or "so long as we both shall live." Most new vows simply leave the question of marital duration unasked and unanswered, as if the issue were either irrelevant or beyond knowing. Other new vows incorporate hopeful but qualified phrases such as "as long as love lasts."

Either way, the underlying philosophy is the same. To pledge marital permanence would be to make a false guarantee. We are in love today, but the future is something that should not or cannot be promised. How long will our love last? We hope forever, but only time will tell. As one bride puts it in a recent book called *Creative Weddings:* "It was important for me not to make promises or to predict the future, but to make intentions and commitments. . . . We avoided using words like 'forever,' but focused on what was honest for the moment and nothing more than that."

The second change is more subtle, but far more profound. Today, growing numbers of couples—perhaps most couples—compose their own vows. My wife and I did in 1986; most couples we know did. I cannot find data to verify the dimensions of this trend, but my sense is that, principally excepting Orthodox Jewish and most Catholic weddings, self-composed vows are more the rule than the exception among newlyweds today. As one wedding book flatly asserts: "The majority of brides and grooms these days are rejecting traditional wedding vows and reciting their own personalized vows instead."

One wedding book by Steven Neel, an ordained minister, advises couples that "Your wedding ceremony can be highly distinctive and individualized if you use your imagination to personalize your expression of love and commitment." Consequently, Neel urges couples today to "accept the challenge of writing your own vows" which "contain the unique expression of your feeling."

It would be hard to exaggerate the symbolic importance of this shift toward self-composed vows. The old vows were created by society and presented to the couple, signifying the goal of conforming the couple to marriage. The new vows are created by the couple and presented to society, signifying the goal of conforming marriage to the couple. The two approaches reflect strikingly divergent views of marriage and of reality itself.

In one view, the vow is prior to the couple. The vow exists on its own, exerting social and sacred authority that is independent of the couple. In this sense, the vow helps to create the couple. For in making the same promise that others before them have made, and that others after them will make, the couple vows on their wedding day to become accountable to an ideal of marriage that is outside of them and bigger than they are.

In the new view, the couple is prior to the promise. The vow is not an external reality, like gravity or the weather, but instead a subjective projection, deriving its meaning solely from the couple. From this perspective, the couple approaches the vow like a painter approaches a canvas. Rather than the vow creating the couple, the couple creates the vow. As a result, each marriage becomes unique, like a painting or a snowflake.

With this one procedural change in the making and exchanging of vows, a ceremony of continuity and idealized forms is displaced by a ceremony of creativity and personal expression. Subject and object trade places. Theologically, the transcendent becomes mundane as couples, in effect, become the gods of their own marriages. A reality in which the marriage is larger than the couple is replaced by a reality in which the couple is larger than the marriage.

Of course, many of the motivating ideas behind the new vows are understandable and even admirable. Couples want to avoid hypocrisy. They want the ceremony to be dramatic and personally meaningful. In part, the new vows represent a practical response to the growing phenomenon of mixed-tradition marriages.

But the essence of this change reflects a dramatic shrinking of our idea of marriage. With the new vows, the robust expectation of marital permanence shrinks to a frail, often unstated hope. Marriage as a vital communal institution shrinks to marriage as a purely private relationship. Marriage as something that defines me shrinks to something that I define.

Finally, as the idea of marriage gets weaker, so does the reality. In this sense, the new vows are important philosophical authorizations for our divorce culture. They are both minor causes and revealing results of a society in which marriage as an institution is decomposing before our eyes.

B. WHY MARRY?
DEFENSES OF MATRIMONY

In most times and places, and in American society until what seems like only yesterday, neither the necessity nor the desirability of marriage was a matter of major cultural debate. Some individuals faced the question "Why marry?" explicitly, but for most people, and for the culture as a whole, marriage was sanctioned and its goodness taken for granted. Most people did as their parents did: they married. Today, because we live under circumstances in which everything is seemingly open to question and is, indeed, articulated as a question— the true meaning of the well-known Chinese curse, "May you live in interesting times"—we have no agreed-upon tacit answer. "Why marry?" is no longer a question for the few; it is now a question for the culture as a whole.

Today, it is marriage, rather than the single life, that is on the defensive. Men, who in past ages were generally more in need of persuasion and cajoling than women, are fearful of financial burdens, emotional commitment, and loss of freedom; especially under our new conditions of easy sex, many are less likely than before to want to accept the sexual restrictions demanded by monogamous marriage. Women, though generally more eager than men for "commitment" and lasting intimacy, worry today about loss of independence, and they fear that marriage may mean submitting to inequality and "patriarchy"; especially under our new conditions of equal opportunity for women, many are concerned about what getting married will mean for their career. Also, to the extent that both men and women now view relations between the sexes in terms of power, they will both be suspicious of genuine partnership; to the extent that they regard themselves as self-contained or amorphous selves, they will be hesitant about promising lasting love or fidelity. Among both sexes, as in the past, the more adventurous and unconventional types often look on marriage as too limiting, mundane, or stifling, as boring, burdensome, or too bourgeois. Now even very conventional men and women are echoing their objections and using them as reasons not to marry.

Though "Why Marry?" has only recently become more of a question for more people, it is, in fact, a very old question. Marriage has long had its rivals and its critics, and past ages have often seen the need to make arguments in favor of marriage, especially to its men. Arguments have been offered over the centuries defending and extolling marriage against the alternatives: pederasty and homosexual love; the competing lives of soldiering and politics, or of philosophy and the arts; celibacy and the religious vocation; or the simple pleasures of the carefree single life. The readings collected in this section contain some of those arguments. It is noteworthy that the reasons offered are multiple, and they do not always agree.

Marriage has been variously defended as good for the community and good for oneself. Communities have seen marriage as a means of containing sexual impulses, of domesticating unruly males, of protecting and providing for women and their children, of nurturing and civilizing the next generation, of giving people a stake in the community and a higher purpose in life, and of putting people on a path toward holiness. Recent arguments by sociobiologists have reinforced, on evolutionary and biological grounds, traditional insights about the differences between female and male attachments to offspring, and the usefulness of marriage as a means of enlisting males in the care of children. In those (more traditional) communities in which people regard themselves primarily in terms of the collective, rather than as autonomous individuals, arguments for marriage appealing to duty and obligation—to the name of the ancestors, to the next generation, to the community, to one's tradition, or to God—have been efficaciously advanced. "Be fruitful and multiply" was God's first injunction to humankind: that it had to be commanded implies that unlike, say, eating and sleeping, human beings may harbor some self-interested resistances to making way for the next generation, resistances that manifest themselves openly in less communitarian times and places.

In modern liberal secular society, with its high premium on freedom and the pursuit of happiness, marriage may remain even more socially important than ever, a brake against run-away individualism. But arguments in its favor can no longer be successfully made in terms of duty. They must now be made increasingly in terms of its benefits for the individuals who marry. To raise one's social status, to gain economic security, and to have a home of one's own, once important individual reasons to marry (especially for women), remain motives for some, as is the desire for children. But for more and more people, the decisive standards are more narrowly personal and psychic. One must be able to see that marriage is good for self-fulfillment, erotic satisfaction, or personal happiness. Or one must be able to see in marriage the possibilities for friendship: avoiding loneliness, sharing common projects and outlooks, protecting and enhancing the personal growth of each partner, expanding the self, enjoying intense and deep intimacy. Or one must be able to see marriage not as boring and banal, but as the high risk, even heroic, adventure that it is, in which one risks one's all in a partnership, filled with hope, 'til death do us part. Or one must be able to see that marriage provides opportunities for self-completion, for the practice of loving and giving, for enjoying what Rousseau called "the sweetest sentiments known to man, conjugal love and paternal love," for being mature and responsible, for making a life, for making one's own life meaningful and worthwhile through committed love.

All the readings gathered in this section explicitly and straightforwardly make one or more of these arguments; most also address arguments against marrying. Arranged roughly chronologically (with one large exception), they happen also to show changes in the reasons people have offered in favor of marrying. Yet even the reasons that now may seem to us dated deserve our serious attention, especially to the extent to which they may help us discover truths about marriage to which we may have become blind.

While thinking about these matters, we should beware the danger of rationalism. Reasons and arguments in favor of marriage surely can shape a cultural outlook and influence individual predilections, but personal decisions to marry—even for very rational men and women—are rarely simply the work of reason. Does the heart have reasons that reason cannot know? Or do the marrying heart and mind sing with one voice?

Darwin, "This is the Question"

We open with this selection (ignoring chronological order) because it offers general arguments for (and against) marriage in the context of an actual, concrete situation of everyday life, the writer's need to decide about his own marriage. Charles Darwin (1809–1882), author of the revolutionary The Origin of Species *(1859), was a rational and careful man, methodical, it seems, even about matters of the heart. These notes, headed "This is the Question" and written in his own hand sometime in 1837 or 1838 (when he was living at Great Marlborough Street, London), compare the consequences of marrying and not marrying. Of special interest for modern readers is the centrality of the issue regarding work (for us, "career"). Soon after writing these notes, Darwin married (he wed Emma Wedgwood on January 29, 1839; their marriage was by all accounts a happy one). The notes, perhaps saved by Emma, were published by Darwin's granddaughter, Nora Barlow, in an appendix to her edition of Darwin's* Autobiography. *Does his rational analysis explain why Darwin married?*

This is the Question

MARRY

Children—(if it please God)—constant companion, (friend in old age) who will feel interested in one, object to be beloved and played with—better than a dog anyhow—
Home, and someone to take care of house—
Charms of music and female chit-chat. These things good for one's health. Forced to visit and receive relations *but terrible loss of time.*

My God, it is intolerable to think of spending one's whole life, like a neuter bee, working, working and nothing after all.—
No, no won't do.—
Imagine living all one's day solitarily in smoky dirty London House.—Only picture to yourself a nice soft wife on a sofa with good fire, and books and music perhaps—

NOT MARRY

No children, (no second life) no one to care for one in old age.—
What is the use of working without sympathy from near and dear friends— who are near and dear friends to the old except relatives.
Freedom to go where one liked—Choice of Society *and little of it.* Conversation of clever men at clubs.—
Not forced to visit relatives, and to bend in every trifle—to have the expense and anxiety of children—perhaps quarreling. *Loss of time*—cannot read in the evenings—fatness and idleness—anxiety and responsibility—less money for books etc— if many children forced to gain one's bread.—
(But then it is very bad for one's health to work too much)
Perhaps my wife won't like London; then the sentence is banishment and degradation with indolent idle fool—

compare this vision with the dingy reality
of Grt Marlboro' St.
Marry—Marry—Marry   Q.E.D.

[On the reverse side of the page comes the summing up]

It being proved necessary to marry—When? Soon or Late. The Governor says soon for otherwise bad if one has children—one's character is more flexible—one's feelings more lively, and if one does not marry soon, one misses so much good pure happiness.—

But then if I married tomorrow: there would be an infinity of trouble and expense in getting and furnishing a house,—fighting about no Society—morning calls—awkwardness—loss of time every day—(without one's wife was an angel and made one keep industrious)—Then how should I manage all my business if I were obliged to go every day walking with my wife.—Eheu!! I never should know French,—or see the Continent,—or go to America, or go up in a Balloon, or take solitary trip in Wales—poor slave, you will be worse than a negro—And then horrid poverty (without one's wife was better than an angel and had money)—Never mind my boy—Cheer up—One cannot live this solitary life, with groggy old age, friendless and cold and childless staring one in one's face, already beginning to wrinkle. Never mind, trust to chance—keep a sharp look out.—There is many a happy slave—

Aquinas, "Of the Marriage Goods"

St. Thomas Aquinas (1225–1274), whose synthesis of Aristotelian philosophy and Christian theology ranks among the greatest intellectual achievements of Western civilization, and whose writings were for centuries regarded as models of rational order and clarity, will seem to most people today an unlikely source of wisdom on the tender subjects of love and marriage. Yet in this selection (Question XLIX, Second and Third Articles) from his Summa Theologica, *"Of the Marriage Goods"* (Bona matrimonii, *variously translated as "marriage goods" or "advantages of marriage"), Aquinas offers a classical Christian understanding of the benefits of marriage. Commenting on the goods of marriage listed in the* Sentences *of Peter Lombard (who is referred to below as "the Master"), he defends and compares three traditional advantages of marriage: faith (meaning here the virtue of living in accord with one's promise), offspring, and sacrament. The first two are regarded as the natural goods of marriage, the last as a specifically Christian good. Readers unfamiliar with Aquinas' dialectical method may be helped by noting that he first states a question and promptly gives, in the form of objections, arguments on both sides, on the one hand, then on the other. Second, he gives his own answer, after which, third, he replies one by one to the original objections. (Readers may find it easiest to begin with Aquinas' answer, and only then proceed to read each objection with his specific reply, taken one at a time.) Despite the strangeness, for us, of this mode of proceeding and of Aquinas' archaic language and unusually precise reasoning, this selection prompts us to consider whether offspring and fidelity are in fact essential goods of marriage and, hence, powerful reasons for marrying. Should one marry for the sake of procreating? Is a childless marriage less a marriage? Can marriage be good if it is not lived under a promise faithfully kept? Could it be an important good of human life to choose to live it under a promise of fidelity? What does it mean to say that marriage is a sacrament, or that marriage reflects the mysterious union of Christ and the Church, or more generally, the union of the divine and the human? How might marital union sanctify one's life?*

Second Article
Whether the goods of marriage are sufficiently enumerated?

We proceed thus to the Second Article:—

Objection I. It would seem that the goods of marriage are insufficiently enumerated by the Master (iv. *Sent.* D. 31), namely *faith, offspring,* and *sacrament.* For the object of marriage among men is not only the begetting and feeding of children, but also the partnership of a common life, whereby each one contributes his share of work to the common stock, as stated in *Ethic.* viii. 12. Therefore as the offspring is reckoned a good of matrimony, so also should the communication of works.

Objection 2. Further, the union of Christ with the Church, signified by matrimony, is the effect of charity. Therefore charity rather than faith should be reckoned among the goods of matrimony.

Objection 3. Further, in matrimony, just as it is required that neither party have intercourse with another, so is it required that the one pay the marriage debt to the other. Now the former pertains to faith according to the Master (iv. *Sent.* D. 31). Therefore justice should also be reckoned among the goods of marriage on account of the payment of the debt.

Objection 4. Further, in matrimony as signifying the union of Christ with the Church, just as indivisibility is required, so also is unity, whereby one man has one wife. But the sacrament which is reckoned among the three marriage goods pertains to indivisibility. Therefore there should be something else pertaining to unity.

Objection 5. On the other hand, it would seem that they are too many. For one virtue suffices to make one act right. Now faith is one virtue. Therefore it was not necessary to add two other goods to make marriage right.

Objection 6. Further, The same cause does not make a thing both useful and virtuous, since the useful and the virtuous are opposite divisions of the good. Now marriage derives its character of useful from the offspring. Therefore the offspring should not be reckoned among the goods that make marriage virtuous.

Objection 7. Further, Nothing should be reckoned as a property or condition of itself. Now these goods are reckoned to be conditions of marriage. Therefore since matrimony is a sacrament, the sacrament should not be reckoned a condition of matrimony.

I answer that, Matrimony is instituted both as an office of nature and as a sacrament of the Church. As an office of nature it is directed by two things, like every other virtuous act. One of these is required on the part of the agent and is the intention of the due end, and thus the *offspring* is accounted a good of matrimony; the other is required on the part of the act, which is good generically through being about a due matter; and thus we have *faith,* whereby a man has intercourse with his wife and with no other woman. Besides this it has a certain goodness as a sacrament, and this is signified by the very word *sacrament.*

Reply to Objection I. Offspring signifies not only the begetting of children, but also their education, to which as its end is directed the entire communion of works that exists between man and wife as united in marriage, since parents naturally *lay up* for their *children* (2 Cor. xii. 14); so that the offspring like a principal end includes another, as it were, secondary end.

Reply to Objection 2. Faith is not taken here as a theological virtue, but as part of justice, in so far as faith (*fides*) signifies the suiting of deed to word (*fiant dicta*) by keeping one's promises; for since marriage is a contract it contains a promise whereby this man is assigned to this woman.

Reply to Objection 3. Just as the marriage promise means that neither party is to have intercourse with a third party, so does it require that they should mutually pay the marriage debt. The latter is indeed the chief of the two, since it follows from the power which each receives over the other. Consequently both these things pertain to faith, although the Book of Sentences mentions that which is the less manifest.

Reply to Objection 4. By sacrament we are to understand not only indivisibility, but all those things that result from marriage being a sign of Christ's union with the Church. We may also reply that the unity to which the objection refers pertains to faith, just as indivisibility belongs to the sacrament.

Reply to Objection 5. Faith here does not denote a virtue, but that condition of virtue which is a part of justice and is called by the name of faith.

Reply to Objection 6. Just as the right use of a useful good derives its rectitude not from the useful but from the reason which causes the right use, so too direction to a useful good may cause the goodness of rectitude by virtue of the reason causing the right direction; and in this way marriage, through being directed to the offspring, is useful, and nevertheless righteous, inasmuch as it is directed aright.

Reply to Objection 7. As the Master says (iv. *Sent.* D. 31), sacrament here does not mean matrimony itself, but its indissolubility, which is a sign of the same thing as matrimony is.

We may also reply that although marriage is a sacrament, marriage as marriage is not the same as marriage as a sacrament, since it was instituted not only as a sign of a sacred thing, but also as an office of nature. Hence the sacramental aspect is a condition added to marriage considered in itself, whence also it derives its rectitude. Hence its sacramentality, if I may use the term, is reckoned among the goods which justify marriage; and accordingly this third good of marriage, the sacrament to wit, denotes not only its indissolubility, but also whatever pertains to its signification.

Third Article
Whether the sacrament is the chief of the marriage goods?

We proceed thus to the Third Article:— *Objection 1.* It would seem that the *sacrament* is not the chief of the marriage goods. For the end is principal in everything. Now the end of marriage is the offspring. Therefore the offspring is the chief marriage good.

Objection 2. Further, In the specific nature the difference is more important than the genus, even as the form is more important than matter in the composition of a natural thing. Now *sacrament* refers to marriage on the part of its genus, while *offspring* and *faith* refer thereto on the part of the difference whereby it is a special kind of sacrament. Therefore these other two are more important than sacrament in reference to marriage.

Objection 3. Further, Just as we find marriage without *offspring* and without *faith,* so do we find it without indissolubility, as in the case where one of the parties enters religion before the marriage is consummated. Therefore neither from this point of view is *sacrament* the most important marriage good.

Objection 4. Further, An effect cannot be more important than its cause. Now consent, which is the cause of matrimony, is often changed. Therefore the marriage also can be dissolved and consequently inseparability is not always a condition of marriage.

Objection 5. Further, The sacraments which produce an everlasting effect imprint a character. But no character is imprinted in matrimony. Therefore it is not conditioned by a lasting inseparability. Consequently just as there is marriage without *offspring* so is there marriage without *sacrament,* and thus the same conclusion follows as above.

On the contrary, That which has a place in the definition of a thing is most essential thereto. Now inseparability, which pertains to sacrament, is placed in the definition of marriage (Q. XLIV., A.3), while offspring and faith are not. Therefore among the other goods sacrament is the most essential to matrimony.

Further, the Divine power which works in the sacraments is more efficacious than human power. But *offspring* and *faith* pertain to matrimony as directed to an office of human nature, whereas *sacrament* pertains to it as instituted by God. Therefore sacrament takes a more important part in marriage than the other two.

I answer that, This or that may be more important to a thing in two ways, either because it is more essential or because it is more excellent. If the reason is because it is more excellent, then *sacrament* is in every way the most important of the three marriage goods, since it belongs to marriage considered as a sacrament of grace; while the other two belong to it as an office of nature; and a perfection of grace is more excellent than a perfection of nature. If, however, it is said to be more important because it is more essential, we must draw a distinction; for *faith* and *offspring* can be considered in two ways. First, in themselves, and thus they regard the use of matrimony in begetting children and observing the marriage compact; while inseparability, which is denoted by *sacrament*, regards the very sacrament considered in itself, since from the very fact that by the marriage compact man and wife give to one another power the one over the other in perpetuity, it follows that they cannot be put asunder. Hence there is no matrimony without inseparability, whereas there is matrimony without *faith* and *offspring*, because the existence of a thing does not depend on its use; and in this sense *sacrament* is more essential to matrimony than *faith* and *offspring*. Secondly, *faith* and *offspring* may be considered as in their principles, so that *offspring* denote the intention of having children, and *faith* the duty of remaining faithful, and there can be no matrimony without these also, since they are caused in matrimony by the marriage compact itself, so that if anything contrary to these were expressed in the consent which makes a marriage, the marriage would be invalid. Taking *faith* and *offspring* in this sense, it is clear that *offspring* is the most essential thing in marriage, secondly *faith*, and thirdly *sacrament*; even as to man it is more essential to be in nature than to be in grace, although it is more excellent to be in grace.

Reply to Objection 1. The end as regards the intention stands first in a thing, but as regards the attainment it stands last. It is the same with *offspring* among the marriage goods; wherefore in a way it is the most important and in another way it is not.

Reply to Objection 2. Sacrament, even as holding the third place among the marriage goods, belongs to matrimony by reason of its difference; for it is called *sacrament* from its signification of that particular sacred thing which matrimony signifies.

Reply to Objection 3. According to Augustine (*De Bono Conjug.* ix), marriage is a good of mortals, wherefore in the resurrection *they shall neither marry nor be married* (Matth. xxii.30). Hence the marriage bond does not last after the life wherein it is contracted, and consequently it is said to be inseparable, because it cannot be sundered in this life, but either by bodily death after carnal union, or by spiritual death after a merely spiritual union.

Reply to Objection 4. Although the consent which makes a marriage is not everlasting materially, i.e. in regard to the substance of the act, since that act ceases and a contrary act may succeed it, nevertheless formally speaking it is everlasting, because it is a consent to an ever lasting bond, else it would not make a marriage, for a consent to take a woman for a time makes no marriage. Hence it is everlasting formally, inasmuch as an act takes its species from its object; and thus it is that matrimony derives its inseparability from the consent.

Reply to Objection 5. In those sacraments wherein a character is imprinted, power is given to perform spiritual actions; but in matrimony, to perform bodily actions. Wherefore matrimony by reason of the power which man and wife receive over one another agrees with the sacraments in which a character is imprinted, and from this it derives its inseparability, as the Master says (*Sent.* iv, D, 31); yet it differs from them in so far as that power regards bodily acts; hence it does not confer a spiritual character.

Erasmus, "A Praise of Marriage"

The great Renaissance humanist, Desiderius Erasmus of Rotterdam (1466?–1536), first published this essay in early 1518, as an example of a letter of persuasion, but it was republished later that year under the title by which it became well known, Encomium matrimonii. *Though the essay enjoyed great success, it embroiled Erasmus in extended controversy with some theologians who regarded it as a veiled attack against ecclesiastical celibacy and monasticism. The letter attempts to persuade a young man, recently orphaned, to marry a noble, beautiful, virtuous woman who is much in love with him, rather than remain celibate. While Erasmus' comprehensive arguments are, in part, crafted specifically against the alternative of celibacy, most of them remain arguments for marriage and against staying single for* any *reason. Considerations of honor, duty, justice, advantage, and pleasure are counted among the advantages of marriage; the alleged disadvantages and counterarguments are rebutted. Erasmus' arguments are, one must note, addressed to a man. Would a woman respond to, or need, the same arguments?*

Although in your exceptional wisdom, my beloved kinsman, you are wise enough of yourself and need no counsel from others, yet I thought I owed it to our long friendship, which, beginning almost from the cradle, has grown through the years, and to your great kindness to me, and lastly to our very close relationship, that I should give you willing and frank advice in matters which I judged to be of great importance for the honour and welfare of you and your family, if indeed I wished to be the grateful and appreciative friend you have always considered me to be. There are times when we perceive others' interests better than our own. I have very often followed your advice in my affairs and have found out that it was as fruitful as it was friendly. Now if you in turn are willing to follow mine in your own affairs, I think that in the outcome I shall not be sorry for having given the advice nor you for having followed it.

On 8 April, when I was at my house in the mountains, Antonius Baldus, who as you know has your interests very much at heart and who has from the first been intimately connected with your family, had dinner with me. It was a joyless and tearful repast. He told me to our great mutual sorrow that your mother, a woman of great virtue, had departed this life; that your sister, overcome with grief and loneliness, had joined a group of women vowed to virginity, and that consequently the hope of prolonging your line had fallen upon you alone. He also informed me that your friends were of one accord in recommending to you, with the offer of a large dowry, a girl of noble birth, exceptional beauty, and excellent character, and who was very much in love with you, but that you, whether from inability to master your grief or from religious scruples, were so set on remaining celibate that neither devotion to your family, nor desire for offspring, nor the advice, prayers, and tears of your friends could induce you to abandon your resolve.

Nevertheless, perhaps on my advice you will change your mind and renounce the single state, a barren way of life hardly becoming to a man, and surrender yourself to holy wedlock. I do not wish in this exhortation to use to my advantage the dearness of your family, which for that matter should have prevailed over your feelings, or my own influence, but I shall show by the clearest of proofs that this alternative would be far more honourable, profitable, and pleasant for you, and, one might add, necessary even in this day and age.

First of all, if you are moved by considerations of honour, which should be a matter of primary importance among men of upright life, what is more honourable than marriage, which was honoured by Christ himself, who not only thought it fit to be present at a wedding[1] together with his mother, but also sanctified the wedding feast with the first fruits of his miracles? What could be holier than that which the father of all creation founded, enjoined, and sanctified, and which nature herself consecrated? What is more worthy of praise, when those who find fault with it are condemned for heresy? Marriage is as honourable as the name of heretic is infamous. What is more just than to return to posterity what we ourselves have received from our forebears? What is more ill-advised than in the pursuit of sanctity to shun as unholy what God himself, the source and father of all holiness, wished to be held most holy? What is more inhuman than to shrink from the laws of the human condition? What is more ungrateful than to deny to one's descendants that which you would not be able to deny if you had not received it from your ancestors?

If we seek the author of marriage, we discover that it was founded and instituted not by Lycurgus, or Moses, or Solon, but by the sovereign maker of all things, and from the same it received praise, and by the same it was made honourable and holy. In the beginning, when he created man out of clay, God realized that man's life would be thoroughly unhappy and unpleasant unless he joined Eve to him as a companion. Therefore he did not bring man's wife out of the clay from which he had brought man, but out of Adam's ribs, so that we might clearly understand that nothing should be dearer to us, nothing more closely joined, nothing more tightly glued to us than a wife.

After the flood, when God was reconciled to the race of mortals, he proclaimed, as we read, as his first law, not that they should embrace celibacy, but

---

[1] At Cana, the scene of Christ's first miracle; John 2:1–11

that should "increase and multiply and replenish the earth." But how could they, unless they gave thought to wedlock? And without adducing the freedom of the Mosaic law or the necessity of those times as a reason, what other meaning can be attributed to the approval of Christ repeated and confirmed in the gospel writings? "For this cause," he says, "shall a man leave father and mother and cleave to his wife." What is more holy than loyalty to one's parents? Yet conjugal fidelity is preferred to this. On whose authority? On God's authority, to be sure. At what time? Not only in the time of Judaism but also during the Christian era.

Father and mother must be abandoned, and one must cleave to one's wife. A son set free begins to be his own master. A son disowned ceases to be a son. But death alone dissolves wedlock, if indeed it does dissolve it. It is only dissolved in the case of those who seek another marriage. As long as wedded love persists, the marriage is not considered to be dissolved.

Now if the other sacraments, which are the chief support of the church of Christ, are observed with scrupulous respect, who cannot see that much reverence is due this one, which was instituted by God before all the others? The rest were instituted upon earth, but this in paradise; the rest for a remedy, this for partnership in happiness. The rest were provided for fallen nature, this alone was granted for its preservation. If we hold as sacrosanct laws passed by mortals, will not the law of wedlock have the most sanctity of all, because we have received it from the giver of life, and because it alone came into existence almost simultaneously with the human race itself?

Finally, to strengthen the law by example, when Christ was invited as a young man to a marriage feast (as was mentioned above), he attended willingly with his mother; and not only did he attend, but he honoured it by an extraordinary favour,[2] choosing no other occasion to inaugurate his miracles. "Why then," you will say, "did Christ himself abstain from wedlock?" As if indeed there were not very many aspects of Christ's life which should excite our wonder rather than our imitation. He was born without a father, was given birth without pain to his mother, and came forth from a sealed sepulchre.

What is there in him that is not above nature? Such attributes belong to him alone. Let us who live under the law of nature look up to those things that are above nature, but emulate what is within our capacity.

"But he chose to be born of a virgin." Yes, of a virgin, but a married virgin. A virgin mother befitted God; the fact that she was married signified the path we should follow. The state of virginity befitted the woman who by the inspiration of the heavenly spirit was to bear, herself immaculate, an immaculate child. Yet Joseph her spouse commends to us the laws of chaste wedlock. How

---

[2]Turning water into wine

could Christ have better commended the union of wedlock than through the mystery of that joining, stupendous even to angelic minds, of divine nature with a human body and soul; or in declaring his amazing and undying love for his church, what greater commendation than to call himself its husband and the church his bride? "Marriage is a great sacrament," says Paul, "in Christ and the church." If there had been any holier bond in the universe, any stricter compact than wedlock, he would certainly have taken his illustration from that. What do we read like this concerning celibacy anywhere in the sacred writings? Wedlock is called honourable, and the marriage bed undefiled by the apostle Paul, but celibacy is never even named there. Nor is it excused except by the compensation of a greater good. In all other respects one who follows the law of nature and procreates children is to be preferred to one who perseveres in the single state simply in order to have a more independent life. We read that men who are truly chaste and virgins are praised, but celibacy in itself receives no praise. Now the law of Moses curses barren wedlock, and we read that some were excluded from the public altars on this account. For what reason then? Simply because like useless drones living for themselves they increased the race by no offspring. In Deuteronomy it is set forth as the greatest proof of God's blessing for the Israelites that no one among them would be barren, neither male nor female. Leah is said to have been despised by her lord for not bearing children. Moreover in the Psalms a wife's fruitfulness is included among the principal portions of blessedness. "Your wife," says the psalmist, "is like a fruitful vine, your sons are like olive shoots round your table." But if the law condemns and stigmatizes a barren marriage, it has condemned the unmarried much more severely. If nature is not exempt from penalty, still less will personal inclination escape it. If those whose good will has been thwarted by nature are subject to condemnation, what do those deserve who have made no efforts to avoid sterility?

The laws of the Hebrews awarded this privilege to marriage, that one who had taken a bride would not be compelled to go to war that same year. The state is in danger unless there are those to protect it by force of arms, but its destruction is assured unless there are those who through the benefit of wedlock make up for the loss of young manhood diminished by death. Roman laws also inflicted a penalty upon those who were unmarried, and excluded them from the offices of the state. But those who had enriched the state with children were decreed a reward from public funds as having served it well. Proof of this is the law of three children,[3] not to mention others. . . .

---

[3]Those who had three legitimate children were accorded certain privileges by Augustus' marriage legislation, including seniority for holding magistracies. Under later emperors these privileges came to be granted as a favour regardless of the number of children.

Lycurgus passed laws that those who did not take wives should be excluded in summer from games and public shows, and in winter should go about the forum without clothing, and admit with curses upon their own heads that they were suffering a just penalty for not obeying the laws.

If you now want to know the value placed on marriage by the ancients, consider the penalty for a violated marriage. The Greeks once decreed that the violation of the rights of marriage had to be vindicated by a ten years' war. In addition, not only Roman law but the laws of the Hebrews and the barbarian nations prescribed capital punishment for adulterers. A thief was penalized by a fourfold repayment; an adulterer's crime was expiated by execution. Among the Hebrews stoning at the hands of the people was the fate of one who violated the institution without which the people would no longer exist. Not content with this, the severity of the laws allowed for an adulterer caught *in flagrante* to be stabbed to death without trial and without legal rights, evidently according to a husband's indignation what it grants only reluctantly to a man defending his own life from danger, which shows that the taking away of a wife was viewed as a more grievous wrong than the taking of a life. Certainly wedlock must be considered an institution of the greatest sanctity if its violation must be expiated by human blood, and the avenging of it need not await laws or judgment, a right which does not exist even in the case of parricide.

Yet why be concerned with written laws? This is the law of nature, not inscribed on any bronze tablets, but deeply implanted in our minds; if anyone does not obey it, he should not even be considered human, much less a good citizen. For if, as the Stoics, the most perceptive of philosophers, maintain, to live rightly is to follow the instigations of nature, what is so consistent with nature as marriage? For nothing has been so firmly implanted by nature, not only in mankind but in all living things, as the instinct in each of them to preserve its own species from destruction and render it in some way immortal by the propagation of offspring. Everyone must know that this cannot come about without the bond of wedlock.

It seems all the more shameful that dumb herds should obey nature's laws, but men, like the giants, should declare war upon nature. If we look at creation with eyes that are not blinded, we shall understand that nature intended that there should be some kind of marital union in all species. I shall say nothing about trees, in which on the sure authority of Pliny, sexual union is found with a clear distinction of sex, particularly in palm trees, so that unless the male tree rests the weight of its branches upon the female trees around it as if with the urge for intercourse these will certainly remain barren. The same writer points out that there are authorities who believe that there is a male and female sex in everything the earth produces. I say nothing about precious stones, in which the same author says sex is to be found, and he is not alone. Has not God linked all things by certain ties so that they seem to need each other? What of the heavens turning with continual motion? Does it not play the part of a husband as it fructifies the earth, parent of all things, beneath it, making it produce every manner of thing by the infusion of its seed?

But it would take too long to run through every detail. What is the point of all this? Simply to have you understand that all things exist and are bound together in the association of wedlock; that without this they all dissolve, perish, and fall away. The tale is devised by those wise poets of antiquity, who took pains to clothe the teaching of philosophy in the wrappings of fable, that giants, the serpent-footed sons of earth, piled up mountains to the sky and waged war with the gods. What is the meaning of this story? Evidently it signifies that some monstrous, savage, and uncivilized men felt a great loathing for the harmony of wedlock, and for this were hurled down by a thunderbolt, that is, they perished utterly, since they shunned the sole means of preserving the human race. The same poets record that Orpheus, poet and luteplayer, moved the hardest of stones with his singing. What did they mean? They meant to show that men as unfeeling as stone, who were living after the manner of wild beasts, were rescued from promiscuity by this wise and eloquent hero and initiated into the holy laws of marriage. It is clear that one who is not affected by the love of matrimony is more like a stone than a human being; he is an enemy of nature, a rebel against God who brings destruction upon himself by his own folly. For a man who plots the destruction of his race is crueler than one who plots only his own destruction. . . .

Surely you are not anxious to appear holier than Abraham himself? He would not have been called "the father of many generations" and that with God's own blessing, if he had shunned cohabitation with a wife. Surely you do not seek to be considered more scrupulous than Jacob, who did not hesitate to purchase the embraces of Rachel by such a lengthy servitude; or wiser than Solomon—yet what a large flock of wives he kept at home! Or more chaste than Socrates, who, we read, put up at home with the shrewish Xanthippe not so much, as he jokingly used to say, that he might learn tolerance at home but that he might not seem to have been delinquent in the service of nature. For the one man judged to be wise by the oracle of Apollo understood that he was begotten under this law, born for this law, and owed this debt to nature. For if what the ancient philosophers said was correct, if it was approved with good reason by our theologians, and if it was deservedly repeated everywhere in the form of a saying that neither God nor nature does anything without purpose, then why did nature assign us these members and add these incitements and this power of reproduction, if celibacy is to be considered praiseworthy? If someone gave you a splendid gift, a bow, or fine raiment, or a sword, you would seem unworthy of what you received if you were unwilling or unable to use it. Since everything else has been designed with a purpose, it hardly seems probable that in this one matter alone nature was asleep.

I have no patience with those who say that sexual excitement is shameful and that venereal stimuli have their origin not in nature, but in sin. Nothing is so far from the truth. As if marriage, whose function cannot be fulfilled without these incitements, did not rise above blame. In other living creatures where do these incitements come from? From nature or from sin? From nature, of course. It must be borne in mind that in the appetites of the body there is very little difference between man and other living creatures. Finally, we defile by our imagination what of its own nature is fair and holy. If we were willing to evaluate things not according to the opinion of the crowd, but according to nature itself, how is it less repulsive to eat, chew, digest, evacuate, and sleep after the fashion of dumb animals, than to enjoy lawful and permitted carnal relations?

"But one must obey virtue rather than nature." As if anything which is at variance with nature could be called virtue! For if it did not proceed from nature, there would be nothing that could be further perfected by training and discipline. But you are attracted by the mode of life of the apostles, who both embraced celibacy themselves and encouraged others to that kind of life. Indeed, let the apostles be imitated by apostolic men, who, since it is their mission to teach and instruct the populace, cannot at one and the same time satisfy both a flock and a wife. Yet it is known that some of the apostles had wives. Let us leave celibacy for bishops. Why do you observe the practice of the apostles when you are far removed from the apostolic function, being in fact a layman and a private individual? They were allowed the privilege of being free from the duties of wedlock, so that they might have more opportunity to produce a more plentiful offspring for Christ. Let that be the prerogative of priests and monks, who evidently have succeeded to the regimen of the Essenes.[4] Your situation is quite different. "But Christ himself," you will say, "declared blessed those who became eunuchs for the kingdom of God's sake." I do not reject the authority of this statement, but I offer an interpretation of its meaning. First, I consider that this dogma of Christ pertains to those times when it was right for an ecclesiastic to be kept as free as possible from all worldly affairs. He had to run about from one country to another, threatened by persecutors on all sides. But nowadays conditions and times are such that you would not find anywhere a less defiled purity of morals than among the married. Let the swarms of monks and virgins exalt their own rule of life as they will, let them

---

[4]A small community of Jews who lived mostly around the Dead Sea, practised extreme asceticism, and were firm believers in celibacy; Erasmus often refers to monks by this term, intended as pejorative.

boast as much as they like of their liturgical functions and their acts of worship, in which they excel all others; the holiest kind of life is wedlock, purely and chastely observed. Besides, it is not only the one who lives unmarried who makes himself a eunuch, but one who in chaste and holy fashion carries out the duties of wedlock. I only wish those who conceal their vices behind the high-sounding name of castration, and under the pretence of chastity gratify worse lusts, were truly castrated. I do not think that it becomes my sense of modesty to describe the disgraceful actions which those who oppose nature often fall into. Lastly, Christ does not impose celibacy on anyone; he does, however, openly forbid divorce. In my view it would not be ill advised for the interests and morals of mankind if the right of wedlock were also conceded to priests and monks, if circumstances required it, especially in view of the fact that there is such a great throng of priests everywhere, so few of whom live a chaste life. How much better it would be to turn concubines into wives, so that the women they now keep dishonourably and with troubled conscience might be retained openly with honourable reputation; then they could beget children whom they could love as truly legitimate offspring and educate conscientiously, to whom they would not be a source of shame, and by whom they might be honoured in turn. And indeed, I think the representatives of the bishops would have seen to this long ago, were it not that concubines are a greater source of revenue than wives.

"But virginity is a divine and angelic prerogative, while wedlock is merely human." I speak now as one man to another, as one commoner to another, as one weak mortal to another. Virginity is certainly worthy of praise, but on the condition that this praise is not transferred to the majority of mankind. If it were to become a general practice, what could be mentioned or imagined more destructive than virginity? Besides, if virginity were to merit special praise in all others, in your case it cannot escape censure, since the duty of preserving from extinction a family that is supremely worthy of immortality will devolve upon you alone. Finally, there is very little distinction between the praise due to virginity and that due to the man who keeps the laws of wedlock unsullied, who keeps a wife for bearing offspring, not for the purpose of lust.

If a brother is bidden to raise up seed for a brother who has died without children, will you allow the hope of your whole line to perish, especially when it has fallen on you alone? I am not unaware that the praise of virginity has repeatedly been sung in huge volumes by the early Fathers, among whom Jerome admires it so much that he all but abuses marriage, and was summoned to recant by some orthodox bishops. However, let us make allowance for the fervour of those times; at the present time, I should wish that those who indiscriminately encourage to celibacy those who are not mature enough to know their own minds should direct similar efforts to presenting a picture of chaste and pure matrimony. The same individuals who are so pleased with virginity are not displeased with warring against the Turks, who outnumber us by so many; if their judgment is correct, it will follow that it should be considered especially right and honourable to strive with all one's might to produce children, and thus provide enough young men to serve in the war. Unless perhaps they think that artillery, missiles, and ships should be provided for this war, but that men are not needed. The same people approve of slaying heathen parents by the sword, so that it may be possible to baptize their children, who are unaware of their newly acquired religion. If that is true, how much more civilized it would be to obtain the same result by the office of wedlock! No nation is so barbarous that it does not execrate the killing of infants. The laws of princes punish with almost equal severity the inducing of abortion and sterility brought on by drugs. Why is that so? Because there is very little difference between the one who cuts short what has begun to be born and one who sees to it that there can be no birth. That which withers away within your body, or is destroyed at great risk to your health, or is ejected in sleep, would have been a human being if only you had been human. The literature of the Hebrews curses the man who, when told to consort with his dead brother's wife, spilled the seed upon the ground so that nothing would be born, and was judged unworthy of life as he had grudged life to a foetus yet to be born.

How very little difference there is between him and those who impose perpetual sterility upon themselves! Does it not seem that they kill as many human beings as would have been born if they had attended to the begetting of children? I ask you, if anyone has a farm with naturally fertile soil that he allows to remain forever uncultivated and barren, should he not be punished by the law, as it is in the country's interests that each one should manage his property well? If a man is punished for neglecting a field that, even if fully cultivated, bears only wheat, or beans, or peas, what penalty does he deserve who refuses to cultivate a farm that when cultivated produces men? In the former case long and hard toil is required, in the latter cultivation is short, and also has the reward of pleasure as an added inducement. So if you are influenced at all by natural feelings, goodness, respect, piety, duty, and virtue, why do you shun what has been instituted by God, sanctioned by nature, prompted by reason, praised in divine and human writings alike, laid down by the law, ratified by the consensus of all peoples, and encouraged by the example of all good men?

But even if many unpleasant things are to be sought after by a good man for no other reason than that they are honourable, then marriage, concerning which it is difficult to determine whether it contains more honour or pleasure, is all the more greatly to be desired. For what is sweeter than living with a woman with whom you are most intimately joined not merely by the bonds of affection but by physical union as well? If we derive much spiritual delight from the kindness of other close relatives and acquaintances, how much more pleasant to have someone with whom to share the secret feelings of the heart, with whom you may talk as if with yourself, to whose loyalty you can safely entrust yourself, who regards your fortune as her own! What happiness there is in the union of husband and wife, than which none greater nor more lasting exists in all of nature! For while we are linked with our other friends by benevolence of mind, with a wife we are joined by the greatest affection, physical union, the bond of the sacrament, and the common sharing of all fortunes. Moreover, how much pretence and bad faith there is in other friendships! Those whom we think to be our dearest friends fail us when fortune's breezes change, like swallows flying away at the end of the summer. At times a more recent friend displaces an old one. I have heard of few whose faithfulness persisted until life's end.

The affection of a wife is not spoilt by faithlessness, is veiled by no pretence, is shattered by no change of fortune; in the end it is severed by death alone, or rather not even by death. She disregards her duties to her parents and sisters and brothers out of love for you, she looks up to you alone, she depends on you, with you she would fain die. If you have wealth, you have someone to look after it and increase it; if you have none, you have someone who can seek it for you. In times of prosperity, happiness is doubled; in adversity there will be someone to console and assist you, to show her devotion, to wish your misfortune hers. Do you think there is any pleasure to be compared with so close a union? If you are at home, she is there to dispel the tedium of solitude; if abroad, she can speed you on your way with a kiss, miss you when you are away, receive you gladly on your return. She is the sweetest companion of your youth, the welcome comfort of your old age. By nature any association is pleasant for man, seeing that nature begot him for kindness and friendship. Then how can this fail to be the most pleasant of all, in which there is nothing that is not shared? On the contrary, if we see that even the wild beasts dread loneliness and are pleased by companionship, in my view anyone who shuns this most honourable and joyful association should not be accounted as human.

For what is more hateful than a man who, as though born for himself alone, lives for himself, looks out for himself, is sparing or lavish for himself, loves no one, and is loved by no one? Indeed, should not such a monster be thought fit to be driven away from the general fellowship of mankind into the midst of the sea along with the notorious Timon of Athens? I should not presume at this point to set before you those pleasures, the sweetest that nature has bestowed upon mankind, which men of great genius, for some reason or other, have chosen to ignore rather than despise. Yet, who has been born with so stern, not to say stolid, a nature as not to be attracted by pleasures of that kind, especially if they can be enjoyed without offence to God or man and without loss of reputation? Truly I should call him not a man, but a stone, even if bodily pleasure is but a small part of the benefits conferred by wedlock. Suppose, however, that you despise this as unworthy of a true man (though without it we do not deserve the name of true man); let it be set, if you wish, among the least advantages of wedlock, then what could be more lovely than chaste love, or, I should say, what more holy and more honourable?

Meanwhile the pleasant throng of relatives grows larger. The number of parents, brothers, sisters, and nephews is doubled. For nature can grant only one mother and one father. By wedlock a second father and second mother are added, who cannot but attend you with unusual devotion, as one to whom they have entrusted their own flesh. Then what joy it will bring you when your beautiful wife makes you the parent of beautiful offspring; when some tiny Aeneas will play in your hall, who will recall your countenance and that of your wife and will call you by the name of "father" with sweet stammering? To the affection of wedlock there will be added a bond as adamant as steel which not even death can sever. "Happy those," says Horace, "three or more times over, / United by an unbroken bond / Whose love, unmarred by bitter strife / Will not release them till their dying day." You have those who will give delight to your old age, close your eyes and perform the obsequies, in whom you may seem to be born again, in whose survival you may even be thought not to have died. What you have amassed for yourself does not pass into the hands of alien heirs. Thus when one has the sense of having performed all of life's duties, not even death itself can seem harsh. Old age threatens all of us willy-nilly. In this manner nature has provided that we should grow young again in our children and grandchildren. For who would find old age a burden when he has seen in his son the very features he had as a young man? Death awaits us all. But in this way alone the providence of nature devises a kind of immortality, as it creates one thing from another in such a way that, just as when a shoot springs up again after a tree has been felled, one who dies leaving offspring behind him does not seem to have perished altogether.

Yet I am well aware of the objections you are raising in the mean time. Wedlock is a blessed institution if all turns out favourably, but what if you end up with a difficult or shameless wife, or the children grow up to be disloyal? Cases of wedlock which brought ruin will come to mind. Magnify them as much as you will, these will prove to be faults of human nature, not of wedlock. Believe me, as a rule, only a bad husband gets a bad wife. Besides, it is within your power to choose a good one. What if she should be corrupted? A good wife can certainly be corrupted by a bad husband; a bad wife is usually reformed by a good husband. The accusations we bring against wives are false. No one, if you have faith in my words, ever had a wicked wife except through his own fault. Further, from good parents similar children are born, as a general rule. In fact, whatever their condition of birth, they turn out very much as one shapes them by education. There is no reason to be afraid of jealousy. That is the disease of those who love foolishly. Chaste and lawful love is innocent of jealousy. . . . You say, "An upright woman is 'a rare bird' upon the earth." Make yourself worthy of a rare wife. As the wise man says, "A good woman is a good inheritance." Dare to hope for one worthy of your character. Much lies in the choice you make, what you make of her, and how you behave towards her.

"But freedom is pleasanter," you will say. "Whoever takes a wife receives fetters that only death can shake off." But what pleasure can there be for a man who is alone? If freedom is pleasant, I think you should take a partner with whom you may be willing to share that benefit. Yet what is more free than a servitude in which each is so subject to the other that neither wishes to be set free? You are bound to one whom you admit to your friendship, but no one claims that his freedom has been taken away on this account. You are afraid that when your children are taken away by death, you may be plunged into grief in your bereavement. If you are afraid of bereavement, you should take a wife for that very reason, since she alone can guarantee your not being childless. Yet why do you inquire so thoroughly, nay, so anxiously, into all the disadvantages of marriage, as if celibacy had no disadvantages? As if there were any form of human existence not liable to all the hazards of fortune! One who wishes to suffer no ills must depart from this life. But if you are thinking of life in heaven, this mortal life must be called death, not life. If, however, you limit your considerations to the life of man, nothing is more secure, more tranquil, more pleasant, more attractive, or more blissful than wedded life.

Consider the matter from its results. How few are there in your experience who, having once made trial of wedlock, are not eager to try it again! My friend Maurice, whose exceptional wisdom is well known to you, entered into matrimony with a new bride a month after the death of the wife whom he dearly loved. This was not because of his inability to resist sexual desire, but he said that life did not seem real to him without a wife to share all his fortunes. Is not our friend Jovius looking for a fourth wife? He was so deeply in love with them when they were alive that he seemed to admit of no consolation. Notwithstanding, when one died, he was quick to fill the loneliness of his marriage-bed, as if he had felt little love for them. But why are we discussing goodness and pleasure when not only advantage induces us, but necessity impels us to wedlock? Take away marriage, and within a very few years all of mankind must perish utterly. They say that when Xerxes, the famous king of the Persians, was gazing from a high place on his mighty array of men, he could not restrain his tears because sixty years from then not a single one of so many thousands would be alive. Why can we not perceive concerning the whole human race what he understood concerning his troops? If wedlock is taken away, of so many regions, provinces, kingdoms, cities, and assemblies how few will be left a century later!

Let us go then and pay our homage to celibacy, since it is destined to visit eternal destruction on our race! What plague or pestilence sent by the gods above or below could be more pernicious? What more bitter consequences could be feared from any flood? . . . In calamities of this kind much remains unharmed, but from the effects of celibacy nothing will be saved. We see what a procession of maladies, how many dangerous situations lie in wait for the meagre race of mankind night and day. How many are carried off by disease, swallowed up by the sea, or snatched away by war? I do not mention the deaths that occur every day. Death hovers all around us: it strikes, seizes, and hastens with all speed to end our race; and yet we admire celibacy and flee from wedlock! . . . Surely we are not waiting for some Jupiter to make us the same gift as he is supposed to have granted to the bees, of having young without intercourse, and gathering the seeds of our descendants from flowers with our mouths? Or do we expect that just as Minerva, as the poets tell, was born from the brain of Jupiter, so children will leap out of our heads? or lastly, trusting the stories of the ancients that men will be produced from the earth, like mice in Egypt, or from the throwing of stones as in the fables, or from the hard trunks of trees? From the bosom of the earth many things are born without our cultivating them. Young shoots often sprout up beneath their parents' shade; but for man nature has willed that there should be this single method of propagation, that by the co-operation of husband and wife the race of mortals should be saved from destruction; but if men were to shun this after your example, not even what you so admire would be able to exist.

Do you admire celibacy and respect virginity? But if you take away the practice of wedlock there will be neither unwedded nor virgins. Why then is virginity preferred and honoured if it involves the abolition of mankind? It has received praise, but in a given period of time and in few individuals. For God wished to show men a kind of picture and likeness of that life in heaven where no women marry or are given in marriage. But for an example a small number is suitable, a large one useless. Not every field, however fertile, is sown to sustain life; but some are neglected, others cultivated to please the eye; for the very abundance allows that in such a vast extent of arable land, a small part may be left barren. But if none were sown, who would not see that we should have to return to acorns? Similarly, amid such a great multitude of men celibacy in a few certainly merits praise, but if extended to all would deserve grievous censure.

Now if in others virginity were to be esteemed a virtue, in your case it would definitely be a vice. For the others will seem to have been interested in leading a pure life; you will be judged the murderer of your line, because, when you were able to have offspring by honourable wedlock, you allowed it to die out through vile celibacy. It would be permissible from a large brood to consecrate a virgin to God. Countrymen offer the first fruits of their crops to the gods, but not the whole yield; you must remember that you are the sole remnant of your line. There is no difference between killing it off or refusing to preserve it, since you are the only one who could preserve it, and easily at that.

But you protest that your sister's example encourages you towards celibacy. This very reason that you cite should have deterred you most of all from the state of celibacy. You are aware that the hope of your family, which previously was divided between the two of you, has now devolved entirely upon you alone. Some indulgence should be granted to her sex and her years. The girl did wrong because she was overcome with grief; at the instance of foolish women or foolish monks she threw herself into it headlong. You who are the elder must remember that you are a man. She has wished to die together with her ancestors; you will make sure that they do not die. Your sister has withdrawn from her duty; consider now that you must play the part of two. The daughters of Lot did not hesitate to consort with their drunken father, judging it better, even through unholy incest, to take thought for the race than to allow it to die off. Will you not, by a marriage that is honourable, holy, modest, without offence, and that promises great satisfaction, take thought for your family, which otherwise is doomed to extinction?

So let us allow those to imitate the example of Hippolytus in the pursuit of celibacy who can be husbands, but not fathers, or whose slender means are insufficient for rearing children, or whose line can be continued through the instrumentality of others, or else is of such a kind that the country is the better for its extinction rather than its continuance, or who by some special favour of the eternal Godhead have been set apart from the general lot of mankind and marked out for some heavenly function—and their number is amazingly small. In your case, on the evidence of a doctor who is quite skilled and honest, you seem to give promise of a large posterity; you have means that are abundant, and an excellent and distinguished line, which cannot be blotted out without the commission of a wicked crime and without grave consequences for the country. Then too your age is sound, good looks are not wanting, and you have the opportunity to take as a wife a girl as virtuous and distinguished as your fellow-citizens have ever seen, pure, modest, respectful, divinely beautiful, with an abundant dowry. Although your friends beg you, your kinsfolk shed tears, your relatives press you, your country requests it, and the very ashes of your ancestors implore this of you from the tomb, do you still hesitate and still contemplate celibacy?

If what was asked of you were something dishonourable or difficult, still the prayers of your kin or the affection of your family should have prevailed over your desire. How much more reasonable it is that the tears of your friends, respect for your country, and your affection for your ancestors should win from you a decision to which you are urged by laws divine and human alike, impelled by nature, led by reason, drawn by honour, attracted by so many advantages, and even compelled by necessity itself? But this is more than enough argument. I am certain that you have long since changed your mind at my prompting, and have turned your thoughts to more useful plans.

Bacon, "Of Marriage and Single Life"

Not everyone who has weighed marriage against remaining single has given the nod unequivocally to marriage. In this famous essay, number eight among The Essays, *the great English philosopher Francis Bacon (1561–1626) considers the relative merits and liabilities of marriage and the single life, not so much from the point of view of the individual as from the perspective of society. Of special interest are the claims that married men, having a greater stake in the future, make better subjects (in democratic regimes, citizens) and soldiers and that "wife and children are a kind of discipline of humanity." What does this mean? Is it a matter of indifference to a community whether its men marry or not? Its women? Are a "husband and children" equally a "discipline of humanity," or do women not require it? What might Bacon say if asked to state the benefits of marriage for women—then and now?*

He that hath wife and children hath given hostages to fortune; for they are impediments to great enterprises, either of virtue or mischief. Certainly the best works, and of greatest merit for the public, have proceeded from the unmarried or childless men; which both in affection and means have married and endowed the public. Yet it were great reason that those that have children should have greatest care of future times; unto which they know they must transmit their dearest pledges. Some there are, who though they lead a single life, yet their thoughts do end with themselves, and account future times impertinences. Nay, there are some other that account wife and children but as bills of charges. Nay more, there are some foolish rich covetous men, that take a pride in having no children, because they may be thought so much the richer. For perhaps they have heard some talk, *Such an one is a great rich man,* and another except to it, *Yea, but he hath a great charge of children;* as if it were an abatement to his riches. But the most ordinary cause of a single life is liberty, especially in certain self-pleasing and humorous minds, which are so sensible of every restraint, as they will go near to think their girdles and garters to be bonds and shackles. Unmarried men are best friends, best masters, best servants; but not always best subjects; for they are light to run away; and almost all fugitives are of that condition. A single life doth well with churchmen; for charity will hardly water the ground where it must first fill a pool. It is indifferent for judges and magistrates; for if they be facile and corrupt, you shall have a servant five times worse than a wife. For soldiers, I find the generals commonly in their hortatives put men in mind of their wives and children; and I think the despising of marriage amongst the Turks maketh the vulgar soldier more base. Certainly wife and children are a kind of discipline of humanity; and single men, though they may be many times more charitable, because their means are less exhaust, yet, on the other side, they are more cruel and hardhearted (good to make severe inquisitors), because their tenderness is not so oft called upon. Grave natures, led by custom, and therefore constant, are commonly loving husbands; as was said of Ulysses, *vetulam suam prætulit immortalitati:* [he preferred his old wife to immortality]. Chaste women are often proud and froward, as presuming upon the merit of their chastity. It is one of the best bonds both of chastity and obedience in the wife, if she think her husband wise; which she will never do if she find him jealous. Wives are young men's mistresses; companions for middle age; and old men's nurses. So as a man may have a quarrel to marry when he will. But yet he was reputed one of the wise men, that made answer to the question, when a man should marry?—*A young man not yet, an elder man not at all.* It is often seen that bad husbands have very good wives; whether it be that it raiseth the price of their husband's kindness when it comes; or that the wives take a pride in their patience. But this never fails, if the bad husbands were of their own choosing, against their friends' consent; for then they will be sure to make good their own folly.

Austen, *Pride and Prejudice:*
For Love or Money?

Jane Austen (1775–1817) described her novels in this way: "I never leave my small square, two inches of ivory." Ivory is associated with instruments of refinement like fans, piano keys, and hair adornments, but it comes from instruments of combat, elephant tusks. Similarly, Austen's novels make vivid the civilized proprieties as well as the harsh necessities of getting wived and husbanded—the small square about which she writes. Austen's women are forever talking, thinking, and scheming about men, for they know full well that only in marriage is their future secure. The situation of the Bennet sisters in Pride and Prejudice *is a case in point: Mr. and Mrs. Bennet live comfortably with their five daughters (Jane, Elizabeth, Mary, Kitty, and Lydia), but as there has been no male issue, the Bennet estate (Longbourn) is due to pass by entail to a distant cousin, the fatuous Mr. Collins. Readers of the novel have always cheered for Elizabeth Bennet's sound rejection of Mr. Collins's proposal of marriage. But no one cheered as much as Elizabeth's still-single, 27-year-old friend, Charlotte Lucas, who immediately saw Elizabeth's refusal as a fresh opportunity and promptly moved in to pursue the quarry. The selections below, excerpted from Volume I, Chapters 19–20 and 22, of* Pride and Prejudice, *cover Mr. Collins's proposal to Elizabeth and its aftermath. They make clear what prompts a Mr. Collins and a Charlotte Lucas to marry, and indirectly and by contrast, what might lead an Elizabeth to marry.*

Chapter 19

The next day opened a new scene at Longbourn. Mr. Collins made his declaration in form. Having resolved to do it without loss of time, as his leave of absence extended only to the following Saturday, and having no feelings of diffidence to make it distressing to himself even at the moment, he set about it in a very orderly manner, with all the observances which he supposed a regular part of the business. On finding Mrs. Bennet, Elizabeth, and one of the younger girls together, soon after breakfast, he addressed the mother in these words,

"May I hope, Madam, for your interest with your fair daughter Elizabeth, when I solicit for the honour of a private audience with her in the course of this morning?"

Before Elizabeth had time for any thing but a blush of surprise, Mrs. Bennet instantly answered,

"Oh dear!—Yes—certainly.—I am sure Lizzy will be very happy—I am sure she can have no objection.—Come, Kitty, I want you up stairs." And gathering her work together, she was hastening away, when Elizabeth called out,

"Dear Ma'am, do not go.—I beg you will not go.—Mr. Collins must excuse me.—He can have nothing to say to me that any body need not hear. I am going away myself."

"No, no, nonsense, Lizzy.—I desire you will stay where you are."—And upon Elizabeth's seeming really, with vexed and embarrassed looks, about to escape, she added, "Lizzy, I insist upon your staying and hearing Mr. Collins."

Elizabeth would not oppose such an injunction—and a moment's consideration making her also sensible that it would be wisest to get it over as soon and as quietly as possible, she sat down again, and tried to conceal by incessant employment the feelings which were divided between distress and diversion. Mrs. Bennet and Kitty walked off, and as soon as they were gone Mr. Collins began.

"Believe me, my dear Miss Elizabeth, that your modesty, so far from doing you any disservice, rather adds to your other perfections. You would have been less amiable in my eyes had there not been this little unwillingness; but allow me to assure you that I have your respected mother's permission for this address. You can hardly doubt the purport of my discourse, however your natural delicacy may lead you to dissemble; my attentions have been too marked to be mistaken. Almost as soon as I entered the house I singled you out as the companion of my future life. But before I am run away with by my feelings on this subject, perhaps it will be advisable for me to state my reasons for marrying—and moreover for coming into Hertfordshire with the design of selecting a wife, as I certainly did."

The idea of Mr. Collins, with all his solemn composure, being run away with by his feelings, made Elizabeth so near laughing that she could not use the short pause he allowed in any attempt to stop him farther, and he continued:

"My reasons for marrying are, first, that I think it a right thing for every clergyman in easy circumstances (like myself) to set the example of matrimony in his parish. Secondly, that I am convinced it will add very greatly to my happiness; and thirdly—which perhaps I ought to have mentioned earlier, that it is the particular advice and recommendation of the very noble lady whom I have the honour of calling patroness. Twice has she condescended to give me her opinion (unasked too!) on this subject; and it was but the very Saturday night before I left Hunsford—between our pools at quadrille, while Mrs. Jenkinson was arranging Miss de Bourgh's foot-stool, that she said, 'Mr. Collins, you must marry. A clergyman like you must marry.—Chuse properly, chuse a gentlewoman for my sake; and for your own, let her be an active, useful sort of person, not brought up high, but able to make a small income go a good way. This is my advice. Find such a woman as soon as you can, bring her to Hunsford, and I will visit her.' Allow me, by the way, to observe, my fair cousin, that I do not reckon the notice and kindness of Lady Catherine de Bourgh as among the least of the advantages in my power to offer. You will find her manners beyond any thing I can describe; and your wit and vivacity I think must be acceptable to her, especially when tempered with the silence and respect which her rank will inevitably excite. Thus much for my general intention in favour of matrimony; it remains to be told why my views were directed to Longbourn instead of my own neighbourhood, where I assure you there are many amiable young women. But the fact is, that being, as I am, to inherit this estate after the death of your honoured father, (who, however, may live many years longer), I could not satisfy myself without resolving to chuse a wife from among his daughters, that the loss to them might be as little as possible, when the melancholy event takes place—which, however, as I have already said, may not be for several years. This has been my motive, my fair cousin, and I flatter myself it will not sink me in your esteem. And now nothing remains for me but to assure you in the most animated language of the violence of my affection. To fortune I am perfectly indifferent, and shall make no demand of that nature on your father, since I am well aware that it could not be complied with; and that one thousand pounds in the 4 per cents. which will not be yours till after your mother's decease, is all that you may ever be entitled to. On that head, therefore, I shall be uniformly silent; and you may assure yourself that no ungenerous reproach shall ever pass my lips when we are married."

It was absolutely necessary to interrupt him now.

"You are too hasty, Sir," she cried. "You forget that I have made no answer. Let me do it without farther loss of time. Accept my thanks for the compliment you are paying me. I am very sensible of the honour of your proposals, but it is impossible for me to do otherwise than decline them."

"I am not now to learn," replied Mr. Collins, with a formal wave of the hand, "that it is usual with young ladies to reject the addresses of the man whom they secretly mean to accept, when he first applies for their favour, and that sometimes the refusal is repeated a second or even a third time. I am therefore by no means discouraged by what you have just said, and shall hope to lead you to the altar ere long."

"Upon my word, Sir," cried Elizabeth, "your hope is rather an extraordinary one after my declaration. I do assure you that I am not one of those young ladies (if such young ladies there are) who are so daring as to risk their happiness on the chance of being asked a second time. I am perfectly serious in my refusal.—You could not make me happy, and I am convinced that I am the last woman in the world who would make you so.—Nay, were your friend Lady Catherine to know me, I am persuaded she would find me in every respect ill qualified for the situation."

"Were it certain that Lady Catherine would think so," said Mr. Collins very gravely—"but I cannot imagine that her ladyship would at all disapprove of you. And you may be certain that when I have the honour of seeing her again I shall speak in the highest terms of your modesty, economy, and other amiable qualifications."

"Indeed, Mr. Collins, all praise of me will be unnecessary. You must give me leave to judge for myself, and pay me the compliment of believing what I say. I wish you very happy and very rich, and by refusing your hand, do all in my power to prevent your being otherwise. In making me the offer, you must have satisfied the delicacy of your feelings with regard to my family, and may take possession of Longbourn estate whenever it falls, without any self-reproach. This matter may be considered, therefore, as finally settled." And rising as she thus spoke, she would have quitted the room, had not Mr. Collins thus addressed her,

"When I do myself the honour of speaking to you next on this subject I shall hope to receive a more favourable answer than you have now given me; though I am far from accusing you of cruelty at present, because I know it to be the established custom of your sex to reject a man on the first application, and perhaps you have even now said as much to encourage my suit as would be consistent with the true delicacy of the female character."

"Really, Mr. Collins," cried Elizabeth with some warmth, "you puzzle me exceedingly. If what I have hitherto said can appear to you in the form of encouragement, I know not how to express my refusal in such a way as may convince you of its being one."

"You must give me leave to flatter myself, my dear cousin, that your refusal of my addresses is merely words of course. My reasons for believing it are briefly these:—It does not appear to me that my hand is unworthy your acceptance, or that the establishment I can offer would be any other than highly desirable. My situation in life, my connections with the family of De Bourgh, and my relationship to your own, are circumstances highly in my favour; and you should take it into farther consideration that in spite of your manifold attractions, it is by no means certain that another offer of marriage may ever be made you. Your portion is unhappily so small that it will in all likelihood undo the effects of your loveliness and amiable qualifications. As I must therefore conclude that you are not serious in your rejection of me, I shall chuse to attribute it to your wish of increasing my love by suspense, according to the usual practice of elegant females."

"I do assure you, Sir, that I have no pretension whatever to that kind of elegance which consists in tormenting a respectable man. I would rather be paid the compliment of being believed sincere. I thank you again and again for the honour you have done me in your proposals, but to accept them is absolutely impossible. My feelings in every respect forbid it. Can I speak plainer? Do not consider me now as an elegant female intending to plague you, but as a rational creature speaking the truth from her heart."

"You are uniformly charming!" cried he, with an air of awkward gallantry; "and I am persuaded that when sanctioned by the express authority of both your excellent parents, my proposals will not fail of being acceptable."

To such perseverance in wilful self-deception Elizabeth would make no reply, and immediately and in silence withdrew; determined, if he persisted in considering her repeated refusals as flattering encouragement, to apply to her father, whose negative might be uttered in such a manner as must be decisive, and whose behaviour at least could not be mistaken for the affectation and coquetry of an elegant female.

Chapter 20

Mr. Collins was not left long to the silent contemplation of his successful love; for Mrs. Bennet, having dawdled about in the vestibule to watch for the end of the conference, no sooner saw Elizabeth open the door and with quick step pass her towards the staircase, than she entered the breakfast-room, and congratulated both him and herself in warm terms on the happy prospect of their nearer connection. Mr. Collins received and returned these felicitations with equal pleasure, and then proceeded to relate the particulars of their interview, with the result of which he trusted he had every reason to be satisfied, since the refusal which his cousin had stedfastly given him would naturally flow from her bashful modesty and the genuine delicacy of her character.

This information, however, startled Mrs. Bennet;—she would have been glad to be equally satisfied that her daughter had meant to encourage him by protesting against his proposals, but she dared not to believe it, and could not help saying so.

"But depend upon it, Mr. Collins," she added, "that Lizzy shall be brought to reason. I will speak to her about it myself directly. She is a very headstrong foolish girl, and does not know her own interest; but I will *make* her know it."

"Pardon me for interrupting you, Madam," cried Mr. Collins; "but if she is really headstrong and foolish, I know not whether she would altogether be a very desirable wife to a man in my situation, who naturally looks for happiness in the marriage state. If therefore she actually persists in rejecting my suit, perhaps it were better not to force her into accepting me, because if liable to such defects of temper, she could not contribute much to my felicity."

"Sir, you quite misunderstand me," said Mrs. Bennet, alarmed. "Lizzy is only headstrong in such matters as these. In every thing else she is as good natured a girl as ever lived. I will go directly to Mr. Bennet, and we shall very soon settle it with her, I am sure."

She would not give him time to reply, but hurrying instantly to her husband, called out as she entered the library,

"Oh! Mr. Bennet, you are wanted immediately; we are all in an uproar. You must come and make Lizzy marry Mr. Collins, for she vows she will not have him, and if you do not make haste he will change his mind and not have *her*."

Mr. Bennet raised his eyes from his book as she entered, and fixed them on her face with a calm unconcern which was not in the least altered by her communication.

"I have not the pleasure of understanding you," said he, when she had finished her speech. "Of what are you talking?"

"Of Mr. Collins and Lizzy. Lizzy declares she will not have Mr. Collins, and Mr. Collins begins to say that he will not have Lizzy."

"And what am I to do on the occasion?—It seems an hopeless business."

"Speak to Lizzy about it yourself. Tell her that you insist upon her marrying him."

"Let her be called down. She shall hear my opinion."

Mrs. Bennet rang the bell, and Miss Elizabeth was summoned to the library.

"Come here, child," cried her father as she appeared. "I have sent for you on an affair of importance. I understand that Mr. Collins has made you an offer of marriage. Is it true?" Elizabeth replied that it was. "Very well—and this offer of marriage you have refused?"

"I have, Sir."

"Very well. We now come to the point. Your mother insists upon your accepting it. Is not it so, Mrs. Bennet?"

"Yes, or I will never see her again."

"An unhappy alternative is before you, Elizabeth. From this day you must be a stranger to one of your parents.—Your mother will never see you again if you do *not* marry Mr. Collins, and I will never see you again if you *do*."

Elizabeth could not but smile at such a conclusion of such a beginning; but Mrs. Bennet, who had persuaded herself that her husband regarded the affair as she wished, was excessively disappointed.

"What do you mean, Mr. Bennet, by talking in this way? You promised me to *insist* upon her marrying him."

"My dear," replied her husband, "I have two small favours to request. First, that you will allow me the free use of my understanding on the present occasion; and secondly, of my room. I shall be glad to have the library to myself as soon as may be."

Not yet, however, in spite of her disappointment in her husband, did Mrs. Bennet give up the point. She talked to Elizabeth again and again; coaxed and threatened her by turns. She endeavoured to secure Jane in her interest, but Jane with all possible mildness declined interfering;—and Elizabeth sometimes with real earnestness and sometimes with playful gaiety replied to her attacks. Though her manner varied however, her determination never did.

Mr. Collins, meanwhile, was meditating in solitude on what had passed. He thought too well of himself to comprehend on what motive his cousin could refuse him; and though his pride was hurt, he suffered in no other way. His regard for her was quite imaginary; and the possibility of her deserving her mother's reproach prevented his feeling any regret.

While the family were in this confusion, Charlotte Lucas came to spend the day with them. She was met in the vestibule by Lydia, who, flying to her, cried in a half whisper, "I am glad you are come, for there is such fun here!— What do you think has happened this morning?—Mr. Collins has made an offer to Lizzy, and she will not have him."

Charlotte had hardly time to answer, before they were joined by Kitty, who came to tell the same news, and no sooner had they entered the breakfast-room, where Mrs. Bennet was alone, than she likewise began on the subject, calling on Miss Lucas for her compassion, and entreating her to persuade her friend Lizzy to comply with the wishes of all her family. "Pray do, my dear Miss Lucas," she added in a melancholy tone, "for nobody is on my side, no-body takes part with me, I am cruelly used, nobody feels for my poor nerves."

Charlotte's reply was spared by the entrance of Jane and Elizabeth. . . .

Chapter 22

The Bennets were engaged to dine with the Lucases, and again during the chief of the day, was Miss Lucas so kind as to listen to Mr. Collins. Elizabeth took an opportunity of thanking her. "It keeps him in good humour," said she, "and I am more obliged to you than I can express." Charlotte assured her friend of her satisfaction in being useful, and that it amply repaid her for the little sacrifice of her time. This was very amiable, but Charlotte's kindness extended farther than Elizabeth had any conception of;—its object was nothing less, than to secure her from any return of Mr. Collins's addresses, by engaging them to-wards herself. Such was Miss Lucas's scheme; and appearances were so favour-able that when they parted at night, she would have felt almost sure of success if he had not been to leave Hertfordshire so very soon. But here, she did injustice to the fire and independence of his character, for it led him to escape out of Longbourn House the next morning with admirable slyness, and hasten to Lucas Lodge to throw himself at her feet. He was anxious to avoid the notice of his cousins, from a conviction that if they saw him depart, they could not fail to conjecture his design, and he was not willing to have the attempt known till its success could be known likewise; for though feeling almost secure, and with reason, for Charlotte had been tolerably encouraging, he was comparatively diffident since the adventure of Wednesday. His reception however was of the most flattering kind. Miss Lucas perceived him from an upper window as he walked towards the house, and instantly set out to meet him accidentally in the lane. But little had she dared to hope that so much love and eloquence awaited her there.

In as short a time as Mr. Collins's long speeches would allow, every thing was settled between them to the satisfaction of both; and as they entered the house, he earnestly entreated her to name the day that was to make him the happiest of men; and though such a solicitation must be waved for the present, the lady felt no inclination to trifle with his happiness. The stupidity with which he was favoured by nature, must guard his courtship from any charm that could make a woman wish for its continuance; and Miss Lucas, who accepted him solely from the pure and disinterested desire of an establishment, cared not how soon that establishment were gained.

Sir William and Lady Lucas were speedily applied to for their consent; and it was bestowed with a most joyful alacrity. Mr. Collins's present circumstances made it a most eligible match for their daughter, to whom they could give little fortune; and his prospects of future wealth were exceedingly fair. Lady Lucas began directly to calculate with more interest than the matter had ever excited before, how many years longer Mr. Bennet was likely to live; and Sir William gave it as his decided opinion, that whenever Mr. Collins should be in possession of the Longbourn estate, it would be highly expedient that both he and his wife should make their appearance at St. James's. The whole family in short were properly overjoyed on the occasion. The younger girls formed hopes of coming out a year or two sooner than they might otherwise have done; and the boys were relieved from their apprehension of Charlotte's dying an old maid. Charlotte herself was tolerably composed. She had gained her point, and had time to consider of it. Her reflections were in general satisfactory. Mr. Collins to be sure was neither sensible nor agreeable; his society was irksome, and his attachment to her must be imaginary. But still he would be her husband.—Without thinking highly either of men or of matrimony, marriage had always been her object; it was the only honourable provision for well-educated young women of small fortune, and however uncertain of giving happiness, must be their pleasantest preservative from want. This preservative she had now obtained; and at the age of twenty-seven, without having ever been handsome, she felt all the good luck of it. The least agreeable circumstance in the business, was the surprise it must occasion to Elizabeth Bennet, whose friendship she valued beyond that of any other person. Elizabeth would wonder, and probably would blame her; and though her resolution was not to be shaken, her feelings must be hurt by such disapprobation. She resolved to give her the information herself, and therefore charged Mr. Collins when he returned to Longbourn to dinner, to drop no hint of what had passed before any of the family. A promise of secrecy was of course very dutifully given, but it could not be kept without difficulty; for the curiosity excited by his long absence, burst forth in such very direct questions on his return, as required some ingenuity to evade, and he was at the same time exercising great self-denial, for he was longing to publish his prosperous love.

As he was to begin his journey too early on the morrow to see any of the family, the ceremony of leave-taking was performed when the ladies moved for the night; and Mrs. Bennet with great politeness and cordiality said how happy they should be to see him at Longbourn again, whenever his other engagements might allow him to visit them.

"My dear Madam," he replied, "this invitation is particularly gratifying, because it is what I have been hoping to receive; and you may be very certain that I shall avail myself of it as soon as possible."

They were all astonished; and Mr. Bennet, who could by no means wish for so speedy a return, immediately said,

"But is there not danger of Lady Catherine's disapprobation here, my good sir?—You had better neglect your relations, than run the risk of offending your patroness."

"My dear sir," replied Mr. Collins, "I am particularly obliged to you for this friendly caution, and you may depend upon my not taking so material a step without her ladyship's concurrence."

"You cannot be too much on your guard. Risk any thing rather than her displeasure; and if you find it likely to be raised by your coming to us again, which I should think exceedingly probable, stay quietly at home, and be satisfied that we shall take no offence."

"Believe me, my dear sir, my gratitude is warmly excited by such affectionate attention; and depend upon it, you will speedily receive from me a letter of thanks for this, as well as for every other mark of your regard during my stay in Hertfordshire. As for my fair cousins, though my absence may not be long enough to render it necessary, I shall now take the liberty of wishing them health and happiness, not excepting my cousin Elizabeth."

With proper civilities the ladies then withdrew; all of them equally surprised to find that he meditated a quick return. Mrs. Bennet wished to understand by it that he thought of paying his addresses to one of her younger girls, and Mary might have been prevailed on to accept him. She rated his abilities much higher than any of the others; there was a solidity in his reflections which often struck her, and though by no means so clever as herself, she thought that if encouraged to read and improve himself by such an example as her's, he might become a very agreeable companion. But on the following morning, every hope of this kind was done away. Miss Lucas called soon after breakfast, and in a private conference with Elizabeth related the event of the day before.

The possibility of Mr. Collins's fancying himself in love with her friend had once occurred to Elizabeth within the last day or two; but that Charlotte could encourage him, seemed almost as far from possibility as that she could encourage him herself, and her astonishment was consequently so great as to overcome at first the bounds of decorum, and she could not help crying out,

"Engaged to Mr. Collins! my dear Charlotte,—impossible!"

The steady countenance which Miss Lucas had commanded in telling her story, gave way to a momentary confusion here on receiving so direct a reproach; though, as it was no more than she expected, she soon regained her composure, and calmly replied,

"Why should you be surprised, my dear Eliza?—Do you think it incredible that Mr. Collins should be able to procure any woman's good opinion, because he was not so happy as to succeed with you?"

But Elizabeth had now recollected herself, and making a strong effort for it, was able to assure her with tolerable firmness that the prospect of their relationship was highly grateful to her, and that she wished her all imaginable happiness.

"I see what you are feeling," replied Charlotte,—"you must be surprised, very much surprised,—so lately as Mr. Collins was wishing to marry you. But when you have had time to think it all over, I hope you will be satisfied with what I have done. I am not romantic you know. I never was. I ask only a comfortable home; and considering Mr. Collins's character, connections, and situation in life, I am convinced that my chance of happiness with him is as fair, as most people can boast on entering the marriage state."

Elizabeth quietly answered "Undoubtedly;"—and after an awkward pause, they returned to the rest of the family. Charlotte did not stay much longer, and Elizabeth was then left to reflect on what she had heard. It was a long time before she became at all reconciled to the idea of so unsuitable a match. The strangeness of Mr. Collins's making two offers of marriage within three days, was nothing in comparison of his being now accepted. She had always felt that Charlotte's opinion of matrimony was not exactly like her own, but she could not have supposed it possible that when called into action, she would have sac-rificed every better feeling to worldly advantage. Charlotte the wife of Mr. Collins, was a most humiliating picture!—And to the pang of a friend disgrac-ing herself and sunk in her esteem, was added the distressing conviction that it was impossible for that friend to be tolerably happy in the lot she had chosen.

Kierkegaard, "Some Reflections on Marriage"

In 1845, the Danish philosopher and theologian, Søren Kierkegaard (1813–1855), wrote, pseudonymously, a profound meditation on the aesthetic, ethical, and religious spheres of human life, Stages on Life's Way: Studies by Various Persons. *The central (of three) parts, written "By a Married Man," is entitled "Some Reflections on Marriage in Answer to Objections," from which several excerpts appear in this anthology. This selection, from the opening pages of "Some Reflections," celebrates the unique kind of association that is marriage, showing forth its defining characteristics. Of special interest are marriage's capacity for transforming the little things of everyday life into moments of glory and faith-in-marriage's capacity for sustaining the best in the love that was present in the original falling in love. Honesty compels us to note that Kierkegaard himself, in a life-wrenching and life-shaping decision, broke off his engagement to the woman he loved, for what were apparently reasons of heeding a higher calling; similarly, in his book, the final "stage" on life's way is not marital (i.e., ethical) but religious. Nevertheless, his pseudonymous "A Married Man" makes a case for marriage whose eloquence is not easily surpassed, and whose power is not easily rejected.*

My dear reader, if you do not have the time and opportunity to take a dozen years of your life to travel around the world to see everything a world traveler is acquainted with, if you do not have the capability and qualifications from years of practice in a foreign language to penetrate to the differences in national characteristics as these become apparent to the research scholar, if you are not bent upon discovering a new astronomical system that will displace both the Copernican and the Ptolemaic—then marry; and if you have time for the first, the capability for the second, the idea for the last, then marry *also.* Even if you did not manage to see the whole globe or to speak in many tongues or to know all about the heavens, you will not regret it, for marriage is and remains the most important voyage of discovery a human being undertakes; compared with a married man's knowledge of life, any other knowledge of it is superficial, for he and he alone has properly immersed himself in life. It is true, of course, that no poet will be able to say of you what the poet says of the wily Ulysses—that he saw many cities of men and learned to know their mentality, but the question is whether he would not have learned just as much and things just as gratifying if he had stayed at home with Penelope. If no one else is of this opinion, my wife is, and if I am not very much in error, every wife agrees. Now that is a bit more than a simple majority, all the more so since he who has the wives on his side no doubt has the men, too. Of course, the traveling companions on this expedition are few; it is not, as on five- and ten-year-long expeditions, a large group, which also, please note, continually remains the same; but then it is reserved for marriage to establish a unique kind of acquaintance, the most wonderful of all, and in which every addition is always the most welcome.

Therefore, praised be marriage, praised be everyone who speaks in its honor. If a beginner may allow himself an observation, then I will say that the reason it seems to me to be so wonderful is that everything revolves around little things that the divine element in marriage nevertheless transforms by a miracle into something significant for the believer. Then, too, all these little things have the remarkable characteristic that nothing can be evaluated in advance, nothing worked out in a rough plan; but while the understanding stands still and the imagination is on a wild-goose chase and calculation calculates wrongly and sagacity despairs, the married life goes along and is transformed from glory unto glory, the insignificant becomes more and more significant by a miracle—for the believer. But a believer one must be, and a married man who is not a believer is a tiresome character, a real household pest. There is nothing more fatal when one goes out in the company of others to enjoy demonstrations and ventures in natural magic than to have a killjoy along who continually disbelieves even though he cannot explain the feats. Yet one puts up with a calamity such as that; after all, it is seldom one goes out that way, and moreover there is the advantage that a fusty spectator like that gets in on the act. Ordinarily the professor of natural magic has it in for him and makes a fool of him by using him to entertain the rest of us with his cleverness . . . But a slug of a married man like that ought to be put in a sack like a patricide and thrown into the water. What agony to see a woman exhaust all her lovableness in persuading him, to see him, after having received the initiation that entitles him to be a believer, only spoil everything—spoil everything—because, jesting aside, marriage in many ways is really a venture in natural magic and a venture in it is truly wonderful. It is nauseating to listen to a pastor who himself does not believe what he says, but it is still more nauseating to see a married man who does not believe in his estate, and all the more shocking because the audience can desert the pastor, but a wife cannot desert her husband, cannot do it, will not do it, does not wish to do it—and even this cannot persuade him.

Ordinarily we speak only of a married man's unfaithfulness, but what is just as bad is a married man's lack of faith. Faith is all that is required, and faith compensates for everything. Just let understanding and sagacity and sophistication reckon, figure out, and describe how a married man ought to be: there is only one attribute that makes him lovable, and that is faith, absolute faith in marriage. Just let experience in life try to define exactly what is required of a married man's faithfulness; there is only one faithfulness, one honesty that is truly lovable and hides everything in itself, and that is the honesty toward God and his wife and his married estate in refusing to deny the miracle.

This is also my consolation when I choose to write about marriage, for while I disclaim any other competence, I do claim just one—conviction. That I have it I know in myself, and I share it with my wife, which to me is of major importance, for even if it behooves the woman to be silent in the congregation and not to be occupied with scholarship and art, what is said about marriage ought essentially to be such that it meets with her approval. It does not follow that she is supposed to know how to evaluate everything critically—that kind of reflection is not suitable for her—but she should have an absolute *veto,* and her approval must be respected as adequately reassuring. My conviction, then, is my one and only justification, and in turn the guarantee for my firm conviction is the weight of the responsibility under which my life, like every married man's life, is placed.

To be sure, I do not feel the weight as a burden but as a blessing; to be sure, I do not feel the bond as binding but as liberating, and yet it is there. The bond? No, the innumerable bonds by which I am bound fast in life as the tree is bound by the multiple branching roots. Suppose everything were to change for me—my God, if that were possible!—suppose I were to feel tied down by being married—what would Laocoön's misery be compared to mine, for no snake, no ten snakes, would be able to wind themselves as alarmingly and tightly around a person's body and squeeze as does the marriage that ties me down in hundreds of ways and consequently would fetter me with a hundred chains. So you see, then—if this is a guarantee—while I feel happy and content and give thanks without ceasing for my happiness here on earth, I also have a presentiment of the terror that can overwhelm a man along this way, of the hell that he builds up who as a husband *adscriptus glebae* [bound to the earth] tries to tear himself loose and thereby continually finds only how impossible it is for him, tries to cut one chain and thereby only discovers one even more elastic that binds him indissolubly—if this is an adequate negative guarantee that what I may have to say is not idle thoughts conceived in a spare moment, is not crafty brain webs designed to trap others, then please do not disdain what I may have to say. . . .

Wherever I am, even if it were in the fiery furnace, when I am to talk about marriage, I notice nothing. An angel is with me, or, more correctly, I am not there, I am with her, her whom I still continue to love with the blessed resolution of youth, I who, although a married man for several years, still have the honor of fighting under the victorious banner of the happy first love alongside her through whom I feel the meaning of my life, that it has meaning and in many ways. For what to the rebel are chains, what to the slave-minded are onerous duties, to me are titles and positions of honor I would not exchange for those of the King, King of the Wends and the Goths, Duke of Slesvig, etc. That is, I do not know whether these titles and positions of honor would have significance in another life, whether they, like so much else, are forgotten in a hundred years, whether it is possible to imagine and clearly ascertain how the idea of such relationships can fill out an eternal consciousness in recollection. I honor the King, as does every good married man, but I would not exchange my titles with his. This is the way I see myself; and I like to think that every other married man does the same, and really, whether the single individual is far away or nearby, I wish that he also would be as I am.

See, I secretly wear on my breast the ribbon of my order, love's necklace of roses. Believe me, its roses are not withered; believe me, its roses do not wither. Even if they change with the years, they still do not fade; even if the rose is not as red, it is because it has become a white rose—it did not fade. And now my titles and positions of honor—what is so glorious about them is that they are so equally apportioned, for only the divine justice of marriage is able continually to give like for like. What I am through her she is through me, and neither of us is anything by oneself, but we are what we are in union. Through her I am Man, for only a married man [*Aegtemand*] is an authentic man [*ægte Mand*]; compared with this any other title is nothing and actually presupposes this. Through her I am Father—any other position of honor is but a human invention, a fad that is forgotten in a hundred years. Through her I am Head of the Family; through her I am Defender of the Home, Breadwinner, Guardian of the Children.

. . . I am her husband, by marriage—that is, by marriage I become eligible for the prize, the race track that is my Rhodes and my dancing place. I am her friend—oh, that I might be that in all sincerity of heart, oh, that she might never feel the need of anyone more sincere. I am her counselor—oh, that my wisdom might be equal to my will. I am her comfort and her encouragement—admittedly not yet summoned—oh, but if I am ever summoned to serve in this capacity, may my strength be equal to the disposition of my heart. I am her debtor, my accounting is honest, and the accounting itself is a blissful task. And finally, this I know, I will be a recollection of her when death one day separates us—oh, that my memory will be faithful, that it will preserve everything when it is lost, an annuity of recollection for my remaining days, that it will give me even the most minor details again and that I may say with the poet when I am anxious about today: *et haec meminisse juvat* [and it is pleasant to recollect these things], and when I am troubled about tomorrow: *et haec meminisse juvabit* [and it will be pleasant to recollect these things]. Alas, like the judge in court, one must at times put up with the dismay of reading again and again a summary of a criminal's *vita ante acta* [earlier life], but with a beloved wife's *vita ante acta* one never becomes bored—neither does one need the accurate printed details in order to recollect. It is certainly true that willing hands make light work, and so it is also with the task of remembrance. It is probably true (when said, it sounds infatuated) that in death the picture of the beloved will be found in the faithful lover's heart, but from the marital point of view a resolution of the will is vigilant in the falling in love so that it does not become lost in the infinite. To be sure, love declares that a moment with the beloved is heavenly bliss, but marriage wishes love well and fortunately is better informed. Suppose it is the case that the first effervescent passion of falling in love, however beautiful it is, cannot be sustained; then marriage knows precisely how the best in the love can be sustained. If a child who has received from his parents a copy of his school book has, so to speak, devoured it even before the year is over, is this a sign that he is to be praised as a pupil for his zeal and delight? So it is with marriage—the married man who from God in heaven received his copy (as beautiful as a gift from God can be!) and read it daily, every day throughout a long life, and when it was laid aside, when night came and the reading had to stop, it was just as beautiful as the day he received it: was not this honest discretion, directly proportionate to the delight of the infatuation, with which he reads again and again, was this not just as praiseworthy, just as strong an expression of falling in love as the strongest expression that falling in love has at its disposal?

Tucker, "Monogamy and Its Discontents"

In this contemporary essay (published in 1993), William Tucker (born in 1942) makes an argument for monogamous marriage from the social point of view. Drawing on sociobiological observations about the different reproductive "strategies" of females and males, Tucker makes a nonreligious and amoral case for the social importance of monogamy, while acknowledging that marriage represents a compromise with built-in sources of discontent. Deserving special attention are the arguments concerning the well-being of children under monogamy and the benefits of social peace and cooperation that flow from reducing sexual competition among males and defusing sexual tensions in social relations between men and women. Are Tucker's social and nonmoral arguments for marriage compatible with the personal and moral arguments made in the other selections? Can marriage be successfully defended only or mainly on these social grounds?

> "It is remarkable that, little as men are able to exist in isolation, they should nevertheless feel as a heavy burden the sacrifices that civilization expects of them in order to make a communal life possible."
>
> —Sigmund Freud, *The Future of an Illusion*

America is in a period of cultural crisis. For as long as we have been a civilization, monogamy, heterosexuality, legitimacy, and the virtues of marital fidelity have been givens of nature. The major religions have sanctioned them, as do four thousand years of Western history. Out-of-wedlock births, homosexuality, and other forms of sexual "deviance" have always existed, but have never laid claim to the mainstream.

All this is now coming under challenge. Part of it may simply be cultural exhaustion—the foolish confidence that the major battles of civilization have been fought and won and that it is now time for a little self-indulgence. Or it may be that the taste for the exotic and forbidden, usually confined to a small minority, has at last become available to the average person.

All this must be tolerated. In a free country, you can't stop people from doing what they want, especially when they have the money and leisure to do it. The situation is complicated, however, by the existence of a vast American "underclass" that does not generally share in the affluence, but is daily exposed to the sirens of self-indulgence. While the abandonment of cultural norms may have an exotic quality for the affluent, it is a palpable threat to the upward aspirations of the poor.

On the matter of single motherhood and illegitimacy, members of the underclass—particularly those of African-American origin—have proved peculiarly susceptible. Single motherhood has virtually become the norm in African-American society. (Over 65 per cent of black children are now born out of wedlock.) The failure to adhere to monogamy and two-parent child-rearing now forms the single greatest obstacle to the advancement of America's underclass.

Yet to speak in favor of monogamy, sexual modesty, fidelity, restraint, and two-parent families in the current cultural climate is to find oneself subject to the charge of being a bigot, a religious nut, or just hopelessly out of touch. The common assumption, particularly among the intelligentsia, is that all the traditional arguments for monogamy and two-parent families are religious and that everything that could be said in their favor was spoken centuries ago.

I cannot agree. For as much as monogamy has been sanctioned by Western culture, I do not believe that its function as the center of our civilization has even been completely understood. There is in everyone a vague awareness that monogamy produces a peaceful social contract that is the framework for cultural harmony and economic advancement. Yet this subconscious recognition has rarely been explored at any great length. There is never any real articulation that monogamy is an ancient compromise whose breakdown only lets loose antagonisms that society has long suppressed. Monogamy, after all, is only one possible outcome of the age-old sexual dance. There are others, whose characteristics may not be quite so appealing.

Yet like all hard-won compromises, monogamy does not produce a perfect outcome for every individual. When examined closely, it proves to be the source of many private dissatisfactions, which form a nagging undercurrent of discontent in any monogamous culture. Ordinarily, these disaffections remain a form of "deviance," generally suppressed and disapproved by the vast majority, although virtually impossible to eradicate. Only when the core ideals of the culture come under attack—when people begin to celebrate these discontents and embrace them within themselves—only then does the underlying architecture of the social contract come into stark relief.

The question that we face today is how much free rein we can give the discontents of monogamy before we risk overturning the central character of our culture. Society, of course, is not without its defenses. The long-standing, almost universal dislike and disapproval of child-bearing out of wedlock, of sexual infidelity, of easy divorce, of public prostitution and pornography, and of widespread, blatant homosexuality—these are not just irrational intolerances. They are the ancient, forgotten logic that holds together a monogamous society. As long as these attitudes remain unexamined, however, they can play little part in the current debate and will be easily dismissed as mere prejudices.

What we need, then, is a defense of monogamy based on a rational understanding of its underlying principles. Here is an attempted beginning.

Let us start with some basic arithmetic. In any reproducing population, the laws of chance dictate that there will be about the same number of males and females. There are thus three ways in which the population can arrange itself for mating purposes: 1) polyandry, in which one female collects several males as mates; 2) polygyny (often called, less precisely, polygamy), in which one male collects several females; and 3) monogamy, in which each female and each male mate with only one other individual.

Of the three possibilities, the first—polyandry—is the rarest in nature. An understanding of the basics of reproduction tells us why.

In nearly all species, the female role in reproduction is the "limiting factor." This has to do with the differences between eggs and sperm. Sperm are small and motile, while eggs are large and relatively immobile. The egg generally comes wrapped in a package of nutrients that will feed the fertilized ovum until "birth." Because eggs are more complex—and therefore harder to manufacture—a female generates far fewer eggs than a male generates sperm. (Among mammals, a single male ejaculation often contains more sperm cells than a female will produce eggs in her lifetime.) Since there are always more sperm than eggs—and since it takes one of each to produce an offspring—eggs are the limiting factor to reproduction.

As a result, females have generally gone on to play a larger role in nurturing offspring as well. The principle that determines this responsibility has been identified by biologists as the "last chance to abandon." Here is how it works.

When fertilization of the egg takes place, one partner is usually left with the egg in his or her possession—often attached to or within his or her body. Most often, this is the female. This leaves the male free to go and seek other mating opportunities. The female, on the other hand, has two basic options: 1) she can abandon the egg and try to mate again (but this will only leave her in the same dilemma); or 2) she can stay with the egg and try to nurture it to maturity. The latter is a better reproductive strategy. As a result, females become "mothers," caring for the fertilized eggs, and often the newborn offspring as well.

The few exceptions prove the rule. Among seahorses, the fertilized egg is nurtured in a kangaroo-like pouch on the *male's* stomach. This makes the male the limiting factor to reproduction. As a result, the sex roles are reversed. Male seahorses become "mothers," nurturing their offspring to maturity, while females abandon their "impregnated" sexual partners and look for new mating opportunities.

The logic of reproduction has produced another universal characteristic in nature, called "female coyness." Males can spread their sperm far and wide, impregnating as many females as possible, while females may get only one mating opportunity per season. Therefore, females must choose wisely. In almost every species, males are the sexual aggressors, while females hold back, trying to select the best mate. Often the male is made to perform some display of strength or beauty, or go through some ritual expression of responsibility (nest-building) before the female agrees to mate with him. With seahorses, once again, the roles are reversed. Males are coy and reluctant, while females are the sexual aggressors.

It is for these reasons that polyandry—one female forming a mating bond with several males—is uncommon and unfavorable. Even though a single female might consort with several males, she can only be impregnated by one or two of them. Thus, most males would be unsuccessful. Moreover, the attachment of several males to one female would mean that other females would be left with no mates. The outcome would be a very slow rate of reproduction. In addition, any male who broke the rules and left his mate for an unmated female would achieve reproductive success, making the whole system extremely unstable. For all these reasons, polyandry is very rare in nature.

Polygyny, on the other hand—the form of polygamy where one male mates with several females—is universally common. (Although "polygamy" can refer to either polyandry or polygyny, it is generally used interchangeably with polygyny.) Polygamy is probably the most "natural" way of mating. It is particularly predominant among mammals, where the fertilized embryo is retained within the female's body, reducing the male's post-conception nurturing to near-zero. Given the differences in size, strength, beauty, or social skills among males, it is inevitable that—in an unregulated sexual marketplace—successful males will collect multiple mating partners while unsuccessful males will be left with none. A successful male lion collects a pride of seven to ten female lions, mating with each of them as they come into heat. A male deer mates with about six to eight female deer. A silverback male gorilla collects a harem of five or six female gorillas. Biologists have even determined that the sexual dimorphism in a species—the size difference between males and females—is directly correlated to the size of the harem: i.e., the bigger the male is in relation to females, the more females he will control. On this scale, we are "slightly polygamous," with male humans outweighing females enough to collect about one and a half mates apiece.

Polygamy creates a clear social order, with distinct winners and losers. Let us look at how this works.

A dominant male wins because he can reproduce with as many females as he can reasonably control. Thus, he can "spread his genes" far and wide, producing many more progeny than he would be able to do under a different sexual regime.

But low-status females are winners, too. This is because: 1) Even the lowest-status females get to mate; there are no "old maids" in a polygamous society. 2) Nearly all females get access to high-status males. Since there are no artificial limits on the number of mates a male can collect, all females can attach themselves to a few relatively desirable males.

The effect upon high-status females is approximately neutral, but the clear losers are low-status males, the "bachelor herd" that is shut out of the mating equation. In some species, like elephants, the bachelor herd forms a dispirited gaggle living relatively meaningless lives on the edge of society. In others, like various monkeys, the subdominants form all-male gangs that combine their efforts to steal females from successful males. In a highly social species, such as baboons, the bachelor herd has been incorporated into the troop. Subdominant males form a "centurion guard" that protects the dominant male and his harem from predators. Among themselves, meanwhile, they engage in endless status struggles, trying to move up the social ladder toward their own mating possibilities.

Altogether, then, polygamy is a very natural and successful reproductive system. Since all females mate, the reproductive capacity of the population is maximized. There is also a strong selective drive toward desirable characteristics. As the operators of stud farms have long known, allowing only the swiftest and strongest males to breed produces the most desirable population.

Yet despite the clear reproductive advantages of polygamy, some species have abandoned it in favor of the more complex and artificially limiting system of monogamy. Why? The answer seems to be that monogamy is better adapted to the task of rearing offspring. This is particularly true where living conditions are harsh or where the offspring go through a long period of early dependency. The task is better handled by *two* parents than one. Quite literally, a species adopts monogamy "for the sake of the children."

Among animals, the most prominent example is birds. Because the fertilized egg is laid outside the female's body, a long period of nesting is required. This ties the male to the task of nurturing. Most bird species are monogamous through each mating season, and many mate for life.

Once mammalian development moved the gestating egg back inside the female's body, however, the need for "nesting" disappeared. With only a few exceptions (beavers, gibbons, orangutans), mammals are polygamous.

Yet as human beings evolved from our proto-chimp ancestors, the record is fairly clear that we reinvented monogamy. Present-day hunter-gatherers—who parallel the earliest human societies—are largely monogamous. Only with the invention of horticulture did many societies around the world revert to polygamy. Then, when animals were harnessed to the plow and urban civilizations were born, human societies again became almost exclusively monogamous. This wandering pattern of development has been the cause of much confusion. When monogamous Western European civilizations discovered the primitive polygamies of Africa and the South Seas in the seventeenth and eighteenth centuries, they assumed that the earliest human civilizations had been polygamous and had later evolved into the "higher" pattern of monogamy. It was only with the discovery of monogamous hunter-gatherers that the mystery was finally resolved. Rather than being an earlier form, polygamy is actually a later development in which many cultures have apparently become sidetracked. Both the earliest and the most advanced (economically successful) human civilizations are generally monogamous.

What has made monogamy so successful a format for human cooperation? First and foremost, monogamy creates a social contract that reduces the sexual competition among males. The underlying assumption of monogamy is that *every male gets a reasonable chance to mate.* As a result, the do-or-die quality of sexual competition among males abates. When one male can collect many females, mating takes on a deadly intensity. With monogamy, however, a more democratic outcome is assured. The bachelor herd disappears.

Second, because monogamy assures the possibility of reproduction to every member of the group, a social contract is born. One need only consider the sultan's harem—where male guards must be eunuchized—to realize that a society that practices polygamy has an inherently non-democratic character. No offer can be extended to marginal or outcast members that entices them to be part of the group. Under monogamy, however, society can function as a cohesive whole.

This is why, under monogamy, other forms of cooperation become possible. Males and females may pair off, but they also maintain other familial and social relationships. Both males and females can form task-oriented groups (in primitive societies, the line between "men's" and "women's work" is always carefully drawn). As society becomes more complex, men and women frequently exchange roles and, although there is always a certain amount of sexual tension, males and females can work together in non-mating settings.

Other social primates have never reached the same level of complexity. Gibbons and orangutans are monogamous—but almost too much so; mated pairs are strongly attached to each other, but live in social isolation, rarely interacting with other members of the species. Gorilla bands generally ignore each other—except when males raid each other's harems. Baboon troops are more organized and task oriented, often encompassing as many as fifty to a hundred individuals. But behavior is rigidly hierarchical. Females are kept at the center of the troop, under close supervision of the alpha male and his associates. Subdominant males guard the periphery. Only the alpha and an occasional close ally mate with females as they come into heat.

Perhaps the most interesting attempt at creating a more complex society is among our closest relatives, the chimpanzees. Chimps practice a polymorphous polygamy, where every female takes care to mate with every male. Sex takes place in public and is relatively non-competitive. When a female comes into estrus, her bottom turns bright pink, advertising her receptivity. Males queue up according to status, but every male, no matter how low on the social ladder, is allowed to copulate.

This creates its own social harmony. For males, it reduces sexual rivalry. Within the "brotherhood" of the tribe, there is little overt sexual competition (although it persists in other subtle ways). As a result, male chimps cooperate in establishing territories to exclude other males and occasionally hunt smaller animals such as monkeys.

The system also creates an advantage for females. Within a polygamous social group, one of the greatest hazards to child-rearing is male jealousy. The male owner of a female harem constantly guards against the possibility that he is wasting energy protecting the offspring of other males. When a new male lion displaces the former owner of a pride, he immediately kills off all the young in order to set the females to work reproducing his own offspring. The heads of polygamous monkey clans do the same thing.

But with chimpanzees, things are different. By taking care to mate with every male, a female assures each male member of the troop that he *might* be the father of her offspring. By "confusing paternity," females create a safe harbor for themselves, within which they are able to raise their offspring in relative tranquillity.

These techniques of unrestricted sexuality and indeterminate paternity have been tried from time to time in small human societies, notably among small religious and political sects. However, they have generally been a failure. The difficulty is that we have eaten too much of the tree of knowledge. We are too good at calculating which progeny are our own and which are not. (Child abuse and infanticide are most common when a man doubts his paternity.)

Rather than living in collective doubt, we have developed complex personalities that allow us to maintain private sexual relationships while sustaining a multi-layered network of relatives, friends, acquaintances, associates, co-workers, and strangers with whom our interactions are mainly non-sexual. The result is the human society in which we all live.

Human monogamy thus holds out distinct advantages. Yet these advantages—as always—are bought at a price. Let us look at where the gains and forfeitures occur.

The winners under polygamy, you will recall, are high-status males and low-status females. Under monogamy, these parties lose their advantages, while compensating advantages are gained by high-status females and low-status males. High-status females no longer have to share their mates with low-status females, a particular advantage where long periods of child-rearing are involved. Low-status males, instead of being consigned to the bachelor herd, get a reasonable chance to a mate.

Perhaps we should pause here a moment to define what we mean by "high" and "low" status. High status usually has to do with desirable characteristics—beauty, strength, swiftness, bright feathers, or intelligence—whatever is admired by the species. In agencies where males fight for control of females (elk, lions, kangaroos), size and strength are usually the deciding factor. In species where females exercise some choice, physical beauty tends to play a greater role. As Darwin first noted, the bright plumage of the male bird is solely the result of generations of female selection.

In almost every species, youth is considered a desirable quality. In females, it implies a long, healthy life in which to raise offspring. In males, youth and vigor also suggest a wide variety of resources for child-rearing. Among the more social species, however, age, intelligence, and experience can play an important role. The alpha baboon is usually quite mature and sustains his access to females not through sheer strength or aggressiveness, but through the skillful formation of political alliances.

Under monogamy, another crucial characteristic is added—the willingness of the male to be a good provider. Yet this creates a dilemma for females. Unfortunately, the two favored characteristics—physical attractiveness and willingness to be a good provider—do not always come together. In fact, they often seem mutually exclusive. The peacock, the most beautiful of male birds, is notoriously a philanderer and a poor provider. With polygamy, females can ignore this problem and attach themselves to the most attractive males. With monogamy, however, females find themselves caught on the horns of the dilemma. Juggling these competing demands become a vexing responsibility—one that, at bottom, most females would ultimately like to escape.

Alternatives have always been available—at least covertly. In the 1950s, a research scientist began a routine experiment concerning natal blood type, trying to figure out which characteristics were dominant. To his astonishment, he found that 11 per cent of the babies born in American hospitals had blood types belonging to neither the mother nor the father—meaning the biological father was not the male listed on the birth certificate. The researcher was so dismayed by these findings that he suppressed them for over twenty years. Even at a time when monogamy was an unquestioned norm, at least 10 per cent of

American women were resolving the female dilemma by tricking one man into providing for the child of another.

With all this in mind, then, let us look at where we should expect to find the major points of dissatisfaction with monogamy.

First and foremost, monogamy limits the mating urges of high-status males. Everywhere in nature, males have an underlying urge to mate with as many females as possible. Studies among barnyard animals have shown that a male that has exhausted himself mating with one female will experience an immediate resurgence of sexual desire when a new female is introduced into his pen. (This is dubbed the "Coolidge effect," after Calvin Coolidge, who once observed it while making a presidential tour of a barnyard.)

"Hogamous, higamous, men are polygamous. Higamous, hogamous, women monogamous," wrote Ogden Nash, and the experience in all societies has been that the male urge to be polygamous is the weakest link in the monogamous chain. This has become particularly true in America's mobile culture, where status-seeking males are often tempted to change wives as they move up the social ladder. "Serial monogamy" is the name we have given it, but a better term might be "rotating polygamy." A serious op-ed article in the *New York Times* a few years ago proposed that polygamy be legalized so that men could be compelled to support their earlier wives even as they move on to younger and more attractive women.

Marital infidelity, the fathering of illegitimate children, the pursuit of younger women, the "bimbo" and "trophy wife" syndromes—all are essential breaches of the monogamous social contract. When a Donald Trump deserts his wife and children for a woman almost twenty years his junior, he is obviously "wrecking a home" and violating monogamy's implicit understanding that children should be supported until maturity. But he is doing something else as well. By mating with a much younger, second woman, he is also limiting the mating possibilities of younger men. One swallow does not make a summer, but repeated over and over, this pattern produces real demographic consequences. In societies that practice polygamy, competition over available females is always more intense.

The problems with male infidelity, then, are fairly clear. What is not always so obvious is that women's commitment to monogamy is also somewhat circumscribed. The difficulties are twofold: 1) the general dissatisfaction of all women in being forced to choose between attractive males and good providers; and 2) the particular dissatisfaction among low-statues women at being confined to the pool of low-status men.

In truth, low-status people of both sexes—or perhaps more significantly, people who are chronically dissatisfied with their status—form a continuing challenge to any monogamous society. Unless there is an overwhelming cultural consensus that marriage and the joint raising of children forms the highest human happiness (which some people think it does), low-status males and females are likely to feel cheated by the relatively narrow pool of mates available to them. Their resentments and underlying desire to disrupt the rules of the game form a constant undercurrent of discontent in any monogamous society.

For males, one obvious way of by-passing the rules is rape. Although feminists, in their never-ending effort to repeal biology, have insisted that rape reflects some amorphous "hatred against women," the more obvious interpretation is that it is a triumph of raw sexual desire over the more complex rules of social conduct. Rape overwhelmingly involves low-status men seeking sex with women who are otherwise inaccessible to them. (Rape is even more of a problem in polygamous societies, because of the more limited options for low-status males.) If "hatred" is involved, it is more likely to be general resentment of monogamy's restrictions, which inaccessible, high-status women may come to represent. But this is all secondary. The basic crime of rape is the violation of a woman's age-old biological right to choose her own sexual partners.

The other avenues for low-status males are prostitution and pornography. Each offers access to higher-status females, albeit under rather artificial circumstances. Individual females may benefit from pornography and prostitution in that they are paid (however poorly) for their participation. There is always a laissez-faire argument for allowing both. But when they become public and widespread, pornography and prostitution become another nagging reminder of the dissatisfactions some people will always feel with monogamy. In other words, they disrupt "family values."

Female dissatisfaction with monogamy, on the other hand, is not always as obvious. Yet the restrictions put upon female—particularly low-status ones—will always be present and, in their own way, form their own undercurrent of discontent.

The principal female dissatisfaction is the dilemma of finding a mate who is *both* physically attractive *and* a good provider. As many and many a woman has discovered, it is much easier to get an attractive male into bed with you for the night than to keep him around in the morning.

There is, however, a practical alternative. This is to return to the greater freedom of polygamy, where females can choose the most attractive males without regard to forming a permanent bond. This, of course, is the essence of "single motherhood."

The rise of single motherhood is basically the expression of female discontent with monogamy. Rising female economic success makes it more practical (social scientists have long noted that marriage becomes more unstable as females become more economically independent). This undoubtedly accounts for the rising rate of divorce and single motherhood among affluent Americans.

But the emergence of almost universal single motherhood among the black underclass undercuts the purely economic argument (except, of course, to the degree that female independence has been subsidized by the welfare system). Black women are not opting for single motherhood because of rising economic success. What the availability of welfare does, however, is enable them to dispense with the courtship rituals of monogamy and choose the most desirable man available to them, regardless of the man's willingness or ability to provide domestic support. It is this dynamic of liberated female sexual choice—and not just the greater economic support offered by welfare—that is driving black single motherhood today.

The essence of single motherhood, then, is status-jumping. By dispensing with the need to make a single choice, a woman can mate with a man who is far more desirable than any she could hope to retain under the artificial restraints of monogamy. The same dynamic is even more obvious among single mothers of the middle and upper classes. When asked to justify their choice, these women refer with surprising regularity to the unavailability of movie stars or other idealized males. ("I know so many women who were waiting for that Alan Alda type to come along," one unwed mother recently told *Newsweek*. "And they were waiting and waiting.") Yet when these women get themselves impregnated by otherwise unattainable men—or artificially inseminate themselves with accomplished doctors and lawyers, talented musicians, or Nobel Prize-winning scientists—what are they practicing but a contemporary form of high-tech polygamy? . . .

To sum up, then, let us admit that no system of monogamy can ever bring complete happiness to everyone. Given the variability among individuals and given the universal desire to be paired with desirable mating partners, there will always be a sizable pool of dissatisfaction under monogamy. The real question is: How far can society allow this pool to grow before these private dissensions begin to rend the social fabric? In short, what can we expect society to look like if the monogamous ideal is abandoned?

It isn't necessary to look very far. Western and Oriental cultures form a monogamous axis that spans the northern hemisphere (Orientals are far more monogamous than Westerners are), but a large part of the remaining world practices polygamy.

Polygamy is tolerated by the Koran—although it should be recognized that, like the principle of "an eye for an eye," the Islamic law that allows a man four wives is a *restriction* from an earlier practice. The Koran requires that a man support all his wives equally, which generally confines the practice to wealthy males. In most Moslem countries, polygamous marriages are restricted to the upper classes and form no more than 4 to 5 per cent of all marriages.

In sub-Saharan Africa, on the other hand, polygamy is far closer to the norm. In parts of West Africa, more than 20 per cent of the marriages are polygamous. Marriage itself is rendered far more fragile by the practice of matrilinearity—tracing ancestry only through the mother's line. In West Africa, a man may sire many children (Chief M. K. O. Abiola, of Nigeria's Yoruba tribe, a self-made billionaire and chairman of ITT Nigeria, has 26 wives), but the paternal claim he can lay upon any of them is far more tenuous than it would be in Oriental or Western societies. In West Africa, women can take their children and leave a marriage at any time, making the institution extremely unstable. In these tribal societies, Christianity and Islam—which teach marital fidelity and permanent unions—are generally regarded as progressive social movements.

What qualities do we find in societies that tolerate polygamy? First, the shortage of women usually leads to the institution of the "bride price," where a young man must pay a sizable sum of money to the bride's family in order to obtain a wife. (The "dowry," in which a sum is attached to an eligible daughter to make her more attractive, is purely a product of monogamy.) This makes wives difficult to obtain for men who come from less well-to-do families.

The numerical imbalance between eligible males and females also forces older men to court younger women. Girls in their teens are often betrothed to men ten and fifteen years their senior. In some South Seas societies, infant females are betrothed to grown men. These strained couplings make marriage itself a distant and unrewarding relationship, far different from the "peer marriages" of Western and Oriental cultures.

Finally, polygamy tends to produce a high level of male violence. Because low-status males are not assured any reasonable chance of mating by the social contract, they are essentially impossible to incorporate into the large work of society. Instead, they form themselves into violent gangs or become the foot soldiers of extremist political groups. In Pakistan, the recent news has been that the country is being overrun by these violent gangs, which have become the competing "parties" in the country's turbulent political system. The head of one of these factions was recently accused of raping dozens of airline stewardesses.

Yet even where polygamy is openly sanctioned, child-rearing is always built around the formation of husband-and-wife households—even if these households may contain several wives. Only among the American underclass has polygamy degenerated into a purely polymorphous variety, where courtship is forgone and family formation has become a virtually forgotten ritual.

In a recent issue of *The Public Interest,* Elijah Anderson, professor of social science at the University of Pennsylvania, described an on-going acquaintance with a 21-year-old black youth whom he called "John Turner." Anderson described the social milieu of Turner's neighborhood as follows:

> [In] Philadelphia,..the young men of many individual streets organize informally bounded areas into territories. They then guard the territories, defending them against the intrusions and whims of outsiders . . .
>
> Local male groups claim responsibility over the women in the area, especially if they are young. These women are seen as their possessions, at times to be argued over and even fought over. When a young man from outside the neighborhood attempts to "go with" or date a young woman from the neighborhood, he must usually answer to the boys' group, negotiating for their permission first . . .
>
> At twenty-one years of age, John was the father of four children out of wedlock. He had two sons who were born a few months apart by different women, one daughter by the mother of one of the sons, and another son by a third woman.

This mating pattern is not uncommon in nature. It has recently been observed in dolphins and of course bears a strong resemblance to the structure of some primate tribes. Yet what works for these species is no longer plausible for human beings. Once again, we have eaten from the tree of knowledge. We have too much intimate knowledge of the details of sexual connection and paternity to be satisfied with this vague collectivism.

Thus "John Turner" explains how his efforts to put some order into his life by creating a bond between two of his sons resulted in his being jailed for assault:

> Well, see, this girl, the girl who's the mother of my one son, Teddy. See, I drove my girlfriend's car by her house with my other son with me. I parked the car down the street from her house and everything. So I took John, Jr., up to the house to see his brother, and we talk for awhile. But when I got ready to leave, she and her girlfriend followed me to the car. I got in the car and put John in. Then she threw a brick through the window.

The unavoidable consequence of polymorphous polygamy among humans is a tangle of competing jealousies and conflicting loyalties that make ordinary life all but impossible. The central institution at the axis of human society— the nuclear family—no longer exists.

Unfortunately, while such a mating system virtually guarantees child abuse (usually involving a "boyfriend"), internal turmoil, and rampant violence, it is also extremely reproductive. While their social life has degenerated into extreme chaos, the American underclass are nonetheless reproducing faster than any other population in the world. This follows a well-known biological principle that when populations come under stress, they attempt to save themselves by reproducing faster, with sexual maturity usually accelerated to a younger age.

The culture of polygamy is also self-reinforcing and self-perpetuating. If men feel there is nothing more to fatherhood than "making babies," then women will feel free to seek the most attractive men, without making any effort to bind them to the tasks of child-rearing. As a cultural pair, the footloose male and the single mother, if not held back by the force of social convention, can easily become the predominant type. The result is a free-for-all in which human society as we know it may become very difficult, if not impossible.

This, then, is the essence of "family values." Family values are basically the belief that monogamy is the most peaceful and progressive way of organizing a human society. Dislike and distaste for anything that challenges the monogamous contract—easy divorce, widespread pornography, legalized prostitution, out-of-wedlock child bearing, blatant homosexuality—are not just narrow or prudish concerns. They come from an intelligent recognition that the monogamous contract is a fragile institution that can easily unravel if dissaffections become too widespread.

What is likely to happen if we abandon these values? People will go on reproducing, you can be sure of that. But families won't be formed ("litters" might be a more appropriate term). And the human beings that are produced in these litters will not be quite the same either. If marriage is a compromise between men and women, then the breakdown of monogamy can only let loose the natural egocentrisms of both.

It is probably not too alarmist to note that societies that have been unable to establish monogamy have also been unable to create working democracies or widely distributed wealth. No society that domesticates too few men can have a stable social order. People who are incapable of monogamy are probably incapable of many other things as well.

As a basically limiting human compact, monogamous marriage is bound to produce its peculiar difficulties. As with any compromise, each individual can argue—based on present or previous deprivation, real or imagined—that he or she should not be bound by the rules.

Yet it should also be clear that, beyond the personal dissatisfactions we all may feel, each of us also retains a permanent, private stake in sustaining a system that creates a peaceful social order and offers to everyone a reasonable chance of achieving personal happiness. If monogamy makes complex demands on human beings, it also offers unique and complex rewards.

Meilaender, "Men and Women— Can We Be Friends?"

Gilbert Meilaender (born in 1946), Christian theologian-moralist and professor of theology at Valparaiso University, is one of our most thoughtful commentators on the moral dimensions of everyday life. This essay (published in 1993) is not obviously, and certainly not to begin with, about marriage, but is rather about friendship. Bringing to the nettlesome question of the possibility of friendship between men and women the insights he has elaborated more fully in his book, Friendship: A Study in Theological Ethics, *Meilaender highlights how the sexual interest, and how "otherness" and "sameness" more generally, both pose obstacles to and provide grounds for deep friendship between man and woman. He concludes in a way that will speak to those for whom the desire for friendship is—or could become—an important motive for marriage.*

In Xenophon's *Oeconomicus,* Socrates and Critobulus are discussing household management, in which the wife plays a major role. The exchange goes this way:

> "Anyhow, Critobulus, you should tell us the truth, for we are all friends here. Is there anyone to whom you commit more affairs of importance than you commit to your wife?"
> "There is not."
> "Is there anyone with whom you talk less?"
> "There are few or none, I confess."

Friendship between husband and wife is, of course, only one possible kind of friendship between the sexes, though an important one. But most classical thinkers—with the exception of Epicurus—were inclined to think friendship between men and women impossible.

No doubt this can be accounted for in part, perhaps large part, by social and cultural circumstances—differences in education, a public life from which most women were excluded, constant warfare that drew males away from home. In my own view, these circumstances have changed considerably, but not everyone agrees. Thus, for example, Mary Hunt author of *Fierce Tenderness: A Feminist Theology of Friendship* (1991), says: "Economic, political, psychological, and other differences between the genders result in the fact that women find it difficult to be friends with men and vice versa." Though I think Hunt is somewhat mistaken about the reasons, it is true that the relation between the sexes is in our society a tense and often anxious one. It still makes sense to ask the classical question: Is friendship possible between men and women? Or, more modestly put, are there reasons why friendship between men and women may be more difficult to sustain than same-sex friendships?

When we ask this question, the first problem that comes to mind is the one raised by Harry Burns in the 1989 movie, *When Harry Met Sally*. In the opening scene, as he and Sally are driving together from Chicago to New York, Harry says: "Men and women can't be friends—because the sex part always gets in the way." Harry has a point—indeed, an important point. And, though I do not think that this is finally the deepest issue that confronts us here, I shall devote a good bit of attention to it.

Aristotle, whose two books on friendship in the *Nicomachean Ethics* are recognized almost universally as the most important piece of writing on the subject, tends to agree with Harry. Aristotle recognizes, of course, that there is a kind of friendship between husband and wife, but it is one example of what he calls friendship between unequals. In such bonds the equality that friendship always requires can be present only if it is "proportionate" rather than "strict"—only, that is, if "the better and the more useful partner . . . [receives] more affection than he gives." Still, of the three types of friendship that Aristotle discusses—based respectively on advantage, pleasure, or character—the highest, based on character, can exist even between unequals as long as the proportion is present. And Aristotle seems to think that, given the necessary proportionate equality, such a character friendship is possible between husband and wife.

More generally, however, Aristotle suggests that a relation grounded in erotic love will not be the highest form of friendship. (When he takes up the question, he has in mind, it would seem, pederastic relationships, but this does not affect his view of the relation between eros and philia.) He distinguishes a bond like friendship, grounded in a trait of character and involving choice, from a bond grounded in an emotion. And, while there can be friendship between lover and beloved, it will not be the highest form of friendship. It will be a friendship grounded not in character but in pleasure—and it is, therefore, likely to fade. "Still," Aristotle grants, noting how one sort of love may grow from another, "many do remain friends if, through familiarity, they have come to love each other's character, [discovering that] their characters are alike."

It is important to note that eros and philia are indeed different forms of love, even if they may sometimes go together. In making a somewhat different point, C. S. Lewis suggested the following thought experiment:

> Suppose you are fortunate enough to have "fallen in love with" and married your Friend. And now suppose it possible that you were offered the choice of two fu-

tures: "*Either* you two will cease to be lovers but remain forever joint seekers of the same God, the same beauty, the same truth, *or else*, losing all that, you will retain as long as you live the raptures and ardors, all the wonder and the wild desire of Eros. Choose which you please."

In recognizing the reality and difficulty of the choice we discern the difference between the loves. That difference Lewis captures nicely in a sentence: "Lovers are normally face to face, absorbed in each other; Friends, side by side, absorbed in some common interest." Friends, therefore, are happy to welcome a new friend who shares their common interest, but eros is a jealous love that must exclude third parties.

Lewis believes that friendship and erotic love may go together, but in many respects he agrees with Harry and with Aristotle that the combination is an unstable one. He suggests that friendship between a man and a woman is likely to slip over into eros unless either they are physically unattractive to each other, or at least one of them already loves another. If neither of these is the case, friendship is "almost certain" to become eros "sooner or later." This is not far from Harry's view of the matter. Having asserted that "men and women can't be friends—because the sex part always gets in the way," Harry adds a corollary when he and Sally meet again five years later: "unless both are involved with other people." But then, in one of his characteristically convoluted pieces of reasoning, he adds: "But that doesn't work. The person you're involved with can't understand why you need to be friends with the other person. She figures you must be secretly interested in the other person—which you probably are. Which brings us back to the first rule." A little more optimistic than Harry, Lewis suggests that lovers who are also friends may learn to share their friendship with others, though not, of course, their eros. Still, that does not address Harry's chief concern: the instability of friendships with members of the opposite sex when those friendships are not shared with one's beloved.

We ought not, I think, deny that friendships between men and women—friendships that are not also marked by erotic love—are possible. We ought not, that is, let a theory lead us to deny the reality we see around us, and we do sometimes see or experience such friendships. Nor need we express the view shared by Harry and Lewis quite as crassly as did Nietzsche: "Women can enter into a friendship with a man perfectly well; but in order to maintain it the aid of a little physical antipathy is perhaps required." Nor, surely, need we hold, as my students sometimes do, that friendship between men and women is possible only if at least one of the friends is homosexual (a view that will make same-sex friendships difficult for those who are homosexual, unless, of course, their experience of eros is in no way jealous or exclusive). At the same time, however, there is no reason to deny some truth to Harry's claim even without the additional support provided by Aristotle and Lewis, for our experience also suggests that there is something to it.

The difficulties of combining eros and philia are the stuff of our daily life. Equalizing the relation of the sexes, bringing women into the academy and the workplace, has not made these difficulties disappear. Indeed, in certain respects they may have been exacerbated. Men and women are radically uncertain about how they are to meet in such shared worlds. Friendship requires an easy spontaneity, a willingness to say what one thinks, talk with few holds barred and few matters off limits—precisely the sort of thing that some will find difficult on occasion to distinguish from sexual harassment.

I have discovered that college students often wish to argue that Harry is wrong, that there need be no obstacle to friendship between the sexes. That, however, may be because they have great difficulty managing erotic attachments (which are quite a different thing from sexual encounters). Fearful of the kind of commitment eros asks of us—fearful of being drawn toward one who is completely other than the self but to whom the most complete self-giving is called for and before whom one therefore becomes vulnerable—they take refuge in groups of friends, hoping thereby to achieve what parents of thirty years ago saw as the advantage of group dating: the domestication of eros. But eros is a wild and unruly deity, unlikely, I think, to be tamed so easily.

It is wiser to grant the point. Friendship between men and women will always have to face certain difficulties that will not be present in same-sex friendships. There will almost always be what J. B. Priestley calls "a faint undercurrent of excitement not present when only one sex is involved." This may even give to the friendship a tone not easily gotten any other way. Thus, as Priestley again puts it: "Probably there is no talk between men and women better than that between a pair who are not in love, have no intention of falling in love, but yet who *might* fall in love, who know one another well but are yet aware of the fact that each has further reserves yet to be explored." Priestley offered this opinion in a little book titled, *Talking: An Essay,* published in 1926 as one of several volumes in "The Pleasures of Life Series." But he might well have been describing what many viewers found appealing in *When Harry Met Sally.* In one scene, Harry and his friend Jess are talking while hitting some balls in a batting cage:

Jess: "You enjoy being with her?"
Harry: "Yeah."
Jess: "You find her attractive?"
Harry: "Yeah."
Jess: "And you're not sleeping with her?"
Harry: "I can just be myself, 'cause I'm not trying to get her into bed."

And yet, of course, not too much later comes the party at which Harry and Sally dance cheek to cheek—and recognize the presence of Priestley's "faint undercurrent," which we call eros. This is, let us face it, a problem for friendships between men and women, even if it may also be enriching. Eros always threatens; for, unlike friendship, eros is a love that is jealous and cannot be shared. . . .

These problems go deeper than the presence of erotic attraction alone. They involve the very nature of the bond of friendship. The friend is, in Aristotle's influential formulation, "another self." At several points, Aristotle considers whether friendship is more probable among those who are like or unlike each other. And, although he notes defenders of each view, he holds that friendship "implies some similarity" and that in the highest form of friendship "the partners are like one another." In arguing that a person of good character should not—and ultimately cannot—remain friends with someone who becomes evil, Aristotle again appeals to the notion that "like is the friend of like."

Anyone who reads Aristotle's discussion of the friend as another self is likely to find it puzzling in certain respects. It grows out of a peculiar treatment of self-love as the basis of friendship, of love for the friend as an extension of the friendly feelings one has for oneself. And there are, in fact, aspects of his discussion that I would not claim fully to understand. What he has in mind, however, in depicting the friend as an alter ego is something we might discuss in terms of the social origins of the self. The friend is the mirror in which I come to know and understand myself. I have no way to look directly at myself and must come to see myself as I am reflected by others—and especially, perhaps, by close friends. In the friend I find that other self in whom I come to know myself. That is why friendship "implies some similarity" and why, at least in the most important kinds of friendship, "the partners are like one another."

Friends wish, Aristotle says, to pursue together activities they enjoy. "That is why some friends drink together or play dice together, while others go in for sports together and hunt together, or join in the study of philosophy: whatever each group of people loves most in life, in that activity they spend their days together." I myself think that Aristotle is largely correct here. We want in the friend someone who cares about the things we care about; yet we want the friend to be "another" who cares about these things, another with whom we can share them and with whom we come to know ourselves (and our concerns) better. The friend must be "another," but not entirely "an-other." Perhaps we do not, therefore, seek from the friend quite that sense of otherness which the opposite sex provides.

This takes us beyond the issue of erotic attraction alone—into much deeper, perhaps unanswerable, questions about what it means to be male or female. I do not know precisely how we can make up our minds about these questions today; we have a hard enough time just discussing them openly and honestly. A child of either sex begins in a kind of symbiotic union with its mother, without any strong sense of differentiation between self and mother. But as that sense of self begins to form, it develops differently for males and females. In attaining a sense of the self as separate and individuated we take somewhat different courses. Thus, psychologist Lillian Rubin argues, boys must repress their emotional identification with their mother, while girls, though repressing any erotic attachment, can leave the larger emotional identification with the mother (and, more generally, other women) intact. The process of becoming a self involves identification with those who can be for us "another self"—those, as it happens, who share our sex.

This does not, in my view, mean that friendship between men and women is impossible. It does mean, though, that J. B. Priestley was right to say of their "talk": "It will be different from the talk of persons of the same sex." These differences are the stuff of best sellers—and of much humor. Thus, for example, Deborah Tannen, who teaches linguistics at Georgetown University, could write a best-seller titled, *You Just Don't Understand: Women and Men in Conversation.* Full of illustrations in which one often sees oneself, Tannen's book suggests that for men life is "a struggle to preserve independence," while for women it is "a struggle to preserve intimacy." The sort of problem this creates is illustrated clearly in a story Tannen recounts:

> Eve had a lump removed from her breast. Shortly after the operation, talking to her sister, she said that she found it upsetting to have been cut into, and that looking at the stitches was distressing because they left a seam that had changed the contour of her breast. Her sister said, "I know. When I had my operation I felt the same way." Eve made the same observation to her friend Karen, who said, "I know. It's like your body has been violated." But when she told her husband, Mark, how she felt, he said, "You can have plastic surgery to cover up the scar and restore the shape of the breast."

Where she felt the need for understanding and sharing, he discerned a problem to be solved.

If this can sometimes be disconcerting, we need not be too serious. And these differences have provided the occasion for much humor. Dave Barry, the columnist, can title a column "Listen up, jerks! Share innermost feelings with her"—and most of us are likely to read it. "We have some good friends," Barry writes,

> Buzz and Libby, whom we see about twice a year. When we get together, Beth and Libby always wind up in a conversation, lasting several days, during which they

discuss virtually every significant event that has occurred in their lives and the lives of those they care about, sharing their innermost feelings, analyzing and probing, inevitably coming to a deeper understanding of each other, and a strengthening of a cherished friendship. Whereas Buzz and I watch the play-offs.

This is not to say Buzz and I don't share our feelings. Sometimes we get quite emotional.

"That's not a FOUL?" one of us will say.

Or: "You're telling me THAT'S NOT A FOUL???"

I don't mean to suggest that all we talk about is sports. We also discuss, openly and without shame, what kind of pizza we need to order. We have a fine time together, but we don't have heavy conversations, and sometimes, after the visit is over, I'm surprised to learn—from Beth, who learned it from Libby—that there has recently been some new wrinkle in Buzz's life, such as that he now has an artificial leg.

Our world is full of attempts, not always terribly humorous, to remove such differences from life. In Tannen's words, "Sensitivity training judges men by women's standards, trying to get them to talk more like women. Assertiveness training judges women by men's standards and tries to get them to talk more like men." Better, perhaps, she suggests, to learn to understand and accept each other.

In this effort, I have found Priestley's old essay quite helpful. If talk between men and women is different from talk between persons of the same sex, it will not give the same kind of pleasure. But it may, Priestley suggests, compensate in other ways. The *first* condition of such talk is, he says, "that sex must be relegated to the background. . . . The man and the woman must be present as individualities, any difference between them being a strictly personal and not a sexual difference. They will then discover, if they did not know it before, how alike the sexes are, once their talk has dug below the level of polite chatter and they are regarding the world and their experience together and not merely flirting." That is, to revert to the terms I drew from Aristotle, they must find in the friend another self, another individuality, but one whose otherness is not so overwhelming as to threaten to engulf or invade their selfhood. No doubt this is not always possible, for reasons we noted earlier when considering the impact of eros on friendship. But when, for whatever reason, "passion is stilled," men and women may meet as individualities who care about the same things or seek the same truth.

There may, however, be something dissatisfying about the suggestion that a crucial aspect of our person—our sexuality—must, as it were, be bracketed for such friendship to be possible. And this *would* be unsatisfactory, I think, were no more to be said. Priestley goes on, though, to suggest that friendship between men and women can go beyond the play of individual personalities. "Secure in this discovery" of how alike they are, men and women "will then go forward and make another one, for at some point they must inevitably discover how unlike the sexes are.... This double play, first of personality and then of sex, is what gives intelligent talk between men and women its curious piquancy..."

In this second movement, when individual personality no longer brackets sexuality, Priestley ultimately discerns something more fundamental still—a third factor, which goes beyond the level of individual identity. "Men frequently complain," he writes, "that women's conversation is too personal." And, even writing in an age that knew not Carol Gilligan, Priestley finds some truth in this judgment. I will quote him at length:

> [Women] remain more personal in their interests and less concerned with abstractions than men on the same level of intelligence and culture. While you are briskly and happily generalizing, making judgments on this and that, and forgetting for the time being yourself and all your concerns, they are brooding over the particular and personal application and are wondering what hidden motive, what secret desire, what stifled memory of joy or hurt, are there prompting your thought. But this habit of mind in women does not spoil talk; on the contrary it improves it, restoring the balance.... It is the habit of men to be overconfident in their impartiality, to believe that they are godlike intellects, detached from desires and hopes and fears and disturbing memories, generalizing and delivering judgment in a serene midair. To be reminded of what lies beyond, now and then, will do them more good than harm. This is what the modern psychologist does, but too often he shatters the illusion of impersonal judgment with a kick and a triumphant bray, like the ass he so frequently is, whereas woman does it, and has done it these many centuries, with one waggle of her little forefinger and one gleam of her eyes, like the wise and witty and tender companion she is. Here, then, is a third kind of play you may have in talk between the sexes, the duel and duet of impersonal and personal interests, making in the end for balance and sanity and, in the progress of the talk, adding to its piquancy.

In this sense, friendship between the sexes may take us not out of ourselves but beyond ourselves—may make us more whole, more balanced and sane, than we could otherwise be.

Indeed, I myself think that this is one of the purposes of friendship. And by such teleological language I mean: one of the purposes God has in giving us friends. We are being prepared ultimately for that vast friendship which is heaven, in which we truly are taken beyond ourselves, and in which all share the love of God. Something like this understanding of friendship, though without the strong theological overtone I have just given it, can be found in Katherine Paterson's *Bridge to Terabithia*—a book about, among other things, friendship, and a book that it would be misleading to describe simply as a children's book.

The friendship in the book is one between a boy and a girl, Jess and Leslie, though they are a little too young for eros yet to have an overt impact on their relationship. In different ways they are both outsiders in the world of their peers at school, and that very fact draws them together. They create—largely at the instigation of Leslie—a "secret country" named Terabithia, in which they are king and queen. This country—a piece of ground on the other side of a creek, to which they swing across on a rope—is, in Leslie's words, "so secret that we would never tell anyone in the whole world about it." And, at least at first, it must be that way. . . . [W]ere no friendships of theirs to be special and particular, were they to have no secret country that others did not share, they would never come to know themselves as fully as they do. Thus, for example, Jess finds that his friendship with Leslie opens up new worlds for him. "For the first time in his life he got up every morning with something to look forward to. Leslie was more than his friend. She was his other, more exciting self— his way to Terabithia and all the worlds beyond."

Jess says that Leslie is his way not only to Terabithia but also to "all the worlds beyond," but he learns that truth only slowly and with great bitterness. When the creek is swollen from a storm and Jess is gone, Leslie still tries to cross to Terabithia on the rope. It breaks, she falls onto the rocks, and is killed. Grief-stricken and alone, without his alter ego, Jess can barely come to terms with what has happened. But he does, finally, and in doing so learns something about the purpose of all friendship.

> It was Leslie who had taken him from the cow pasture into Terabithia and turned him into a king. He had thought that was it. Wasn't king the best you could be? Now it occurred to him that perhaps Terabithia was like a castle where you came to be knighted. After you stayed for a while and grew strong you had to move on. For hadn't Leslie, even in Terabithia, tried to push back the walls of his mind and make him see beyond to the shining world—huge and terrible and beautiful and very fragile?

To learn to see beyond our own secret countries—to what is at the same time both terrible and beautiful—is, from the perspective of Christian faith, the purpose of friendship. And to the degree that friendship not only with those of our own sex but with those of the opposite sex may more fully enable such vision, we have every reason to attempt it, despite its inherent difficulties.

We should not, therefore, underestimate the importance of the most obvious location for friendship between men and women: the bond of marriage. There are many differences between our world and that shared by Socrates and Critobulus. By no means least of them is the formative influence of Christian culture, with its exaltation of marriage as the highest of personal bonds. To be sure, precisely because the husband or wife as friend is not only "another self" but as fully "an-other" as we can experience, friendship in marriage cannot be presumed. If there is any truth in Lillian Rubin's analysis, each spouse may fear the otherness of the partner and the loss of self that intimacy requires. The man fears engulfment, "losing a part of himself that he's struggled to maintain over the years." The woman fears invasiveness that threatens the boundary she has struggled to maintain between her self and others. Each is tempted to avoid such otherness, to settle for a friend more like the self. But if we can overcome that temptation—in this case, perhaps, with the aid of eros—we may find a bond that truly helps us see beyond ourselves.

When Harry finally realizes that he loves Sally and wants to marry her, he ticks off the reasons: the way she's cold when it's 71 degrees outside; the way it takes her an hour-and-a-half to order a sandwich; the way she crinkles up her nose when she looks at him. All these might be only the signs of an infatuated lover looking at the beloved, not of a friend who stands beside the friend and looks outward. But last in Harry's litany of reasons is that Sally is "the last person I want to talk to before I go to bed at night." And J. B. Priestley—though worrying that spouses' lives may be "so intertwined, that they are almost beyond talk as we understand it"—has a view not unlike Harry's: "Talk demands that people should begin, as it were, at least at some distance from one another, that there should be some doors still to unlock. Marriage is partly the unlocking of those doors, and it sets out on its happiest and most prosperous voyages when it is launched on floods of talk."

In marriage, if we are patient and faithful, we may find that "balance and sanity" which friendship between men and women offers, and we may find it in a context where eros too may be fulfilled without becoming destructive. Against the view of Critobulus we may, therefore, set the wisdom of Ben Sira: "A friend or companion is always welcome, but better still to be husband and wife."

Borowitz, "Speaking Personally"

Rabbi Eugene B. Borowitz (born in 1924), professor of education and Jewish religious thought at Hebrew Union College–Jewish Institute of Religion in New York City, is one of the leading thinkers of Reform Judaism in the United States, specializing in contemporary Jewish thought and ethics. This short extract is taken from the concluding chapter, "Speaking Personally," of his book, Choosing a Sex Ethic: A Jewish Inquiry *(1969), where it forms part of an argument for why marriage is the "most right context" for sexual intimacy. What does Borowitz mean by "personal fulfillment" and "becoming a person"? How does marriage make these possible? Though Borowitz speaks from within the Jewish tradition, he claims that his discussion is "deeply Jewish and deeply human at the same time." Is his more than a parochial view?*

I believe—again my Jewish faith asserts itself—that man can only be man through time and in responsibility. Becoming a whole person must include not just what one is and can enjoy but equally the enduring relationships and continuing commitments through which alone one can mature. The friendships which increase in understanding as in demand, the love that deepens to obligate as to quicken us over the years, these are what make men fully human. Integrity of self is not merely the work of moments or periods but the hard-won result of pursuing a continuity in our lives. Momentary genuineness is splendid, but we have not become true persons unless we can extend occasional authenticity to a lifetime of trying to be true. Experiment has its place, and joy must not be underrated. Still it is in what we do with our lives in the long run that we show how human we are. Marriage and a family are not an eventual necessity—an attitude that invites disaster before the vows are spoken!—but the preferred path of personal fulfillment. Without their intense commitment, demanding trust, unrelenting involvement, it is difficult to become fully human. They are worth working and waiting for, and this includes cultivating the values and attitudes that can make it possible for them to succeed.

Let me illustrate the difference between these two attitudes toward life by proposing a choice between two possible situations. Neither is really satisfactory, yet they represent what life offers to many people. In one case we will find love, rich and moving, but never great enough to result in marriage. Thus, while such affairs last months or even years, each inevitably ends, and the lovers go their separate ways. The other possibility is of a life spent in a marriage but one not initiated because of love. The couple has very genuine regard for one another, but it cannot be said to rise to that level of empathy and passion we call love. Yet knowing themselves to be unlikely to have a much richer emotional experience or to have a better partner with whom to spend their lives, they marry. Would you prefer a life of love that never comes to marriage over a life of marriage that knows regard but not love? The choice is, of course, odious, and one should not be forced into such an undesirable situation. Yet many people are. I like that choice no better than anyone else because I feel that life is best fulfilled in love-for-life and, therefore, marriage. Yet, seen from the perspective of time and of a whole life, if there must be a choice, then being married, even only in deep friendship, seems to me far more personally significant than being in love from time to time. If forced to choose, I confess I am not ultimately a romantic who thinks high moments are more important than continual personal growth. I value ecstasy, but I believe in almost every case becoming a person is more truly bound up with perseverance.

Muir, "The Annunciation"

In this lyric poem, whose title alludes to the famous announcement of the birth of a redeemer, the Scottish-born poet, Edwin Muir (1887–1959), announces the new birth of freedom, the new wealth of heart and mind, the more than mortal grace, and the wholeness of spirit that each bestows on each through love. Though he does not speak specifically of the marital union of husband and wife but rather of soul to soul, Muir indicates that the union of which he speaks is lived "in this iron reign," that is, it is lived under restraint, under a vow or promise. Moreover, it is precisely such restraint that is liberating and self-fulfilling: in such union each asks—requests, does not command—of each to give precisely what each most wants to give. We are granted the opportunity to become most completely, most fully, ourselves.

Now in this iron reign
I sing the liberty
Where each asks from each
What each most wants to give
And each awakes in each
What else would never be,
Summoning so the rare
Spirit to breathe and live.

Then let us empty out
Our hearts until we find
The last least trifling toy,
Since now all turns to gold,
And everything we have
Is wealth of heart and mind,
That squandered thus in turn
Grows with us manifold.

Giving, I'd give you next
Some more than mortal grace,
But that you deifying
Myself I might deify,
Forgetting love was born
Here in a time and place,

And robbing by such praise
This life we magnify.

Whether the soul at first
This pilgrimage began,
Or the shy body leading
Conducted soul to soul
Who knows? This is the most
That soul and body can,
To make us each for each
And in our spirit whole.

C. WHAT ABOUT SEX?
MAN, WOMAN, AND SEXUALITY

If you are one of those readers who have turned immediately to this part of the book, you are going to be disappointed. The readings in this section are not about whether, how, or when one might, can, may, should, or must "have sex": they are neither titillating nor moralizing. Rather, they are intended to make us thoughtful about *what it means* that we *are* sexual beings, differentiated into male and female sexes and filled with sexual desire. The great power of sexual desire, and the intensity of sexual pleasure, may make it seem that the point or meaning of it all is simply self-evident. But, for the very same reasons, the opposite may well be the case. The meaning of sexual desire turns out to be an extremely interesting and complicated matter, but it can only be properly approached precisely when the desire itself is not upon us. As Aristotle remarked, offering evidence of our divided nature, "no one can think about anything while in the midst of the aphrodisiac pleasure"—not even, we might add, about sexual pleasure itself.

As background for the readings in this section, we remind ourselves of what is naturally or biologically given, of some richly laden facts presupposed by all our selections. Sexual desire first comes to sight as the desire for sexual coupling. Sex and the existence of two sexes are, to begin with, defined relative to the sex act, in which the male and female partners play distinctive yet complementary roles, the male (more) active and aggressive, the female (more) passive and receptive. Somehow, strength and yielding, war and peace, overcome each other, as desire is sated or relieved, at least for a brief while (see the selections from Homer and Rousseau). But sexual appetite, unlike hunger or thirst, also serves a goal that is partly hidden from the sexually active partners, a goal that exists beyond their own well-being and pleasure. Whether the participants know it or not, the sex act itself takes its primary biological meaning from sexual reproduction, the activity to which all sexually desiring beings, males and females alike, are indebted for their very existence. Sexual desire both presupposes and disposes to procreation.

Sexual reproduction—the generation of new life from two complementary elements, one female, one male, (usually) through coitus—is the natural way of all mammalian reproduction. By nature, each child has two complementary biological progenitors; each child thus stems from and unites exactly two lineages. Moreover, the precise genetic being of the resulting offspring is determined by a combination of nature and chance: each human child shares the common natural human species genotype, each child is genetically and equally kin to each parent, yet each child is also—thanks to the lottery of sex—genetically unique. These biological truths about our origins, not surprisingly, foretell deep truths about our identity and about our human condition altogether; every one of us is at once equally human, equally enmeshed in a particular familial nexus of origin, and equally individuated in our trajectory from birth to death—and, if all goes well, equally capable (despite our mortality) of participating, with a complementary other, in the very same renewal of such human possibility through procreation.

Human beings caught up in sexual passion are generally, like the animals, utterly oblivious to the natural connection between sex and procreation, and nature herself seems to have arranged things to keep the connection veiled. Nature cleverly gets us to do "her work" of procreation by having us ardently pursue "our work" of copulation. Yet this gap between act and consequence assures that what is for nature a means can be regarded by us as an end-in-itself, or less radically, as a means to or aspect of some end other than procreation: pleasure, sport, solace, communion, diversion, self-revelation, adoration, domination—the list is endless (see selection by William May). The polymorphousness and perversity of human sexuality is a consequence of the freedom that lurks in the detachability of the sexual act from its procreative intention.

These natural facts about sex and sexual reproduction also have profound social significance. Human societies virtually everywhere have sought to channel and direct sexual desire, both to tame its excesses and to support its procreative purpose. Human societies virtually everywhere have structured male-female relationships, child-rearing responsibilities, and systems of identity and kinship on the basis of the deep natural facts of begetting. The pregnant possibilities in male-female union are ratified by customs protecting the intimacies of marriage and by laws against adultery, since everyone needs to be clear about who belongs with whom (see selection from Herodotus). The mysterious yet ubiquitous "love of one's own" is everywhere culturally exploited, to make sure that children are not just produced but well-cared-for and to create for everyone clear ties of meaning, belonging, and obligation. Such naturally-rooted social practices are not mere cultural constructs (like left- or right-driving, or like the difference between burying and cremating the dead) that we can alter with little human cost. What would kinship be without its clear natural grounding? And what would identity be without kinship? At the same time, the incest taboo and the practice of exogamy ("leave his father and mother and cleave to his wife") everywhere thwart and restrain the extremes and excesses of the love of one's own flesh and bone (see selection from Genesis). The *natural* meaning of sexuality turns out to be *humanly* profound, and in yet more wonderful ways.

The emergence of sex is not a trivial innovation, but a matter of deep ontological significance. Indeed, it is, we submit, impossible for there to have been the human kind of life—or even the higher forms of animal life—in the absence of sexuality and sexual reproduction. Sexuality brings with it a new and enriched relationship to the world. Only sexual animals can seek and find complementary others with whom to pursue a goal that transcends their own existence. For a sexual being, the world is no longer an indifferent and largely homogeneous *otherness,* in part edible, in part dangerous. It also contains some very special and related and complementary beings, of the same kind but of opposite sex, toward whom one reaches out with special interest and intensity. In higher birds and mammals, the outward gaze keeps a lookout not only for food and predators, but also for prospective mates; the beholding of the many-splendored world is suffused with desire for union, the animal antecedent of human *eros* and the germ of sociality, consciousness of which desire becomes central to our humanity (see selections from Genesis and Kant). Not by accident is the human animal both the sexiest animal—whose females do not go into heat but are receptive throughout the estrus cycle and whose males must therefore have greater sexual appetite and energy in order to reproduce successfully—and also the most aspiring, the most social, the most open, and the most intelligent animal.

According to one explanation, the soul-elevating power of sexuality is, at bottom, rooted in its strange connection to mortality, which it simultaneously accepts and tries to overcome. Asexual reproduction may be seen as a continuation of the activity of self-preservation: when one organism buds or divides to become two, the original being is (doubly) preserved, and nothing dies. Sexuality, by contrast, as such means perishability and serves replacement; the two that come together to generate one soon will die. Sexual desire, in human beings as in animals, thus serves an end that transcends the self-serving individual; in essence self-sacrificing, it simultaneously holds the promise of life's answer to mortality.

According to another explanation, the soul-elevating power of sexuality is rooted in its strange connection to beauty, by which sexual desire is aroused and with which it seeks to fuse (see selection from Homer) or toward which sexual desire, restrained and sublimated, inspires and leads us (see selection from Kant). Yet a third explanation credits the psychic restlessness (including confusion and shame) which results from the sex act's failure to quiet our experience of needy incompleteness or to answer fully the less than obvious deeper aspirations of sexual desire ("What does it really want of us?"). But whatever the explanation, in the sexually self-conscious animal, sexual desire can become eros, lust can become love. Sexual desire *humanly* regarded can become an erotic longing for wholeness, completion, and immortality, which then can drive us knowingly into the embrace and its generative fruit—as well as into all the higher human possibilities of deed and speech, song and worship. These erotic and higher possibilities (more fully explored in the next section of the anthology, "Is This Love?") appear to be connected with the phenomena of shame and modesty, that enable an impulse for "having sex" to become a power for "love-making," and more. It is no coincidence that the animal that knows sexual shame and sexual restraint is also the animal that knows awe and reverence (see selections from Genesis, Rousseau, Kant, and Riezler).

In human beings, sex and procreation are not simply matters of bodily instinct and physiology. Neither are they simply activities of our rational wills. They are more complete activities precisely because they engage us bodily, erotically, mentally, aesthetically, and even spiritually. There thus appears to be wisdom in the mystery of nature that has joined the pleasure of sex, the inarticulate longing for union, the communication of the loving embrace, the deep-seated and only partly articulate desire for children, and even an openness to the divine in the very activity by which we continue the chain of human existence and participate in the renewal of human possibility.

This section begins with three selections (one ancient Greek and poetic, one biblical, one modern and philosophic) that address the male-female sexual difference and its complementarity, as well as the complex natural character of human sexual desire. These and (especially) the next three selections (one ancient Greek and historical, one modern philosophical, one contemporary psychological) explore the meaning of the connections between sex, shame, and awe. The final essay (contemporary and theological), by William May, differs from the others. It deals less with the native structure of human sexuality, more with competing evaluative attitudes towards sex; it also touches on the possible connection between human sexuality and monogamous marriage.

Homer, The Coupling of Ares and Aphrodite

Homer (circa 8th century BC), the first Greek poet of whom we know, is often regarded as the poet or maker of the Greeks. For he taught the Greeks how to think about the gods and, hence, about their own human possibilities and limitations. In his epic poems, the gods, who often assume human shape, are not only characters who influence the course of human events but are (at least in some cases) also incarnations of powerful natural forces that dominate human life. For instance, the different aspects of femaleness and maleness are associated with different divinities: femininity as virginal purity is associated with Artemis, commanding wifeliness with Hera, concrete intelligence and prudence, artfulness, and the ferocious defense of one's own with Athena, the hearth with Hestia; masculinity as remote and abstract intelligence is connected with Apollo, law, rule, and dominion with Zeus, shamelessness, stealth, and mischief with Hermes, craft and technique with Hephaestus. But regarding female and male sexually considered, the prototypical pair are Aphrodite and Ares, she the goddess of beauty, who inspires sexual desire and who gives birth to Eros, he the lustful, manly, murderous god who breeds war and strife. In the Odyssey *(Book VIII, lines 301–410), Homer gives us the classic story of their "relationship," which is, in essence, a paradigmatic story of sex. In this tale, Aphrodite, the lawful wife of the lame divine craftsman, Hephaestus, lies in adulterous union with the daring and dashing Ares. Hephaestus uses his art to avenge the adultery, weaving a subtle but invisible web that ensnares and immobilizes the lovers, just when they have had enough of each other. Proudly, he summons the other gods to observe his craftsmanship—at the same time, thus exposing also his cuckoldry—and each of the gods reacts in character (compare the rational Apollo, the shameless Hermes, the wild and unruly Poseidon, and the reticent and modest goddesses who refuse out of shame [aidos] to attend). This paradigmatic story invites many questions: Why does warlike maleness lust after female beauty? Does she inspire his boldness? Does he conquer her, or does she tame and pacify him? Is this really a union of opposites or is there something warlike in naked sexual desire? What does this desire really want, and can it be satisfied? Can such a lusty union last, on its own? Can it be—does it seek to be—fruitful? Can it be made enduring by means of craft? Can anyone permanently hold the beautiful? Can a man—or a woman—who relies solely on craft hope to sustain a stable marriage? Is primal (natural) sexual desire necessarily the enemy of (lawful) marriage?*

> [N]ow the bard struck up an irresistible song:
> The Love of Ares and Aphrodite Crowned with Flowers . . .

how the two had first made love in Hephaestus' mansion,
all in secret. Ares had showered her with gifts
and showered Hephaestus' marriage bed with shame
but a messenger ran to tell the god of fire—
Helios, lord of the sun, who'd spied the couple
lost in each other's arms and making love.
Hephaestus, hearing the heart-wounding story,
bustled toward his forge, brooding on his revenge—
planted the huge anvil on its block and beat out chains,
not to be slipped or broken, all to pin the lovers on the spot.
This snare the Firegod forged, ablaze with his rage at War,
then limped to the room where the bed of love stood firm
and round the posts he poured the chains in a sweeping net
with streams of others flowing down from the roofbeam,
gossamer-fine as spider webs no man could see,
not even a blissful god—
the Smith had forged a masterwork of guile.
Once he'd spun that cunning trap around his bed
he feigned a trip to the well-built town of Lemnos,
dearest to him by far of all the towns on earth.
But the god of battle kept no blind man's watch.
As soon as he saw the Master Craftsman leave
he plied his golden reins and arrived at once
and entered the famous god of fire's mansion,
chafing with lust for Aphrodite crowned with flowers.
She'd just returned from her father's palace, mighty Zeus,
and now she sat in her rooms as Ares strode right in
and grasped her hand with a warm, seductive urging:
"Quick, my darling, come, let's go to bed
and lose ourselves in love! Your husband's away—
by now he must be off in the wilds of Lemnos,
consorting with his raucous Sintian friends."

                                                        So he pressed
and her heart raced with joy to sleep with War
and off they went to bed and down they lay—
and down around them came those cunning chains
of the crafty god of fire, showering down now
till the couple could not move a limb or lift a finger—
then they knew at last: there was no way out, not now.
But now the glorious crippled Smith was drawing near . . .
he'd turned around, miles short of the Lemnos coast,
for the Sungod kept *his* watch and told Hephaestus all,

so back he rushed to his house, his heart consumed with anguish.
Halting there at the gates, seized with savage rage
he howled a terrible cry, imploring all the gods,
"Father Zeus, look here—
the rest of you happy gods who live forever—
here is a sight to make you laugh, revolt you too!
Just because I am crippled, Zeus's daughter Aphrodite
will always spurn me and love that devastating Ares,
just because of his stunning looks and racer's legs
while I am a weakling, lame from birth, and who's to blame?
Both my parents—who else? If only they'd never bred me!
Just look at the two lovers . . . crawled inside my bed,
locked in each other's arms—the sight makes me burn!
But I doubt they'll want to lie that way much longer,
not a moment more—mad as they are for each other.
No, they'll soon tire of bedding down together,
but then my cunning chains will bind them fast
till our Father pays my bride-gifts back in full,
all I handed *him* for that shameless bitch his daughter,
irresistible beauty—all unbridled too!"
                                   So Hephaestus wailed
as the gods came crowding up to his bronze-floored house.
Poseidon god of the earthquake came, and Hermes came,
the running god of luck, and the Archer, lord Apollo,
while modesty [shame; *aidos*] kept each goddess to her mansion.
The immortals, givers of all good things, stood at the gates,
and uncontrollable laughter burst from the happy gods
when they saw the god of fire's subtle, cunning work.
One would glance at his neighbor, laughing out,
"A bad day for adultery! Slow outstrips the Swift."

     "Look how limping Hephaestus conquers War,
quickest of all the gods who rule Olympus!"

     "The cripple wins by craft."

                                   "The adulterer,
he will pay the price!"

                              So the gods would banter
among themselves but lord Apollo goaded Hermes on:
"Tell me, Quicksilver, giver of all good things—

even with those unwieldy shackles wrapped around you,
how would you like to bed the golden Aphrodite?"

"Oh Apollo, if only!" the giant-killer cried.
"Archer, bind me down with triple those endless chains!
Let all you gods look on, and all you goddesses too—
how I'd love to bed that golden Aphrodite!"

A peal of laughter broke from the deathless ones
but not Poseidon, not a smile from him; he kept on
begging the famous Smith to loose the god of war,
pleading, his words flying, "Let him go!
I guarantee you Ares will pay the price,
whatever you ask, Hephaestus,
whatever's right in the eyes of all the gods."

But the famous crippled Smith appealed in turn,
"God of the earthquake, please don't urge this on me.
A pledge for a worthless man is a worthless pledge indeed.
What if he slips out of his chains—his debts as well?
How could I shackle *you* while all the gods look on?"

But the god of earthquakes reassured the Smith,
"Look, Hephaestus, if Ares scuttles off and away,
squirming out of his debt, I'll pay the fine myself."

And the famous crippled Smith complied at last:
"Now *there's* an offer I really can't refuse!"

With all his force the god of fire loosed the chains
and the two lovers, free of the bonds that overwhelmed them so,
sprang up and away at once, and the Wargod sped to Thrace
while Love with her telltale laughter sped to Paphos,
Cyprus Isle, where her grove and scented altar stand.
There the Graces bathed and anointed her with oil,
ambrosial oil, the bloom that clings to the gods
who never die, and swathed her round in gowns
to stop the heart . . . an ecstasy—a vision.

Genesis 2:4–4:2: The Anthropology of Sex

Few stories have exercised greater power on Western imagination and sensibility than the story of the Garden of Eden, the story of human disobedience, the loss of innocence, and the emergence of human freedom and moral self-consciousness, paradise lost and our entrance upon a burdened mortal existence. Embedded in this tale is also our civilization's foundational story of man and woman. Human sexuality, here seen as encompassing more than the coupling of Ares and Aphrodite, thus acquires much of its meaning from the larger context of our humanity.

Everyone knows the story. But precisely because of its familiarity, it is rarely read with sufficient alertness and care. To help remedy this situation, we offer an over-long (but far from exhaustive) series of questions, intended to slow down the reading and to provoke reflection. We do so not merely for the sake of understanding this story. The questions this story raises are in fact central to the entire subject of this volume, as well as to many of the particular readings.

First, the origin of woman from out of man (2:21–22). Does this leave man wounded, no longer whole? Will the man know what he is now lacking and, therefore, what he desires? Is woman's origin higher or lower than man's? What does it mean that she comes from a rib, from a place close to the heart? Why might God have seen fit to remedy the problem of man's aloneness by sending him a counter-part, an "other"?

Next, the text locates at least three different aspects of sexuality, the first connected with the man's speech upon first seeing the woman (2:23). Is his speech the expression of carnal and possessive desire, or of tender feeling, or of delight in companionship? Does the man seek union of body or of soul? What does the woman want? What does it mean that we are not told what she says, upon first seeing the man? Is her sexual interest less strong or just less focused? (Does this have any bearing on why she is more open to the speech of the serpent [3:1–6]?) Why does the teller of the story interrupt to draw the inference about cleaving to one's wife and becoming one flesh (2:24)? What does it mean to become one flesh?

Sexual self-consciousness is the first discovery of the knowledge of good and evil (3:7). What is the meaning of nakedness, and what is shameful about sexuality? Why do the pair seek—in partnership—to cover their nakedness? How might their self-consciousness alter their relationship? What might clothing do to or for sexual desire? for love? Is there any connection between their discovering their nakedness and their hearing God's voice (3:8)? Is shame (or sex) connected with awe?

Third, sex is disclosed to have something to do with bearing children (3:16).

Why does the man rename the woman, and, this time, without reference to himself (3:20)? How might this generative "division of labor" change their relationship? How might the fact of giving birth be connected with attaching a woman's desire to her husband? with his ruling over her?

Finally, in the first act outside the Garden, the man knew his wife and she conceived and bore a son (4:1). What kind of knowledge is sexual knowing? What is the woman's reaction to childbirth? Is it the same as the man's? What does it mean that we are not told what he says?

The story read with these questions in mind may not be the same story you knew before.

One final point: In addition to reading the story descriptively (as we suggest), finding phenomena for anthropological reflection, the story can be read and has traditionally been read prescriptively, as a source of moral evaluation and instruction. Many traditional interpretations see in the provision of woman for man, and especially in the remark " . . . cleave to his wife and they shall be one flesh," the divine establishment of, and sanction for, monogamous marriage. How far does natural sexuality point to marriage? Does it do so only under divine authority and command?

Chapter 2

4. These are the generations of the heaven and of the earth when they were created, in the day that the Lord God made earth and heaven.

5. No shrub of the field was yet in the earth, and no herb of the field had yet sprung up; for the Lord God had not caused it to rain upon the earth, and there was not a man [*adam*] to till the ground; 6. but there went up a mist from the earth, and watered the whole face of the ground. 7. Then the Lord God formed man of the dust of the ground, and breathed into his nostrils the breath of life; and man became a living soul. 8. And the Lord God planted a garden eastward, in Eden; and there He put the man whom He had formed. 9. And out of the ground made the Lord God to grow every tree that is pleasant to the sight, and good for food; the tree of life also in the midst of the garden and the tree of the knowledge of good and evil. 10. And a river went out of Eden to water the garden; and from thence it was parted, and became four heads. 11. The name of the first is Pishon; that is it which compasseth the whole land of Havilah, where there is gold; 12. and the gold of that land is good; there is bdellium and the onyx stone. 13. And the name of the second river is Gihon; the same is it that compasseth the whole land of Cush. 14. And the name of the third river is Tigris; that is it which goeth toward the east of Asshur. And the fourth river is the Euphrates. 15. And the Lord God took the man and put him into the garden of Eden to dress it and to keep it. 16. And the Lord God

commanded the man, saying: 'Of every tree of the garden thou mayest freely eat; 17. but of the tree of the knowledge of good and evil, thou shalt not eat of it; for in the day that thou eatest thereof thou shalt surely die.'

18. And the Lord God said: 'It is not good that man should be alone; I will make him a help opposite him.' 19. And out of the ground the Lord God formed every beast of the field, and every fowl of the air; and brought them unto the man to see what he would call them; and whatsoever the man would call every living creature, that was to be the name thereof. 20. And the man gave names to all cattle, and to the fowl of the air, and to every beast of the field; but for the man there was not found a help opposite him. 21. And the Lord God caused a deep sleep to fall upon the man, and he slept; and He took one of his ribs, and closed up the place with flesh instead thereof. 22. And the rib, which the Lord God had taken from the man, made He a woman, and brought her unto the man. 23. And the man said: 'This, now, is bone of my bones, and flesh of my flesh; she shall be called Woman [ishah], because from Man [ish] this was taken.' 24. Therefore shall a man leave his father and his mother, and shall cleave unto his wife, and they shall be one flesh. 25. And they were both naked, the man and his wife, and were not ashamed.

Chapter 3

1. Now the serpent was more subtle than any beast of the field which the Lord God had made. And he said unto the woman: 'Yea, hath God said: Ye shall not eat of any tree of the garden?' 2. And the woman said unto the serpent: 'Of the fruit of the trees of the garden we may eat; 3. but of the fruit of the tree which is in the midst of the garden, God hath said: Ye shall not eat of it, neither shall ye touch it, lest ye die.' 4. And the serpent said unto the woman: 'Ye shall not surely die; 5. for God doth know that in the day ye eat thereof, then your eyes shall be opened, and ye shall be as God, knowing good and evil.' 6. And when the woman saw that the tree was good for food, and that it was a delight to the eyes, and that the tree was to be desired to make one wise, she took of the fruit thereof, and did eat; and she gave also unto her husband with her, and he did eat. 7. And the eyes of them both were opened, and they knew that they were naked; and they sewed fig-leaves together, and made themselves girdles. 8. And they heard the voice of the Lord God walking in the garden toward the cool of the day; and the man and his wife hid themselves from the presence of the Lord God amongst the trees of the garden. 9. And the Lord God called unto the man, and said unto him: 'Where art thou?' 10. And he said: 'I heard Thy voice in the garden, and I was afraid, because I was naked; and I hid myself.' 11. And He said: 'Who told thee that thou wast naked? Hast thou eaten of the tree, whereof I commanded thee that thou shouldest not eat?'

12. And the man said: 'The woman whom Thou gavest to be with me, she gave me of the tree, and I did eat.' 13. And the Lord God said unto the woman: 'What is this thou hast done?' And the woman said: 'The serpent beguiled me, and I did eat.' 14. And the Lord God said unto the serpent: 'Because thou hast done this, cursed art thou from among all cattle, and from among all beasts of the field; upon thy belly shalt thou go, and dust shalt thou eat all the days of thy life. 15. And I will put enmity between thee and the woman, and between thy seed and her seed; they shall bruise thy head, and thou shalt bruise their heel.'

16. Unto the woman He said: 'I will greatly multiply thy pain and thy travail; in pain thou shalt bring forth children; and thy desire shall be to thy husband, and he shall rule over thee.'

17. And unto the man He said: 'Because thou hast hearkened unto the voice of thy wife, and hast eaten of the tree, of which I commanded thee, saying: Thou shalt not eat of it; cursed is the ground for thy sake; in toil shalt thou eat of it all the days of thy life. 18. Thorns also and thistles shall it bring forth to thee; and thou shalt eat the herb of the field. 19. In the sweat of thy face shalt thou eat bread, till thou return unto the ground; for out of it wast thou taken; for dust thou art, and unto dust shalt thou return.' 20. And the man called his wife's name Eve [*Chavah*], because she was the mother of all living [*chai*]. 21. And the Lord God made for man and for his wife garments of skins, and clothed them.

22. And the Lord God said: 'Behold, the man is become as one of us, to know good and evil; and now, lest he put forth his hand, and take also of the tree of life, and eat, and live for ever.' 23. Therefore the Lord God sent him forth from the garden of Eden, to till the ground from whence he was taken. 24. So He drove out the man; and He placed at the east of the garden of Eden the cherubim and the flaming sword which turned every way, to keep the way to the tree of life.

Chapter 4

1. And the man knew Eve his wife; and she conceived and bore Cain, and said: 'I have gotten [*kanah*] a man with the Lord.' 2. And again she bore his brother Abel . . .

Rousseau, *Emile:* Sexual Complementarity

More than any modern political philosopher, Jean-Jacques Rousseau (1712–1778) paid special attention in his writings to matters of love and sexuality. This should not be attributed to his own notorious erotic adventures. On the contrary, Rousseau sought to combat the heartless acquisitiveness and personal loneliness of bourgeois society, as well as the repressive and inegalitarian teachings of the an-cien régime and traditional Christianity, by articulating a new view of mar-riage, founded on romantic love, perfectly suited to democratic man (see especially his novel Julie *or* Nouvelle Heloise, *published in 1760). His most philosophical treatment of the subject is found in* Emile *or* On Education *(1762)—according to Rousseau, his greatest work—a work that describes how to rear independent, re-sponsible, uncorrupted, and unself-conflicted human beings. The wholeness man seeks is to be found not in political community, through citizenship, but more likely in marriage, through love. Accordingly, the culmination of Emile's education is his preparation for love and marriage. The courtship of Emile and Sophie ap-pears later in this anthology. Here we excerpt (from the beginning of Book V) Rousseau's profound and provocative discussion of the natural differences between male and female sexuality, and the implication of these differences for the rela-tionship between man and woman. The text is difficult, the argument subtle, and the speech blunt; and the teachings about natural sex differences are no doubt today uncongenial to those who believe in androgyny or who regard gender dif-ferences as entirely the work of cultural construction and prejudice. Still, Rousseau makes us think hard about the psychology of the sex act, about the reasons for the so-called moral double-standard, about the need for and power of female modesty, and, most important, about how, precisely through the complementary sexual dif-ference, two human beings could come to live as one, without either surrendering his or her autonomy or will.*

Now we have come to the last act in the drama of youth, but we are not yet at the dénouement. It is not good for man to be alone. Emile is a man. We have promised him a companion. She has to be given to him. That companion is Sophie. In what place is her abode? Where shall we find her? To find her, it is necessary to know her. Let us first learn what she is; then we shall better judge what places she inhabits. And even when we have found her, everything will still not have been done. "Since our young gentleman," says Locke, "is ready to marry, it is time to leave him to his beloved." And with that he finishes his work. But as I do not have the honor of raising a gentleman [but a lover], I shall take care not to imitate Locke on this point.

Sophie
Or The Woman

Sophie ought to be a woman as Emile is a man—that is to say, she ought to have everything which suits the constitution of her species and her sex in order to fill her place in the physical and moral order. Let us begin, then, by examining the similarities and the differences of her sex and ours.

In everything not connected with sex, woman is man. She has the same organs, the same needs, the same faculties. The machine is constructed in the same way; its parts are the same; the one functions as does the other; the form is similar; and in whatever respect one considers them, the difference between them is only one of more or less.

In everything connected with sex, woman and man are in every respect related and in every respect different. The difficulty of comparing them comes from the difficulty of determining what in their constitutions is due to sex and what is not. On the basis of comparative anatomy and even just by inspection, one finds general differences between them that do not appear connected with sex. They are, nevertheless, connected with sex, but by relations which we are not in a position to perceive. We do not know the extent of these relations. The only thing we know with certainty is that everything man and woman have in common belongs to the species, and that everything which distinguishes them belongs to the sex. From this double perspective, we find them related in so many ways and opposed in so many other ways that it is perhaps one of the marvels of nature to have been able to construct two such similar beings who are constituted so differently.

These relations and these differences must have a moral[1] influence. This conclusion is evident to the senses; it is in agreement with our experience; and it shows how vain are the disputes as to whether one of the two sexes is superior or whether they are equal—as though each, in fulfilling nature's ends according to its own particular purpose, were thereby less perfect than if it resembled the other more! In what they have in common, they are equal. Where they differ, they are not comparable. A perfect woman and a perfect man ought not to resemble each other in mind any more than in looks, and perfection is not susceptible of more or less.

In the union of the sexes each contributes equally to the common aim, but not in the same way. From this diversity arises the first assignable difference in the moral relations of the two sexes. One ought to be active and strong, the

---

[1]"Moral" is here understood to mean humanly social or interpersonal, as opposed to merely natural or physical, that is, moral as opposed to non-moral. [eds.]

other passive and weak. One must necessarily will and be able; it suffices that the other put up little resistance.

Once this principle is established, it follows that woman is made specially to please man. If man ought to please her in turn, it is due to a less direct necessity. His merit is in his power; he pleases by the sole fact of his strength. This is not the law of love, I agree. But it is that of nature, prior to love itself.

If woman is made to please and to be subjugated,[2] she ought to make herself agreeable to man instead of arousing him. Her own violence is in her charms. It is by these that she ought to constrain him to find his strength and make use of it. The surest art for animating that strength is to make it necessary by resistance. Then *amour-propre*[3] unites with desire, and the one triumphs in the victory that the other has made him win. From this there arises attack and defense, the audacity of one sex and the timidity of the other, and finally the modesty and the shame with which nature armed the weak in order to enslave the strong.

Who could think that nature has indiscriminately prescribed the same advances to both men and women, and that the first to form desires should also be the first to show them? What a strange depravity of judgment! Since the undertaking has such different consequences for the two sexes, is it natural that they should have the same audacity in abandoning themselves to it? With so great an inequality in what each risks in the union, how can one fail to see that if reserve did not impose on one sex the moderation which nature imposes on the other, the result would soon be the ruin of both, and mankind would perish by the means established for preserving it? If there were some unfortunate region on earth where philosophy had introduced this practice—especially in hot countries, where more women are born than men—men would be tyrannized by women. For, given the ease with which women arouse men's senses and reawaken in the depths of their hearts the remains of ardors which are almost extinguished, men would finally be their victims and would see themselves dragged to death without ever being able to defend themselves.

If females among the animals do not have the same shame, what follows from that? Do they have, as women do, the unlimited desires to which this shame serves as a brake? For them, desire comes only with need. When the need is satisfied, the desire ceases. They no longer feign to repulse the male[4]

---

[2] Rousseau is speaking about the sex act. He is, perhaps, also offering a gloss on Genesis 3:16, "thy desire shall be to thy husband, and he shall rule over thee."

[3] or "vanity"

[4] I have already noticed that affected and provocative refusals are common to almost all females, even among animals, even when they are most disposed to give themselves. One has to have never observed their wiles not to agree with this. [JJR]

but really do so. They do exactly the opposite of Augustus' daughter; they accept no more passengers when the ship has its cargo. Even when they are free, their times of good will are short and quickly pass. Instinct impels them, and instinct stops them. What will be the substitute for this negative instinct when you have deprived women of modesty? To wait until they no longer care for men is equivalent to waiting until they are no longer good for anything.

The Supreme Being wanted to do honor to the human species in everything. While giving man inclinations without limit, He gives him at the same time the law which regulates them, in order that he may be free and in command of himself. While abandoning man to immoderate passions, He joins reason to these passions in order to govern them. While abandoning woman to unlimited desires, He joins modesty to these desires in order to constrain them. In addition, He adds yet another real recompense for the good use of one's faculties—the taste we acquire for decent things when we make them the rule of our actions. All this, it seems to me, is worth more than the instinct of beasts.

Whether the human female shares man's desires or not and wants to satisfy them or not, she repulses him and always defends herself—but not always with the same force or, consequently, with the same success. For the attacker to be victorious, the one who is attacked must permit or arrange it; for does she not have adroit means to force the aggressor to use force? The freest and sweetest of all acts does not admit of real violence. Nature and reason oppose it: nature, in that it has provided the weaker with as much strength as is needed to resist when it pleases her; reason, in that real rape is not only the most brutal of all acts but the one most contrary to its end—either because the man thus declares war on his companion and authorizes her to defend her person and her liberty even at the expense of the aggressor's life, or because the woman alone is the judge of the condition she is in, and a child would have no father if every man could usurp the father's rights.

Here, then, is a third conclusion drawn from the constitution of the sexes—that the stronger appears to be master but actually depends on the weaker. This is due not to a frivolous practice of gallantry or to the proud generosity of a protector, but to an invariable law of nature which gives woman more facility to excite the desires than man to satisfy them. This causes the latter, whether he likes it or not, to depend on the former's wish and constrains him to seek to please her in turn, so that she will consent to let him be the stronger. Then what is sweetest for man in his victory is the doubt whether it is weakness which yields to strength or the will which surrenders. And the woman's usual ruse is always to leave this doubt between her and him. In this the spirit of women corresponds perfectly to their constitution. Far from blushing at their weakness, they make it their glory. Their tender muscles are without resistance. They pretend to be unable to lift the lightest burdens. They would be ashamed to be strong. Why is that? It is not only to appear delicate; it is due to a shrewder precaution. They prepare in advance excuses and the right to be weak in case of need. . . .

Observe how the physical leads us unawares to the moral, and how the sweetest laws of love are born little by little from the coarse union of the sexes. Women possess their empire not because men wanted it that way, but because nature wants it that way. It belonged to women before they appeared to have it. The same Hercules who believed he raped the fifty daughters of Thespitius was nevertheless constrained to weave while he was with Omphale; and the strong Samson was not so strong as Delilah. This empire belongs to women and cannot be taken from them, even when they abuse it. If they could ever lose it, they would have done so long ago.

There is no parity between the two sexes in regard to the consequences of sex. The male is male only at certain moments. The female is female her whole life or at least during her whole youth. Everything constantly recalls her sex to her; and, to fulfill its functions well, she needs a constitution which corresponds to it. She needs care during her pregnancy; she needs rest at the time of childbirth; she needs a soft and sedentary life to suckle her children; she needs patience and gentleness, a zeal and an affection that nothing can rebuff in order to raise her children. She serves as the link between them and their father; she alone makes him love them and gives him the confidence to call them his own. How much tenderness and care is required to maintain the union of the whole family! And, finally, all this must come not from virtues but from tastes, or else the human species would soon be extinguished.

The strictness of the relative duties of the two sexes is not and cannot be the same. When woman complains on this score about unjust man-made inequality, she is wrong. This inequality is not a human institution—or, at least, it is the work not of prejudice but of reason. It is up to the sex that nature has charged with the bearing of children to be responsible for them to the other sex. Doubtless it is not permitted to anyone to violate his faith, and every unfaithful husband who deprives his wife of the only reward of the austere duties of her sex is an unjust and barbarous man. But the unfaithful woman does more; she dissolves the family and breaks all the bonds of nature. In giving the man children which are not his, she betrays both. She joins perfidy to infidelity. I have difficulty seeing what disorders and what crimes do not flow from this one. If there is a frightful condition in the world, it is that of an unhappy father who, lacking confidence in his wife, does not dare to yield to the sweetest sentiments of his heart, who wonders, in embracing his child, whether he is embracing another's, the token of his dishonor, the plunderer of his own children's property. What does the family become in such a situation if not a society of secret enemies whom a guilty woman arms against one another in forcing them to feign mutual love?

It is important, then, not only that a woman be faithful, but that she be judged to be faithful by her husband, by those near her, by everyone. It is important that she be modest, attentive, reserved, and that she give evidence of her virtue to the eyes of others as well as to her own conscience. If it is important that a father love his children, it is important that he esteem their mother. These are the reasons which put even appearances among the duties of women, and make honor and reputation no less indispensable to them than chastity. There follows from these principles, along with the moral difference of the sexes, a new motive of duty and propriety which prescribes especially to women the most scrupulous attention to their conduct, their manners, and their bearing. To maintain vaguely that the two sexes are equal and that their duties are the same, is to lose oneself in vain declaiming; it is to say nothing so long as one does not respond to these considerations. . . .

Once it is demonstrated that man and woman are not and ought not to be constituted in the same way in either character or temperament, it follows that they ought not to have the same education. In following nature's directions, man and woman ought to act in concert, but they ought not to do the same things. The goal of their labors is common, but their labors themselves are different, and consequently so are the tastes directing them. After having tried to form the natural man, let us also see how the woman who suits this man ought to be formed so that our work will not be left imperfect.

Do you wish always to be well guided? Then always follow nature's indications. Everything that characterizes the fair sex ought to be respected as established by nature. You constantly say, "Women have this or that failing which we do not have." Your pride deceives you. They would be failings for you; they are their good qualities. Everything would go less well if they did not have these qualities. Prevent these alleged failings from degenerating, but take care not to destroy them.

For their part, women do not cease to proclaim that we raise them to be vain and coquettish, that we constantly entertain them with puerilities in order to remain more easily their masters. They blame on us the failings for which we reproach them. What folly! And since when is it that men get involved in the education of girls? Who prevents their mothers from raising them as they please? They have no colleges. What a great misfortune! Would God that there were none for boys; they would be more sensibly and decently raised! Are your daughters forced to waste their time in silliness? Are they made in spite of themselves to spend half their lives getting dressed up, following the example you set them? Are you prevented from instructing them and having them instructed as you please? Is it our fault that they please us when they are pretty, that their mincing ways seduce us, that the art which they learn from you attracts us and pleases us, that we like to see them tastefully dressed, that we let them sharpen at their leisure the weapons with which they subjugate us? So, decide to raise them like men. The men will gladly consent to it! The more women want to resemble them, the less women will govern them, and then men will truly be the masters.

All the faculties common to the two sexes are not equally distributed between them: but taken together, they balance out. Woman is worth more as woman and less as man. Wherever she makes use of her rights, she has the advantage. Wherever she wants to usurp ours, she remains beneath us. One can respond to this general truth only with exceptions, the constant mode of argument of the gallant partisans of the fair sex.

To cultivate man's qualities in women and to neglect those which are proper to them is obviously to work to their detriment. Crafty women see this too well to be duped by it. In trying to usurp our advantages, they do not abandon theirs. But it turns out that they are unable to manage both well—because the two are incompatible—and they remain beneath their own level without getting up to ours, thus losing half their value. Believe me, judicious mother, do not make a decent man of your daughter, as though you would give nature the lie. Make a decent woman of her, and be sure that as a result she will be worth more for herself and for us.

Does it follow that she ought to be raised in ignorance of everything and limited to the housekeeping functions alone? Will man turn his companion into his servant? Will he deprive himself of the greatest charm of society with her? In order to make her more subject, will he prevent her from feeling anything, from knowing anything? Will he make her into a veritable automaton? Surely not. It is not thus that nature has spoken in giving women such agreeable and nimble minds. On the contrary, nature wants them to think, to judge, to love, to know, to cultivate their minds as well as their looks. These are the weapons nature gives them to take the place of the strength they lack and to direct ours. They ought to learn many things but only those that are suitable for them to know.

Whether I consider the particular purpose of the fair sex, whether I observe its inclinations, whether I consider its duties, all join equally in indicating to me the form of education that suits it. Woman and man are made for one another, but their mutual dependence is not equal. Men depend on women because of their desires; women depend on men because of both their desires and their needs. We would survive more easily without them than they would without us. For them to have what is necessary to their station, they depend on us to give it to them, to want to give it to them, to esteem them worthy of it. They depend on our sentiments, on the value we set on their merit, on the importance we attach to their charms and their virtues. By the very law of nature women are at the mercy of men's judgments, as much for their own sake as for that of their children. It is not enough that they be estimable; they must be esteemed. It is not enough for them to be pretty; they must please. It is not enough for them to be temperate; they must be recognized as such. Their honor is not only in their conduct but in their reputation; and it is not possible that a woman who consents to be regarded as disreputable can ever be decent. When a man acts well, he depends only on himself and can brave public judgment; but when a woman acts well, she has accomplished only half of her task, and what is thought of her is no less important to her than what she actually is. From this it follows that the system of woman's education ought to be contrary in this respect to the system of our education. Opinion is the grave of virtue among men and its throne among women.

The good constitution of children initially depends on that of their mothers. The first education of men depends on the care of women. Men's morals, their passions, their tastes, their pleasures, their very happiness also depend on women. Thus the whole education of women ought to relate to men. To please men, to be useful to them, to make herself loved and honored by them, to raise them when young, to care for them when grown, to counsel them, to console them, to make their lives agreeable and sweet—these are the duties of women at all times, and they ought to be taught from childhood. So long as one does not return to this principle, one will deviate from the goal, and all the precepts taught to women will be of no use for their happiness or for ours.

But although every woman wants to please men and should want to, there is quite a difference between wanting to please the man of merit, the truly lovable man, and wanting to please those little flatterers who dishonor both their own sex and the one they imitate. Neither nature nor reason can bring a woman to love in men what resembles herself; nor is it by adopting their ways that she ought to seek to make herself loved.

Herodotus, The Story of
Candaules and Gyges

*The story (Book I, Chapters 8–12) with which the Greek historian Herodotus
(circa 484–circa 420 BC) begins his* Histories *concerns the violation of sexual
shame and modesty. It features a conflict between the king, Candaules, who asserts the principle of the superiority of seeing (the beautiful) for yourself, and his
bodyguard, Gyges, who subscribes to the superiority of harkening to (the beautiful) ancient customs, including the teaching that restricts gazing—including erotic
gazing—to the things of one's own. The queen finds an ingenious way to vindicate
her modesty, to avenge its violation, and to restore the customary principle, to
each (only) his own. Herodotus seems, in Chapter 10, to imply that only the barbarians—the non-Greeks—care greatly about the uncovering of nakedness. Be this
as it may, what do we make of this story, the deeds and motives of each of its three
characters, and its view of the importance of sexual shame-awe-reverence?*

8. Now this Candaules loved his own wife, and loving her, deemed her to be
far the most beautiful woman of all. So that deeming these things, since there
was among his bodyguards one most pleasing to him, Gyges, son of Daskulus,
and to this Gyges Candaules used to communicate even more weighty matters,
he used to rave to him about the looks of his wife. After not a long time passed
(as it was necessary that it turn out badly for Candaules), he spoke to Gyges as
follows: "Gyges, as it seems to me that you are not persuaded by my speaking
about the looks of my wife (for ears happen to be for human beings less credulous than eyes), bring it about that you will gaze upon her naked." That one
[i.e., Gyges], crying out, said: "Master, what an unhealthy speech you speak,
commanding me to gaze upon my own mistress naked? At the same time with
the putting off of the tunic, a woman puts off together also her shame/awe/
reverence (*aidôs*). Long ago, the noble [or beautiful] things (*ta kala*) were discovered by human beings, from which one ought to learn; among these there
is this one, 'Let each one look upon the things of his own.' I am persuaded that
she is the most beautiful of all women, and I beg of you not to ask [of me]
lawless things." 9. The very one, saying such things, declined, fearing lest something evil come to him from these things [or these people]; the other answered
in these words. "Take courage, Gyges, and do not fear, neither me, that I say
that speech making trial of you, nor my wife, lest some harm come to you from
her. For, to begin with, I will so contrive that she does not learn that she has
been seen by you. For I will set you in the bedchamber in which we sleep behind the opened door. After I have entered, my wife will also arrive at the bed.

Set near the entrance is a chair. Upon this, she will place her clothes, one by one as each is removed, and you will be able to behold quite at leisure. But when she walks away from the chair toward the bed and you are opposite her back, take care for yourself that she does not see you going through the door. 10. This very one [i.e., Gyges], as he was not able to escape, he was ready; and Candaules, when he judged it to be the time for bed, led Gyges into the bedchamber, and immediately after this his wife also arrived. When she entered and while putting down her clothes, Gyges gazed upon her. And as he came opposite to the back of the woman going to her bed, having slipped out, he went outside, but the woman looked upon him going out. Understanding the thing done by her husband, she neither cried out, having been shamed, nor did she appear to understand, having in her mind to avenge herself on Candaules. For with the Lydians, and, roughly speaking, also with the other barbarians, even for a man to be seen naked leads to great shame [disgrace]. 11. Thus, for the time being revealing nothing, she kept silent; but as soon as day had come she saw those of her household that were especially faithful to her, and making them ready, she called Gyges. He, supposing that she knew nothing of the business, came when called; for he was used to come regularly before her, whenever the queen might call. When Gyges came, the woman said the following. "Now, Gyges, to you I give a choice of two ways available; which do you wish to take? For either, slaying Candaules, you must have both me and the kingdom of the Lydians, or there is need for you yourself right now thus to die, so that, obeying Candaules in all things, you will not hereafter look upon the things you ought not. But it is necessary either that he who planned these things perish or you who saw me naked and who did not keep our customs/laws (*nomoi*)." Gyges for a while marveled much at the things said, but then he beseeched her not to bind him perforce to make such a choice. In no way could he persuade her, but he saw that necessity truly set before him either to kill his master or to be killed himself by others; he preferred to survive himself. He asked, saying the following: "Since you compel me to kill my master unwillingly, come, I will hear also in what manner we will make an attack on him." Answering, she said, "The attack will be from the same place where indeed he exhibited me naked, and when he is sleeping the attack will be." 12. When they had prepared the plot and night had come (for Gyges was not released nor was there for him any escape at all, but it was necessary that either he or Candaules perish), he followed with the woman into the bedchamber, and she, giving him a dagger, hid him behind the same door. And thereafter, when Candaules was sleeping, he slipped out and killed him, and Gyges got control of both the woman and the kingdom . . .

Kant, On Shame and Love

In his essay, "Conjectural Beginning of Human History" (published in 1786), the German philosopher Immanuel Kant (1724–1804) speculates on the stages through which mankind acquired its humanity and by means of which human beings became the psychic, spiritual, social, and moral beings we are today. Kant offers his anthropological conjectures in what is, in effect, a philosophical commentary on the early chapters of the book of Genesis (though without making any reference to the role of God). The transgression in eating the forbidden fruit Kant treats as the first stage of humanization, as human desire is freed, through the suggestions of reason and imagination (the serpent), from the limits of fixed appetites (or instinct). The second stage, discussed in the excerpt below, on the fig leaf (Genesis 3:7), concerns the restraint of (sexual) appetite by means of reason. Clothing, an obstacle to the immediate gratification of lust, allows the imagination to embellish and, hence, love to grow in the space opened by sexual shame and ratified by covering it up.

Next to the instinct for food, by means of which nature preserves the individual, the greatest prominence belongs to the sexual instinct, by means of which she preserves the species. Reason, once aroused, did not delay in demonstrating its influence here as well. In the case of animals, sexual attraction is merely a matter of transient, mostly periodic impulse. But man soon discovered that for him this attraction can be prolonged and even increased by means of the imagination—a power which carries on its business, to be sure, the more moderately, but at once also the more constantly and uniformly, the more its object is removed from the senses. By means of the imagination, he discovered, the surfeit was avoided which goes with the satisfaction of mere animal desire. The fig leaf (3:7), then, was a far greater manifestation of reason than that shown in the earlier stage of development. For the one [i.e., desiring the forbidden fruit] shows merely a power to choose the extent to which to serve impulse; but the other—rendering an inclination more inward [*inniglich*] and constant by removing its object from the senses—already reflects consciousness of a certain degree of mastery of reason over impulse. *Refusal* was the feat which brought about the passage from merely sensual [*empfundenen*] to spiritual [*idealischen*] attractions, from mere animal desire gradually to love, and along with this from the feeling of the merely agreeable to a taste for beauty, at first only for beauty in man but at length for beauty in nature as well. In addition, there came a first hint at the development of man as a moral creature. This came from the sense of decency [*Sittsamkeit*], which is an inclination to inspire others to respect by proper manners, i.e., by concealing all that which might arouse low esteem. Here, incidentally, lies the real basis of all true sociability [*Geselligkeit*].

This may be a small beginning. But if it gives a wholly new direction to thought, such a beginning is epoch-making. It is then more important than the whole immeasurable series of expansions of culture which subsequently spring from it.

Riezler, "Comment on the Social Psychology of Shame"

In this remarkable discussion of shame, the twentieth-century German-American social theorist and philosopher, Kurt Riezler (1882–1955), shows how shame everywhere plays a crucial role in the process by which we human beings build up our individual and social "selves." Though shame is not confined to sexual matters, sexual shame plays a crucial role in the humanization of sexuality and in the growth and protection of love. Riezler also notes the deep connection between shame and awe, between what makes us ashamed and what we revere and look up to. Though our culture may no longer recognize it, Riezler suggests that there is something naturally awe-ful in sexuality and that shame in matters sexual tacitly points to something mysterious and venerable. What might this be? What does Riezler mean when he says that shame protects love in sex? Is love itself—or what it aspires to—something venerable?

I

Anthropologists, in comparing cultures, find different tribes ashamed of different things. Obviously they could not make such comparisons unless they had a certain knowledge of an attitude called shame as distinct from the contents of shame, the *pudenda*. The variations the anthropologists report seem to concern the content, not the attitude. In many a study of the genesis of social norms man is a clean slate on which different conditions write different stories. Shame, we are told, has to do with habits. Habits are products of yesterday's conditions. But how is it that each of the different stories has a chapter about shame? Everywhere man blushes and conceals. Human life, under all conditions, seems to move within the frame of a fundamental pattern in which an attitude called shame may have a hidden place.

The phenomenon called shame is broad. Man, as his own observer, can be ashamed of things of which no one knows. It is not a matter of course that the individual is ashamed of merely violating the moral code of the group to which he belongs. Nor is it a matter of course that shame should be tied up with sex. A human being can be ashamed of a cowardly or mean act that even the psychoanalyst may fail to connect with sex. Man can be ashamed of himself and his actions or of others—friends, parents, children—and their actions, ashamed even of his country.

At the threshold of any inquiry into human attitudes and emotions we stumble over a difficulty that concerns the relations between things and their names. In different languages the same things have different names: stone, flower, horse. The name, then, does not alter the thing. But emotions or attitudes merge into one another in countless nuances, transitions, and mixtures. There are no sharp, unmistakable frontiers. Different languages do not draw exactly the same distinctions. Where the human heart is concerned, languages seem to be attempts to lay hands on an evasive subject matter. Each tries to solve an unsolvable problem in its own, and never entirely satisfactory, manner. We admire the subtleness of one for the shades of emotion it can express and deplore the clumsiness of another.

Names lead our thinking, but they do not create things; whenever they seem to create things, these things are not necessarily the right ones. At any rate, we do not determine what shame is by determining the meaning of the term, that is, the conventional use of "shame" in English. English and German have one word for "shame"—*Scham;* French and Greek each have two: *pudeur* and *honte, Aischyne* and *Aidos.* The use of two words emphasizes a difference; the use of one, in blurring the difference, stresses a kinship. Each usage may have its strength and its weakness.

Let us begin with a simple case. A mother scolds her child for a mean act. "Aren't you ashamed of yourself?" "Schämst du dich nicht?" "N'as-tu pas honte?" Mothers in all civilizations talk in this or a similar manner to their children, whatever moral or social code determines the things of which the child should be ashamed. The attitude called shame may be the same, though the content may be different.

A boy is eager to ride on a pony. A little afraid, he hesitates. The mother reproves him: "Aren't you ashamed?" Even if she adds, "Imagine if someone saw that you are afraid," she wants her son to be ashamed of himself as his own observer. Do we really need the social group and its moral code demanding courage? There is something in the soul of the boy that corresponds to the moral code of courage and to the motherly reprimand; without this something the boy would hardly respond.

Perhaps the mother can teach him merely the things of which he should be ashamed, thus directing his shame toward certain contents. To an entirely shameless being, shame cannot be taught. The teacher of such a being could only substitute fear for shame.

What part in an appeal to shame does the observer play? He does not represent merely a social or moral code imposed from without. The boy is anxious lest someone see that he is afraid. He tries to conceal his fear, at least from others; not because shame is merely social and always with respect to others, but because, if others know, the fact is established and his image of himself is put beyond his own power of forgetting and remembering. One cannot prevent others from knowing unless one possesses the power of killing. A powerful man, wishing to save his own image of himself, may on that ground alone cause another man to die.

Though not "merely" social, shame is still a social phenomenon. The individual himself is a social phenomenon. The boy builds up an image of himself for others as well as for himself. He cannot help being to himself what he is to others. His life in others is part of himself. He wants to be something to others. If he cannot be what he wants to be, he tries to appear to be what he cannot be. If he is not contented with himself as others see him, he tries to console himself with his own self-image; if he does not approve of his self-image, he seeks consolation in what others think about him. We adjust ourselves to the norms of others and try to adjust others to our norms. Our "being-to-others" and our "being-to-ourselves" are not side by side. They have been correlated ever since man's beginning. Life is their give and take, the play of their concord and discord.

Shame is a phenomenon as old, if not older, than man. What is its function?

Man, in being something to himself, behaves toward himself. Even in behaving toward others, he cannot help behaving toward himself. He can love and hate, respect and despise himself. He can be content and angry with himself. He can be truthful and a liar to himself. This behaving toward himself does not presuppose introspection, self-observation, a conscious act in which a man directs his attention toward his self. The phenomenon springs the bounds of these terms. Man is a finite creature, in need and danger. He is moved and acted upon. But in being moved he moves; in being acted upon he acts. He builds up his world in relation to himself, himself in relation to his world. Since he is finite, his world is never quite the world. The self he builds is never quite his self. He is both creator and creatum. There is a double nature in man, but the creator is not necessarily the creatum. When we say that man builds up his "self" we should realize that the builder is not the building. We can differentiate the I and the Me. At any moment the I puts another Me, which should be and perhaps never will be actual, ahead of the actual Me. The I may even draw beyond all actual Me's an image of a Me for his own eyes or for the eyes of others, believing and making believe. The distinction between an unconscious and a conscious ego by no means corresponds to this distinction between the I and the Me. Both the unconscious and the conscious have their share in this formative process and a part in both the I and the Me. In this process, in which a finite creator builds up his self as his creatum, shame resides. It covers and conceals the vulnerable spots and protects man against himself and against others. The root of the English "shame" and the German "Scham" is in a Gothic word "Schama" which signifies cover and which is also the root of the German "Hemd," shirt, and the English and French "chemise." . . .

III

Shame is so closely connected with sex that many seem almost to forget that there are things apart from sex of which man can be ashamed. Our Christian tradition suggests that sexual matters are sinful and therefore things to be ashamed of. The association of a bad conscience with sexuality as such is a Christian peculiarity. But it was not Christianity that brought shame into sex.

We ought to be very careful ere we assume that there are "shameless" tribes. Numerous tribes seem shameless according to our codes. They have their own codes, however, within which our acts do not have our meanings. Their codes, however shameless they may seem to us, differentiate as well as ours between shame and shamelessness. Nature herself seems to connect sex with shame. Every inquiry into this problem meets great difficulties. The preconceptions in our theories of sex prevent us from discovering the facts. Some people even distort the facts before trying to observe them.

A few undeniable facts that concern different functions of shame in matters of sex may help to articulate the problem, at least in a preliminary way. The phenomena are tender; words are harsh.

1. Shame asks for the concealment of our sexual actions. It guards their privacy. All peoples exclude the observer. The observer or he who consents to being observed is shameless. Thus shame seems to be concerned less with the sexual actions themselves than with their observation. Talk offends more than action. Mephisto states in Faust:

> Du darfst es nicht vor keuschen Ohren nennen,
> Was keusche Herzen nicht entbehren koennen.[1]

The devil, shameless by nature, sneers at what he fails to understand. Though codes differ widely, we may say that within each the offense to shame by talk is greater the less familiar people are with one another. Societies that admit, relish, or even cultivate a way of talking about sex that to puritans seems utterly shameless have their own way of bowing before shame. They usually develop a code of their own which stipulates at least that the veil shall not be removed unless with wit or grace.

---

[1] One should not name before innocent ears what innocent hearts cannot forbear. [eds.]

2. All peoples require a sense of shame in youngsters, especially in young girls. Shame suits youth and protects the growth of sexual maturity. It plays a role in the selection of the first sexual companion. The nurse upbraids Juliet: "Have you no modesty, no maiden shame?" Everyone makes allowance to Juliet for the strength of her passion. She may violate the social code as interpreted by nurses; she does not violate the human code. Each of her sweet words is full of "modesty and maiden shame." Obviously our judgment of whether an attitude is shameless or not depends on the presence or absence of a mysterious something called "love," whatever it may be.

In Sanskrit the word for shame means the reserve and defense that in the game of love is appropriate to the female part even in the eyes of the libidinous male. Poets of most ages and countries praise this sort of shame. As males writing for audiences of males, they suggest that to love alone should shame yield through love.

Obviously we cannot deal with shame in sex without introducing love. Love is not coextensive with sex. There is sex without love and perhaps even love without sex. Since, however, man has fancied that he could reduce love, as a sublimation of a biological urge, to sex, a few words in defense of my view are a necessity today. I am not sure whether the word "sublimation" has a definite meaning. It seems to me that its role is to desublimate love by suggesting that love is nothing but sex, i.e., a biological urge. Armed with such a preconception, the psychologist does not have to describe the sublimation and look at what really happens between a man and a woman in love besides the satisfaction of a biological urge. Hence the blindness in the modern scientific literature concerning matters of Eros. I do not dare to set forth a theory of love. When I use the word, I refer to the plain fact that relations between human beings can be such that the I and the You build up a We as the whole of an intimate world in which they are obliged to be to themselves what they are to each other and are permitted to be to each other what they are to themselves. This phenomenon cannot be reduced to sex, though it may require and create, or be required and created by, sexual intercourse. Shame seems to safeguard the youthful genesis of love against the biological urge and thus to watch over the sublimation of sex.

3. The further role shame plays between two sexual companions depends on love. Mutual love banishes shame. In a sexual intercourse that we imagine to be the mere satisfaction of a biological urge and without a tinge of love shame insists on being present; without love, the companion becomes the observer. Shame decreases with increasing love, increases with decreasing love. It takes its leave when love reaches its peak and reappears when love takes its leave. Shame protects love in sex against sex without love.

The matter is so delicate, however, that the more precise one tries to be the more inadequate the description becomes. It seems to shun bright light. Are we really right in saying that shame disappears in passionate love? Perhaps we should say that it merely changes its code. Intimacy seems to prescribe and create its special code, a subtle thing, which guards the I against the You as well as the You against the I and perhaps even the We against both the I and the You. We may say that this fragile thing is not shame but tact. Tact, however, implies shame. Mutual tact respects mutual shame.

These meager remarks merely indicate a diversity of function under different conditions. Even they, however, give an outline that thorough analysis can certainly enrich but scarcely alter. I am aware of the countless variations in each civilization or period that enliven the story of shame with unique shades and inflections. But historic interest should not induce the student of human nature to miss the sameness of the theme. The melody is faint but audible.

The melody, the same despite all the variable *pudenda* and their diverse manifestations, compels us to admit a meaning of shame that is not a creation of man-made moral codes or of interests of social groups. This shame is not a *creatum* but part of the inner structure of a creative process in which men build up their selves and their countless worlds. The contents of shame, the *pudenda,* depend upon the different worlds man creates; shame itself preserves the sameness of its function provided we are careful to determine it in terms of an inner structure of human life instead of using the identities of a material world as the frame of reference.

Although Nature dislikes to divulge her secret, I may inquire whether the language is right in using one and the same word for shame both in and outside sex.

We react to both kinds of shame in one and the same way: we blush and we conceal. Since the reaction does not depend upon social codes or historical changes we might follow the lead Nature seems to indicate. In and outside sex shame prevents us from doing what, if done, would make us blush and conceal. Shame guides a process of formation and shields its vulnerable spots, solicitous for what is frail and fragile. This may be our own Self, the Me or the image of the Me in our own eyes or in the eyes of others. It may even be another self, in whose name we feel shame or whom we avoid putting to shame. It may be the privacy of our sexual life, the mysterious something called love, its growth or its intimacy, the We and its barriers. Shame stresses the secret. Every creator has his secret, beyond his *creata.*

Both the French and the Greek use two words. Their distinction, however, does not correspond to the distinction between sexual and nonsexual matters. *Pudeur* means a kind of shame that tends to keep you from an act, whereas you may feel *honte* after an act. Customary loose usage tends to blur the distinction and to forget that you may feel *pudeur* outside sex and *honte* within sex.

IV

The Greek distinction between *Aidos* and *Aischyne* does not correspond to the French between *pudeur* and *honte;* nor has it anything to do with a distinction between sexual and nonsexual matters. The old grammarians define: "*Aidos* est pudor profectus ex verecundia. *Aischyne* est pudor profectus ex turpitudine."[2] The origin of *Aischyne* is dishonor, of *Aidos,* awe. Dishonor puts the emphasis on man-made codes. If you are ashamed of violating or having violated such codes, the Greeks use the verb that corresponds to the noun *Aischyne. Aidos* is not concerned merely with man-made codes. You feel *Aidos* when confronted with things nature tells you to revere and not violate. Shame in sexual matters is *Aidos,* not *Aischyne.* In the *Odyssey* Hephaistos catches his wife, Aphrodite, with her lover, Ares, in nets he spread around Aphrodite's bed. He calls all the gods and goddesses to look at the adulterous couple. The gods hurry to the place, but the goddesses stay at home out of shame. Homer calls this shame *Aidos.*

A mighty personality, be it a king, poet, or philosopher, is *Aidoios. Aidoia* is the word for the sexual organs. You feel *Aidos* when you enter a temple, a holy grove, the shadow of a cave, the dark of a wood. These things have a secret you should respect. In the courts of Attica the defendant had his place beside a stone dedicated to *Aidos;* the stone on the opposite side, the place of the prosecutor, was dedicated to *Anaideia,* shamelessness. The one is entitled to conceal, the other obliged to unmask.

In Euripides' tragedy, *Hippolytos,* the pure youth, Hippolytos, enters the holy grove of Artemis at dawn and offers the goddess a crown of flowers.

> My Goddess Mistress, I bring you ready woven
> This garland. It was I that plucked and wove it,
> Plucked it for you in your Inviolate Meadow.
> No shepherd dares to feed his flock within it:
> No reaper plies a busy scythe within it:
> Only the bees in springtime haunt the Inviolate Meadow.
> Its gardener is the *Spirit Reverence* who
> Refreshes it with water from the river.

---

[2] *Aidos* is shame (or modesty/decency) derived from a natural feeling of awe or reverence; *aischyne* is shame (or modesty/decency) derived from disgrace or baseness.

Not those who by instruction have profited
To learn, but in whose very soul the seed
Of Chastity towards all things alike
Nature has deeply rooted, they alone
May gather flowers there! the wicked may not.[3]

The *Spirit Reverence* of the translation is *Aidos*. These lines, I think, are eloquent enough to disclose the particular flavor of the term. We should not disregard the wisdom of such wording as an arbitrariness of a language, or a
Greek peculiarity that may interest the historian alone. *Aidos* links shame to
awe: this link may be in the things themselves, whether or not the language
retains it in the connotations of its words.

Shame is rooted, as I have said, in the formative process we call the life of
man. So is awe. Shame protects, awe guides this process. Man is a being directed toward a whither—creative but finite. As he is finite, he is in need and
danger, dependent on things that are beyond his power. Thus he is bound to
take heed lest he go astray. As he is creative he is bound to revere consciously
or unconsciously, building up before himself an image and tending to transcend every present actuality of his Self. It is in the name of such an image
that shame warns, protects, and conceals. As a finite being endowed with a bit
of creativity gropes its way, it is, in any phase, both limping behind and running ahead of itself: between shame and awe. Neither a noncreative finite being
nor an infinite creator can feel either shame or awe. Both God and the devil,
the infinite creator and the infinite destroyer, are beyond shame and awe.

V

If a boy is ashamed of wearing childish pants, he looks up to another kind
of pants he or his group holds in higher esteem. *Pudenda* and *veneranda* imply
each other. Behind every *pudendum* is hidden a *venerandum,* though man may
refuse to recognize it as such. *Pudenda* may lose their *veneranda.* You may inherit a *pudendum;* its origin may be a *venerandum* of a social group of times
forgotten. *Pudenda,* in outliving their *veneranda,* outlive themselves.

History tells a tale of impervious complexity. Civilizations, social groups
of all kinds, individuals as they grow, build up systems of *pudenda* and *veneranda.* These systems may be called moral, social, or religious codes, rules of taboo and mana, or have no name at all. They may be conscious, half-conscious,
or unconscious. They tend to be systems. Man tends to build up himself and

---

[3]Translation by David Grene, *Three Greek Tragedies* (Chicago: University of Chicago Press, 1942).

his world as consistent wholes, not as aggregates. As a social group or an individual develops, aggregates converge toward a focus. An elaborate whole is shaped. In this process man adjusts conditions to himself as well as himself to conditions. An "environment" becomes a "world." In achieving a personality man drops those of his *pudenda* and *veneranda,* opinions or lines of behavior which were merely casual, or alters their functions and meanings, relates the one to the other, or shapes new habits that are less casual, thus building up himself, his "world," the conscious or unconscious norms of his behavior as a consistent whole. A civilization tends to follow the same pattern. The focus of this unity remains beyond our conscious thinking. In both a strong personality and a high civilization we recognize the fact by admiring its secret.

As civilizations decay *pudenda* and *veneranda* become anemic; systems disintegrate into aggregates. Life quits the fragments. Man inherits petrified habits. Mothers still transmit to children pieces of a forgotten whole. Children outgrow fear and learn to disregard the lifeless pieces. Rules of mana and taboo in primitive tribes often seem to us but aggregates of unconnected superstitions. The tribes may have still better excuses for the inconsistency of their *pudenda* and *veneranda* than we have for ours. They may be very old, stabilized products of a long history they do not remember.

Growth and decay, however, are interwoven; most periods are both young and old at the same time. The official system of *pudenda* and *veneranda* need not be the real system; it may be but the system of yesterday and still govern institutions and terms, though no longer acts. Moreover, the real system governing the acts of parents and teachers may not be the real system of their children. While parents complain that their children have neither shame nor reverence, children may be shaping a system of their own, which sometimes promises to be both more consistent and more honest.

Since the individual shapes his self and builds his world in relation to others to whom he wants to be what he is to himself and cannot help that his being-to-others is part of his being-to-himself, growth and decay of individual and social systems are interlocked. The individual itself is a social, and sociability an individual, phenomenon. In a tensile civilization the system of *pudenda* and *veneranda* is the framework of the particular social systems built by individuals or groups; in a loosened civilization they are often merely *disjecta membra* thrown together into jerry-built edifices. During all the phases of this indefatigable process of dependency and creation, shame and awe hold hands. Wherever there is still some creativity they are present. "Shameless" times, if there are any, are periods of destruction. So are times without any kind of awe. But even in such times shame and awe are present by their very absence—as need and want in human hearts.

As we move, the mental, social, or moral space in which we live goes on moving. Nevertheless, the codes of shame and awe may change; shame and awe themselves are not products of history but structural elements of the process itself and therefore neither younger nor older than man, though probably older than God and the devil.

May, "Four Mischievous Theories of Sex"

Nature may be responsible for the "facts of life," but what we make of those facts, and especially how we evaluate them morally, is largely up to us. In this short but provocative paper, most of it prepared for a 1984 conference on "Passionate Attachments," Protestant theologian and ethicist William F. May (born in 1927) explores four conflicting attitudes toward and assessments of sexual intercourse: sex as demonic, divine, casual, or nuisance. Giving each its due, May, giving reasons, nonetheless finds all of them finally not only inadequate but also mischievous. The final section, on "covenanted sexual love" (prepared for a 1993 meeting on the Ethics of Everyday Life), looks into the question of whether and how far the nature of the human sex act, and especially its expressive and revelatory character, points toward and supports monogamous marriage as its fulfillment and proper home.

Several conflicting attitudes toward sex beset us today. We loosely associate these attitudes with the behavior of different cultural groups. Whether these groups actually behaved in these ways poses a descriptive question that will not preoccupy me for the moment. I am interested more in the attitudes than in the historical accuracy of the symbols. The Victorian prude feared sex as demonic; romantics, such as D. H. Lawrence, elevated sex to the divine; liberals tend to reduce sex to the casual; and the British, as the satirists relentlessly portray them, pass it off as a nuisance. I will argue that all these views of sex contain an element of truth; all are ultimately mischievous; and most can be found conflicting and concurrent in ourselves.

Sex as Demonic

Those who fear sex as the demon in the groin reckon with sex as a power which, once let loose, tends to grip and destroy its host; it is self-destructive and destructive of others, a loose cannon, as it were, in human affairs. Our movies and drugstore paperbacks relentlessly mock this view, which we tend to assign remotely to our Victorian forebears and proximately to our parents. While parents, in fact, may fear the explosive power of sex in their adolescent children, it is doubtful whether most parents are quite the Victorians their children assume them to be. Children impute this view to their elders because at some level of their being they partly hold to this attitude themselves.

In any event, this pessimism that emphasizes the runaway destructiveness of sex hardly originated with the Victorians. Religiously, it dates back to the Manichaean dualists of the Third Century of the Common Era. Manichaeans divided all reality and power into two rival kingdoms: the Kingdom of God pitted against the Kingdom of Satan, Good versus Evil, Light versus Darkness. They associated the Absolute Good with Spirit and Absolute Evil with Matter. Originally Spirit and Matter existed in an uneasy separation from one another; but through the aggressive strategies of Satan, the present world and human-kind came into existence, a sad commingling of them both—Spirit and Flesh. The world is a kind of battleground between these two rival kingdoms. Man's only hope rests in disengaging himself from the pain and confusion and muck of life in the flesh, and allying himself with the Kingdom of Spirit. I say "man" deliberately because the Manichaeans tended to associate women with the in-tentions of the Devil; that is, with his strategy to perpetuate this present age of confusion and commingling through the device of sex and offspring. Quite literally, marriage in their view is an invention of the Devil, a scheme for per-petuating the human race and the messy world that we know. Man should achieve a final state of metaphysical *Apartheid,* a clean separation from the toils of the flesh, women, and all their issue.

Manichaean sex counselors thus urged on their followers a rigorous ethic of sexual denial—with, however, an antinomian escape clause since not every-one could lead the wholly ascetic life. If one couldn't totally abstain—here is the twist—the Manichaeans believed it was better to engage in "unnatural sex" so as to avoid the risk of progeny. In the Manichaean vision of things, sex is bad, but children are worse. Reproduction should be avoided at all costs since it only perpetuates the grim, woe-beset world that we know. (The mythology sounds strange to the modern ear, but the Manichaeans have served as a sym-bol of pessimism in later Western theology, and rightly so. A reluctance to have children usually blurts out the pessimism—whatever its causes—of those who think little of the world's present and future prospects.)

Christianity rejected this Manichaean pessimism, and thereby confirmed the religious vision it derived largely from the Scriptures of Israel and from the New Testament. Its monotheism differs from a dualism that takes evil too se-riously and that identifies evil too readily with the flesh. Its scriptures highly esteem sexual love (the erotic Song of Solomon would jar in a Manichaean scripture); it grants a sacramental status to marriage; and it describes the body as the temple of the Lord. The lowly, needy, hungering, flatulent body is noth-ing less than the real estate where the resurrection will occur.

But dualism kept reappearing in the Western tradition, often nesting in Christianity itself or appearing in an alluring alternative, the cult of roman-tic love. On the surface, the ideal of romantic love, Denis de Rougemont once shrewdly argued, appears to be sexually vigorous; it celebrates God's good green gift of sex. But, in fact, it secretly despairs of sex; it always directs itself to the faraway princess—not to the partner you've got, but to the dream person, the remote figure not yet yours. Sex slips its focus on actual contacts between people and transposes to the realm of the imagination. To possess her is to lose one's appetite for her. Love, therefore, feeds best on obstacles. "We love each other, but you're a Capulet and I'm a Montague." And so it goes from Romeo and Juliet, backward to the Tristan and Iseult myth, and forward to Noel Coward's "Brief Encounter" and the mawkish "Love Story." The poignancy of passion depends upon separation, ultimately upon death.[1] The cult of romantic love locates passion in the teased imagination. The flesh kills; the spirit alone endures; thus Manichaean pessimism hides in its alluring garb.

The post-Renaissance world offered a somewhat drabber version of this dualist suspicion of sex. Social diseases assaulted the Western countries and associated sex with forces that abuse the mind and body. Further, a concept of marriage emerged with middle-class careerism that encourages a Manichaean wariness toward sex. The bourgeois family depended for its stability and life on the career and the property of the male provider. Premarital sex, which distracts a man from his career and leads him prematurely into marriage, severely limits his prospects. Extramarital sex spoils the marriage itself and public reputation. And marital sex leads to too many children with a cramping effect on the careers of those already arrived. Thus, all told, sex severely inconveniences a careerist-oriented society that depends throughout on deferred gratification.

But not surprisingly, bourgeois culture produced not only repression, but also a pornographic fascination with sex. Sex became, at one and the same time, unmentionable in polite society but also an unshakable obsession in fantasy. Geoffrey Gorer, the English social anthropologist, in his often plagiarized article, "The Pornography of Death," nicely defined all such pornographic preoccupation with sex as an obsession with the sex act abstracted from its natural human emotion, which is *affection*. This definition helps explain the inevitable structure of pornographic novels and films. Invariably, they must proliferate and escalate the varieties of sexual performance. When the sex act separates from its natural human emotion of affection, it loses its tie with the concrete lives of the two persons performing the act; it becomes *boring*. Inevitably, one must reinvest one's interest in the variety of ways and techniques with which the act is performed—one on one, then two on one, then in all possible permutations and combinations, culminating in the orgy. When affection isn't there, it won't do to have bodies perform the act in the age-old ways. Sad variety alone compensates. . . .

This ambivalent attitude toward sex that generates both repression and obsession is basically religious—not Jewish or Christian, to be sure, but religious,

---

[1] De Rougemont's treatment of this matter can be found in the next section, "Is This Love?" [eds.]

specifically Manichaean—in its root. It religiously preoccupies itself with sex as a major evil in human affairs.

Sex as Divine

The second of the four attitudes toward sex also qualifies as religious; in this case, however, one elevates sex from the demonic to the divine. D. H. Lawrence offers the definitive expression of this sex-mysticism; let his views stand for the type. *Lady Chatterley's Lover* is a religious book. That assessment didn't occur to people of my generation who, before laying hands on the book, assumed its title was *Lady Chatterley's Lovers,* and settled down for the inevitable orgy. The book offered, however, religion in a very traditional sense, for religion consists of some sort of experience of sacred power perceived in contest with other powers. The sacred grips the subject as overwhelming, alluring, and mysterious, and eventually orders the rest of life for the person or community so possessed. (Exodus 3, for example, describes the contest between Yahveh, God of the Jews, and the power of the Pharaoh. God liberates his people from Egypt and orders their life at Mt. Sinai; God prevails.)

Just so, the novel focuses on a woman who experiences in her own being a contest of the powers—those opposingly symbolized by Lord Clifford, her husband, and Oliver Mellors, her husband's gamekeeper. Her husband possessed those several powers which the English highly prized—status, money, and talent. He was at once an aristocrat, an industrial captain, and an author—an ironmonger and wordmonger. He wielded economic power and word power. Leaving such a man for his gamekeeper would utterly confound the commitments of Lady Chatterley's class. Lord Clifford's only trouble, his fatal trouble, however, was a war wound that left him dead from the waist down, a state of affairs which was but the natural issue of the kind of destructive power which he wields. Lady Chatterley discovers in the gamekeeper and in the grove where he breeds pheasants, a different kind of power, a growing power in the pheasant and the phallus, and this power prevails.

Lawrence's novel celebrates not random sex but a sex-mysticism. The grove where Lady Chatterley and Oliver meet serves as a sacred precinct removed from the grimy, profane, sooty, industrial midlands of England where men like Lord Clifford ruled. Lawrence explicitly uses the coronation Psalms of Israel to describe the act of sexual intercourse. "Open up, ye everlasting gates, and let the king of glory enter in." In using royal language, Lawrence advocated not sexual promiscuity, as the hungering undergraduates of my generation supposed. Far from it! Lawrence disdained the merely casual affair: he exalted sexual union into a sacred encounter. Tenderhearted sex is the closest we come to salvation in this life. It provides contact with all that nurtures and fulfills.

Americans in the 1950s relied on a sentimental marital version of this religious expectation. As the song of the times put it, "love and marriage go together like a horse and carriage." In the oft-called "age of conformity" one tended to look to the sanctuary of marriage to provide respite from the loneliness and pressures of the outer world to which one conformed but which one found unfulfilling.

Sex as Casual

W. H. Auden once observed that the modern liberal offended Lawrence more than the Puritan. The Puritan mistakenly viewed sex as an outsize evil, but the liberal made the even greater mistake of reducing sex to the casual—to one of the many incidental goods which in our liberty we take for granted. Some have called this the drink-of-water theory of sex.

This casual attitude toward sex reflects a liberal industrial culture that prizes autonomy above all else, that reduces nature to raw material to be manipulated and transformed into products of man's own choosing, and that correspondingly reduces the body to the incidental—not to the prison house of the dualists, or to the Lord's temple of the monotheists, or to the sacred grove of the mystics, but to a playground pure and simple.

Some observers argue that this third attitude toward sexual experience dominates our time. Is not D. H. Lawrence, despite his flamboyance, actually somewhat quaint and old-fashioned, the reverse side, if you will, of the Victorian prude? Don't both the prude and the romantic make the mistake of taking sex too seriously? One elevates sex into the satanic, and the other celebrates it as divine. Have we not succeeded in desacralyzing sex and reducing it now to the casual?

This third and apparently prevailing theory of sex today, the so-called new sex ethic, takes two forms. First and most notoriously, its earlier, male chauvinist version converts sex into an instrument of domination. It reduces sex to the casual by converting women into bunnies and by replacing heterosexuality with a not so latent male orientation. In its magazine formula, it condemns women, flatters the young male, and lavishes on him advice on how to dress, talk, choose his cars, and handle his women—all without involvement. The women's movement has shown proper contempt for this view.

The second version of the new sex ethic avoids the more obvious criticisms of the woman's movement; indeed, it seeks to join it by offering easy access, easy departure, and no long term ties, but with equal rights for both partners. One of our entertainers best summarized this casual, tentative, experimental attitude toward sex and marriage by referring to his decision to do the "marriage bit"—a phrase from show biz. It suggests that marriage offers a role one chooses to play rather than a relationship by which one is permanently al-tered—not necessarily a one-night stand, but then not likely, either, to run as long as "Life With Father."

This reading of the social history of our time—from the religious to the secular—only apparently persuades. We are not quite as casual about sex as this analysis would suggest. Our popular magazines—men's and women's—may have evangelized for a cool attitude toward sex; but they would not have sold millions of copies if, underneath it all, in the steamy depths of our desires, we could toy with it that easily.

Denis de Rougemont neatly skewers our irrepressible fascination with sex in *The Devil's Share,* a book that included chapters on such topics as the "Devil and Betrayal," the "Devil and War," and the "Devil and Lying." His first sen-tence in his essay on the "Devil and Sex" reads, in effect: "To the adolescent amongst my readers who have turned to this chapter first . . . " I read de Rougemont's book when I was 32, but the age makes little difference. There one is—young or old—caught red-handed, eyes riveted, imagination stirred, ready for fresh rivulets of knowledge on that most fascinating of topics. Casual cu-riosity? Yes. But the lure of mystery as well. Elements of the religious as well as the casual characterize our attitude toward the subject.

Sex as a Nuisance

So far, this essay has covered three views of sex; symmetry alone would demand a fourth to complete two sets of paired attitudes. Dualists inflate sex into a transcendent evil; mystics view it as a transcendent good; and casualists reduce it to a trivial good. The demands of symmetry, then, would posit the existence of a fourth group composed of those prosaic folk who dismiss sex as a minor evil, a nuisance. Comic writers have rounded up this particular popu-lation and located them in Great Britain under the marquee: "No Sex, Please. We're British." Copulation is, at best, a burdensome ritual to be endured for the sake of a few lackluster goods. One has visions therewith of an underblooded, overarticulate clutch of aristocrats in whom the life force runs thin. But a re-port in one of the most popular of American syndicated newspaper columns (in the *Washington Post,* June 14 and 15, 1985) suggests that the number of people occupying the quadrant of petty pessimists may be surprisingly large. Ann Landers asked her reading audience to send a postcard or letter with a reply to the question: "Would you be content to be held close and treated ten-derly and forget about 'the act'? Reply YES or NO and please add one line: 'I am over (or under) 40 years of age.' No signature is necessary." Even discount-ing for the fact that the disgruntled find more time to write than the contented, the percentage of those replying to Landers' inquiry who deemed themselves to be sexually burdened was impressive. More than 70 percent replied YES and 40 percent of those affirmatives were under 40 years of age. Clearly the people who find sex to be a burden transcend the boundaries of the British Isles. Over 90,000 letters poured in from the US and other places where Landers' column appears (in Canada, Europe, Tokyo, Hong Kong, Bangkok, Mexico). This out-pouring has exceeded every inquiry that Landers has directed to her readers, except for the pre-fab letter to be sent to President Reagan on the subject of nuclear war. "This sex survey beats . . . the poll asking parents, 'If you had to do it over again, would you have children?'" (Seventy percent said NO.) (Some astute historians of religion have argued that Manichaeaism persists as the ranking heresy in the West.)

Critics of the Landers report have warned that her results are not scientific. Her respondents are self-selective and her question tips the responses nega-tively. By placing the term for intercourse in quotation marks and calling it "the act," she tends to separate the sex act from tenderness. Still, the gram-mar of her question does not force an either/or response: tenderness or sex. However parsed, Landers uncovers a great deal of dissatisfaction amongst women . . . "it's a burden, a bore, no satisfaction . . . " Her letter-writers largely blame men for this state of affairs, but her survey and the ensuing discussion leave untouched the question as to whether the male failure to satisfy reflects a deeper masculine version of the experience of sex as a nuisance. One thinks here not of the occasionally impotent male who is agonizingly aware of sex as a nuisance, but, of the robust stallion who prides himself on his efficient performance but who finds foreplay, afterplay, tenderness, and gratitude an in-comprehensible and burdensome detail.

Theological Interpretation

Since I am a trained Protestant theologian, not a social commentator, I will close with a few comments about each of these four attitudes on the basis of the biblical tradition. In these matters I don't think I stray too far from what my colleagues in the rabbinate and priesthood might say.

1. Whatever criticisms the biblical tradition might deliver against the casu-alist approach to sex, that approach has an element of truth to it. Not all sexual encounters should carry the weight of an ultimate significance. Sometimes sex is merely recreational, a way to fall asleep, a *jeu d'esprit*, to say nothing of a *jeu de corps*. But at the same time, the interpretation of a particular episode should not exhaust the full meaning of the activity. At first glance, the ideology of the casualist seems virile, optimistic, and pleasure-oriented. But a latent melan-choly pervades it. The fantasy of transient pleasure as an interpretation of the full meaning of the act requires a systematic elimination of everything that

might shadow the fantasy. The sacred grove trivializes into a playpen. Hugh Hefner's original policy of never accepting a story for his magazine [Playboy] on the subject of death betrays the pathos of the approach. The fact of human frailty and death shatters the illusion upon which Hefner's world depends. By comparison, a sturdy optimism underlies a tradition that invites a couple to exchange vows that can stretch across the stark events of plenty and want, sickness and health, until death parts them. Since life is no playpen, it lets the world as it is flood in upon the lovers in the very content of their pledge.

Further, the casual outlook tends to ignore the inevitable complications of most sexual relationships. It lapses into a kind of emotional prudery. We are inclined to apply the word prudish to those who deny their sexual being. The modern casualist, however, is an emotional prude; that is, he tries to deny those emotions that cluster around his sexual life: affection, but not affection alone, loneliness in absence, jealousy, envy, preoccupation, restlessness, anger, and hopes for the future. The emotional prude dismisses all these or assumes that sincerity and honesty provide a kind of solvent that breaks down chemically any and all inconvenient and messy feelings: You hope for the future? But I never promised you a future. Why complain? I am emotionally clean, drip-dry. Why not you? This antiseptic view overlooks the element of dirt farming in sex and marriage. Caesar ploughed her and she cropped. Put another way, this view overlooks the comic in sex; adopting the pose of the casual it lacks a comic sense. It overlooks the way sex gets out of control. Sex refuses to stay in the playpen. It tends to defy our advance formulae. It mires each side down in complications that need to be respected.

If sex is a great deal more important, complicated, and consequential for the destiny of each partner than the committed casualists are wont to pretend, then it may not be out of place to subject it to a deliberateness, to submit it to a discipline to let sexual decisions be *decisions* instead of resolving sexual ties by the luck of the draw, opportunity, and drift. The Hebrew tradition emphasized and symbolized the element of deliberateness in sexual life when it imposed the rite of circumcision. The rite does not deny the natural (as castration does with a vengeance) but neither does it accept the natural vitalities without their conforming to purposes that transcend them. Human sexual life is properly itself only when it is drawn into the self's deeper identity. Thus, against those who reduce sex to the casual, the tradition says sex is *important*, and should be subjected to discipline like anything important and consequential in human affairs.

2. The approach of the dualists to sex, either those who elevate it to a transcendental evil or those who reduce it to a doggish burden, hold to an element of truth. Sometimes, sexual activity can be abysmally self-destructive and destructive of others; at other times, it is merely a burdensome obligation. But,

from the biblical perspective, both approaches wrongly estimate sexual love: they confuse the abuse of an activity with the activity itself. Sexual love is a good rather than an evil. God created man in his own image, *male and female* created He them. Genesis provides quite an exalted theory of sexual identity. Not divine, but in the image of God.

This differing estimate of sexual love shifts dramatically the meaning and warrants for discipline in one's sexual life. The Manichaeans disciplined sexual activity in the sense that they sought to eradicate it altogether; they justified radical denial on the ground that sex is inherently *evil*. The Jew and Christian, on the other hand, justify discipline on the basis of the goodness of sexual power.

Unfortunately, most popular justifications of discipline, especially in the perspective of the young, rest on the evilness of an activity or a faculty. Discipline the child because he is evil. Renounce your sexuality because it corrupts. This is the Manichaean way.

We may need to recover the vastly more important warrant for discipline that we already recognize in education and that the biblical tradition largely supports. The goodness and promise of the human mind, not its evilness, justifies the lengthy discipline of an education. Because the child has worthwhile potentialities, we consider it worth our while to develop her to the maximum. Because the piano is a marvelously versatile and expressive instrument, we think it worth the labors of the talented person to realize the full potentialities of the instrument rather than trivialize its capabilities with "Chopsticks." Some sexual encounters are not so much wicked as trivial, less than the best.

3. Finally, the sex-mystics also have an element of truth on their side. The event of sexual intercourse does supply us with one of our privileged contacts with ecstasy—the possibility of being beside ourselves, of moving beyond ourselves, experiencing a level of energy and urgency that both suspends and restores the daily round. But when all is said and done, sexuality, though a good, is only a *human* good, not *divine* as such. Despite Lawrence's perorations on the subject of love and the mountains atremble for Robert Jordan and his mate in Hemingway's *For Whom the Bell Tolls,* the act of sexual intercourse falls short of Exodus-Mount Sinai, death-resurrection. Intercourse is not an event of salvation; neither is marriage another name for redemption.

Biblical realism requires us to acknowledge three ways of abusing sex—to malign it with the dualists, to underestimate it with the casualists, but also to overestimate it with the sentimentalists and therefore to get angry, frustrated, and retaliatory when it fails to transcend the merely human. As a sexologist St. Augustine had his faults, but he recognized that people tend to engage in a double torture when they elevate the human into the divine—whether it be sex, marriage, children, or any other creaturely good.

First, they condemn themselves to disappointment; they torture themselves. If men and women look for the resolution to all their problems in marriage, if they look to it for salvation, they are bound to discover that neither sex nor marriage converts an ordinary human being into someone sublime. They let themselves in for a letdown. Second, one not only tortures oneself, one also tortures the partner to whom one has turned. One places on the mate too heavy a burden. Dostoevsky tells of a dream in which a driver flogs a horse, forcing it to drag an overloaded wagon until the horse collapses under too much weight. We similarly overburden another when we look to him for too much. We expect others to function as a surrogate for the divine. Thus parents drive their thwarted ambitions through their children like a stake through the heart. Some marriages break up not because people expected too little from marriage, but because they have expected too much.

This biblical realism need not produce the sort of pessimism that expects little of the world and savors even less. Indeed, it should free us a little for enjoyment. Once we free our relationships to others from the impossible pressure to rescue us or redeem us, perhaps we can be free to enjoy them for what they are. Specifically, we can enjoy without shame and with delight a sexual relationship for the pleasurable, companionable, and fertile human good that it is.

Covenanted Sexual Love

Christian theologians have chosen different starting points in developing a theology of sexual love. Some begin with the natural tendencies of the act of sexual intercourse; others with the significance of the act in the setting of Scripture. The first approach hardly ignores Scripture; indeed it takes such Biblical injunctions as, "be fruitful and multiply," very seriously. But it seeks to show that the restraints under which the tradition places sexual congress are not unnatural; they are profoundly congruent with the human.

An approach that begins with the act of sexual intercourse can take two forms, emphasizing the procreative and/or the expressive character of the act.

According to natural law theorists in the Catholic tradition, sexual intercourse for human, as for all living, beings serves the natural end of reproducing the species. Thus the Church has opposed contraception and, of course, abortion as thwarting that end. Since, moreover, the end of procreation is not fully realized in human beings except that the young enjoy extended care, nurture, and education, the Church argued the necessity of the monogamous family for carrying out these tasks. Indeterminate copulation of the sexes, though natural to some species, compromises the continuing collaboration required of both human parents. Fornication, adultery, onanism, sodomy, and all other sins of lust distract from the natural ordering of sex to the human family and the positive commands of Scripture to "be fruitful and multiply."

Other interpreters of the tradition also begin with the sex act, but question whether the purpose or purposes of the act follow solely from its procreative power without due regard for its further meaning for the sexual partners themselves. The sex act expresses as well as engenders. It reveals love between the partners. A further end of sexual intercourse is a love union.

In due course, the hierarchical Church conceded that conjugal love, as well as procreation, is an essential end of sexual intercourse. But, on the basis of this position, the Church has not softened its opposition to the use of contraceptives or withdrawn its objections to artificial insemination. While conjugal love is an essential end of sexual intercourse, it does not independently justify the act of love-making apart from the end of procreation. Thus the official Church continues to prohibit the use of contraceptives. At the same time, the status of conjugal love as an essential end reinforces the Church's opposition to artificial insemination inasmuch as artificial insemination pursues the end of procreation apart from a specific act of conjugal love.

Some Catholic theologians, trying to work within the framework of the official language, have suggested that procreation be accepted and honored as essential and primary in marriage without requiring that this end control a couple's intention and practice in every act of sexual intercourse. The marriage itself must be procreative—open to procreation—but not every act need be procreative. Thus contraceptives may be used on occasion without compromising the overarching primary end. Similarly, some theologians have suggested that the overarching reality of conjugal love in a marriage suffices to provide for the principled presence of sexual love in conception even though the couple may have had to resort to artificial insemination in order to have a baby. So far, the official Church has rejected these interpretations.

In what follows, I want to explore whether the expressive/revelatory character of sexual intercourse argues for its restriction to marriage. Argument for this restriction can be developed in two ways.

The first argument appeals to the distinctiveness of the act as a revelatory event. Love-making—just like a smile, a shrug of the shoulders, a smirk on the lips, or raised eyebrows—gestures. Gestures can modify their meaning somewhat, but, on the whole, human community depends upon some stability in their meaning. For example, a shrug signifies resignation; a smirk, contempt; and a smile, friendliness or amusement. Such gestures, given and received, make possible human community. Correspondingly, when a discrepancy develops between the inner and the outer person, human community suffers strains. The smile says one thing, but it masks a person who thinks and feels something else. Under these circumstances, gestures no longer establish and nourish community, quite the contrary, they distort it.

The potential for distortion intensifies in the case of sexual intercourse. It is the most intimate, complete, and unconditional unveiling of which two human beings are capable. . . . Further, the self-giving which the act conveys reflects more than a sincere feeling at the time of performance. For better or for worse, temporality distinguishes human beings from other creatures. They cannot live in the present alone. They always cast ahead of themselves into the morrow, and they bring along with themselves their yesterdays. The self does not fully give itself—however fervent the act—if it withholds the future.

Admittedly, a couple can hedge against a misleading gesture by candid and mutual acknowledgment that the act does not carry its usual freight of meaning. While such honesty is better than dishonesty, it quickly sounds the false note of pomposity. It is not easy to make a gesture—whether it is a handshake or a smile—and launch into an explanation that the gesture does not carry its ordinary meaning. The pomposity intensifies in the case of a gesture that purportedly exposes the self, while the accompanying language turns self-protective. A person ought not inflict such a heavy pedagogical load on a sexual partner preceding or following intercourse. Only an emotional prig would pretend to reconfigure the act and ignore the awkwardness, the groping, the reticence, and the importuning that characterizes the act as a human unveiling.

This argument, however, from the ultimate revelatory power of sexual intercourse has its limitations. It lapses into a sex-mysticism whenever it sentimentalizes intercourse as a final breakthrough between human beings, a unique, once-for-all event so consummate in character as never again to need repeating. Quite the contrary, sexual intercourse is an eminently repeatable event, enriched by its very repeating under the varied conditions that make up married life. It is not the sovereign triumph and breakthrough of a single act of love, but rather it is triumph edged with incompleteness which calls for its continuing context in covenant love. Love remains still needy even while expressed. Love asks for the continuance of love. So goes a second, somewhat less ecstatic, line of argument for marriage as the normative context for love-making. It depends less upon the *ultimate* expressive power of the act than upon its power to awaken a further thirst even while it slakes. That is the grandeur and the misery of sexual love, a doubleness which the covenant of marriage honors.

When all has been said, however, it is doubtful whether an analysis of the sex act leads unambiguously to the monogamous marriage and family. The proponents of the so-called new morality had a point when they eschewed its procreative and revelatory powers and settled for its obvious pleasures. Sexual intercourse, after all, offers self-satisfaction whatever its powers of self-communication and engendering may be. Not that the desire for pleasure contradicts the expression and nurture of love. Partners can nourish love even when each partner intends only immediate satisfaction in the body of the other. But, to say the least, the impulse to pleasure is a rambunctious tendency, which, though it may serve—and serve exuberantly—the ends of love and procreation, nevertheless, in no man or woman is it smoothly coincident and subordinate to these two.

It would seem therefore that prior commitments, rather than an independent analysis of sexual intercourse, prompt the Christian to subordinate the varied and vagrant impulses that inform sexuality to the ends of covenant love and the family. The value of such independent analysis is not that it produces a fully transparent natural law of sexuality and achieves thereby a prior consent for the Christian standpoint, but that it makes clear that Christian, unlike Manichaean, morality understands itself to be congruent with the natural. There are, in truth, tendencies in the act to the expression and nurturing of love, the begetting of children, as well as the pursuit of bodily pleasure. Meanwhile, the lively and somewhat discordant relations of these three tendencies to one another reminds the Christian of the element of spiritual pride in pretending to a "position" on the subject wholly free of travail, a pomposity today at least as evident in the evangelists for sexual freedom.

D. IS THIS LOVE?
EROS AND ITS AIMS

In the general introduction to this anthology, we explored the ambiguity in the meaning of "love," distinguishing erotic love from two other loves, friendship (*philia*) and love of neighbor (*agape*). While remembering these other loves, this section concentrates almost entirely on *eros*, on passionate or romantic love that preoccupies the lover with his beloved, the soul-searing desire that drives lovers pell-mell into one another's presence. It is this love—intense, focused, exclusive, coupling—that is generally regarded as the love which points to marriage and which is itself the germ of marital love, at least in those cultures such as our own in which people wish to marry for love. As the old ditty had it, "First comes love, then comes marriage, then comes Sally with the baby carriage."

But things are not so simple, not now, not ever. The nature of erotic love and what it wants for us and from us have always been deeply puzzling and mysterious matters, not least to those under its sway. Not without reason did the ancient Greeks (among others) describe love as a form of madness and ascribe falling in love to supernatural causes, indeed, to divine possession ("struck by Aphrodite," "smitten by Cupid's [Eros's] arrows"). Precisely because this "madness" often comes and goes inexplicably and without warning, it has on its own no necessary connection to the stable and enduring relationship sought for in marriage; yet, at the same time, love tends to feel and speak in tones of "always" and "forever." In this respect, love aims higher than mere sexual desire, with which it is, nevertheless, intimately entangled and sometimes confused. It is not always clear whether someone has fallen in love or fallen in lust. Yet distinguishing these states of soul is frequently crucial for everyday life: men and women, especially those hungry for love, do not wish to be deceived about the other person's feelings or self-deceived about their own. No matter how casually they treat sexual encounters, most people know and care about the difference between being in love and being "turned on." Most people are still eager to love and be loved, and want to be sure they are getting the real thing (see the story by Divakaruni that opens this section).

But what exactly is the "real thing," and what does it seek? The readings collected in this section address these questions and more. There are, to begin with, questions about the object of *eros*. Why, for example, do we love those we love? Do we love them because they are lovable (e.g., beautiful or good, in looks or in soul) or because they are ours (e.g., because they appear to love us as theirs)? The possible tension between these two accounts could be stretched to the breaking point: on the principle that love is the love of one's own, one would love oneself most, and when push comes to shove, one would be likely to sacrifice the beloved to self-love. (See Aristophanes' speech from the *Symposium*.) On the other hand, if love is the love of the good, the greatest love would be the love of the very best, which might turn out to be incapable of returning the affection because, being so much better than the lover, it could not find him lovable. Today, we are inclined to insist that love must be mutual and reciprocated in order to *be* love; but equal and mutual love would appear to be paradoxical if love loves what is better, whereas being loved is the deserved fate only of the good. (See Socrates' speech from the *Symposium*.)

There are questions about the character of *eros*. Is love a needy passion or a generous one? Does it mainly seek our own good or the good of our beloved? Does its activity consist mainly in receiving or in giving? Is love a desire born of lack or emptiness, like hunger, which, if satisfied or filled, disappears? Or is it a condition born of excess or fullness, like pregnancy, which, the more it is nurtured, the more it overflows with generous issue?

There are questions about the connection between love and beauty. The phenomenon of "love at first sight" is only one sign of the mysterious connection between visible beauty and erotic passion. But what does this connection mean? Does one hope through attachment to the beautiful beloved to become more beautiful oneself? Can one "have" the beautiful, and if so, what will one get when one has it (her/him)? Or is the beautiful loved rather as a promise, an advertisement, "the skin of the good"? Is it a reliable promise? Does a beautiful surface faithfully reveal beautiful depths, for example, fine character? Or is the beautiful rather a trigger that releases certain overflowing powers of the lover's soul, that inspires the lover toward his or her own excellence?

What indeed is love's goal with the beloved: his or her presence, companionship, or return of love? Possession or appreciation? Capture or surrender, mastery or service? Merging and union—of bodies? of souls? Contemplation and admiration? Or rather, protection of separate solitudes (see Rilke)? Something temporal or something eternal? Earthly happiness or transcendent blessedness? What has love to do with death and human longings for immortality? Many of the readings in this section explore these mysterious matters.

The readings also suggest that the character and goals of erotic love may change over time as a result of cultural influences. Though native to the human soul, love and the capacity to love are apparently also subject to education. For example, romantic love in its classical form is apparently very different from the *eros* of the Greeks. According to De Rougemont, romantic love, the child of medieval European love poetry, is fundamentally tragic, not because a sought-for union with the beloved is physically impossible (Aristophanes' speech), but because love does not really want the beloved but rather prefers the condition of being-in-love, the state of unfulfilled longing (see also the selection from *Romeo and Juliet*). Later, a different kind of love poetry, providing a different education of the imagination, presented romantic love not as tragic but as a realizable ideal (see selections from Rousseau's *Emile* and Shakespeare's Sonnets). Mindful of the changing faces of *eros*, we wonder about the character of romantic and passionate love under present-day conditions. What kind of love are we now talking about when we "fall in love," when we want to be loved by someone special, when we want to marry only for love?

Finally, there are questions about *eros* and the other loves: friendship, love of neighbor, love of the divine. Are these loves all compatible? Does *eros* need the help of the other loves? Can it lead to them? And what, if any, are the connections between the love of one person and the love of God? If love is "divine possession" or "divine madness," the divine would appear to be "in" the lover; but would this not mean, paradoxically, that it is the beloved—in whom the divine is not—who becomes the object of "divinely inspired" reverence? Is there then some connection between the divine and the beloved, such that the love of the latter may lead toward the former? The selections from Socrates' speech, from *The Song of Songs,* and from C. S. Lewis help us think about these (and other) deepest wonders of the power of love.

Divakaruni, "The Word Love"

This poignant story appears in Arranged Marriage, *a collection of short stories (published in 1995), written by Indian-born poet and writer, Chita Banerjee Divakaruni (born in 1956), who now lives in California. The nameless young Indian woman in this story comes from a traditional culture that still widely practices arranged marriage. (Advertisements regularly placed in major newspapers in India are carefully scrutinized by parents of daughters, and the prospective grooms are rated according to caste, educational achievement, and economic prospects; the young couple often do not meet until the wedding day.) She studies romantic literature in the (for her) "alien" or "liberated" territory of the University of California at Berkeley, where she is a graduate student in English (apparently in postmodernist fashion: a class on "a deconstructionist critique of the Sonnets"). Adapting to her new culture, her relations to men have also become "untraditional." Caught between two worlds, she struggles to make the words that she studies have meaning in her life, and to give words to her deepest desires: to love and to be loved. Why is she so confused about the meaning of love? Who loves her? Whom does she love? Was her boyfriend lovable? Why could she not read his character the way the reader can? Is she better off—or any wiser about love—at the end of the story? What does she learn about the word 'love'? About love? Is there anything in the way she lives or in what she studies that can help her find what she is looking for? What do you think are her prospects for love and happiness, and for a good marriage?*

You practice them out loud for days in front of the bathroom mirror, the words with which you'll tell your mother you're living with a man. Sometimes they are words of confession and repentance. Sometimes they are angry, defiant. Sometimes they melt into a single, sighing sound. *Love.* You let the water run so he won't hear you and ask what those foreign phrases you keep saying mean. You don't want to have to explain, don't want another argument like last time.

"Why are you doing this to yourself?" he'd asked, throwing his books down on the table when he returned from class to find you curled into a corner of the sagging sofa you'd bought together at a Berkeley garage sale. You'd washed your face but he knew right away that you'd been crying. Around you, wads of paper crumpled tight as stones. (This was when you thought writing would be the best way.) "I hate seeing you like this." Then he added, his tone darkening, "You're acting like I was some kind of a criminal."

You'd watched the upside-down titles of his books splaying across the table. *Control Systems Engineering. Boiler Operations Guide. Handbook of Shock and Vibration.* Cryptic as tarot cards, they seemed to be telling you something. If only you could decipher it.

"It isn't you," you'd said, gathering up the books guiltily, smoothing their covers. Holding them tight against you. "I'd have the same problem no matter who it was."

You tried to tell him about your mother, how she'd seen her husband's face for the first time at her wedding. How, when he died (you were two years old then), she had taken off her jewelry and put on widow's white and dedicated the rest of her life to the business of bringing you up. *We only have each other,* she often told you.

"So?"

"She lives in a different world. Can't you see that? She's never traveled more than a hundred miles from the village where she was born; she's never touched cigarettes or alcohol; even though she lives in Calcutta, she's never watched a movie."

"Are you serious!"

"I love her, Rex." *I will not feel apologetic,* you told yourself. You wanted him to know that when you conjured up her face, the stern angles of it softening into a rare smile, the silver at her temples catching the afternoon sun in the back-yard under the pomegranate tree, love made you breathless, as though someone had punched a hole through your chest. But he interrupted.

"So don't tell her," he said, "that you're living in sin. With a foreigner, no less. Someone whose favorite food is sacred cow steak and Budweiser. Who pops a pill now and then when he gets depressed. The shock'll probably do her in."

You hate it when he talks like that, biting off the ends of words and spitting them out. You try to tell yourself that he wants to hurt you only because *he's* hurting, because he's jealous of how much she means to you. You try to remember the special times. The morning he showed up outside your Shakespeare class with violets the color of his eyes. The evening when the two of you drove up to Grizzly Peak and watched the sunset spreading red over the Bay while he told you of his childhood, years of being shunted between his divorced parents till he was old enough to move out. How you had held him. The night in his apartment (has it only been three months?) when he took your hands in his warm strong ones, asking you to move in with him, please, because he really needed you. You try to shut out the whispery voice that lives behind the ache in your eyes, the one that started when you said yes and he kissed you, hard.

Mistake, says the voice, whispering in your mother's tones.

Sometimes the voice sounds different, not hers. It is a rushed intake of air, as just before someone asks a question that might change your life. You don't want to hear the question, which might be *how did you get yourself into this mess,* or perhaps *why,* so you leap in with that magic word. *Love,* you tell yourself, *lovelovelove.* But you know, deep down, that words solve nothing.

And so you no longer try to explain to him why you *must* tell your mother. You just stand in the bathroom in front of the crooked mirror with tarnished edges and practice the words. You try not to notice that the eyes in the mirror are so like her eyes, that same vertical line between the brows. The line of your jaw slants up at the same angle as hers when she would lean forward to kiss you goodbye at the door. Outside a wino shouts something. Crash of broken glass and, later, police sirens. But you're hearing the street vendor call out *momphali, momphali, fresh and hot,* and she's smiling, handing you a coin, saying, *yes, baby, you can have some.* The salty crunch of roasted peanuts fills your mouth, the bathroom water runs and runs, endless as sorrow, the week blurs past, and suddenly it's Saturday morning, the time of her weekly call.

She tells you how Aunt Arati's arthritis isn't getting any better in spite of the turmeric poultices. It's so cold this year in Calcutta, the *shiuli* flowers have all died. You listen, holding on to the rounded *o*'s, the long liquid *e*'s, the *s*'s that brush against your face soft as night kisses. She's trying to arrange a marriage for cousin Leela who's going to graduate from college next year, remember? She misses you. Do you like your new apartment? How long before you finish the Ph.D. and come home for good? Her voice is small and far, tinny with static. "You're so quiet. . . . Are you OK, *shona?* Is something bothering you?" You want to tell her, but your heart flings itself around in your chest like a netted bird, and the words that you practiced so long are gone.

"I'm fine, Ma," you say. "Everything's all right."

*

The first thing you did when you moved into his apartment was to put up the batik hanging, deep red flowers winding around a black circle. The late summer sun shone through the open window. Smell of California honeysuckle in the air, a radio next door playing Mozart. He walked in, narrowing his eyes, pausing to watch. You waited, pin in hand, the nubs of the fabric pulsing under your palm, erratic as a heart. "Not bad," he nodded finally, and you let out your breath in a relieved shiver of a laugh.

"My mother gave it to me," you said. "A going-away-to-college gift, a talisman. . . . " You started to tell him how she had bought it at the Maidan fair on a day as beautiful as this one, the buds just coming out on the mango trees, the red-breasted bulbuls returning north. But he held up his hand, *later.* Swung you off the rickety chair and carried you to the bed. Lay on top, pinning you down. His eyes were sapphire stones. His hair caught the light, glinting like warm sandstone. Surge of electric (love or fear?) up your spine, making you shiver, making you forget what you wanted to say.

At night after lovemaking, you lie listening to his sleeping breath. His arm falls across you, warm, *protective,* you say to yourself. Outside, wind rattles the panes. A dry wind. (There hasn't been rain for a long time.) *I am cherished.*

But then the memories come.

Once when you were in college you had gone to see a popular Hindi movie with your girlfriends. Secretly, because Mother said movies were frivolous, decadent. But there were no secrets in Calcutta. When you came home from classes the next day, a suitcase full of your clothes was on the doorstep. A note on it, in your mother's hand. *Better no daughter than a disobedient one, a shame to the family.* Even now you remember how you felt, the dizzy fear that shriveled the edges of the day, the desperate knocking on the door that left your knuckles raw. You'd sat on the doorstep all afternoon, and passersby had glanced at you curiously. By evening it was cold. The numbness crept up your feet and covered you. When she'd finally opened the door after midnight, for a moment you couldn't stand. She had pulled you up, and you had fallen into her arms, both of you crying. Later she had soaked your feet in hot water with boric soda. You still remember the softness of the towels with which she wiped them.

Why do you always focus on the bad things, you wonder. Is it some flaw in yourself, some cross-connection in the thin silver filaments of your brain? So many good things happened, too. Her sitting in the front row at your high school graduation, face bright as a dahlia above the white of her sari. The two of you going for a bath in the Ganga, the brown tug of the water on your clothes, the warm sleepy sun as you sat on the bank eating curried potatoes wrapped in hot *puris.* And further back, her teaching you to write, the soft curve of her hand over yours, helping you hold the chalk, the smell of her newly washed hair curling about your face.

But these memories are wary, fugitive. You have to coax them out of their dark recesses. They dissipate, foglike, even as you are looking at them. And suddenly his arm feels terribly heavy. You are suffocating beneath its weight, its muscular, hairy maleness. You slip out and step into the shower. The wind snatches at the straggly nasturtiums you planted on the little strip of balcony. *What will you remember of him when it is all over?* whispers the papery voice inside your skull. Light from the bathroom slashes the floor while against the dark wall the hanging glows fire-red.

The first month you moved in with him, your head pounded with fear and guilt every time the phone rang. You'd rush across the room to pick it up while he watched you from his tilted-back chair, raising an eyebrow. (You'd made him promise never to pick up the phone.) At night you slept next to the bedside extension. You picked it up on the very first ring, struggling up out of layers of sleep heavy as water to whisper a breathless hello, the next word held in readiness, *mother*. But it was never her. Sometimes it was a friend of yours from the graduate program. Mostly it was for him. Women. Ex-girl-friends, he would explain with a guileless smile, stressing the *ex*. Then he would turn toward the window, his voice dropping into a low murmur while you pretended sleep and hated yourself for being jealous.

She always called on Saturday morning, Saturday night back home. The last thing before she went to bed. You picture her sitting on the large mahogany bed where you, too, had slept when you were little. Or when you were sick or scared. Outside, crickets are chanting. The night watchman makes his rounds, calling out the hour. The old *ayah* (she has been there from before you were born) stands behind her, combing out her long hair which lifts a little in the breeze from the fan, the silver in it glimmering like a smile. It is the most beautiful hair in the world.

And so you grew less careful. Sometimes you'd call out from the shower for him to answer the phone. And he would tease you (*you sure now?*) before picking it up. At night after the last kiss your body would slide off his damp, glistening one—and you didn't care which side of the bed it was as long as you had him to hold on to. *Or was it that you wanted her, somehow, to find out?* the voice asks. But you are learning to not pay attention to the voice, to fill your mind with sensations (how the nubs of his elbows fit exactly into your cupped palms, how his sleeping breath stirs the small hairs on your arm) until its echoes dissipate.

So when the phone rang very early that Tuesday morning you thought nothing of it. You pulled sleep like a furry blanket over your head, and even when you half heard his voice, suddenly formal, saying *just one moment, please,* you didn't get it. Not until he was shaking your shoulder, handing you the phone, mouthing the words silently, *your mother.*

Later you try to remember what you said to her, but you can't quite get the words right. Something about a wonderful man, getting married soon (although the only time you'd discussed marriage was when he had told you it wasn't for him). She'd called to let you know that cousin Leela's wedding was all arranged—a good Brahmin boy, a rising executive in an accounting firm. Next month in Delhi. The whole family would travel there. She'd bought your ticket already. *But now of course you need not come.* Her voice had been a spear of ice. Did you cry out, *Don't be angry, Mother, please?* Did you beg forgiveness?

Did you whisper (again that word) *love?* You do know this: you kept talking, even after the phone went dead. When you finally looked up, he was watching you. His eyes were opaque, like pebbles.

All through the next month you try to reach her. You call. The *ayah* answers. She sounds frightened when she hears your voice. *Memsaab* has told her not to speak to you, or else she'll lose her job.

"She had the lawyer over yesterday to change her will. What did you do, Missybaba, that was so bad?"

You hear your mother in the background. "Who are you talking to, Ayah? What? How can it be my daughter? I don't *have* a daughter. Hang up right now."

"Mother . . . " you cry. The word ricochets through the apartment so that the hanging shivers against the wall. Its black center ripples like a bottomless well. The phone goes dead. You call again. Your fingers are shaking. It's hard to see the digits through the tears. Your knees feel as though they have been broken. The phone buzzes against your ear like a trapped insect. No one picks it up. You keep calling all week. Finally a machine tells you the number has been changed. There is no new number.

Here is a story your mother told you when you were growing up:

There was a girl I used to play with sometimes, whose father was the roof thatcher in your grandfather's village. They lived near the women's lake. She was an only child, pretty in a dark-skinned way, and motherless, so her father spoiled her. He let her run wild, climbing trees, swimming in the river. Let her go to school, even after she reached the age when girls from good families stayed home, waiting to be married. (You know already this is a tale with an unhappy end, a cautionary moral.) *He would laugh when the old women of the village warned him that an unmarried girl is like a firebrand in a field of ripe grain. She's a good girl, he'd say. She knows right and wrong. He found her a fine match, a master carpenter from the next village. But a few days before the wedding, her body was discovered in the women's lake. We all thought it was an accident until we heard about the rocks she had tied in her sari.* (She stops, waits for the question you do not want to ask but must.) *Who knows why? People whispered that she was pregnant, said they'd seen her once or twice with a man, a traveling actor who had come to the village some time back. Her father was heartbroken, his good name ruined. He had to leave the village, all those tongues and eyes. Leave behind the house of his forefathers that he loved so much. No, no one knows what happened to him.*

For months afterward, you lie awake at night and think of the abandoned house, mice claws skittering over the floors, the dry papery slither of snakes, bats' wings. When you fall asleep you dream of a beautiful dark girl knotting stones into her *palloo* and swimming out to the middle of the dark lake. The water is cool on her heavying breasts, her growing belly. It ripples and parts for her. Before she goes under, she turns toward you. Sometimes her face is a blank oval, featureless. Sometimes it is your face.

*

Things are not going well for you. At school you cannot concentrate on your classes, they seem so disconnected from the rest of your life. Your advisor calls you into her office to talk to you. You stare at the neat rows of books behind her head. She is speaking of missed deadlines, research that lacks innovation. You notice her teeth, large and white and regular, like a horse's. She pauses, asks if you are feeling well.

"Oh yes," you say, in the respectful tone you were always taught to use with teachers. "I feel just fine."

But the next day it is too difficult to get up and get dressed for class. What difference would it make if you miss a deconstructionist critique of the Sonnets? you ask yourself. You stay in bed until the postal carrier comes.

You have written a letter to Aunt Arati explaining, asking her to please tell your mother that you're sorry. *I'll come home right now if she wants.* Every day you check the box for Aunt's reply, but there's nothing. Her arthritis is acting up, you tell yourself. It's the wedding preparations. The letter is lost.

Things are not going well between him and you either. Sometimes when he is talking, the words make no sense. You watch him move his mouth as though he were a character in a foreign film someone has forgotten to dub. He asks you a question. By the raised tone of his voice you know that's what it is, but you have no idea what he wants from you. He asks again, louder.

"What?" you say.

He walks out, slamming the door.

You have written a letter to your mother, too. A registered letter, so it can't get lost. You run outside every day when you hear the mail van. Nothing. You glance at the carrier, a large black woman, suspiciously. "Are you sure?" you ask. You wonder if she put the letter into someone else's box by mistake. After she leaves, you peer into the narrow metal slots of the other mailboxes, trying to see.

At first he was sympathetic. He held you when you lay sleepless at night. "Cry," he said. "Get it out of your system." Then, "It was bound to happen sooner or later. You must have known that. Maybe it's all for the best." Later, "Try to look at the positive side. You had to cut the umbilical cord *sometime.*"

You pulled away when he said things like that. What did *he* know, you thought, about families, about (yes) love. He'd left home the day he turned eighteen. He only called his mother on Mother's Day and, if he remembered, her birthday. When he told her about you she'd said, "How *nice*, dear. We really must have you both over to the house for dinner sometime soon."

Lately he has been angry a lot. "You're blaming me for this mess between your mother and yourself," he shouted the other day at dinner although you hadn't said anything. He shook his head. "You're driving yourself crazy. You need a shrink." He shoved back his plate and slammed out of the apartment again. The dry, scratchy voice pushing at your temples reminded you how he'd watched the red-haired waitress at the Mexican restaurant last week, how he was laughing, his hand on her shoulder, when you came out of the rest room. How, recently, there had been more late-night calls.

When he came back, very late, you were still sitting at the table. Staring at the hanging. He took you by the arms and brought his face close to yours.

"Sweetheart," he said, "I want to help you but I don't know how. You've become obsessed with this thing. You're so depressed all the time I hardly know you anymore. So your mother is behaving irrationally. *You* can't afford to do the same."

You looked past his head. He has a sweet voice, you thought absently. A voice that charms. An actor's voice.

"You're not even listening," he said.

You tried because you knew he was trying, too. But later in bed, even with his lips pressing hot into you, a part of you kept counting the days. How many since you mailed the letter? He pulled away with an angry exclamation and turned the other way. You put out your hand to touch the nubs of his backbone. *I'm sorry.* But you went on thinking, something *must* be wrong. A reply should have reached you by now.

The letter came today. You walked out under a low, gray-bellied sky and there was the mail-woman, holding it up, smiling—the registered letter to your mother, with a red ink stamp across the address. *Not accepted. Return to sender.*

Now you are kneeling in the bathroom, rummaging in the cabinet behind the cleaning supplies. When you find the bottles, you line them up along the sink top. You open each one and look at the tablets: red, white, pink. You'd found them one day while cleaning. You remember how shocked you'd been, the argument the two of you'd had. He'd shrugged and spread his hands, palms up. You wish now you'd asked him which ones were the sleeping pills. No matter. You can take them all, if that's what you decide to do.

You'd held the letter in your hand a long time, until it grew weightless, transparent. You could see through it to another letter, one that wasn't written yet. His letter.

You knew what it would say.

Before he left for class this morning he had looked at you still crumpled on the sofa where you'd spent the night. He looked for a long time, as though he'd never really seen you before. Then he said, very softly, "It was never me, was it? Never love. It was always you and her, her and you."

He hadn't waited for an answer.

Wind slams a door somewhere, making you jump. It's raining outside, the first time in years. Big swollen drops, then thick silver sheets of it. You walk out to the balcony. The rain runs down your cheeks, the tears you couldn't shed. The nasturtiums, washed clean, are glowing red. Smell of wet earth. You take a deep breath, decide to go for a long walk.

As you walk you try to figure out what to do. (And maybe the meaning of what you have done.) The pills are there, of course. You picture it: the empty bottles by the bed, your body fallen across it, a hand flung over the side. The note left behind. Will he press repentant kisses on your pale palm? Will she fly across the ocean to wash your stiff eyelids with her tears?

Or—what? *what?* Surely there's another choice. But you can't find the words to give it shape. When you look down the empty street, the bright leaves of the newly-washed maples hurt your eyes.

So you continue to walk. Your shoes darken, grow heavy. Water swirls in the gutters, carrying away months of dust. Coming toward you is a young woman with an umbrella. Shoulders bunched, she tiptoes through puddles, trying hard to stay dry. But a gust snaps the umbrella back and soaks her. She is shocked for a moment, angry. Then she begins to laugh. And you are laughing too, because you know just how it feels. Short, hysterical laugh-bursts, then quieter, drawing the breath deep into yourself. You watch as she stops in the middle of the sidewalk and tosses her ruined umbrella into a garbage can. She spreads her arms and lets the rain take her: hair, paisley blouse, midnight-blue skirt. Thunder and lightning. It's going to be quite a storm. You remember the monsoons of your childhood. There are no people in this memory, only the sky, rippling with exhilarating light.

You know then that when you return to the apartment you will pack your belongings. A few clothes, some music, a favorite book, the hanging. No, not that. You will not need it in your new life, the one you're going to live for yourself.

And a word comes to you out of the opening sky. The word *love.* You see that you had never understood it before. It is like rain, and when you lift your face to it, like rain it washes away inessentials, leaving you hollow, clean, ready to begin.

Plato, *Symposium:*
Aristophanes' Speech on *Eros*

In the Symposium, *Plato (circa 428–348 or 347 BC) dramatizes a celebratory gathering of the intellectual elite of Athens at which various speakers deliver speeches in praise of the god Eros. This is the only Platonic dialogue that has as its explicit theme the nature of a god and that features a direct contest between Socrates and the poets. Two speeches stand out, one given by the comic poet Aristophanes (presented here), the other by Socrates (presented next in this anthology). Aristophanes' speech, like those of his two predecessors in the dialogue (Pausanias and Eryximachus), is among other things an attempt to justify pederasty. But its enduring appeal comes from its comic caricature of embracing lovers and, more important, its serious presentation of love as the desire for self-sufficient wholeness attainable through coupling, for union with one's own, perfectly fitting, missing other half. Among the speech's many significant suggestions, we note the following: humanity owes its upright, civilized bearing to the (surgical) shaping of the gods; eros, in its aspiration to heal our dividedness, is therefore a force in opposition to the rule of Zeus (i.e., to civilizing law and custom); eros is fundamentally separate from sexuality and procreation; lovers cannot say what they truly want from one another, though it is clearly more than just sexual intercourse; love is simply the love of one's own, or the love of being loved back. Aristophanes makes no mention of any connection between love and the beautiful, love and speech, love and generation, love and immortality, or love and any higher aspirations of the human soul. The whole mutually sought by the lovers—is it union of only bodies or also souls?—is radically "self-ish."*

This account of the emergence of love following divine division of an originally unified nature should be compared and contrasted with the similar account in the Garden of Eden story. One should also consider to what extent Aristophanes' tale reveals the truth about eros, and about what it seeks.

"Well, Eryximachus," Aristophanes said, "I do intend to speak in a somewhat different vein from that in which you and Pausanias spoke. Human beings, in my opinion, have been entirely unaware of the power of Eros, since if they were aware of it, they would have provided the greatest sanctuaries and altars for him, and would be making him the greatest sacrifices, and not act as they do now when none of this happens to him, though it most certainly should. For Eros is the most philanthropic of gods, a helper of human beings as well as a physician dealing with an illness the healing of which would result in the greatest happiness for the human race. So I shall try to initiate you into his power; and you will be the teachers of everyone else. But you must first understand human nature and its afflictions. Our nature in the past was not the same as now but of a different sort. First of all, the races of human beings were three, not two as now, male and female; for there was also a third race that shared in both, a race whose name still remains, though it itself has vanished. For at that time one race was androgynous, and in looks and name it combined both, the male as well as the female; but now it does not exist except for the name that is reserved for reproach. Secondly, the looks of each human being were as a whole round, with back and sides in a circle. And each had four arms, and legs equal in number to his arms, and two faces alike in all respects on a cylindrical neck, but there was one head for both faces—they were set in opposite directions—and four ears, and two sets of genitals, and all the rest that one might conjecture from this. Each used to walk upright too, just as one does now, in whatever direction he wanted; and whenever he had the impulse to run fast, then just as tumblers with their legs straight out actually move around as they tumble in a circle, so did they, with their eight limbs as supports, quickly move in a circle. It is for this reason that the races were three and of this sort: because the male was in origin the offspring of the sun; the female, of the earth; and the race that shared in both, of the moon—since the moon also shares in both. And they themselves were globular, as was their manner of walking, because they were like their parents. Now, they were awesome in their strength and robustness, and they had great and proud thoughts, so they made an attempt on the gods. And what Homer says about Ephialtes and Otus,[1] is said about them—that they attempted to make an ascent into the sky with a view to assaulting the gods. Then Zeus and the other gods deliberated as to what they should do with them. And they were long perplexed, for the gods knew neither how they could kill them and (just as they had struck the giants with lightning) obliterate the race—for, in that case, their own honors and sacrifices from human beings would vanish—nor how they could allow them to continue to behave licentiously. Then Zeus thought hard and says, 'In my own opinion,' he said, 'I have a device whereby human beings would continue to exist and at the same time, having become weaker, would stop their licentiousness. I shall now cut each of them in two,' he said; 'and they will be both weaker and more useful to us through the increase in their numbers. And they will walk upright on two legs. But if they are thought to behave licentiously still, and are unwilling to keep quiet, then I shall cut them again in two,' he said, 'so that they will go hopping on one leg.' As soon as he said this he began to cut human beings in two, just like those who cut sorb-apples in preparation for pickling, or those who cut eggs with hairs. And whenever he cut someone,

---

[1]Homer, *Odyssey*, 11.305-320: *Iliad*, 5.385-391.

he had Apollo turn the face and half the neck around to face the cut, so that in beholding his own cutting the human being might be more orderly; and he had him heal all the rest. Apollo turned the face around; and by drawing together the skin from everywhere toward what is now called the belly (just like drawstring bags) he made one opening, which he tied off in the middle of the belly, and that is what they call the navel. He shaped up the chest and smoothed out many of the other wrinkles, with somewhat the same kind of tool as shoemakers use in smoothing the wrinkles in leather on the last; but he left a few wrinkles, those on the belly itself and the navel, to be a reminder of our ancient affliction. When its nature was cut in two, each—desiring its own half—came together; and throwing their arms around one another and entangling themselves with one another in their desire to grow together, they began to die off due to hunger and the rest of their inactivity, because they were unwilling to do anything apart from one another; and whenever one of the halves did die and the other was left, the one that was left tried to seek out another and entangle itself with that, whether it met the half of the whole woman—and that is what we now call a woman—or of a man; and so they continued to perish. But Zeus took pity on them and supplied another device: He rearranged their genitals toward the front—for up till then they had them on the outside, and they generated and gave birth not in one another but in the earth, like cicadas—and for this purpose, he changed this part of them toward the front, and by this means made generation possible in one another, by means of the male in the female; so that in embracing, if a man meets with a woman, they might generate and the race continue; and if male meets with male there might at least be satiety in their being together; and they might pause and turn to work and attend to the rest of their livelihood. So it is really from such early times that human beings have had, inborn in themselves, Eros for one another—Eros, the bringer-together of their ancient nature, who tries to make one out of two and to heal their human nature. Each of us, then, is a token of a human being, because we are sliced like fillets of sole, two out of one; and so each is always in search of his own token. Now all who are the men's slice from the common genus, which was then called androgynous, are lovers of women; and many adulterers have been of this genus; and, in turn, all who are women of this genus prove to be lovers of men and adulteresses. And all women who are sliced off from woman hardly pay attention to men but are rather turned toward women, and lesbians arise from this genus. But all who are male slices pursue the males, and while they are boys—because they are cutlets of the male—they are friendly to men and enjoy lying down together with and embracing men; and these are the best of boys and lads, because they are naturally the manliest. Some, to be sure, assert that such boys are shameless, but they lie. For it is not out of shamelessness that they do this but out of boldness, manliness, and masculinity, feeling affection for what is like to themselves. And there is a great proof of this, for once they have reached maturity, only men of this kind go off to political affairs. When they are fully grown men, they are pederasts and naturally pay no attention to marriage and procreation, but are compelled to do so by the law; whereas they would be content to live unmarried with one another. Now it is one of this sort who wholly becomes a pederast and passionate lover, always feeling affection for what is akin to himself. And when the pederast or anyone else meets with that very one who is his own half, then they are wondrously struck with friendship, attachment, and love, and are just about unwilling to be apart from one another even for a short time. And here you have those who continue through life with one another, though they could not even say what they want to get for themselves from one another. For no one would be of the opinion that it was sexual intercourse that was wanted, as though it were for this reason—of all things—that each so enjoys being with the other in great earnestness; but the soul of each plainly wants something else. What it is, it is incapable of saying, but it divines what it wants and speaks in riddles. If Hephaestus with his tools were to stand over them as they lay in the same place and were to ask, 'What is it that you want, human beings, to get for yourselves from one another?'—and if in their perplexity he were to ask them again, 'Is it this you desire, to be with one another in the very same place, as much as is possible, and not to leave one another night and day? For if you desire that, I am willing to fuse you and make you grow together into the same thing, so that—though two—you would be one; and as long as you lived, you would both live together just as though you were one; and when you died, there again in Hades you would be dead together as one instead of as two. So see if you love this and would be content if you got it.' We know that there would not be even one who, if he heard this, would refuse, and it would be self-evident that he wants nothing else than this; and he would quite simply believe he had heard what he had been desiring all along: in conjunction and fusion with the beloved, to become one from two. The cause of this is that this was our ancient nature and we were wholes. So love is the name for the desire and pursuit of the whole. And previously, as I say, we were one; but now through our injustice we have been dispersed by the god, just as the Arcadians were dispersed by the Spartans. There is the fear, then, that if we are not orderly in our behavior to the gods, we shall be split again and go around like those who are modeled in relief on stelae, sawed through our nostrils, like dice. For this reason every real man must be exhorted to be pious toward the gods in all his acts, so that we may avoid the one result and get the other, as Eros is our guide and general. Let no one act contrary to Eros—and he acts contrary whoever incurs the enmity of the gods—for if we become friends and reconciled to the gods, we shall find out and meet with our own favorites, which few at the moment do. And please don't let Eryximachus suppose, in making a comedy of my speech, that I mean Pausanias and Agathon—perhaps they have found their own and are both naturally born males. For whatever the case may be with them, I am referring to all men and women: our race would be happy if we were to bring our love to a consummate end, and each of us were to get his own favorite on his return to his ancient nature. And if this is the best, it must necessarily be the case that, in present circumstances, that which is closest to it is the best; and that is to get a favorite whose nature is to one's taste. And were we to hymn the god who is the cause of this we should justly hymn Eros, who at the present time benefits us the most by leading us to what is our own; and in the future he offers the greatest hopes, while we offer piety to the gods, to restore us to our ancient nature and by his healing make us blessed and happy.

Plato, *Symposium:* Socrates' Speech on *Eros*

In this celebrated reflection on eros, Plato's Socrates articulates a view of love that shows its connection to the beautiful and the good, mortality and immortality, the animal, the human, and the divine. Discovering the riches of the speech requires careful and patient exegesis and interpretation; we here hazard a few general remarks to help orient the reader. Whereas Aristophanes had suggested that love is the selfish love of one's own, or the love of the one who loves you back, Socrates argues that love is a unidirectional, upward-seeking love of the good, the true, and the eternal—and, finally, in the usual sense of "self", self-forgetting. The speech is in three major parts. First, there is a purely mythic account of the origins and character of Eros which reveals that Eros (love) is not born of Aphrodite (beauty) and, more important, that Eros is not a god but rather a daemonic, "intermediate" power that mediates between the mortal and immortal, the human and the divine, and that strives to link what is perishable to what is eternal. Second (beginning with Socrates' question to Diotima, "Of what use is he [Eros] for human beings?"), there is the most serious and strictly philosophical argument that concludes, first, that "love is of the good to be one's own always," and, second, that "love is also of immortality." This second conclusion is tied to the important observation that love is expressive not merely of a needy emptiness seeking to be filled, but rather, of an appreciative fullness seeking to give birth, both in body and in soul. The final part of the speech (beginning with Diotima's question to Socrates about "the cause of this eros and desire") discusses the three leading modes by which individuals, spurred by love, seek their own immortality: bearing one's own children; performing great and noble deeds or composing great and beautiful poems; beholding the eternal and unchanging ideas, the goal of the philosophical quest. This last section, with its beautification of philosophy, contains the famous poetic image of the ladder of love, with its powerful suggestion that all earthly loves are, rightly understood, continuous with and, finally, but a vehicle for the love of Being itself and of its highest principles.

Is this too rosy, too lofty, too impersonal, or too philosophical a picture of eros? Can eros lead to happiness? Or is it, as Aristophanes' speech has it, always tragically unfulfilled? Can or should eros be so little interested in particularity, in the individual human beloved? Or is it only through loving the good (or the divine) that we can properly love individual persons? Conversely, are we able through loving individual human beings to see beyond the particular and the perishable? Does it matter if the beloved does not love back? Is love really the power that unifies the world?

"And I shall let you go for now, and turn to the speech about Eros that I once heard from a woman, Diotima of Mantineia. She was wise in these and many other things; when the Athenians once made a sacrifice before the plague, she caused the onset of the disease to be delayed ten years; and she is the very one who taught me erotics. The speech that she was wont to make, I shall now try to tell you all on the basis of what has been agreed on between Agathon and myself; and I shall try to do it on my own, as best I can. For just as you explained, Agathon, one must first tell who Eros himself is and what sort he is, and then tell his deeds. In my opinion, it is easiest to do this in just the same way that the stranger once did in quizzing me. For I came pretty near, in speaking to her, to saying the same sort of things that Agathon said to me now—that Eros was a great god, and was the love of beautiful things. She then went on to refute me with those same arguments with which I refuted him—that he is neither beautiful, according to my argument, nor good.

"And I said, 'How do you mean it, Diotima? Is Eros after all ugly and bad?'

"And she said, 'Hush! Or do you believe that whatever is not beautiful must necessarily be ugly?'

"'Absolutely.'

"'And whatever is not wise, without understanding? Or were you unaware that there is something in between wisdom and lack of understanding?'

"'What is this?'

"'Don't you know,' she said, 'that to opine correctly without being able to give an account [logos] is neither to know expertly (for how could expert knowledge be an unaccounted for [alogon] matter?) nor lack of understanding (for how could lack of understanding be that which has hit upon what is)? But surely correct opinion is like that, somewhere between intelligence and lack of understanding.'

"'What you say is true,' I said.

"'Then do not compel what is not beautiful to be ugly, or what is not good, to be bad. So too since you yourself agree that Eros is not good or beautiful, do not at all believe that he must be ugly and bad,' she said, 'but something between the two of them.'

"'And yet,' I said, 'it is agreed on by all that he is a great god.'

"'Do you mean by all who do not know,' she said, 'or by those who know?'

"'No, by all together.'

"And she said with a laugh, 'And how, Socrates, could he be agreed to be a great god by those who deny even that he is a god?'

"'Who are these?' I said.

"'You are one,' she said, 'and I am one.'

"And I said, 'How can you say this?' I said.

"And she said, 'It's easy. Tell me, don't you assert that all gods are happy and beautiful? Or would you dare to deny that any one of the gods is beautiful and happy?'

"'By Zeus, I would not,' I said.

"'But don't you mean by the happy precisely those who possess the good things and the beautiful things?'

"'Of course.'

"'And do you hold to the agreement that Eros out of need for the good and beautiful things desires those very things of which he is in need?'

"'Yes, I hold to it.'

"'How then could he who is without a share in the beautiful and good things be a god?'

"'In no way, it seems.'

"'Do you see then,' she said, 'that you too hold that Eros is not a god?'

"'What would Eros then be?' I said. 'A mortal?'

"'Hardly that.'

"'Well, what then?'

"'Just as before,' she said, 'between mortal and immortal.'

"'What is that, Diotima?'

"'A great daemon, Socrates, for everything daemonic[1] is between god and mortal.'

"'With what kind of power?' I said.

"'Interpreting and ferrying to gods things from human beings and to human beings things from gods: the requests and sacrifices of human beings, the orders and exchanges-for-sacrifices of gods; for it is in the middle of both and fills up the interval so that the whole itself has been bound together by it. Through this proceeds all divination and the art of the priests who deal with sacrifices, initiatory rituals, incantations, and every kind of soothsaying and magic. A god does not mingle with a human being; but through this occurs the whole intercourse and conversation of gods with human beings while they are awake and asleep. And he who is wise in things like this is a daemonic man; but he who is wise in anything else concerning either arts or handicrafts is vulgar and low. These daemons are many and of all kinds; and one of them is Eros.'

"'Who is his father?' I said, 'And who is his mother?'

"'It is rather long,' she said, 'to explain; but I shall tell you all the same. When Aphrodite was born, all the other gods as well as Poros [Resource] the

---

[1]Daemonic (*daimonion*) is either a neuter diminutive of *daimon* or a neuter adjective, related to *daimon* as divine (*theion*) is to god (*theos*). This neuter, in any case, is the theme of the dialogue up to Socrates' speech that concludes with "vulgar and low."

son of Metis [Intelligence] were at a feast;[2] and when they had dined, Penia [Poverty] arrived to beg for something—as might be expected at a festivity—and she hung about near the door. Then Poros got drunk on nectar—for there was not yet wine—and, heavy of head, went into the garden of Zeus and slept. Then Penia, who because of her own lack of resources was plotting to have a child made out of Poros, reclined beside him and conceived Eros. It is for this reason that Eros has been the attendant and servant of Aphrodite, as he was conceived on her birthday; for he is by nature a lover in regard to the beautiful, and Aphrodite is beautiful. So because Eros is the son of Poros and Penia, his situation is in some such case as this. First of all, he is always poor; and he is far from being tender and beautiful, as the many believe, but is tough, squalid, shoeless, and homeless, always lying on the ground without a blanket or a bed, sleeping in doorways and along waysides in the open air; he has the nature of his mother, always dwelling with neediness. But in accordance with his father he plots to trap the beautiful and the good, and is courageous, stout, and keen, a skilled hunter, always weaving devices, desirous of practical wisdom and inventive, philosophizing through all his life, a skilled magician, druggist, sophist. And his nature is neither immortal nor mortal, but sometimes on the same day he flourishes and lives, whenever he has resources; and sometimes he dies, but gets to live again through the nature of his father. And as that which is supplied to him is always gradually flowing out, Eros is never either without resources nor wealthy, but is in between wisdom and lack of understanding. For here is the way it is: No one of the gods philosophizes and desires to become wise—for he is so—nor if there is anyone else who is wise, does he philosophize. Nor, in turn, do those who lack understanding philosophize and desire to become wise; for it is precisely this that makes the lack of understanding so difficult—that if a man is not beautiful and good, nor intelligent, he has the opinion that that is sufficient for him. Consequently, he who does not believe that he is in need does not desire that which he does not believe he needs.'

" 'Then who, Diotima, are the philosophizers,' I said, 'if they are neither the wise nor those who lack understanding?'

" 'By now it is perfectly plain even to a child,' she said, 'that they are those between them both, of whom Eros would be one. For wisdom is one of the most beautiful things, and Eros is love in regard to the beautiful; and so Eros is—necessarily—a philosopher; and as a philosopher he is between being wise and being without understanding. His manner of birth is responsible for this, for he is of a wise and resourceful father, and an unwise and resourceless

---

[2]Metis is the first goddess Zeus marries after the wars among the gods are over. He is warned in time not to allow her child Athena to be born, lest Athena's children overthrow him; he swallows Metis, and Athena is later born from the head of Zeus (see Hesiod, *Theogony*, 886–900).

mother. Now the nature of the daemon, dear Socrates, is this; but as for the one whom you believed to be Eros, it is not at all surprising that you had this impression. You believed, in my opinion, as I conjecture from what you say, that the beloved is Eros, and is not that which loves. It is for this reason, I believe, that Eros seemed to you to be wholly beautiful. For the beloved thing is truly beautiful, delicate, perfect, and most blessed; but that which loves has another kind of look, the sort that I just explained.'

"And I said, 'All right, stranger, what you say is fine. If Eros is of this sort, of what use is he for human beings?'

"'It is this, Socrates,' she said, 'that I shall next try to teach you. Now, Eros is of that sort and was born in that way; and he is of the beautiful things, as you assert. But what if someone were to ask us, "What about those beautiful things of which Eros is, Socrates and Diotima?" It is more clearly expressed as follows: He who loves the beautiful things loves—what does he love?'

"And I said, 'That they be his.'

"'But the answer,' she said, 'still longs for the following sort of question: What will he have who gets the beautiful things?'

"I said that I was hardly capable of giving a ready answer to this question.

"'Well,' she said. 'What if someone changed his query and used the good instead of the beautiful? Come, Socrates, the lover of the good things loves: what does he love?'

"'That they be his,' I said.

"'And what will he who gets the good things have?'

"'This,' I said, 'I can answer more adequately: he will be happy.'

"'That,' she said, 'is because the happy are happy by the acquisition of good things; and there is no further need to ask, "For what consequence does he who wants to be happy want to be so?" But the answer is thought to be a complete one.'

"'What you say is true,' I said.

"'This wanting and this eros, do you suppose they are common to all human beings, and all want the good things to be theirs always, or how do you mean it?'

"'That way,' I said. 'They are common to all.'

"'Why is it, then, Socrates,' she said, 'that we deny that everyone loves—given, that is, that everyone loves the same things and always—but we say that some love and some do not?'

"'I too,' I said, 'am amazed.'

"'Well,' she said, 'don't persist in your amazement; for we detach from eros a certain kind of eros and give it the name eros, imposing upon it the name of the whole; while in the other cases we employ several different names.'

"'What are those?' I said.

" 'Like the following: You know that "making" [*poiesis*] has a wide range; for, you see, every kind of making is responsible for anything whatsoever that is on the way from what is not to what is. And thus all the productions that are dependent on the arts are makings, and all the craftsmen engaged in them are makers.'

" 'What you say is true.'

" 'But nevertheless,' she said, 'you know that not all craftsmen are called makers but have other names; and one part is separated off from all of making—that which is concerned with music and meters—and is addressed by the name of the whole. For this alone is called poetry; and those who have this part of making are poets.'

" 'What you say is true,' I said.

" 'So too in the case of eros. In brief, eros is the whole desire of good things and of being happy, "the greatest and all-beguiling eros." But those who turn toward it in many other ways, in terms of either money-making, love of gymnastics, or philosophy, are neither said to love nor called lovers; whereas those who earnestly apply themselves to a certain single kind, get the name of the whole, love, and are said to love and called lovers.'

" 'What you say is probably true,' I said.

" 'And there is a certain account,' she said, 'according to which those who seek their own halves are lovers. But my speech denies that eros is of a half or of a whole—unless, comrade, that half or whole can be presumed to be really good; for human beings are willing to have their own feet and hands cut off, if their opinion is that their own are no good. For I suspect that each does not cleave to his own (unless one calls the good one's own and belonging to oneself, and the bad alien to oneself) since there is nothing that human beings love other than the good. Or is it your opinion that they do?'

" 'No, by Zeus,' I said, 'that is not my opinion.'

" 'Then,' she said, 'is it to be said unqualifiedly that human beings love the good?'

" 'Yes,' I said.

" 'What about this? Mustn't it be added,' she said, 'that they love the good to be theirs?'

" 'It must be added.'

" 'And not only that it be theirs,' she said, 'but always as well?'

" 'This too must be added.'

" 'So, in sum,' she said, 'eros is of the good's being one's own always.'

" 'What you say is most true,' I said.

" 'Since eros is always this,' she said, 'then in what manner and in what activity would the earnestness and intensity of those who pursue the good be called eros. What in fact are they doing when they act so? Can you tell?'

"'If I could, Diotima, then I should not, you know, in admiration of your wisdom,' I said, 'resort to you to learn this very thing.'

"'Well, I shall tell you,' she said. 'Their deed is bringing to birth in beauty both in terms of the body and in terms of the soul.'

"'Whatever it is that you mean,' I said, 'is in need of divination, and I do not begin to understand.'

"'Well, I shall speak more clearly,' she said. 'All human beings, Socrates,' she said, 'conceive both in terms of the body and in terms of the soul, and whenever they are at a certain age, their nature desires to give birth; but it is incapable of giving birth in ugliness, but only in beauty, for the being together of man and woman is a bringing to birth. This thing, pregnancy and bringing to birth, is divine, and it is immortal in the animal that is mortal. It is impossible for this to happen in the unfitting; and the ugly is unfitting with everything divine, but the beautiful is fitting. So Kallone [Beauty] is the Moira [Fate] and Eileithyia[3] for birth. It is for these reasons that whenever the pregnant draws near to beauty, it becomes glad and in its rejoicing dissolves and then gives birth and produces offspring; but whenever it draws near to ugliness, then, downcast and in pain, it contracts inwardly, turns away, shrinks up, and does not produce offspring, but checking the course of the pregnancy, has a hard time of it. So this is why someone who is pregnant, with breasts already swelling, flutters so much around the beautiful, because the one who has the beautiful releases him from great labor pains. For eros is not, Socrates,' she said, 'of the beautiful, as you believe.'

"'Well, what then?'

"'It is of engendering and bringing to birth in the beautiful.'

"'All right,' I said.

"'It is more than all right,' she said. 'And why is eros of engendering? Because engendering is born forever and is immortal as far as that can happen to a mortal being. From what has been agreed to, it is necessary to desire immortality with good, provided eros is of the good's always being one's own. So it is necessary from this argument that eros be of immortality too.'

"All of these things she used to teach me whenever she made her speeches about erotics. And once she also asked, 'What do you believe, Socrates, is the cause of this eros and desire? Or aren't you aware how uncanny is the disposition of all the beasts (the footed as well as the winged) whenever they desire to produce offspring? They are all ill and of an erotic disposition, first concerning actual intercourse with one another, then later concerning the nurture of

---

[3]Fate and Eileithyia are goddesses who preside over birth, and Kallone is a cult name of Artemis-Hecate.

what is generated. And they are ready to fight to the finish, the weakest against the strongest, for the sake of those they have generated, and to die on their behalf; and they are willingly racked by starvation and stop at nothing to nourish their offspring. One might suppose,' she said, 'that human beings do this from calculation; but as for the beasts, what is the cause of their erotic disposition's being of this sort? Can you say?'

"And I again said that I did not know; and she said, 'Do you really think you will ever become skilled in erotics, if you do not understand this?'

"'But you see, Diotima, that is the reason—as I said just now—why I have come to you: I know I am in need of teachers. But do tell me the cause of these things as well as of the rest that concern erotics.'

"'If you put your trust,' she said, 'in the statement that by nature eros is of that which we have often agreed to, don't persist in your amazement. For in the eros of the beasts, in terms of the same argument as that concerning men, the mortal nature seeks as far as possible to be forever and immortal. Mortal nature is capable of immortality only in this way, the way of generation, because it is always leaving behind another that is young to replace the old. For while each one of the animals is said to live and be the same (for example, one is spoken of as the same from the time one is a child until one is an old man; and though he never has the same things in himself, nevertheless, he is called the same), he is forever becoming young in some respects as he suffers losses in other respects: his hair, flesh, bones, blood, and his whole body. And this is so not only in terms of the body but also in terms of the soul; his ways, character, opinions, desires, pleasures, pains, fears, each of these things is never present as the same for each, but they are partly coming to be and partly perishing. And what is far stranger still is that in the case of our sciences [or "knowledges"; *episteme*] too not only are some coming to be while others are perishing (and we are never the same in terms of the sciences either); but also each single one of the sciences is affected in the same way. For studying, as it is called, is done on the grounds that the science is passing out from us; for forgetfulness is the exiting of science; and studying, by instilling a fresh memory again to replace the departing one, preserves the science, so that it may be thought to be the same. For in this way every mortal thing is preserved; not by being absolutely the same forever, as the divine is, but by the fact that that which is departing and growing old leaves behind another young thing that is as it was. By this device, Socrates,' she said, 'the mortal shares in immortality, both body and all the rest; but the immortal has a different way. So do not be amazed if everything honors by nature its own offshoot; for it is for the sake of immortality that this zeal and eros attend everything.'

"And when I had heard her speech I was amazed and said 'Really!' I said. 'Wisest Diotima, is it truly like this?'

"And she, like the perfect Sophists, said, 'Know it well Socrates,' she said, 'inasmuch as in the case of human beings, if you were willing to glance at their love of honor, you would be amazed at their irrationality unless you understand what I have said and reflect how uncanny their disposition is made by their love of renown, "and their setting up immortal fame for eternity"; and for the sake of fame even more than for their children, they are ready to run all risks, to exhaust their money, to toil at every sort of toil, and to die. For do you suppose,' she said, 'that Alcestis would have died for Admetus' sake, or Achilles would have died after Patroclus, or your own Codrus would have died before his sons for the sake of their kingship, if they had not believed that there would be an immortal remembering of their virtue, which we now retain? Far from it,' she said, 'but I believe that all do all things for the sake of immortal virtue and a famous reputation of that sort; and the better they are, so much the more is it thus; for they love the immortal. Now there are those who are pregnant in terms of their bodies,' she said, 'and they turn rather to women and are erotic in this way, furnishing for themselves through the procreation of children immortality, remembrance, and happiness (as they believe) for all future time. But there are others who are pregnant in terms of the soul—for these, in fact,' she said, 'are those who in their souls even more than in their bodies conceive those things that it is appropriate for soul to conceive and bear. And what is appropriate for soul? Prudence and the rest of virtue; it is of these things that all the poets and all the craftsmen who are said to be inventive are procreators; and by far the greatest and most beautiful part of prudence,' she said, 'is the arranging and ordering of the affairs of cities and households. Its name is moderation and justice. So whenever someone from youth onward is pregnant in his soul with these virtues, if he is divine and of suitable age, then he desires to give birth and produce offspring. And he goes round in search, I believe, of the beautiful in which he might generate, for he will never generate in the ugly. So it is beautiful bodies rather than ugly ones to which he cleaves because he is pregnant; and if he meets a beautiful, generous, and naturally gifted soul, he cleaves strongly to the two (body and soul) together. And to this human being he is at once fluent in speeches about virtue—of what sort the good man must be and what he must practice—and he tries to educate him. So in touching the one who is beautiful, I suspect, and in association with him, he engenders and gives birth to offspring with which he was long pregnant; and whether the [lover] is present or absent he holds the beautiful one in memory, and nurtures with him that which has been generated in common. Therefore, those of this sort maintain a greater association and firmer friendship with one another than do those who have children in common, because the children they share in common are more beautiful and more immortal. And everyone would choose to have for himself children like these rather than the human kind; and if one looks at Homer, Hesiod, and the other good poets, one envies them: what offspring of themselves they have left behind! For as these offspring are in their own right immortal, they supply the poets with immortal fame and memory. And if you want,' she said, 'think of the children that Lycurgus left behind in Sparta, the preservers of Sparta and, to exaggerate a little, of Greece. Solon too is honored among you through his engendering of the laws; and other men as well in many other regions, among Greeks and among barbarians, by their showing forth of many beautiful deeds, have engendered every kind of virtue. It is to these that many sanctuaries are now dedicated through children of this kind; while through the human sort there are no sanctuaries for anyone yet.

" 'Now perhaps, Socrates, you too might be initiated into these erotics; but as for the perfect revelations—for which the others are means, if one were to proceed correctly on the way—I do not know if you would be able to be initiated into them. Now I shall speak.' she said. 'I shall not falter in my zeal; do try to follow, if you are able. He who is to move correctly in this matter must begin while young to go to beautiful bodies. And first of all, if the guide is guiding correctly, he must love one body and there generate beautiful speeches. Then he must realize that the beauty that is in any body whatsoever is related to that in another body; and if he must pursue the beauty of looks, it is great folly not to believe that the beauty of all bodies is one and the same. And with this realization he must be the lover of all beautiful bodies and in contempt slacken this [erotic] intensity for only one body, in the belief that it is petty. After this he must believe that the beauty in souls is more honorable than that in the body. So that even if someone who is decent in his soul has only a slight youthful charm, the lover must be content with it, and love and cherish him, and engender and seek such speeches as will make the young better: in order that [the lover], on his part, may be compelled to behold the beautiful in pursuits and laws, and to see that all this is akin to itself, so that he may come to believe that the beauty of the body is something trivial. And after these pursuits, he must lead [the beloved] on to the sciences, so that he [himself, the lover] may see the beauty of sciences, and in looking at the beautiful, which is now so vast, no longer be content like a lackey with the beauty in one, of a boy, of some human being, or of one practice, nor be a sorry sort of slave and petty calculator; but with a permanent turn to the vast open sea of the beautiful, behold it and give birth—in ungrudging philosophy—to many beautiful and magnificent speeches and thoughts; until, there strengthened and increased, he may discern a certain single philosophical science, which has as its object the following sort of beauty. Try to pay as close attention as you can,' she said. 'Whoever has been educated up to this point in erotics, beholding successively and correctly the beautiful things, in now going to the perfect end of erotics shall suddenly glimpse something wonderfully beautiful in its nature—that very thing, Socrates, for whose sake alone all the prior labors were undertaken—something that is, first of all, always being and neither coming to be nor perishing, nor increasing nor passing away; and secondly, not beautiful in one respect and ugly in another, nor at one time so, and at another time not—either with respect to the beautiful or the ugly—nor here beautiful and there ugly, as being beautiful to some and ugly to others; nor in turn will the beautiful be imagined by him as a kind of face or hands or anything else in which body shares, nor as any speech nor any science, and not as being somewhere in something else (for example, in an animal, or in earth, or in heaven, or in anything else), but as it is alone by itself and with itself, always being of a single form; while all other beautiful things that share in it do so in such a way that while it neither becomes anything more or less, nor is affected at all, the rest do come to be and perish. So whenever anyone begins to glimpse that beauty as he goes on up from these things through the correct practice of pederasty, he must come close to touching the perfect end. For this is what it is to proceed correctly, or to be led by another, to erotics—beginning from these beautiful things here, always to proceed on up for the sake of that beauty, using these beautiful things here as steps: from one to two, and from two to all beautiful bodies; and from beautiful bodies to beautiful pursuits; and from pursuits to beautiful lessons; and from lessons to end at that lesson, which is the lesson of nothing else than the beautiful itself; and at last to know what is beauty itself. It is at this place in life, in beholding the beautiful itself, my dear Socrates,' the Mantinean stranger said, 'that it is worth living, if—for a human being—it is [worth living] at any place. Should you ever see the beautiful itself, it will be your opinion that it is not to be compared to gold and garments and the beautiful boys and youths at whose sight you are now thunderstruck. And you and many others are prepared, in seeing the beloved and in always being with him, neither to eat nor drink, if it were somehow possible, but only to behold him and be with him. What then,' she said, 'do we believe happens to one, if he gets to see the beautiful itself, pure, clean, unmixed, and not infected with human flesh, colors, or a lot of other mortal foolishness, and can glimpse the divine beautiful itself as being of a single shape? Do you believe,' she said, 'that life would prove to be a sorry sort of thing, when a human being gazes in the direction of the beautiful and beholds it with the instrument with which he must and is together with it? Or don't you realize,' she said, 'that only here, in seeing in the way the beautiful is seeable, will he get to engender not phantom images of virtue—because he does not lay hold of a phantom—but true, because he lays hold of the true; and that once he has given birth to and cherished true virtue, it lies within him to become dear to god and, if it is possible for any human being, to become immortal as well?'

"Here, Phaedrus and you others, is what Diotima declared and what I am convinced of. And in this state of conviction, I try to persuade others that for this possession one could not easily get a better co-worker with human nature than Eros. Accordingly, I assert that every real man must honor Eros, as I myself honor erotics and train myself exceptionally in them; and I urge it on the rest, and now and always I eulogize the power and courage of Eros as far as I am able. Regard this speech, then, Phaedrus, if you want to, as spoken in eulogy of Eros; but if not, and your pleasure is to give it some other kind of name, so name it."

The Song of Songs

Eros is a pagan deity, but the love he is said to cause is not foreign to the ancient biblical tradition. Indeed, the Hebrew Bible contains the Song of Songs (also known as the Song of Solomon), one of the most beautiful love poems in Western literature. The book comprises what appear to be some twenty-five distinct lyric poems of love, rich in sensuous and erotic imagery, and scholars differ on the question of their possible interrelation and unity. Although the Song of Songs contains no explicit divine or religious references, Jewish and Christian interpreters over the centuries have read the text theologically. For example, Jewish mystical readers see in the images of erotic longing the expression of the soul's longing for God. And, in some Orthodox Jewish communities, all the men—young and old, single and married—together sing the Song of Songs in the synagogue on Friday night, welcoming the Sabbath bride. In contrast, Christian tradition has interpreted the song as an allegory of the love of Christ for his bride, the Church, or as symbolizing the experience of God's love in the individual human soul. The editors of this anthology, far from feeling the need to choose between sensualist and mystical or religious interpretations, are moved rather to wonder whether and how passionate, sensuous love of man and woman may be related, not merely symbolically, to the love for and from the divine. What, to take only one example, is responsible for this remarkable erotic fact: the wondrous appearance—"leaping upon the mountains, skipping upon the hills" or "coming up out of the wilderness"—only to me, of the one whom I encounter as my beloved? What, or who, sent her (him) to me?

1

The song of songs, which is Solomon's.
²Let him kiss me with the kisses of his mouth—
³Thine ointments have a goodly fragrance;
⁴Draw me, we will run after thee;
The king hath brought me into his chambers;
We will be glad and rejoice in thee,
We will find thy love more fragrant than wine!
Sincerely do they love thee.
⁵"I am black, but comely,
O ye daughters of Jerusalem,
As the tents of Kedar,
As the curtains of Solomon.

⁶Look not upon me, that I am swarthy,
That the sun has tanned me;
My mother's sons were incensed against me,
They made me keeper of the vineyards;
But mine own vineyard have I not kept.'
⁷Tell me, O thou whom my soul loveth,
Where thou feedest, where thou makest thy flock to rest at noon;
For why should I be as one that veileth herself
Beside the flocks of thy companions?
⁸If thou know not, O thou fairest among women,
Go thy way forth by the footsteps of the flock
And feed thy kids, beside the shepherds' tents.
⁹I have compared thee, O my love,
To a steed in Pharaoh's chariots.
¹⁰Thy cheeks are comely with circlets,
Thy neck with beads.
¹¹We will make thee circlets of gold
With studs of silver.

¹²While the king sat at his table,
My spikenard sent forth its fragrance.
¹³My beloved is unto me as a bag of myrrh,
That lieth betwixt my breasts.
¹⁴My beloved is unto me as a cluster of henna
In the vineyards of En-gedi.

¹⁵Behold, thou art fair, my love; behold, thou art fair;
Thine eyes are as doves.
¹⁶Behold, thou art fair, my beloved, yea, pleasant;
Also our couch is leafy.
¹⁷The beams of our houses are cedars,
And our panels are cypresses.

2

I am a rose of Sharon,
A lily of the valleys.

²As a lily among thorns,
So is my love among the daughters.

[3]As an apple-tree among the trees of the wood,
So is my beloved among the sons.
Under its shadow I delighted to sit,
And its fruit was sweet to my taste.
[4]He hath brought me to the banqueting-house,
And his banner over me is love.
[5]'Stay ye me with dainties, refresh me with apples;
For I am love-sick.'
[6]Let his left hand be under my head,
And his right hand embrace me.
[7]'I adjure you, O daughters of Jerusalem,
By the gazelles, and by the hinds of the field,
That ye awaken not, nor stir up love,
Until it please!'

[8]Hark! my beloved! behold, he cometh,
Leaping upon the mountains, skipping upon the hills.
[9]My beloved is like a gazelle or a young hart;
Behold, he standeth behind our wall,
He looketh in through the windows,
He peereth through the lattice.
[10]My beloved spoke, and said unto me:
'Rise up, my love, my fair one, and come away.
[11]For, lo, the winter is past,
The rain is over and gone;
[12]The flowers appear on the earth;
The time of singing is come,
And the voice of the turtledove is heard in our land;
[13]The fig-tree putteth forth her green figs,
And the vines in blossom give forth their fragrance.
Arise, my love, my fair one, and come away.

[14]O my dove, that art in the clefts of the rock, in the covert of the cliff,
Let me see thy countenance, let me hear thy voice;
For sweet is thy voice, and thy countenance is comely.'
[15]'Take us the foxes, the little foxes, that spoil the vineyards;
For our vineyards are in blossom.'

[16]My beloved is mine, and I am his,
That feedeth among the lilies.
[17]Until the day breathe, and the shadows flee away,

Turn, my beloved, and be thou like a gazelle or a young hart
Upon the mountains of spices.

3

By night on my bed I sought him whom my soul loveth;
I sought him, but I found him not.
²'I will rise now, and go about the city,
In the streets and in the broad ways,
I will seek him whom my soul loveth,'
I sought him, but I found him not.
³The watchmen that go about the city found me:
'Saw ye him whom my soul loveth?'
⁴Scarce had I passed from them,
When I found him whom my soul loveth:
I held him, and would not let him go,
Until I had brought him into my mother's house,
And into the chamber of her that conceived me.
⁵'I adjure you, O daughters of Jerusalem,
By the gazelles, and by the hinds of the field,
That ye awaken not, nor stir up love,
Until it please.'

⁶Who is this that cometh up out of the wilderness
Like pillars of smoke,
Perfumed with myrrh and frankincense,
With all powders of the merchant?
⁷Behold, it is the litter of Solomon;
Threescore mighty men are about it,
Of the mighty men of Israel.
⁸They all handle the sword,
And are expert in war;
Every man hath his sword upon his thigh,
Because of dread in the night.

⁹King Solomon made himself a palanquin
Of the wood of Lebanon.
¹⁰He made the pillars thereof of silver,
The top thereof of gold,
The seat of it of purple,
The inside thereof being inlaid with love,

From the daughters of Jerusalem.
[11]Go forth, O ye daughters of Zion,
And gaze upon king Solomon,
Even upon the crown wherewith his mother hath crowned him in the day of
   his espousals,
And in the day of the gladness of his heart.

4

Behold, thou art fair, my love; behold, thou art fair;
Thine eyes are as doves behind thy veil;
Thy hair is as a flock of goats
That trail down from mount Gilead.
[2]Thy teeth are like a flock of ewes all shaped alike,
Which are come up from the washing;
Whereof all are paired,
And none faileth among them.
[3]Thy lips are like a thread of scarlet,
And thy mouth is comely;
Thy temples are like a pomegranate split open
Behind thy veil.
[4]Thy neck is like the tower of David
Builded with turrets,
Whereon there hang a thousand shields,
All the armour of the mighty men.
[5]Thy two breasts are like two fawns
That are twins of a gazelle,
Which feed among the lilies.
[6]Until the day breathe,
And the shadows flee away,
I will get me to the mountain of myrrh,
And to the hill of frankincense.
[7]Thou art all fair, my love;
And there is no spot in thee.
[8]Come with me from Lebanon, my bride,
With me from Lebanon;
Look from the top of Amana,
From the top of Senir and Hermon,
From the lions' dens,
From the mountains of the leopards.

[9]Thou hast ravished my heart, my sister, my bride;
Thou hast ravished my heart with one of thine eyes,
With one bead of thy necklace.
[10]How fair is thy love, my sister, my bride!
How much better is thy love than wine!
And the smell of thine ointments than all manner of spices!
[11]Thy lips, O my bride, drop honey—
Honey and milk are under thy tongue;
And the smell of thy garments is like the smell of Lebanon.
[12]A garden shut up is my sister, my bride;
A spring shut up, a fountain sealed.
[13]Thy shoots are a park of pomegranates,
With precious fruits;
Henna with spikenard plants,
[14]Spikenard and saffron, calamus and cinnamon,
With all trees of frankincense;
Myrrh and aloes, with all the chief spices.
[15]Thou art a fountain of gardens,
A well of living waters,
And flowing streams from Lebanon.

[16]Awake, O north wind;
And come, thou south;
Blow upon my garden,
That the spices thereof may flow out.
Let my beloved come into his garden,
And eat his precious fruits.

5

I am come into my garden, my sister, my bride;
I have gathered my myrrh with my spice;
I have eaten my honeycomb with my honey;
I have drunk my wine with my milk.

Eat, O friends;
Drink, yea, drink abundantly, O beloved.

[2]I sleep, but my heart waketh;
Hark! my beloved knocketh:

'Open to me, my sister, my love, my dove, my undefiled;
For my head is filled with dew,
My locks with the drops of the night.'
[3]I have put off my coat;
How shall I put it on?
I have washed my feet;
How shall I defile them?
[4]My beloved put in his hand by the hole of the door,
And my heart was moved for him.
[5]I rose up to open to my beloved;
And my hands dropped with myrrh,
And my fingers with flowing myrrh,
Upon the handles of the bar.
[6]I opened to my beloved;
But my beloved had turned away, and was gone.
My soul failed me when he spoke.
I sought him, but I could not find him;
I called him, but he gave me no answer.
[7]The watchmen that go about the city found me,
They smote me, they wounded me;
The keepers of the walls took away my mantle from me.
[8]'I adjure you, O daughters of Jerusalem,
If ye find my beloved,
What will ye tell him?
That I am love-sick.'

[9]'What is thy beloved more than another beloved,
O thou fairest among women?
What is thy beloved more than another beloved,
That thou dost so adjure us?'

[10]'My beloved is white and ruddy,
Pre-eminent above ten thousand.
[11]His head is the most fine gold,
His locks are curled,
And black as a raven.
[12]His eyes are like doves
Beside the water-brooks;
Washed with milk,
And fitly set.
[13]His cheeks are as a bed of spices,

As banks of sweet herbs;
His lips are as lilies,
Dropping with flowing myrrh.
[14]His hands are as rods of gold
Set with beryl;
His body is as polished ivory
Overlaid with sapphires.
[15]His legs are as pillars of marble,
Set upon sockets of fine gold;
His aspect is like Lebanon,
Excellent as the cedars.
[16]His mouth is most sweet;
Yea, he is altogether lovely.
This is my beloved, and this is my friend,
O daughters of Jerusalem.'

6

'Whither is thy beloved gone,
O thou fairest among women?
Whither hath thy beloved turned him,
That we may seek him with thee?'
[2]'My beloved is gone down to his garden,
To the beds of spices,
To feed in the gardens,
And to gather lilies.
[3]I am my beloved's, and my beloved is mine,
That feedeth among the lilies.'

[4]'Thou are beautiful, O my love, as Tirzah,
Comely as Jerusalem,
Terrible as an army with banners.
[5]Turn away thine eyes from me,
For they have overcome me.
Thy hair is as a flock of goats,
That trail down from Gilead.
[6]Thy teeth are like a flock of ewes,
Which are come up from the washing;
Whereof all are paired,
And none faileth among them.
[7]Thy temples are like a pomegranate split open

Behind thy veil.
[8]There are threescore queens,
And fourscore concubines,
And maidens without number.
[9]My dove, my undefiled, is but one;
She is the only one of her mother;
She is the choice one of her that bore her.
The daughters saw her, and called her happy;
Yea, the queens and the concubines, and they praised her.'

[10]Who is she that looketh forth as the dawn,
Fair as the moon,
Clear as the sun,
Terrible as an army with banners?

[11]I went down into the garden of nuts,
To look at the green plants of the valley,
To see whether the vine budded,
And the pomegranates were in flower.
[12]Before I was aware, my soul set me
Upon the chariots of my princely people.

7

Return, return, O Shulammite;
Return, return, that we may look upon thee.

What will ye see in the Shulammite?
As it were a dance of two companies.

[2]How beautiful are thy steps in sandals,
O prince's daughter!
The roundings of thy thighs are like the links of a chain,
The work of the hands of a skilled workman.
[3]Thy navel is like a round goblet,
Wherein no mingled wine is wanting;
Thy belly is like a heap of wheat
Set about with lilies.
[4]Thy two breasts are like two fawns
That are twins of a gazelle.
[5]Thy neck is as a tower of ivory;

Thine eyes as the pools in Heshbon,
By the gate of Bath-rabbim;
Thy nose is like the tower of Lebanon
Which looketh toward Damascus.
⁶Thy head upon thee is like Carmel,
And the hair of thy head like purple;
The king is held captive in the tresses thereof.
⁷How fair and how pleasant art thou,
O love, for delights!
⁸This thy stature is like to a palm-tree,
And thy breasts to clusters of grapes.
⁹I said: 'I will climb up into the palm-tree,
I will take hold of the branches thereof;
And let thy breasts be as clusters of the vine,
And the smell of thy countenance like apples;
¹⁰And the roof of thy mouth like the best wine,
That glideth down smoothly for my beloved,
Moving gently the lips of those that are asleep.'

¹¹I am my beloved's,
And his desire is toward me.
¹²Come, my beloved, let us go forth into the field;
Let us lodge in the villages.
¹³Let us get up early to the vineyards;
Let us see whether the vine hath budded,
Whether the vine-blossom be opened,
And the pomegranates be in flower;
There will I give thee my love.
¹⁴The mandrakes give forth fragrance,
And at our doors are all manner of precious fruits,
New and old,
Which I have laid up for thee, O my beloved.

8

Oh that thou wert as my brother,
That sucked the breasts of my mother!
When I should find thee without, I would kiss thee;
Yea, and none would despise me.
²I would lead thee, and bring thee into my mother's house,
That thou mightest instruct me;

I would cause thee to drink of spiced wine,
Of the juice of my pomegranate.

[3]His left hand should be under my head,
And his right hand should embrace me.
[4]'I adjure you, O daughters of Jerusalem:
Why should ye awaken, or stir up love,
Until it please?'

[5]Who is this that cometh up from the wilderness,
Leaning upon her beloved?
Under the apple-tree I awakened thee;
There thy mother was in travail with thee,
There was she in travail and brought thee forth.

[6]Set me as a seal upon thy heart,
As a seal upon thine arm;
For love is strong as death,
Jealousy is cruel as the grave;
The flashes thereof are flashes of fire,
A very flame of the LORD.
[7]Many waters cannot quench love,
Neither can the floods drown it;
If a man would give all the substance of his house for love,
He would utterly be contemned.

[8]We have a little sister,
And she hath no breasts;
What shall we do for our sister
In the day when she shall be spoken for?
[9]If she be a wall,
We will build upon her a turret of silver;
And if she be a door,
We will enclose her with boards of cedar.
[10]I am a wall,
And my breasts like the towers thereof;
Then was I in his eyes
As one that found peace.

[11]Solomon had a vineyard at Baal-hamon;
He gave over the vineyard unto keepers;

Every one for the fruit thereof
Brought in a thousand pieces of silver.
[12]My vineyard, which is mine, is before me;
Thou, O Solomon, shalt have the thousand,
And those that keep the fruit thereof two hundred.

[13]Thou that dwellest in the gardens,
The companions hearken for thy voice:
'Cause me to hear it.'
[14]Make haste, my beloved,
And be thou like to a gazelle or to a young hart
Upon the mountains of spices.

De Rougemont, "The Tristan Myth"

In his magisterial work, Love in the Western World *(published in 1940), the Swiss philosopher Denis De Rougemont (1906–1985) explores the psychology of romantic love as presented in Western myth and literature, from its origins in the songs of the troubadours in the twelfth century up to the present age. The guiding theme is what De Rougemont regards as the unavoidable conflict between passionate eros or romantic love and marriage, the latter connected to political, moral, and religious responsibilities, the former free, chaotic, and unfulfillable. The point of departure of his account is the myth of Tristan and Iseult, which De Rougemont treats as the prototype of courtly love and its romanticist successors. In the two extracts taken from Book I, "The Tristan Myth" (Chapter 4, and Chapters 8 and 9), we get first a summary of the myth and then De Rougemont's interpretation.*

What the Tristan Romance[1] Seems to Be About

Amors par force vos demeine![2]—Béroul

Tristan is born in misfortune. His father has just died, and Blanchefleur, his mother, does not survive his birth. Hence his name, the sombre hue of his life, and the lowering stormy sky that hangs over the legend. King Mark of Cornwall, Blanchefleur's brother, takes the orphan into his castle at Tintagel and brings him up there.

Tristan presently performs an early feat of prowess. He vanquishes the Morholt. This Irish giant has come like a Minotaur to exact his tribute of Cornish maidens or youths. Tristan is of an age for knighthood—that is, he has just reached puberty—and he obtains leave to fight him. The Morholt is killed, but not before he has wounded Tristan with a poisoned barb. Having no hope of recovery, Tristan begs to be put on board a boat that is cast adrift with neither sail nor oar. He takes his sword and harp with him.

He lands in Ireland. There is only one remedy that can save him, and, as it happens, the Queen of Ireland is alone in knowing its secret. But the giant

---

[1]In summing up the chief episodes of the Romance, I shall make use (except here and there) of M. Bédier's *Concordance* (contained in his study of Thomas's poem) for the five twelfth-century versions—those by Béroul, Thomas and Eilhart together with *La Folie Tristan and Le Roman en prose*. The later versions by Gottfried of Strasbourg, or by German, Italian, Danish, Russian, Czech, and other imitators, are all derived from those five. I also take into account the more recent critical undertakings of Messrs. F Muret and E. Vinaver.

[2]'Love by force dominates you!'

Morholt was this queen's brother, and so Tristan is careful not to disclose his name or to explain how he has come by his wound. Iseult, the queen's daughter, nurses him and restores him to health. That is the Prologue.

A few years later a bird has brought to King Mark a golden hair. The king determines to marry the woman from whose head the hair has come. It is Tristan whom he selects to go in quest of her. A storm causes the hero to be cast ashore once again in Ireland. There he fights and kills a dragon that was threatening the capital. (This is the conventional motif of a virgin delivered by a young paladin.) Having been wounded by the dragon, Tristan is again nursed by Iseult. One day she learns that the wounded stranger is no other than the man who killed her uncle. She seizes Tristan's sword and threatens to transfix him in his bath. It is then that he tells her of the mission on which he has been sent by King Mark. And Iseult spares him, for she would like to be a queen. (According to some of the authors, she spares him also because she then finds him handsome.)

Tristan and the princess set sail for Cornwall. At sea the wind drops and the heat grows oppressive. They are thirsty. Brengain, Iseult's maid, gives them a drink. But by mistake she pours out the 'wine of herbs' which the queen, Iseult's mother, has brewed for King Mark and his bride after they shall have wed. Tristan and Iseult drink it. The effect is to commit them to a fate from 'which they can never escape during the remainder of their lives, *for they have drunk their destruction and death*'. They confess that they are now in love, and fall into one another's arms.

(Let it be noted here that according to the archetypal version, which Béroul alone has followed, the effect of the love-potion is limited to three years. Thomas, a sensitive psychologist and highly suspicious of marvels, which he considers crude, minimizes the importance of the love-potion as far as possible, and depicts the love of Tristan and Iseult as having occurred spontaneously. Its first signs he places as early as the episode of the bath. On the other hand, Eilhart, Gottfried, and most of the others attribute unlimited effect to the magic wine. Nothing could be more significant than these variations, as we shall see.)

Thus the fault is perpetrated. *Yet Tristan is still in duty bound to fulfil the mission with which King Mark has entrusted him.* So, notwithstanding his betrayal of the king, he delivers Iseult to him. On the wedding night Brengain, thanks to a ruse, takes Iseult's place in the royal bed, thus saving her mistress from dishonour and at the same time expiating the irretrievable mistake she made in pouring out the love-potion.

Presently, however, four 'felon' barons of the king's go and tell their sovereign that Tristan and Iseult are lovers. Tristan is banished to Tintagel town. But thanks to another trick—the episode of the pine-tree in the orchard—Mark is convinced of his innocence and allows him to return to the castle. Then Frocin the Dwarf, who is in league with the barons, lays a trap in order to establish the lovers' guilt. In the spear-length between Tristan's bed and the queen's he scatters flour, and persuades Mark to order Tristan to ride to King Arthur at Carduel the next morning at dawn. Tristan is determined to embrace his mistress once more before he rides away. To avoid leaving his foot-marks in the flour he leaps across from his own bed to the queen's. But the effort reopens a wound in his leg inflicted the previous day by a boar. Led by Frocin, the king and the barons burst into the bedchamber. They find the flour blood-stained. Mark is satisfied with this evidence of adultery. Iseult is handed over to a party of a hundred lepers, and Tristan is sentenced to the stake. On the way to execution, however, he is allowed to go into a chantry on the cliff's edge. He forces a window and leaps over the cliff, thus effecting his escape. He rescues Iseult from the lepers, and together they go and hide in the depths of the Forest of Morrois. There for three years they lead a life 'harsh and hard'. It happens one day that Mark comes upon them while they are asleep. But on this occasion Tristan has put between Iseult and himself his drawn sword. Moved by this evidence of innocence, as he supposes it to be, the king spares them. Without waking them, he takes up Tristan's sword and sets his own in its place.

At the end of three years the potency of the love-potion wears off (according to Béroul and the common ancestor of the five versions). It is only then that Tristan repents, and that Iseult wishes she were a queen again. Together they seek out the hermit Ogrin, through whom Tristan offers peace to the king, saying he will surrender Iseult. Mark promises forgiveness. As the royal procession approaches, the lovers part. But before this happens Iseult has besought Tristan to stay in the neighbourhood till he has made certain that Mark is treating her well. Then, with a final display of feminine wiles, she follows up her advantage in having persuaded Tristan to agree to this, and declares she will join him at the first sign he makes, for nothing shall stop her from doing his will, 'neither tower, nor wall, nor stronghold'.

They have several secret meetings in the hut of Orri the Woodman. But the felon barons are keeping watch and ward over the queen's virtue. She asks and is granted 'a Judgement of God'. Thanks to a subterfuge, the ordeal is a success. Before she grasps the red-hot iron which will not harm one who has spoken the truth, she swears that no man has ever held her in her arms except the king and a poor pilgrim who has just carried her ashore from a boat. And the poor pilgrim is Tristan in disguise.

However, fresh adventures carry Tristan far away from Iseult, and he then comes to suppose that she no longer loves him. So he agrees to marry 'for her beauty and her name' another Iseult, Iseult 'of the White Hand'. And indeed this Iseult remains unstained, for after their marriage Tristan still sighs for 'Iseult the Fair'.

At last, wounded by a poisoned spear and about to die, Tristan sends for the queen from Cornwall, she who alone can save his life. She comes, and as her ship draws near it hoists a white sail as a sign of hope. But Iseult of the White Hand has been on the look-out, and, tormented by jealousy, she runs to Tristan and tells him that the sail is black. Tristan dies. As he does so, Iseult the Fair lands, and on arriving at the castle, she lies down beside her dead lover and clasps him close. Then she dies too.

At this point, De Rougemont notes some peculiarities in the myth that beg for explanation, among them the following: Why does not Tristan take advantage of his superior strength to win the princess? Why the sword of chastity placed between the two sleepers in the forest? Why, if the lovers repent their adultery, do they agree to meet again in the moment they undertake to part? Why does Tristan marry another Iseult whom he does not love, does not touch, and will not make his wife, putting himself in a position from which the only escape is death? De Rougemont argues that courtly or romantic love is at odds not only with feudal society and its loveless marriages, but also with the fulfillment of its own passion in the possession and union of the lovers. Lovers put obstacles in the way of their love in order that love may be intensified—but at the cost of their happiness and even of their lives. Thus, according to De Rougemont, eros is the enemy not only of marriage but also of happiness; moreover, it finally cares not for the beautiful or worthy beloved but for its own burning fire and the transfigured death to which it necessarily leads.

The Love of Love

'*De tous les maux, le mien diffère; il me plaît; je me réjouis de lui; mon mal est ce que je veux et ma douleur est ma santé. Je ne vois donc pas de quoi je me plains; car mon mal me vient de ma volonté; c'est mon vouloir qui devient mon mal; mais j'ai tant d'aise à vouloir ainsi que je souffre agréablement, et tant de joie dans ma douleur que je suis malade avec délices.*'—Chrétien de Troyes.[3]

It is only 'silly' questions that can enlighten us; for behind whatever seems obvious lurks something that is not. Let us then boldly ask: Does Tristan care for Iseult, and she for him? The lovers do not seem to be brought together in any normal *human* way. On the contrary, at their first encounter they confine

---

[3]'From all other ills doth mine differ. It pleaseth me; I rejoice at it; my ill is what I want and my suffering is my health. So I do not see what I am complaining about; for my ill comes to me by my will; it is my willing that becomes my ill; but I am so pleased to want thus that I suffer agreeably, and have so much joy in my pain that I am sick with delight.'

themselves to having ordinary polite relations; and later, when Tristan returns to Ireland to fetch Iseult, the politeness, it will be remembered, gives place to open hostility. Everything goes to show that they would never have chosen one another were they acting *freely*. But no sooner have they drunk the love-potion than passion flares between them. Yet that any fondness supervenes to unite them as a result of the magic spell I have found, among the thousands of lines of the Romance, only a single indication. When, following Tristan's escape, it has been told how they have gone to live in the Forest of Morrois, there occur these lines:

> Aspre vie meinent et dure:
> Tant s'entraiment de bone amor
> L'un por l'autre ne sent dolor.[4]

If it should be imagined that poets in the Middle Ages were less emotional than we have grown to be and felt no need to insist on what goes without saying, let the account of the three years in the forest be read attentively. Its two finest passages—which are no doubt also the most profound passages in the whole legend—describe the lovers' two visits to the hermit Ogrin. The first time they go to see him, it is in order to make confession. But instead of confessing their sin and asking for absolution, they do their best to convince him that they are not to blame for what has befallen, since after all *they do not care for one another!*

> Q'el m'aime, c'est par la poison
> Ge ne me pus de lié partir,
> N'ele de moi—[5]

So speaks Tristan, and Iseult says after him:

> Sire, por Deu omnipotent,
> Il ne m'aime pas, ne je lui,
> Fors par un herbé dont je bui
> Et il en but: ce fu pechiez.[6]

They are thus in a thrillingly contradictory position. They love, but not one another. They have sinned, but cannot repent; for they are not to blame.

---

[4]'Harsh life led they and hard, so entertaining good love for one another. One by the other was ne'er exposed to pain.'

[5]'If she loves me, it is by the poison which holds me from leaving her and her from leaving me.'

[6]'Lord, by almighty God, he loves me not, nor I him; except for a herb potion which I drank and which he drank; it was a sin.'

They make confession, but wish neither to reform nor even to beg forgiveness. Actually, then, like all other great lovers, they imagine that they have been ravished 'beyond good and evil' into a kind of transcendental state outside ordinary human experience, into an ineffable absolute irreconcilable with the world, but that they feel to be *more real than the world.* Their oppressive fate, even though they yield to it with wailings, obliterates the antithesis of good and evil, and carries them away beyond the source of moral values, beyond pleasure and pain, beyond the realm of distinctions—into a realm where opposites cancel out.

Their admission is explicit enough: 'Il ne m'aime pas, ne je lui.' Everything happens as if they could neither see nor recognize one another. They are the prisoners of 'exquisite anguish' owing to something which neither controls—some alien power independent of their capacities, or at any rate of their conscious wishes, and of their being in so far as they are aware of being. Both characters, the man as much as the woman, are depicted physically and psychologically in an entirely conventional and rhetorical manner. He is 'the strongest'; she, 'the most beautiful'; he, the knight; she, the princess; and so on. It is impossible to believe that any human feeling can grow between two such rudimentary characters. The friendship mentioned in connexion with the length of time the effect of the love-potion lasts is the opposite of a true friendship; and, what is still more striking, if moral friendship does at last appear, it is at the moment their passion declines. And the immediate consequence of their nascent friendship, far from being to knit them more closely together, is to make them feel that they have everything to gain from a separation. This last point deserves to be considered more closely.

> L'endemain de la saint Jehan
> Aconpli furent li troi an.[7]

Tristan is out in the forest after game. Suddenly he is reminded of the world. He sees in his mind's eye King Mark's castle. He sighs for 'the vair and grey' and for the pomp of chivalry. He thinks of the high rank he might hold among his uncle's barons. He thinks too of his beloved—apparently for the first time! But for him she might be 'in fine rooms . . . hung with cloth of silk'. Simultaneously Iseult is filled with similar regrets. In the evening they are together and they confess to one another what is newly agitating them—'en mal uson nostre jovente'. It does not take them long to agree to part. Tristan talks of making off to Brittany. But first they will seek out Ogrin the Hermit and beg his forgiveness and at the same time King Mark's forgiveness of Iseult.

---

[7]'On the morrow of St John's Day, the three years were accomplished.'

It is at this point that there occurs a highly dramatic short dialogue between the hermit and the two penitents:

> Amors par force vos demeine!
> Conbien durra vostre folie?
> Trop avez mené ceste vie.[8]

So Ogrin admonishes them.

> Tristan li dist: or escoutez
> Si longuement l'avons menee
> Itel fu nostre destinee.[9]

On top of this comes one more feature. When Tristan hears that the king agrees to Iseult's return:

> Dex! dist Tristan, quel departie!
> Molt est dolenz qui pert s'amie![10]

It is with his own pain that he commiserates; not a thought for 's'amie'! And she too, we are made to feel, finds it much more pleasant to be back with the king than she ever did with her lover—happier in the unhappiness of love than she ever was in the life they led together in the Morrois.

For that matter, later on—as we have seen—passion seizes the lovers again, notwithstanding that the effect of the love-potion has worn off, and this time they are so carried away that they die—'he by her, she by him'. The seeming *selfishness* of their love is enough to account for the many 'chance' happenings and tricks of fate that obstruct their attainment of happiness. But this selfishness, in its profound ambiguity, still wants explaining. Selfishness, it is said, always ends in death. But that is as a final defeat. Theirs, on the contrary, requires death for its perfect fulfilment and triumph. To the problem this raises there is only one answer worthy of the myth.

Tristan and Iseult do not love one another. They say they don't, and everything goes to prove it. *What they love is love and being in love.* They behave

---

[8] 'Love by force dominates you. How long will your folly last? Too long you have been leading this life.' *Amors par force vos demeine*—the most poignant description of passion ever penned by a poet! We must pause to admire it. In a single line the whole of passion is summed up with a vigour of expression making all romanticism look pallid! Shall we ever recover this sturdy 'dialect of the heart'?

[9] 'Tristan quoth to him: 'Now hearken, if for long we have been leading this life, that is because it was our destiny.'

[10] 'God!' quoth Tristan, 'What a fate! Wretched he who loseth his mistress.'

as if aware that whatever obstructs love must ensure and consolidate it in the heart of each and intensify it infinitely in the moment they reach the absolute obstacle, which is death. Tristan loves the awareness that he is loving far more than he loves Iseult the Fair. And Iseult does nothing to hold Tristan. All she needs is her passionate dream. Their need of one another is in order to be aflame, and they do not need one another as they are. What they need is not one another's presence, but one another's absence. *Thus the partings of the lovers are dictated by their passion itself,* and by the love they bestow on their passion rather than on its satisfaction or on its living object. That is why the Romance abounds in obstructions, why when mutually encouraging their joint dream in which each remains solitary they show such astounding indifference, and why events work up in a romantic climax to a fatal apotheosis.

The duality is at once irrevocable and deliberate. 'Molt est dolenz qui pert s'amie,' Tristan sighs: and yet he then already sees, glimmering in the depths of the approaching night, that hidden flame which absence rekindles.

The Love of Death

But we must push on further still. Augustine's *amabam amare* [I loved to love] is a poignant phrase with which he himself was not content. I have repeatedly referred to *obstruction,* and there is the way in which the passion of the two lovers *creates obstruction,* its effects coinciding with those of narrative necessity and of the reader's suspense. Is this obstruction not simply a *pretext* needed in order to enable the passion to progress, or is it connected with the passion in some far more profound manner? If we delve into the recesses of the myth, we see that this obstruction is what passion really *wants*—its true object.

I have shown that the Romance is given its motive power by the repeated partings and reunions of the lovers. For convenience, here once more, briefly, is what happens. Tristan, having landed in Ireland, meets Iseult and then parts from her without being in love. He turns up in Ireland again, and this time Iseult wants to kill him. They take ship together and drink the love-potion, and then sin. Next, Iseult is delivered up to Mark, and Tristan is banished from the castle. He and Iseult meet under a pine-tree, their talk being overheard by Mark. Tristan comes back to the castle, and Frocin and the barons discover evidence of his crime. They are parted. They meet again, and for three years go to live in the forest. Then, once more, they part. They meet at the hut of Orri the Woodman. Tristan goes away. He comes back, disguised as a poor pilgrim. He goes away again. The separation this time is prolonged, and he marries Iseult of the White Hand. Iseult the Fair is about to rejoin him when he dies. She dies too. More briefly still: They have one long spell together ('L'aspre vie'—'The harsh life'), to which corresponds a lengthy separation—and Tristan's marriage. First, the love-potion; lastly, the death of both. In between, furtive meetings.

They are led to part so often either by adverse external circumstances or by hindrances which Tristan devises; and it is to be noted that Tristan's behaviour varies according to which kind of cause is operating. When social circumstances—for example, Mark's presence, the barons' suspiciousness, the Judgement of God—threaten the lovers, Tristan leaps over the obstruction (this is symbolized by his leap from his own bed to the queen's). He then does not mind pain (his wound reopens) nor the danger to his life (he knows he is being spied upon). Passion is then so violent—so brutish, it might be said—that in the intoxication of his *déduit* (or delight) he is oblivious to pain and perils alike. Nevertheless, the blood flowing from his wound betrays him. This is the 'red stain' that apprises the king of what is happening. And it also apprises the reader of the lovers' secret—that they are seeking peril for its own sake. But so long as the peril comes from without, Tristan's prowess in overcoming it is an affirmation of life. At this stage Tristan is simply complying with the feudal practice of knights. He has to prove his 'valour' and show he is either the stronger or the more wily. We have seen that if he persevered in this direction he would carry off the queen, and that established law is only respected here because this gives the tale an excuse to rebound.

But the knight's demeanour becomes quite different when nothing external any longer separates the two lovers. Indeed, it becomes the opposite of what it has been. When Tristan puts his drawn sword between himself and Iseult although they are lying down fully clothed, this is again prowess, but on this occasion against himself, *to his own cost*. Since he himself has set up the obstruction, it is no longer one *he can overcome!* It must not be overlooked that the hierarchy of events corresponds closely to the hierarchy of both the storyteller's and the reader's *preferences*. The most serious obstruction is thus the one preferred above all. It is the one most suited to intensifying passion. At this extreme, furthermore, the wish to part assumes an emotional value *greater than that of passion itself*. Death, in being the goal of passion, kills it.

Yet the drawn sword is not the ultimate expression of the dark desire and of the actual *end* of passion (in both senses of the word 'end'). The admirable episode of the exchange of swords makes this clear. When the king comes upon the lovers lying asleep in the cave, he substitutes his own sword for that of his rival. The meaning of this is that in place of the obstruction which the lovers have wanted and have deliberately set up he puts the sign of his social prerogative, a legal and objective obstruction. Tristan accepts the challenge, and thereby enables the *action* of the tale to rebound. At this point the word 'action' takes on a symbolical meaning. Action prevents 'passion' from being complete, for passion is 'what is suffered'—and its limit is death. In other words, the action here is a fresh postponement of passion, which means a delaying of Death.

There is the same shift as regards the two marriages in the Romance, that of Iseult the Fair to the king and that of Iseult of the White Hand to Tristan. The first is an obstruction in fact. The concrete existence of a *husband* symbolizes its character, husbands being despised in courtly love. Making the obstruction that leads to adultery a husband is unimaginative, the excuse most readily thought of, and *most* in keeping with everyday experience.[11] See how Tristan shoves the husband aside, and enjoys making sport of him! But for the existence of a husband, the love of Tristan and Iseult would not have lasted beyond three years! And old Béroul showed his good sense in limiting the effect of the love-potion to that length of time:

> La mere Yseut, qui le bolli,
> A trois anz d'amistié le fist.[12]

But for the existence of a husband, the lovers would have had to get married; and it is unbelievable that Tristan should ever be in a position to marry Iseult. She typifies the woman a man does not marry; for once she became his wife she would no longer be what she is, and he would no longer love her. Just think of a Mme Tristan! It would be the negation of passion—at least of the passion we are concerned with here. The spontaneous ardour of a love crowned and not thwarted is essentially of short duration. It is a flare-up doomed not to survive the effulgence of its fulfilment. But its *branding* remains, and this is what the lovers want to prolong and indefinitely to renew. That is why they go on summoning fresh perils. But these the knight's valour drives him to overcome, and so he has to go away, in quest of more profound and more intimate—and it even seems, more interior—experiences.

When Tristan is sighing quietly for his lost Iseult, the brother of Iseult of the White Hand thinks his friend must be in love with his sister. This confusion—produced by identity of name—is the sole 'cause' of Tristan's marrying. It is obvious that he could easily have cleared up the misunderstanding. But here again honour supervenes—of course, as a mere pretext—to prevent him from drawing back. The reason is that he foresees, in this new ordeal which is *self-imposed,* the opportunity of a decisive advance. This merely formal marriage with a woman he finds beautiful is an obstruction which he can remove only by achieving a victory *over himself* (as well as over the institution of marriage, which he thus damages from within). This time his prowess goes against

---

[11]Romanticism was later on to devise more refined excuses.

[12]'Mother Yseut, who brewed it, made it to three years of love.'

him. His chastity now he is married corresponds to the placing of the drawn sword between himself and the other Iseult. But a self-imposed chastity is a symbolical suicide (here is the hidden meaning of the sword)—a victory for the courtly ideal over the sturdy Celtic tradition which proclaimed its pride in life. It is a way of purifying desire of the spontaneous, brutish, and active elements still encumbering it. 'Passion' triumphs over desire. Death triumphs over life.

Hence Tristan's inclination for a *deliberate obstruction* turns out to be a desire for death and an advance in the direction of Death! But this death is for love, a deliberate death coming at the end of a series of ordeals thanks to which he will have been purified; a death that means transfiguration, and is in no way the result of some violent chance. Hence the aim is still to unite an external with an internal fate, which the lovers deliberately embrace. *In dying for love they redeem their destiny and are avenged for the love-potion.* So that at the last the struggle between passion and obstruction is inverted. At this point the obstruction is no longer serving irresistible passion, but has itself become the goal and end wished for its own sake. Passion has thus only played the part of a purifying ordeal, it might almost be said of a penance, in the service of this transfiguring death. Here we are within sight of the ultimate secret.

The love of love itself has concealed a far more awful passion, a desire altogether unavowable, something that could only be 'betrayed' by means of symbols such as that of the drawn sword and that of perilous chastity. Unawares and in spite of themselves, the lovers have never had but one desire—the desire for death! Unawares, and passionately deceiving themselves, they have been seeking all the time simply to be redeemed and avenged for 'what they have suffered'—the passion unloosed by the love-potion. In the innermost recesses of their hearts they have been obeying the fatal dictates of a wish for death; they have been in the throes of *the active passion of Darkness.* . . .

Shakespeare, *Romeo and Juliet*

The tragedy of great love, discussed by De Rougement, finds expression in the plays of Shakespeare (1564–1616), most notably in Antony and Cleopatra. *But the charm and innocence of intense young love is perhaps nowhere better portrayed than in* Romeo and Juliet. *Romeo, son of a Veronese nobleman, Montague, despondent over his unrequited love of one Rosaline, arrives at a masked ball given by his family's sworn enemy, Capulet. There he falls in love at first sight with Capulet's daughter, Juliet, a girl, though not yet fourteen, who is on the cusp of womanhood. The first excerpt, taken from Act I, Scene v and Act II, Scene ii, portrays the germ of their love at the ball and its mutual declaration later that night in the famous balcony scene. Even older and wiser readers respond sympathetically to the ardent and idealistic expression of their passion. Yet given the ease with which Romeo's love shifts from Rosaline to Juliet, might he not be more in love with love than with either beloved?*

From the start, Shakespeare calls Romeo and Juliet a "pair of star-crossed lovers" who enjoy a "death-marked love." We wonder, therefore, whether their love is doomed only because of the obstacles erected by the feuding enmity of their families. Could there instead be something ill-fated and deadly in the kind of love they suffer? Could this love, under better circumstances in which it might have been disciplined by open courtship and custom, in the context and with the blessings of their families, become the basis of lasting marriage? Or is the enmity of the lovers' families meant to show that this kind of love is in principle at odds both with family ties and with marriage? Is such love necessarily incompatible with the happinesses of everyday life? Further evidence that Romeo and Juliet *represents a return of the Tristan myth is provided in Romeo's last speech, in Act V, Scene iii, delivered at the tomb containing the sleeping but, to Romeo, apparently dead Juliet, whom he seeks to join in death. Excerpts from this speech form our second selection.*

Act I, Scene v, lines 16–144. Location: a ball in the home of the Capulets
Stage Directions: Enter Capulet, his wife, Juliet, Tybalt (Lady Capulet's Nephew), Juliet's Nurse, and all the Guests and Gentlewomen to the Maskers.

Capulet. Welcome, gentlemen! Ladies that have their toes
    Unplagued with corns will walk a bout[1] with you.
    Ah ha, my mistresses! which of you all
    Will now deny to dance? She that makes dainty,[2]

---

[1] **walk a bout** dance a turn
[2] **makes dainty** pretends to hesitate

She I'll swear hath corns. Am I come near ye now?
Welcome, gentlemen! I have seen the day
That I have worn a visor and could tell
A whispering tale in a fair lady's ear,
Such as would please. 'Tis gone, 'tis gone, 'tis gone!
You are welcome, gentlemen! Come, musicians, play.

Music plays, and they dance.

A hall, a hall![3] give room! and foot it, girls
More light, you knaves! and turn the tables up,
And quench the fire, the room is grown too hot.
Ah, sirrah, this unlooked-for sport[4] comes well.
Nay, sit, nay, sit, good cousin Capulet,
For you and I are past our dancing days.
How long is't now since last yourself and I
Were in a mask ?

2. *Capulet.*   By'r Lady, thirty years.[5]

Capulet. What, man? 'Tis not so much, 'tis not so much;
          'Tis since the nuptial of Lucentio,
          Come Pentecost as quickly as it will,
          Some five-and-twenty years, and then we masked.

2. *Capulet.* 'Tis more, 'tis more. His son is elder, sir;
          His son is thirty.

Capulet.   Will you tell me that?
          His son was but a ward two years ago.

Romeo. [*to a Servingman*] What lady's that, which doth
               enrich the hand
          Of yonder knight?

Servingman. I know not, sir.

Romeo. O, she doth teach the torches to burn bright!
          It seems she hangs upon the cheek of night
          As a rich jewel in an Ethiop's ear—
          Beauty too rich for use, for earth too dear!
          So shows a snowy dove trooping with crows
          As yonder lady o'er her fellows shows.
          The measure done, I'll watch her place of stand
          And, touching hers, make blessèd my rude[6] hand.

---

[3] **a hall** clear the hall for dancing
[4] **unlooked for sport** (a dance was not originally planned)
[5] **thirty years** (indicating Capulet's advanced age)
[6] **rude** coarse-skinned

Did my heart love till now? Forswear it, sight!

For I ne'er saw true beauty till this night.

Tybalt. This, by his voice, should be a Montague.

Fetch me my rapier, boy. What, dares the slave

Come hither, covered with an antic face,[7]

To fleer[8] and scorn at our solemnity?[9]

Now, by the stock and honor of my kin,

To strike him dead I hold it not a sin.

Capulet. Why, how now, kinsman? Wherefore storm you

so?

Tybalt. Uncle, this is a Montague, our foe;

A villain, that is hither come in spite

To scorn at our solemnity this night.

Capulet. Young Romeo is it?

Tybalt.   'Tis he, that villain Romeo.

Capulet. Content thee, gentle coz, let him alone.

'A bears him like a portly[10] gentleman,

And, to say truth, Verona brags of him

To be a virtuous and well-governed youth.

I would not for the wealth of all this town

Here in my house do him disparagement.

Therefore be patient, take no note of him.

It is my will, the which if thou respect,

Show a fair presence and put off these frowns.

An ill-beseeming semblance for a feast.

Tybalt. It fits when such a villain is a guest.

I'll not endure him.

Capulet.   He shall be endured.

What, goodman boy! I say he shall. Go to!

Am I the master here, or you? Go to!

You'll not endure him, God shall mend my soul![11]

You'll make a mutiny[12] among my guests!

You will set cock-a-hoop,[13] you'll be the man![14]

---

[7]**antic face** comic mask

[8]**fleer** mock

[9]**solemnity** dignified feast

[10]**portly** of good carriage

[11]**God . . . soul** (an expression of impatience)

[12]**mutiny** violent disturbance

[13]**set cock-a-hoop** take the lead

[14]**be the man** play the big man

Tybalt. Why, uncle, 'tis a shame.

Capulet.   Go to, go to!

You are a saucy boy. Is't so, indeed?

This trick may chance to scathe you. I know what.[15]

You must contrary me! Marry, 'tis time[16]—

Well said,[17] my hearts![18]—You are a princox[19]—go!

Be quiet, or—More light, more light!—For shame!

I'll make you quiet; what!—Cheerly, my hearts!

Tybalt. Patience perforce[20] with willful choler meeting

Makes my flesh tremble in their different greeting.

I will withdraw; but this intrusion shall,

Now seeming sweet, convert to bitt'rest gall.   [*Exit*]

Romeo. If I profane with my unworthiest hand

This holy shrine,[21] the gentle sin[22] is this;

My lips, two blushing pilgrims,[23] ready stand

To smooth that rough touch with a tender kiss.

Juliet. Good pilgrim, you do wrong your hand too much,

Which mannerly devotion shows in this;

For saints have hands that pilgrims' hands do touch,

And palm to palm is holy palmers'[24] kiss.[25]

Romeo. Have not saints lips, and holy palmers too?

Juliet. Ay, pilgrim, lips that they must use in prayer.

Romeo. O, then, dear saint, let lips do what hands do![26]

They pray; grant thou, lest faith turn to despair.

Juliet. Saints do not move,[27] though grant for prayers' sake.

Romeo. Then move not while my prayer's effect I take.

Thus from my lips, by thine my sin is purged.   [*Kisses her.*]

Juliet. Then have my lips the sin that they have took.

Romeo. Sin from my lips? O trespass sweetly urged!

---

[15]**what** what I am doing

[16]**'tis time** it's time you learned your place [?]

[17]**said** done

[18]**my hearts** (addressed to the dancers)

[19]**princox** saucy boy

[20]**Patience perforce** enforced self-restraint

[21]**shrine** Juliet's hand

[22]**sin** roughening her soft hand with his coarser one

[23]**pilgrims** (so called because pilgrims visit shrines)

[24]**palmers** religious pilgrims

[25]**Good . . . kiss** your touch is not rough, to heal it with a kiss is unnecessary, a handclasp is sufficient greeting

[26]**do what hands do** press each other (in a kiss)

[27]**move** take the initiative

Give me my sin again.   [*Kisses her*]

Juliet. You kiss by th' book.[28]

Nurse. Madam, your mother craves a word with you.

Romeo. What is her mother?

Nurse.   Marry, bachelor,

Her mother is the lady of the house,

And a good lady, and a wise and virtuous.

I nursed her daughter that you talked withal

I tell you, he that can lay hold of her

Shall have the chinks.[29]

Romeo.   Is she a Capulet?

O dear account! my life is my foe's debt.[30]

Benvolio. Away, be gone; the sport is at the best.

Romeo. Ay, so I fear; the more is my unrest.

Capulet. Nay, gentlemen, prepare not to be gone;

We have a trifling foolish banquet towards.[31]

Is it e'en so? Why then, I thank you all.

I thank you, honest gentlemen. Good night.

More torches here! Come on then, let's to bed.

Ah, sirrah, by my fay,[32] it waxes late;

I'll to my rest.   [*Exeunt all but Juliet and Nurse.*]

Juliet. Come hither, nurse. What is yond gentleman?

Nurse. The son and heir of old Tiberio.

Juliet. What's he that now is going out of door?

Nurse. Marry, that, I think, be young Petruchio.

Juliet. What's he that follows there, that would not dance?

Nurse. I know not.

Juliet. Go ask his name.—If he be married,

My grave is like to be my wedding bed.

Nurse. His name is Romeo, and a Montague,

The only son of your great enemy.

Juliet. My only love, sprung from my only hate!

Too early seen unknown, and known too late!

Prodigious[33] birth of love it is to me

That I must love a loathed enemy.

---

[28]**book** book of etiquette

[29]**chinks** money

[30]**my foe's debt** owed to my foe

[31]**banquet towards** light refreshments in preparation

[32]**fay** faith

[33]**prodigious** monstrous

Nurse. What's this? what's this?

Juliet.   A rhyme I learnt even now
    Of one I danced withal. [*One calls within,* 'Juliet.']

Nurse. Anon, anon!
    Come, let's away; the strangers all are gone.   *Exeunt.*

*

Act II, Scene ii. Location: orchard of the Capulets' home.
Stage Directions: Romeo enters

Romeo. [*coming forward*] He jests at scars that never felt a
    wound.

[*Enter Juliet above at a window.*]

                But soft! What light through yonder window breaks?
                It is the East, and Juliet is the sun!
                Arise, fair sun, and kill the envious moon,
                Who is already sick and pale with grief
                That thou her maid art far more fair than she.
                Be not her maid,[34] since she is envious.
                Her vestal livery[35] is but sick and green,[36]
                And none but fools do wear it. Cast it off.
                It is my lady; O, it is my love!
                O that she knew she were!
                She speaks, yet she says nothing. What of that?
                Her eye discourses; I will answer it.
                I am too bold; 'tis not to me she speaks.
                Two of the fairest stars in all the heaven,
                Having some business, do entreat her eyes
                To twinkle in their spheres[37] till they return.
                What if her eyes were there, they in her head?
                The brightness of her cheek would shame those stars
                As daylight doth a lamp; her eyes in heaven
                Would through the airy region stream so bright
                That birds would sing and think it were not night.
                See how she leans her cheek upon her hand!
                O that I were a glove upon that hand,

[34]**her maid** (Diana, moon-goddess, was patroness of virgins)
[35]**vestal livery** virginity (after Vesta, another virgin goddess)
[36]**green** anemic
[37]**spheres** orbits

That I might touch that cheek!

Juliet.   Ay me!

Romeo.   She speaks.

O, speak again, bright angel! for thou art

As glorious to this night, being o'er my head,

As is a winged messenger of heaven

Unto the white-upturnèd[38] wond'ring eyes

Of mortals that fall back to gaze on him

When he bestrides the lazy-pacing clouds

And sails upon the bosom of the air.

Juliet. O Romeo, Romeo! wherefore art thou Romeo?

Deny thy father and refuse thy name;

Or, if thou wilt not, be but sworn my love,

And I'll no longer be a Capulet.

Romeo. [*aside*] Shall I hear more, or shall I speak at this?

Juliet. 'Tis but thy name that is my enemy.

Thou art thyself, though not a Montague.

What's Montague? It is nor hand, nor foot,

Nor arm, nor face, nor any other part

Belonging to a man. O, be some other name!

What's in a name ? That which we call a rose

By any other name would smell as sweet.

So Romeo would, were he not Romeo called,

Retain that dear perfection which he owes[39]

Without that title. Romeo, doff thy name;

And for thy name, which is no part of thee,

Take all myself.

Romeo.   I take thee at thy word.

Call me but love, and I'll be new baptized;

Henceforth I never will be Romeo.

Juliet. What man art thou that, thus bescreened in night,

So stumblest on my counsel?

Romeo.   By a name

I know not how to tell thee who I am.

My name, dear saint, is hateful to myself,

Because it is an enemy to thee.

Had I it written, I would tear the word.

Juliet. My ears have yet not drunk a hundred words

---

[38]**white-upturnèd** (the whites show when the eyes are turned upward)

[39]**owes** owns

Of thy tongue's uttering, yet I know the sound.

Art thou not Romeo, and a Montague?

Romeo. Neither, fair maid, if either thee dislike.

Juliet. How camest thou hither, tell me, and wherefore?

The orchard walls are high and hard to climb,

And the place death, considering who thou art,

If any of my kinsmen find thee here.

Romeo. With love's light wings did I o'erperch[40] these walls;

For stony limits cannot hold love out,

And what love can do, that dares love attempt.

Therefore thy kinsmen are no stop to me.

Juliet. If they do see thee, they will murder thee.

Romeo. Alack, there lies more peril in thine eye

Than twenty of their swords! Look thou but sweet,

And I am proof against their enmity.

Juliet. I would not for the world they saw thee here.

Romeo. I have night's cloak to hide me from their eyes;

And but thou love me, let them find me here.

My life were better ended by their hate

Than death proroguèd,[41] wanting of[42] thy love.

Juliet. By whose direction found'st thou out this place?

Romeo. By love, that first did prompt me to inquire.

He lent me counsel, and I lent him eyes.

I am no pilot; yet, wert thou as far

As that vast shore washed with the farthest sea,

I should adventure for such merchandise.

Juliet. Thou knowest the mask of night is on my face;

Else would a maiden blush bepaint my cheek

For that which thou hast heard me speak to-night.

Fain would I dwell on form—fain, fain deny

What I have spoke; but farewell compliment![43]

Dost thou love me? I know thou wilt say 'Ay';

And I will take thy word. Yet, if thou swear'st,

Thou mayst prove false. At lovers' perjuries,

They say Jove laughs. O gentle Romeo,

If thou dost love, pronounce it faithfully.

[40] o'erperch fly over
[41] proroguèd postponed
[42] wanting of lacking
[43] compliment etiquette

Or if thou thinkest I am too quickly won,
I'll frown, and be perverse, and say thee nay,
So thou wilt woo; but else, not for the world.
In truth, fair Montague, I am too fond,
And therefore thou mayst think my havior[44] light;
But trust me, gentleman, I'll prove more true
Than those that have more cunning to be strange.[45]
I should have been more strange, I must confess,
But that thou overheard'st, ere I was ware,[46]
My true-love passion. Therefore pardon me,
And not impute this yielding to light love,
Which the dark night hath so discoverèd.[47]

Romeo. Lady, by yonder blessed moon I vow,
That tips with silver all these fruit-tree tops—

Juliet. O, swear not by the moon, th' inconstant moon,
That monthly changes in her circled orb,
Lest that thy love prove likewise variable.

Romeo. What shall I swear by?

Juliet.   Do not swear at all;
Or if thou wilt, swear by thy gracious self,
Which is the god of my idolatry,
And I'll believe thee.

Romeo.   If my heart's dear love—

Juliet. Well, do not swear. Although I joy in thee,
I have no joy of this contract to-night.
It is too rash, too unadvised, too sudden;
Too like the lightning, which doth cease to be
Ere one can say 'It lightens.' Sweet, good night!
This bud of love, by summer's ripening breath,
May prove a beauteous flow'r when next we meet.
Good night, good night! As sweet repose and rest
Come to thy heart as that within my breast!

Romeo. O, wilt thou leave me so unsatisfied?

Juliet. What satisfaction canst thou have to-night?

Romeo. Th' exchange of thy love's faithful vow for mine.

Juliet. I gave thee mine before thou didst request it;

---

[44]**havior** behavior
[45]**strange** aloof, distant
[46]**ware** aware of you
[47]**discoverèd** revealed

And yet I would it were to give again.

Romeo. Wouldst thou withdraw it? For what purpose, love?

Juliet. But to be frank[48] and give it thee again.

And yet I wish but for the thing I have.

My bounty[49] is as boundless as the sea,

My love as deep; the more I give to thee,

The more I have, for both are infinite.

I hear some noise within. Dear love, adieu!

                                        [*Nurse calls within.*]

Anon, good nurse! Sweet Montague, be true.

Stay but a little, I will come again.   [*Exit*]

Romeo. O blessed, blessed night! I am afeard,

Being in night, all this is but a dream,

Too flattering-sweet to be substantial.

[*Enter Juliet above.*]

Juliet. Three words, dear Romeo, and good night indeed.

If that thy bent of love be honorable,

Thy purpose marriage, send me word to-morrow,

By one that I'll procure to come to thee,

Where and what time thou wilt perform the rite;

And all my fortunes at thy foot I'll lay

And follow thee my lord throughout the world

Nurse. [within] Madam!

Juliet. I come, anon.—But if thou meanest not well

I do beseech thee—

Nurse. [*within*] Madam!

Juliet.   By and by I come.—

To cease thy suit and leave me to my grief

To-morrow will I send.

Romeo.   So thrive my soul—

Juliet. A thousand times good night!   [*Exit.*]

Romeo. A thousand times the worse, to want thy light!

Love goes toward love as schoolboys from their books;

But love from love, toward school with heavy looks.

                Enter Juliet [above] again.

[48]**frank** generous
[49]**bounty** wish to give (love)

Juliet. Hist! Romeo, hist! O for a falc'ner's voice
    To lure this tassel-gentle[50] back again!
    Bondage[51] is hoarse and may not speak aloud,
    Else would I tear the cave where Echo lies
    And make her airy tongue more hoarse than mine
    With repetition of 'My Romeo!'
Romeo. It is my soul that calls upon my name.
    How silver-sweet sound lovers' tongues by night,
    Like softest music to attending ears!
Juliet. Romeo!
Romeo. My sweet?
Juliet.   At what o'clock to-morrow
    Shall I send to thee?
Romeo.   By the hour of nine.
Juliet. I will not fail. 'Tis twenty years till then.
    I have forgot why I did call thee back.
Romeo. Let me stand here till thou remember it.
Juliet. I shall forget, to have thee still stand there,
    Rememb'ring how I love thy company.
Romeo. And I'll still stay, to have thee still forget,
    Forgetting any other home but this.
Juliet. 'Tis almost morning. I would have thee gone—
    And yet no farther than a wanton's[52] bird,
    That lets it hop a little from her hand,
    Like a poor prisoner in his twisted gyves,[53]
    And with a silken thread plucks it back again,
    So loving-jealous of his liberty.
Romeo. I would I were thy bird.
Juliet.   Sweet, so would I.
    Yet I should kill thee with much cherishing.[54]
    Good night, good night! Parting is such sweet sorrow
    That I shall say good night till it be morrow.   [*Exit*]
Romeo. Sleep dwell upon thine eyes, peace in thy breast!
    Would I were sleep and peace, so sweet to rest!

[50]**tassel-gentle** tercel-gentle or male falcon
[51]**Bondage** (she feels imprisoned by the nearness of her kinsman)
[52]**wanton** spoiled child
[53]**gyves** fetters
[54]**cherishing** caressing

Hence will I to my ghostly[55] father's cell,
His help to crave and my dear hap[56] to tell.   [*Exit*]

* * *

Act V. Scene iii. Lines 88–120. Location: a churchyard, at a tomb in a monument belonging to the Capulets

[*Romeo and Juliet were secretly married by the obliging Friar Laurence within days of their first meeting. By chance, Tybalt, Juliet's cousin, learned of their marriage and swore to kill Romeo on his return from the wedding. Romeo's friend, Mercutio, intervened and was killed by Tybalt. Romeo, to avenge Mercutio, challenged Tybalt to a duel and killed him, for which deed Romeo was then banished. To console Juliet, whom he mistakenly thought was grieving for Tybalt, Juliet's father arranged to marry her to Paris, a young count. Juliet appealed to Friar Laurence for help; he gave her a sleeping potion which would enable her to feign death and thus avoid the marriage. The sleeping Juliet was laid in a tomb, where she is visited by the grieving would-be bridegroom, Paris. Here Romeo comes upon him, the two of them fight, and Romeo kills Paris. Romeo lays Paris in the tomb with the "dead" Juliet and speaks as follows:*]

Romeo. . . .

How oft when men are at the point of death
Have they been merry! which their keepers[57] call
A lightning before death. O, how may I
Call this a lightning? O my love! my wife!
Death, that hath sucked the honey of thy breath,
Hath had no power yet upon thy beauty.
Thou art not conquered. Beauty's ensign[58] yet
Is crimson in thy lips and in thy cheeks,
And death's pale flag is not advancèd there.
                              . . . Ah, dear Juliet,
Why art thou yet so fair? Shall I believe
That unsubstantial Death is amorous,
And that the lean abhorrèd monster keeps
Thee here in dark to be his paramour?
For fear of that I will stay with thee
And never from this pallet dim night

---

[55]**ghostly** spiritual
[56]**dear hap** good luck
[57]**keepers** jailers
[58]**ensign** banner

Depart again. Here, here will I remain
With worms that are thy chambermaids. O, here
Will I set up my everlasting rest
And shake the yoke of inauspicious stars
From this world-wearied flesh. Eyes, look your last!
Arms, take your last embrace! and lips, O you
The doors of breath, seal with a righteous kiss
A dateless bargain to engrossing death!
Come, bitter conduct;[59] come, unsavory guide!
Thou desperate pilot,[60] now at once run on
The dashing rocks thy seasick weary bark![61]
Here's to my love! [*Drinks.*] O true apothecary!
Thy drugs are quick. Thus with a kiss I die.   [*Falls.*]

[59]**conduct** guide, i.e., the poison
[60]**pilot** i.e., Romeo's soul
[61]**bark** i.e., Romeo's body

Rousseau, *Emile:* Educating for Love

Rousseau, a partisan of romantic love, sought to transform it so as to overcome its tragic tendencies and to make it—for the first time—the basis of happy and durable marriage. The secret of this transformation lies in the right kind of sex education, one very different from the kind now in vogue. For Rousseau, sex education is neither about the human body, biologically understood, nor about how to make love, but about the capacity to love, which, for him, entirely depends upon the prior development of the imagination. In the two selections below (excerpted from early and late in Book IV), Rousseau begins by distinguishing natural (or instinctual) sexual attraction, which is generalized and indeterminate, from love, an acquired feeling, based on preference and choice, directed toward the one beloved. It is this passion that requires careful education. Accordingly, Rousseau begins by discussing how one should teach the mere "facts of life" to a child in order not to spoil the child's future prospects for love. In the second excerpt, Rousseau indicates how to render chastity desirable and, thereby, true love possible. He argues that one must join to the idea of the allure of the sex act "the idea of the exclusive attachment which makes it delicious, and the idea of the duties of fidelity and of modesty which surround it and redouble its charm in fulfilling its object." He further maintains that one must depict marriage—the union of hearts—as the "sweetest of associations and most inviolable and holiest of all contracts." In preparing Emile for this "supreme happiness," Rousseau vividly evokes the ideal woman (given the name Sophie) for whom Emile will then wish to search, caring little, it seems, whether the object he so depicts is merely imaginary. "What is true love itself," Rousseau provocatively asks, "if not chimera, lie, and illusion?"

This selection raises many important questions. Can one learn to be capable of love? If so, by what kinds of speech and stories, images and opinions? Does it matter, for the capacity to love, how and when one learns the "facts of life"? Does one learn to love by first loving an ideal, that is, by loving someone who does not really exist? Does fueling the imagination by providing an ideal sustain one's innocence or merely one's ignorance? Is love an illusion? If it is not itself an illusion, does it require illusions to sustain itself? If what one looks for is one's own ideal, that is, a projection of what one most desires oneself, can one's love for one's beloved (should one find him or her) ever be truly generous (that is, not merely narcissistic)?

As soon as man has need of a companion, he is no longer an isolated being. His heart is no longer alone. All his relations with his species, all the affections of his soul are born with this one. His first passion soon makes the others ferment.

The inclination of instinct is indeterminate. One sex is attracted to the other; that is the movement of nature. Choice, preferences, and personal attachments are the work of enlightenment, prejudice, and habit. Time and knowledge are required to make us capable of love. One loves only after having judged; one prefers only after having compared. These judgments are made without one's being aware of it, but they are nonetheless real. True love, whatever is said of it, will always be honored by men; for although its transports lead us astray, although it does not exclude odious qualities from the heart that feels it—and even produces them—it nevertheless always presupposes estimable qualities without which one would not be in a condition to feel it. This choosing, which is held to be the opposite of reason, comes to us from it. Love has been presented as blind because it has better eyes than we do and sees relations we are not able to perceive. For a man who had no idea of merit or beauty, every woman would be equally good, and the first comer would always be the most lovable. Far from arising from nature, love is the rule and the bridle of nature's inclinations. It is due to love that, except for the beloved object, one sex ceases to be anything for the other.

One wants to obtain the preference that one grants. Love must be reciprocal. To be loved, one has to make oneself lovable. To be preferred, one has to make oneself more lovable than another, more lovable than every other, at least in the eyes of the beloved object. This is the source of the first glances at one's fellows; this is the source of the first comparisons with them; this is the source of emulation, rivalries, and jealousy. A heart full of an overflowing sentiment likes to open itself. From the need for a mistress is soon born the need for a friend. He who senses how sweet it is to be loved would want to be loved by everyone; and all could not want preference without there being many malcontents. With love and friendship are born dissensions, enmity, and hate. From the bosom of so many diverse passions I see opinion raising an unshakable throne, and stupid mortals, subjected to its empire, basing their own existence on the judgments of others. . . .

If the age at which man acquires knowledge of his sex differs as much due to the effect of education as to the action of nature, it follows that this age can be accelerated or retarded according to the way in which children are raised; and if the body gains or loses consistency to the extent that this progress is retarded or accelerated, it follows again that the greater the effort made to retard it, the more a young man acquires vigor and force. I am still speaking only of purely physical effects. It will soon be seen that the effects are not limited to these.

From these reflections I draw the solution to the question so often debated—whether it is fitting to enlighten children early concerning the objects of their curiosity, or whether it is better to put them off the trail with little falsehoods? I think one ought to do neither the one nor the other. In the first place, this curiosity does not come to them without someone's having provided the occasion for it. One must therefore act in such a way that they do not have such curiosity. In the second place, questions one is not forced to answer do not require deceiving the child who asks them. It is better to impose silence on him than to answer him by lying. He will be little surprised by this law if care has been taken to subject him to it in inconsequential things. Finally, if one decides to answer, let it be with the greatest simplicity, without mystery, without embarrassment, without a smile. There is much less danger in satisfying the child's curiosity than there is in exciting it.

Let your responses always be solemn, short, and firm, without ever appearing to hesitate. I do not need to add that they ought to be true. One cannot teach children the danger of lying to men without being aware of the greater danger, on the part of men, of lying to children. A single proved lie told by the master to the child would ruin forever the whole fruit of the education. An absolute ignorance concerning certain matters is perhaps what would best suit children. But let them learn early what is impossible to hide from them always. Either their curiosity must not be aroused in any way, or it must be satisfied before the age at which it is no longer without danger. Your conduct with your pupil in this respect depends a great deal on his particular situation, the societies which surround him, the circumstances in which it is expected that he might find himself, etc. It is important here to leave nothing to chance; and if you are not sure of keeping him ignorant of the difference between the sexes until he is sixteen, take care that he learn it before he is ten.

I do not like it when too pure a language is affected with children or when long detours, which they notice, are made to avoid giving things their true names. Good morals in these matters always contain much simplicity, but imaginations soiled by vice make the ear delicate and force a constant refinement of expression. Coarse terms are inconsequential; it is lascivious ideas which must be kept away.

Although modesty is natural to the human species, naturally children have none. Modesty is born only with the knowledge of evil, and how could children, who do not and should not have this knowledge, have the sentiment which is its effect? To give them lessons in modesty and decency is to teach them that there are shameful and indecent things. It is to give them a secret desire to know those things. Sooner or later they succeed, and the first spark which touches the imagination inevitably accelerates the inflammation of the senses. Whoever blushes is already guilty. True innocence is ashamed of nothing. . . .

I see only one good means of preserving children in their innocence; it is for all those who surround them to respect and to love it. Without that, all the restraint one tries to use with them is sooner or later belied. A smile, a wink, a careless gesture, tells them everything one seeks to hide from them. To learn it, they need only see that one wanted to hide it from them. The delicacy of the turns of phrase and of the expressions which polite people use with one another is completely misplaced in relation to children since it assumes an enlightenment they ought not to have; but when one truly honors their simplicity, one easily takes on, in speaking to them, the simplicity of the terms which suit them. There is a certain naïveté of language which fits and pleases innocence. This is the true tone which turns a child away from a dangerous curiosity. In speaking simply to him about everything, one does not let him suspect that anything remains to be told him. In joining to coarse words the displeasing ideas suitable to them, the first fire of imagination is smothered. He is not forbidden to pronounce these words and to have these ideas; but without his being aware of it, he is made to have a repugnance against recalling them. And how much embarrassment this naïve freedom spares those who, drawing such freedom from their own hearts, always say what should be said and always say just what they feel!

"Where do children come from?" An embarrassing question which comes naturally enough to children, and to which an indiscreet or a prudent answer is sometimes decisive for their morals and their health for their whole lives. The most expeditious way that a mother can imagine for putting it off without deceiving her son is to impose silence on him. That would be good if one had accustomed him to it for a long time in regard to unimportant questions and he did not suspect mysteries in this new tone. But rarely does she leave it at that. "That's the secret of married people," she will tell him. "Little boys shouldn't be so curious." This is very good for getting the mother out of trouble. But she should know that the little boy, stung by this contemptuous air, will not have a moment's rest before he has learned the secret of married people, and that he will not be long in learning it.

Permit me to report a very different answer which I heard given to the same question, one which was all the more striking as it came from a woman as modest in her speech as in her manners. When necessary, however, she knew how to trample on the false fear of blame and the vain remarks of mockers for the sake of virtue and her son's good. Not long before the child had passed in his urine a little stone which had torn his urethra but had been forgotten when the illness passed. "Mama," said the giddy little fellow, "where do children come from?" "My child," answered the mother without hesitation, "women piss them out with pains which sometimes cost them their lives." Let madmen laugh and fools be scandalized; but let the wise consider whether they can ever find a more judicious answer or one that better achieves its purposes.

In the first place, the idea of a need which is natural and known to the child turns aside that of a mysterious process. The accessory ideas of pain and death cover this process with a veil of sadness which deadens the imagination and represses curiosity. Everything turns the mind toward the consequences of the delivery and not toward its causes. The infirmities of human nature, distasteful objects, images of suffering—these are the clarifications to which this answer leads, if the repugnance it inspires permits the child to ask for them. How will the restlessness of the desires be awakened in conversations thus directed? And, nevertheless, you see that the truth has not been adulterated and there was no need to take advantage of one's pupil instead of instructing him.

Your children read. From their reading they get knowledge they would not have if they had not read. If they study, the imagination catches fire and intensifies in the silence of their rooms. If they live in society, they hear odd talk; they see things that strike them. They have been well persuaded that they are men; therefore, whatever men do in their presence serves as the occasion for them to investigate how it applies to them. The actions of others must surely serve as models for them when the judgments of others serve as laws for them. The domestics who are made dependent on them, and are consequently interested in pleasing them, pay their court to them at the expense of good morals. Laughing governesses make remarks to them at four which the most brazen women would not dare to make to them at fifteen. Soon the governesses forget what they said, but the children do not forget what they heard. Naughty conversations prepare the way for libertine morals. The rascally lackey debauches the child, and the latter's secret acts as a guarantee for the former's. . . .

Do you wish to put order and regularity in the nascent passions? Extend the period during which they develop in order that they have the time to be arranged as they are born. Then it is not man who orders them; it is nature itself. Your care is only to let it arrange its work. If your pupil were alone, you would have nothing to do. But everything surrounding him influences his imagination. The torrent of prejudices carries him away. To restrain him, he must be pushed in the opposite direction. Sentiment must enchain imagination, and reason silence the opinion of men. The source of all the passions is sensibility; imagination determines their bent. Every being who has a sense of his relations ought to be affected when these relations are altered, and he imagines, or believes he imagines, others more suitable to his nature. It is the errors of imagination which transform into vices the passions of all limited beings—even those of angels, if they have any, for they would have to know the nature of all beings in order to know what relations best suit their nature.

This is, then, the summary of the whole of human wisdom in the use of the passions: (1) To have a sense of the true relations of man, with respect to the species as well as the individual. (2) To order all the affections of the soul according to these relations.

* * *

I even think that reflections on the true purity of speech and on the false delicacy of vice could have a useful place in the discussions about morality to which this subject leads us; for in learning the language of decency, Emile must also learn that of seemliness, and it is quite necessary that he learn why these two languages are so different. However that may be, I maintain that if one waits, instead of hammering vain precepts into the ears of the young before the proper time—precepts which they then mock at the age when they would be opportune; if one prepares the moment for making oneself understood; if one then expounds the laws of nature in all their truth; if one shows him the sanction of these same laws in the physical and moral ills that their infraction brings down upon the guilty; if in speaking of this inconceivable mystery of generation, one joins to the idea of the allure given to this act by the Author of nature the idea of the exclusive attachment which makes it delicious, and the idea of the duties of fidelity and of modesty which surround it and redouble its charm in fulfilling its object; if, in depicting marriage to him not only as the sweetest of associations but as the most inviolable and holiest of all contracts, one tells him forcefully all the reasons which make so sacred a bond respectable to all men, and which bring hatred and maledictions to whoever dares to stain its purity; if one presents him with a striking and true picture of the horrors of debauchery, of its foolish degradation, of the gradual decline by which a first disorder leads to them all and finally drags to destruction whoever succumbs to it; if, I say, one shows him clearly how the taste for chastity is connected with health, strength, courage, the virtues, love itself, and all the true goods of man, I maintain that one will then render this chastity desirable and dear to him and that his mind will be amenable to the means he will be given for preserving it; for, so long as chastity is preserved, it is respected; it is despised only after having been lost. . . .

Those who want to guide the young soberly, in order to preserve them from the traps of the senses, make love disgusting to them and would gladly make it a crime for them to think of it at their age, as though love were made for the old. All these deceitful lessons, to which the heart gives the lie, are not persuasive. The young man, guided by a surer instinct, secretly laughs at the gloomy maxims to which he feigns acquiescence, and all he waits for is the occasion to discard them. All this is contrary to nature. By following an opposite route, I shall more surely arrive at the same goal. I shall not be afraid to indulge him in the sweet sentiment for which he has such a thirst. I shall depict it to him as the supreme happiness of life, because in fact it is. In depicting it to him, I want him to yield to it. In making him sense how much charm the union of hearts adds to the attraction of the senses, I shall disgust him with libertinism, and I shall make him moderate by making him fall in love.

How limited one must be to see only an obstacle to the lessons of reason in the nascent desires of a young man! I see in them the true means of making him amenable to these very lessons. One has a hold on the passions only by means of the passions. It is by their empire that their tyranny must be combated; and it is always from nature itself that the proper instruments to regulate nature must be drawn.

Emile is not made to remain always solitary. As a member of society he ought to fulfill its duties. Since he is made to live with men, he ought to know them. He knows man in general; it remains for him to know individuals. He knows what is done in society; it remains for him to see how one lives in it. It is time to show him the exterior of this great stage, all of whose hidden mechanisms he already knows. He will bring to it no longer the stupid admiration of a giddy young man, but the discernment of a sound and exact mind. His passions will doubtless be able to lead him astray. When do they not lead astray those who yield to them? But at least he will not be deceived by the passions of others. If he sees them, it will be with the eyes of the wise man, and he will not be carried away by the example of others or seduced by their prejudices.

Just as there is a proper age for the study of the sciences, there is a proper age for getting a good grasp of social practices. Whoever learns these practices too young follows them throughout his whole life without selectivity, without reflection, and—despite his competence—without ever having clear knowledge of what he does. But he who learns these practices and sees the reasons for them follows them with more discernment and, consequently, with more exactness and grace. Give me a child of twelve who knows nothing at all; I should return him at fifteen to you as knowledgeable as the child you have instructed from the earliest age—but with the difference that your child's knowledge will be only in his memory, while mine's will be in his judgment. Similarly, introduce a young man of twenty into society; if he is well guided, in a year he will be more amiable and more judiciously polite than a young man who has been reared in society from childhood; for the former, capable of sensing the reasons for all the forms of conduct related to a given age, station, and sex—which constitute social custom—can reduce them to principles and extend them to unforeseen cases; whereas the latter, having nothing but his routine as a guiding rule, is in trouble as soon as he departs from it. . . .

. . . My expedient by itself provides for everything. "Your heart," I say to the young man, "needs a companion. Let us go seek her who suits you. We shall not easily find her perhaps. True merit is always rare. But let us neither be in a hurry nor become disheartened. Doubtless there is such a woman and in the end we shall find her, or at least the one who is most like her." With a project that is so appealing to him, I introduce him into society. What need have I to say more? Do you not see that I have done everything?

Imagine whether I shall know how to get his ear when I depict the beloved whom I destine for him. Imagine whether I shall know how to make agreeable and dear to him the qualities he ought to love, whether I shall know how to make all his sentiments properly disposed with respect to what he ought to seek or to flee? I would have to be the clumsiest of men not to be able to make him passionate in advance of his knowing about whom. It is unimportant whether the object I depict for him is imaginary; it suffices that it make him disgusted with those that could tempt him; it suffices that he everywhere find comparisons which make him prefer his chimera to the real objects that strike his eye. And what is true love itself if it is not chimera, lie, and illusion? We love the image we make for ourselves far more than we love the object to which we apply it. If we saw what we love exactly as it is, there would be no more love on earth. When we stop loving, the person we loved remains the same as before, but we no longer see her in the same way. The magic veil drops, and love disappears. But, by providing the imaginary object, I am the master of comparisons, and I easily prevent my young man from having illusions about real objects.

For all that, I do not want to deceive a young man by depicting for him a model of perfection which cannot exist. But I shall choose such defects in his beloved as to suit him, as to please him, and to serve to correct his own. Nor do I want to lie to him by falsely affirming that the object depicted for him exists. But if he takes pleasure in the image, he will soon hope that it has an original. From the hope to the supposition, the path is easy; it is a matter of some skillful descriptions which clothe this imaginary object with features he can grasp with his senses and give it a greater air of truth. I would go so far as to give her a name. I would say, laughing, "Let us call your future beloved Sophie. The name Sophie augurs well. If the girl whom you choose does not bear it, she will at least be worthy of bearing it. We can do her the honor in advance." If, after giving all these details, you neither affirm nor deny her existence but slip out of it by evasions, his suspicions will turn into certainty. He will believe that you are keeping a secret about the spouse who is intended for him and that he will see her when the time has come. Once he is at that point, and if you have chosen well the features he should be showed, all the rest is easy. He can be exposed to society almost without risk. Defend him only against his senses; his heart is safe.

But whether or not he believes the model I have succeeded in making lovable to him is a real person, this model, if well made, will nonetheless attach him to everything resembling it and will estrange him from everything not resembling it, just as if his passion had a real object. What an advantage this is for preserving his heart from the dangers to which his person must be exposed; for repressing his senses by his imagination; and especially for tearing him away from those ladies who give an education that is purchased so dearly and who teach a young man good manners only by taking all decency from him! Sophie is so modest! How will he view their advances? Sophie has so much simplicity! How will he like their airs? Too great a distance separates his ideas from his observations for the latter ever to be dangerous to him.

All those who speak of the governance of children adhere to the same prejudices and the same maxims, because they observe badly and reflect still worse. It is due to neither temperament nor the senses that the wildness of youth begins; it is due to opinion. . . . Take a young man soberly raised in his father's home in the country, and examine him at the moment he arrives in Paris or enters society. You will find that he is right-thinking about decent things and even that his will is as healthy as his reason. You will find in him contempt for vice and horror of debauchery. At the very mention of a prostitute you will see scandalized innocence in his eyes. I maintain that there is not one such young man who can resolve to enter by himself the gloomy abodes of these unfortunate women, even if he were to know their use and to feel the need of them.

Consider the same young man again six months later. You will no longer recognize him. The easy talk, the fashionable maxims, the jaunty bearing would cause him to be taken for a different man, if his jokes about his former simplicity, and his shame when it is recalled to him, did not show that he is the same man and that this fact makes him blush. O how much he has been educated in so short a time! Whence comes so great and so sudden a change? From the progress of temperament? Would his temperament not have made the same progress in his paternal home? And there, surely, he would have acquired neither this style nor these maxims. From the first pleasures of the senses? On the contrary. When one begins to yield to these pleasures, one is fearful and uneasy; one flees broad daylight and gossip. The first delights are always mysterious. Modesty seasons them and hides them. His first mistress makes a man not brazen but timid. Totally absorbed in a condition so new for him, the young man withdraws into himself to enjoy it and constantly dreads losing it. If he is loud, he is neither voluptuous nor tender. So long as he boasts, he has not enjoyed.

New ways of thinking have by themselves produced these differences. His heart is still the same, but his opinions have changed. His sentiments, slower to alter, will eventually be spoiled by these opinions, and it is only then that he will be truly corrupted. He has hardly entered society when he receives there a second education completely opposed to his first, an education from which he learns to despise what he esteemed and to esteem what he despised. He is made to regard the lessons of his parents and his masters as a pedantic jargon and the duties they have preached to him as a puerile morality that ought to be disdained when one has grown up. He believes himself honor-bound to change his conduct. He becomes a seducer without desires and a fop out of fear of ridicule. He mocks good morals before having gotten the taste for bad ones and prides himself on debauchery without knowing how to be debauched. I shall never forget the admission of a young officer in the Swiss Guards who was greatly bored by the brazen pleasures of his comrades but did not dare to abstain for fear of being ridiculed. "I am getting practice at that," he said, "as I am at taking tobacco in spite of my repugnance. The taste will come from habit. One must not remain a child forever."

Thus, a young man entering society must be preserved less from sensuality than from vanity. He yields more to the inclinations of others than to his own, and *amour-propre* produces more libertines than love does.

Therefore I ask whether there is a young man on the entire earth who is better armed than Emile against everything that can attack his morals, his sentiments, or his principles? Whether there is one better prepared to resist the torrent? For against what seduction is he not on guard? If his desires lead him to women, he does not find what he is looking for, and his preoccupied heart holds him back. If his senses agitate and impel him, where will he find the means of satisfying them? His horror of adultery and debauchery keeps him away from both prostitutes and married women, and it is always with one of these two classes of women that the disorders of youth begin. A marriageable girl may be coquettish, but she will not be brazen; she will not throw herself at a young man who might marry her if he believes her to be chaste. Besides, she will have someone looking after her. Nor will Emile be left completely to himself. Both will at least be guarded by fear and shame, which are inseparable from our first desires. They will not immediately proceed to extreme familiarities, and they will not have the time to get to them by degrees without hindrance. To go about it otherwise, Emile would have to have already taken lessons from his comrades, to have learned from them to regard his restraint as ridiculous, and to have become insolent in imitation of them. But who in the world is less of an imitator than Emile? Who is less governed by ridicule than the man who has no prejudices and does not know how to concede anything to those of others? I have worked for twenty years to arm Emile against mockers. They will need more than a day to make him their dupe; for in his eyes ridicule is only the argument of fools, and nothing makes one more insensitive to mockery than being above opinion. Instead of jokes, he has to have reasons; and so long as that is the case, I am not afraid that wild young men are going to take him from me. I have conscience and truth on my side. If prejudice has to be mixed in, an attachment of twenty years is also something. Emile will never be made to believe that I bored him with vain lessons; and in an honest and sensitive heart, the voice of a faithful and true friend can surely drown out the cries of twenty seducers. Since it then becomes only a question of showing him that they deceive him and that, in feigning to treat him as a man, they really treat him as a child, I shall always use arguments that are simple but grave and clear, so that he will sense that it is I who treat him like a man. I shall say to him, "You see that your interest alone, which is also mine, dictates my speeches; I can have no other interest. But why do these young people want to persuade you? It is because they want to seduce you. They do not love you. They take no interest in you. Their whole motive is a secret spite at seeing that you are better than they are. They want to bring you down to their low level, and they reproach you for letting yourself be governed only in order to govern you themselves. Can you believe that there would be any profit for you in this change? Is their wisdom, then, so superior, and is their brief attachment to you stronger than mine? To give some weight to their ridicule, one would have to be able to give some weight to their authority; but what experience do they have that would make their maxims superior to ours? All they have done is to imitate other giddy fellows, just as they want to be imitated in their turn. To set themselves above the alleged prejudices of their fathers, they enslave themselves to those of their comrades. I do not see what they gain by that, but I do see that they surely lose two great advantages: paternal affection, which provides tender and sincere advice; and experience, which allows one to judge what one knows; for fathers have been children, and children have not been fathers.

"But do you believe that they are at least sincere in their rash maxims? Not even that, dear Emile. They deceive themselves in order to deceive you. They are not in harmony with themselves. Their hearts constantly give them the lie, and their mouths often contradict them. One man derides everything decent but would be in despair if his wife thought as he does. Another will extend his indifference about morals to those of the wife he does not yet have or—the crown of infamy—to those of the wife he already has. But go farther; speak to him of his mother, and see if he will gladly be looked upon as a child of adultery and the son of a woman of easy virtue, as one who has wrongfully assumed a family name, as a thief of the natural heir's patrimony; finally, see if he will patiently allow himself to be called a bastard! Who among them will want to have his own daughter dishonored as he dishonors the daughter of another? There is not one of them who would not make an attempt upon your very life if in practice you adopted toward him all the principles he makes an effort to teach you. It is thus that they finally disclose their inconsistency and that one senses that none of them believes what he says. These are my arguments, dear Emile. Weigh them against theirs, if they have any, and compare them. If I wanted to use contempt and ridicule as they do, you would see that they leave themselves open to ridicule as much as and perhaps more than I do. But I am not afraid of a serious examination. The triumph of mockers does not last long. Truth remains, and their foolish laughter vanishes."

Shakespeare, Sonnets 18, 115, and 116

Romantic love and poetry are so closely linked that each is given credit as the source of the other: love inspires the poet, whose paeans to love feed the imagination, without which love is thought not to be possible. Yet in his sonnets (first printed together in 1609), as in his romantic comedies, Shakespeare suggests alternatives to the tragic form of romantic love that, like Romeo's and Juliet's, is actualized only in death. His meaning is conveyed as much by the brevity and form of the sonnets, as by their pregnant similes and pithy concluding couplets. For example, the fixed rhyme scheme—ababcdcdefefgg—of these fourteen-line, ten-syllable-per-line poems about love tacitly suggests that orderly speech and formal convention can discipline and educate passion and, by acknowledging the necessary ravages of time, can save love from life's unavoidable decay. In the three sonnets selected here, the lover-poet implies that the poems themselves—their writing, as well as their having been written, the reading of them, as well as their having been read—are acts of love, enabling lovers to (respectively) preserve, augment, and elevate their love. Addressing himself to a particular beloved, the lover-poet of Sonnet 18 extols the beauty of his beloved—indeed, he seems to love her for her beauty— which he seeks to hold fast by means of his "eternal lines." The seemingly more mature lover-poet of Sonnet 115 corrects an earlier belief which celebrated youthful love in favor of a view which holds that love can grow and burn with clearer flame despite—perhaps because of—the ravages of time. For the more philosophical poet of Sonnet 116, lasting love is regarded as a marriage of true (that is, loyal and fitting) minds. In none of these sonnets does love seem tragic. Do any of them describe a love suitable for marriage?

Sonnet 18

Shall I compare thee to a summer's day?
Thou art more lovely and more temperate.
Rough winds do shake the darling buds of May,
And summer's lease hath all too short a date.
Sometime too hot the eye of heaven shines,
And often is his gold complexion dimmed.
And every fair from fair sometime declines,
By chance or nature's changing course untrimmed.
But thy eternal summer shall not fade,
Nor lose possession of that fair thou owest,
Nor shall Death brag thou wander'st in his shade

When in eternal lines to time thou grow'st.
>   So long as men can breathe, or eyes can see,
>   So long lives this, and this gives life to thee.

Sonnet 115

Those lines that I before have writ do lie,
Even those that said I could not love you dearer.
Yet then my judgment knew no reason why
My most full flame should afterward burn clearer.
But reckoning Time, whose millioned accidents
Creep in 'twixt vows, and change decrees of kings,
Tan sacred beauty, blunt the sharp'st intents,
Divert strong minds to the course of alterning things—
Alas, why, fearing of Time's tyranny,
Might I not then say, "Now I love you best,"
When I was certain o'er incertainty,
Crowning the present, doubting of the rest?
>   Love is a babe, then might I not say so,
>   To give full growth to that which still doth grow?

Sonnet 116

Let me not to the marriage of true minds
Admit impediments. Love is not love
Which alters when it alteration finds,
Or bends with the remover to remove.
Oh no! It is an ever-fixèd mark
That looks on tempests and is never shaken.
It is the star to every wandering bark,
Whose worth's unknown, although his height be taken.
Love's not Time's fool, though rosy lips and cheeks
Within his bending sickle's compass come.
Love alters not with his brief hours and weeks,
But bears it out even to the edge of doom.
>   If this be error and upon me proved,
>   I never writ, nor no man ever loved.

Rilke, Letters on Love

Love was a central theme of the poems and letters of the early twentieth-century German poet, Rainer Maria Rilke (1875–1926). His thoughts on the subject are unconventional, radical, hard-headed yet full-hearted. In the first of these three selections from his letters, he offers favorable comment on Socrates' speech on eros in Plato's Symposium. *In the second, he criticizes the youthful or romantic passion that seeks merging and togetherness, that wants to make one out of two. Love, according to Rilke, is rather the difficult work of preserving and nurturing in the beloved a deep, wide, and rich individuality—in Rilke's terms, "solitude." It is, in fact, this kind of love Rilke recommends for marriage, the subject of the third selection. What is the difference between "loneness" of solitude and loneliness? Is respect for such solitude a mark of true love and compatible with marriage?*

I

Do you know what I felt like, leafing through Plato's *Symposium* for the first time in a long while? When I first read it, I dwelt alone in Rome in a tiny house deep in an ancient park. . . . My friend, I grasped one thing then, predisposed as I may have been—there is no beauty in Eros; and when Socrates said so and in his cautious way waited for his younger and more volatile conversational antagonist to block all other paths, one by one, leaving but the one way open—that Eros is not beautiful—Socrates himself then walking that path toward his god, serene and pure in heart—how then my innermost nature took fire that Eros could not be fair! I saw him just as Socrates had invoked him, lean and hard and always a little out of breath, sleepless, troubled day and night about the two between whom he trod, to and fro, hither and yon, ceaselessly accosted by both: yes, that was Eros. Truly, how they mistook him who thought he was fair, envied his soft life. Ah, he was slender and tanned and covered with the dust of the road, but there was no peace for him amid the two of them (for when, I say, is there not distance left between them?); and when he came he spoke with fervor of the other's beauty, teasing each heart to grow fairer, goading it on. Surely there is much in the book—we do not grasp it yet: once upon a time it *was* grasped—who lost it? How do we spend the centuries? Where is he among us who dare speak of *love?*

II

At bottom no one in life can help anyone else in life; this one experiences over and over in every conflict and every perplexity: that one is alone.

All companionship can consist only in the strengthening of two neighboring solitudes, whereas everything that one is wont to call giving oneself is by
nature harmful to companionship: for when a person abandons himself, he is
no longer anything, and when two people both give themselves up in order to
come close to each other, there is no longer any ground beneath them and their
being together is a continual falling.

There is scarcely anything more difficult than to love one another. That it
is work, day labor, day labor, God knows there is no other word for it. And
look, added to this is the fact that young people are not prepared for such difficult loving; for convention has tried to make this most complicated and ultimate relationship into something easy and frivolous, has given it the appearance of everyone's being able to do it. It is not so. Love is something difficult
and it is more difficult than other things because in other conflicts nature herself enjoins men to collect themselves, to take themselves firmly in hand with
all their strength, while in the heightening of love the impulse is to give oneself
wholly away. But just think, can that be anything beautiful, to give oneself
away not as something whole and ordered, but haphazard rather, bit by bit, as
it comes? Can such giving away, that looks so like a throwing away and dis-
memberment, be anything good, can it be happiness, joy, progress? No, it cannot. . . . When you give someone flowers, you arrange them beforehand, don't
you? But young people who love each other fling themselves to each other in
the impatience and haste of their passion, and they don't notice at all what a
lack of mutual esteem lies in this disordered giving of themselves; they notice
it with astonishment and indignation only from the dissension that arises between them out of all this disorder. And once there is disunity between them,
the confusion grows with every day; neither of the two has anything unbroken,
pure, and unspoiled about him any longer, and amid the disconsolateness of a
break they try to hold fast to the semblance of their happiness (for all that was
really supposed to be for the sake of happiness). Alas, they are scarcely able to
recall any more what they meant by happiness. In his uncertainty each becomes
more and more unjust toward the other; they who wanted to do each other
good are now handling one another in an imperious and intolerant manner,
and in the struggle somehow to get out of their untenable and unbearable state
of confusion, they commit the greatest fault that can happen to human relationships: they become impatient. They hurry to a conclusion; to come, as they
believe, to a final decision, they try once and for all to establish their relationship, whose surprising changes have frightened them, in order to remain the
same now and *forever* (as they say). That is only the last error in this long chain
of errings linked fast to one another. What is dead cannot even be clung to (for
it crumbles and changes its character); how much less can what is living and
alive be treated definitively, once and for all. Self-transformation is precisely
what life is, and human relationships, which are an extract of life, are the most

changeable of all, rising and falling from minute to minute, and lovers are those in whose relationship and contact no one moment resembles another. People between whom nothing accustomed, nothing that has already been present before ever takes place, but many new, unexpected, unprecedented things. There are such relationships which must be a very great, almost unbearable happiness, but they can occur only between very rich natures and between those who, each for himself, are richly ordered and composed; they can unite only two wide, deep, individual worlds.—Young people—it is obvious—cannot achieve such a relationship, but they can, if they understand their life properly, grow up slowly to such happiness and prepare themselves for it. They must not forget, when they love, that they are beginners, bunglers of life, apprentices in love,—must *learn* love, and that (like *all* learning) wants peace, patience, and composure!

To take love seriously and to bear and to learn it like a task, this it is that young people need.—Like so much else, people have also misunderstood the place of love in life, they have made it into play and pleasure because they thought that play and pleasure were more blissful than work; but there is nothing happier than work, and love, just because it is the extreme happiness, can be nothing else but work.—So whoever loves must try to act as if he had a great work: he must be much alone and go into himself and collect himself and hold fast to himself; he must work: he must become something!

For believe me, the more one is, the richer is all that one experiences. And whoever wants to have a deep love in his life must collect and save for it and gather honey.

To love is good, too: love being difficult. For one human being to love another: that is perhaps the most difficult of all our tasks, the ultimate, the last test and proof, the work for which all other work is but preparation. For this reason young people, who are beginners in everything, cannot yet know love: they have to learn it. With their whole being, with all their forces, gathered close about their lonely, timid, upward-beating heart, they must learn to love. But learning-time is always a long, secluded time, and so loving, for a long while ahead and far on into life, is—solitude, intensified and deepened loneness for him who loves. Love is at first not anything that means merging, giving over, and uniting with another (for what would a union be of something unclarified and unfinished, still subordinate—?); it is a high inducement to the individual to ripen, to become something in himself, to become world, to become world for himself for another's sake; it is a great exacting claim upon him, something that chooses him out and calls him to vast things. Only in this sense, as the task of working at themselves ("to hearken and to hammer day and night"), might young people use the love that is given them. Merging and surrendering and every kind of communion is not for them (who must save and gather for a long, long time still), is the ultimate, is perhaps that for which human lives as yet scarcely suffice.

But young people err so often and so grievously in this: that they (in whose nature it lies to have no patience) fling themselves at each other, when love takes possession of them, scatter themselves, just as they are, in all their untidiness, disorder, confusion. . . . And then what? What is life to do to this heap of half-battered existence which they call their communion and which they would gladly call their happiness if it were possible, and their future? Thus each loses himself for the sake of the other and loses the other and many others that wanted still to come. And loses the expanses and the possibilities, exchanges the approach and flight of gentle, divining things for an unfruitful perplexity out of which nothing can come any more, nothing save a little disgust, disillusionment and poverty, and rescue in one of the many conventions that have been put up in great number like public refuges along this most dangerous road. No realm of human experience is so well provided with conventions as this: life-preservers of most varied invention, boats and swimming-bladders are here; the social conception has managed to supply shelters of every sort, for, as it was disposed to take love-life as a pleasure it had also to give it an easy form, cheap, safe and sure, as public pleasures are.

It is true that many young people who wrongly, that is, simply with abandon and unsolitarily (the average will of course always go on doing so), feel the oppressiveness of a failure and want to make the situation in which they have landed viable and fruitful in their own personal way—; for their nature tells them that, less even than all else that is important, can questions of love be solved publicly and according to this or that agreement; that they are questions, intimate questions from one human being to another, which in any case demand a new, special, *only* personal answer—: but how should they, who have already flung themselves together and no longer mark off and distinguish themselves from each other, who therefore no longer possess anything of their own selves, be able to find a way out of themselves, out of the depth of their already shattered solitude?

They act out of common helplessness, and then, if, with the best intentions, they try to avoid the convention that occurs to them (say, marriage), they land in the tentacles of some less loud, but equally deadly conventional solution; for then everything far around them is—convention; where people act out of a prematurely fused, turbid communion, *every* move is convention: every relation to which such entanglement leads has its convention, be it ever so unusual (that is, in the ordinary sense immoral); why, even separation would here be a conventional step, an impersonal chance decision without strength and without fault.

Whoever looks seriously at it finds that neither for death, which is difficult, nor for difficult love has any explanation, any solution, any hint or way yet been discerned; and for these two problems that we carry wrapped up and hand on without opening, it will not be possible to discover any general rule resting in agreement. But in the same measure in which we begin as individuals to put life to the test, we shall, being individuals, meet these great things at closer range. The demands which the difficult work of love makes upon our development are more than life-size, and as beginners we are not up to them. But if we nevertheless hold out and take this love upon us as burden and apprenticeship, instead of losing ourselves in all the light and frivolous play, behind which people have hidden from the most earnest earnestness of their existence—then a little progress and an alleviation will perhaps be perceptible to those who come long after us; that would be much.

III

I hold this to be the highest task of a bond between two people: that each should stand guard over the solitude of the other. For, if it lies in the nature of indifference and of the crowd to recognize no solitude, then love and friendship are there for the purpose of continually providing the opportunity for solitude. And only those are the true sharings which rhythmically interrupt periods of deep isolation. . . .

I am of the opinion that "marriage" as such does not deserve as much emphasis as it has acquired through the conventional development of its nature. It does not occur to anyone to expect a single person to be "happy,"—but if he marries, people are much surprised if he *isn't!* (And for that matter it really isn't at all important to be happy, whether single or married.) Marriage is, in many respects, a simplification of one's way of life, and the union naturally combines the forces and wills of two young people so that, together, they seem to reach farther into the future than before.—Only, those are sensations by which one cannot live. Above all, marriage is a new task and a new seriousness,—a new challenge to and questioning of the strength and generosity of each partner and a great new danger for both.

It is a question in marriage, to my feeling, not of creating a quick community of spirit by tearing down and destroying all boundaries, but rather a good marriage is that in which each appoints the other guardian of his solitude, and shows him this confidence, the greatest in his power to bestow. A *togetherness* between two people is an impossibility, and where it seems, nevertheless, to exist, it is a narrowing, a reciprocal agreement which robs either one party or both of his fullest freedom and development. But, once the realization is accepted that even between the *closest* human beings infinite distances continue to exist, a wonderful living side by side can grow up, if they succeed in loving the distance between them which makes it possible for each to see the other whole and against a wide sky!

Therefore this too must be the standard for rejection or choice: whether one is willing to stand guard over the solitude of a person and whether one is inclined to set this same person at the gate of one's own solitude, of which he learns only through that which steps, festively clothed, out of the great darkness.

Lewis, "Eros"

In an accessible and beautifully written book, The Four Loves *(published in 1960), the prolific English novelist, essayist, and Christian humanist, C. S. Lewis (1898–1963), compares and contrasts the fundamental species of human loving: Affection, Friendship, Eros, and Charity. The chapter on Eros, reproduced here in its entirety, illuminates many familiar yet puzzling aspects of being in love. Lewis explores the place of Venus (or sex) within erotic love; exposes both the seriousness and the humor in erotic love; compares what he calls the pagan sacrament of love with the Christian one; and makes vivid how eros can set itself up as a god to be worshipped. His account invites us to ask whether he is right in maintaining that eros is necessarily fickle or in implying that one can have multiple relationships based on love (rather than lust). For our present purposes, it is useful also to observe how, for Lewis, eros can indeed be a healthy seed of marriage, but only if it is finally brought under the rule of a higher love, charity, to which Lewis believes eros points. What does Lewis mean by suggesting that eros, left to itself, cannot be itself or keep the promises it makes, outside the larger context of charity and fidelity?*

By Eros I mean of course that state which we call "being in love"; or, if you prefer, that kind of love which lovers are "in." Some readers may have been surprised when, in an earlier chapter, I described Affection as the love in which our experience seems to come closest to that of the animals. Surely, it might be asked, our sexual functions bring us equally close? This is quite true as regards human sexuality in general. But I am not going to be concerned with human sexuality simply as such. Sexuality makes part of our subject only when it becomes an ingredient in the complex state of "being in love." That sexual experience can occur without Eros, without being "in love," and that Eros includes other things besides sexual activity, I take for granted. If you prefer to put it that way, I am inquiring not into the sexuality which is common to us and the beasts or even common to all men but into one uniquely human variation of it which develops within "love"—what I call Eros. The carnal or animally sexual element within Eros, I intend (following an old usage) to call Venus. And I mean by Venus what is sexual not in some cryptic or rarefied sense—such as a depth-psychologist might explore—but in a perfectly obvious sense; what is known to be sexual by those who experience it; what could be proved to be sexual by the simplest observations.

Sexuality may operate without Eros or as part of Eros. Let me hasten to add that I make the distinction simply in order to limit our inquiry and without any moral implications. I am not at all subscribing to the popular idea that it is the absence or presence of Eros which makes the sexual act "impure" or "pure," degraded or fine, unlawful or lawful. If all who lay together without being in the state of Eros were abominable, we all come of tainted stock. The times and places in which marriage depends on Eros are in a small minority. Most of our ancestors were married off in early youth to partners chosen by their parents on grounds that had nothing to do with Eros. They went to the act with no other "fuel," so to speak, than plain animal desire. And they did right; honest Christian husbands and wives, obeying their fathers and mothers, discharging to one another their "marriage debt," and bringing up families in the fear of the Lord. Conversely, this act, done under the influence of a soaring and iridescent Eros which reduces the role of the senses to a minor consideration, may yet be plain adultery, may involve breaking a wife's heart, deceiving a husband, betraying a friend, polluting hospitality and deserting your children. It has not pleased God that the distinction between a sin and a duty should turn on fine feelings. This act, like any other, is justified (or not) by far more prosaic and definable criteria; by the keeping or breaking of promises, by justice or injustice, by charity or selfishness, by obedience or disobedience. My treatment rules out mere sexuality—sexuality without Eros—on grounds that have nothing to do with morals; because it is irrelevant to our purpose.

To the evolutionist Eros (the human variation) will be something that grows out of Venus, a late complication and development of the immemorial biological impulse. We must not assume, however, that this is necessarily what happens within the consciousness of the individual. There may be those who have first felt mere sexual appetite for a woman and then gone on at a later stage to "fall in love with her." But I doubt if this is at all common. Very often what comes first is simply a delighted pre-occupation with the Beloved—a general, unspecified pre-occupation with her in her totality. A man in this state really hasn't leisure to think of sex. He is too busy thinking of a person. The fact that she is a woman is far less important than the fact that she is herself. He is full of desire, but the desire may not be sexually toned. If you asked him what he wanted, the true reply would often be, "To go on thinking of her." He is love's contemplative. And when at a later stage the explicitly sexual element awakes, he will not feel (unless scientific theories are influencing him) that this had all along been the root of the whole matter. He is more likely to feel that the incoming tide of Eros, having demolished many sand-castles and made islands of many rocks, has now at last with a triumphant seventh wave flooded this part of his nature also—the little pool of ordinary sexuality which was there on his beach before the tide came in. Eros enters him like an invader, taking over and reorganising, one by one, the institutions of a conquered country. It may have taken over many others before it reaches the sex in him; and it will reorganise that too.

No one has indicated the nature of that reorganisation more briefly and accurately than George Orwell, who disliked it and preferred sexuality in its native condition, uncontaminated by Eros. In *Nineteen Eighty-Four* his dreadful hero (how much less human than the four-footed heroes of his excellent *Animal Farm!*), before towsing the heroine, demands a reassurance, "You like doing this?" he asks, "I don't mean simply me; I mean the thing in itself." He is not satisfied till he gets the answer, "I adore it." This little dialogue defines the reorganisation. Sexual desire, without Eros, wants *it*, the *thing in itself*; Eros wants the Beloved.

The *thing* is a sensory pleasure; that is, an event occurring within one's own body. We use a most unfortunate idiom when we say, of a lustful man prowling the streets, that he "wants a woman." Strictly speaking, a woman is just what he does not want. He wants a pleasure for which a woman happens to be the necessary piece of apparatus. How much he cares about the woman as such may be gauged by his attitude to her five minutes after fruition (one does not keep the carton after one has smoked the cigarettes). Now Eros makes a man really want, not a woman, but one particular woman. In some mysterious but quite indisputable fashion the lover desires the Beloved herself, not the pleasure she can give. No lover in the world ever sought the embraces of the woman he loved as the result of a calculation, however unconscious, that they would be more pleasurable than those of any other woman. If he raised the question he would, no doubt, expect that this would be so. But to raise it would be to step outside the world of Eros altogether. The only man I know of who ever did raise it was Lucretius, and he was certainly not in love when he did. It is interesting to note his answer. That austere voluptuary gave it as his opinion that love actually impairs sexual pleasure. The emotion was a distraction. It spoiled the cool and critical receptivity of his palate. (A great poet; but "Lord, what beastly fellows these Romans were!")

The reader will notice that Eros thus wonderfully transforms what is *par excellence* a Need-pleasure into the most Appreciative of all pleasures. It is the nature of a Need-pleasure to show us the object solely in relation to our need, even our momentary need. But in Eros, a Need, at its most intense, sees the object most intensely as a thing admirable in herself, important far beyond her relation to the lover's need.

If we had not all experienced this, if we were mere logicians, we might boggle at the conception of desiring a human being, as distinct from desiring any pleasure, comfort, or service that human being can give. And it is certainly hard to explain. Lovers themselves are trying to express part of it (not much) when they say they would like to "eat" one another. Milton has expressed more when he fancies angelic creatures with bodies made of light who can achieve total interpenetration instead of our mere embraces. Charles Williams has said something of it in the words, "Love you? I *am* you."

Without Eros sexual desire, like every other desire, is a fact about ourselves. Within Eros it is rather about the Beloved. It becomes almost a mode of perception, entirely a mode of expression. It feels objective; something outside us, in the real world. That is why Eros, though the king of pleasures, always (at his height) has the air of regarding pleasure as a by-product. To think about it would plunge us back in ourselves, in our own nervous system. It would kill Eros, as you can "kill" the finest mountain prospect by locating it all in your own retina and optic nerves. Anyway, whose pleasure? For one of the first things Eros does is to obliterate the distinction between giving and receiving.

Hitherto I have been trying merely to describe, not to evaluate. But certain moral questions now inevitably arise, and I must not conceal my own view of them. It is submitted rather than asserted, and of course open to correction by better men, better lovers and better Christians.

It has been widely held in the past, and is perhaps held by many unsophisticated people to-day, that the spiritual danger of Eros arises almost entirely from the carnal element within it; that Eros is "noblest" or "purest" when Venus is reduced to the minimum. The older moral theologians certainly seem to have thought that the danger we chiefly had to guard against in marriage was that of a soul-destroying surrender to the senses. It will be noticed, however, that this is not the Scriptural approach. St. Paul, dissuading his converts from marriage, says nothing about that side of the matter except to discourage prolonged abstinence from Venus (*I Cor.* VII, 5). What he fears is pre-occupation, the need of constantly "pleasing"—that is, considering—one's partner, the multiple distractions of domesticity. It is marriage itself, not the marriage bed, that will be likely to hinder us from waiting uninterruptedly on God. And surely St. Paul is right. If I may trust my own experience, it is (within marriage as without) the practical and prudential cares of this world, and even the smallest and most prosaic of those cares, that are the great distraction. The gnat-like cloud of petty anxieties and decisions about the conduct of the next hour have interfered with my prayers more often than any passion or appetite whatever. The great, permanent temptation of marriage is not to sensuality but (quite bluntly) to avarice. With all proper respect to the medieval guides, I cannot help remembering that they were all celibates, and probably did not know what Eros does to our sexuality; how, far from aggravating, he reduces the nagging and addictive character of mere appetite. And that not simply by satisfying it. Eros, without diminishing desire, makes abstinence easier. He tends, no doubt, to a pre-occupation with the Beloved which can indeed be an obstacle to the spiritual life; but not chiefly a sensual pre-occupation.

The real spiritual danger in Eros as a whole lies, I believe, elsewhere. I will return to the point. For the moment, I want to speak of the danger which at present, in my opinion, especially haunts the act of love. This is a subject on which I disagree, not with the human race (far from it), but with many of its gravest spokesmen. I believe we are all being encouraged to take Venus too seriously; at any rate, with a wrong kind of seriousness. All my life a ludicrous and portentous solemnisation of sex has been going on.

One author tells us that Venus should recur through the married life in "a solemn, sacramental rhythm." A young man to whom I had described as "pornographic" a novel that he much admired, replied with genuine bewilderment, "Pornographic? But how can it be? It treats the whole thing so seriously"—as if a long face were a sort of moral disinfectant. Our friends who harbour Dark Gods, the "pillar of blood" school, attempt seriously to restore something like the Phallic religion. Our advertisements, at their sexiest, paint the whole business in terms of the rapt, the intense, the swoony-devout; seldom a hint of gaiety. And the psychologists have so bedevilled us with the infinite importance of complete sexual adjustment and the all but impossibility of achieving it, that I could believe some young couples now go to it with the complete works of Freud, Kraft-Ebbing, Havelock Ellis and Dr. Stopes spread out on bed-tables all round them. Cheery old Ovid, who never either ignored a mole-hill or made a mountain of it, would be more to the point. We have reached the stage at which nothing is more needed than a roar of old-fashioned laughter.

But, it will be replied, the thing *is* serious. Yes; quadruply so. First, theologically, because this is the body's share in marriage which, by God's choice, is the mystical image of the union between God and Man. Secondly, as what I will venture to call a sub-Christian, or Pagan or natural sacrament our human participation in, and exposition of, the natural forces of life and fertility—the marriage of Sky-Father and Earth-Mother. Thirdly, on the moral level, in view of the obligations involved and the incalculable momentousness of being a parent and ancestor. Finally it has (sometimes, not always) a great emotional seriousness in the minds of the participants.

But eating is also serious; theologically, as the vehicle of the Blessed Sacrament; ethically in view of our duty to feed the hungry; socially, because the table is from time immemorial the place for talk; medically, as all dyspeptics know. Yet we do not bring bluebooks to dinner nor behave there as if we were in church. And it is gourmets, not saints, who come nearest to doing so. Animals are always serious about food.

We must not be totally serious about Venus. Indeed we can't be totally serious without doing violence to our humanity. It is not for nothing that every language and literature in the world is full of jokes about sex. Many of them may be dull or disgusting and nearly all of them are old. But we must insist that they embody an attitude to Venus which in the long run endangers the Christian life far less than a reverential gravity. We must not attempt to find an absolute in the flesh. Banish play and laughter from the bed of love and you may let in a false goddess. She will be even falser than the Aphrodite of the Greeks; for they, even while they worshipped her, knew that she was "laughter-loving." The mass of the people are perfectly right in their conviction that Venus is a partly comic spirit. We are under no obligation at all to sing all our love-duets in the throbbing, world-without-end, heart-breaking manner of Tristan and Isolde; let us often sing like Papageno and Papagena instead.

Venus herself will have a terrible revenge if we take her (occasional) seriousness at its face value. And that in two ways. One is most comically—though with no comic intention—illustrated by Sir Thomas Browne when he says that her service is "the foolishest act a wise man commits in all his life, nor is there anything that will more deject his cool'd imagination, when he shall consider what an odd and unworthy piece of folly he hath committed." But if he had gone about that act with less solemnity in the first place he would not have suffered this "dejection." If his imagination had not been misled, its cooling would have brought no such revulsion. But Venus has another and worse revenge.

She herself is a mocking, mischievous spirit, far more elf than deity, and makes game of us. When all external circumstances are fittest for her service she will leave one or both the lovers totally indisposed for it. When every overt act is impossible and even glances cannot be exchanged—in trains, in shops, and at interminable parties—she will assail them with all her force. An hour later, when time and place agree, she will have mysteriously withdrawn; perhaps from only one of them. What a pother this must raise—what resentments, self-pities, suspicions, wounded vanities and all the current chatter about "frustration"—in those who have deified her! But sensible lovers laugh. It is all part of the game; a game of catch-as-catch-can, and the escapes and tumbles and head-on collisions are to be treated as a romp.

For I can hardly help regarding it as one of God's jokes that a passion so soaring, so apparently transcendent, as Eros, should thus be linked in incongruous symbiosis with a bodily appetite which, like any other appetite, tactlessly reveals its connections with such mundane factors as weather, health, diet, circulation, and digestion. In Eros at times we seem to be flying; Venus gives us the sudden twitch that reminds us we are really captive balloons. It is a continual demonstration of the truth that we are composite creatures, rational animals, akin on one side to the angels, on the other to tom-cats. It is a bad thing not to be able to take a joke. Worse, not to take a divine joke; made, I grant you, at our expense, but also (who doubts it?) for our endless benefit.

Man has held three views of his body. First there is that of those ascetic Pagans who called it the prison or the "tomb" of the soul, and of Christians like Fisher to whom it was a "sack of dung," food for worms, filthy, shameful, a source of nothing but temptation to bad men and humiliation to good ones. Then there are the Neo-Pagans (they seldom know Greek), the nudists and the sufferers from Dark Gods, to whom the body is glorious. But thirdly we have the view which St. Francis expressed by calling his body "Brother Ass." All three may be—I am not sure—defensible; but give me St. Francis for my money.

Ass is exquisitely right because no one in his senses can either revere or hate a donkey. It is a useful, sturdy, lazy, obstinate, patient, lovable and infuriating beast; deserving now the stick and now a carrot; both pathetically and absurdly beautiful. So the body. There's no living with it till we recognise that one of its functions in our lives is to play the part of buffoon. Until some theory has sophisticated them, every man, woman and child in the world knows this. The fact that we have bodies is the oldest joke there is. Eros (like death, figure-drawing, and the study of medicine) may at moments cause us to take it with total seriousness. The error consists in concluding that Eros should always do so and permanently abolish the joke. But this is not what happens. The very faces of all the happy lovers we know make it clear. Lovers, unless their love is very short-lived, again and again feel an element not only of comedy, not only of play, but even of buffoonery, in the body's expression of Eros. And the body would frustrate us if this were not so. It would be too clumsy an instrument to render love's music unless its very clumsiness could be felt as adding to the total experience its own grotesque charm—a sub-plot or anti-masque miming with its own hearty rough-and-tumble what the soul enacts in statelier fashion. (Thus in old comedies the lyric loves of the hero and heroine are at once parodied and corroborated by some much more earthy affair between a Touchstone and an Audrey or a valet and a chambermaid.) The highest does not stand without the lowest. There is indeed at certain moments a high poetry in the flesh itself; but also, by your leave, an irreducible element of obstinate and ludicrous unpoetry. If it does not make itself felt on one occasion, it will on another. Far better plant it foursquare within the drama of Eros as comic relief than pretend you haven't noticed it.

For indeed we require this relief. The poetry is there as well as the unpoetry; the gravity of Venus as well as her levity, the *gravis ardor* or burning weight of desire. Pleasure, pushed to its extreme, shatters us like pain. The longing for a union which only the flesh can mediate while the flesh, our mutually excluding bodies, renders it forever unattainable can have the grandeur of a metaphysical pursuit. Amorousness as well as grief can bring tears to the eyes. But Venus does not always come thus "entire, fastened to her prey," and the fact that she sometimes does so is the very reason for preserving always a hint of playfulness in our attitude to her. When natural things look most divine, the demoniac is just round the corner.

This refusal to be quite immersed—this recollection of the levity even when, for the moment, only the gravity is displayed—is especially relevant to a certain attitude which Venus, in her intensity, evokes from most (I believe, not all) pairs of lovers. This act can invite the man to an extreme, though short-lived, masterfulness, to the dominance of a conqueror or a captor, and the woman to a correspondingly extreme subjection and surrender. Hence the roughness, even fierceness, of some erotic play; the "lover's pinch which hurts and is desired." How should a sane couple think of this? or a Christian couple permit it?

I think it is harmless and wholesome on one condition. We must recognise that we have here to do with what I called "the Pagan sacrament" in sex. In Friendship, as we noticed, each participant stands for precisely himself—the contingent individual he is. But in the act of love we are not merely ourselves. We are also representatives. It is here no impoverishment but an enrichment to be aware that forces older and less personal than we work through us. In us all the masculinity and femininity of the world, all that is assailant and responsive, are momentarily focused. The man does play the Sky-Father and the woman the Earth-Mother; he does play Form, and she Matter. But we must give full value to the word *play*. Of course neither "plays a part" in the sense of being a hypocrite. But each plays a part or role in—well, in something which is comparable to a mystery-play or ritual (at one extreme) and to a masque or even a charade (at the other).

A woman who accepted as literally her own this extreme self-surrender would be an idolatress offering to a man what belongs only to God. And a man would have to be the coxcomb of all coxcombs, and indeed a blasphemer, if he arrogated to himself, as the mere person he is, the sort of sovereignty to which Venus for a moment exalts him. But what cannot lawfully be yielded or claimed can be lawfully enacted. Outside this ritual or drama he and she are two immortal souls, two free-born adults, two citizens. We should be much mistaken if we supposed that those marriages where this mastery is most asserted and acknowledged in the act of Venus were those where the husband is most likely to be dominant in the married life as a whole; the reverse is perhaps more probable. But within the rite or drama they become a god and goddess between whom there is no equality—whose relations are asymmetrical.

Some will think it strange I should find an element of ritual or masquerade in that action which is often regarded as the most real, the most unmasked and sheerly genuine, we ever do. Are we not our true selves when naked? In a sense, no. The word *naked* was originally a past participle; the naked man was the man who had undergone a process of *naking,* that is, of stripping or peeling (you used the verb of nuts and fruit). Time out of mind the naked man has seemed to our ancestors not the natural but the abnormal man; not the man who has abstained from dressing but the man who has been for some reason undressed. And it is a simple fact—anyone can observe it at a men's bathing place—that nudity emphasises common humanity and soft-pedals what is individual. In that way we are "more ourselves" when clothed. By nudity the lovers cease to be solely John and Mary; the universal He and She are emphasised. You could almost say they *put* on nakedness as a ceremonial robe—or as the costume for a charade. For we must still beware—and never more than when we thus partake of the Pagan sacrament in our love passages—of being serious in the wrong way. The Sky-Father himself is only a Pagan dream of One far greater than Zeus and far more masculine than the male. And a mortal man is not even the Sky-Father, and cannot really wear his crown. Only a copy of it, done in tinselled paper. I do not call it this in contempt. I like ritual; I like private theatricals; I even like charades. Paper crowns have their legitimate, and (in the proper context) their serious, uses. They are not in the last resort much flimsier ("if imagination mend them") than all earthly dignities.

But I dare not mention this Pagan sacrament without turning aside to guard against any danger of confusing it with an incomparably higher mystery. As nature crowns man in that brief action, so the Christian law has crowned him in the permanent relationship of marriage, bestowing—or should I say, inflicting?—a certain "headship" on him. This is a very different coronation. And as we could easily take the natural mystery too seriously, so we might take the Christian mystery not seriously enough. Christian writers (notably Milton) have sometimes spoken of the husband's headship with a complacency to make the blood run cold. We must go back to our Bibles. The husband is the head of the wife just in so far as he is to her what Christ is to the Church. He is to love her as Christ loved the Church—read on—*and give his life for her* (*Eph.* V, 25). This headship, then, is most fully embodied not in the husband we should all wish to be but in him whose marriage is most like a crucifixion; whose wife receives most and gives least, is most unworthy of him, is—in her own mere nature—least lovable. For the Church has no beauty but what the Bridegroom gives her; he does not find, but makes her, lovely. The chrism of this terrible coronation is to be seen not in the joys of any man's marriage but in its sorrows, in the sickness and sufferings of a good wife or the faults of a bad one, in his unwearying (never paraded) care or his inexhaustible forgiveness: forgiveness, not acquiescence. As Christ sees in the flawed, proud, fanatical or lukewarm Church on earth that Bride who will one day be without spot or wrinkle, and labours to produce the latter, so the husband whose headship is Christ-like (and he is allowed no other sort) never despairs. He is a King Cophetua who after twenty years still hopes that the beggar-girl will one day learn to speak the truth and wash behind her ears.

To say this is not to say that there is any virtue or wisdom in making a marriage that involves such misery. There is no wisdom or virtue in seeking unnecessary martyrdom or deliberately courting persecution; yet it is, none the less, the persecuted or martyred Christian in whom the pattern of the Master is most unambiguously realised. So, in these terrible marriages, once they have come about, the "headship" of the husband, if only he can sustain it, is most Christ-like.

The sternest feminist need not grudge my sex the crown offered to it either in the Pagan or in the Christian mystery. For the one is of paper and the other of thorns. The real danger is not that husbands may grasp the latter too eagerly; but that they will allow or compel their wives to usurp it.

From Venus, the carnal ingredient within Eros, I now turn to Eros as a whole. Here we shall see the same pattern repeated. As Venus within Eros does not really aim at pleasure, so Eros does not aim at happiness. We may think he does, but when he is brought to the test it proves otherwise. Everyone knows that it is useless to try to separate lovers by proving to them that their marriage will be an unhappy one. This is not only because they will disbelieve you. They usually will, no doubt. But even if they believed, they would not be dissuaded. For it is the very mark of Eros that when he is in us we had rather share unhappiness with the Beloved than be happy on any other terms. Even if the two lovers are mature and experienced people who know that broken hearts heal in the end and can clearly foresee that, if they once steeled themselves to go through the present agony of parting, they would almost certainly be happier ten years hence than marriage is at all likely to make them—even then, they would not part. To Eros all these calculations are irrelevant—just as the coolly brutal judgment of Lucretius is irrelevant to Venus. Even when it becomes clear beyond all evasion that marriage with the Beloved cannot possibly lead to happiness—when it cannot even profess to offer any other life than that of tending an incurable invalid, of hopeless poverty, of exile, or of disgrace—Eros never hesitates to say, "Better this than parting. Better to be miserable with her than happy without her. Let our hearts break provided they break together." If the voice within us does not say this, it is not the voice of Eros.

This is the grandeur and terror of love. But notice, as before, side by side with this grandeur, the playfulness. Eros, as well as Venus, is the subject of countless jokes. And even when the circumstances of the two lovers are so tragic that no bystander could keep back his tears, they themselves—in want, in hospital wards, on visitors' days in jail—will sometimes be surprised by a merriment which strikes the onlooker (but not them) as unbearably pathetic.

Nothing is falser than the idea that mockery is necessarily hostile. Until they have a baby to laugh at, lovers are always laughing at each other.

It is in the grandeur of Eros that the seeds of danger are concealed. He has spoken like a god. His total commitment, his reckless disregard of happiness, his transcendence of self-regard, sound like a message from the eternal world.

And yet it cannot, just as it stands, be the voice of God Himself. For Eros, speaking with that very grandeur and displaying that very transcendence of self, may urge to evil as well as to good. Nothing is shallower than the belief that a love which leads to sin is always qualitatively lower—more animal or more trivial—than one which leads to faithful, fruitful and Christian marriage. The love which leads to cruel and perjured unions, even to suicide-pacts and murder, is not likely to be wandering lust or idle sentiment. It may well be Eros in all his splendour; heart-breakingly sincere; ready for every sacrifice except renunciation.

There have been schools of thought which accepted the voice of Eros as something actually transcendent and tried to justify the absoluteness of his commands. Plato will have it that "falling in love" is the mutual recognition on earth of souls which have been singled out for one another in a previous and celestial existence. To meet the Beloved is to realise "We loved before we were born." As a myth to express what lovers feel this is admirable. But if one accepted it literally one would be faced by an embarrassing consequence. We should have to conclude that in that heavenly and forgotten life affairs were no better managed than here. For Eros may unite the most unsuitable yokefellows; many unhappy, and predictably unhappy, marriages were love-matches.

A theory more likely to be accepted in our own day is what we may call Shavian—Shaw himself might have said "metabiological"—Romanticism. According to Shavian Romanticism the voice of Eros is the voice of the *élan vital* or Life Force, the "evolutionary appetite." In overwhelming a particular couple it is seeking parents (or ancestors) for the superman. It is indifferent both to their personal happiness and to the rules of morality because it aims at something which Shaw thinks very much more important: the future perfection of our species. But if all this were true it hardly makes clear whether—and if so, why—we should obey it. All pictures yet offered us of the superman are so unattractive that one might well vow celibacy at once to avoid the risk of begetting him. And secondly, this theory surely leads to the conclusion that the Life Force does not very well understand its (or her? or his?) own business. So far as we can see the existence or intensity of Eros between two people is no warrant that their offspring will be especially satisfactory, or even that they will have offspring at all. Two good "strains" (in the stockbreeders' sense), not two good lovers, is the recipe for fine children. And what on earth was the Life Force doing through all those countless generations when the begetting of children depended very little on mutual Eros and very much on arranged marriages, slavery, and rape? Has it only just thought of this bright idea for improving the species?

Neither the Platonic nor the Shavian type of erotic transcendentalism can help a Christian. We are not worshippers of the Life Force and we know nothing of previous existences. We must not give unconditional obedience to the voice of Eros when he speaks most like a god. Neither must we ignore or attempt to deny the god-like quality. This love is really and truly like Love Himself. In it there is a real nearness to God (by Resemblance); but not, therefore and necessarily, a nearness of Approach. Eros, honoured so far as love of God and charity to our fellows will allow, may become for us a means of Approach. His total commitment is a paradigm or example, built into our natures, of the love we ought to exercise towards God and Man. As nature, for the nature-lover, gives a content to the word *glory,* so this gives a content to the word *Charity.* It is as if Christ said to us through Eros, "Thus—just like this—with this prodigality—not counting the cost—you are to love me and the least of my brethren." Our conditional honour to Eros will of course vary with our circumstances. Of some a total renunciation (but not a contempt) is required. Others, with Eros as their fuel and also as their model, can embark on the married life. Within which Eros, of himself, will never be enough—will indeed survive only in so far as he is continually chastened and corroborated by higher principles.

But Eros, honoured without reservation and obeyed unconditionally, becomes a demon. And this is just how he claims to be honoured and obeyed. Divinely indifferent to our selfishness, he is also demoniacally rebellious to every claim of God or Man that would oppose him. Hence as the poet says:

> People in love cannot be moved by kindness,
> And opposition makes them feel like martyrs.

Martyrs is exactly right. Years ago when I wrote about medieval love-poetry and described its strange, half make-believe, "religion of love," I was blind enough to treat this as an almost purely literary phenomenon. I know better now. Eros by his nature invites it. Of all loves he is, at his height, most god-like; therefore most prone to demand our worship. Of himself he always tends to turn "being in love" into a sort of religion.

Theologians have often feared, in this love, a danger of idolatry. I think they meant by this that the lovers might idolise one another. That does not seem to me to be the real danger; certainly not in marriage. The deliciously plain prose and businesslike intimacy of married life render it absurd. So does the Affection in which Eros is almost invariably clothed. Even in courtship I question whether anyone who has felt the thirst for the Uncreated, or even dreamed of feeling it, ever supposed that the Beloved could satisfy it. As a fellow-pilgrim pierced with the very same desire, that is, as a Friend, the Beloved may be gloriously and helpfully relevant; but as an object for it—well (I would not be rude), ridiculous. The real danger seems to me not that the lovers will idolise each other but that they will idolise Eros himself.

I do not of course mean that they will build altars or say prayers to him. The idolatry I speak of can be seen in the popular misinterpretation of Our Lord's words "Her sins, which are many, are forgiven her, for she loved much" (*Luke* VII, 47). From the context, and especially from the preceding parable of the debtors, it is clear that this must mean: "The greatness of her love for Me is evidence of the greatness of the sins I have forgiven her." (The *for* here is like the *for* in "He can't have gone out, *for* his hat is still hanging in the hall"; the presence of the hat is not the cause of his being in the house but a probable proof that he is). But thousands of people take it quite differently. They first assume, with no evidence, that her sins were sins against chastity, though, for all we know, they may have been usury, dishonest shopkeeping, or cruelty to children. And they then take Our Lord to be saying, "I forgive her unchastity because she was so much in love." The implication is that a great Eros extenuates—almost sanctions—almost sanctifies—any actions it leads to.

When lovers say of some act that we might blame, "Love made us do it," notice the tone. A man saying, "I did it because I was frightened," or "I did it because I was angry," speaks quite differently. He is putting forward an excuse for what he feels to require excusing. But the lovers are seldom doing quite that. Notice how tremulously, almost how devoutly, they say the word *love,* not so much pleading an "extenuating circumstance" as appealing to an authority. The confession can be almost a boast. There can be a shade of defiance in it. They "feel like martyrs." In extreme cases what their words really express is a demure yet unshakable allegiance to the god of love.

"These reasons in love's law have passed for good," says Milton's Dalila. That is the point; *in love's law.* "In love," we have our own "law," a religion of our own, our own god. Where a true Eros is present resistance to his commands feels like apostasy, and what are really (by the Christian standard) temptations speak with the voice of duties—quasi-religious duties, acts of pious zeal to love. He builds his own religion round the lovers. Benjamin Constant has noticed how he creates for them, in a few weeks or months, a joint past which seems to them immemorial. They recur to it continually with wonder and reverence, as the Psalmists recur to the history of Israel. It is in fact the Old Testament of Love's religion; the record of love's judgments and mercies towards his chosen pair up to the moment when they first knew they were lovers. After that, its New Testament begins. They are now under a new law, under what corresponds (in this religion) to Grace. They are new creatures. The "spirit" of Eros supersedes all laws, and they must not "grieve" it.

It seems to sanction all sorts of actions they would not otherwise have dared. I do not mean solely, or chiefly, acts that violate chastity. They are just as likely to be acts of injustice or uncharity against the outer world. They will seem like proofs of piety and zeal towards Eros. The pair can say to one another in an almost sacrificial spirit, "It is for love's sake that I have neglected my parents—left my children—cheated my partner—failed my friend at his greatest need." These reasons in love's law have passed for good. The votaries may even come to feel a particular merit in such sacrifices; what costlier offering can be laid on love's altar than one's conscience?

And all the time the grim joke is that this Eros whose voice seems to speak from the eternal realm is not himself necessarily even permanent. He is notoriously the most mortal of our loves. The world rings with complaints of his fickleness. What is baffling is the combination of this fickleness with his protestations of permanency. To be in love is both to intend and to promise lifelong fidelity. Love makes vows unasked; can't be deterred from making them. "I will be ever true," are almost the first words he utters. Not hypocritically but sincerely. No experience will cure him of the delusion. We have all heard of people who are in love again every few years; each time sincerely convinced that "*this* time it's the real thing," that their wanderings are over, that they have found their true love and will themselves be true till death.

And yet Eros is in a sense right to make this promise. The event of falling in love is of such a nature that we are right to reject as intolerable the idea that it should be transitory. In one high bound it has overleaped the massive wall of our selfhood; it has made appetite itself altruistic, tossed personal happiness aside as a triviality and planted the interests of another in the centre of our being. Spontaneously and without effort we have fulfilled the law (towards one person) by loving our neighbour as ourselves. It is an image, a foretaste, of what we must become to all if Love Himself rules in us without a rival. It is even (well used) a preparation for that. Simply to relapse from it, merely to "fall out of" love again, is—if I may coin the ugly word—a sort of *disredemption*. Eros is driven to promise what Eros of himself cannot perform.

Can we be in this selfless liberation for a lifetime? Hardly for a week. Between the best possible lovers this high condition is intermittent. The old self soon turns out to be not so dead as he pretended—as after a religious conversion. In either he may be momentarily knocked flat; he will soon be up again; if not on his feet, at least on his elbow, if not roaring, at least back to his surly grumbling or his mendicant whine. And Venus will often slip back into mere sexuality.

But these lapses will not destroy a marriage between two "decent and sensible" people. The couple whose marriage will certainly be endangered by them, and possibly ruined, are those who have idolised Eros. They thought he had the power and truthfulness of a god. They expected that mere feeling would do for them, and permanently, all that was necessary. When this expectation is disappointed they throw the blame on Eros or, more usually, on their partners. In reality, however, Eros, having made his gigantic promise and shown you in glimpses what its performance would be like, has "done his stuff." He, like a godparent, makes the vows; it is we who must keep them. It is we who must labour to bring our daily life into even closer accordance with what the glimpses have revealed. We must do the works of Eros when Eros is not present. This all good lovers know, though those who are not reflective or articulate will be able to express it only in a few conventional phrases about "taking the rough along with the smooth," not "expecting too much," having "a little common sense," and the like. And all good Christian lovers know that this programme, modest as it sounds, will not be carried out except by humility, charity and divine grace; that it is indeed the whole Christian life seen from one particular angle.

Thus Eros, like the other loves, but more strikingly because of his strength, sweetness, terror and high port, reveals his true status. He cannot of himself be what, nevertheless, he must be if he is to remain Eros. He needs help; therefore needs to be ruled. The god dies or becomes a demon unless he obeys God. It would be well if, in such case, he always died. But he may live on, mercilessly chaining together two mutual tormentors, each raw all over with the poison of hate-in-love, each ravenous to receive and implacably refusing to give, jealous, suspicious, resentful, struggling for the upper hand, determined to be free and to allow no freedom, living on "scenes." Read *Anna Karenina*, and do not fancy that such things happen only in Russia. The lovers' old hyperbole of "eating" each other can come horribly near to the truth.

E. HOW CAN I FIND AND WIN THE RIGHT ONE? COURTSHIP

We come now to the heart of this anthology, the readings on courtship itself. Even for those who are convinced that they wish and ought to marry, even for people who are thoughtful about the meaning of human sexuality and who seek to make a life based on lasting love—who want adventurous permanence, not perpetual adventuring—the big question still remains, indeed, becomes most pressing: How do I find and win the right one to marry? The big question has littler parts: Where do I look? How do I recognize a likely prospect? What, in fact, should I be looking for? looking at? What are the telling and revealing signs that he (she) is right for me? Assuming I have found her (him), how do I win her (him)? How to proceed through the delicate steps that, if all goes well, will lead not just to a wedding but to a flourishing married life?

To be sure, courtship, if it happens naturally, does not proceed by means of asking and answering these or other such explicit questions. Courtship is surely not primarily an intellectual matter, though it always begs for keen attention, accurate discernment, and astute judgment. It is more a matter of the heart, of character, of intuition and imagination, poise and tact, sense and sensibility. Such matters are notoriously hard to describe, much less to reduce to rules and prescriptions. In more stable times, "knowledge" about courtship, like other important matters of everyday life, would normally be acquired tacitly and indirectly.

Nevertheless, in the present cultural confusions about this subject, people are looking for advice about how to proceed. Practical-minded Americans, especially in the present age, are likely to turn to the "experts"—advice columnists (like Ann Landers), psychologists, communications consultants, "couples therapists," and the like—to gain the missing "know-how." And the experts are not shy in attempting to fill the vacuum. For example, in his most recent book, *Mars and Venus on a Date,* psychologist and counselor John Gray provides "a guide for navigating the 5 stages of dating [attraction, uncertainty, exclusivity, intimacy, engagement] to create a loving and lasting relationship." The advice, a mixture of common sense and current popular psychology, rests entirely on the assumption, developed in Gray's earlier best-seller, *Men Are from Mars, Women Are from Venus*, that men and women have fundamentally different ways of thinking and expressing themselves, and hence fundamentally different approaches to life's journey. Learning how to understand the stereotyped other sex—as if it were entirely "alien"—is thus the key to this "how-to" manual. In addition, all discussion centers on the partners solely in relation to one another; they are regarded one-dimensionally, in complete isolation and abstraction from the rest of their lives—from family ties and other personal associations, from religious and ethnic connections, from work and community involvements and responsibilities, indeed, even from matters of character and taste. Nothing is said that could truly educate the sentiments or furnish the imagination. In consequence, by narrowing the gaze in an effort to improve "communication," Gray's book—because it *is* merely a "practical" manual—finally constricts rather than enlarges our vision of courtship.

The readings collected here have been gathered in a different spirit and toward a different end. They address not the mechanics of the process, but the nature of courtship itself. Taken together, they seek to shed light on its character, its motions and rhythms, its nuances and subtleties, its mysteries, its mysteriousness. None of the selections are ideological, almost none are explicitly didactic. Most offer concrete examples from literature which will, like courtship itself, engage the sentiments as well as the mind. Many of the selections will at first glance probably strike readers reared only on contemporary culture as alien or quaint. But it is precisely this strangeness that can awaken us to what we are missing and enable us to see more clearly and feel more deeply when we go a'courting. Our ability to respond to these texts, even now, proves that they speak to enduring human concerns and feelings.

Remembering C. S. Lewis's remark that erotic love is both profound and funny, we begin with a contemporary selection from Judith Martin's *Miss Manners' Guide to Excruciatingly Correct Behavior*, a book in the long tradition of works on etiquette; here the modern reader should feel very much at home. We then move far back to two biblical examples, taken from Genesis, which help us think about the question "Is this the right one?" in the *absence* of typical courtship. With a contemporary short story by Pearl Abraham, we present the alternative of arranged marriage as a counterpoise to the subsequent examples. An anthropological study of courtship practices in rural Spain, *The People of the Sierra*, shows how courtship takes place today in societies with well-defined gender identities and roles.

Thereafter the selections turn largely to examples of courtship, taken mainly from literature. A fictive colloquy by Erasmus illuminates many of the important concerns in courtship, classically understood. Two Shakespearean examples of courtship, one (from the *Tempest*) regulated by paternal authority, the other (from *As You Like It*) managed by the would-be bride in male disguise, dramatize the ways and means of disciplining romanticism. The sober Benjamin Franklin, looking to marriage built not on romance or erotic passion but on friendship and what one might call "rational love," offers practical advice—advice very different in tone and substance from the "how-to" guidance offered by our current "experts"; we include also a letter ("The Elysian Fields") showing Franklin himself paying court. Rousseau, in contrast to Franklin, places erotic desire, suitably shaped by looking up to an imaginary ideal, at the center of both courtship and marriage; the long selection recounting the finely controlled courtship of Emile and Sophie shows how *eros* can be disciplined and rendered sublime, and how it can then lead to a marriage of free, equal, and uncorrupted lovers. Corruption by living among sophisticates and by living too much in the opinions of others—or perhaps simply just too much uneducated lust—leads foolish Pierre into a disastrous marriage; while open, natural, and nearly speechless affection seals a wonderful marriage between Levin and Kitty—the subjects of the next two selections, both from Tolstoy, a man who shared much of Rousseau's outlook on private life and personal happiness. Finally, lengthy extracts from Jane Austen's *Pride and Prejudice* chronicle the tortuous courtship of Darcy and Elizabeth, richly located in the complexities of family and social life; here, pride, prejudice, and the other vices born of the imagination need to be corrected by an accurate reading of character if one is truly to find and win the right one.

Martin, Miss Manners'
Advice on Courtship

Over the past twenty years, through her regular newspaper columns, public lectures, and very popular books, Judith Martin (born in 1938) has almost single-handedly revived American attention to the important, yet still sadly underappreciated, subjects of etiquette and manners. No subject of social life escapes her knowing eye and keen wit. Her purpose is high-minded, yet her approach is down-to-earth; her style is light and humorous, yet her advice is often "no-nonsense" and straight-shooting, though masked by a tone of ironic self-mockery. She appears to have found the perfect voice for teaching manners in irreverent times. Touting neither old traditions nor newfangled theories, shunning both moralism and (especially) psychologism, Miss Manners sees both what is continuous and what is novel in the various dramas of everyday life, including the vexed subject of modern courtship. In these selections from the section on Courtship, in the chapter on "Rites de Passage," from Miss Manners' Guide to Excruciatingly Correct Behavior (1983), *she addresses familiar questions of romance: Who should take the initiative? Should I tell him how I feel? How can I make her like me? What should I say to him when he has nothing to say? How affectionate may we be in public? How do I know if she really cares for me? How can I get him to "commit"?*

Are all the topics discussed rightly regarded as aspects of courtship? *What is the goal of courtship as Miss Manners understands it? She seems to offer androgynous advice, recommending the same behavior for men and women. To what extent is this sensible?*

Age-Old Problems

Diligently as Miss Manners has been doing her research, she has been unable to discover any true innovations in the relations between the genders during the twentieth century. Sex seems to have been invented quite a few generations ago, contrary to the popular belief that it first occurred on the evening after one's own parents' wedding, but that its full potential was realized only when one came of age oneself. Apparently even primitive people long ago managed to catch on to the general idea and even the standard variations.

Therefore when Miss Manners is asked about the horrendous problems arising from Modern Sex, she has a difficult time concealing a weary little smile. The only modern development she has observed is the custom of self-gossip—that is, of making one's own activities so public as to force people who had been perfectly aware what was happening but essentially uninvolved to take stances of approval or disapproval. In Miss Manners' opinion, this contribution has not made the world go around any faster.

Other so-called inventions turn out to be cases of historical ignorance. Take, for example, the "modern" matter of ladies asking gentlemen for dates. Have you never heard of "I find I have an extra theater ticket for Thursday night"? Yet one is constantly hearing of ladies who are puzzled about how to take the initiative and gentlemen who are bewildered about how to respond. Many ladies are unable to take no for an answer, and many gentlemen unable to give it.

The roles of the pursuer and the pursued are well known in society, and there is no excuse for those who have practiced one side to botch things and plead ignorance when playing the opposite part. Miss Manners has no objection to a lady's initiating a social engagement, provided she does so in the dignified, straightforward way that ladies have always appreciated in gentlemen. This means that one suggests a specific date and activity, and is gracious if it is declined. After three separate refusals, one stops asking. Gentlemen should realize that it is perfectly proper to refuse such an invitation politely if one is not interested, and that elaborate excuses need not be given.

Why is it, then, that a lady who knows what it is to be pestered with unwanted attentions does not know how to shrug and accept fate when her advances do not meet with success? Neither continued pursuit nor bitter behavior is gentlemanly, she should know. A gentleman, who knows what a rebuff is, will sometimes yield to the attentions of someone he doesn't really enjoy simply because he feels put on the spot at having been asked. He should know that it is a lady's prerogative to say no. They should both know that sexual attentions should never be demanded or given out of the disgusting notion that they are a return to the person who pays the entertainment bills. You see, Miss Manners has nothing at all against modern trivial variations on behavior, provided the traditions are observed.

For Young Lovers and Others

DEAR MISS MANNERS:

I am a sixteen-year-old girl. I like this guy a lot, and I am faced with having to tell him how I feel. I can't come right out and tell him, because I'm really the shy type when it comes to this sort of thing. Also, it seems to me that I talk a lot around him. Before I see him, I always tell myself, "I'm not going to talk too much." But no matter what I tell myself, I always seem to run off at the mouth and act silly. Please give me some advice that I can follow, so I can act more ladylike. I don't want him or anyone else to feel that I am a person who doesn't have any control over myself.

GENTLE READER:

The first thing you must learn to control is that impulse to tell the young gentleman exactly how you feel. This is difficult, but to learn it will be of value to you later in life. One reason is that he already knows. Or at least, he has a pretty good idea. Even a gentleman of sixteen can recognize the cause of such heightened behavior as you describe.

If you can teach yourself to tone down that behavior, it would be a good idea. Your task is to make him less certain, not more, about how deeply you care, until such time as you are led to believe that your feelings are reciprocated. Miss Manners is not telling you this because you are a girl who should be ladylike. She would advise all boys, girls, women, and men to put some ambiguity into their behavior in the early stages of courtship. For reasons she does not pretend to understand, the obvious adoration of someone to whom you have not already been forming your own feeling of love produces distaste, rather than reciprocation.

If you cannot teach yourself to get that clear message of love out of your behavior, a skill that requires great practice, at least do not reinforce it with declarations. Cheerful friendliness, along with the vaguest of looks that suggest one's feelings could grow, is the standard at which to aim.

There is no certainty in love, especially these days. Therefore pressing to find out if someone "really cares" is always a mistake. If you have to ask, you don't want to hear the answer. Nevertheless, Miss Manners sympathizes with the wish of ladies—and gentlemen, too—to be assured that their love will be requited before they give it freely. In fact, she considers that the only sensible and civilized way to behave. Handing over your heart to someone who may, for all you know, scream "Yuck!" and drop it in disgust is not a good idea.

The trouble is that the world could easily come to an end if everyone waited for everyone else to speak first. This is why we have developed other ways of knowing, such as the meaningful glance, the small attention, the reduction of conventional distance between bodies (translation: sitting closer on the sofa than the spacing of the cushions), and so on. If these signals are in working order, the romance should progress evenly, so that the person who first says "I love you" is pretty well assured of getting a me-too. If it is progressing slowly, or not at all, the more interested person can, by holding back his or her pace, at least save the embarrassment of dramatic failure. The only way to increase the other person's pace is to slow one's own to a near standstill. Uncertainty and ambiguity are as exciting in courtship as they are tedious in marriage.

Pushy tactics are self-defeating. The real skill, in courtship, is to be able to play just slightly more slowly than one's partner

. . .

The Secret of Popularity

DEAR MISS MANNERS:

I am almost fifteen years old, and I would be happy if I had a girl friend. Some of the boys in my class date, but so far, I haven't had any luck. My reason for wanting a girl friend is not only what you probably already think. I am talking about a special girl I could talk to all the time. My parents just manage to tolerate me, sometimes not even that. School is even worse. If I had a girl I could tell all this to, I could get along, and maybe I wouldn't mind so much about the others. So far, I'm a long way from it. I go to the school dances, where there are a lot of girls and not too many boys, but when I ask a girl to dance, they'll make some dumb excuse, or the girls give each other funny looks and laugh instead of talking to me. I can't stand much more of that. I don't think there is anything wrong with me. I just don't know what the secret is of being popular, and it doesn't have to be popular with lots of girls. Just one would do if she's the right one.

GENTLE READER:

Many people who are older but no wiser than you also believe one can attract love by looking badly in need of it. This is a mistaken notion. At best, you may attract someone with a social worker approach to romance who will therefore, immediately after making you happy, want to move on. If looking like a problem in search of a solution is not sexually irresistible, looking like someone with a solution is. The secret to popularity is looking as if you had discovered the secret of a happy life, whether or not you have. You may then, once someone has fallen in love with you, have a sudden relapse into misery and expect her sympathy and help.

The Silent Type

DEAR MISS MANNERS

My boyfriend is very shy, and we never seem to have anything to talk about. On the phone—he calls me every night before bedtime—the silences are awful. Can you suggest something I could say to him?

GENTLE READER:

"Do you have any nice friends?"

. . .

Newer Problems

Displaying Affection

The birds are singing, the flowers are budding, and it is time for Miss Manners to tell young lovers to stop necking in public.

It's not that Miss Manners is immune to romance. Miss Manners has been known to squeeze a gentleman's arm while being helped over a curb, and, in her wild youth, even to press a dainty slipper against a foot or two under the dinner table. Miss Manners also believes that the sight of people strolling hand in hand or arm in arm or arm in hand dresses up a city considerably more than the more familiar sight of people shaking umbrellas at one another. What Miss Manners objects to is the kind of activity that frightens the horses on the streets, although it is not the horses' sensibilities she is considering. It's the lovers', and their future.

Heavy romances—we are speaking of the kind in which the participants can hardly keep their hands to themselves, not the kind in which they have nothing better to do with them—can progress in only two ways:

They can (1) end. In this case, if you have displayed the height of the romance publicly, the public will take pleasure in seeking you out in the depths. Just when you are being very careful not to move suddenly because you have your heart tied together only with bits of old string, it will spring at you and demand to know, "Where's Rock? I thought you were inseparable?" or "How come I saw Hope out with three other guys last night?"

That is not the worst that can happen, however. Romances can also (2) not end. The participants can get married and live happily ever after. Then they are in trouble. This is because one day they will stop behaving conspicuously. Then everyone will notice. The cause may not be that the romance will have gone out of the marriage, but that it will have a home to go to. With more opportunities to express affection, the couple no longer seizes the opportunity to do so on other people's sofas. The other people will then have a good snicker which, unlike the original snickers, cannot be passed off by the loving couple as jealousy. The Duchess of Windsor once said that she hated to have dinner in a restaurant alone with her husband because if they failed for one minute to chatter sparklingly at each other—taking, say, a moment to chew their food, instead—everyone in the restaurant would be saying, "You see? That's what he gave up a throne for, and now look how bored they are."

"I Love You"

DEAR MISS MANNERS:

My boyfriend and I are having an argument about what the response should be when someone says "I love you." He once replied, "Thank you," and I said that one does not say "Thank you" when someone says "I love you." What can one say in response, besides, "I love you, too"?

GENTLE READER:

There is no doubt that "I love you, too," is the only really acceptable reply to "I love you." Acceptable to the lover, that is.

However, making the other person feel good is not, as Miss Manners keeps telling you, always the object of etiquette. If you do not love the person making the original statement, replying kindly could lead to all sorts of dreadful complications, not the least of which is further and even more unfortunate questions, such as "But do you really love me?" or "More than you've ever loved anyone before?" or "How can I believe you?"

One needs, therefore, to make the lack of reciprocation clear while showing gratitude for the other person's good taste. Your boyfriend's suggestion is not bad, although Miss Manners prefers "You do me great honor." If, however, his object was merely to give variety to the conversation of happy lovers, "Thank you" is a little stiff, as it is firmly attached, in most people's minds to "You're welcome," and that has a kind of finality that rounds off the conversation, rather than leading it to "Let's run off to Paris for the weekend."

If he doesn't want to keep saying "I love you, too," let him offer one of the many restatements of this remark in every true lover's icky vocabulary. But Miss Manners has never understood why lovers can't keep saying the same thing over and over. They keep doing the same thing over and over, don't they?

A Simple Question

DEAR MISS MANNERS:

I am a twenty-eight-year-old male and have been seeing a twenty-three-year-old woman for almost one year. We work together and see no one else. My problem is that I am in love with her, but she is unable to verbalize any feelings at all for me. She has never had a relationship last for more than a few weeks and says she has never been in love. All of her friends and relatives like me and she is well liked by everyone I know. Many of her friends often say, "When are you two getting married?" She says she cares for me a great deal; but I feel I could very easily lose her. Every six weeks or so, I become depressed and get the feeling I am being used.

Is there a way for me to get her to express her true feelings? Even if they were negative, I would at least know how she felt and I would then have to deal with that.

GENTLE READER:

Yes, there is, but it is so simple that people lose sight of it while they are busy with such complicated things as feeling used, being unable to verbalize, or getting depressed. Ask her: "Will you marry me?" If she says "Yes," it will mean that she cares for you as more than temporary companionship, and if she says "No," it means that she doesn't.

. . .

Increasing the Rate of Romance

DEAR MISS MANNERS:

I have been dating a fellow for a year and one half, during which we only saw each other on weekends, due to the distance involved. During that time, we were both basically happy and he told me he loved me. Recently during our one and only big argument, I brought up "commitments" and felt that our relationship should be more integrated after this period of time. His response was that he cared but that something tells him that he wants something different, which would include more freedom and the possibility of dating other women. He wants to be friends. We are still dating occasionally. I can tell that the feelings are still present, but neither one of us has discussed the outcome of our argument.

What do you do when you still care just as much as ever, but now are only seeing him occasionally, not knowing if in between times he is seeing others? I feel that if I give him an ultimatum and question him, he'll know it bothers me. Do you think the advice in your article about being a cheerful loser would still apply when they tell you they care? I would appreciate any advice that could be given because the situation is driving me crazy and I'm just not sure how to handle it.

GENTLE READER:

Of course the situation is driving you crazy. The slow jilt is bad enough, but it is at least clear that one must not hang around waiting to get the last possible twitch of torture. When there is real hope that a slow courtship, rather than a slow jilt, is what is going on, the response is more difficult.

You are actually doing quite well. Miss Manners knows that it is fear, and not understanding, that keeps you from blurting out, "Why can't you make a commitment? Don't you love me? If you really loved me, you'd want to," and all those tedious remarks. Whatever the motivation, the action required in this situation is no action. A commitment is made when both people want certainty. Pressing an unwilling person to make a commitment is giving that person the certainty without extracting it. It thereby removes his incentive of securing certainty by giving it freely. Miss Manners apologizes if this sounds like the old keep-'em-guessing routine. She is well aware how exhausting, degrading, and debilitating such antics are for the sure and loving heart. That is why God invented marriage: to give people a rest. Miss Manners wishes you the best and only asks that should you live through this courtship to marriage, you appreciate certainty and not start whining about how there is no more magic in your life.

Genesis 24: Finding a Wife for Isaac

The life of the patriarch Abraham is drawing to a close. He has completed his numerous trials, been rewarded (at age 99!) with the birth of a son (Isaac) through his beloved, long-barren wife, Sarah, survived the test of the binding of Isaac, and buried Sarah in a cave, purchased from the natives, in the promised land. In order to provide for the perpetuation of the new way of life to which God had called him as founder, Abraham needs to arrange for a proper wife for Isaac, who, for unstated reasons, is apparently not fit to go looking on his own behalf. Abraham's servant is up to the task of finding and winning the right one: We know from the sequel that Rebekah will play a crucial role in securing the perpetuation of God's new way, leading her misguided husband (at first, by means of guile) to bless their more suitable son, Jacob, while also avoiding the danger of fratricide between her twin sons. Why is it important that the wife come from Abraham's own clan? How does the servant identify "the right woman"? What virtues of Rebekah are revealed in this story? How is she won? What do we make of her decisive (in Hebrew, one-word) choice, in verse 58, "I-will-go"? What about the portraits of Isaac and Rebekah that anticipate their meeting (vv. 62–65)? Why does Rebekah veil herself? And what do we make of this suggested (and, perhaps, preferred) sequence: first, he installed her in his mother's place, then he "took her" so that she became (de facto) his wife, and (only) then "he loved her"? Do the answers to these questions regarding this ancient "courtship-by-proxy" hold any lessons for wooing and wedding on one's own? For us today?

And Abraham was old, well stricken in age; and the Lord had blessed Abraham in all things. ²And Abraham said unto his servant, the elder of his house, that ruled over all that he had: 'Put, I pray thee, thy hand under my thigh. ³And I will make thee swear by the Lord the God of heaven and the God of the earth, that thou shalt not take a wife for my son of the daughters of the Canaanites, among whom I dwell. ⁴But thou shalt go unto my country, and to my kindred, and take a wife for my son, even for Isaac.' ⁵And the servant said unto him: 'Peradventure the woman will not be willing to follow me unto this land; must I needs bring thy son back unto the land from whence thou camest?' ⁶And Abraham said unto him: 'Beware thou that thou bring not my son back thither. ⁷The Lord, the God of heaven, who took me from my father's house, and from the land of my nativity, and who spoke unto me, and who swore unto me, saying: Unto thy seed will I give this land; He will send His angel before thee, and thou shalt take a wife for my son from thence. ⁸And if the woman be not willing to follow thee, then thou shalt be clear from this my oath; only thou shalt not bring my son back thither.' ⁹And the servant put his hand under the thigh of Abraham his master, and swore to him concerning this matter. ¹⁰And the servant took ten camels, of the camels of his master, and departed; having all goodly things of his master's in his hand; and he arose, and went to ªAram-naharaim, unto the city of Nahor. ¹¹And he made the camels to kneel down without the city by the well of water at the time of evening, the time that women go out to draw water. ¹²And he said: 'O LORD, the God of my master Abraham, send me, I pray Thee, good speed this day, and show kindness unto my master Abraham. ¹³Behold, I stand by the fountain of water; and the daughters of the men of the city come out to draw water. ¹⁴So let it come to pass, that the damsel to whom I shall say: Let down thy pitcher, I pray thee, that I may drink; and she shall say: Drink, and I will give thy camels drink also; let the same be she that Thou hast appointed for Thy servant, even for Isaac; and thereby shall I know that Thou hast shown kindness unto my master.' ¹⁵And it came to pass, before he had done speaking, that, behold, Rebekah came out, who was born to Bethuel the son of Milcah, the wife of Nahor, Abraham's brother, with her pitcher upon her shoulder. ¹⁶And the damsel was very fair to look upon, a virgin, neither had any man known her; and she went down to the fountain, and filled her pitcher and came up. ¹⁷And the servant ran to meet her, and said: 'Give me to drink, I pray thee, a little water of thy pitcher.' ¹⁸And she said: 'Drink, my lord'; and she hastened, and let down her pitcher upon her hand, and gave him drink. ¹⁹And when she had done giving him drink, she said: 'I will draw for thy camels also, until they have done drinking.' ²⁰And she hastened, and emptied her pitcher into the trough, and ran again unto the well to draw, and drew for all his camels. ²¹And the man looked stedfastly on her; holding his peace, to know whether the LORD had made his journey prosperous or not. ²²And it came to pass, as the camels had done drinking, that the man took a golden ring of half a shekel weight, and two bracelets for her hands of ten shekels weight of gold; ²³and said: 'Whose daughter art thou? tell me, I pray thee. Is there room in thy father's house for us to lodge in?' ²⁴And she said unto him: 'I am the daughter of Bethuel the son of Milcah, whom she bore unto Nahor.' ²⁵She said moreover unto him: 'We have both straw and provender enough, and room to lodge in.' ²⁶And the man bowed his head and prostrated himself before the LORD. ²⁷And he said: 'Blessed be the LORD, the God of my master Abraham, who hath not forsaken His mercy and His truth toward my master; as for me, the LORD hath led me in the way to the house of my master's brethren.' ²⁸And the damsel ran, and told her mother's house according to these words. ²⁹And Rebekah had a brother, and his name was Laban; and Laban ran out unto the man, unto the fountain. ³⁰And it came to pass,

---

ªThat is, *Mesopotamia*

when he saw the ring, and the bracelets upon his sister's hands, and when he heard the words of Rebekah his sister, saying: 'Thus spoke the man unto me,' that he came unto the man; and, behold, he stood by the camels at the fountain. ³¹And he said: 'Come in, thou blessed of the Lord; wherefore standest thou without? for I have cleared the house, and made room for the camels.' ³²And the man came into the house, and he ungirded the camels; and he gave straw and provender for the camels, and water to wash his feet and the feet of the men that were with him. ³³And there was set food before him to eat; but he said: 'I will not eat, until I have told mine errand.' And he said: 'Speak on.' ³⁴And he said: 'I am Abraham's servant. ³⁵And the Lord hath blessed my master greatly; and he is become great; and He hath given him flocks and herds, and silver and gold, and men-servants and maid-servants, and camels and asses. ³⁶And Sarah my master's wife bore a son to my master when she was old; and unto him hath he given all that he hath. ³⁷And my master made me swear, saying: Thou shalt not take a wife for my son of the daughters of the Canaanites, in whose land I dwell. ³⁸But thou shalt go unto my father's house, and to my kindred, and take a wife for my son. ³⁹And I said unto my master: Peradventure the woman will not follow me. ⁴⁰And he said unto me: The Lord, before whom I walk, will send His angel with thee, and prosper thy way; and thou shalt take a wife for my son of my kindred, and of my father's house, ⁴¹then shalt thou be clear from my oath, when thou comest to my kindred; and if they give her not to thee, thou shalt be clear from my oath. ⁴²And I came this day unto the fountain, and said: O Lord, the God of my master Abraham, if now Thou do prosper my way which I go: ⁴³behold, I stand by the fountain of water; and let it come to pass, that the maiden that cometh forth to draw, to whom I shall say: Give me, I pray thee, a little water from thy pitcher to drink; ⁴⁴and she shall say to me: Both drink thou, and I will also draw for thy camels; let the same be the woman whom the Lord hath appointed for my master's son. ⁴⁵And before I had done speaking to my heart, behold, Rebekah came forth with her pitcher on her shoulder; and she went down unto the fountain, and drew. And I said unto her: Let me drink, I pray thee. ⁴⁶And she made haste, and let down her pitcher from her shoulder, and said: Drink, and I will give thy camels drink also. So I drank, and she made the camels drink also. ⁴⁷And I asked her, and said: Whose daughter art thou? And she said: The daughter of Bethuel, Nahor's son, whom Milcah bore unto him. And I put the ring upon her nose, and the bracelets upon her hands. ⁴⁸And I bowed my head, and prostrated myself before the Lord, and blessed the Lord, the God of my master Abraham, who had led me in the right way to take my master's brother's daughter for his son. ⁴⁹And now if ye will deal kindly and truly with my master, tell me; and if not, tell me; that I may turn to the right hand or to the left.' ⁵⁰Then Laban and Bethuel answered and said: 'The thing proceedeth from the

Lord; we cannot speak unto thee bad or good. [51]Behold, Rebekah is before thee, take her, and go, and let her be thy master's son's wife, as the Lord hath spoken.' [52]And it came to pass, that, when Abraham's servant heard their words, he bowed himself down to the earth unto the Lord. [53]And the servant brought forth jewels of silver, and jewels of gold, and raiment, and gave them to Rebekah; he gave also to her brother and to her mother precious things. [54]And they did eat and drink, he and the men that were with him, and tarried all night; and they rose up in the morning, and he said: 'Send me away unto my master.' [55]And her brother and her mother said: 'Let the damsel abide with us a few days, at the least ten; after that she shall go.' [56]And he said unto them: 'Delay me not, seeing the Lord hath prospered my way; send me away that I may go to my master.' [57]And they said: 'We will call the damsel, and inquire at her mouth.' [58]And they called Rebekah, and said unto her: 'Wilt thou go with this man?' And she said: 'I will go.' [59]And they sent away Rebekah their sister, and her nurse, and Abraham's servant, and his men. [60]And they blessed Rebekah, and said unto her: 'Our sister, be thou the mother of thousands of ten thousands, and let thy seed possess the gate of those that hate them.' [61]And Rebekah arose, and her damsels, and they rode upon the camels, and followed the man. And the servant took Rebekah, and went his way. [62]And Isaac came from the way of Beer-lahai-roi; for he dwelt in the land of the South. [63]And Isaac went out to meditate in the field at the eventide; and he lifted up his eyes, and saw, and, behold, there were camels coming. [64]And Rebekah lifted up her eyes, and when she saw Isaac, she alighted from her camel. [65]And she said unto the servant: 'What man is this that walketh in the field to meet us?' And the servant said: 'It is my master.' And she took her veil, and covered herself. [66]And the servant told Isaac all the things that he had done. [67]And Isaac brought her into his mother Sarah's tent, and took Rebekah, and she became his wife; and he loved her. And Isaac was comforted for his mother.

Genesis 29–31: Jacob Finds a Wife

Sent out by his father, Isaac, to find a wife from among the daughters of his mother's (Rebekah's) brother, Laban, Jacob goes courting on his own. Unlike Abraham's servant, to whose journey the present episode is fruitfully compared, Jacob goes empty-handed, without gifts or bride-price. We wonder whether he will fare well in his choice of wife. Jacob, it seems, falls in love at first sight with Rachel at the well and labors seven years for her. But, thanks to Laban's deception on his wedding night, Jacob winds up with two wives, his extraordinarily beautiful and beloved Rachel, who will be barren, and her soft- or tender-eyed but unloved sister Leah, who will bear Jacob many children. The story thus naturally provokes the question of which woman makes Jacob the better wife. Is falling in love with visible beauty a reliable guide for a good marriage? If eyes are windows to the soul, are they perhaps more revealing and relevant than beauteous form? Does Rachel's attachment to the (visible) household gods of her father (Chapter 31) have any bearing on the wisdom of Jacob's love? What does Jacob's response to Rachel's demand for children reveal about his own—and about Rachel's—understanding of marriage?

Genesis 29

Then Jacob went on his journey, and came to the land of the children of the east. ²And he looked, and behold, a well in the field, and lo, three flocks of sheep lying there by it.—For out of that well they watered the flocks. And the stone upon the well's mouth was great. ³And thither were all the flocks gathered; and they rolled the stone from the well's mouth, and watered the sheep, and put the stone back upon the well's mouth in its place.—⁴And Jacob said unto them: 'My brethren, whence are ye?' And they said: 'Of Haran are we.' ⁵And he said unto them: 'Know ye Laban the son of Nahor?' And they said: 'We know him.' ⁶And he said unto them: 'Is it well with him?' And they said: 'It is well; and, behold, Rachel his daughter cometh with the sheep.' ⁷And he said: 'Lo, it is yet high day, neither is it time that the cattle should be gathered together; water ye the sheep, and go and feed them.' ⁸And they said: 'We cannot, until all the flocks be gathered together, and they roll the stone from the well's mouth; then we water the sheep.' ⁹While he was yet speaking with them, Rachel came with her father's sheep; for she tended them. ¹⁰And it came to pass, when Jacob saw Rachel the daughter of Laban his mother's brother, and the sheep of Laban his mother's brother, that Jacob went near, and rolled the stone from the well's mouth, and watered the flock of Laban his mother's brother. ¹¹And

Jacob kissed Rachel, and lifted up his voice, and wept. [12]And Jacob told Rachel that he was her father's brother, and that he was Rebekah's son; and she ran and told her father. [13]And it came to pass, when Laban heard the tidings of Jacob his sister's son, that he ran to meet him, and embraced him, and kissed him, and brought him to his house. And he told Laban all these things. [14]And Laban said to him: 'Surely thou art my bone and my flesh.' And he abode with him the space of a month. [15]And Laban said unto Jacob: 'Because thou art my brother, shouldest thou therefore serve me for nought? tell me, what shall thy wages be?' [16]Now Laban had two daughters: the name of the elder was Leah, and the name of the younger was Rachel. [17]And Leah's eyes were soft; but Rachel was of beautiful form and beautiful to look upon. [18]And Jacob loved Rachel; and he said: 'I will serve thee seven years for Rachel thy younger daughter.' [19]And Laban said: 'It is better that I give her to thee, than that I should give her to another man; abide with me.' [20]And Jacob served seven years for Rachel; and they seemed unto him but a few days, for the love he had to her. [21]And Jacob said unto Laban: 'Give me my wife, for my days are fulfilled, that I may go in unto her.' [22]And Laban gathered together all the men of the place, and made a feast. [23]And it came to pass in the evening, that he took Leah his daughter, and brought her to him; and he went in unto her. [24]And Laban gave Zilpah his handmaid unto his daughter Leah for a handmaid. [25]And it came to pass in the morning that, behold, it was Leah; and he said to Laban: 'What is this thou hast done unto me? did not I serve with thee for Rachel? wherefore then hast thou beguiled me?' [26]And Laban said: 'It is not so done in our place, to give the younger before the first-born. [27]Fulfil the week of this one, and we will give thee the other also for the service which thou shalt serve with me yet seven other years.' [28]And Jacob did so, and fulfilled her week; and he gave him Rachel his daughter to wife. [29]And Laban gave to Rachel his daughter Bilhah his handmaid to be her handmaid. [30]And he went in also unto Rachel, and he loved Rachel more than Leah, and served with him yet seven other years.

[31]And the Lord saw that Leah was hated, and he opened her womb; but Rachel was barren. [32]And Leah conceived, and bore a son, and she called his name Reuben; for she said: 'Because the LORD [a]hath looked upon my affliction; for now my husband will love me.' [33]And she conceived again, and bore a son; and said: 'Because the LORD [b]hath heard that I am hated, He hath therefore given me this son also.' And she called his name [c]Simeon. [34]And she conceived again, and bore a son; and said: 'Now this time will my husband be [d]joined

[a]Heb. *raah beonji.*
[b]Heb. *shama.*
[c]Heb. *Shimeon.*
[d]From the Heb. root *lavah*

unto me, because I have borne him three sons.' Therefore was his name called Levi. [35]And she conceived again, and bore a son; and she said: 'This time will I [e]praise the LORD.' Therefore she called his name [f]Judah; and she left off bearing.

Genesis 30

And when Rachel saw that she bore Jacob no children, Rachel envied her sister; and she said to Jacob: 'Give me children, or else I die.' [2]And Jacob's anger was kindled against Rachel; and he said: 'Am I in God's stead, who hath withheld from thee the fruit of the womb?' [3]And she said: 'Behold my maid Bilhah, go in unto her; that she may bear upon my knees, and I also may be builded up through her.' [4]And she gave him Bilhah her handmaid to wife; and Jacob went in unto her. [5]And Bilhah conceived, and bore Jacob a son. [6]And Rachel said: 'God hath [g]judged me, and hath also heard my voice, and hath given me a son.' Therefore called she his name Dan. [7]And Bilhah Rachel's handmaid conceived again, and bore Jacob a second son. [8]And Rachel said: 'With mighty wrestlings have I [h]wrestled with my sister, and have prevailed.' And she called his name Naphtali. [9]When Leah saw that she had left off bearing, she took Zilpah her handmaid, and gave her to Jacob to wife. [10]And Zilpah Leah's handmaid bore Jacob a son. [11]And Leah said: 'Fortune is come!' And she called his name [i]Gad. [12]And Zilpah Leah's handmaid bore Jacob a second son. [13]And Leah said: 'Happy am I! for the daughters will call me happy.' And she called his name [j]Asher. [14]And Reuben went in the days of wheat harvest, and found mandrakes in the field, and brought them unto his mother Leah. Then Rachel said to Leah: 'Give me, I pray thee, of thy son's mandrakes.' [15]And she said unto her: 'Is it a small matter that thou hast taken away my husband? and wouldest thou take away my son's mandrakes also?' And Rachel said: 'Therefore he shall lie with thee to-night for thy son's mandrakes.' [16]And Jacob came from the field in the evening, and Leah went out to meet him, and said: 'Thou must come in unto me; for I have surely hired thee with my son's mandrakes.' And he lay with her that night. [17]And God hearkened unto Leah, and she conceived, and bore Jacob a fifth son. [18]And Leah said: 'God hath given me my [k]hire, because I gave my handmaid to my husband.' And she called his name Issachar. [19]And Leah conceived again, and bore a sixth son to Jacob. [20]And Leah said: 'God hath

---

[e]From the Heb. *hodah.*
[f]Heb. *Jehudah*
[g]Heb. *dan,* he judged.
[h]Heb. *naphtal,* he wrestled.
[i]That is, *Fortune.*
[j]That is, *Happy.*
[k]Heb. *sachar.*

endowed me with a good dowry; now my husband [l]dwell with me, because I have borne him six sons.' And she called his name Zebulun. [21]And afterwards she bore a daughter, and called her name Dinah. [22]And God remembered Rachel, and God hearkened to her, and opened her womb. [23]And she conceived, and bore a son, and said: 'God [m]hath taken away my reproach.' [24]And she called his name Joseph, saying: 'The Lord [n]add to me another son.'

[25]And it came to pass, when Rachel had borne Joseph, that Jacob said to Laban: 'Send me away, that I may go unto mine own place, and to my country. [26]Give me my wives and children for whom I have served thee, and let me go, for thou knowest my service wherewith I have served thee.' [27]And Laban said unto him: 'If now I have found favour in thine eyes—I have observed the signs, and the LORD hath blessed me for thy sake.' [28]And he said: 'Appoint me thy wages, and I will give it.' [29]And he said unto him: 'Thou knowest how I have served thee, and how thy cattle have fared with me. [30]For it was little which thou hadst before I came, and it hath increased abundantly; and the LORD hath blessed thee whithersoever I turned. And now when shall I provide for mine own house also?' [31]And he said: 'What shall I give thee?' And Jacob said: 'Thou shalt not give me aught; if thou wilt do this thing for me I will again feed thy flock and keep it. [32]I will pass through all thy flock to-day, removing from thence every speckled and spotted one, and every dark one among the sheep, and the spotted and speckled among the goats; and of such shall be my hire. [33]So shall my righteousness witness against me hereafter, when thou shalt come to look over my hire that is before thee: every one that is not speckled and spotted among the goats, and dark among the sheep, that if found with me shall be counted stolen.' [34]And Laban said: 'Behold, would it might be according to thy word.' [35]And he removed that day the he-goats that were streaked and spotted, and all the she-goats that were speckled and spotted, every one that had white in it, and all the dark ones among the sheep, and gave them into the hand of his sons. [36]And he set three days' journey betwixt himself and Jacob. And Jacob fed the rest of Laban's flocks. [37]And Jacob took him rods of fresh poplar, and of the almond and of the planetree; and peeled white streaks in them, making the white appear which was in the rods. [38]And he set the rods which he had peeled over against the flocks in the gutters in the watering-troughs where the flocks came to drink; and they conceived when they came to drink. [39]And the flocks conceived at the sight of the rods, and the flocks brought forth streaked, speckled, and spotted. [40]And Jacob separated the

[l]Heb. *zabal,* he dwelt.
[m]Heb. *asaph.*
[n]Heb. *joseph.*

lambs—he also set the faces of the flocks toward the streaked and all the dark in the flock of Laban—and put his own droves apart, and put them not unto Laban's flock. [41]And it came to pass, whensoever the stronger of the flock did conceive, that Jacob laid the rods before the eyes of the flock in the gutters, that they might conceive among the rods; [42]but when the flock were feeble, he put them not in; so the feebler were Laban's, and the stronger Jacob's. [43]And the man increased exceedingly, and had large flocks, and maid-servants and men-servants, and camels and asses.

Genesis 31

And he heard the words of Laban's sons, saying: 'Jacob hath taken away all that was our father's; and of that which was our father's hath he gotten all this wealth.' [2]And Jacob beheld the countenance of Laban, and, behold, it was not toward him as beforetime. [3]And the LORD said unto Jacob: 'Return unto the land of thy fathers, and to thy kindred; and I will be with thee.' [4]And Jacob sent and called Rachel and Leah to the field unto his flock, [5]and said unto them: 'I see your father's countenance, that it is not toward me as beforetime; but the God of my father hath been with me. [6]And ye know that with all my power I have served your father. [7]And your father hath mocked me, and changed my wages ten times; but God suffered him not to hurt me. [8]If he said thus: The speckled shall be thy wages; then all the flock bore speckled; and if he said thus: The streaked shall be thy wages; then bore all the flock streaked. [9]Thus God hath taken away the cattle of your father, and given them to me. [10]And it came to pass at the time that the flock conceived, that I lifted up mine eyes, and saw in a dream, and, behold, the he-goats which leaped upon the flock were streaked, speckled, and grizzled. [11]And the angel of God said unto me in the dream: Jacob; and I said: Here am I. [12]And he said: Lift up now thine eyes, and see, all the he-goats which leap upon the flock are streaked, speckled, and grizzled; for I have seen all that Laban doeth unto thee. [13]I am the God of Beth-el, where thou didst anoint a pillar, where thou didst vow a vow unto Me. Now arise, get thee out from this land, and return unto the land of thy nativity.' [14]And Rachel and Leah answered and said unto him: 'Is there yet any portion or inheritance for us in our father's house? [15]Are we not accounted by him strangers? for he hath sold us, and hath also quite devoured our bride price. [16]For all the riches which God hath taken away from our father, that is ours and our children's. Now then, whatsoever God hath said unto thee, do.' [17]Then Jacob rose up, and set his sons and his wives upon the camels; [18]and he carried away all his cattle, and all his substance which he had gathered, the cattle of his getting, which he had gathered in Paddan-aram, to go to Isaac his father unto the land of Canaan. [19]Now Laban was gone to shear his sheep. And Rachel stole the °teraphim that were her father's. [20]And Jacob outwitted Laban the Aramean, in that he told him not that he fled. [21]So he fled with all that he had; and he rose up, and passed over the River, and set his face toward the mountain of Gilead.

[22]And it was told Laban on the third day that Jacob was fled. [23]And he took his brethren with him, and pursued after him seven days' journey; and he overtook him in the mountain of Gilead. [24]And God came to Laban the Aramean in a dream of the night, and said unto him: 'Take heed to thyself that thou speak not to Jacob either good or bad.' [25]And Laban came up with Jacob. Now Jacob had pitched his tent in the mountain; and Laban with his brethren pitched in the mountain of Gilead. [26]And Laban said Jacob: 'What hast thou done that thou hast outwitted me, and carried away my daughters as though captives of the sword? [27]Wherefore didst thou flee secretly, and outwit me; and didst not tell me, that I might have sent thee away with mirth and with songs, with tabret and with harp; [28]and didst not suffer me to kiss my sons and my daughters? now hast thou done foolishly. [29]It is in the power of my hand to do you hurt; but the God of your father spoke unto me yesternight, saying: Take heed to thyself that thou speak not to Jacob either good or bad. [30]And now that thou art surely gone, because thou sore longest after thy father's house, wherefore hast thou stolen my gods?' [31]And Jacob answered and said to Laban: 'Because I was afraid; for I said: Lest thou shouldest take thy daughters from me by force. [32]With whomsoever thou findest thy gods, he shall not live; before our brethren discern thou what is thine with me, and take it to thee.'—For Jacob knew not that Rachel had stolen them.—[33]And Laban went into Jacob's tent, and into Leah's tent, and into the tent of the two maid-servants; but he found them not. And he went out of Leah's tent, and entered into Rachel's tent. [34]Now Rachel had taken the teraphim, and put them in the saddle of the camel, and sat upon them. And Laban felt about all the tent, but found them not. [35]And she said to her father: 'Let not my lord be angry that I cannot rise up before thee; for the manner of women is upon me.' And he searched, but found not the teraphim. [36]And Jacob was wroth, and strove with Laban. And Jacob answered and said to Laban: 'What is my trespass? what is my sin, that thou hast hotly pursued after me? [37]Whereas thou hast felt about all my stuff, what has thou found of all thy household stuff? Set it here before my brethren and thy brethren, that they may judge betwixt us two. [38]These twenty years have I been with thee; thy ewes and thy she-goats have not cast their young, and the rams of thy flocks have I not eaten. [39]That which was torn of beasts I brought not unto thee; I bore the loss of it; of my hand didst thou require it, whether stolen

°The household gods

by day or stolen by night. ⁴⁰Thus I was: in the day the drought consumed me, and the frost by night; and my sleep fled from mine eyes. ⁴¹These twenty years have I been in thy house: I served thee fourteen years for thy two daughters, and six years for thy flock; and thou has changed my wages ten times. ⁴²Except the God of my father, the God of Abraham, and the Fear of Isaac, had been on my side, surely now hadst thou sent me away empty. God hath seen mine affliction and the labour of my hands, and gave judgment yesternight.' ⁴³And Laban answered and said unto Jacob: 'The daughters are my daughters, and the children are my children, and the flocks are my flocks, and all that thou seest is mine; and what can I do this day for these my daughters, or for their children whom they have borne? ⁴⁴And now come, let us make a covenant, I and thou; and let it be for a witness between me and thee.' ⁴⁵And Jacob took a stone, and set it up for a pillar. ⁴⁶And Jacob said unto his brethren: 'Gather stones'; and they took stones, and made a heap. And they did eat there by the heap. ⁴⁷And Laban called it ᴾJegar-sahadutha; but Jacob called it ᑫGaleed. ⁴⁸And Laban said: 'This heap is witness between me and thee this day.' Therefore was the name of it called Galeed; ⁴⁹and ᴿMizpah, for he said: 'The LORD watch between me and thee, when we are absent one from another. ⁵⁰If thou shalt afflict my daughters, and if thou shalt take wives beside my daughters, no man being with us; see, God is witness betwixt me and thee.' ⁵¹And Laban said to Jacob: 'Behold this heap, and behold the pillar, which I have set up betwixt me and thee. ⁵²This heap be witness, and the pillar be witness, that I will not pass over this heap to thee, and that thou shalt not pass over this heap and this pillar unto me, for harm. ⁵³The God of Abraham, and the God of Nahor, the God of their father, judge betwixt us.' And Jacob swore by the Fear of his father Isaac. ⁵⁴And Jacob offered a sacrifice in the mountain, and called his brethren to eat bread; and they did eat bread, and tarried all night in the mountain.

ᴾThat is, *The heap of witness*, in Aramaic.
ᑫThat is, *The heap of witness*, in Hebrew.
ᴿThat is, *The watch-post*.

Abraham, "The Engagement: A Story"

For most people living in the West, arranged marriage is a thing of the distant past. And though one hears today, as one would never have heard thirty years ago, the occasional half-serious nostalgic remark to the effect that parents arranging marriage for their children could hardly do worse than the children are now doing on their own, secular and enlightened opinion condemns the very idea as a violation of both personal freedom and the proper erotic foundation of matrimony. But in some strongly traditional subcultures, even in America, the matchmaking ways followed by the patriarch Abraham are still being practiced, indeed, precisely to ensure that the traditional ways get perpetuated by means of households expressly constituted with that primary end in view. In these communities, when young men and young women are brought together, everyone understands that serious matters are at stake. In this story, adapted from her first novel, The Romance Reader *(1995), Pearl Abraham (born in 1960) tells of a match arranged for a young Jewish woman who is more independent and less tradition-minded than her rabbinical family, and who has acquired certain romantic notions about love and marriage from her reading. The arrangement makes no pretense of finding "one's heart's desire"—a tall, dark man in boots—or, in general, of living up to imaginary portraits of erotic longings, but of finding a good-enough match, taking into account the idiosyncrasies of the man and the woman. What is won is not so much the woman's heart but her consent; love, if it comes, comes later, born from a shared familial life informed by common tradition and cares. Why does the heroine, Rachel, choose as she does? Does the system work to get her a suitable husband? Will she be happy or fulfilled? Is reading about love dangerous? What do we think of the opinions voiced by the other characters, especially her friend Elke, who insists that love comes only after marriage: "Everyone I know says so"? Is there something to be said for the view that "Maybe it's better doing things the way everyone does. You know exactly how it goes"?*

"What kind of man do you want me to look for?" Ma asks when we're walking. "You'll have to rely on me to find the right one; your father has no idea."

This is her favorite subject these days.

"Not a man like Father," I tell her. "Not a man with a synagogue that no one needs, and who walks around not knowing what day it is."

"No; I wouldn't wish on anyone a man like your father," Ma agrees. "You need iron nerves to live with a man like your father. Mine are shattered. But what did I know? I liked him. Girls today are smarter. They know more."

Liked or loved? The Yiddish word for like is the same as for love. I wonder, is there a difference?

I say, "I need someone who gets things done someone who's on time."

"Yes, a *geshikter,* like Mr. Lebowitz. In that family, it's just the opposite. Mrs. Lebowitz is the slow one. Her husband is always quick, quick. The way I am."

"I don't want someone exactly like Mr. Lebowitz; just lively like him."

"You're right," Ma says. "Your husband should have a head like your father and should be *geshikt* like Mr. Lebowitz."

I don't answer. I can think of better heads than Father's. Heads that work more thoroughly, clearly. Heads that don't care about hasidic dynasties. Heads too involved in Torah to worry about what people say.

Ma looks at me. "What, you don't think your father has a good head?"

"It's not that," I say slowly, carefully. "I just don't want someone like Father. I want a plain person, not a hasidic rabbi."

Ma shakes her head. "Father will only accept a *rebbishe* family for his first daughter. That's what he told the *shadkhan.*[1] He says the first one is most important. The first marriage sets the pattern for the others."

"The *shadkhan?*" I say. "You mean you spoke to a *shadkhan?* I told you I'm not interested until after I graduate. I won't even hear of anyone before then."

"I know, I know. But it doesn't hurt to start feeling around. Graduation is not so far away. Chayie Brecher is already engaged. Soon there'll be others in your class."

"Chayie is an orphan. She needs a home. She doesn't count."

"The *shadkhan* called Father," Ma says. "It's better that they call than that we should have to call them. This way you know someone put him up to it. Someone's interested." She looks at me. "Don't you wonder who?"

Her eyes sparkle. She's so excited that someone called. All she wants is a married daughter; she's excited about having a married daughter and a son-in-law. With David right after me, she'll soon have a daughter-in-law too. Then Leah will get married; and still there will be Levi, Sarah, Aaron, and Esther.

"No, I'm not interested," I say. "I told you already. I want to teach for at least a year before getting married. I've said this at least ten times. Why didn't you tell Father to say that to the *shadkhan?*"

She waves her hand, making nothing I say matter. "There's no reason to say it. Let the *shadkhan* do his work. A year goes quickly. I wasn't supposed to tell you. Father said not to mention it. Maybe he was right. You go for your interview and get the job. We'll take care of things."

[1]A *shadkhan* is a matchmaker.

"What, and surprise me one day when I come home? Tell me a boy's here to see me? You better not pull any *shtick* like that."

Ma laughs. "Who said anything about a boy coming to see you? It's all talk now. The boys aren't lining up at your door. Don't worry. You're not so desirable. The *shadkhan* said there are rumors that you're modern; he asked what kind of stockings you wear. Father convinced him you wear the thickest seams, nothing see-through. Don't worry. It won't go so smoothly, it won't be one-two-three."

She knows how to go from one side to the other with just a snap of her fingers. First a compliment, then an insult. I don't trust Father. I think he's planning to pull something off. He wants to hurry me into marriage before I know what's what. I'm only a daughter, and not one who will bring honor to this family. He wants to get to David. For David he can choose from the best.

I wear my new pale-blue mohair sweater, a long, straight gray-flannel skirt, and my black shoe-boots to my interview with Rabbi Nathan. He tells me he has two grades for me, second and sixth. He wants every teacher to teach one grade in the morning and the other in the afternoon, a full day. I was looking forward to half-days off, but I agree to teach both. There'll be a few meetings before the summer, he says. Before everyone goes away. This will be his first year in this school, too, he says, so everything will be as new to him as to me. We'll learn about the place together, he says.

I like him. He smokes a pipe, and every time he starts to talk, he fumbles, almost drops it, trying to take it out. Sometimes he leaves it in and talks out of the side of his mouth.

He says there will be two other English teachers, both a year older than I am, both from Beth Yaakov, a better school than mine. Based on their experience, he says, their salaries will be higher.

"You don't drive, do you? I can pick you up and bring you back, since I'll be driving there anyway. The first teachers' meeting is two weeks away. The other principal wants to meet us; we're what they call the *goyishe*[2] staff." He laughs. "I understand you know more about these hasidic people than I do. Perhaps you can help me out."

We don't shake hands at the end of the interview, even though it seems as if we should. I smile, and he walks me to the door of his house. I walk down the stairs stiffly, like a teacher, and, at the bottom, turn and see him still standing there, chewing on the end of his pipe watching me. He waves. "See you in two weeks," he says.

I walk home wondering whether he shook the other teachers' hands,

[2]Gentile; non-Jewish

whether he made an exception for me, knowing who Father is. People always act as if I am like Father. It is expected that I will be what my parents are.

At home, everyone surrounds me at the kitchen table. Father strokes my cheek the way he did when I was little. He's happy to have me teaching in a hasidic school, even if it's only English subjects. "Teaching is the most honored, the highest profession in the world," he says. "It's the job of every mother. A child learns his first lessons, his first words, even, from his mother."

I'm not sure I like Father being so proud. I tell him two girls from modern Beth Yaakov are teaching with me. He nods, not caring. He's thinking about what he can say to the *shadkhan:* my daughter teaches at the best hasidic school in the world.

Seeing Father happy pleases Ma. Leah's excited about my becoming a teacher, imagining herself graduating and becoming a teacher too. Esther pulls her finger out of her mouth long enough to say, "Imagine if one day you become my teacher."

"It could happen," Ma says. "If Rachel likes teaching, she can continue doing it after she's married. Even after she has a baby. Nowadays young women work after their first baby. They get a baby-sitter. It's better than staying home all day, cleaning and cooking. Laundry can wait. Besides, with a husband who studies, the money has to come from somewhere."

All this talk about me married, me with babies. As if I'm already engaged. As if it's all happening tomorrow. Right now I have a history test to study for. I have still to graduate high school.

The *shadkhan* calls back and tells Father people inform him I do not wear stockings with seams. That I've never worn seams. Father says, "I see her every morning and evening. She's wearing seams. I bought them for her myself. People don't know what they're saying."

Ma looks at me, into me, seeing what I don't want her to see. She walks behind Father and beckons me into the hallway.

"Tell me the truth, once and for all. What do you wear?"

I don't answer.

"Listen, it's too late to change anyway. Your reputation is your own. But don't make fools of your parents. Don't have them saying one thing when people know another."

"I wear what I want to wear. What I feel comfortable wearing. I don't wear seams."

Ma takes a deep breath. "So you don't wear seams. Do you at least wear thick stockings, stockings you can't see through?"

I nod. "Yes, I wear opaque beige and taupe stockings."

Ma leaves the room. I open my stocking drawer. She won't find anything there I don't want her to find. She'll see two old pairs of opaque tights without seams. Maybe she's already seen them.

Father comes into the room and closes the door behind him. He sits on the bed.

"Again you didn't listen to your father. For years now you've been walking around wearing what you want and not what your father wants."

"I told you then, I'll never wear stockings with seams. You want stockings with seams, you wear them." Having to tell him this makes me angry. I'm trembling. Why should a daughter wear what her father wants her to wear?

He doesn't answer. He sits for a moment, not saying anything, and then gets up slowly and walks to the door. Before he closes the door, he turns back and says, "I'm very proud of David. The *shadkhan* tells me the head of his yeshiva wants him for a son-in-law."

So that's why Father's in a hurry to get me married.

In the morning, I wear opaque panty hose over my sheer. I don't have to make believe I'm wearing seams anymore. The double layer, opaque over sheer, makes my stockings look even thicker, and Ma's satisfied.

She advises Father. "Tell the *shadkhan* it was your mistake. That it's your wife who wears the seams. You're a man; what do you know about what girls wear? Tell him she wears thick, modest stockings. No seams. Tell him the girls here don't wear seams."

Father keeps his head down. "Who'd want to marry a girl who lies to her own parents, tell me. We'll have to be satisfied with whatever comes. The first that comes."

Ma looks at me, bites her lip, and wrings her hands, to show me how bad things are. I don't stay to listen. I can't stand this constant talk about whom I'll marry. No matter what I say, the talk goes on. I don't care whom I marry. Once married, I at least won't have to worry about it. Married, I'll do and wear what I want. I'll be who I am.

It's October. I walk in from teaching, and Ma says, "The Sklars are breaking a plate tonight. Elke called to invite us."

I sit on my bed. There were only sixteen girls in my graduating class, but every month there's another party or wedding. And with it comes all the well-wishing: God willing, soon we'll be celebrating yours.

Should I say, Not ever, God willing? That would cause a scandal, and then it might be never. I don't know what I want.

"You don't want to be one of the last ones," Ma says, "Like that Landau girl. Who knows how her children will be?"

Henna Landau waited too long, people say. First her twin brothers were in the way, then she was too picky. The *shadkhan* stopped calling. Soon she turned twenty-six and had little choice. She married the only normal one in the Rosenbaum family.

"What about the girls I teach with? They're still single."

"So you're comparing yourself to them now," Ma says. "They come from modern homes. They wait longer. And remember David. We're not going to let Rabbi Blau's daughter go, waiting for you."

David's not yet seventeen, and already his engagement is all set. They're just waiting for me. Only David knows nothing about it.

Father says, "There's no need to tell a yeshiva boy. Why disturb his studies? If we tell him, he'll get nervous, lose sleep. Without sleep, he won't study."

I wonder if David knows anything about girls and babies. About sex. Do boys in yeshiva talk about anything?

Ma says, "If we marry him off before you, you'll have real problems. As if you don't have enough. The *shadkhan* keeps saying to forget about a rabbi's son for you."

"This is why you have to be careful of your reputation," Fatner says, pulling his beard so hard it is no wonder it's thin. "The Talmud says a father has a responsibility: he must give his daughter to a scholar and to a good family. It doesn't say anything about a daughter who's given herself a reputation, a daughter who's made things impossible for her father, a daughter who's better known to strangers than to her own father."

He speaks of me the way the prophets speak of whores. As if I've walked the streets, invited men into my bed.

I talk to Ma privately. "I don't need a rabbi's son. I want someone who'll work and earn a living. I don't want to be poor all my life."

She says, "Right away, as soon as you're married, you want him to go off to work? Like some coarse factory worker? Let him study for a few years. Then, after two or three children, I can understand. I also wanted your father to get a real job, bring in a salary. But not right away."

There's a lot to be said for reputations. My reputation will help the *shadkhan* find someone for me, not for Father. How else would he know whom to bring?

Ma says, "Elke's groom is no big deal. He's no great scholar, and his father isn't either. They're plain workers and always will be."

Father would never say this, but he thinks it, he agrees. He and Ma work together, they're a team, with Ma as the bad tongue, as if it's more seemly coming from a woman.

There are advantages to coming from a regular family, like Elke's. She's free. She doesn't have to be a model for the community, to live for what people think and say. And they have a regular income. Her father works for a living; they don't have to count pennies, or depend like Father on book sales and donations. They don't have to wait for the mail, to see if there will be enough to pay for groceries. I don't want gifts all my life. Giving feels better than getting. The Midrash says those who give, love. A wife gives to her husband and grows to love him. A mother gives life to her children and loves them. Takers never learn to love.

During the party, Elke takes me into her bedroom to show me what she's already bought. She's been shopping mostly in Brooklyn, where the groom is from. She shows me a Christian Dior set of sheets I've seen before, orange flowers on a white background. And towels to match. She also bought a set of white eyelet linens.

"I need two more," she says. "Everyone gets married with four sets these days."

The best thing about being engaged is shopping. A bride gets everything new, like starting life all over again. Elke's room is full of bags. I don't think I'll get as much.

"Did you see him?" she asks.

"Yes. He's so tall, and he's handsome." What I don't say is that he's not romantic. Maybe a man with a beard, a hasidic man, can never be.

Elke smiles and doesn't say anything. She's in love with this man she just met, like love at first sight. Will it happen to me?

On the floor is a box containing the Sanyo vacuum cleaner Ma told me about. Elke opens the box to show me. It's a new design, beige and very shiny. Very Japanese. It looks too clean to clean with.

"It's the lightest vacuum in the world," Elke says. "Lift it."

"It *is* light," I say. "My mother would like it. Instead of that heavy blue Electrolux she drags around."

"I think your mother wants it for you, not for herself," Elke says. She opens the door to her room, still carrying the vacuum, and beckons Ma over. I look at her, a bride dressed in pale-peach chiffon, carrying a shiny beige vacuum cleaner.

Ma takes it from Elke and raises it, using one hand. "It is very pretty. And light. Like a toy. Will it last?"

Elke nods. "It has a two-year warranty, and it's only $110. On special." She turns to me. "You should get one now. Before it goes up."

I don't answer. Elke looks toward Ma, as if I am too young to understand.

"I'll call King's Appliances and order it," Ma says.

A few days later, the box is on the floor in my closet. Ma paid for it out of her own money. I open it and imagine cleaning my own, very clean apartment. Elke found a place a few blocks away, and she's starting to decorate it. I helped her paint a coffeepot pattern on the kitchen walls one night. It was fun.

Ma's excited. She wants to start buying things and making trips to the city. She says to use my money for clothes and linens, and she and Father will pay for the rest.

"I'm not engaged yet, remember?"

"You could be. Father talked to the *shadkhan* yesterday."

"About what?"

"What do you mean, about what? About a boy. For you."

"I don't want a boy. I want a man."

Ma laughs. "You know what I mean. Anyway, how could he be a man, at your age? But the one we're talking about is a little older. His name is Israel Mittelman."

I look at her.

"He's already twenty-one."

"What's wrong with him?"

"Nothing. He's twenty-one. You just said you want a man, yes?"

Who wants to marry a boy? But asking for a man is as good as agreeing to see one. I hear Father on the phone. They're setting something up, and I'm letting them. It's Elke's apartment. I'm beginning to want things of my own. I want to live on my own. Married is the only way I can be on my own. I have to become Mrs. Someone, Mrs. Mittelman. I try the name out on paper, Mrs. Rachel Mittelman. That's not bad. I want to fall in love, like Elke, like a woman in a novel.

It's all set up for Saturday night at eight. The Mittelmans live in Brooklyn, and they're taking the first bus up north after sundown.

"Everyone says the best things about this young man," Father says. "And the family: I know the father way back from Romania; he's a good man, and the family has always had an excellent reputation."

For Father, knowing the family makes up for their not being rabbinical.

I'm trying not to show my excitement. I don't want to seem eager, but I am. I'll finally find out what it's like, meeting a man. Ma's excited too.

I act as if it's no big deal. "I'm only meeting him. I'm not getting engaged."

"What if you really like him? You'll say no?" Ma asks.

"Everyone gets married," Leah says every time we talk about it. "Then you can leave the dishes in the sink all day. When I'm married, we can do things together, go shopping without anyone's permission." She looks at me. "What? You'd rather live with Ma and Father forever?"

We've talked about this so much, we sound like broken records. What she says is true; I can't live here forever. Still, I need her persuasion. I want to be, I let myself be, persuaded. I thought I'd never get married. That I'd just move into my own house and live by myself. But that can't happen.

"Seventeen-year-old girls don't go and live by themselves," Leah says.

"But why not?" I ask. "Why can't I just do what I want?"

"You know that's not possible," Leah says. "You always want what's impossible. Concentrate on what you can get."

She plans to marry a wealthy boy from Brooklyn and wear designer clothes and high heels. This is the country, and people here look it. Leah wants to be like the hasidic girls in Williamsburg, the ones who wear mascara so lightly you can hardly tell. I am sick of lightly.

Ma talks about nothing else all Shabbat. She and I go for our walk after eating, and she's mostly too out of breath to talk. We just walk. We get along better now that I'm out of school. Maybe because I'm older. She bought me a white silk blouse with French cuffs, and on Friday we had to go and buy cuff links at the Men's Store. No one in our family has ever worn cuff links.

On our way back we slow down and Ma says, "I'll call Mrs. Fogel. She can send us some fine embroidered tablecloths and napkins from Montreal. Like mine. It's cheaper there."

"I'm not engaged yet, Ma. I'm just seeing someone. And only the first one."

"How many do you think girls see? Ten? Twenty?"

"Ten is a lot more than one. There is an in-between."

"It doesn't matter. You'll need tablecloths someday. And you'll need some nice clothes. It's a good thing you've got some money saved."

Ma's so excited about tonight, about having a married daughter, I finally just let her be. I'm starting to believe I'll just get married, that this is it, that Israel Mittelman's the one.

At sundown, Leah and Sarah offer to do the dishes and clean up so I can go right into the shower. I blow-dry my hair, straight, shoulder-length, with bangs. I put on my new blouse and a navy wool skirt. Ma helps with the cuff links. She's wearing her green wool dress with a matching print silk kerchief.

Ma hurries Leah, Sarah, Esther, and Aaron out to a cab. They're going to 99 Lanes on Route 59. No one's told Ma yet that bowling is modern. We took her there once, and she swung the ball hard and clean and knocked all the pins down, even though she'd never before held a bowling ball in her hand. She and Leah have always been great at sports.

The Mittelman family arrives five minutes after eight. The grandmother and an aunt too. As if we're having an engagement party. Ma leads them to the table in the dining room, and we all sit. Israel sits near Father. I can see him without looking straight at him. He is thin and well-groomed. His beard is perfectly combed. He wears a black hat like Father's. And a good wool suit coat, better than Father's. His hands are on the edge of the table, only his fingertips show, and they're pink with pressure. I can tell he's very nervous, and I feel sorry for him. I wonder if he's seen any other girls. It's harder to be the man, I think. He has to start talking.

There's a silver bowl filled with fruit on the table and a pitcher of water. Father sits in his regular place, at the head of the table. He peels a tangerine and serves it to Mr. Mittelman. Ma quarters an apple and passes it to Mrs. Mittelman. They talk about the one-and-a-half-hour ride from Brooklyn. There's no bus home tonight, so they're staying over with their friends, the Kleins from Klein's Fruit.

"Do you know them? Do you buy your fruits and vegetables there?" Mrs. Mittelman asks.

Ma nods. "For the most part."

She looks at me and bites her lip. We're both thinking the same thing. Too many people know about this. These meetings should be kept secret until both sides are agreed and an engagement is announced. The Mittelmans should have rented a car or taken a taxi.

Mrs. Mittelman asks about my teaching. She says one of my students is a relative of theirs, Gitty Loeb.

So the Loebs know, too.

During a moment of silence, Ma says, "Let's leave the children alone for a few minutes."

They make a lot of noise pushing their chairs back. Ma's the last one out, and before she shuts the door, she smiles and winks. I wait for Israel to speak. I won't be the first one.

"What do you do?" he asks. His teeth are perfectly white.

"I teach the second and sixth grades."

"What do you teach them?"

"All subjects taught in English: math, literature, history, science."

"Would you prefer teaching religious subjects?" he asks.

"No. There are plenty of girls who are good at that. I'm good at English; I like literature."

It would help my reputation if I taught Jewish subjects. I know this is something the Mittelmans have discussed. The *shadkhan* called to ask Ma about it. I was sitting at the kitchen table with her, listening.

Ma rolled her eyes to indicate trouble. She said, "Rachel is smart and she likes to read, like her father. No matter how many Yiddish books we had in the house, there were never enough. For a while, my husband even considered teaching her some Talmud, but they say women shouldn't. Anyway, it can't hurt to marry a smart girl; think of the children."

The way Ma talked, anyone would have thought she'd supported my reading all along.

Israel and I are talking as if neither one of us has heard anything about the other. It's all so set up. His lips, I notice, are very pink. Not like my thick brown lips. He has small features, a small nose, and thin lips, unlike mine. He's quiet, and I realize it's my turn to speak.

"Which yeshiva do you go to?"

"I'm not in yeshiva anymore. I study with the older men, in the synagogue."

I should've known that. He's already twenty-one, past yeshiva age. Most boys get married at eighteen. I can't ask, Why did you wait so long? "Do you like being out of yeshiva?"

He nods, I wait for more, for a reason. He doesn't say anything.

"Why? What's good about it?" I ask.

He says slowly, "I like not having to report to anyone and not being tested every week. I like coming and going like an adult." I watch his mouth, the way his mustache spreads so straight and black above his lips.

He mentions Gitty Loeb, who told his mother about the games I have them play in class to help them memorize. He says, "Tell me the rules of the game."

I explain the rules of *Go Fish* and *Twister* for learning body parts and colors.

He smiles. "Where do you get such good ideas?"

"From *Teacher's Magazine.* I subscribe."

"You sound like a very good teacher."

I know he says this to flatter me. Still, it works; I am flattered.

We talk about our families. He has two brothers and one sister. He tells me his youngest brother slipped and told a friend about tonight. Before they left home the phone rang. It was the boy's mother, calling to wish the Mittelmans a *mazel tov.*[3] Israel laughs.

I don't think it's funny. I don't even smile. He's too sure of tonight. Who said anything about getting engaged?

We actually talk about the weather.

Then we're both quiet for what seems like forever, and I push my chair back slightly as a sign that our meeting is over.

He gets up too. I walk into the kitchen, and he goes down the hall, to the boys' room, which today serves as a living room.

I find Ma behind the kitchen door; she's been listening in.

"Well?" she asks, her face happy and hopeful.

"Well, what?"

"Is it a yes or a no?"

"I don't know."

---

[3] Congratulations (literally, "good fortune")

"You can't send them home like that, not knowing. They came all this way. Especially the old grandmother."

"She shouldn't have come," I say.

"You can't blame her. She's old; she wants to be at her first grandchild's engagement. They're expecting to break a plate tonight."

Father walks in. "*Nu?* What do you say?"

"She doesn't know," Ma says.

"That's not saying no," Father says.

"I'm not giving an answer tonight," I announce in a loud voice so the Mittelmans will hear. "I need time. Send them home."

"Shhh," Ma says and closes the door. "We can wait till tomorrow," Father says, looking at Ma. I can tell he's warning her not to push too hard. "But you'll have to decide by tomorrow."

I say good-night to the Mittelmans and to Israel, and just as they're finally leaving, Leah and the kids arrive home. Sarah and Aaron are arguing loudly about who's better at bowling.

Leah comes in. "He looks OK," she says. "Skinny but kind of cute. Not manly. A little like Father, don't you think? Did you say yes?"

In books, the men are always tall and dark, or tall, strong, and blond. Not at all like Israel. He does look like Father, thin and sensitive. His hair is black, too. But his face is pale, unlike Father's brown skin.

"That's what I fell in love with," Ma always says. "His dark skin like a Yemenite."

After the Mittelmans are gone, Father prods again, "*Nu?* What do you say?"

"Stop asking so much, or I'll just say no."

"What don't you like about him?" Father asks.

"Nothing. There's nothing wrong with him. He's fine."

"Do you still want to see another boy?" Ma asks. "Even though it won't look good for you to say no to the Mittelmans. Too many people know about this. And if you see someone else, you'll have to say yes."

"And meet another whole family? Mothers and grandmothers? Why did they have to bring the grandmother? It's embarrassing."

"There's no need to meet another family. Make this one the one. God sent you this family, a good family," Father says, smiling and trying to catch my eye.

I don't smile back, and look away. He's worse than Ma. He doesn't want to give me any choice. He wants this to happen. I could say no just to show I'm in control. But I don't know what I want. Saying no to the Mittelmans would mean that I'd have to say yes to the next one. And who knows who the next boy will be. By then the Mittelmans will be insulted. Or Israel will get engaged to someone else. He's older than most boys; his parents want him to get married.

And if I say no to the next one, people will say I refuse boys for no reason, like the Adler girl. Everyone was saying, Who does she think she is, a princess? She finally married a boy who'd been turned down by at least ten girls because he's short and fat. Serves her right, people said. About me, they'd say worse.

I expect some sign from God all night. I don't deserve it, only the most virtuous people can hope for that, but still I expect it. I fall asleep imagining being held and kissed, and I wake up feeling thrilled. I don't remember any dreams; there's nothing to tell me what to do. But I'm excited. I try to imagine Israel in bed with me and can't. He's not the type. I wonder how he would start. How does anyone start such things?

In the kitchen Ma's at the counter. Father's in the synagogue. The others are in school. "Should I see another man?" I ask her.

"Not if you like Israel. After your father, I refused to see anyone else. There was a Belgian boy, from a wealthy family, and I said no because I'd already made up my mind to marry your father."

Ma had an opportunity to marry a Belgian boy, a foreigner. I'm seeing someone from regular old Brooklyn, even if he is from fancy Borough Park.

"Do you think you made the right choice?" I ask.

She looks at me, surprised. "You mean marrying your father? Of course. Look at what a beautiful family I have. Do you know how many women envy me all this?"

"What about all your complaints? You used to complain a lot. About not having enough money. About being a rabbi's wife."

She waves her hand, making none of that matter, and sips her coffee. "Those first years were hard; it was a hard life. Feeding, clothing, and educating seven of you."

"You might have had it easier with a wealthy Belgian husband."

Ma sips and swallows. "I love your father."

Father comes home, and we eat breakfast together. We both dunk our bread in the soft-boiled egg yolk. Ma started a new diet today; she's had her wheat germ and milk already, and now she's on her second cup of coffee. She wants to fit into her raw-silk dress for the engagement party. She wants to look as good as thin Mrs. Mittelman, with her blond wig and her little black hat on top. Ma can never look as good in the kerchief she wears. When I'm married I'm expected to wear a wig with a hat, like Mrs. Mittelman. Father says why not do even better, wear what your mother wears. He doesn't know that after I'm married, when he and Ma can't tell me what to do, I won't even wear the hat.

Ma knows. She says, "Let her wear a covered wig, and at least you'll know she'll stay with it. Not change after. Like Borough Park girls. They're more concerned with how they look than with God or their parents. It's hard to believe that after their first night with their husband they can be so hard, so unchanged, so concerned with just looks."

As if sex with a man is supposed to make you better, softer, more religious. Ma thinks that after I'm married I'll start wearing seams if Israel asks me.

She says, "Wait and see. Plenty of girls do. They're in love with their husband, and he just has to ask them at the right moment and they do it. A smart boy asks right after the first night; it's the best time to get the girl to agree."

I plan not to change one bit. I don't even want to wear a wig. I think if all women refused to shave and cover their heads, the rabbis would have to rethink the laws, change them. But I don't know anyone who agrees with me.

Leah says, "That's ridiculous. It will never happen."

When I talk to Elke, she says, "I don't mind shaving my hair. Everyone does it. You should be happy to get rid of yours. You're always complaining about how fine it is."

"I talked to Mr. Mittelman in the synagogue this morning," Father says. "He's very understanding. He suggests another meeting this afternoon, and if it's yes, we can break the plate and they can take the four- or six-o'clock bus home. He says he understands a young girl wanting to be more certain."

I like Mr. Mittelman for understanding. Still, what is there I could see better the second time around? You don't get to know a person sitting at a table and talking or going out on a date. It takes time. It takes forgetting that you're doing it.

Father looks at me. "So what do you say to a second time?"

"What for?" I say. "What else is there to see?"

He smiles and looks satisfied. He knows I'm interested. He reaches over and puts his hand on top of mine and says, "Then make this second meeting the engagement."

I call Elke's house. Her mother says she's at her new apartment.

I walk over. She's painting the woodwork in the bathroom. I sit on the edge of the tub and watch.

"Are you at all nervous, Elke?"

She puts her head to the side.

"I mean, how did you know he was the one you wanted? He was the only one you saw."

"I just did," Elke says. "He's good-looking. And he was funny when we talked. And I knew I didn't want him to see any other girls."

Things seem so easy for her. I'm too serious. Elke would have laughed with Israel about the phone call before he left home, she would've thought it funny.

She sits back with the brush in her hand and leans against the sink. "It's not the newest thing in the world, you know. People get engaged and married. It's not such a big deal. Just do it. We'll have fun being newlyweds."

"What about love?"

"It comes after. Everyone I know says so." We look at each other. "You think too modern," she says. "You always did. You always did things that were too modern for your family. Too modern even for the most modern girls in our class. And you're from a *rebbishe*[4] family. Everyone in school talked about it. Even Leah thinks so. She says you just never know when to stop, that you have no limits."

I think it's easier for Elke because she doesn't think about love in novels. She hates reading. She doesn't know any tall, dark men in boots. She thinks only about the hasidic way, real life. For the first time, I see a reason not to read.

I say, "It's not as if I'm about to get engaged. I'm just thinking about seeing him again."

"That's getting engaged, in hasidic families. It happens very quickly. One day you meet, the next day you're engaged. Sometimes the same day. Just do it; you'll have to do it sooner or later anyway."

Elke is always ahead, a veteran. I used to think things would be different for me. That my life would be different. But it isn't. I teach grade school like all the others. I'll get engaged like all the others. Get married. Maybe it's better doing things the way everyone does. You know exactly how it goes. Besides, I don't even know what I really want to do that's different. Or what there is to do. Even modern girls get married eventually. They just do it later. They go out on dates instead of sitting in. Then they get engaged and married. I thought there'd be more things a person could do, more choices. But there's nothing else. People get married and start living their own lives. Married is the only way to live on my own, in my own apartment.

At four, Israel comes again. He looks exactly the same, and I wonder if he's even changed his shirt. This time, only his father is with him. The women are waiting at the Kleins'. Maybe Ma said something.

We talk. Today he looks into my eyes, and I notice his deep-blue eyes. They're beautiful. I don't know how I missed them last night. I ask him where he wants to live. We're looking at each other. I can see myself in his eyes, and I think maybe this is love.

He answers slowly. "Wherever you decide."

I wish his answer were more definite, a name, Borough Park. I want him to take me away to another city. I want him to be strong, a man in a novel. He isn't. But his mind is made up about one thing: he wants to be engaged to me.

[4]Rabbinical

My reputation isn't stopping him. My hesitation, seeing him a second time, hasn't upset him. Maybe it's the family I come from. He wants to marry into a rabbinical family.

"I think I want to live in Borough Park," I tell him. "Somewhere different."

He nods. "We can. But for the summer, we should rent an apartment here. The city empties out in the summer. My parents move out to the country. It's not very nice there in the hot summer."

I think that's a good idea. I was a lifeguard last summer, and I could do it again. I could continue earning money. I tell him that, and he asks me about lifeguarding.

"You must swim very well," he says, looking at me, admiring me.

When I come into the kitchen, Ma has that question on her face, and I know I don't want to say no, I'm tired of saying no. I don't wait for her to ask. I decide to trust her. I can trust her more than Father. "You think I should say yes?" I ask.

She nods.

"OK, yes," I say, thinking how easy it is to say it. Yes, yes, yes. There's nothing else to say when you say yes.

Ma kisses me on the cheek and calls Father. He kisses me on the forehead. Mr. Mittelman telephones his wife. I call Elke, and she quickly comes over.

Ma brings out the chipped china plate she's been saving for me, her first daughter, and wraps it in a dish towel. For some reason, we're all standing in the kitchen.

When Mrs. Mittelman, the grandmother, and Mr. and Mrs. Klein arrive, Ma hands the plate to the old lady as an honor. She looks around slowly and lifts her hands up as if she's too close to the ground. A plate that doesn't break is a bad omen. If it doesn't break, I think it will be a sign from God. A sign to say no. The plate crashes to the floor, and we hear it shatter. Everyone says *mazel tov*. The fathers shake hands, the mothers kiss. The Mittelmans kiss their son. The grandmother kisses her grandson, my future husband, Israel. I watch how he bends down to help her reach him. Elke hugs me. The phone rings. Everyone arrives home from school, and Leah and Sarah take turns answering and making calls. Mrs. Mittelman also gets on the phone. Aaron and Esther are underfoot.

Esther wants to know if I'm going to have a baby now. Elke explains that it takes a while. Listening to her, I remember David and Levi in yeshiva. They know nothing about this. I send Aaron to tell Leah to call them. She's so excited, she's calling everyone she can think of. Leah looks at me from across the room and points to her watch to indicate it's not the right time to call. They have set hours for everything there. I wonder how long before David gets engaged, whether Father will even wait until after my wedding. I'm almost eighteen. David is already seventeen, and Father says a boy should be under the wedding canopy before he's eighteen.

Ma unties the dish towel and hands everyone a piece of the plate. She saves the largest piece, a piece from the center, for me. It has three tiny pink flowers. Mrs. Mittelman asks if I want it set in gold as a necklace charm. We look at my piece of the plate. It's large enough for a round or oval setting. All the brides in Brooklyn are doing it now, she says. I give it to her, and she puts it in her fancy black purse with a long strap, like younger women wear, not like Ma's old-lady bag with handles.

Ma tells Mrs. Mittelman my ring size is five. For my engagement party, I will receive a diamond ring and a big silver vase filled with roses. That's what Elke got. Bridal gifts conform to the latest trends, because mothers-in-law are afraid to differ. Receiving fewer or cheaper gifts could be taken as an insult. As a bride, I can expect a gift for every holiday that comes up between now and my wedding. I don't care about any of this, but Ma says to keep my mouth shut. She received a pearl instead of a diamond ring, and she will never let anyone forget it. Grandfather said it was because he'd seen dirt under her fingernails.

"A complete lie," Ma says. "Can you imagine me with dirty fingernails? He just needed an excuse, that stingy old man."

Ma and Mrs. Mittelman discuss a date for the engagement party and decide on a month from now, on a Sunday, my day off from school. Ma says we'll do it in the new synagogue next door, the women in the women's section and the men in theirs. She explains that things are still a little raw, construction isn't entirely finished, but it's large enough for the party, if not the wedding, and it's bright.

Before they all leave, Israel comes over, and Leah and Elke move away quickly. With his eyes lowered for modesty, he wishes me *mazel tov* and a good night. This is impressing Ma, I know. At the last minute, he looks into my face and smiles.

I wonder if he's thinking of what I'm thinking. Of us kissing. Of us in bed. I can't imagine us together. I'm not sure what men think about. I always knew what the women in stories felt, I could understand what they felt, but I don't know anything about men.

Mr. and Mrs. Mittelman wish me a good night; Mrs. Mittelman kisses me, then I kiss the grandmother. Mr. Mittelman bows his head and smiles. Until I'm married, Father is the only man allowed to kiss me. Then my husband.

From the kitchen window, I watch them pile into Father's car. He's driving them to Route 59, where the bus to New York City stops. Ma is at the front door, waving. It's a starry dark night, the moon is full and round, at the beginning of her month. I'll have to start keeping track of my month, count the days to my period and away from it. Husband and wife are allowed to touch each other only two weeks of the month. There are five to seven days of menstruating, a seven-day count of clean days, then the ritual bath. I have to find the right day for my wedding, before my period begins again.

In the Talmud, there are three kinds of virtuous women: girl, wife, and mother. I will be a girl for four more months.

Pitt-Rivers, *The People of the Sierra*

In his book, The People of the Sierra *(1961), the English social anthropologist, J. A. Pitt-Rivers (born in 1919), examines the social structure of a contemporary rural community—Alcala—located in the mountains of southern Spain. Unlike the many fictional and philosophical accounts of courtship provided in this volume, Pitt-Rivers' account is based on his own empirical field research. More vividly than do the stories of individual courtship, this study makes clear how courtship practices are connected with fundamental community values, including especially those regarding masculinity and femininity, honor and shame, and the importance of marriage. The selections presented here (excerpted from Chapters 6 through 8) address these issues. Though a tradition-bound community regarding courtship practices, as well as regarding beliefs about what constitutes a good marriage, the people of Alcala are surprisingly romantic. They believe, for example, that young "sweethearts" must talk the talk of love to one another in order to "bind the emotions of each to the other so securely that the attachment will last a lifetime." Recognizing the importance of love for marriage, they believe that love is an illusion that must be fostered through talk. The courtship practices of Alcala are usefully compared to Rousseau's philosophically-inspired reflections on the same subject, presented later in this section of the anthology.*

"The Values of the Male"

To attempt to define the standards of behaviour between the sexes in terms of prohibitions and obligations would be difficult. Conversation is free and no subject is taboo, provided it is not discussed indelicately in the presence of the opposite sex. The restraints in behaviour proceed from the conceptions which the situation brings into play. In the organisation of conduct, not only in situations where a member of the opposite sex is present, a primordial importance attaches to the ideal types of either sex. It would be tedious to attempt to enumerate the moral qualities attaching to manliness or womanliness for in general they are the same as in our own traditional culture: "Knights are bold and ladies are fair." Courage and strength are emphasised as male attributes. Beauty and frailty are for women. The saying: "El hombre como el oso, mientras más feo más hermoso" ("Man like the bear, the uglier the handsomer") expresses this aspect of manliness, while the grace of the women in carriage and gesture reveals the value which is given to delicacy and beauty in the feminine ideal. . . .

The quintessence of manliness is fearlessness, readiness to defend one's own pride and that of one's family. It is ascribed directly to a physical origin and the idiom in which it is expressed is frankly physiological. To be manly is to have *cojones* (testicles), and the farmyard furnishes its testimony in support of the theory. Castrated animals are *manso* (tame), a castrated ox is not dangerous like a bull. A castrated dog, it is thought, will always run away from an uncastrated one. A man who fails to show fearlessness is lacking in manliness and, by analogy, castrated or *manso*. While it is not supposed that he is literally devoid of the male physiological attributes, he is, figuratively, so. That part of his person does not possess the moral qualities properly associated with it. . . .

The word which serves literally to translate manliness (*hombría*) also contributes to the same conception:

"The modern race is degenerate," said a friend once, "in the days of our grandfathers there was more manliness than today." To be "muy hombre" is to have an abundance of that moral quality which we have been discussing, and, through it, to command the respect of one's fellows. . . .

Clearly, such a conceptual evaluation of sexual virility leads to a certain proclivity to justify manliness literally, and the moral precepts taught in education tend to be outweighed by the desire for such justification. Success with women is a powerful gratification to the self-esteem of the Andalusian. The appreciation of feminine beauty and the attitude of ready courtship which it inspires are expressed in the *piropo,* a word which means literally a ruby and also means a compliment paid to a lady. It is a tribute paid disinterestedly to one whose presence is a source of joy and, theoretically at any rate, without any ulterior motive. It may be paid publicly to an unknown lady as she passes down the street, for it requires no response from her, and the freedom and charm of such a custom has done much to recommend the cities of Andalusia to the pretty tourist. Opportunities for this kind of *piropo* barely exist in the pueblo where everyone is known, but an appreciation of feminine attractiveness is nevertheless not scant in Alcala. The restraints upon the sexually aggressive behaviour of men derive, it appears, from sanctions of a social nature rather than from the prohibitions of the individual conscience. . . .

"The Values of the Female"

. . . The male social personality has been related to the conception of manliness. The feminine counterpart of the conception, which expresses the essence of womanhood, is *vergüenza,* or shame. In certain of its aspects only, for the word has first of all a general sense not directly related to the feminine sex and it is this which must first be explained.

It means shame, the possibility of being made to blush. It is a moral quality, like manliness, and it is persistent, though like manliness or like innocence, which it more closely resembles, it may be lost. Once lost it is not, generally speaking, recoverable, though a feeling remains that it is only lost by those whose shame was not true shame but a deceptive appearance of it. It is the essence of the personality and for this reason is regarded as something permanent.

... The code of ethics to which *vergüenza* is related is that which incurs the moral stricture of the community. To use Marett's distinction, it relates to "external moral sanctions" not to "internal moral sanctions" or conscience.[1] Thus, to do a thing blatantly makes a person a *sin vergüenza* (shameless one); but to have done it discreetly, would only have been wrong. This, then, is the difference. Shamelessness faces the world, faces people in particular situations. Wrong faces one's conscience. Let me now try a definition:

"*Vergüenza* is the regard for the moral values of society, for the rules whereby social intercourse takes place, for the opinion which others have of one. But this, not purely out of calculation. True *vergüenza* is a mode of feeling which makes one sensitive to one's reputation and thereby causes one to accept the sanctions of public opinion."

Thus a *sin vergüenza* is a person who either does not accept or who abuses those rules. And this may be either through a lack of understanding or through a lack of sensitivity. One can perceive these two aspects of it.

First as the result of understanding, upbringing, education. "Lack of education" is a polite way of saying "lack of *vergüenza*". It is admitted that if the child is not taught how to behave it cannot have *vergüenza*. It is sometimes necessary to beat a child "to give him *vergüenza*", and it is the only justifiable excuse for doing so. Failure to inculcate *vergüenza* into one's children brings doubt to bear upon one's own *vergüenza*.

But, in its second aspect as sensitivity, it is truly hereditary. A person of bad heredity cannot have it since he has not been endowed with it. He can only behave out of calculation as though he had it, simulating what to others comes naturally. A normal child has it in the form of shyness, before education has developed it. When a two-year-old hides its face from a visitor it is because of its *vergüenza*. Girls who refuse to dance in front of an assembled company do so because of their *vergüenza*. *Vergüenza* takes into consideration the personalities present. It is *vergüenza* which forbids a boy to smoke in the presence of his father. In olden times people had much more *vergüenza* than today, it is said. Another polite form illustrates this aspect of shame. To be shameless in this sense is to be *descarado* or *cara dura* (hard-faced), and this is a far more serious matter than to be "thick-skinned", the nearest expression in English to it.

---

[1] R. R. Marett: "The beginnings of morals and culture," in *An Outline of Modern Knowledge* (London, 1931).

It is in this second sense, as a moral quality innate and hereditary, that the term *sin vergüenza* reaches its full force as an insult, that the epithet used to a man's face is tantamount to insulting the purity of his mother. . . .

It will hardly surprise the reader to learn that *vergüenza* is closely associated with sex. While to cheat, lie, betray or otherwise behave in an immoral manner shows a lack of shame, sexual conduct is particularly liable to exhibit shamelessness, and particularly in the female sex. Lack of shame exhibited in other behaviour is, as it were, derived from a fundamental shamelessness which could be verifiable if one were able to know about such matters in the person's sexual feelings. It is highly significant that the more serious insults which can be directed at a man refer not to him at all but to a female member of his elementary family and in particular to his mother. Personal reproach, while it refers to a man's character or actions, is answerable, but when it concerns a man's mother then his social personality is desecrated. At that point, if he has manliness, he fights. Up till that point matters can be argued. A man must make a living for his family, and this will lead him into conflict with other men. To fail to meet his family responsibilities would appear more shameless than to take advantage of people for whom he was not responsible. A certain licence is conceded to the male sex, so that a man is not judged so severely either in matters relating to business or in his sexual conduct, where the need to justify his manliness provides an understandable explanation of his short-comings. "Men are all shameless", women say. The essence of his shame will be seen in his heredity, however. And therefore a reflection upon his mother's shame is far more vital than a reflection upon his own conduct. By extension, any reflection upon his sister's shame is important to him since it derives from his mother's. The whole family is attained by the shamelessness of one of its female members.

Just as the official and economic relations of the family are conducted in the name of its head, the husband, who has legal responsibility for and authority over its members, so the moral standing of the family within the community derives from the *vergüenza* of the wife. The husband's manliness and the wife's *vergüenza* are complementary. Upon the conjunction of these two values the family, as a moral unity, is founded. From it the children receive their names, their social identity and their own shame. Shameless behaviour on the part of their mother—marital unfaithfulness is the most serious example of this, though one form of shamelessness implies the others and is implied by them, since *vergüenza* is something which either one possesses or one lacks—brings doubt to bear upon their paternity. They are no longer the children of their father. He is no longer father of his children. The importance of a woman's *vergüenza* in relation to the social personality of her children and of her husband rests upon this fact. Adultery on the husband's part does not affect the structure of the family. This is recognised in the law of the land in the distinction which it makes between adultery on the part of the husband or wife. A husband's infidelity is only legally adultery if it takes place in the home or scandalously outside it.

A wife's *vergüenza* involves a man, then, in quite a different way to his mother's. Her unfaithfulness is proof only of her, not of his, shamelessness, but it defiles his manliness. In a sense it testifies to his lack of manliness, since had he proved an adequate husband and kept proper authority over her she would not have deceived him. This much is implied, at any rate, in the language which appears to throw the blame for his misfortune on the deceived husband himself. In English, the word "cuckold" is thought to derive from cuckoo, the bird which lays its egg in the nest of another. Yet the word refers not to him who plays the part of the cuckoo, that is, the cuckolder, but to the victim whose role he usurps. The same curious inversion is found in Spanish. The word *cabrón* (a he-goat), the symbol of male sexuality in many contexts, refers not to him whose manifestation of that quality is the cause of the trouble but to him whose implied lack of manliness has allowed the other to replace him. To make a man a cuckold is in the current Spanish idiom, "to put horns on him". I suggest that the horns are figuratively placed upon the head of the wronged husband in signification of his failure to defend a value vital to the social order. He has fallen under the domination of its enemy and must wear his symbol.

The word *cabrón* is considered so ugly that it is never mentioned in its literal sense in Alcala. Even shepherds refer to the billy-goat of the herd by the euphemism *el cabrito* (the kid). Yet, figuratively, the pueblo uses the word in a wider sense than is general. It applies there to both the cuckold and the cuckolder, to any male, in fact, who behaves in a sexually shameless manner. . . . The best translation of *cabrón* as the pueblo uses it is "one who is on the side of anti-social sex".

While the greatest importance is attached to female continence—and the Andalusian accent upon virginity illustrates this—incontinence in the male has been shown to carry quite different implications. Sexual activity enhances the male prestige, it endangers the female, since through it a woman may lose her *vergüenza* and thereby taint that of her male relatives and the manliness of her husband. Yet *vergüenza* in a woman is not synonymous with indifference or frigidity towards the opposite sex. Quite the contrary, it is the epitome of womanhood and as such finds itself allied in the ideal of woman with the beauty and delicacy which are most admired. The sacred imagery of Seville or the Saints of Murillo illustrate this point abundantly. . . .

In the juxtaposition of these two conceptions, manliness and *vergüenza*, there are two possible bases of interrelation: one social, the other anti-social. In marriage, the wife's *vergüenza* ratifies the husband's manliness and combined with her fertility proves it. Through his manliness he gives her children, thereby raising her to the standing of mother and enabling her to pass her *vergüenza* on. The instincts implanted by nature are subordinated to a social end. But if these instincts seek satisfaction outside marriage then they threaten the institution of the family. Extra-marital manifestations of female sexuality threaten the *vergüenza* of her own kin. On the other hand, the male attempt to satisfy his self-esteem in a sexually aggressive way is also anti-social but for a different reason. If he approaches a woman who has *vergüenza,* he involves her in its loss and through that loss in that of another man's manliness, a husband's or a future husband's. Within the community of the pueblo this cannot but be a serious matter, and Chapter XI [not included here] will show how the pueblo reacts to such a threat. Expressed in moral terms, *vergüenza* is the predominant value of the home. It involves restraint of individual desires, the fulfilment of social obligations, altruism within the family, personal virtue and social good. Masculinity, on the other hand, unharnessed to female virtue and the values of the home which it upholds and economically supports, means the conquest of prestige and individual glory, the pursuit of pleasure, a predatory attitude towards the female sex and a challenging one towards the male; hence social evil and personal vice. According to the values of the pueblo it is only a force of good as long as it remains within, or potentially within, the institution of marriage.

"Courtship"

The only institution which binds the sexes together is the family. Primarily through marriage, but also through all the relationships established by it. The form of the individual family is continually changing in time, but we may take as its starting-point the moment when the young person abandons the companionship of his own sex and family, and seeks to establish an individual relationship with a person of the opposite sex and another family.

As the children grow up through adolescence the segregation of the sexes takes a new turn. The interest in the opposite sex, unrelated hitherto to structural issues, begins to offer the possibility of a lasting attachment which will alter the standing of the couple radically. The boy deserts the "dirty-story-telling" group of his fellows to go courting his girl. Typically, the farming families of the valley, in contrast to wealthier families of the pueblo, tend to form attachments of a serious nature as early as fifteen to eighteen years, and to regard each other thenceforward as *novios* (sweethearts), in all the structural implications of the term. *Novios* are boy and girl who will eventually be man and wife. The *noviazgo* (courtship) is the prelude to the foundation of the family. It is characteristically long in this society, always of a few years' duration, though the length depends on the age of the participants and also on their economic position. Yet it should not be regarded as a time of delay necessary for the establishment of the economic foundations of the family, though it fulfils that function. It is, rather, a steadily developing relationship which ends in marriage. The degrees of seriousness which attach to the term and give it at times a certain ambiguity derive from the fact that it covers all the stages of courtship from acquaintance to marriage. The dog which deserts the farm at night in search of a bitch is said to go "buscando la novia" ("searching for a *novia*") and the word may even be used as a euphemism for a married person's lover. But the term does not imply sexual intimacy when referring to an established relationship between boy and girl. It is thought proper to "respect" the woman who will be your wife.

The first step in the formation of this relationship is made when two young people leave the group in order to talk to one another alone. They sit together or go for a walk apart at some reunion, and this establishes a tentative beginning. If this behaviour recurs then people say that they are "talking to one another". The expression is important for it sums up an aspect of the *noviazgo*. It covers all the period of informal relations, extending from the first stage up till the "demand for the hand". During this time the relationship deepens but it is not yet irrevocable. Andres V., speaking of his former *novia*, said: "I spoke with her for twelve years and at the end she turned out a whore." This period of twelve years was exceptionally long owing to the fecklessness of the speaker and his inability to follow with one job for any length of time. When finally it became evident that he would not marry her, he laid the blame on her.

The idea of this talking together is that the *novios* get to know each other really well. The swiftness of the men to enter a sexual relationship of no structural importance contrasts with the care and delay with which they enter into matrimony. But the nature of this talk, though it inevitably varies, has a particular quality associated with courtship and which serves to forward the purpose of that institution. Its purpose is to bind the emotions of each to the other so securely that the attachment will last a lifetime. The word *camelar* expresses this kind of talk. It means—and it is above all the man who does the talking—"to compliment", "to show gallantry to", "to cause to fall in love". It is assumed that adulation is what causes people to fall in love, and this theory is found in the secondary meaning of the word: "to deceive with adulation". In this way the nominal form *camelo* comes in the end to mean: "nonsense", "line-shooting", "a tall story", "a tale which no one but a fool would be taken in by". It is generally asserted that the essential attribute for success with women is knowledge of how to talk to them. The Don Juan must know how to deceive women with words. However, in the case of courtship, this knowledge is put to the service of matrimony. Love is an essential to a happy marriage. And this is not only the opinion of romantic *señoritas*. Andrés el Baño, a hardheaded and intelligent small farmer says: "You can see clearly which marriages were made for money. They spend their whole lives quarreling. Sensible people marry for love." "How is a man to spend all his life working for a woman if he has no *ilusión* for her?" For it is admitted that love, like all terrestrial delights, is an illusion—to fall out of love is *quitarse la ilusión*. But in marriage it is a necessary illusion. Each person knows that he or she is not in fact the most wonderful person in the world, but through *camelos* one can be made to feel it and to feel the same about the other. The attachment formed by this mutually inspired self-esteem bridges the gulf of sex-differentiation and forms the bond on which the family is built.[2]

Courting takes place traditionally, in Andalusia, at the *reja* (the grill which covers every window), and sentimental numbers in the music-halls and the romantic postcards sold on news-stalls portray a *novio* so ardent that only iron bars can safeguard the purity of his love. The reality is less theatrical, of course. In summer the *novios* can go for walks together in the immediate vicinity of the town. To stray too far, to be out after dark, excites suspicious comment in the pueblo. Men who work and are away until dusk must do their courting after nightfall, and upon Thursdays and Sundays, the days for courting, boys will walk five or six miles, even after the day's work, in order to keep a rendezvous with a girl. Courting takes place at the girl's home. In Alcala the doorway is used rather than the window. The visiting *novio* stands on the threshold to talk to his girl while she stands within. The girl's family pay no attention to the couple. If the father comes out he pretends not to notice the *novio*. Formerly it was considered an affront to the father to be seen by him courting his daughter.[3] The suitor would retire while the father was in sight, but today he separates slightly from the girl and lets go her hand. To hold hands is considered proper behaviour for *novios,* save in the presence of a member of her family.

When the couple decide to get married, the *novio* makes a formal call upon the father of his *novia* in order to ask for her hand. His mother calls upon her mother. The girl's father is supposed not to answer but finally to allow himself to be persuaded by her mother. When the request is granted the young man hands over a sum of money to the girl with which she is to buy the requirements and furniture of the house, and the wedding day is fixed—usually for a

---

[2]The word *ilusión* is most commonly heard in the sense of ambition or hope, but it is also used with conscious cynicism as a euphemism for "lust".

[3]The avoidance between the girl's father and her *novio* is explained [in this way]. Until the young man marries her and thereby becomes a member of her family and therefore a person concerned in her *vergüenza,* he represents a threat to it and through it to that of her family. The avoidance may be seen to relate to the ambiguity of his position as, at the same time, both the potential future son-in-law and also as a threat to the family's *vergüenza*.

date three or four months ahead. The *noviazgo* then enters upon its final stage and although it remains theoretically repudiable, it would by now be extremely difficult for the *novio* to escape. The parents have been brought in who will become linked in the relationship of *consuegro* (co-parent-in-law). The money has been paid. From that moment onwards the marriage is assured. But until the demand for the hand the ties which bind the two together are purely personal. The longer an engagement lasts the stronger becomes the obligation to marry, the worse a repudiation would appear if there were no excuse for it but faithlessness. The danger is above all one for the girl, because once a long engagement is broken off it may not be easy for her to find a second suitor. The girl who has had other *novios* is not sought after in the same way, for the pride of the second *novio* must, to a greater or lesser extent, be sacrificed if he is to follow in the footsteps of another. If his *novia* were not a virgin it would make him a retrospective cuckold, but even if this is not believed, she would nevertheless be a less attractive proposition than previously. Girls whose first engagement is broken off tend to marry less easily subsequently.

It can be seen, then, that a girl of, say, twenty-five, whose engagement falls through after a long courtship is in a difficult position. If she has beauty or the prospect of inheritance, she will have no difficulty in finding a new *novio*. But if not, then she may have missed her opportunity. Andres V.'s *novia* remained a spinster. The moral feelings of the pueblo supply a powerful sanction against such faithlessness, for it involves the other members of both families. But *noviazgos* are in danger above all when boys go to work elsewhere for a time, and thereby escape the sanctions of the pueblo. They sometimes do not return but break with the *novia* of their home town and marry in the place where they are working, where they may never admit having had a previous *novia*, and where in any case the matter will have little importance.

Faced with this danger for which, should it materialise, the society offers no redress, it is not surprising to find the supernatural coming into play. There is a wealth of folklore which relates to finding and holding *novios*, and much of the practice of the *sabia* (wise woman) is devoted to resolving this problem. The girl whose *novio* begins to look at other girls with interest, visits her less regularly or writes to her less frequently, in short, gives her reason to believe that her hold over him is weakening, may go to the *sabia*. For the *sabia* has power to discover whether he still loves her or not, and is also able to perform love-magic in order to secure his constancy. She uses her love-magic, in this context, in support of the social order. . . .

"Marriage and the Family"

. . . A man reaches his full manliness in fatherhood; a woman in motherhood attains her full social standing. The change which marriage brings in the relationship of *novios is* reflected by changed attitudes. Marriage marks the end of romantic love, the beginning of the preparation for parenthood. This transition is reflected in the nostalgia of married people for the days when they were *novios*. "That is when everyone is happiest."

The change of attitude is not always complete. Few are the men who do not retain something of the boy, and there are opportunities for many members of the pueblo for justifying their manliness while away from home. But the fleeting infidelity need not detain us. We are concerned with premarital and extra-marital relations within the community.

It is generally conceded that girls' morals are not what they used to be. Babies are not infrequently born to the unmarried *novia*. Provided that her *novio* will marry her there is no harm done and no great shame attaches to her plight, at any rate among the people with no "social pretensions". The sanctions of public opinion are strongly exerted to force the boy to honour his obligation to marry her. Salvador D. was father to his *novia's* child while he was still writing to another *novia* whom, he maintained, he preferred but who lived elsewhere (he had met her in Jerez during his military service). His widowed mother, a very forceful character, went to the family of the girl and demanded that the baby should be named after her, as was her right if the marriage were to take place. As both grandmothers were called Maria a happy ambiguity prevailed, but soon afterwards the mother made a demand for the girl's hand on her son's behalf and paid some money for the setting up of the house. When the child was nearly eighteen months old they were finally married. The delay was partly due to the fact that his elder brother had to get married first. In most cases the parents of children born prematurely marry. However, in another case the *novio* rebelled, said the father of the child was not he but his uncle, and there was a very ugly row which would have ended in the courts had not the papers been mysteriously mislaid. The child had no father, took the same surnames as its mother, and its uncle was *padrino*.

In neither of these instances was the courtship really well established. In other cases, as we have seen, poor couples set up house together without the formality of a marriage ceremony and raise a family. During the years before the Civil War many families abandoned the rites of the Church, but in the eyes of the pueblo this is not important. If they live together faithfully and raise a family then they are married. "I don't know whether they are married by the Church, but they are a married couple", is how the matter is explained. Today many pressures are brought to bear in order to get them married. Both the Church societies and also the Town Hall use their influence. In certain cases, the need to register the child in order to get it a ration-card at the time of weaning is seen to be the conclusive moment. It is then said that: "Les echan las bendiciones" ("The marriage is sanctified").

No doubt on account of a pregnancy, there are a number of couples who marry very young, some even before the boy has done his military service. While, in addition to these cases, it sometimes happens that young *novios* wish to force the issue and run away together, establishing themselves in a house in the pueblo—very often in a house belonging to parents who are farmers in the valley. Sometimes the parents react by recovering their daughter and, if she is still under their tutelage, bringing the forces of Justice into action against the young man; but in other instances they accept the *fait accompli* and attempt to enable the young couple to set up a home and get married.

In short, the situation presents no grave problem as long as the parties are unmarried. If, on the other hand, they are either of them married and are not content to observe discretion but set up house together, then the pueblo finds itself threatened in one of its vital structural principles.

Erasmus, "Courtship": A Colloquy

In this colloquy (published in 1523), Erasmus presents a classic instance of the disciplining of manly erotic ardor by womanly wit and modesty. Many of the ideas treated in his "A Praise of Marriage" (see Section B, above) are here given dramatic enactment. Maria, a most charming and intelligent young woman, is in command throughout. Pamphilus (whose name means "loved by all" or "all-loving" or "loving all") woos after the conventions of love poetry, and while it seems he is willing to marry, he is eager to win Maria (named after the Virgin) here and now. Maria, however, is governed by modesty and the conventions of marriage, and though she clearly welcomes and encourages his suit, she uses refusal to bring Pamphilus to do the honorable thing. She needs to know whether he is not only a loving but also a marrying man, and she maneuvers him to proceed toward marriage in the proper way. Of special interest are the way the speech moves from the conventions of love poetry toward the conventions of marriage; Pamphilus' reasons for believing that they are well-matched; and Maria's understanding of the seriousness of declaring a vow ("I am yours") or of offering her kiss. What's in a kiss? Does it make sense for Maria, who though more restrained and confined by convention is still free to exercise her choice, to deliberately hold back her heart no less than her lips? Why does she insist that Pamphilus first accept marriage? Why must he first secure the blessings of her family? Who, then, is the wooer and who the wooed? Should we be sanguine about the prospects for this union?

Pamphilus. Hello, hello, and hello—you cruel, hardhearted, unyielding creature!

Maria.   Hello yourself, Pamphilus, as often and as much as you like, and by whatever name you please. But sometimes I think you've forgotten my name. It's Maria.

Pamphilus. Well, you should have been named Martia.

Maria.   Why so? What have I to do with Mars?

Pamphilus. You slay men for sport, as the god does. Except that you're more pitiless than Mars: you kill even a lover.

Maria.   Mind what you're saying. Where's this heap of men I've slain? Where's the blood of the slaughtered?

Pamphilus. You've only to look at me to see one lifeless corpse.

Maria.   What do I hear? You talk and walk when you're dead? I hope I never meet more fearsome ghosts!

Pamphilus. You're joking, but all the same you're the death of poor me, and you kill more cruelly than if you pierced with a spear. Now, alas, I'm just skin and bones from long torture.

Maria. Well, well! Tell me, how many pregnant women have miscarried at the sight of you?

Pamphilus. But my pallor shows I've less blood than any ghost.

Maria. Yet this pallor is streaked with lavender. You're as pale as a ripening cherry or a purple grape.

Pamphilus. Shame on you for making fun of a miserable wretch!

Maria. But if you don't believe me, bring a mirror.

Pamphilus. I want no other mirror, nor do I think any could be brighter than the one in which I'm looking at myself now.

Maria. What mirror are you talking about?

Pamphilus. Your eyes.

Maria. Quibbler! Just like you. But how do you prove you're lifeless? Do ghosts eat?

Pamphilus. Yes, but they eat insipid stuff, as I do.

Maria. What do they eat, then?

Pamphilus. Mallows, leeks, and lupins.

Maria. But you don't abstain from capons and partridges.

Pamphilus. True, but they taste no better to my palate than if I were eating mallows, or beets without pepper, wine, and vinegar.

Maria. Poor you! Yet all the time you're putting on weight. And do dead men talk too?

Pamphilus. Like me, in a very thin, squeaky voice.

Maria. When I heard you wrangling with your rival not long ago, though, your voice wasn't so thin and squeaky. But I ask you, do ghosts even walk? Wear clothes? Sleep?

Pamphilus. They even sleep together—though after their own fashion.

Maria. Well! Witty fellow, aren't you?

Pamphilus. But what will you say if I demonstrate with Achillean proofs that I'm dead and you're a murderer?

Maria. Perish the thought, Pamphilus! But proceed to your argument.

Pamphilus. In the first place, you'll grant, I suppose, that death is nothing but the removal of soul from body?

Maria. Granted.

Pamphilus. But grant it so that you won't want to take back what you've given.

Maria. I won't want to.

Pamphilus. Then you won't deny that whoever robs another of his soul is a murderer?

Maria. I allow it.

Pamphilus. You'll concede also what's affirmed by the most respected authors and endorsed by the assent of so many ages: that man's soul is not where it animates but where it loves?

Maria. Explain this more simply. I don't follow your meaning well enough.

Pamphilus. And the worse for me that you don't see this as clearly as I do.

Maria. Try to make me see it.

Pamphilus. As well try to make adamant see!

Maria. Well, I'm a girl, not a stone.

Pamphilus. True, but harder than adamant.

Maria. But get on with your argument.

Pamphilus. Men seized by a divine inspiration neither hear nor see nor smell nor feel, even if you kill them.

Maria. Yes, I've heard that.

Pamphilus. What do you suppose is the reason?

Maria. You tell me, professor.

Pamphilus. Obviously because their spirit is in heaven, where it possesses what it ardently loves, and is absent from the body.

Maria. What of it?

Pamphilus. What of it, you unfeeling girl? It follows both that I'm dead and that you're the murderer.

Maria. Where's your soul, then?

Pamphilus. Where it loves.

Maria. But who robbed you of your soul?—Why do you sigh? Speak freely; I won't hold it against you.

Pamphilus. Cruelest of girls, whom nevertheless I can't hate even if I'm dead!

Maria. Naturally. But why don't you in turn deprive her of *her* soul—tit for tat, as they say?

Pamphilus. I'd like nothing better if the exchange could be such that her spirit migrated to my breast, as my spirit has gone over completely to her body.

Maria. But may I, in turn, play the sophist with you?

Pamphilus. The sophistress.

Maria. It isn't possible for the same body to be living and lifeless, is it?

Pamphilus. No, not at the same time.

Maria. When the soul's gone, then the body's dead?

Pamphilus. Yes.

Maria. It doesn't animate except when it's present?

Pamphilus. Exactly.

Maria.　　　Then how does it happen that although the soul's there where it loves, it nevertheless animates the body left behind? If it animates that body even when it loves elsewhere, how can the animated body be called lifeless?

Pamphilus. You dispute cunningly enough, but you won't catch me with such snares. The soul that somehow or other governs the body of a lover is incorrectly called soul, since actually it consists of certain slight remnants of soul—just as the scent of roses remains in your hand even if the rose is taken away.

Maria.　　　Hard to catch a fox with a noose, I see. But answer me this: doesn't one who kills perform an act?

Pamphilus. Of course.

Maria.　　　And the one who's killed suffers?

Pamphilus. Yes indeed.

Maria.　　　Then how is it that although the lover is active and the beloved passive, the beloved is said to kill—when the lover, rather, kills himself?

Pamphilus. On the contrary, it's the lover who suffers; the beloved does the deed.

Maria.　　　You'll never win this case before the supreme court of grammarians.

Pamphilus. But I'll win it before the congress of logicians.

Maria.　　　Now don't begrudge an answer to this, too: do you love willingly or unwillingly?

Pamphilus. Willingly.

Maria.　　　Then since one is free not to love, whoever loves seems to be a self-murderer. To blame the girl is unjust.

Pamphilus. Yet the girl doesn't kill by being loved but by failing to return the love. Whoever can save someone and refrains from doing so is guilty of murder.

Maria.　　　Suppose a young man loves what is forbidden, for example another man's wife or a Vestal Virgin? She won't return his love in order to save the lover, will she?

Pamphilus. But *this* young man loves what it's lawful and right, and reasonable and honourable, to love; and yet he's slain. If this crime of murder is trivial, I'll bring a charge of poisoning too.

Maria.　　　Heaven forbid! Will you make a Circe of me?

Pamphilus. Something more pitiless than that. For I'd rather be a hog or a bear than what I am now, a lifeless thing.

Maria.　　　Well, just what sort of poison do I kill men with?

Pamphilus. You bewitch them.

Maria.　　　Then you want me to keep my poisonous eyes off you hereafter?

Pamphilus. Don't say such things! No, turn them on me more and more.

Maria. If my eyes are charmers, why don't the other men I look at languish too? So I suspect this witchcraft is in your own eyes, not in mine.

Pamphilus. Wasn't it enough to slay Pamphilus without mocking him besides?

Maria. A handsome corpse! But when's the funeral?

Pamphilus. Sooner than you think—unless you rescue me.

Maria. Have I so much power?

Pamphilus. You can bring a dead man back to life, and that with little trouble.

Maria. If someone gave me a cure-all.

Pamphilus. No need of medicines; just return his love. What could be easier or fairer? In no other way will you be acquitted of the crime of homicide.

Maria. Before which court shall I be tried? That of the Areopagites?

Pamphilus. No, the court of Venus.

Maria. She's an easygoing goddess, they say.

Pamphilus. Oh, no, her wrath's the most terrible of all.

Maria. Has she a thunderbolt?

Pamphilus. No.

Maria. A trident?

Pamphilus. By no means.

Maria. Has she a spear?

Pamphilus. Not at all, but she's goddess of the sea.

Maria. I don't go sailing.

Pamphilus. But she has a boy.

Maria. Not old enough to scare me.

Pamphilus. He's vengeful and wilful.

Maria. What will he do to me?

Pamphilus. What will he do? Heaven avert it! I wouldn't want to predict calamity to one whose welfare I have at heart.

Maria. Tell me anyway. I'm not superstitious.

Pamphilus. Then I'll tell you. If you reject this lover—who, unless I'm mistaken, is not altogether unworthy of having his love returned—the boy may, at his mother's bidding, shoot you with a dreadfully poisonous dart. As a result you'd fall desperately in love with some low creature who wouldn't return your love.

Maria. You tell me of a horrible punishment. For my part, I'd rather die than be madly in love with a man who's ugly or wouldn't return love for love.

Pamphilus. Yet there was recently a much publicized example of this misfortune, involving a certain girl.

Maria.   Where?

Pamphilus. At Orleans.

Maria.   How many years ago was this?

Pamphilus. How many years? Scarcely ten months ago.

Maria.   What was the girl's name? Why do you hesitate?

Pamphilus. Never mind. I know her as well as I do you.

Maria.   Why don't you tell me her name, then?

Pamphilus. Because I don't like the omen. I only wish she'd had some other name! Hers was the very same as yours.

Maria.   Who was her father?

Pamphilus. He's still living. Eminent lawyer and well-to-do.

Maria.   Give me his name.

Pamphilus. Maurice.

Maria.   Family name?

Pamphilus. Bright.

Maria.   Is the mother living?

Pamphilus. Died recently.

Maria.   What illness did she die of?

Pamphilus. What illness, you ask? Grief. And the father, though one of the hardiest of men, was in mortal danger.

Maria.   May one know the mother's name too?

Pamphilus. Of course. Everybody knew Sophronia. But why this questioning? Do you think I'm spinning some yarn?

Maria.   Would I suspect that of *you?* More commonly this suspicion is directed against our sex. But tell me what happened to the girl.

Pamphilus. She was a girl of respectable, wealthy background, as I said, and extremely beautiful—in short, worthy to marry a prince. She was courted by a certain young man whose social standing was similar to hers.

Maria.   What was his name?

Pamphilus. Alas, a bad omen for me! Pamphilus was his name too. He tried everything, but she obstinately turned him down. The young man wasted away with sorrow. Not long afterwards she fell desperately in love with one who was more like an ape than a man.

Maria.   What's that you say?

Pamphilus. So madly in love it's inexpressible.

Maria.   So attractive a girl in love with so hideous a man?

Pamphilus. He had a peaked head, thin hair—and that torn and unkempt, full of scurf and lice. The mange had laid bare most of his scalp; he was cross-eyed, had flat, wide-open nostrils like an ape's, thin mouth, rotten teeth, a stuttering tongue, pocky chin; he was hunchbacked, potbellied, and had crooked shanks.

Maria.   You describe some Thersites to me.

Pamphilus. What's more, they said he had only one ear.

Maria.   Perhaps he lost the other in war.

Pamphilus. Oh, no, in peace.

Maria.   Who dared do that to him?

Pamphilus. Denis the hangman.

Maria.   Maybe a large family fortune made up for his ugliness.

Pamphilus. Not at all; he was bankrupt and head over heels in debt. With this husband, so exceptional a girl now spends her life and is often beaten.

Maria.   A wretched tale you tell.

Pamphilus. But a true one. Thus it pleased Nemesis to avenge the injury to the youth who was spurned.

Maria.   I'd rather be destroyed by a thunderbolt than put up with such a husband.

Pamphilus. Then don't provoke Nemesis: return your lover's love.

Maria.   If that's enough, I do return it.

Pamphilus. But I'd want this love to be lasting and to be mine alone. I'm courting a wife, not a mistress.

Maria.   I know that, but I must deliberate a long time over what can't be revoked once it's begun.

Pamphilus. I've thought it over a very long time.

Maria.   See that love, who's not the best adviser, doesn't trick you. For they say he's blind.

Pamphilus. But one who proceeds with caution is keen-sighted. You don't appear to me as you do because I love you; I love you because I've observed what you're like.

Maria.   But you may not know me well enough. If you wore the shoe, you'd feel then where it pinched.

Pamphilus. I'll have to take the chance; though I infer from many signs that the match will succeed.

Maria.   You're a soothsayer too?

Pamphilus. I am.

Maria.   Then by what auguries do you infer this? Has the night owl flown?

Pamphilus. That flies for fools.

Maria.   Has a pair of doves flown from the right?

Pamphilus. Nothing of the sort. But the integrity of your parents has been known to me for years now. In the first place, good birth is far from a bad sign. Nor am I unaware of the wholesome instruction and godly examples by which you've been reared; and good education is better than good birth. That's another sign. In addition, between my family—not an altogether contemptible one, I believe—and yours there has long been intimate friendship. In fact, you and I have known each other from our cradle days, as they say, and our temperaments are pretty much the same. We're nearly equal in age; our parents, in wealth, reputation, and rank. Finally—and this is the special mark of friendship, since excellence by itself is no guarantee of compatibility—your tastes seem to fit my temperament not at all badly. How mine agree with yours, I don't know.

Obviously, darling, these omens assure me that we shall have a blessed, lasting, happy marriage, provided you don't intend to sing a song of woe for our prospects.

Maria. What song do you want?

Pamphilus. I'll play 'I am yours'; you chime in with 'I am yours.'

Maria. A short song, all right, but it has a long finale.

Pamphilus. What matter how long, if only it be joyful?

Maria. I'm so prejudiced about you that I wouldn't want you to do something you might be sorry for afterwards.

Pamphilus. Stop looking on the dark side.

Maria. Maybe I'll seem different to you when illness or old age has changed this beauty.

Pamphilus. Neither will I always be as handsome as I am now, my dear. But I don't consider only this dwelling place, which is blooming and charming in every respect. I love the guest more.

Maria. What guest?

Pamphilus. Your mind, whose beauty will forever increase with age.

Maria. Truly you're more than a Lynceus if you see through so much make-up!

Pamphilus. I see your mind through mine. Besides, we'll renew our youth repeatedly in our children.

Maria. But meantime my virginity is gone.

Pamphilus. True, but see here: if you had a fine orchard, would you want it never to bear anything but blossoms or would you prefer, after the blossoms have fallen, to see the trees heavy with ripe fruit?

Maria. How he prattles!

Pamphilus. Answer this at least: which is the prettier sight, a vine rotting on the ground or encircling some post or elm tree and weighing it down with purple grapes?

Maria. *You* answer *me* in turn: which is the more pleasing sight, a rose gleaming white on its bush or plucked and gradually withering?

Pamphilus. In my opinion the rose that withers in a man's hand, delighting his eyes and nostrils the while, is luckier than one that grows old on a bush. For that one too would wither sooner or later. In the same way, wine is better if drunk before it sours. But a girl's flower doesn't fade the instant she marries. On the contrary, I see many girls who before marriage were pale, run-down, and as good as gone. The sexual side of marriage brightened them so much that they began to bloom at last.

Maria. Yet virginity wins universal approval and applause.

Pamphilus. A maiden is something charming, but what's more unnatural than an old maid? Unless your mother had been deflowered, we wouldn't have this blossom here. But if, as I hope, our marriage will not be barren, we'll pay for one virgin with many.

Maria. But they say chastity is a thing most pleasing to God.

Pamphilus. And therefore I want to marry a chaste girl, to live chastely with her. It will be more a marriage of minds than of bodies. We'll reproduce for the state; we'll reproduce for Christ. By how little will this marriage fall short of virginity! And perhaps some day we'll live as Joseph and Mary did. But meantime we'll learn virginity; for one does not reach the summit all at once.

Maria. What's this I hear? Virginity to be violated in order to be learned?

Pamphilus. Why not? As by gradually drinking less and less wine we learn temperance. Which seems more temperate to you, the person who, sitting down in the midst of dainties, abstains from them or the one secluded from those things that invite intemperance?

Maria. I think the man whom abundance cannot corrupt is more steadfastly temperate.

Pamphilus. Which more truly deserves praise for chastity, the man who castrates himself or the one who, while sexually unimpaired, nevertheless abstains from sexual love?

Maria. My vote would go to the latter. The first I'd regard as mad.

Pamphilus. But don't those who renounce marriage by a strict vow castrate themselves, in a sense?

Maria. Apparently.

Pamphilus. Now to abstain from sexual intercourse isn't a virtue.

Maria. Isn't it?

Pamphilus. Look at it this way. If it were a virtue *per se* not to have intercourse, intercourse would be a vice. Now it happens that it is a vice not to have intercourse, a virtue to have it.

Maria. When does this 'happen'?

Pamphilus. Whenever the husband seeks his due from his wife, especially if he seeks her embrace from a desire for children.

Maria. What if from lust? Isn't it right for him to be denied?

Pamphilus. It's right to reprove him, or rather to ask him politely to refrain. It's not right to refuse him flatly—though in this respect I hear few husbands complain of their wives.

Maria.   But liberty is sweet.

Pamphilus. Virginity, on the other hand, is a heavy burden. I'll be your king, you'll be my queen; we'll rule a family at our pleasure. Or does this seem servitude to you?

Maria.   The public calls marriage a halter.

Pamphilus. But those who call it that really deserve a halter themselves. Tell me, I beg you, isn't your soul bound to your body?

Maria.   Evidently.

Pamphilus. Like a little bird in a cage. And yet ask him if he desires to be free. He'll say no, I think. Why? Because he's willingly confined.

Maria.   Our fortune is modest.

Pamphilus. So much the safer. You'll increase it at home by thrift, which is not unreasonably called a large source of income; I'll increase it away from home by my industry.

Maria.   Children bring countless cares with them.

Pamphilus. But they bring countless delights and often repay the parents' devotion with interest many times over.

Maria.   Loss of children is a miserable experience.

Pamphilus. Aren't you childless now? But why expect the worst in every uncertainty? Tell me, which would you prefer, never to be born or to be born to die?

Maria.   I'd rather be born to die, of course.

Pamphilus. As those who have lived are more fortunate than those who never were born and never will be born, so is childlessness the more miserable in never having had and never expecting to have offspring.

Maria.   Who are these who are not and will not be?

Pamphilus. Though one who refuses to run the risks of human life—to which all of us, kings and commoners alike, are equally liable—ought to give up life, still, whatever happens, you'll bear only half. I'll take over the larger share, so that if we have good luck the pleasure will be double; if bad, companionship will take away half the pain. As for me, if heaven summons, it will be sweet to die in your arms.

Maria.   Men bear more readily what nature's universal laws decree. But I observe how much more distressed some parents are by their children's conduct than by their death.

Pamphilus. Preventing that is mostly up to us.

Maria.   How so?

Pamphilus. Because, with respect to character, good children are usually born of good parents. Kites don't come from doves. We'll try, therefore, to be good ourselves. Next, we'll see that our children are imbued from birth with sacred teachings and beliefs. What the jar is filled with when new matters most. In addition, we'll see that at home we provide an example of life for them to imitate.

Maria.   What you describe is difficult.

Pamphilus. No wonder, because it's good. (And you're difficult too, for the same reason!) But we'll labour so much the harder to this end.

Maria.   You'll have tractable material to work with. See that you form and fashion me.

Pamphilus. But meanwhile say just three words.[1]

Maria.   Nothing easier, but once words have flown out they don't fly back. I'll give better advice for us both: confer with your parents and mine, to get the consent of both sides.

Pamphilus. You bid me ask for your hand in marriage, but in three words you can make success certain.

Maria.   I don't know whether I could. I'm not a free agent. In former times marriages were arranged only by the authority of elders. But however that may be, I think our marriage will have more chance of success if it's arranged by our parents' authority. And it's your part to make the proposal; that isn't appropriate to our sex. We girls like to be swept off our feet, even if sometimes we're deeply in love.

Pamphilus. I won't be hesitant in making the proposal. Only don't let your decision alone defeat me.

Maria.   It won't. Cheer up, Pamphilus dear!

Pamphilus. You're more strait-laced towards me in this business than I should like.

Maria.   But first ponder your own private decision. Judge by your reason, not your feeling. What emotion decides is temporary; rational choice generally pleases forever.

Pamphilus. Indeed you philosophize very well, so I'm resolved to take your advice.

Maria.   You won't regret it. But see here: a disturbing difficulty has turned up.

Pamphilus. Away with these difficulties!

Maria.   You wouldn't want me to marry a dead man?

Pamphilus. By no means; but I'll revive.

Maria.   You've removed the difficulty. Farewell, Pamphilus darling.

Pamphilus. That's up to you.

---

[1]"I am yours." In canon law, the exchange of such a pledge, in the present tense, was regarded as binding and accepted as a valid marriage, whether spoken publicly or privately.[Eds.]

Maria.   I bid you good night. Why do you sigh?

Pamphilus. 'Good night,' you say? If only you'd grant what you bid!

Maria.   Don't be in too great a hurry. You're counting chickens before they're hatched.

Pamphilus. Shan't I have anything from you to take with me?

Maria.   This sachet, to gladden your heart.

Pamphilus. Add a kiss at least.

Maria.   I want to deliver to you a virginity whole and unblemished.

Pamphilus. Does a kiss rob you of your virginity?

Maria.   Then do you want me to bestow my kisses on others too?

Pamphilus. Of course not. I want your kisses kept for me.

Maria.   I'll keep them for you. Though there's another reason why I wouldn't dare give away kisses just now.

Pamphilus. What's that?

Maria.   You say your soul has passed almost entirely into my body and that there's only the slightest particle left in yours. Consequently, I'm afraid this particle in you would skip over to me in a kiss and you'd then become quite lifeless. So shake hands, a symbol of our mutual love; and farewell. Persevere in your efforts. Meanwhile I'll pray Christ to bless and prosper us both in what we do.

Shakespeare, *The Tempest*

The courtship of the young lovers Ferdinand and Miranda in Shakespeare's The Tempest *(first published in the Folio of 1623) is carefully arranged and fully or-chestrated by Miranda's father, Prospero. To those who reject the importance of fa-milial intervention in such matters, the play seems to offer a cautionary warning. For Shakespeare depicts these young lovers much as he does Romeo and Juliet—Miranda is as innocent as Juliet, Ferdinand as spirited, as star-crossed, as impetu-ous as Romeo—and in a situation similar to theirs: their parents are inveterate enemies. But here tragedy is averted, thanks largely to the wisdom and foresight of Miranda's father. True, Prospero has much to gain from their union, person-ally and politically. Twelve years earlier, Prospero, then Duke of Milan, was ousted from his throne, turned adrift on the sea with his three-year old daughter, and cast upon the island, where he and Miranda have lived ever since, virtually alone. Just prior to the opening of the play, an "accident most strange" brings a ship car-rying Prospero's enemies—principally, his usurper brother Antonio and his ally, the King of Naples, Ferdinand's father—as well as Ferdinand, to the shores of his island home, and Prospero sees in the union of the young pair a fitting way of avenging himself upon his enemies and providing for his own succession. But, were he reckoning only for himself, father Prospero has much to lose in this plan (as he is well aware): he must say good-bye to the young child whom he has cared for and loved all these years. Yet Prospero's actions are not just self-regarding. Now that Miranda has come of age, fatherly care obliges him to put her welfare first. The measures he takes seem directed to his daughter's future happiness, even more than to his own. He seeks to protect and preserve her trusting innocence, at the same time as he deliberately helps to awaken her independence and desire. In his fatherly way, he prepares his daughter, and himself, for her entrance not only into love but into marriage.*

The first selection (from Act I, Scene ii) shows the first meeting of Ferdinand and Miranda. As we observe, though Prospero made all the arrangements, the love of Ferdinand and Miranda immediately grows wings of its own. Ferdinand knows Miranda long enough to speak a mere four lines when he proclaims her a "wonder" and wonders himself about whether she "be maid or no." And Miranda, though moments earlier (in the very same scene) listened with pity and rapt at-tention to her father's tale of his earlier woes, and had reason to believe that the tempest, which she knows to have been staged by her father, brought his enemies ashore, immediately throws all caution to the wind. Sighingly, pityingly, she de-fends Ferdinand against her father. Are Prospero's concerns about their hasty pas-

sion warranted? Is it reasonable for him to fear that "too light winning make the prize light"? Why, and for whose sake, does Prospero insist that Ferdinand submit to his rule?

> *Act I. Scene ii. Lines 375–503.*
> *Stage Directions: Enter Ferdinand and Ariel (the island sprite who enacts Prospero's orders). Ariel is invisible as he sings, beckoning the forlorn Ferdinand toward Miranda. (Ferdinand was separated from his father and the rest of the crew during Prospero's tempest and is of the opinion that he is the ship's sole survivor.) Awaiting him, as he steps forward, are Prospero and Miranda.*

Ariel's Song.

Come unto these yellow sands,
   And then take hands.
Curtsied when you have and kissed,
   The wild waves whist,[1]
Foot it featly[2] here and there;
And, sweet sprites, the burden[3] bear.
   Hark, hark!
                  Burden, dispersedly. Bowgh, wawgh!
   The watchdogs bark.
                  Burden, dispersedly. Bowgh, wawgh!
   Hark, hark I hear
   The strain of strutting chanticleer
      Cry cock-a-diddle-dowe.

Ferdinand. Where should this music be? I' th' air or th' earth?
   It sounds no more; and sure it waits upon
   Some god o' th' island. Sitting on a bank,
   Weeping again the King my father's wreck,
   This music crept by me upon the waters,
   Allaying both their fury and my passion[4]
   With its sweet air. Thence I have followed it,
   Or it hath drawn me rather; but 'tis gone.
   No, it begins again.

---

[1] **whist** being hushed
[2] **featly** nimbly
[3] **burden** undersong, refrain
[4] **passion** lamentation

Ariel's Song.

Full fathom five thy father lies;
　　Of his bones are coral made;
Those are pearls that were his eyes;
　　Nothing of him that doth fade
But doth suffer a sea-change
Into something rich and strange.
Sea nymphs hourly ring his knell:
　　　　　Burden. Ding-dong.
Hark! now I hear them—Ding-dong bell.

Ferdinand. The ditty does remember[5] my drowned father.
　　This is no mortal business, nor no sound
　　That the earth owes.[6] I hear it now above me.
Prospero. The fringèd curtains of thine eye advance[7]
　　And say what thou seest yond.
Miranda.　　　　　　　　What is't? a spirit?
　　Lord, how it looks about! Believe me, sir,
　　It carries a brave form. But 'tis a spirit.
Prospero. No, wench: it eats, and sleeps, and hath such senses
　　As we have, such. This gallant which thou seest
　　Was in the wreck; and, but he's something stained[8]
　　With grief (that's beauty's canker), thou mightst call him
　　A goodly person. He hath lost his fellows
　　And strays about to find 'em.
Miranda.　　　　　　　　I might call him
　　A thing divine; for nothing natural
　　I ever saw so noble.
Prospero.　　　　　　*[aside]* It goes on, I see,
　　As my soul prompts[9] it. Spirit, fine spirit, I'll free thee
　　Within two days for this.
Ferdinand. [seeing Miranda] Most sure,[10] the goddess
　　On whom these airs attend! Vouchsafe my prayer
　　May know if you remain[11] upon this island,

---

[5]**remember** allude to
[6]**owes** owns
[7]**advance** raise
[8]**stained** disfigured
[9]**prompts** would like
[10]**most sure** this is certainly
[11]**remain** dwell

And that you will some good instruction give
How I may bear me[12] here. My prime request,
Which I do last pronounce, is—O you wonder!—
If you be maid or no?

Miranda.   No wonder, sir,
But certainly a maid.

Ferdinand.   My language? Heavens!
I am the best of them that speak this speech,
Were I but where 'tis spoken.

Prospero.   How? the best?
What wert thou if the King of Naples heard thee?

Ferdinand. A single[13] thing, as I am now, that wonders
To hear thee speak of Naples.[14] He does hear me;
And that he does I weep. Myself am Naples,
Who with mine eyes, never since at ebb, beheld
The King my father wrecked.

Miranda.   Alack, for mercy!

Ferdinand. Yes, faith, and all his lords, the Duke of Milan
And his brave son being twain.

Prospero.   [aside] The Duke of Milan
And his more braver daughter could control[15] thee,
If now 'twere fit to do't. At the first sight
They have changed eyes.[16]—Delicate Ariel,
I'll set thee free for this.—[To Ferdinand] A word, good sir.
I fear you have done yourself some wrong.[17] A word!

Miranda. Why speaks my father so ungently? This
Is the third man that e'er I saw; the first
That e'er I sighed for. Pity move my father
To be inclined my way!

Ferdinand.   O, if a virgin,
And your affection not gone forth, I'll make you
The Queen of Naples.

Prospero.   Soft, sir! one word more.
[Aside] They are both in either's pow'rs. But this swift business
I must uneasy make, lest too light winning

---

[12]**bear me** conduct myself
[13]**single** (1) solitary (2) weak or helpless
[14]**Naples** King of Naples
[15]**control** refute
[16]**changed eyes** exchanged love looks
[17]**done . . . wrong** told a lie

Make the prize light.—*[To Ferdinand]* One word more! I charge thee
That thou attend me. Thou dost here usurp
The name thou ow'st[18] not, and hast put thyself
Upon this island as a spy, to win it
From me, the lord on't.

Ferdinand.   No, as I am a man!

Miranda. There's nothing ill can dwell in such a temple.
If the ill spirit have so fair a house,
Good things will strive to dwell with't.

Prospero.   Follow me.—
Speak not you for him; he's a traitor.—Come!
I'll manacle thy neck and feet together;
Sea water shalt thou drink; thy food shall be
The fresh-brook mussels, withered roots, and husks
Wherein the acorn cradled. Follow!

Ferdinand.   No.
I will resist such entertainment[19] till
Mine enemy has more power.

                              He draws, and is charmed from moving.

Miranda.   O dear father,
Make not too rash a trial[20] of him, for
He's gentle,[21] and not fearful.[22]

Prospero.   What, I say,
My foot my tutor?[23]—Put thy sword up, traitor!
Who mak'st a show but dar'st not strike, thy conscience
Is so possessed with guilt. Come, from thy ward![24]
For I can here disarm thee with this stick
And make thy weapon drop.

Miranda.   Beseech you, father!

Prospero. Hence! Hang not on my garments.

Miranda.   Sir, have pity.
I'll be his surety.

Prospero.   Silence! One word more
Shall make me chide thee, if not hate thee. What,

---

[18]**ow'st** ownest
[19]**entertainment** treatment
[20]**trial** judgment
[21]**gentle** noble
[22]**fearful** cowardly
[23]**My . . . tutor** i.e., instructed by my underling
[24]**ward** fighting posture

An advocate for an impostor? Hush!

Thou think'st there is no more such shapes as he,

Having seen but him and Caliban. Foolish wench!

To th' most of men this is a Caliban,

And they to him are angels.

Miranda.   My affections[25]

Are then most humble. I have no ambition

To see a goodlier man.

Prospero.   Come on, obey![26]

Thy nerves[27] are in their infancy again

And have no vigor in them.

Ferdinand.   So they are.

My spirits, as in a dream, are all bound up.

My father's loss, the weakness which I feel,

The wreck of all my friends, nor this man's threats

To whom I am subdued, are but light to me,

Might I but through my prison once a day

Behold this maid. All corners else o' th' earth

Let liberty make use of. Space enough

Have I in such a prison.

Prospero.   *[aside]* It works. *[to Ferdinand]*

Come on.—

Thou hast done well, fine Ariel! *[to Ferdinand]* Follow

me.

[To Ariel] Hark what thou else shalt do me.

Miranda.   Be of comfort.

My father's of a better nature, sir,

Than he appears by speech. This is unwonted

Which now came from him.

Prospero. [To Ariel]   Thou shalt be as free

As mountain winds; but then exactly do

All points of my command.

Ariel.   To th' syllable.

Prospero. Come, follow.—*[To Miranda]* Speak not for him.   *Exeunt*

* * *

---

[25]**affections** inclinations

[26]**obey** follow

[27]**nerves** sinews, tendons

The second selection (Act III, Scene i) is the central episode in the courtship of Ferdinand and Miranda (and the central scene in the play as a whole). Ferdinand is hard at work at the log-bearing task set for him by Prospero. From the outset of the scene, he seems chastened and transformed, and his subsequent conversation with Miranda affirms this impression. Even more remarkable, Miranda, tempted at first by desire and independence and in rebellion against her father, is slowly recalled to her sense of propriety. The very moment she realizes that her love and desire for Ferdinand are reciprocated she does not forget herself but rather disciplines herself, eliciting from him the promise of marriage. The two lovers then plight their troths. Many a contemporary reader will no doubt wonder at Miranda's self-command. (It seems even Prospero does so.) Is she, and is their mutual agreement, believable? How did the log-bearing task set by Prospero contribute to this end? Was it important that that task be carrying logs? What is it about these two lovers that makes them so educable? Why does Prospero, who seems completely responsible for bringing the lovers together, call upon the Heavens to "rain grace on that which breeds between 'em"?

Act III. Scene i.

Stage Directions: Enter Ferdinand, bearing a log. (Miranda and Prospero enter shortly thereafter, though, neither of the lovers knows that Prospero is present.)

Ferdinand. There be some sports are painful,[28] and their labor
    Delight in them sets off;[29] some kinds of baseness
    Are nobly undergone, and most poor matters[30]
    Point to rich ends. This my mean task
    Would be as heavy to me as odious, but
    The mistress which I serve quickens[31] what's dead
    And makes my labors pleasures. O, she is
    Ten times more gentle than her father's crabbèd;
    And he's composed of harshness! I must remove
    Some thousands of these logs and pile them up,
    Upon a sore injunction.[32] My sweet mistress
    Weeps when she sees me work, and says such baseness
    Had never like executor. I forget;

---

[28] **painful** strenuous
[29] **sets off** makes greater by contrast
[30] **matters** affairs
[31] **quickens** brings to life
[32] **sore injunction** grievous command

But these sweet thoughts do even refresh my labors
Most busy least[33] when I do it.

Enter Miranda; and Prospero [behind, unseen].

Miranda.   Alas, now pray you
Work not so hard! I would the lightning had
Burnt up those logs that you are enjoined to pile!
Pray set it down and rest you. When this burns,
'Twill weep[34] for having wearied you. My father
Is hard at study: pray now rest yourself.
He's safe for these three hours.
Ferdinand.   O most dear mistress,
The sun will set before I shall discharge
What I must strive to do.
    Miranda.   If you'll sit down,
I'll bear your logs the while. Pray give me that:
I'll carry it to the pile.
Ferdinand.   No, precious creature:
I had rather crack my sinews, break my back,
Than you should such dishonor undergo
While I sit lazy by.
Miranda.   It would become me
As well as it does you; and I should do it
With much more ease; for my good will is to it,
And yours it is against.
Prospero.   *[aside]* Poor worm, thou art infected!
This visitation[35] shows it.
Miranda.   You look wearily.
Ferdinand. No, noble mistress: 'tis fresh morning with me
When you are by at night. I do beseech you—
Chiefly that I might set it in my prayers—
What is your name?
Miranda.   Miranda.—O my father,
I have broke your hest[36] to say so!
Ferdinand   Admired Miranda!
Indeed the top of admiration,[37] worth

---

[33]**least** i.e., least conscious of being busy
[34]**weep** i.e., exude resin
[35]**visitation** (1) visit (2) attack of plague (in the metaphor of 'infected')
[36]**hest** command
[37]**admiration** wonder, astonishment (the name Miranda means wonderful woman; Cf. I, ii, 427)

What's dearest to the world! Full many a lady
I have eyed with best regard,[38] and many a time
The harmony of their tongues hath into bondage
Brought my too diligent ear; for several[39] virtues
Have I liked several women; never any
With so full soul[40] but some defect in her
Did quarrel with the noblest grace she owed,[41]
And put it to the foil.[42] But you, O you,
So perfect and so peerless, are created
Of every creature's best!

Miranda.   I do not know
One of my sex; no woman's face remember,
Save, from my glass, mine own; nor have I seen
More that I may call men than you, good friend,
And my dear father. How features are abroad[43]
I am skilless[44] of; but, by my modesty
(The jewel in my dower), I would not wish
Any companion in the world but you;
Nor can imagination form a shape,
Besides yourself, to like of.[45] But I prattle
Something too wildly, and my father's precepts
I therein do forget.

Ferdinand.   I am, in my condition,[46]
A prince, Miranda; I do think, a king
(I would not so), and would no more endure
This wooden slavery than to suffer
The fleshfly blow my mouth. Hear my soul speak!
The very instant that I saw you, did
My heart fly to your service; there resides,
To make me slave to it; and for your sake
Am I this patient log-man.

Miranda.   Do you love me?

Ferdinand. O heaven, O earth, bear witness to this sound,

---

[38]**best regard** highest approval
[39]**several** different
[40]**with. . . . soul** i.e., so wholeheartedly
[41]**owed** owned
[42]**foil** (1) overthrow (2) contrast
[43]**abroad** elsewhere
[44]**skilless** ignorant
[45]**like of** compare to
[46]**condition** situation in the world

And crown what I profess with kind event[47]
If I speak true! if hollowly, invert
What best is boded me to mischief! I,
Beyond all limit of what else i' th' world,
Do love, prize, honor you.

Miranda.   I am a fool
To weep at what I am glad of.

Prospero.   [aside] Fair encounter
Of two most rare affections! Heavens rain grace
On that which breeds between 'em!

Ferdinand.   Wherefore weep you?

Miranda. At mine unworthiness, that dare not offer
What I desire to give, and much less take
What I shall die to want.[48] But this is trifling;
And all the more it seeks to hide itself,
The bigger bulk it shows. Hence, bashful cunning,[49]
And prompt me, plain and holy innocence!
I am your wife, if you will marry me;
If not, I'll die your maid. To be your fellow[50]
You may deny me; but I'll be your servant,
Whether you will or no.

Ferdinand.   My mistress, dearest,
And I thus humble ever.

Miranda.   My husband then?

Ferdinand. Ay, with a heart as willing
As bondage e'er of freedom.[51] Here's my hand.

Miranda. And mine, with my heart in't; and now farewell
Till half an hour hence.

Ferdinand.   A thousand thousand!

                    Exeunt [Ferdinand and Miranda severally].

Prospero. So glad of this as they I cannot be,
Who are surprised withal;[52] but my rejoicing
At nothing can be more. I'll to my book;
For yet ere supper time must I perform
Much business appertaining.[53]   *Exit.*

---

[47]**kind event** favorable outcome
[48]**want** lack
[49]**bashful cunning** i.e. coyness
[50]**fellow** equal
[51]**of freedom** i.e., to win freedom
[52]**surprised withal** taken unaware by it
[53]**appertaining** relevant

Shakespeare, *As You Like It*

In Shakespeare's As You Like It *(first published in the Folio of 1623), as in* The Tempest, *a young nobleman, here named Orlando, and a young maiden, here named Rosalind, fall in love at first sight. But as each has been separated from the tutelage of parents or mentors, the courtship that proceeds is here directed by Rosalind herself, who, of the pair, is by far the more worldly-wise and self-aware and, practically from the start, consciously directed toward marriage. The five excerpts presented here trace the full development of their courtship.*

As the play opens, spirited young Orlando, youngest son of the late nobleman Sir Rowland de Boys, is chafing under the tyrannical rule of his older brother Oliver. Held back in childhood, deprived of both education and cultivation, he has decided out of frustration to take matters into his own hands. But he knows not what to do. Thus, he impetuously attacks his older brother, then recklessly resolves to go up against Charles, wrestler extraordinaire to Duke Frederick. As he enters the Duke's palace to take on the mighty adversary, he meets Rosalind, who, like Orlando, also suffers from familial displacement. Rosalind's father, Duke Senior, has been displaced and banished from his dukedom by his brother, Duke Frederick, who has kept Rosalind in the palace as company for his daughter Celia. The selections begin with the first meeting of Orlando and Rosalind, noteworthy not least for its revelation of the deep love that once existed between their two absent fathers.

> Act I. Scene ii. Lines 141–280. Location: before the Duke's Palace.
> Stage Directions: Flourish. Enter Duke Frederick, Lords, Orlando, Charles and attendants. (Already present on stage are Rosalind, Celia and Le Beau, a courtier attending on Frederick.)

Duke Frederick. Come on. Since the youth will not be
    entreated, his own peril on his forwardness.[1]
Rosalind. Is yonder the man?
Le Beau. Even he, madam.
Celia. Alas, he is too young! Yet he looks successfully.[2]
Duke Frederick. How now, daughter and cousin? Are
    you crept hither to see the wrestling?
Rosalind. Ay, my liege, so please you give us leave.[3]
Duke Frederick. You will take little delight in it, I can

---

[1] **entreated ... forwardness** i.e., entreated to desist, let the risk be blamed upon his own rashness
[2] **successfully** i.e., as if he would be successful
[3] **so ... leave** if you will permit us

tell you, there is such odds[4] in the man.[5] In pity of the
challenger's youth I would fain[6] dissuade him, but he
will not be entreated. Speak to him, ladies; see if you
can move him.

Celia. Call him hither, good Monsieur Le Beau.

Duke Frederick. Do so. I'll not be by. *[He steps aside.]*

Le Beau. Monsieur the challenger, the princess calls for
you.

Orlando. *[Approaching the ladies]* I attend them with all
respect and duty.

Rosalind. Young man, have you challenged Charles the
wrestler?

Orlando. No, fair princess; he is the general challenger.
I come but in, as others do, to try with him the
strength of my youth.

Celia. Young gentleman, your spirits are too bold for
your years. You have seen cruel proof of this man's
strength. If you saw yourself with your eyes or knew
yourself with your judgment,[7] the fear of your adventure would counsel you to a more equal[8] enterprise. We
pray you, for your own sake, to embrace your own
safety and give over this attempt.

Rosalind. Do, young sir. Your reputation shall not
therefore[9] be misprized.[10] We will make it our suit to the
Duke that the wrestling might not go forward.

Orlando. I beseech you, punish me not with your hard
thoughts, wherein I confess me much guilty to deny
so fair and excellent ladies anything. But let your fair
eyes and gentle wishes go with me to my trial;
wherein if I be foiled, there is but one shamed that was
never gracious;[11] if killed, but one dead that is willing to
be so. I shall do my friends no wrong, for I have none
to lament me; the world no injury, for in it I have

---

[4]**odds** superiority

[5]**the man** i.e., Charles

[6]**fain** willingly

[7]**If ... judgment** i.e., if you saw yourself objectively, using your observation and your judgment

[8]**equal** i.e., where the odds are

[9]**therefore** on that account.

[10]**misprized** despised

[11]**gracious** looked upon with favor

nothing. Only in the world I[12] fill up a place, which may
be better supplied when I have made it empty.

Rosalind. The little strength that I have, I would it were
with you.

Celia. And mine, to eke out hers.

Rosalind. Fare you well. Pray heaven I be deceived
in you![13]

Celia. Your heart's desires be with you!

Charles. Come, where is this young gallant that is so
desirous to lie with his mother earth?

Orlando. Ready, sir, but his will hath in it a more
modest working.[14]

Duke Frederick. You shall try but one fall.

Charles. No, I warrant Your Grace, you shall not en-
treat him to a second, that have so mightily persuaded
him from a first.

Orlando. You mean to mock me after; you should not
have mocked me before. But come your ways.[15]

Rosalind. Now Hercules be thy speed,[16] young man!

Celia. I would I were invisible, to catch the strong fellow by the leg.   *[Orlando and Charles wrestle.]*

Rosalind. O excellent young man!

Celia. If I had a thunderbolt in mine eye, I can tell who
should down.[17]   *Shout. [Charles is thrown.]*

Duke Frederick. No more, no more.

Orlando. Yes, I beseech Your Grace. I am not yet well
breathed.[18]

Duke Frederick. How dost thou, Charles?

Le Beau.   He cannot speak, my lord.

Duke Frederick.

Bear him away. What is thy name, young man?

[Exeunt some with Charles.]

---

[12]**Only, . . . I** in the world I merely

[13]**deceived in you** i.e., mistaken in fearing you will lose

[14]**modest working** decorous endeavor (than to lie with one's mother earth—an endeavor, Orlando
implies, with sexual overtones)

[15]**come your ways** come on

[16]**Hercules be thy speed** may Hercules help you

[17]**down** fall

[18]**well breathed** warmed up

Orlando. Orlando, my liege, the youngest son of Sir
    Rowland de Boys.
Duke Frederick.
    I would thou hadst been son to some man else.
    The world esteemed thy father honorable,
    But I did find him still[19] mine enemy.
    Thou shouldst have better pleased me with this deed
    Hadst thou descended from another house.
    But fare thee well; thou art a gallant youth.
    I would thou hadst told me of another father.

*Exit Duke [with train, and others. Rosalind and Celia remain; Orlando stands
apart from them].*

Celia. [*To Rosalind*]
    Were I my father, coz, would I do this?
Orlando. [*To no one in particular*]
    I am more proud to be Sir Rowland's son,
    His youngest son, and would not change that calling[20]
    To be adopted heir to Frederick.
Rosalind. [To *Celia*]
    My father loved Sir Rowland as his soul,
    And all the world was of my father's mind.
    Had I before known this young man his son,
    I should have given him tears unto[21] entreaties
    Ere he should thus have ventured.
Celia. [*To Rosalind*] Gentle cousin,
    Let us go thank him and encourage him.
    My father's rough and envious[22] disposition
    Sticks[23] me at heart.—Sir, you have well deserved.
    If you do keep your promises in love
    But justly[24] as you have exceeded all promise,
    Your mistress shall be happy.
Rosalind.   Gentleman,
              [Giving him a chain from her neck]

---

[19]**still** continually
[20]**calling** position, status
[21]**unto** in addition to
[22]**envious** malicious
[23]**Sticks** stabs
[24]**But justly** exactly

Wear this for me, one out of suits with fortune,[25]

That could[26] give more, but that her hand lacks means.

[To Celia] Shall we go, coz?

Celia.   Ay. Fare you well, fair gentleman.

[Rosalind and Celia start to leave.]

Orlando. [Aside]

He calls us back. My pride fell with my fortunes;
Can I not say, "I thank you"? My better parts

Are all thrown down, and that which here stands up

Is but a quintain,[27] a mere lifeless block.

Rosalind.

He calls us back. My pride fell with my fortunes;

I'll ask him what he would.[28]—Did you call, sir?

Sir, you have wrestled well and overthrown

More than your enemies.

Celia. Will you go, coz?

Rosalind. Have with you.[29]—Fare you well.

Exit [with Celia].

Orlando.

What passion hangs these weights upon my tongue?

I cannot speak to her, yet she urged conference.

O poor Orlando, thou art overthrown!

Or Charles or something weaker masters thee.

Enter Le Beau.

Le Beau.

Good sir, I do in friendship counsel you

To leave this place. Albeit you have deserved

High commendation, true applause, and love,

Yet such is now the Duke's condition[30]

That he misconsters[31] all that you have done.

The Duke is humorous.[32] What he is indeed

More suits you to conceive than I to speak of.

---

[25] **out . . . fortune** (1) whose petitions to Fortune are rejected (2) not wearing the livery of Fortune, not in her service

[26] **could** would be disposed to

[27] **quintain** wooden figure used as a target in tilting

[28] **would** wants

[29] **Have with you** I'll go with you

[30] **condition** state of mind, disposition

[31] **misconsters** misconstrues

[32] **humorous** temperamental, capricious

Orlando.

>   I thank you, sir. And, pray you, tell me this:
>   Which of the two was daughter of the Duke
>   That here was at the wrestling?

Le Beau.

>   Neither his daughter, if we judge by manners,
>   But yet indeed the taller is his daughter.
>   The other is daughter to the banished Duke,
>   And here detained by her usurping uncle
>   To keep his daughter company, whose loves
>   Are dearer than the natural bond of sisters.
>   But I can tell you that of late this Duke
>   Hath ta'en displeasure 'gainst his gentle niece,
>   Grounded upon no other argument[33]
>   But that the people praise her for her virtues
>   And pity her for her good father's sake;
>   And, on my life, his malice 'gainst the lady
>   Will suddenly[34] break forth. Sir, fare you well.
>   Hereafter, in a better world[35] than this,
>   I shall desire more love and knowledge of you.

Orlando.

>   I rest much bounden[36] to you. Fare you well.
>
>   *[Exit Le Beau.]*
>   Thus must I from the smoke into the smother,[37]
>   From tyrant Duke unto a tyrant brother.
>   But heavenly Rosalind!   *Exit.*

Act I. Scene iii. Lines 1–35. Location: an apartment in Duke Frederick's court.
Stage Directions: Enter Celia and Rosalind.

Celia. Why, cousin, why, Rosalind! Cupid have mercy!
>   Not a word?

Rosalind. Not one to throw at a dog.

Celia. No, thy words are too precious to be cast away
>   upon curs; throw some of them at me. Come, lame me
>   with reasons.[38]

---

[33]**argument** reason

[34]**suddenly** very soon

[35]**world** i.e., state of affairs

[36]**bounden** indebted

[37]**smoke into the smother** i.e., out of the frying pan into the fire. (*Smother* means "a dense suffocating smoke")

[38]**lame ... reasons** i.e., throw some explanations (for your silence) at me

Rosalind. Then there were two cousins laid up, when
the one should be lamed with reasons and the other
mad without any.

Celia. But is all this for your father?

Rosalind. No, some of it is for my child's father.[39] O,
how full of briers is this working-day world!

Celia. They are but burrs, cousin, thrown upon thee in
holiday foolery. If we walk not in the trodden paths,
our very petticoats will catch them.

Rosalind. I could shake them off my coat; these burrs
are in my heart.

Celia. Hem[40] them away.

Rosalind. I would try, if I could cry "hem"[41] and have
him.

Celia. Come, come, wrestle with thy affections.

Rosalind. O, they take the part of a better wrestler than
myself!

Celia. O, a good wish upon you! You will try in time,
in despite of a fall.[42] But, turning these jests out of service,[43] let us talk in good earnest. Is it possible, on such
a sudden, you should fall into so strong a liking with
old Sir Rowland's youngest son?

Rosalind. The Duke my father loved his father dearly.

Celia. Doth it therefore ensue that you should love his
son dearly? By this kind of chase,[44] I should hate him,
for my father hated his father dearly; yet I hate not
Orlando.

Rosalind. No, faith, hate him not, for my sake.

Celia. Why should I not? Doth he not deserve well?[45]

Rosalind. Let me love him for that, and do you love him because I do. . . .

* * *

*Duke Frederick, learning that Orlando is the son of Sir Rowland, a friend
of his exiled brother, revives his anger against the latter and proceeds to banish*

[39]**my child's father** one who might sire my children, i.e., Orlando

[40]**Hem** cough (since you say they are in the chest)

[41]**cry "hem"** clear away with a "hem" or a cough (with a play on *him*)

[42]**You . . . fall** i.e., you'll undertake to wrestle with Orlando sooner or later, despite the danger of
your being thrown down. (Contains sexual suggestion.)

[43]**turning . . . service** i.e., dismissing this banter

[44]**chase** argument that is pursued

[45]**deserve well** i.e., well deserve to be hated. (But Rosalind interprets in the sense of "deserve favor.")

Rosalind from his court. Celia, as well as Touchstone, the Duke's fool, accompanies Rosalind into exile. Meanwhile, Orlando, after hearing that Oliver is determined to kill him, also goes into exile. Disguising herself as a young countryman, Rosalind takes the name Ganymede, while Celia passes as Ganymede's sister, Aliena. All the exiles go to live in the Forest of Arden, a place meant to remind of the Garden of Eden. Lovelorn and fancy-free, Orlando spends his time roaming the forest, hanging love verses on the trees. The verses and, shortly thereafter, the young man himself are discovered by Rosalind, who, though beside herself with joy and fully as lovesick as her lover, nevertheless maintains her disguise, determined, she says, "to play the knave with him." Orlando's dismissive response to the first question she puts to him—"[W]hat is 't o'clock?"—precipitates a discussion about the relation between time and love; later, Rosalind suggests that Orlando woo her, to begin with by making a date with her, allegedly so that she can cure him of his love-madness. Does she really want him cured? Why the disguise? Is Rosalind merely being knavish? Why does she seem to attach such importance to time? How can keeping time help cure—?alleviate ?solidify—the passion of love?

> *Act III. Scene ii. Lines 1–10. Location: the forest of Arden*
> *Stage Directions: Enter Orlando with a paper, which he hangs on a tree.*

Orlando.

> Hang there, my verse, in witness of my love;
>> And thou, thrice-crownèd queen[46] of night, survey
> With thy chaste eye, from thy pale sphere above,
>> Thy huntress'[47] name that my full life doth sway.[48]
> O Rosalind! These trees shall be my books,
>> And in their barks my thoughts I'll character,[49]
> That every eye which in this forest looks
>> Shall see thy virtue witnessed everywhere.
> Run, run, Orlando, carve on every tree
> The fair, the chaste, and unexpressive[50] she.   *Exit.*

> *Act III. Scene ii. Lines 86–247, 290–423. Same location.*
> *Stage Directions: Enter Rosalind, who, unaware of the presence of Touchstone and*

---

[46]**thrice-crownèd queen** i.e., Diana in the three aspects of her divinity: as Luna or Cynthia, goddess of the moon; as Diana, goddess on earth; and as Hecate or Proserpina, goddess in the lower world

[47]**Thy huntress'** i.e., Rosalind's, who is here thought of as a chaste huntress accompanying Diana, patroness of the hunt

[48]**sway** control

[49]**character** inscribe

[50]**unexpressive** inexpressible

the shepherd Corin, comes up, sees Orlando's paper on the tree, removes it and begins to read it.

Rosalind.

> "From the east to western Ind
> No jewel is like Rosalind.
> Her worth, being mounted on the wind,
> Through all the world bears Rosalind.
> All the pictures fairest lined
> Are but black to Rosalind.
> Let no face be kept in mind
> But the fair of Rosalind."

Touchstone. I'll rhyme you so eight years together, dinners and suppers and sleeping hours excepted. It is the right butter-women's rank to market.[51]

Rosalind. Out, Fool!

Touchstone. For a taste:

> If a hart do lack a hind,
> Let him seek out Rosalind.
> If the cat will after kind,
> So be sure will Rosalind.
> Wintered[52] garments must be lined,
> So must slender Rosalind.
> They that reap must sheaf and bind;
> Then to cart[53] with Rosalind.
> Sweetest nut hath sourest rind;
> Such a nut is Rosalind.
> He that sweetest rose will find
> Must find love's prick[54] and Rosalind.

This is the very false gallop[55] of verses. Why do you infect yourself with them?

Rosalind. Peace, you dull fool! I found them on a tree.

Touchstone. Truly, the tree yields bad fruit.

Rosalind. I'll graft it with you,[56] and then I shall graft it

---

[51]**It is ... market** i.e., the rhymes, all alike, follow each other precisely like a line of butter-women or dairywomen jogging along to market

[52]**Wintered** prepared for winter

[53]**to cart** (1) onto the harvest can (2) onto the can used to carry delinquent women through the streets, exposing them to public ridicule

[54]**prick** thorn. (With bawdy suggestion, as elsewhere in Touchstone's verses: *will after kind* etc.)

[55]**false gallop** canter

[56]**you** (with a pun on yew)

with a medlar.[57] Then it will be the earliest fruit i' the
country; for you'll be rotten ere you be half ripe, and
that's the right virtue[58] of the medlar.

Touchstone. You have said; but whether wisely or no,
let the forest judge.

Enter Celia, with a writing.

Rosalind. Peace, here comes my sister, reading. Stand
aside.

Celia. [Reads]

"Why should this a desert be?
For it is unpeopled? No!
Tongues I'll hang on every tree,
That shall civil sayings[59] show:
Some, how brief the life of man
Runs his erring[60] pilgrimage,
That the stretching of a span[61]
Buckles in[62] his sum of age;
Some, of violated vows
Twixt the souls of friend and friend;
But upon the fairest boughs,
Or at every sentence end,
Will I 'Rosalinda' write,
Teaching all that read to know
The quintessence[63] of every sprite[64]
Heaven would in little[65] show.
Therefore heaven Nature charged
That one body should be filled
With all graces wide-enlarged.[66]

---

[57]**medlar** a fruit like a small brown-skinned apple that is eaten when it starts to decay (with a pun on *meddler*)

[58]**right virtue** true quality

[59]**civil sayings** maxims of civilized life

[60]**his erring** its wandering

[61]**That . . . span** so that the distance across an open-spread hand

[62]**Buckles in** encompasses

[63]**quintessence** highest perfection. (Literally, the fifth essence or element of the medieval alchemists, purer even than fire.)

[64]**sprite** spirit

[65]**in little** in small space, i.e., in one person, Rosalind. (Alludes probably to the idea of man as the microcosm; the heavenly bodies would be composed of quintessence, which is here thought of as the supreme quality of a person.)

[66]**wide-enlarged** widely distributed (i.e., that had been spread through the world but now are concentrated in Rosalind)

Nature presently distilled
Helen's cheek, but not her heart,[67]
Cleopatra's majesty,
Atalanta's better part,[68]
Sad Lucretia's[69] modesty.
Thus Rosalind of many parts
By heavenly synod[70] was devised,
Of many faces, eyes, and hearts,
To have the touches[71] dearest prized.
Heaven would that she these gifts should have,
And I to live and die her slave."

Rosalind. O most gentle Jupiter,[72] what tedious homily
of love have you wearied your parishioners withal,
and never cried, "Have patience, good people!"

Celia. How now? Back,[73] friends. Shepherd, go off a little. Go with him, sirrah.[74]

Touchstone. Come, shepherd, let us make an honorable retreat, though not with bag and baggage,[75] yet
with scrip and scrippage.[76]   *Exit [with Corin].*

Celia. Didst thou hear these verses?

Rosalind. O, yes, I heard them all, and more too, for
some of them had in them more feet than the verses
would bear.

Celia. That's no matter. The feet might bear the verses.

Rosalind. Ay, but the feet were lame and could not
bear themselves without[77] the verse and therefore stood
lamely in the verse.

Celia. But didst thou hear without wondering how thy
name should be hanged and carved upon these trees?

---

[67]**Helen's . . . heart** i.e., the beauty of Helen of Troy but not her false heart
[68]**Atalanta's better part** i.e., her fleetness of foot, not her scornfulness and greed. (She refused to marry any man who was unable to defeat her in a foot race and, when challenged by Hippomenes, lost to him because Hippomenes dropped in her way three apples of the Hesperides.)
[69]**Lucretia** honorable Roman lady raped by Tarquin (whose story Shakespeare tells in The Rape of Lucrece)
[70]**synod** assembly
[71]**touches** traits
[72]**Jupiter** (Often emended to *pulpiter*.)
[73]**Back** i.e., move back, away. (Addressed to Corin and Touchstone.)
[74]**sirrah** (Form of address to inferiors; here, Touchstone.)
[75]**bag and baggage** i.e., equipment appropriate to a retreating army
[76]**scrip and scrippage** shepherd's pouch and its contents
[77]**without** (1) without the help of (2) outside

Rosalind. I was seven of the nine days out of the wonder[78] before you came; for look here what I found on a
palm tree. I was never so berhymed since Pythagoras'[79]
time, that[80] I was an Irish rat,[81] which I can hardly remember.

Celia. Trow you[82] who hath done this?

Rosalind. Is it a man?

Celia. And a chain[83] that you once wore about his neck.
Change you color?

Rosalind. I prithee, who?

Celia. O Lord, Lord, it is a hard matter for friends to
meet; but mountains may be removed with earthquakes and so encounter.[84]

Rosalind. Nay, but who is it?

Celia. Is it possible?

Rosalind. Nay, I prithee now with most petitionary ve-
hemence, tell me who it is.

Celia. O wonderful, wonderful, and most wonderful
wonderful! And yet again wonderful, and after that,
out of all whooping![85]

Rosalind. Good my complexion![86] Dost thou think,
though I am caparisoned[87] like a man, I have a doublet
and hose in my disposition? One inch of delay more
is a South Sea of discovery.[88] I prithee, tell me who is it
quickly, and speak apace. I would thou couldst stam-
mer, that thou mightst pour this concealed man out of
thy mouth, as wine comes out of a narrow-mouthed
bottle, either too much at once or none at all. I prithee,
take the cork out of thy mouth that I may drink thy tidings.

---

[78] **seven . . . wonder** (A reference to the common phrase "a nine days' wonder.")

[79] **Pythagoras** Greek philosopher credited with the doctrine of the transmigration of souls

[80] **that** when

[81] **Irish rat** (Refers to a current belief that Irish enchanters could rhyme rats and other animals to death.)

[82] **Trow you** have you any idea

[83] **And a chain** i.e., and with a chain

[84] **friends . . . encounter** (A playful inversion of the proverb, "Friends may meet, but mountains never greet." Celia appears to be teasing Rosalind's eagerness to meet Orlando.)

[85] **out . . . whooping** beyond all whooping, i.e., power to utter

[86] **Good my complexion** O my (feminine) temperament, my woman's curiosity

[87] **caparisoned** bedecked (Usually said of a horse.)

[88] **a South Sea of discovery** i.e., as tedious as the long delays on exploratory voyages to the South Seas

Celia. So you may put a man in your belly.[89]

Rosalind. Is he of God's making?[90] What manner of
    man? Is his head worth a hat, or his chin worth a beard?

Celia. Nay, he hath but a little beard.

Rosalind. Why, God will send more, if the man will be
    thankful. Let me stay[91] the growth of his beard, if thou
    delay me not the knowledge of his chin.

Celia. It is young Orlando, that tripped up the wrestler's
    heels and your heart both in an instant.

Rosalind. Nay, but the devil take mocking. Speak sad
    brow and true maid.[92]

Celia. I faith, coz, tis he.

Rosalind. Orlando?

Celia. Orlando.

Rosalind. Alas the day, what shall I do with my dou-
    blet and hose? What did he when thou sawst him?
    What said he? How looked he? Wherein went he?[93]
    What makes he here? Did he ask for me? Where re-
    mains he? How parted he with thee? And when shalt
    thou see him again? Answer me in one word.

Celia. You must borrow me Gargantua's mouth[94] first;
    'tis a word too great for any mouth of this age's size.
    To say ay and no to these particulars is more than to
    answer in a catechism.[95]

Rosalind. But doth he know that I am in this forest and
    in man's apparel? Looks he as freshly as he did the
    day he wrestled?

Celia. It is as easy to count atomies[96] as to resolve the
    propositions[97] of a lover. But take a taste of my finding
    him, and relish it with good observance. I found him

---

[89]**belly** (1) stomach (2) womb

[90]**of God's making** i.e., a real man, not of his tailor's making

[91]**stay** wait for

[92]**sad . . . maid** seriously and truthfully

[93]**Wherein went he** in what clothes was he dressed

[94]**Gargantua's mouth** (Gargantua is the giant of popular literature who, in Rabelais's novel, swallowed five pilgrims in a salad.)

[95]**To . . . catechism** to give even yes and no answers to these questions would take longer than to go through the catechism (i.e., the formal questioning used in the Church to teach the principles of faith)

[96]**atomies** motes, specks of dirt

[97]**propositions** questions

     under a tree, like a dropped acorn.

Rosalind. It may well be called Jove's tree,[98] when it
     drops forth such fruit.

Celia. Give me audience, good madam.

Rosalind. Proceed.

Celia. There lay he, stretched along, like a wounded
     knight.

Rosalind. Though it be pity to see such a sight, it well
     becomes[99] the ground.

Celia. Cry "holla"[100] to thy tongue, I prithee; it curvets[101]
     unseasonably. He was furnished[102] like a hunter.

Rosalind. O, ominous! He comes to kill my heart.[103]

Celia. I would sing my song without a burden.[104] Thou
     bring'st[105] me out of tune.

Rosalind. Do you not know I am a woman? When I
     think, I must speak. Sweet, say on. . . .

*Stage Directions: Orlando enters speaking to Jacques, a lord attending Duke
Senior. After Jacques leaves, Rosalind continues.*

Rosalind. *[Aside to Celia]* I will speak to him like a
     saucy lackey and under that habit[106] play the knave with
     him.—Do you hear, forester?

Orlando. Very well. What would you?

Rosalind. I pray you, what is 't o'clock?

Orlando. You should ask me what time o' day. There's
     no clock in the forest.

Rosalind. Then there is no true lover in the forest, else
     sighing every minute and groaning every hour would
     detect[107] the lazy foot of Time as well as a clock.

Orlando. And why not the swift foot of Time? Had not
     that been as proper?

Rosalind. By no means, sir. Time travels in divers

[98]**Jove's tree** the oak
[99]**becomes** adorns
[100]**holla** stop
[101]**curvets** prances
[102]**furnished** equipped, dressed
[103]**heart** (with pun on *hart*)
[104]**burden** undersong, bass part
[105]**Thou bring'st** you put
[106]**habit** guise
[107]**detect** reveal

paces with divers persons. I'll tell you who Time ambles withal, who Time trots withal, and who Time gallops
withal, and who he stands still withal.

Orlando. I prithee, who doth he trot withal?

Rosalind. Marry, he trots hard[108] with a young maid between the contract of her marriage and the day it is
solemnized. If the interim be but a se'nnight,[109] Time's
pace is so hard that it seems the length of seven year.

Orlando. Who ambles Time withal?

Rosalind. With a priest that lacks Latin and a rich man
that hath not the gout, for the one sleeps easily because he cannot study and the other lives merrily because he feels no pain, the one lacking the burden of
lean and wasteful[110] learning, the other knowing no burden of heavy tedious penury. These Time ambles
withal.

Orlando. Who doth he gallop withal?

Rosalind. With a thief to the gallows, for though he go
as softly[111] as foot can fall, he thinks himself too soon
there.

Orlando. Who stays it still withal?

Rosalind. With lawyers in the vacation; for they sleep
between term and term,[112] and then they perceive not
how Time moves.

Orlando. Where dwell you, pretty youth?

Rosalind. With this shepherdess, my sister; here in the
skirts of the forest, like fringe upon a petticoat.

Orlando. Are you native of this place?

Rosalind. As the coney[113] that you see dwell where she is
kindled.[114]

Orlando. Your accent is something finer than you
could purchase[115] in so removed a dwelling.

Rosalind. I have been told so of many. But indeed an

---

[108]**hard** slowly, with uneven pace
[109]**se'nnight** week
[110]**wasteful** making one waste away
[111]**go as softly** walk as slowly
[112]**term** court session
[113]**coney** rabbit
[114]**kindled** littered, born
[115]**purchase** acquire

old religious[116] uncle of mine taught me to speak, who
was in his youth an inland[117] man, one that knew courtship[118] too well, for there he fell in love. I have heard him
read many lectures against it, and I thank God I am
not a woman, to be touched[119] with so many giddy
offences as he hath generally taxed their whole sex
withal.

Orlando. Can you remember any of the principal evils
that he laid to the charge of women?

Rosalind. There were none principal; they were all like
one another as halfpence are, every one fault seeming
monstrous till his fellow fault came to match it.

Orlando. I prithee, recount some of them.

Rosalind. No, I will not cast away my physic but on
those that are sick. There is a man haunts the forest
that abuses our young plants with carving "Rosalind"
on their barks, hangs odes upon hawthorns, and elegies
on brambles, all, forsooth, deifying the name of
Rosalind. If I could meet that fancy-monger,[120] I would
give him some good counsel, for he seems to have the
quotidian[121] of love upon him.

Orlando. I am he that is so love-shaked. I pray you, tell
me your remedy.

Rosalind. There is none of my uncle's marks upon you.
He taught me how to know a man in love, in which
cage of rushes[122] I am sure you are not prisoner.

Orlando. What were his marks?

Rosalind. A lean cheek, which you have not; a blue eye[123]
and sunken, which you have not; an unquestionable[124]
spirit, which you have not; a beard neglected, which
you have not—but I pardon you for that, for simply
your having in beard is a younger brother's revenue.[125]

---

[116] **religious** i.e., member of a religious order

[117] **inland** from a center of civilization

[118] **courtship** (1) wooing (2) knowledge of courtly manners

[119] **touched** tainted

[120] **fancy-monger** dealer or advertiser of love

[121] **quotidian** fever recurring daily

[122] **cage of rushes** i.e., flimsy prison

[123] **blue eye** i.e., having dark circles

[124] **unquestionable** unwilling to converse

[125] **simply . . . revenue** what beard you have is like a younger brother's inheritance (i.e., small)

Then your hose should be ungartered, your bonnet unbanded,[126] your sleeve unbuttoned, your shoe untied,
and everything about you demonstrating a careless
desolation. But you are no such man; you are rather
point-device[127] in your accoutrements, as loving yourself,
than seeming the lover of any other.

Orlando. Fair youth, I would I could make thee believe
I love.

Rosalind. Me believe it? You may as soon make her
that you love believe it, which I warrant she is apter
to do than to confess she does. That is one of the
points in the which women still[128] give the lie to their
consciences. But in good sooth,[129] are you he that hangs
the verses on the trees wherein Rosalind is so
admired?

Orlando. I swear to thee, youth, by the white hand of
Rosalind, I am that he, that unfortunate he.

Rosalind. But are you so much in love as your rhymes
speak?

Orlando. Neither rhyme nor reason can express how
much.

Rosalind. Love is merely[130] a madness and, I tell you,
deserves as well a dark house and a whip[131] as madmen
do; and the reason why they are not so punished and
cured is that the lunacy is so ordinary that the whippers
are in love too. Yet I profess curing it by counsel.

Orlando. Did you ever cure any so?

Rosalind. Yes, one, and in this manner. He was to
imagine me his love, his mistress; and I set him every
day to woo me. At which time would I, being but a
moonish[132] youth, grieve, be effeminate, changeable,
longing and liking, proud, fantastical, apish, shallow,
inconstant, full of tears, full of smiles, for every passion
something and for no passion truly anything, as boys

---

[126]**bonnet unbanded** hat lacking a band around the crown
[127]**point-device** faultless, correct
[128]**still** continually
[129]**good sooth** honest truth
[130]**merely** utterly
[131]**dark . . . whip** (The common treatment of lunatics.)
[132]**moonish** changeable

and women are for the most part cattle of this color;
would now like him, now loathe him; then entertain
him, then forswear him; now weep for him, then spit
at him; that I drave[133] my suitor from his mad humor of
love to a living humor of madness,[134] which was to forswear
the full stream of the world and to live in a nook
merely monastic. And thus I cured him; and this way
will I take upon me to wash your liver[135] as clean as a
sound sheep's heart, that there shall not be one spot of
love in 't.

Orlando. I would not be cured, youth.

Rosalind. I would cure you, if you would but call me
Rosalind and come every day to my cote[136] and woo me.

Orlando. Now by the faith of my love, I will. Tell me
where it is.

Rosalind. Go with me to it, and I'll show it you; and
by the way you shall tell me where in the forest you
live. Will you go?

Orlando. With all my heart, good youth.

Rosalind. Nay, you must call me Rosalind.—Come, sister,
will you go?   *Exeunt.*

* * *

In the next selection Rosalind, still in male disguise, greets Orlando, who has
arrived, alas, an hour late for their first official date. Rosalind rebukes him with
rather heavy-handed allusions to adultery, then insists they enact a mock wedding, in which vows are exchanged. Like much of the play, the scene is very funny,
and some readers find it silly. Is it? Does Rosalind, physician to the lovesick soul,
know what she is doing?

Act IV. Scene i. Lines 37–210. Location: the forest.
Stage Directions: Enter Orlando [who joins Rosalind and Celia, already present]

Rosalind.
Why, how now, Orlando, where have you been all
this while? You a lover? An[137] you serve me such another

---

[133] **drave** drove
[134] **mad . . . madness** mad fancy of love to a real madness
[135] **liver** (Supposed seat of the emotions, especially love.)
[136] **cote** cottage
[137] **An** if

trick, never come in my sight more.

Orlando. My fair Rosalind, I come within an hour of
    my promise.

Rosalind. Break an hour's promise in love? He that will
    divide a minute into a thousand parts and break but
    a part of the thousandth part of a minute in the affairs
    of love, it may be said of him that Cupid hath clapped
    him o' the shoulder,[138] but I'll warrant him heart-whole.

Orlando. Pardon me, dear Rosalind.

Rosalind. Nay, an you be so tardy, come no more in
    my sight. I had as lief[139] be wooed of a snail.

Orlando. Of a snail?

Rosalind. Ay, of a snail; for though he comes slowly,
    he carries his house on his head—a better jointure,[140] I
    think, than you make a woman. Besides, he brings his
    destiny with him.

Orlando. What's that?

Rosalind. Why, horns,[141] which such as you are fain[142] to
    be beholding to your wives for. But he comes armed in
    his fortune[143] and prevents the slander of his wife.

Orlando. Virtue is no horn maker, and my Rosalind is
    virtuous.

Rosalind. And I am your Rosalind.

Celia. It pleases him to call you so; but he hath a Rosalind
    of a better leer[144] than you.

Rosalind. Come, woo me, woo me, for now I am in a
    holiday humor and like enough to consent. What
    would you say to me now, an I were your very, very
    Rosalind?

Orlando. I would kiss before I spoke.

Rosalind. Nay, you were better speak first, and when
    you were graveled[145] for lack of matter, you might take
    occasion to kiss. Very good orators, when they are out,[146]

---

[138]**clapped . . . shoulder** i.e., accosted or arrested him
[139]**lief** willingly
[140]**jointure** marriage settlement
[141]**horns** (1) snails' horns (2) cuckold's horns, signs of an unfaithful wife
[142]**fain** willing
[143]**armed . . . fortune** i.e., with the horns of a cuckold, which it was his fate to earn
[144]**of . . . leer** better-looking
[145]**graveled** stuck, at a standstill (Literally, run aground on a shoal.)
[146]**out** i.e., at a loss through forgetfulness or confusion

they will spit; and for lovers lacking—God warrant[147] us!—
matter, the cleanliest shift[148] is to kiss.

Orlando. How if the kiss be denied?

Rosalind. Then she puts you to entreaty, and there
begins new matter.

Orlando. Who could be out, being before his beloved
mistress?

Rosalind. Marry, that should you, if I were your
mistress, or I should think my honesty[149] ranker[150] than
my wit.

Orlando. What, of my suit?[151]

Rosalind. Not out of your apparel, and yet out of your
suit. Am not I your Rosalind?

Orlando. I take some joy to say you are, because I
would be talking of her.

Rosalind. Well, in her person I say I will not have you.

Orlando. Then in mine own person I die.

Rosalind. No, faith, die by attorney.[152] The poor world is
almost six thousand years old,[153] and in all this time
there was not any man died in his own person, videlicet,[154]
in a love cause. Troilus[155] had his brains dashed out
with a Grecian club,[156] yet he did what he could to die
before, and he is one of the patterns of love. Leander,[157]
he would have lived many a fair year though Hero
had turned nun, if it had not been for a hot mid-

---

[147]**warrant** defend

[148]**cleanliest shift** cleverest device

[149]**honesty** chastity

[150]**ranker** even more corrupt. (Rosalind playfully interprets being out *before one's mistress,* as not being inside her, not having sex with her; she says her lover will have to stay out, and thus will not obtain his suit.)

[151]**of my suit** (Orlando means "out of my suit," at a loss for words in my wooing; but Rosalind puns on the meaning "suit of clothes"; to be out of apparel would be to be undressed.)

[152]**attorney** proxy

[153]**six ... old** (A common figure in biblical calculation.)

[154]**videlicet** namely

[155]**Troilus** hero of the story of Troilus and Cressida in which he remains faithful to her but she is faithless in love

[156]**had ... club** (Troilus was slain by Achilles; Rosalind's account of his death is calculatedly unromantic.)

[157]**Leander** hero of the story of Hero and Leander, who lost his life swimming the Hellespont to visit his sweetheart. (Rosalind's account of the cramp is more undercutting of romantic idealism.)

summer night; for, good youth, he went but forth to
wash him in the Hellespont and being taken with the
cramp was drowned; and the foolish chroniclers of that
age found it was[158]—Hero of Sestos. But these are all
lies. Men have died from time to time, and worms
have eaten them, but not for love.

Orlando. I would not have my right[159] Rosalind of this
mind, for I protest her frown might kill me.

Rosalind. By this hand, it will not kill a fly. But come,
now I will be your Rosalind in a more coming-on[160]
disposition, and ask me what you will, I will grant it.

Orlando. Then love me, Rosalind.

Rosalind. Yes, faith, will I, Fridays and Saturdays
and all.

Orlando. And wilt thou have me?

Rosalind. Ay, and twenty such.

Orlando. What sayest thou?

Rosalind. Are you not good?

Orlando. I hope so.

Rosalind. Why then, can one desire too much of a good
thing? Come, sister, you shall be the priest and marry
us. Give me your hand, Orlando. What do you say,
sister?

Orlando. Pray thee, marry us.

Celia. I cannot say the words.

Rosalind. You must begin, "Will you, Orlando—"

Celia. Go to. Will you, Orlando, have to wife this
Rosalind?

Orlando. I will.

Rosalind. Ay, but when?

Orlando. Why now, as fast as she can marry us.

Rosalind. Then you must say, "I take thee, Rosalind,
for wife."

Orlando. I take thee, Rosalind, for wife.

Rosalind. I might ask you for your commission;[161] but I

---

[158]**found it was** arrived at the verdict that the cause (of his death) was

[159]**right** real

[160]**coming-on** compliant

[161]**ask . . . commission** ask you what authority you have for taking her (since no one is here to give the bride away)

do take thee, Orlando, for my husband. There's a girl
goes before[162] the priest, and certainly a woman's
thought runs before her actions.

Orlando. So do all thoughts, they are winged.

Rosalind. Now tell me how long you would have her
after you have possessed her.

Orlando. For ever and a day.

Rosalind. Say "a day," without the "ever." No, no, Orlando,
men are April when they woo, December when
they wed. Maids are May when they are maids, but
the sky changes when they are wives. I will be more
jealous of thee than a Barbary cock-pigeon[163] over his
hen, more clamorous than a parrot against[164] rain, more
newfangled[165] than an ape, more giddy in my desires
than a monkey. I will weep for nothing,[166] like Diana in
the fountain,[167] and I will do that when you are disposed
to be merry; I will laugh like a hyena, and that when
thou art inclined to sleep.

Orlando. But will my Rosalind do so?

Rosalind. By my life, she will do as I do.

Orlando. O, but she is wise.

Rosalind. Or else she could not have the wit to do this;
the wiser, the waywarder. Make[168] the doors upon a
woman's wit, and it will out at the casement; shut
that, and 'twill out at the keyhole; stop that, 'twill fly
with the smoke out at the chimney.

Orlando. A man that had a wife with such a wit, he
might say, "Wit, whither wilt?"[169]

Rosalind. Nay, you might keep that check[170] for it till you
met your wife's wit going to your neighbor's bed.

---

[162]**goes before** (who) anticipates

[163]**Barbary cock-pigeon** an ornamental pigeon originally from the Barbary (north) coast of Africa. (Following Pliny, the cock-pigeon's jealousy was often contrasted with the mildness of the hen.)

[164]**against** before, in expectation of

[165]**newfangled** infatuated with novelty

[166]**for nothing** for no apparent reason

[167]**Diana in the fountain** (Diana frequently appeared as the centerpiece of fountains. Stow's *Survey of London* describes the setting up of a fountain with a Diana in green marble in the year 1596.)

[168]**Make** make fast, shut

[169]**Wit, whither wilt** wit, where are you going. (A common Elizabethan expression implying that one is talking fantastically, with a wildly wandering wit.)

[170]**check** retort

Orlando. And what wit could wit have to excuse that?

Rosalind. Marry, to say she came to seek you there.
You shall never take her without her answer, unless
you take her without her tongue. O, that woman that
cannot make her fault her husband's occasion,[171] let her
never nurse her child herself, for she will breed it like
a fool!

Orlando. For these two hours, Rosalind, I will leave
thee.

Rosalind. Alas, dear love, I cannot lack thee two hours!

Orlando. I must attend the Duke at dinner. By two
o'clock I will be with thee again.

Rosalind. Ay, go your ways, go your ways; I knew
what you would prove. My friends told me as much,
and I thought no less. That flattering tongue of yours
won me. 'Tis but one cast away,[172] and so, come, death!
Two o'clock is your hour?

Orlando. Ay, sweet Rosalind.

Rosalind. By my troth, and in good earnest, and so
God mend me, and by all pretty oaths that are not
dangerous, if you break one jot of your promise or
come one minute behind your hour, I will think you
the most pathetical[173] break-promise, and the most
hollow lover, and the most unworthy of her you call
Rosalind, that may be chosen out of the gross band[174] of the
unfaithful. Therefore beware my censure and keep
your promise.

Orlando. With no less religion[175] than if thou wert indeed
my Rosalind. So adieu.

Rosalind. Well, Time is the old justice that examines all
such offenders, and let Time try.[176] Adieu.

Exit [Orlando].

Celia. You have simply misused[177] our sex in your love

---

[171]**make . . . occasion** i.e., turn a defense of her own conduct into an accusation against her husband

[172]**but one cast away** only one woman jilted

[173]**pathetical** pitiable, miserable

[174]**gross band** whole troop

[175]**religion** strict fidelity

[176]**try** determine

[177]**simply misused** absolutely slandered

prate. We must have your doublet and hose plucked
over your head and show the world what the bird
hath done to her own nest.[178]

Rosalind. O coz, coz, coz, my pretty little coz, that thou
didst know how many fathom deep I am in love! But
it cannot be sounded;[179] my affection hath an unknown
bottom, like the Bay of Portugal.

Celia. Or rather, bottomless, that as fast as you pour
affection in, it runs out.

Rosalind. No, that same wicked bastard of Venus,[180] that
was begot of thought,[181] conceived of spleen,[182] and born of
madness, that blind rascally boy that abuses[183]
everyone's eyes because his own are out, let him be judge
how deep I am in love. I'll tell thee, Aliena, I cannot be
out of the sight of Orlando. I'll go find a shadow[184]
and sigh till he come.

Celia. And I'll sleep.   *Exeunt.*

* * *

Rosalind is once again impatiently awaiting the arrival of the tardy Orlando.
Oliver, Orlando's older brother, shows up instead of Orlando, and rehearses the
story of the events that led him there. This episode was clearly not part of
Rosalind's own wooing strategy, but it seems, nevertheless, important for its suc-
cessful outcome. Why?

Act IV. Scene iii. Lines 1–5, 76–183. Location: the forest.
Stage Directions: Enter Rosalind and Celia [joined by Oliver later on]

Rosalind. How say you now? Is it not past two o clock?
And here much[185] Orlando!

Celia. I warrant[186] you, with pure love and troubled

---

[178]**We . . . nest** i.e., we must expose you for what you are, a woman, and show everyone how a
woman has defamed her own kind just as a foul bird proverbially fouls its own nest

[179]**sounded** measured for depth

[180]**bastard of Venus** i.e., Cupid, son of Venus and Mercury rather than Vulcan, Venus' husband

[181]**thought** fancy

[182]**spleen** i.e., impulse

[183]**abuses** deceives

[184]**shadow** shady spot

[185]**much** (Said ironically: A fat lot we see of Orlando!)

[186]**warrant** assure

brain, he hath ta'en his bow and arrows and is gone
forth—to sleep.

Enter Oliver.

Oliver. Good morrow, fair ones. Pray you, if you know,
    Where in the purlieus[187] of this forest stands
    A sheepcote fenced about with olive trees?
Celia.
    West of this place, down in the neighbor bottom;[188]
    The rank of osiers[189] by the murmuring stream
    Left[190] on your right hand brings you to the place.
    But at this hour the house doth keep itself;
    There's none within.
Oliver.
    If that an eye may profit by a tongue,
    Then should I know you by description,
    Such garments and such years: "The boy is fair,
    Of female favor,[191] and bestows[192] himself
    Like a ripe[193] sister; the woman, low
    And browner than her brother." Are not you
    The owner of the house I did inquire for?
Celia.
    It is no boast, being asked, to say we are.
Oliver.
    Orlando doth commend him to you both,
    And to that youth he calls his Rosalind
    He sends this bloody napkin.[194] Are you he?
                    [He produces a bloody handkerchief.]
Rosalind.
    I am. What must we understand by this?
Oliver.
    Some of my shame, if you will know of me

---

[187]**purlieus** tracts of land on the border of a forest
[188]**neighbor bottom** neighboring dell
[189]**rank of osiers** row of willows
[190]**Left** left behind, passed
[191]**favor** features
[192]**bestows** behaves
[193]**ripe** mature or elder
[194]**napkin** handkerchief

What man I am, and how, and why, and where
This handkerchief was stained.

Celia.   I pray you, tell it.

Oliver.

When last the young Orlando parted from you
He left a promise to return again
Within an hour, and, pacing through the forest,
Chewing the food of sweet and bitter fancy,[195]
Lo, what befell! He threw his eye aside,
And mark what object did present itself:
Under an old oak, whose boughs were mossed with age
And high top bald with dry antiquity,
A wretched ragged man, o'ergrown with hair,
Lay sleeping on his back. About his neck
A green and gilded snake had wreathed itself,
Who with her head nimble in threats approached
The opening of his mouth; but suddenly,
Seeing Orlando, it unlinked[196] itself
And with indented[197] glides did slip away
Into a bush, under which bush's shade
A lioness, with udders all drawn dry,[198]
Lay couching, head on ground, with catlike watch,
When[199] that the sleeping man should stir; for 'tis
The royal disposition of that beast
To prey on nothing that doth seem as dead.
This seen, Orlando did approach the man
And found it was his brother, his elder brother.

Celia.

O, I have heard him speak of that same brother,
And he did render him[200] the most unnatural
That lived amongst men.

Oliver.   And well he might so do,
For well I know he was unnatural.

Rosalind.

But to Orlando: did he leave him there,

---

[195]**fancy** love
[196]**unlinked** uncoiled
[197]**indented** zigzag
[198]**udders . . . dry** (It would therefore be fierce with hunger.)
[199]**When** for the moment
[200]**render him** describe him as

Food to the sucked and hungry lioness?

Oliver.

> Twice did he turn his back and purposed so;
> But kindness, nobler ever than revenge,
> And nature, stronger than his just occasion,[201]
> Made him give battle to the lioness,
> Who quickly fell before him; in which hurtling[202]
> From miserable slumber I awaked.

Celia.

> Are you his brother?

Rosalind.   Was't you he rescued?

Celia.

> Was't you that did so oft contrive to kill him?

Oliver.

> 'Twas I; but 'tis not I. I do not shame[203]
> To tell you what I was, since my conversion
> So sweetly tastes, being the thing I am.

Rosalind.

> But for the bloody napkin?

Oliver.   By and by.

> When from the first to last betwixt us two
> Tears our recountments had most kindly bathed,
> As how I came into that desert place,
> In brief, he led me to the gentle Duke,
> Who gave me fresh array and entertainment,[204]
> Committing me unto my brother's love;
> Who led me instantly unto his cave,
> There stripped himself, and here upon his arm
> The lioness had torn some flesh away,
> Which all this while had bled; and now he fainted
> And cried, in fainting, upon Rosalind.
> Brief, I recovered[205] him, bound up his wound,
> And, after some small space, being strong at heart,
> He sent me hither, stranger as I am,
> To tell this story, that you might excuse
> His broken promise, and to give this napkin

---

[201] **just occasion** fair chance (or revenge)
[202] **hurtling** clatter, tumult
[203] **do not shame** am not ashamed
[204] **entertainment** hospitality, provision
[205] **recovered** revived

Dyed in his blood unto the shepherd youth
That he in sport doth call his Rosalind.
                              [Rosalind swoons.]
Celia.
    Why, how now, Ganymede, sweet Ganymede!
Oliver.
    Many will swoon when they do look on blood.
Celia.
    There is more in it.—Cousin Ganymede!
Oliver. Look, he recovers.
Rosalind. I would I were at home.
Celia. We'll lead you thither.—
        I pray you, will you take him by the arm?
                              [They help Rosalind up.]
Oliver. Be of good cheer, youth. You a man? You lack
    a man's heart.
Rosalind. I do so, I confess it. Ah, sirrah, a body would
    think this was well counterfeited. I pray you, tell your
    brother how well I counterfeited. Heigh-ho!
Oliver. This was not counterfeit. There is too great
    testimony in your complexion that it was a passion of
    earnest.
Rosalind. Counterfeit, I assure you.
Oliver. Well then, take a good heart and counterfeit to
    be a man.
Rosalind. So I do; but i' faith, I should have been a
    woman by right.
Celia. Come, you look paler and paler. Pray you, draw
    homewards.—Good sir, go with us.
Oliver.
    That will I, for I must bear answer back
    How you excuse my brother, Rosalind.
Rosalind. I shall devise something. But, I pray you,
    commend my counterfeiting to him. Will you go?
                              Exeunt.

* * *

*Filled with remorse for his earlier cruelty to his brother, Oliver's newly awak-
ened piteous heart is ripe for romance as well. He falls in love with Celia (still
disguised as Aliena) and promptly arranges to marry her. Listening to Oliver's
report of his love and intentions, Orlando too suddenly feels a sense of urgency*

and he is no longer content to play the part of a suitor: "I can live no longer by thinking," he announces. Rosalind (still disguised as Ganymede), hearing this, promises to weary him no longer and abruptly proceeds to bring the charade to a end. Beckoning Orlando to prepare to marry on the morrow, she and we leave the young lovers. But as we watch this culminating scene unfold, we are again invited to ask what Rosalind has seen. How does she now know that Orlando is the just right one for her to marry? Is she right? Is there reason to believe that she is as right for Orlando as she thinks he is for her? Should we be sanguine about her prospects as a wife?

Act V. Scene ii. Lines 1–73. Location: the forest.
Stage Directions: Enter Orlando and Oliver [joined by Rosalind later on]

Orlando. Is 't possible that on so little acquaintance
    you should like her? That but seeing you should love
    her? And loving woo? And, wooing, she should
    grant? And will you persevere to enjoy her?
Oliver. Neither call the giddiness[206] of it in question, the
    poverty of her, the small acquaintance, my sudden
    wooing, nor her sudden consenting; but say with me,
    "I love Aliena"; say with her that she loves me; consent
    with both that we may enjoy each other. It shall be to
    your good; for my father's house and all the revenue
    that was old Sir Rowland's will I estate[207] upon you, and
    here live and die a shepherd.

Enter Rosalind.

Orlando. You have my consent. Let your wedding be
    tomorrow. Thither will I invite the Duke and all 's
    contented followers. Go you and prepare Aliena;
    for look you, here comes my Rosalind.
Rosalind. God save you, brother.[208]
Oliver. And you, fair sister.[209]   *[Exit.]*
Rosalind. O my dear Orlando, how it grieves me to
    see thee wear thy heart in a scarf![210]

---

[206] **giddiness** sudden speed
[207] **estate** settle as an estate, bestow
[208] **brother** i.e., brother-in-law to be
[209] **sister** (Rosalind is still dressed as a man, but Oliver evidently adopts the fiction that Ganymede is Orlando's Rosalind.)
[210] **wear . . . scarf** (Perhaps she suggests that Orlando has been wearing his heart on his sleeve; literally, she refers to the scarf or bandage for his wounded arm.)

Orlando. It is my arm.

Rosalind. I thought thy heart had been wounded with
    the claws of a lion.

Orlando. Wounded it is, but with the eyes of a lady.

Rosalind. Did your brother tell you how I counterfeited
    to swoon when he showed me your handkerchief?

Orlando. Ay, and greater wonders than that.

Rosalind. O, I know where you are.[211] Nay, 'tis true.
    There was never anything so sudden but the fight of
    two rams and Caesar's thrasonical[212] brag of "I came,
    saw, and overcame." For your brother and my sister
    no sooner met but they looked, no sooner looked
    but they loved, no sooner loved but they sighed, no sooner
    sighed but they asked one another the reason, no
    sooner knew the reason but they sought the remedy;
    and in these degrees[213] have they made a pair of stairs to
    marriage which they will climb incontinent,[214] or else be
    incontinent before marriage. They are in the very
    wrath[215] of love, and they will together. Clubs cannot
    part them.

Orlando. They shall be married tomorrow, and I will
    bid the Duke to the nuptial. But O, how bitter a thing
    it is to look into happiness through another man's
    eyes! By so much the more shall I tomorrow be at the
    height of heart-heaviness, by how much I shall think
    my brother happy in having what he wishes for.

Rosalind. Why then tomorrow I cannot serve your
    turn for Rosalind?

Orlando. I can live no longer by thinking.

Rosalind. I will weary you then no longer with idle
    talking. Know of me then, for now I speak to some
    purpose, that I know you are a gentleman of good conceit.[216]
    I speak not this that you should bear a good opinion
    of my knowledge, insomuch I say I know you are;

---

[211]**where you are** i.e., what you mean

[212]**thrasonical** boastful

[213]**degrees** (Plays on the original meaning, steps.)

[214]**incontinent** immediately (followed by a pun on the meaning "unchaste or sexually unrestrained")

[215]**wrath** impetuosity, ardor

[216]**conceit** intelligence, understanding

neither do I labor for a greater esteem than may in
some little measure draw a belief[217] from you, to do
yourself good and not to grace me.[218] Believe then, if you
please, that I can do strange things. I have, since I was
three years old, conversed[219] with a magician, most profound
in his art and yet not damnable.[220] If you do love
Rosalind so near the heart as your gesture[221] cries it out,
when your brother marries Aliena, shall you marry
her. I know into what straits of fortune she is driven;
and it is not impossible to me, if it appear not
inconvenient[222] to you, to set her before your eyes tomorrow,
human[223] as she is, and without any danger.[224]

Orlando. Speak'st thou in sober meanings?[225]

Rosalind. By my life I do, which I tender dearly,
though I say I am a magician.[226] Therefore, put you in
your best array; bid your friends; for if you will be
married tomorrow, you shall, and to Rosalind, if you
will.

---

[217]**belief** i.e., confidence in my ability

[218]**grace me** bring favor on myself

[219]**conversed** associated

[220]**not damnable** not a practicer of forbidden or black magic, worthy of damnation

[221]**gesture** bearing

[222]**inconvenient** inappropriate

[223]**human** i.e., the real Rosalind

[224]**danger** i.e., the danger to the soul from one's involvement in magic or witchcraft

[225]**in sober meanings** seriously

[226]**though . . . magician** (According to Elizabethan antiwitchcraft statutes, some forms of witch-craft were punishable by death; Rosalind thus endangers her life by what she has said.)

Franklin, "Reflections on Courtship and Marriage"

In 1746, Benjamin Franklin (1706–1790) published "Reflections on Courtship and Marriage: In Two Letters to a Friend. Wherein a Practicable Plan is Laid Down for Obtaining and Securing Conjugal Felicity." The first letter, excerpted here as an example of early American thinking on the subject, concerns what to look for in a wife, in light of Franklin's view that marriage is properly founded upon friendship and mutual esteem and regarded as an equal partnership of a like-minded and sensible couple. (The second letter, not here anthologized, offers advice for promoting felicity after the marriage takes place.) Despite the archaic language (and spelling and punctuation), Franklin's remarks are far ahead of his time; indeed, his major emphases are decidedly modern. Early in the letter (in passages not here selected) Franklin dismisses those who argue that women are incapable of being a man's lifelong friend and companion; he celebrates the equality of women and men, and he blames women's foibles on the silliness of their (then current) education and on the flattering attentions of equally foolish men. The excerpted material is less about the actual practice of courting, more about what to look for and about the concerns that should (and should not) guide one's search for the right one. With his eye firmly fixed on partnership as the key to marital happiness, he warns equally against both the mercenary or economic and the passionate or romantic views of marriage. Courtship should proceed without artifice, flattery, coquetry, or romanticism. Instead, "conversations of sober Reason and Good Sense" are to disclose and cultivate a high like-mindedness upon which the best conjugal friendship can subsequently be built. Also of interest is Franklin's delicately written but still very liberal postscript on the limits of parental authority over the marriages of their children. Is Franklin's 250-year-old advice still useful? Is he right in turning courtship into the cultivation of friendship? Is his view of husband-wife friendship too high-minded? Are there important matters he neglects?

. . . I am then of that Gentleman's Opinion..:

THAT unhappy Matches are often occasioned by meer *mercenary Views* in one or *both* of the Parties; or by the *headstrong* Motives of *ill conducted Passion.*

THAT by a *prudent* and *judicious* Proceeding, in our Addresses to a young Lady of a good natural Temper, a probable Foundation may be laid for making her an agreeable Companion, a steady Friend, and a good Wife.

AND that after Marriage, by continuing in the Road of *Prudence* and *Judgment,* we may erect a Superstructure of as much real Felicity, and as refined an Enjoyment of Life, to its latest Period, as any other Scheme can justly lay claim to.

I shall give you my deliberate Thoughts on these four Particulars; the *first, second* and *third,* will be the Subject of *this,* the *fourth* that of *another Letter;* and, to be the less confused, I shall put them under a Sort of Method.

Sect. I. Many unhappy Matches are occasioned by mercenary Views in one or both of the Parties.

THAT Luxury, and an expensive Manner of Life, is not less the Attention than the Ambition of most People in their several Classes; and that such a Turn of Mind must naturally and necessarily carry with it a violent and insatiable Thirst for Riches; to any Person of Observation and Reflection, is as obvious, on the one Hand, as 'tis consequential on the other.

'TIS as certain, that a Passion so prevalent, will, of course, weigh down and stifle every noble, generous, and disinterested Sentiment.

WE see but too often, like a destructive Torrent, it hurries away all the Principles of Humanity, Friendship and Honour.

In short—whenever *Luxury,* and an Ambition for *Show* and *Grandeur,* becomes our *ruling Passion,* the *Love of Money,* as being the necessary Means for attaining the other, will be proportionly strong: And whatever be our *ruling Passion,* it will swallow up all the rest, and be the *governing Principle* of our Actions.

A great Philosopher, and a Poet, that has, I think, no Equal in our Language, tell us,

> *The ruling Passion, be it what it will,*
> *The ruling Passion conquers Reason still.*[1]

EVERY Man of Observation and Thought does, I believe, find, that *exterior Show,* and the Possession of Wealth, is become the common Standard of Merit; that a *slavish Obsequiousness* is paid to it, at the Expence of all that is *truly Great and Manly.*

THE same *little, sneaking,* and *selfish* Spirit, is crept into our matrimonial Pursuits; and not, I think, less with the Fair than our own Sex.

WHAT abominable *Prostitutions* of Persons and Minds are daily to be seen in many of our Marriages! How little a Share has *real Friendship* and *Esteem* in most of them! How many *play the Harlot,* for a good Settlement, under

[1] Pope's Epist. to Lord *Bathurst.*

the *legal Title* of a Wife! And how many the *Stallion,* to repair a broken Fortune, or to gain one.

ARE these *Muckworms* to expect any *social Happiness* with each other?
shall their *wretched Experience* be quoted as Instances to prove Matrimony unworthy our Choice? . . .

The real Felicity of Marriage does undoubtedly consist in a *Union of
Minds,* and a *Sympathy of Affections; in a mutual Esteem and Friendship* for
each other in the highest Degree possible. But in that Alliance, where Interest
and Fortune *only* is considered, those refined and tender Sentiments are neither
felt or known. And what are they exchanged for? Why, to make a glare in the
Eyes of the little and great Vulgar; to be hurried thro' Scenes of ridiculous and
treacherous Ceremony; to raise Envy in the weak and silly Part of the World,
Pity and Contempt in the Wise and Judicious.

AND what are the Consequences to the Parties themselves? Why, at best a
cold, flat, and *insipid* Intercourse; void of the exquisite Relish of a sincere Esteem, and the divine Pleasures of a reasonable and honourable Friendship.—
But more frequently the *Iniquity* of their *interested* Views, in one or both appears undisguised, is succeeded by Contempt and Disdain, and throws such a
Fire of Contention and Uneasiness between them, as gives too just a Cause for
that direful Simile, a *Hell upon Earth.*

IF the Happiness of a married Life does, as it most certainly *must,* arise
from an *unfeigned Esteem,* and *sincere Friendship* for each other: how is it possible for such *godlike Effects* to flow from such *diabolical Causes,* as *Avaricious,
mercenary,* and *selfish* Views? Do such Dispositions, and can such *dirty Souls,*
ever feel the *pure* and *delicate* Flame of a *sincere Love?* Of that *mysterious Affection* which *swells* the Heart, and *overflows* in the *gentle Streams* of an *anxious
Fondness?* Can interested Designs, can those *Slaves* to *Dross* be animated with
the *Spirit* of a *generous,* an *elevated* and *inflexible Friendship?* 'Tis inconsistent
and repugnant to Reason and Nature: *Gold* is their *Idol,* 'tis that they wed.

To conclude, 'tis a Truth of the plainest Demonstration, that *Slaves to Fortune,* or the Gratification of their own selfish Passions, who center their Views
in Life within themselves, independant on the Feelings of others, are *incapable*
of a sincere and steady Friendship; nor can their Hearts *glow* with the *warm
benevolence of a tender Affection.*

DOES it not then very evidently appear, that Marriages which are made
on the meer motives of Interest, will naturally turn out, insipid, unhappy, and
fatal Situations. . . .

IT must not be inferred from the foregoing, that Prudence and Discretion
with regard to Fortune, are to be banish'd from our Consideration. That wou'd
be an Extream, on the other Hand, equally, or more subversive of our Happiness.

To talk of a Competence, is, in Effect, saying Nothing at all; what may be so to one Man, is not so to another. But this is certain: The nearer we bring our Desires of Living, and our Relishes of Pleasure, to the Necessities of our Nature, the more easy and certain will our Happiness be: And undoubtedly Splendor and Magnificence, are more *imaginary* than *real* and *necessary* Ingredients to human Felicity.

How much, or *how little* a Fortune will content us, depends chiefly on our own Way of Thinking. Be this as it will, it should seem very proper before all Marriages, for both parties to know truly and fairly, what they have to *expect* on this Head, and seriously to consider with themselves, whether it will be sufficient so far to answer their Desires, as to prevent future Murmurings and Anxieties, and prudently allow them to enjoy Life as they intend. All *Deceit* herein should be *carefully avoided,* we may otherwise impose on our selves, and ruin all our future Felicity.

Sect. II. Unhappy Marriages are often occasioned from the Headstrong Motives of ungoverned Passion.

THE cool and considerate Views of *Interest,* have taken so deep a Root even in very young Minds, that those *feverish Marriages* are not very common; and we are, I think, now a days, more liable to them in our Dotage than our Bloom.

An amorous Complexion, a lively Imagination, and a generous Temper, are so apt to be charm'd with an agreeable Person, the insinuating Accomplishments of Musick and Dancing, *un bon Grace,* and a *Gaietè de Coeur,* that it is instantly transported, sighs, languishes, dies for Possession. In this *distempered* Condition, and *amorous Fit* of Madness, his sanguine and heated Imagination paints her out to him, in all the romantick Lights of an *Arcadian Princess,* an *Angel Form,* and a *heavenly Mind,* the *Pride of Nature,* and the *Joy of Man,* a Source of *immortal Pleasures, Raptures* that will *never satiate, Bliss uninterrupted,* and *Transports too big for Expression.*—Bloated with all these nonsensical Ideas or *Chimeras,* worked up to a raging Fit of Enthusiasm, he falls down and worships this *Idol* of his own intoxicated Brain, runs to her, talks Fustian and Tragedy by wholesale. Miss blushes, looks down, admires his Eloquence, pities the dying Swain, catches the Infection, and *consents,* if *Papa* and *Mamma* will give theirs.

THE old People strike the *Bargain;* the young Ones are mad and lightheaded with those ravishing Scenes their warm Constitutions and distempered Fancies present to their View.

WELL, they are married, and have taken their Full of Love. The young Spark's Rant is over, he finds his imaginary Goddess *meer Flesh and Blood* with the Addition of a *vain, affected, silly Girl;* and when his Theatrical Dress is off, she finds he was a *lying, hot-brain'd Coxcomb.*

THUS come to their Senses, and the mask thrown off, they look at one another like utter Strangers, and Persons just come out of a Trance; he finds by Experience he fell in Love with his own Ideas, and she with her own Vanity. Thus pluckt from the soaring Heights of their warm and irregular Passions, they are vext at, and ashamed of themselves *first,* and heartily hate each other *afterwards.* From hence arise *Reproaches, Contradictions,* &c. Thus all their *fantastick Bliss* ends in *Shame* and *Repentance.*

IN serious Truth how can it be otherwise?

PASSIONS are extreamely transient and unsteady, and *Love,* with no other Support, will ever be short liv'd and fleeting. 'Tis a *Fire* that is *soon extinguished,* and where there is no solid Esteem and well cemented Friendship to *blow it up,* it rarely *lights* again, but from some accidental Impulses, by no Means to be depended on; which a Contrariety of Tempers, the Fatalities of Sickness, or the Frowns of Fortune, may, for ever, prevent, as Age most certainly will.

BESIDES, in Marriages of this Kind, there is neither *Time* nor *Coolness* sufficient, for fixing an Esteem and Friendship; and therefore the very *Foundations* for its *lasting* Happiness are wanting. May they follow, do you think? Alas how uncertain is that! and so many Probabilities on the contrary Side, that none surely but the most daring and *inconsiderate* People would run the Risque.

WHAT has been observed seems to point out, that a *blind,* a sudden and *intoxicating* Passion, has a natural Tendency, under its own Direction, to occasion *unhappy Marriages,* and produce Scenes of *Grief* and *Repentance.*

LET us, on the contrary, proceed with Deliberation and Circumspection. Let *Reason* and *Thought* be summoned before we engage in the Courtship of a Lady. Endeavour as much as possible, to stifle all those passionate and amorous Emotions, that wou'd *cloud* and *bribe* our Judgments. Let us *seriously* reflect, that Engagements of this Kind, are of the *greatest* Moment and Import to our future Happiness in Life. That Courtship brings on Marriage, and that makes all the Peace and Welfare of our Lives dependant on the Behaviour and Disposition of another; a Matter of the *utmost* Consequence, and of which we cannot well think too long or too much. Let not therefore our *Eyes* or *Passions* prevail with us, to barter away all that is truly valuable in our Existence for their Gratification.

SOME Women have infinite Art, being early bred to disguise and dissemble; yet by a skilful Attention, Calmness, and Impartiality, we may form a Judgment of their Characters in the main: Which we should endeavor to do, and compare them fairly with our own; see how they will *correspond:* Be rationally convinced of a Similitude in our Ways of Thinking, a *Harmony* in our Minds and Tempers, before we venture to change the Name of Mistress into that of wife.

THUS let us deliberate, thus let us proceed, and thus arm our selves with Reason and Reflection in this great Affair. Lest by too much *Warmth* and *Precipitancy,* we draw those Miseries on our selves, which Repentance will neither assuage or remove.

HAVING now drove the *mercenary Herd* to their native Mines, and made evident their Unfitness for breathing the pure and generous air of matrimonial Felicity; left the *Inamoratoes* to float in their Fool's Paradise with Novels and Romances; let us endeavor to fix our selves on the *true Basis* of conjugal Happiness, and see if we can hit upon the Path wherein an agreeable Companion, a steady friend, and a good Wife, may be found.

AND this we must enter upon by a *prudent and judicious Courtship,* which as 'twas before observed, is laying the foundation of *a happy Marriage.*

Sect. III. In our Addresses, let our Conduct be sincere, and Tempers undisguised; let us use no Artifices to cover or conceal our natural Frailties and Imperfections; but be outwardly, what we really are within, and appear such as we design stedfastly to continue.

IN the gay Time of Courtship, it seems to be a general Practice with both Sexes, to conceal all personal Defects by every Artifice of Dress, &c.

THIS is not so politick; and may be attended with future Consequences very prejudicial. By so intimate an Union as that of Marriage, all bodily Defects will soon be discovered; and as Hypocrisy in the minutest Matters amongst Friends, is extreamly odious, those Defects will carry a Sting and Guilt with them, to which perhaps we may be never reconciled. Whereas had no Art been used for their Concealment, they might have caused little or no concern.

NOTHING to a generous Mind is more ungrateful, than any Sort of *Imposition* from a Friend.

LOVE and Friendship are of so *nice* and *delicate* a Texture, that *Disingenuity* in the smallest Matters should be avoided.

THESE Remarks may appear but of little Importance, to People of a coarse and unpolished Taste, but I am persuaded they will have their Weight with those of a contrary Turn.

FOR my own Part, I wou'd, if any thing, be rather *less* careful and exact in my personal Appearance, *before* than *after* Marriage, because the difficulty of *raising* an Affection, is not so great, as that of *preserving* it; as every little personal Embellishment may be serviceable in the former Case, so it undoubtedly will in the latter.—But the Care of our Persons, will come under a more particular Observation in my second Letter; and tho' 'tis seldom neglected *before*, yet 'tis often so notoriously *after* Marriage, that I believe many unhappy Ones are caused by it.

HOWEVER it be as to the Spruceness and Decoration of our *Persons*, I must affirm it a most dangerous Folly, an Imposition highly culpable, to mask our *Tempers*, and appear what we really are not; to exhibit a *forged Draught* of our Minds and Dispositions in order to win the Affections.

I am really at a Loss to judge, whether the Absurdity or Iniquity of such a Scheme be the greatest.

Is this Courtship? Is this laying a Foundation for our future Happiness? Monstrous! But this is sometimes, too often the Case with both Sexes. 'Tis really amazing how People can be so *preposterously* wicked, in a Correspondence of the most *sacred* and tender Kind, in the Consequences of which, all the future Happiness of their Lives may depend. How *stupid*, thus to study our own Ruin, by the infamous Deception of One, we choose for the Partner of our Joys and our Cares, the Companion of our Days and our Nights! How *shocking* to set out with Fraud, and proceed with Deceit in such solemn Engagements! How *shallow* is the Cunning of such inconsiderate Minds! Must not all the Pleasures of Marriage be unanimous and inseparable? Do they not flow from *real* and *unaffected* Loveliness? Can we think the Cheat will lie long concealed in a Society so intimate? When Time and Experience unmasks our *assumed* Appearances, shows us in our *native Colours*, and *exposes* that Reality we have so industriously laboured to *cover;* can we expect Love and Esteem from any One whom we have so *shamefully over-reached* and ensnared? Surely *no*. On the contrary we shall entail on our selves, *certain* Indignation, and *lasting* Contempt.

We have raised and supported an Affection by *false Appearances;* when those are seen thro', as most certainly they will be, what Title have we to Love or Friendship? NONE, and consequently no Prospect of social Happiness.

LET us, my Friend, on the contrary, observe a *religious Sincerity*, appear in our *Native Characters*, undisguised and unaffected. If under those we gain Esteem and Friendship, our Prospects of maintaining them, are as secure, as our own Minds and Dispositions may be lasting.—Let us be *outwardly*, what we really are *within*, and appear in such a Character as we stedfastly design to continue. Hereby we shall lay a strong Foundation for our future Happiness in Marriage.

Sect. IV. Let our Manner of conversing with a Mistress be void of fulsome Flattery, and the ridiculous Bombast of Novels and Romances.

IT was an Objection, you may remember, made against Matrimony; that the Education of young Ladies, gave such a trifling Turn to their Tempers, and

Manner of Thinking, as rendered them unfit for the rational Pleasures of Society and Conversation.

ALLOWING this to be true, and in general but too true it really is, how prejudicial and fatal must *Flattery* be to such? And how completely must that foppish Rant, called *Gallantry*, poison their understandings, and tend to destroy the Possibility of inspiring them with Sentiments of Reason and good Sense.

BY such a Proceeding, a Man naturally forms a young Creature, for a *vain* and *insipid Companion;* and if by that Means, he finds Matrimony to be an irksome and disagreeable Scene, what Wonder, and where does the Blame lye?

NOTHING more naturally carries us beyond our selves, and puffs us up with an over-rating Opinion of our own Merit; swells every Appearance of Desert; so strongly intrenches our Frailties and Imperfections, that Reason and Reflection are too much enervated to dislodge them; nothing more effectually spoils our Tempers, and corrupts our Judgments, than FLATTERY: It renders us positive in our Ignorance, and impatient of Contradiction.

THEN that Hodge-Podge of Nonsense, which many call *Making Love*[2] is using a Woman to such intemperate and frothy Sallies of Fancy, such romantick and unmeaning Impressions; that sober Thought, and plain good sense, are foreign to her Taste; and an Entertainment, to which being not used, she has no *Gout* or Relish.

WHAT an agreeable and pretty Sort of a Companion, what a comfortable Wife do we hereby contrive for our selves? And how ingeniously do we thus labour to make her a positive and empty, a conceited and fantastical Simpleton? thus modelled, we soon come to despise her, and curse our Marriage.

BUT some say this is the most certain and expeditious Way to gain the Affections of a young Lady, and that a Man would make but a dull and heavy Figure in their Eyes without it, and finds his Attacks very unsuccessful.

This may be true with some, and 'tis no less a Mark of *Merit*, than a Point of great *good Fortune*, to meet with Insensibility from them.—

BUT 'tis far from being so with all; there are young Ladies, and many with whom I am persuaded a Man would find himself more acceptable and successful by a contrary Method: And to such only should every Man apply himself, for the valuable and lasting Felicities of a Conjugal Life.

If we allow a Man may make a more speedy Conquest by Fustian and Flattery, yet whoever, methinks, reflects on the Consequences, should be convinced, that it must be fatal to the future Repose and Tranquility of his Life.— Let Coxcombs boast of such Triumphs, but Men of Sense will ever despise and shun them.

[2]Wooing or courting [eds.]

**Sect. V. Let us my Friend, on the contrary, use [i.e.,
accustom] her we design for a Wife and Companion, to the
Conversations of sober Reason and good Sense: Endeavour by
every probable Method, to inspire her with the Sentiments of
rational Esteem, a generous and stedfast Friendship for us.—**

HEREBY we have a great Probability, and well grounded Expectations of securing to our selves an agreeable and entertaining Companion.

BY seasonably introducing into Conversation useful Subjects on human Life and Characters; by making solid and practical Reflections thereon, and engaging the Attention by a polite, an easy and lively Manner; we shall correct and strengthen the Judgment, enlarge the Faculties of the Mind, and raise the Soul to a free and generous Way of Thinking; drive out and extirpate, that childish, that little narrow-spirited Way of Thinking, that mean and injudicious Distrust; those low and pitiful Artifices, and that lurking Sort of Cunning, which is too much the Characteristick of many Women, is the Detestation of every great Mind, and the Abhorrence of all ingenuous Spirits.

THERE is no Friendship or Confidence to be had with such *dirty, tricking, low Minds;* they are an utter Privation to all social Happiness, and when carried into a married Life, are insuperable Obstacles to its Welfare.

MANY proper Opportunities may likewise be found, for recommending the Perusal of elegant and improving Books, which by a good Choice and a judicious Taste, will have a very beneficial Effect on the Mind and Understanding.

BUT in all this, great Delicacy and a good judgment is very essential; to distinguish nicely and to manage with Discretion, are highly necessary. We should be careful to cover our good Intentions with so engaging an Artifice, as by no Means to shock the Passions; render every Thing as a Matter rather of Choice and Taste than Prescription.

YOU will not, I am persuaded, so greatly misapprehend my Meaning, under these Reflections, as to imagine I am pleading up for what is commonly understood by a *learned* and *bookish Character* in a young Lady; such a One as Mr. *Pope* points out, a

> *"Wise Fool! with Pleasures too refin'd to please,*
> *"With too much Thinking to have common Thought.*

I am far from designing any such ridiculous Extreams. Nothing in Nature is, I think, more odious and contemptible than a *female Pedant,* a formal, a conceited and affected Wit; whose Brain is loaded with a Heap of indigested Stuff, and is eternally throwing up her confused Nonsense, in hard Words ill pronounced, jumbled Quotations misapplyed, and a Jargon of Common-Places; in order to let you know she is a Woman of Reading; whereby she convinces you, she has taken a great deal of Pains to render herself a Fool of the first Class, and of the most irreclaimable Kind.

—THE Barking of a Lap-dog is not more grating to the Ear, than the Gibberish of their impertinent Clacks; and the Chatter of a Parrot infinitely more entertaining. In short, such Women are the Mountebanks of their own, the Dread and Contempt of our Sex.

BUT must these jingling Pretenders to Wit and Sense, exclude us from the delightful Harmony, the amiable Conversation of a modest and unaffected Fair One, in whom a good Understanding is joined with a good Mind.

HOW engaging are the Graces of such a Character! How insinuating are its Charms! How imperceptibly does it win on the Mind! What a Flow of tender Sentiments, it diffuses thro' the Heart! Calms each rougher Passion, and swells the Breast with those exquisite Emotions that rise above all Description.

THUS to imitate, and if possible to equal this Character it is, that I wou'd have Conversation and Books tend. And I cannot but think, if thus adapted and directed, they wou'd have a great Efficacy towards it.

HOW great a Prospect, and what reasonable Hopes of Happiness, there must be with such a Companion, requires surely no Arguments to prove.

But the Truth is, we are either actuated by other Motives than a Regard to and Desire of social Happiness, or that we are hurried thro' Courtship, by an intemperate and unthinking Warmth: Hereby our Conversation is rendered either Designing or Ridiculous.

NOR is it less necessary to inspire our Mistress with the Sentiments of a rational Esteem, of a stedfast and generous Friendship.

IT has been already observed, that Love considered meerly as a Passion, will naturally have but a short Duration; like all other Passions 'tis changeable, transient and accidental. But Friendship and Esteem are derived from Principles of Reason and Thought, and when once truly fixed in the Mind, are lasting Securities of an Attachment to our Persons and Fortunes; participate with, and refine all our Joys; simpathize with, and blunt the Edge of every adverse Occurrence.—In vain should I endeavour to make an Elogium on true *Friendship*, in any measure equal to its sublime and exalted Value: There is no Good in Life comparable to it; neither are any, or all of its other Enjoyments worth desiring without it. 'Tis the Crown to all our Felicities; the Glory, and I think, the Perfection of our Natures. Life's a Wilderness without a Friend, and all its gilded Scenes but barren and tasteless.

HERE have I a copious Subject, to reflect on the many false Friendships there are in the World!—How few real and sincere ones!—How much talk'd of, how little meant, and less understood! No *generous* and *disinterested* Feelings of Mind, (the Essence of Friendship) can possibly display themselves, whilst *mercenary* Views, and *selfish Designs* are the Principles of Action. But this is a Digression:

HOWEVER it be in *common Life,* there cannot certainly be any steady or lasting Happiness in a *married One,* where a mutual Esteem and Friendship, of the strongest and noblest Kind, does not subsist. Let it therefore be the sacred Business of our Courtship to cultivate One, and on no Account engage our selves in Wedlock without it.

I know of no Method, more likely to promote and secure it, than by being prepossessed with it our selves.

THERE is a Sort of attractive Force in similar Minds, as there is in Matter.

> Great Minds by Instinct to each other turn,
> Demand Alliance, and in Friendship burn.
> —Mr. Addison's Campaign

'TIS a common Saying, that *Love begets Love;* that is not always true. But where there is any Similitude of Minds, *Sentiments of Friendship, will beget Friendship.*

LET us then take every Opportunity of testifying our Esteem and Friendship: Court the Understanding, the Principles of Thought, and conciliate them to our own.

HEREBY we shall as it were enter into the Soul, and take Possession of all its Powers; this should be the Ground-work of Love, this will be a vital Principal to that, and make our Concord as lasting as our Minds are unchangeable.

THIS Subject should be often that of our Conversation; and we should particularly endeavour to fix *right* and *just* Notions concerning it. To inspire a certain Greatness of Mind, that *scorns the least Falshood or Treachery;* which no Distress can possibly shake, and which no Prosperity can ever relax. We should, endeavour to *fire the Soul* (if you will allow me the Expression) with a Sort of *heroick Enthusiasm,* that no Decoys of Pleasure, no *Terrors* of Pain, should ever be capable of extinguishing, and rather to dare *Martyrdom* than *Apostacy.*

THUS should we fortify the Principles of Friendship, in her we choose for a Wife, and, by every possible Method in our Power, fix the root deep in her Soul. For unless both Minds *burn* with this *noble* and *essential Flame,* our Happiness in Marriage will have but a weak Basis, and a very slender Tye; every little Flurry of Humour, every little Blast of Adversity, will go near to overset the Bark of our Felicity: We shall at best toss about without a Rudder and without a Compass.

BUT a fix'd Principle of Friendship will steady and secure us, and we shall glide o'er the Waves of Life, with Serenity and Confidence; prepared for Rocks and Quicksands, with unshaken Courage, and an equal Mind.—Thus chearful, happy, and resigned, steer a virtuous and invariable Course of Affection, 'till the Port of Mortality puts an End to our Voyage, having already anticipated that Heaven in each other's Love and Friendship, which we then go more fully to possess. . . .

Postscript

You may perhaps think me guilty of an Omission in the foregoing Reflections, in having said nothing with regard to the *Consent of Parents*. I shall therefore deliver you my Opinion in relation thereto as concisely as possible.

THAT there is a certain *Authority* lodged in Parents over their Children, and in consequence thereof, a certain *Obedience* due from Children to their Parents, are Truths derived from Nature, and founded in Reason, and have had the Concurrence of all Ages and all Nations.

History gives us Instances of this Obedience paid to Parents, in some of the most illustrious Characters of Antiquity; and even in respect of Marriage, as you may remember in the Life of Cyrus the Great.

WE have likewise many past and living Examples, where the Authority of Parents over their Children in Marriages, has been most tyrannically and fatally exerted.

WITHOUT entering into a Train of Reasoning, I may venture to take it for granted;

THAT no parental Authority, that is *repugnant* to the Dictates of *Reason* and *Virtue*, or (which is the same Thing) the *moral Happiness* of our Natures, is any ways binding on Children.

To marry without a *Union of Minds*, a Sympathy of Affections, a mutual Esteem and Friendship for each other, is contrary to Reason and Virtue, the Moral Happiness of our Natures.

IT follows therefore that no parental Authority, thus to make ourselves unhappy by marrying, is any ways binding on Children.

To marry with a Union of Minds &c. being therefore agreeable to Reason and Virtue, and the Moral Happiness of our Natures; 'tis evident that Parents have no Authority, founded in Truth or Nature, to hinder their Children from so doing.

THO' these Propositions, and the Inferences drawn from them, are, I believe, just and true; yet Children should undoubtedly be *extreamly tender* in thwarting the Wills of their Parents: Should be *very careful*, that their *Passions* do not *blind*, or their *Caprice mislead* them: Should with great Calmness and Impartiality reason with themselves: Appeal to their Parents, with great Deference and Humility: Consult with some wise and unbiassed Friend: Desire their Interposition. In short, do every Thing in their Power to convince and persuade: and nothing but a manifest and conscious Violation of Reason and their real Happiness, should force them to oppose or disobey the Will of their Parents; especially to such as have ever behaved kindly, carefully and friendly to them: They have the *greatest Authority* over Children, that one Mortal *can have* over another.

How far it may be our *Interest* to obey or not, is another Consideration. What has been said on the Article of mercenary Views, may serve to determine us.

I conclude with the Lines of an anonymous Author,

> *Let no dire Threats, no kind Entreaties move,*
> *To give thy Person where thou canst not love.*

Franklin, "The Elysian Fields"

Benjamin Franklin not only gave advice about courtship; he also practiced it. Late in his life, after the death of his wife of nearly fifty years, Franklin proposed marriage to the widow of Claude-Adrien Helvétius, the French philosopher (1715– 1771). Mme. Helvétius refused him. The next day (December 7, 1778), Franklin again pressed his suit with the following letter. The editors report, sadly, that he was no more successful on this attempt. Did Mme. Helvétius make a mistake?

M. Franklin to Madame Helvétius

Vexed by your barbarous resolution, announced so positively last evening, to remain single all your life in respect to your dear husband, I went home, fell on my bed, and, believing myself dead, found myself in the Elysian Fields.

I was asked if I desired to see anybody in particular. Lead me to the home of the philosophers.—There are two who live nearby in the garden: they are very good neighbors, and close friends of each other.—Who are they?— Socrates and H—.—I esteem them both prodigiously; but let me see first H—, because I understand a little French, but not one word of Greek. He received me with great courtesy, having known me for some time, he said, by the reputation I had there. He asked me a thousand things about the war, and about the present state of religion, liberty, and the government in France.—You ask nothing then of your dear friend Madame H—; nevertheless she still loves you excessively and I was at her place but an hour ago. Ah! said he, you make me remember my former felicity.—But it is necessary to forget it in order to be happy here. During several of the early years, I thought only of her. Finally I am consoled. I have taken another wife. The most like her that I could find. She is not, it is true, so completely beautiful, but she has as much good sense, a little more of Spirit, and she loves me infinitely. Her continual study is to please me; and she has actually gone to hunt the best Nectar and the best Ambrosia in order to regale me this evening; remain with me and you will see her. I perceive, I said, that your old friend is more faithful than you: for several good offers have been made her, all of which she has refused. I confess to you that I myself have loved her to the point of distraction; but she was hard-hearted to my regard, and has absolutely rejected me for love of you. I pity you, he said, for your bad fortune; for truly she is a good and beautiful woman and very loveable. But the Abbé de la R—, and the Abbé M—, are they not still sometimes at her home? Yes, assuredly, for she has not lost a single one of your friends. If you had won over the Abbé M— (with coffee and cream) to speak for you, perhaps you would have succeeded; for he is a subtle logician like Duns Scotus or St. Thomas; he places his arguments in such good order that they become nearly irresistible. Also, if the Abbé de la R— had been bribed (by some beautiful edition of an old classic) to speak against you, that would have been better: for I have always observed, that when he advises something, she has a very strong penchant to do the reverse.—At these words the new Madame H— entered with the Nectar: at which instant I recognized her to be Madame F—, my old American friend. I reclaimed to her. But she told me coldly, "I have been your good wife forty-nine years and four months, nearly a half century; be content with that. Here I have formed a new connection, which will endure to eternity."

Offended by this refusal of my Eurydice, I suddenly decided to leave these ungrateful spirits, to return to the good earth, to see again the sunshine and you. Here I am! Let us revenge ourselves.

Rousseau, *Emile:* The Courtship of Emile and Sophie

From the start of the Emile, *Rousseau tells us that he aims to educate his young charge to be free and independent, undivided and unself-conflicted (see earlier selections from* Emile, *above). Later, he adds, his aim will be fully achieved, and young Emile will attain supreme happiness, through love in marriage. Through the courtship of Emile and Sophie (excerpted here in selections from Book V), we learn how these seemingly opposite goals—independence and happiness in love and marriage—can be achieved. This courtship is the culmination of Emile's education.*

The young lovers are brought together in the heart of Sophie's family's country home, at the dinner table, under the watchful gaze of parents and tutor. Well before dinner is completed, the couple find themselves completely and mutually absorbed in one another. Sophie has been moved by the tenderness Emile shows toward her parents, and Emile, first by her name (Sophie is the name earlier suggested by his tutor for the ideal woman whom he has been in search of for many months), then by her features, gestures, and "natural and timid voice." Neither then nor during their early subsequent visits does a word pass directly between them, but no word seems possible or necessary. Emile, we are told, acts as if his very soul is animated by Sophie and, as we observe, Sophie acts likewise. The once free and independent young Emile becomes literally enthralled, so much so that for the first time in his life he even resorts to guile to achieve his end: to be in Sophie's presence. Their courtship, which proceeds in earnest after these initial meetings, is primarily designed to enable Emile, now very much in love, to regain his independence and thereby to become, according to Rousseau, a worthy husband for the estimable Sophie. As in the rest of the Emile, *the education that constitutes the courtship is especially directed at Emile, but its lessons seem clearly meant for Sophie as well. The courtship unfolds like a carefully orchestrated fugue in which each voice passes, in turn, between the ecstasy of apparent acceptance and the agony of apparent rejection. Each stage is designed to allow the young lovers to reveal themselves as they are, by nature and rearing, to each other and, most importantly, to themselves. The self-consciousness and self-governance thus achieved mark the completion of Emile's education. Their passion, now disciplined by courtship, also gains for both Emile and Sophie an equal entrance into what Rousseau believes is the only kind of human association that is natural, free, pleasant, and not founded on exploitative or mercenary interests. Together they become a natural whole, precisely as they choose to do so freely, equally, and lovingly.*

Rousseau, master of detail, not only shows us the joys and sorrows the young couple are made to endure; he explicitly reminds us that no part of their courtship occurs by chance. Our lives are not so carefully arranged; and most readers are repelled by the tutor's manipulation of Emile. Nevertheless, these very contrivances, part of Rousseau's pedagogical artfulness, alert us to certain crucial concerns and questions everyone might face, tutor or no tutor. The questions Rousseau pointedly puts to his readers invite us to reflect on how the various episodes in the courtship contribute to their overall purpose. For those of us who value our freedom and yet still want to be married, they invite, as well, reflection on our own assumptions and practices. To paraphrase Rousseau's questions: Why does Emile find Sophie far from the city, in the depths of a distant retreat? Why is he made to meet her in the way, and at the place, he does? Why must he find a dwelling far away from hers? Why is he allowed to see her so rarely and, even then, forced to purchase the pleasure of seeing her with so much exertion? To add questions of our own: Why must Emile, whom we learn is a wealthy man, be gainfully employed? Why must Sophie visit him at work? What do Emile and Sophie learn about themselves? Why might their hard-won self-knowledge be conducive to lasting love and marriage? Why, even after they pledge their troths, must they part? Finally, why does Rousseau say that courtship is really the best time of one's life?

One day, after having strayed more than usual in valleys and mountains where no path can be perceived, we can no longer find our way again. It makes little difference to us. All paths are good, provided one arrives. But, still, one has to arrive somewhere when one is hungry. Happily we find a peasant who takes us to his cottage. We eat his meager dinner with great appetite. On seeing us so tired and famished, he says to us, "If the good Lord had led you to the other side of the hill you would have been better received . . . you would have found a house of peace . . . such charitable people . . . such good people . . . They are not better-hearted than I am, but they are richer, although it is said that they were previously much more so . . . they are not suffering, thank God, and the whole countryside feels the effects of what remains to them."

At this mention of good people, the good Emile's heart gladdens. "My friend," he says, looking at me, "let us go to that house whose masters are blessed in the neighborhood. I would be glad to see them. Perhaps they will be glad to receive us, too. I am sure they will receive us well. If they are of our kind, we shall be of theirs."

Having received good directions to the house, we leave and wander through the woods. On the way heavy rain surprises us. It slows us up without stopping us. Finally we find our way, and in the evening we arrive at the designated house. In the hamlet which surrounds it, this house alone, although simple, stands out. We present ourselves. We ask hospitality. We are taken to speak to the master. He questions us, but politely. Without telling him the subject of our trip, we tell him the reason for our detour. From his former opulence he has retained a facility for recognizing the station of people by their manners. Whoever has lived in high society is rarely mistaken about that. On the basis of this passport we are admitted.

We are shown to a very little, but clean and comfortable apartment. A fire is made. We find linen, garments, everything we need. "What!" says Emile. "It is as though we were expected! Oh how right the peasant was! What attention, what goodness, what foresight! And for unknowns! I believe I am living in Homer's time." "Be sensitive to all this," I say to him, "but don't be surprised. Wherever strangers are rare, they are welcome. Nothing makes one more hospitable than seldom needing to be. It is the abundance of guests which destroys hospitality. In the time of Homer people hardly traveled, and travelers were well received everywhere. We are perhaps the only transients who have been seen here during the whole year." "It makes no difference," he replies. "That itself is praise—to know how to get along without guests and always to receive them well."

After we have dried ourselves and straightened up, we go to rejoin the master of the house. He presents his wife to us. She receives us not only politely but with kindness. The honor of her glances belongs to Emile. A mother in her situation rarely sees a man of that age enter her home without uneasiness or at least curiosity.

For our sake they have supper served early. On entering the dining room, we see five settings. We are seated, but an empty place remains. A girl enters, curtseys deeply, and sits down modestly without speaking. Emile, busy with his hunger or his answers, greets her and continues to speak and eat. The principal object of his trip is as distant from his thoughts as he believes himself to be still distant from its goal. The discussion turns to the travelers' losing their way. "Sir," the master of the house says to him, "you appear to me to be a likable and wise young man, and that makes me think that you and your governor have arrived here tired and wet like Telemachus and Mentor on Calypso's island." "It is true," Emile answers, "that we find here the hospitality of Calypso." His Mentor adds, "And the charms of Eucharis."[1] But although Emile knows the *Odyssey*, he has not read *Telemachus*. He does not know who Eucharis is. As for the girl, I see her blush up to her eyes, lower them toward her plate, and not dare to murmur. Her mother, who notices her embarrassment, gives a sign to her father, and he changes the subject. In speaking of his solitude, he gradually gets involved in the story of the events which confined him to it: the misfortunes of his life, the constancy of his wife, the consolations

---

[1]A character in Fénelon's *Telemachus*, one of the two books Sophie has read.

they have found in their union, the sweet and peaceful life they lead in their retreat—and still without saying a word about the girl. All this forms an agreeable and touching story which cannot be heard without interest. Emile, moved and filled with tenderness, stops eating in order to listen. Finally, at the part where the most decent of men enlarges with great pleasure on the attachment of the worthiest of women, the young traveler is beside himself; with one hand he grips the husband's hand, and with the other he takes the wife's hand and leans toward it rapturously, sprinkling it with tears. The young man's naïve vivacity enchants everyone, but the girl, more sensitive than anyone to this mark of his good heart, believes she sees Telemachus affected by Philoctetes' misfortunes. She furtively turns her eyes toward him in order to examine his face better. She finds nothing there which denies the comparison. His easy bearing is free without being arrogant. His manners are lively without being giddy. His sensitivity makes his glance gentler, his expression more touching. The girl, seeing him cry, is ready to mingle her tears with his. But even with so fair a pretext, a secret shame restrains her. She already reproaches herself for the tears about to escape her eyes, as though it were bad to shed them for her family.

Her mother, who from the beginning of the supper has not stopped watching her, sees her constraint and delivers her from it by sending her on an errand. A minute later the young girl returns, but she is so little recovered that her disorder is visible to all eyes. Her mother gently says to her, "Sophie, pull yourself together. Will you never stop crying over the misfortunes of your parents? You, who console them for their misfortunes, must not be more sensitive to them than they are themselves."

At the name Sophie, you would have seen Emile shiver. Struck by so dear a name, he is wakened with a start and casts an avid glance at the girl who dares to bear it. "Sophie, O Sophie! Is it you whom my heart seeks? Is it you whom my heart loves?" He observes her and contemplates her with a sort of fear and distrust. He does not see exactly the face that he had depicted to himself. He does not know whether the one he sees is better or worse. He studies each feature; he spies on each movement, each gesture. In all he finds countless confused interpretations. He would give half his life for her to be willing to speak a single word. Uneasy and troubled, he looks at me. His eyes put a hundred questions to me and make a hundred reproaches all at once. He seems to say to me with each look, "Guide me while there is time. If my heart yields and is mistaken, I shall never recover in all my days."

Emile is worse at disguising his feelings than any man in the world. How would he disguise them in the greatest disturbance of his life, in the presence of four spectators who examine him and of whom the most distracted in appearance is actually the most attentive? His disorder does not escape Sophie's penetrating eyes. Moreover, his eyes teach her that she is the cause of his disorder. She sees that this apprehensiveness is not yet love. But what difference does it make? He is involved with her, and that is enough. She will be most unlucky if he becomes involved with her with impunity.

Mothers have eyes just as their daughters do, and they have experience to boot. Sophie's mother smiles at the success of our projects. She reads the hearts of the two young people. She sees that it is time to captivate the heart of the new Telemachus. She gets her daughter to speak. Her daughter responds with her natural gentleness in a timid voice which makes its effect all the better. At the first sound of this voice Emile surrenders. It is Sophie. He no longer doubts it. If it were not she, it would be too late for him to turn back.

It is then that the charms of this enchanting girl flow in torrents into his heart, and he begins to swallow with deep draughts the poison with which she intoxicates him. He no longer speaks, he no longer responds; he sees only Sophie, he hears only Sophie. If she says a word, he opens his mouth; if she lowers her eyes, he lowers his; if he sees her breathe, he sighs. It is Sophie's soul which appears to animate him. How his own soul has changed in a few instants! It is no longer Sophie's turn to tremble; it is Emile's. Farewell freedom, naïveté, frankness! Confused, embarrassed, fearful, he no longer dares to look around him for fear of seeing that he is being looked at. Ashamed to let the others see through him, he would like to make himself invisible to everyone in order to sate himself with contemplating her without being observed. Sophie, on the contrary, is reassured by Emile's fear. She sees her triumph. She enjoys it:

Nol mostra già, ben che in suo cor ne rida.[2]

Her countenance has not changed. But in spite of this modest air and these lowered eyes, her tender heart palpitates with joy and tells her that Telemachus has been found.

If I enter here into the perhaps too naïve and too simple history of their innocent love, people will regard these details as a frivolous game, but they will be wrong. They do not sufficiently consider the influence which a man's first liaison with a woman ought to have on the course of both their lives. They do not see that a first impression as lively as that of love, or the inclination which takes its place, has distant effects whose links are not perceived in the progress of the years but do not cease to act until death. We are given treatises on education consisting of useless, pedantic, bloated verbiage about the chimerical duties of children, and we are not told a word about the most important and most difficult part of the whole of education—the crisis that serves as a passage from childhood to man's estate. If I have been able to make these essays

---

[2] "She does not show it, although she rejoices in her heart." Tasso *Jerusalem Delivered* IV 33.

useful in some respect, it is especially by having expanded at great length on this essential part, omitted by all others, and by not letting myself be rebuffed in this enterprise by false delicacies or frightened by difficulties of language. If I have said what must be done, I have said what I ought to have said. It makes very little difference to me if I have written a romance. A fair romance it is indeed, the romance of human nature. If it is to be found only in this writing, is that my fault? This ought to be the history of my species. You who deprave it, it is you who make a romance of my book.

Another consideration which strengthens the first is that I am dealing here not with a young man given over from childhood to fear, covetousness, envy, pride, and all the passions that serve as instruments for common educations, but with a young man for whom this is not only his first love but his first passion of any kind. On this passion, perhaps the only one he will feel intensely in his whole life, depends the final form his character is going to take. Once fixed by a durable passion, his way of thinking, his sentiments, and his tastes are going to acquire a consistency which will no longer permit them to deteriorate.

One can conceive that for Emile and me the night following such an evening is not spent entirely in sleeping. What? Ought the mere agreement of a name to have so much power over a wise man? Is there only one Sophie in the world? Do they all resemble one another in soul as they do in name? Are all the Sophies he will see his? Is he mad, getting passionate in this way about an unknown girl to whom he has never spoken? Wait, young man. Examine. Observe. You do not even know yet whose house you are in, and to hear you one would believe you are already in your own home.

This is not the time for lessons, and such lessons are not going to be heard. They only have the effect of giving the young man a new interest in Sophie out of the desire to justify his inclination. This resemblance of names, this meeting (which he believes is fortuitous), and my very reserve have only the effect of exciting his vivacity. Already Sophie appears too estimable for him not to be sure of making me love her.

I suspect that the next morning Emile will try to dress himself up more carefully in his sorry traveling outfit. He does not fail to do so. But I laugh at his eagerness to make use of the household linen. I see through his thought. I realize with pleasure that, by seeing to it that there are things to be returned or exchanged, he seeks to establish for himself a sort of connection which gives him the right to send things back here and come back himself.

I had also expected to find Sophie a bit more dressed up. I was mistaken. This vulgar coquetry is good for those whom one only wants to please. The coquetry of true love is more refined; it has very different pretensions. Sophie is dressed up even more simply and casually than the day before, although still with scrupulous cleanliness. I see coquetry in this casualness only because I see affectation in it. Sophie knows that more studied adornment is a declaration, but she does not know that more casual adornment is also a declaration. She shows that she is not content to please by her dress, that she also wants to please by her person. What difference does it make to her lover how she is dressed provided that he sees that she is concerned with him? Already sure of her empire, Sophie does not content herself with appealing to Emile's eyes with her charms; his heart must seek them out. It is no longer enough for her that he see her charms; she wants him to suppose them. Has he not seen enough of them to be obliged to guess the rest?

It may be believed that, during the time of our discussions that night, Sophie and her mother also did not remain silent. There were confessions extracted, instructions given. The next day's gathering has been well prepared. It is not yet twelve hours since our young people saw each other for the first time. They have not yet said a single word to each other, and already one sees that they have reached an understanding. Their manner is not familiar; it is embarrassed and timid; they do not speak to each other. Their eyes are lowered and seem to avoid each other; that is itself a sign of communication; they avoid each other, but by agreement. They already sense the need of mystery before having said anything to each other. As we leave, we ask permission to come back ourselves to return what we are taking away with us. Emile's mouth asks this permission from the father and the mother, while his apprehensive eyes, turned to the daughter, ask it from her much more insistently. Sophie says nothing, makes no sign, appears to see nothing and hear nothing. But she blushes, and this blush is a still clearer answer than her parents'.

We are permitted to return without being invited to stay over. This conduct is suitable. Board is given to passers-by who are at a loss for lodging, but it is not seemly for a lover to sleep in his beloved's home.

We hardly are out of this dear house before Emile thinks of establishing ourselves in the neighborhood. Even the nearest cottage seems too distant. He would like to sleep in the ditches of the manor. "Giddy young man!" I say to him in a tone of pity. "What, does passion already blind you? Do you already no longer see either propriety or reason? Unfortunate one! You believe you are in love, and you want to dishonor your beloved! What will be said when it is known that a young man who leaves her home sleeps in the vicinity? You love her, you say! Will you then ruin her reputation? Is that the payment for the hospitality her parents have granted you? Will you cause the disgrace of the girl from whom you expect your happiness?" "Well," he answers, "what difference do the vain talk of men and their unjust suspicions make? Haven't you yourself taught me to take no notice of it? Who knows better than I how much I honor Sophie, how much I want to respect her? My attachment will not cause her shame; it will cause her glory; it will be worthy of her. If my heart and my attentions everywhere render her the homage she deserves, how can I insult her?" "Dear Emile," I respond, embracing him, "you reason for yourself. Learn to reason for her. Do not compare the honor of one sex to that of the other. They have entirely different principles. These principles are equally solid and reasonable because they derive equally from nature; and the same virtue which makes you despise men's talk for yourself obliges you to respect it for your beloved. Your honor is in you alone, and hers depends on others. To neglect it would be to wound your own honor; and you do not render yourself what you owe yourself if you are the cause of her not being rendered what is owed her."

Then I explain the reasons for these differences to him, making him sense what an injustice it would be to take no account of these differences. Who has told him that he will be the husband of Sophie, whose sentiments he is ignorant of, whose heart (or whose parents) has perhaps made prior commitments, whom he does not know, and who perhaps suits him in none of the ways which can make for a happy marriage? Does he not know that for a girl every scandal is an indelible stain, which even her marriage to the man who caused it does not remove? What sensitive man wants to ruin the girl he loves? What decent man wants to make an unfortunate girl weep forever for the misfortune of having pleased him?

The young man, who is always extreme in his ideas, is frightened by the consequences I make him envisage, and he now believes he is never far enough away from Sophie's dwelling. He doubles his pace to flee more quickly. He looks around to see whether we are overheard. He would sacrifice his happiness a thousand times for the honor of the one he loves. He would rather not see her again in his life than cause her any displeasure. This is the first fruit of the cares I took in his youth to form in him a heart that knows how to love.

We have to find, then, an abode that is distant but within range. We seek, and we make inquiries; we learn that two leagues away there is a town. We go to find lodging there rather than in nearer villages, where our stay would become suspect. The new lover finally arrives there full of love, hope, joy, and, especially, good sentiments. And this is how, by directing his nascent passion little by little toward what is good and decent, without his being aware of it I dispose all of his inclinations to take the same bent.

I approach the end of my career. I already see it in the distance. All the great difficulties are overcome. All the great obstacles are surmounted. Nothing difficult is left for me to do, except not to spoil my work by hurrying to consummate it. In the uncertainty of human life, let us avoid above all the false prudence of sacrificing the present for the future; this is often to sacrifice what is for what will not be. Let us make man happy at all ages lest, after many cares, he die before having been happy. Now, if there is a time to enjoy life, it is surely the end of adolescence when the faculties of body and soul have acquired their greatest vigor. Man is then in the middle of his course, and he sees from the greatest distance the two end points which make him feel its brevity. If imprudent youth makes mistakes, it is not because it wants enjoyment; it is because it seeks enjoyment where it is not, and because, while preparing a miserable future for itself, it does not even know how to use the present moment.

Consider my Emile—now past twenty, well formed, well constituted in mind and body, strong, healthy, fit, skillful, robust, full of sense, reason, goodness, and humanity, a man with morals and taste, loving the beautiful, doing the good, free from the empire of cruel passions, exempt from the yoke of opinion, but subject to the law of wisdom and submissive to the voice of friendship, possessing all the useful talents and some of the agreeable ones, caring little for riches, with his means of support in his arms, and not afraid of lacking bread whatever happens. Now he is intoxicated by a nascent passion. His heart opens itself to the first fires of love. Its sweet illusions make him a new universe of delight and enjoyment. He loves a lovable object who is even more lovable for her character than for her person. He hopes for, he expects a return that he feels is his due. It is from the similarity of their hearts, from the conjunction of decent sentiments that their first inclination was formed. This inclination ought to be durable. He yields confidently, even reasonably, to the most charming delirium, without fear, without regret, without remorse, without any other worry than that which is inseparable from the sentiment of happiness. What is lacking to his happiness? Look, consider, imagine what he still needs that can accord with what he has. He enjoys together all the goods that can be obtained at once. None can be added except at the expense of another. He is as happy as a man can be. Shall I at this moment shorten so sweet a destiny? Shall I trouble so pure a delight? Ah, the whole value of life is in the felicity he tastes! What could I give him which was worth what I had taken away from him? Even in putting the crown on his happiness, I would destroy its greatest charm. This supreme happiness is a hundred times sweeter to hope for than to obtain. One enjoys it better when one looks forward to it than when one tastes it. O good Emile, love and be loved! Enjoy a long time before possessing. Enjoy love and innocence at the same time. Make your paradise on earth while awaiting the other one. I shall not shorten this happy time of your life. I shall spin out its enchantment for you. I shall prolong it as much as possible. Alas, it has to end, and end soon. But I shall at least make it last forever in your memory and make you never repent having tasted it.

Emile does not forget that we have things to return. As soon as they are ready, we take horses and set out at full speed; this one time, Emile would like to have arrived as soon as we leave. When the heart is opened to the passions, it is opened to life's boredom. If I have not wasted my time, his whole life will not pass in this way.

Unhappily there is a severe break in the road and the countryside proves heavy going. We get lost. He notices it first, and without impatience and without complaint he gives all his attention to finding his way again. He wanders for a long time before knowing where he is, always with the same coolness. This means nothing to you but a great deal to me, since I know his hot nature. I see the fruit of the care I have taken since his childhood to harden him against the blows of necessity.

Finally we arrive. The reception given us is far more simple and more obliging than the first time. We are already old acquaintances. Emile and Sophie greet each other with a bit of embarrassment and still do not speak to each other. What would they say to each other in our presence? The conversation they require has no need of witnesses. We take a walk in the garden. It has as its parterre a very well-arranged kitchen garden; as its park it has an orchard covered with large, beautiful fruit trees of every kind, interspersed with pretty streams and beds full of flowers. "What a beautiful place," cries out Emile, full of his Homer and always enthusiastic. "I believe I see the garden of Alcinous." The daughter would like to know who Alcinous is, and the mother asks. "Alcinous," I tell them, "was a king of Corcyra whose garden, described by Homer, is criticized by people of taste for being too simple and without enough adornment. This Alcinous had a lovable daughter who dreamed, on the eve of a stranger's receiving hospitality from her father, that she would soon have a husband." Sophie is taken aback and blushes, lowers her eyes, bites her tongue. One cannot imagine such embarrassment. Her father, who takes pleasure in increasing it, joins in and says that the young princess herself went to wash the linen in the river. "Do you believe," he continues, "that she would have disdained to touch the dirty napkins, saying that they smelled of burnt fat?" Sophie, against whom the blow is directed, forgets her natural timidity and excuses herself with vivacity: her papa knows very well that all the small linen would have no other laundress than her if she had been allowed to do it, and that she would have done more of it with pleasure if she had been so directed. While speaking these words, she looks at me on the sly with an apprehensiveness which I cannot help laughing at, reading in her ingenuous heart the alarm which makes her speak. Her father is cruel enough to pick up this bit of giddiness by asking her in a mocking tone what occasion she has for speaking on her own behalf here, and what she has in common with Alcinous' daughter? Ashamed and trembling, she no longer dares to breathe a word or look at anyone. Charming girl, the time for feigning is past. You have now made your declaration in spite of yourself.

Soon this little scene is forgotten, or appears to be. Very happily for Sophie, Emile is the only one who has understood nothing of it. The walk continues, and our young people, who at first were at our sides, have difficulty adjusting themselves to the slowness of our pace. Imperceptibly they move ahead of us, approach each other, and finally meet, and we see them rather far in front of us. Sophie seems attentive and composed. Emile speaks and gesticulates with fire. Their discussion does not appear to bore them. At the end of a solid hour we turn back; we call them, and they return, but now they are the slow ones, and we see that they use the time profitably. Finally their conversation suddenly stops before we are within range of hearing them, and they speed up in order to rejoin us. Emile approaches us with an open and caressing air. His eyes sparkle with joy; however, he turns them with a bit of apprehensiveness toward Sophie's mother to see the reception she will give him. Sophie is far from having so relaxed a bearing; as she approaches, she seems quite embarrassed to be seen in a tête-à-tête with a young man—she who has so often been with other young men without being bothered by it and without its ever having been treated as wrong. Hurrying to reach her mother, she is a bit out of breath; she says a few words which do not mean a great deal, as if to give the impression of having been there for a long time.

From the serenity visible on the faces of these lovable children one sees that this conversation has relieved their young hearts of a great weight. They are no less reserved with one another, but it is a less embarrassed reserve. It now comes only from Emile's respect, Sophie's modesty, and the decency of both. Emile dares to address a few words to her; sometimes she dares to respond, but never does she open her mouth for that purpose without casting her eyes toward her mother's. She changes most palpably in her behavior toward me. She gives evidence of a more eager regard for me. She looks at me with interest; she speaks to me affectionately. She is attentive to what might please me. I see that she honors me with her esteem, and that she is not indifferent to obtaining mine. I understand that Emile has spoken to her about me. One would say that they have already plotted to win me over. Nothing of the kind has happened, however, and Sophie herself is not won so quickly. He will perhaps need my favor with her more than hers with me. Charming couple! ... In thinking that my young friend's sensitive heart has given me a great part in his first discussion with his beloved, I enjoy the reward for my effort. His friendship has repaid everything.

The visits are repeated. The conversations between our young people become more frequent. Intoxicated by love, Emile believes he has already attained his happiness. However, he does not get Sophie's formal consent. She listens to him and says nothing to him. Emile knows the extent of her modesty. He is not very surprised by so much restraint. He senses that he does not stand badly with her. He knows that it is fathers who marry off children. He supposes that Sophie is waiting for an order from her parents. He asks her permission to solicit it. She does not oppose his doing so. He speaks to me about it; I speak for him in his own presence. What a surprise for him to learn that it is up to Sophie alone, and that to make him happy she has only to want to do so. He begins no longer to understand anything about her conduct. His confidence diminishes. He is alarmed; he sees that he has not gotten as far as he thought he had. And it is then that his tenderest love employs its most touching language to sway her.

Emile is not the kind of man who can guess what is hindering him. If he is not told, he will never find out, and Sophie is too proud to tell him. The difficulties which are holding her back would only make another girl more eager. She has not forgotten her parents' lessons. She is poor, and Emile is rich; she knows it. He has a great deal to do in order to gain her esteem! What merit must he possess in order to wipe away this inequality? But how could he dream of these obstacles? Does Emile know he is rich? Does he even deign to inquire about it? Thank heaven he has no need to be rich. He knows how to be beneficent without riches. The good he does is drawn from his heart and not from his purse. He gives his time, his care, his affections, and his person to the unhappy; and in estimating his benefactions, he hardly dares to count the money he scatters among the indigent.

Not knowing what to blame for his disgrace, he attributes it to his own fault: for who would dare to accuse the object of his adoration of caprice? The humiliation of his *amour-propre* increases his regret that his love has been spurned. He no longer approaches Sophie with that lovable confidence of a heart which feels it is worthy of hers. He is fearful and trembling before her. He no longer hopes to touch her by tenderness. He seeks to sway her by pity. Sometimes his patience wearies, and vexation is ready to take its place. Sophie seems to foresee these storms, and glances at him. This glance alone disarms and intimidates him. He is more thoroughly subjected than before.

Troubled by this obstinate resistance and this invincible silence, he opens his heart to his friend. He confides to him the pain of a heart broken by sadness. He implores his assistance and his counsel. "What an impenetrable mystery! She is interested in my fate; I cannot doubt it. Far from avoiding me, she enjoys being with me. When I arrive, she gives signs of joy, and when I leave, of regret. She receives my attentions kindly. My services appear to please her. She deigns to give me advice, sometimes even orders. Nevertheless, she rejects my entreaties and my prayers. When I dare to speak of union, she imperiously imposes silence on me; and if I add another word, she leaves me on the spot. For what strange reason does she want me to be hers without wanting to hear a word about her being mine? You whom she honors, you whom she loves and whom she will not dare to silence, speak, make her speak. Serve your friend. Crown your work. Do not make all your care fatal to your pupil. Ah, what he has gotten from you will cause his misery if you do not complete his happiness!"

I speak to Sophie, and with little effort I extract from her a secret I knew before she told it to me. I have more difficulty in obtaining permission to inform Emile. Finally, I do obtain it and make use of it. This explanation sends him into a state of astonishment from which he cannot recover. He understands nothing of this delicacy. He cannot imagine what effect a few *écus* more or less have on character and merit. When I make him understand what they do to prejudices, he starts laughing, and, transported with joy, he wants to leave on the spot to go and tear up everything, throw out everything, renounce everything in order to have the honor of being as poor as Sophie and to return worthy of being her husband.

"What!" I say, stopping him and laughing in turn at his impetuosity. "Will this young mind never become mature; and after having philosophized your whole life, will you never learn to reason? How can you not see that, in following your insane project, you are going to make your situation worse and Sophie more intractable? It is a small advantage to have a bit more property than she does, but it would be a very big advantage to have sacrificed it all for her; and if her pride cannot resolve to accept the former obligation to you, how will it resolve to accept the latter? If she cannot endure that a husband be able to reproach her for having enriched her, will she endure that he be able to reproach her with having impoverished himself for her? O unhappy fellow, tremble lest she suspect you of having had this project! Instead, become economical and careful for love of her, lest she accuse you of wanting to win her by trickery and of voluntarily sacrificing to her what you lose by neglect.

"Do you believe that at bottom great property frightens her and that it is precisely wealth that is the source of her opposition? No, dear Emile, it has a more solid and weightier cause—namely, the effect that wealth has on the soul of the possessor. She knows that fortune's goods are always preferred over everything else by those who have them. The rich all count gold before merit. In regard to the family resources constituted by the contribution of money and services, they always find that the latter never compensate for the former; they think that someone is still in their debt when he has spent his life serving them while eating their bread. What is there for you to do, Emile, to reassure her about her fears? Make yourself well known to her. That is not the business of a day. Show her treasures in your noble soul that are sufficient to redeem those with which you have the misfortune to be endowed. By dint of constancy and time surmount her resistance. By dint of great and generous sentiments force her to forget your riches. Love her, serve her, serve her respectable parents.

Prove to her that these efforts are the effect not of a mad and fleeting passion but of ineffaceable principles engraved in the depths of your heart. Give proper honor to merit that has been insulted by fortune. This is the only means of reconciling her to merit favored by fortune."

One may conceive what transports of joy this speech gives to the young man, how much confidence and hope it gives him. His decent heart is delighted that in order to please Sophie he has to do exactly what he would do on his own if Sophie did not exist or if he were not in love with her. However little one has understood his character, who will not be able to imagine his conduct on this occasion?

Now I am the confidant of my two good young people and the mediator of their loves! A fine employment for a governor! So fine that never in my life have I done anything which raised me so much in my own eyes and made me so satisfied with myself. Moreover, this employment does not fail to have its agreeable aspects. I am not unwelcome in the house. I am entrusted with the care of keeping the lovers in order. Emile, who is constantly trembling for fear of displeasing me, was never so docile. The little girl overwhelms me with friendliness by which I am not deceived, and I take for myself only what is intended for me. It is thus that she compensates herself indirectly for the respect she imposes on Emile. Through me she gives him countless tender caresses which she would rather die than give to him directly. And Emile, who knows that I do not want to harm his interests, is charmed that I am on good terms with her. When she refuses his arm in walking, he consoles himself with the fact that it is to prefer mine to his. He leaves without complaint, grasping my hand, and saying softly to me with his eyes as well as his voice, "Friend, speak for me." His eyes follow us with interest. He tries to read our sentiments in our faces and to interpret our speeches by our gestures. He knows that nothing of what is said between us is inconsequential for him. Good Sophie, how your sincere heart is at ease when, without being heard by Telemachus, you can converse with his Mentor! With what lovable frankness you let him read everything going on in your tender heart! With what pleasure you show him all your esteem for his pupil! With what touching ingenuousness you let him discern even sweeter sentiments! With what feigned anger you send the importunate Emile away when impatience forces him to interrupt you! With what charming vexation you reproach him for his tactlessness when he comes and prevents you from speaking well of him, from hearing good things about him, and from always drawing some new reason for loving him from my responses!

Having thus gotten himself tolerated as a suitor, Emile takes advantage of all the rights of that position. He speaks, he urges, he entreats, he importunes. If he is spoken to harshly or if he is mistreated, it makes little difference to him provided that he make himself heard. Finally, though not without effort, he induces Sophie to be kind enough to assume openly a beloved's authority over him—to prescribe to him what he must do, to order instead of to ask, to accept instead of to thank, to regulate the number and the time of his visits, to forbid him to come until this day or to stay past that hour. All this is not done as a game but very seriously. Although it was an effort to get her to accept these rights, she makes use of them with a rigor that often reduces poor Emile to regret that he has given them to her. But whatever she commands, he does not reply, and often, when leaving to obey her, he looks at me with eyes full of joy telling me: "You see that she has taken possession of me." Meanwhile, the proud girl observes him stealthily and smiles secretly at her slave's pride.

Albani and Raphael, loan me the brush with which to paint sensuous delight. Divine Milton, teach my coarse pen to describe the pleasures of love and innocence. But, no, hide your lying arts before the holy truth of nature. You need only have sensitive hearts and decent souls; then let your imagination wander without constraint in contemplating the transports of two young lovers who—under the eyes of their parents and their guides—are untroubled as they yield themselves to the sweet illusion delighting them; in the intoxication of their desires they advance slowly toward their goal, weaving flowers and garlands around the happy bond which is going to unite them until the grave. So many charming images intoxicate me that I bring them together without order and without coherence; the delirium they cause prevents me from connecting them. Oh, who has a heart and does not know how to depict for himself the delicious scenes of the father, the mother, the daughter, the governor, and the pupil in their various situations and their respective contributions to the union of the most charming couple that can be made happy by love and virtue?

Having become truly eager to please, Emile now begins to sense the value of the agreeable talents with which he has provided himself. Sophie loves to sing. He sings with her. He does more; he teaches her music. She is lively and light, and she likes to jump. He dances with her; he turns her jumps into steps; he trains her. These lessons are charming. Rollicking gaiety animates them, and it mitigates the timid respect of love. A lover is permitted to give these lessons voluptuously. He is permitted to be his mistress's master.

They have an old harpsichord that is in very bad shape. Emile fixes it and tunes it. He is a maker of keyboard and stringed instruments as well as a carpenter. His maxim was always to learn to do without the help of others in regard to everything he could do himself. The house is in a picturesque setting. He draws different views of it—to which Sophie sometimes puts her hand—and she ornaments her father's study with them. Their frames are not gilded and do not need to be. By watching Emile sketch and imitating him, she becomes more skillful from following his example. She cultivates all the talents, and her charm embellishes them all. Her father and mother recall their former opulence in seeing the fine arts, which alone made opulence dear to them, flourishing around them again. Love has adorned their entire home. Without expense and without effort, love alone establishes there the reign of the same pleasures which they previously assembled only by dint of money and boredom.

As the idolater enriches the object of his worship with treasures that he esteems and adorns on the altar the God he adores, so the lover—although he may very well see his mistress as perfect—constantly wants to add new ornaments to her. She does not need them in order to please him, but he needs to adorn her. It is a new homage he believes he is doing her and a new interest he adds to the pleasure of contemplating her. It seems to him that nothing beautiful is in its place when it is not ornamenting the supreme beauty. It is both a touching and a laughable spectacle to see Emile eager to teach Sophie all he knows, without considering whether what he wants to teach her is to her taste or is suitable for her. He tells her about everything, he explains everything to her with a puerile eagerness. He believes he has only to speak and she will understand on the spot. He fancies beforehand the pleasure he will have in reasoning and in philosophizing with her. He regards as useless all the attainments he cannot display to her eyes. He almost blushes at knowing something she does not know.

Therefore, he gives her lessons in philosophy, physics, mathematics, history—in a word, in everything. Sophie lends herself with pleasure to his zeal and tries to profit from it. When he can obtain permission to give his lessons on his knees before her, how content Emile is! He believes he sees the heavens opened. However this position, more constricting for the student than for the master, is not the most favorable for instruction. On such occasions she does not know exactly what to do with her eyes to avoid those that are pursuing them; and when they meet, the lesson does not gain by it.

. . . Sometimes on their walks, as they contemplate nature's marvels, their innocent and pure hearts dare to lift themselves up to its Author. They do not fear His presence. They open their hearts jointly before Him.

"What, two lovers in the flower of age use their tête-à-tête to speak of religion? They spend their time saying their catechism?" Why must you debase something sublime? Yes, no doubt they do say it, under the influence of the illusion which charms them. They see each other as perfect; they love one another; they converse with each other enthusiastically about what gives virtue its reward. The sacrifices they make to virtue render it dear to them. In the midst of transports that they must vanquish, they sometimes shed tears together purer than heaven's dew, and these sweet tears constitute the enchantment of their life. They are in the most charming delirium that human souls have ever experienced. Their very privations add to their happiness and do them honor in their own eyes for their sacrifices. Sensual men, bodies without souls, one day they will know your pleasures, and for their whole lives they will regret the happy time during which they denied them to themselves.

Despite their being on such good terms, they do not fail to have some disagreements, even some quarrels. The mistress is not without caprice nor the lover without anger. But these little storms pass rapidly and only have the effect of strengthening their union. Experience even teaches Emile not to fear them so much; the reconciliations are always more advantageous to him than the spats are harmful. The fruit of their first spat made him hope for as much from the others. He was wrong. But, in the end, if he does not always take away so palpable a profit, he always gains from these spats by seeing Sophie confirm her sincere interest in his heart. People will want to know what this profit is. I will gladly consent to tell them, for this example gives me the occasion to expound a most useful maxim and to combat a most baneful one.

Emile loves. Therefore, he is not bold. And it can even more readily be conceived that the imperious Sophie is not the girl to overlook his familiarities. Since moderation has its limits in all things, she could be charged with too much harshness rather than too much indulgence; and her father himself sometimes fears that her extreme pride will degenerate into haughtiness. In their most secret tête-à-têtes Emile would not dare to solicit the least favor nor even to appear to aspire to one. When she is so kind as to take his arm during a walk—a favor she does not allow to be turned into a right—he hardly dares occasionally to sigh and press this arm against his breast. Nevertheless, after long constraint he furtively ventures to kiss her dress, and several times he is lucky enough for Sophie to be so kind as not to notice it. One day when he wants to take the same liberty a bit more openly, she decides to take it amiss. He persists. She gets irritated. Vexation dictates a few stinging words. Emile does not endure them without reply. The rest of the day is passed in pouting, and they separate very discontented.

Sophie is ill at ease. Her mother is her confidant. How could she hide her chagrin from her? It is her first spat, and a spat that lasts an hour is so great a business! She repents her mistake. Her mother permits her to make amends. Her father orders her to do so.

The next day Emile is apprehensive and returns earlier than usual. Sophie is in her mother's dressing room. Her father is also there. Emile enters respectfully but with a sad air. Sophie's father and mother have hardly greeted him when Sophie turns around and, extending her hand, asks him in a caressing tone how he is. It is clear that this pretty hand has been extended only in order to be kissed. He takes it and does not kiss it. Sophie is a bit ashamed, and she withdraws her hand with as good grace as is possible for her. Emile, who is not experienced in women's ways and does not know the purpose of their caprices, does not forget easily and is not so quickly appeased. Sophie's father, seeing her embarrassment, succeeds in disconcerting her by mockery. The poor girl is confused and humiliated; she no longer knows what she is doing and would give anything in the world to dare to cry. The more she constrains herself, the more her heart swells. A tear finally escapes her in spite of her efforts. Emile sees this tear, rushes to her knees, takes her hand, and kisses it several times, entranced. "Really, you are too good," says her father, bursting out laughing. "I would have less indulgence for all these mad girls, and I would punish the mouth that offended me." Emboldened by this speech, Emile turns a suppliant eye toward Sophie's mother and, believing he sees a sign of consent, tremblingly approaches Sophie's face. She turns her head away and, in order to save her mouth, exposes a rosy cheek. The tactless boy is not satisfied. She resists feebly. What a kiss, if it were not stolen under a mother's eyes! Severe Sophie, take care. He will often ask you for permission to kiss your dress, provided that you sometimes refuse it.

After this exemplary punishment Sophie's father leaves to attend to some business; her mother sends Sophie away under some pretext, and then she addresses Emile and says to him in quite a serious tone: "Monsieur, I believe that a young man as well born and as well raised as you, who has sentiments and morals, would not want to repay the friendship a family has showed him by dishonoring it. I am neither unsociable nor a prude. I know what must be overlooked in the wildness of youth, and what I have tolerated under my eyes sufficiently proves it to you. Consult your friend about your duties. He will tell you what a difference there is between the games authorized by the presence of a father and mother and the liberties taken far away from them, liberties which abuse their confidence and turn into traps the same favors which are innocent under their eyes. He will tell you, sir, that my daughter has done you no other wrong than that of not noticing at the outset a practice she ought never to have tolerated. He will tell you that everything taken to be a favor becomes one, and that it is unworthy of a man of honor to abuse a young girl's simplicity to usurp in secret the same liberties that she can permit before everyone. One knows what propriety can permit in public; but no one knows where the man who sets himself up as the sole judge of his whims will stop himself in the shadows of secrecy."

After this just reprimand, addressed much more to me than to my pupil, this wise mother departs and leaves me admiring her rare prudence, which takes little account of one's kissing her daughter's mouth in front of her but is frightened of someone's daring to kiss her daughter's dress in private. Reflecting on the folly of our maxims, which always sacrifice true decency to propriety, I understand why language is more chaste as hearts become more corrupted and why rules of conduct are more exact as those subject to them become more dishonest.

In using this occasion to fill Emile's heart with the duties I ought to have dictated to him earlier, I am struck by a new reflection which perhaps honors Sophie the most and which I am nevertheless very careful not to communicate to her lover. It is clear that this pretended pride for which others reproach her is only a very wise precaution to protect her from herself. Since she has the misfortune to sense a combustible temperament within herself, she dreads the first spark and keeps it at a distance with all her power. It is not from pride that she is severe; it is from humility. She assumes an empire over Emile which she fears she does not have over Sophie. She uses the one to fight the other. If she were more confident, she would be much less proud. Apart from this one point, what girl in the world is more yielding and sweeter? Who endures an offense more patiently? Who is more fearful of committing one against others? Who makes fewer claims of every kind, except for the claim of virtue? Furthermore, it is not her virtue of which she is proud; she is proud only in order to preserve it. And when she can yield to the inclination of her heart without risk, she caresses even her lover. But her discreet mother does not relate all these details even to her father. Men ought not to know everything.

Far from seeming to have become proud as a result of her conquest, Sophie has become still more affable and less demanding with everyone—except perhaps with him who is the cause of this change. The sentiment of independence no longer swells her noble heart. She triumphs with modesty, winning a victory which costs her her freedom. Her bearing is less free and her speech is more timid now that she no longer hears the word *lover* without blushing. But contentment pierces through her embarrassment, and this very shame is not a disagreeable sentiment. It is especially with other young men that the difference in her conduct is most easily sensed. Since she no longer fears them, the extreme reserve that she used to have with them has been much relaxed. Now that she has made her choice, she has no qualms about acting graciously toward those to whom she is indifferent. Since she no longer takes any interest in them, she is less demanding about their merits, and she finds them always likable enough for people who will never mean anything to her.

If true love could make use of coquetry, I would even believe that I see some traces of it in the way Sophie behaves with these young men in the presence of her lover. One would say that, not content with the ardent passion which she kindles in him by means of an exquisite mixture of reserve and endearment, she is not sorry if she excites this passion still more by means of a bit of anxiety. One would say that by purposely making her young guests merry, she intends to torment Emile with the charms of a playfulness she does not dare to indulge in with him. But Sophie is too attentive, too good, and too judicious actually to torment him. Love and decency take the place of prudence for her in tempering this dangerous stimulant. She knows how to alarm him and to reassure him precisely when it is necessary. And if she sometimes makes him anxious, she never makes him sad. Let us pardon the concern she causes the man she loves by attributing it to her fear that he is never bound to her closely enough. . . .

Emile loves Sophie. But what are the chief charms which have attached him to her? Sensitivity, virtue, love of decent things. While loving this love in his mistress, will he have lost it in himself? For what price did Sophie in turn give herself? She was won by all the sentiments natural to her lover's heart: esteem of true goods, frugality, simplicity, generous disinterestedness, contempt for show and riches. Emile had these virtues before love imposed them on him. How, then, has Emile truly changed? He has new reasons to be himself. This is the single point where he differs from what he was.

I do not imagine that anyone reading this book with some attention could believe that all the circumstances of the situation in which Emile finds himself have been gathered around him by chance. Is it by chance that, although the cities furnish so many lovable girls, the one who pleases him is to be found only in the depths of a distant retreat? Is it by chance that he meets her? Is it by chance that they suit one another? Is it by chance that they cannot lodge in the same place? Is it by chance that he finds a dwelling so far from her? Is it by chance that he sees her so rarely and that he is forced to purchase the pleasure of seeing her once in a while with so much exertion? He is becoming effeminated, you say? On the contrary, he is hardening himself. He has to be as robust as I have made him to withstand the exertion Sophie makes him endure. . . .

The first times that we went to see Sophie, we had traveled on horseback in order to go more quickly. We find this expedient convenient, and the fifth time we are still traveling on horseback. We are expected. At more than half a league from the house we perceive people on the path. Emile observes them, his heart throbs, he approaches; he recognizes Sophie, leaps from his horse, dashes off, and is quickly at the feet of the lovable family. Emile loves fine horses. His own horse is lively; when it becomes aware that it is free, it takes off through the fields. I follow it, catch it with some effort, and bring it back. Unhappily Sophie is afraid of horses; I do not dare to approach her. Emile sees nothing. But Sophie informs him in a whisper of the effort he has let his friend make. Quite ashamed, Emile runs up to take the horses and stays back. It is just for each to have his turn. He leaves first in order to get rid of our mounts. On leaving Sophie behind him in this way, he no longer finds the horse so convenient a vehicle. He returns out of breath and meets us halfway.

On our next trip Emile no longer wants to use horses. "Why?" I say to him. "We have only to take a lackey to care for them." "Ah," he says, "are we to burden Sophie's respectable family in this way? You see that they want to feed everyone, both men and horses." "It is true," I respond, "that they have the noble hospitality of indigence. The rich, who are miserly amidst their ostentation, lodge only their friends, but the poor also lodge their friends' horses." "Let us go on foot," he says. "Don't you have the courage, you who so goodheartedly share your child's fatiguing pleasures?" "Very gladly," I respond at once." Moreover, it seems to me that love prefers to go about its business without so much stir."

On approaching, we find mother and daughter still farther out on the path than the first time. We have traveled like a thunderbolt. Emile is all in a sweat. A dear hand deigns to wipe his cheeks with a handkerchief. There would have to be a lot of horses in the world before we would be tempted to make use of them again.

However, it is quite cruel for Emile and Sophie never to be able to spend the evening together. Summer advances. The days begin to get shorter. No matter what we say, we are never permitted to wait until nightfall before going home; and if we do not come early in the morning, we have to leave practically as soon as we have arrived. As a result of pitying us and being anxious about us, Sophie's mother concludes that although in truth they could not properly lodge us in their house, a bed in which to sleep could sometimes be found for us in the village. At these words Emile claps his hands and shivers with joy. And Sophie, without being aware of it, kisses her mother a little more often on the day she comes up with this expedient. . . .

From the arrangements I have made, one sees that my young man is far from spending his life near Sophie and seeing her as much as he would want. A trip or two a week are all that he receives permission to make, and his visits, which are often limited to a single half day, are rarely extended to the next day. He employs far more time in hoping to see Sophie or in congratulating himself on having seen her than in actually seeing her. And of the time devoted to his trips he spends less of it with her than in getting there or going back. His pleasures, which are true, pure, and delicious but less real than imaginary, exacerbate his love without effeminating his heart.

On the days when he does not see her, he is not idle and sedentary. On those days he is Emile again. He has not been transformed at all. Most often he roams through the surrounding countryside. He pursues his natural history; he observes and examines the earth, its products, and its cultivation; he compares the way of farming he sees to the ones he knows; he seeks the reasons for the differences. When he judges other methods preferable to the local ones, he gives them to the farmers. If he proposes a better form of plow, he has it made according to his designs. If he finds a marl quarry, he teaches them its use which is unknown in these parts. Often he puts his hand to the work himself. The farmers are all surprised to see him handle their tools more easily than they do themselves, dig furrows deeper and straighter than theirs, sow more evenly, and lay out embankments with more intelligence. They do not make fun of him as a fine talker about agriculture. They see that he actually knows about it. In a word, he extends his zeal and his care to everything which is of primary and general utility. He does not even limit himself to that. He visits the peasants' houses, inquires about their condition, their families, the number of their children, the quantity of their lands, the nature of their produce, their market, their means, their expenses, their debts, etc. He does not give them much money, knowing that they usually employ it badly; but he directs its employment himself and makes it useful to them in spite of themselves. He provides them with workers and often pays them wages themselves to do the work they need. He gets one farmer to rebuild or roof his cottage which is half in ruins; he gets another to clear his land which has been abandoned for want of means; he provides a third with a cow, a horse, and livestock of all kinds to replace those he has lost. Two neighbors are ready to enter into litigation; he wins them over and reconciles them. A peasant falls ill; he has him cared for; he cares for him himself. Another is harassed by a powerful neighbor; he protects and advises him. Two poor young people want to be united; he helps them to get married. A good woman has lost her dear child; he goes to see her and consoles her; he does not leave as soon as he has gone in. He does not disdain the indigent, and he is not in a hurry to get away from the unhappy. He often takes his meal with the peasants he assists. He also accepts a meal from those who do not need him. In becoming the benefactor of some and the friend of the others, he does not cease to be their equal. Finally, he always does as much good with his person as with his money.

Sometimes he takes his walks in the direction of the happy dwelling. He could hope to see Sophie on the sly, to see her taking her walk without himself being seen. But Emile's conduct is never devious; he does not know how to be evasive and does not want to be. He has that amiable delicacy which flatters and feeds *amour-propre* with the good witness of oneself. He rigorously sticks to his banishment and never approaches near enough to get from chance what he wants to owe only to Sophie. On the other hand, he wanders with pleasure in her neighborhood, seeking for traces of his beloved's steps, touched by the efforts she has taken and the errands she has been kind enough to run for the sake of obliging him. On the eve of the days when he is going to see her, he will go to some neighboring farm to order a snack for the next day. Their walk is directed toward this place without appearing to be. They enter as though by chance; they find fruits, cakes, and custard. The dainty Sophie is not insensitive to these attentions and gladly gives us credit for our foresight; for I always get a share of the compliment, although I had no share in the effort that elicits it. This is the evasion used by a little girl to feel less embarrassed in giving thanks. . . .

To these various occupations is added the trade we have learned. At least one day a week and on all those days when bad weather does not permit us to stay out in the countryside, Emile and I go to work at a master's. We work there not for form's sake, as men above this station, but as true workers. Once when Sophie's father comes to see us, he finds us at work and does not fail to report with admiration to his wife and his daughter what he has seen. "Go and see this young man in the workshop," he says, "and you will see whether he despises the condition of the poor!" One can imagine whether Sophie is glad to hear this speech! They talk about it again; they would like to surprise him at work. They question me without giving any indication of what they are about, and after making sure about one of our workdays, mother and daughter take a calèche and come to the city on that day.

On entering the shop, Sophie perceives at the far end a young man in a jacket who has his hair carelessly bound up and is so busy with what he is doing that he does not see her. She stops and gives her mother a sign. Emile, with a chisel in one hand and the mallet in the other, is completing a mortise. Then he saws a plank and fixes one piece in the vise to polish it. This sight does not make Sophie laugh. It touches her; it is respectable. Woman, honor the head of your house. It is he who works for you, who wins your bread, who feeds you. This is man.

While they are attentively observing Emile, I notice them and tug on Emile's sleeve. He turns around, sees them, drops his tools, and darts toward them with a shout of joy. After having yielded to his initial transports, he makes them sit down and picks up his work again. But Sophie cannot stay seated. She gets up with vivacity, roams the shop, examines the tools, touches the polished surfaces of the planks, gathers shavings from the floor, looks at our hands, and then says that she likes this trade because it is clean. The silly girl even tries to imitate Emile. With her frail white hand she pushes a plane along the plank. The plane slides and does not bite. I believe I see Love in the air laughing and beating his wings. I believe I hear him let out shouts of gladness and say, "Hercules is avenged." . . .

After having spent some time chatting with us but without distracting us, the mother says to her daughter, "Let us go; it is late, and we must not keep people waiting." Then, approaching Emile, she gives him a little pat on the cheek and says to him, "Well, good worker, don't you want to come with us?"

He answers in a very sad tone, "I am committed. Ask the master." The master is asked if he would be kind enough to do without us. He answers that he cannot. "I have pressing work which must be delivered the day after tomorrow," he says. "Counting on these gentlemen, I have turned away other workers who showed up. If these two fail me, I do not know where to find others, and I will not be able to deliver the work on the promised day." The mother makes no reply. She expects Emile to speak. Emile lowers his head and keeps quiet. "Sir," she says, a bit surprised by this silence, "have you nothing to say to this?" Emile looks tenderly at her daughter and answers with only these words, "You see that I have to stay." At that the ladies depart and leave us. Emile accompanies them to the door, follows them with his eyes as far as he can, sighs, returns without speaking, and sets to work.

Sophie's mother is piqued, and on the way she speaks to her daughter about the strangeness of this behavior. "What?" she says. "Was it so difficult to satisfy the master without being obliged to stay? Doesn't this young man, who is so prodigal and who pours out money without necessity, any longer know how to find money on suitable occasions?" "O mother," Sophie answers, "God forbid that Emile put so much emphasis on money that he use it to break a personal commitment, to violate his word with impunity, and to cause someone else's word to be violated! I know that he could easily compensate the worker for the slight harm his absence would cause him. But meanwhile he would enslave his soul to riches; he would accustom himself to putting his riches in the place of his duties and to believing that one is excused from everything provided one pays. Emile has other ways of thinking, and I hope not to be the cause of his changing them. Do you believe it cost him nothing to stay? Mama, don't deceive yourself. It is for me that he stays. I saw it in his eyes."

It is not that Sophie is easygoing in regard to the true attentions of love. On the contrary, she is imperious and exacting. She would rather not be loved than be loved moderately. She has that noble pride based on merit which is conscious of itself, esteems itself, and wants to be honored as it honors itself. She would disdain a heart which did not feel the full value of her heart, which did not love her for her virtues as much as, and more than, for her charms, and which did not prefer its own duty to her and her to everything else. She did not want a lover who knew no law other than hers. She wants to reign over a man whom she has not disfigured. . . .

But apart from this inviolable and sacred right, Sophie is excessively jealous of all her rights and watches to see how scrupulously Emile respects them, how zealously he accomplishes her will, how skillfully he guesses it, and how vigilant he is to arrive at the prescribed moment. She wants him to be neither late nor early. She wants him to be on time. To be early is to prefer himself to her; to be late is to neglect her. Neglect Sophie! That would not happen twice. The unjust suspicion that it happened once came close to ruining everything. But Sophie is equitable, and she knows how to make amends for her wrongs.

One evening we are awaited. Emile has received the order. They come out to meet us. We do not arrive. "What became of them? What misfortune has befallen them? Why haven't they sent anyone?" The evening is spent waiting for us. Poor Sophie believes us dead. She is desolate; she torments herself; she spends the night crying. In the evening they had sent a messenger to inquire after us and report news of us the next morning. The messenger returns accompanied by another messenger from us who makes our excuses orally and says that we are well. A moment later we ourselves appear. Then the scene changes. Sophie dries her tears; or if she sheds any, they are tears of rage. Her haughty heart has not profited from being reassured about our lives. Emile lives and has kept her waiting needlessly.

At our arrival she wants to closet herself. She is asked to stay. She has to stay. But, making her decision on the spot, she affects a tranquil and contented air intended to make an impression on others. Her father comes out to meet us and says, "You have kept your friends in a state of distress. There are people here who will not easily pardon you." "Who is that, papa?" says Sophie, affecting the most gracious smile she can. "What difference does it make to you," her father answers, "provided it is not you?" Sophie does not reply and lowers her eyes to her work. Her mother receives us with a cold and composed air. Emile is embarrassed and does not dare approach Sophie. She speaks to him first, asks him how he is, invites him to sit down, and counterfeits so well that the poor young man, who still understands nothing of the language of the violent passions, is taken in by this coolness and as a result is about to get piqued himself.

To disabuse him, I go and take Sophie's hand. I want to bring it to my lips as I sometimes do. She withdraws it briskly, saying the word "Monsieur!" in such a singular manner that this involuntary movement at once opens Emile's eyes.

Seeing that she has betrayed herself, Sophie is less constrained. Her apparent coolness changes into an ironical contempt. She responds to everything said to her in monosyllables pronounced in a slow and unsure voice, as though she is afraid to let the accent of indignation pierce through too much. Emile, who is half-dead with fright, looks at her sorrowfully and tries to get her to cast her eyes on his so that he can better read her true sentiments. Sophie is further irritated by his confidence and casts a glance at him which takes away his desire to solicit a second one. Taken aback and trembling, Emile no longer dares—very fortunately for him—to speak to her or look at her; for even were he not guilty, she would never have pardoned him if he had been able to bear her anger.

Seeing that it is my turn and that it is time to explain ourselves, I return to Sophie. I take her hand which she no longer withdraws, for she is about to faint. I tell her gently, "Dear Sophie, we are luckless fellows, but you are reasonable and just, and you will not judge us without hearing us. Listen to us." She does not answer, and I speak as follows:

"We left yesterday at four o'clock. We were told to arrive at seven o'clock, and we always set aside more time than we need so that we can rest before approaching here. We had already come three-quarters of the way when we heard pained laments. They came from a gorge between the hills at some distance from us. We ran toward the cries. We found an unfortunate peasant who had been a bit drunk as he rode back from the city and had fallen off his horse so heavily that he broke his leg. We shouted for help. No one answered. We tried to put the injured man back on his horse, but did not succeed; at the slightest movement the luckless fellow suffered horrible pain. We decided to tie up his horse out of the way in the woods. Then, making a stretcher of our arms, we set the injured man on it and carried him as gently as possible, following his directions about the route to be taken in order to get to his home. The way was long. We had to rest several times. We finally arrived, completely worn out. We found with bitter surprise that we already knew the house, and that this poor fellow whom we were carrying back with such effort was the same man who had received us so cordially the day of our first arrival here. In our mutual distress we had not recognized each other until that moment.

"He had only two little children. His wife, who was about to give him a third, was so overwhelmed at the sight of him that she felt sharp pains and gave birth a few hours later. What was to be done in this situation in an isolated cottage where one could not hope for any help? Emile decided to go and get the horse that we had left in the woods, to mount it and to ride at full gallop to look for a surgeon in the city. He gave the horse to the surgeon. As he was not able to find a nurse quickly enough, he returned on foot with a domestic after having sent you a messenger. Meanwhile in the house I was at a loss, as you can believe, between a man with a broken leg and a woman in labor; but I readied everything which I could foresee might be necessary to help them both.

"I shall not give you the rest of the details. That is not now the question. It was two hours past midnight before either of us had a moment's respite. Finally, we returned before dawn to our rooms near here, where we awaited the hour of your rising in order to give you an account of our accident."

I stop speaking without adding anything. But before anyone speaks, Emile approaches his beloved, raises his voice, and says to her with more firmness than I would have expected, "Sophie, you are the arbiter of my fate. You know it well. You can make me die of pain. But do not hope to make me forget the rights of humanity. They are more sacred to me than yours. I will never give them up for you."

At these words Sophie, instead of responding, rises, puts an arm around his neck, and gives him a kiss on the cheek. Then, extending her hand with inimitable grace, she says to him, "Emile, take this hand. It is yours. Be my husband and master when you wish. I will try to merit this honor." . . .

I will not describe the common joy. Everyone ought to sense it. After dinner Sophie asks whether those poor sick people are too far away for us to go to see them. Sophie desires it, and it is a good deed. We go. We find them in two separate beds. Emile had had a second bed brought in. We find them surrounded by people who are there to help them. Emile had provided for that. But both husband and wife are lying in such disorder that they suffer as much from discomfort as from their conditions. Sophie gets one of the good woman's aprons and goes to settle the wife in her bed. Next she does the same for the man. Her gentle and light hand knows how to get at everything that hurts them and to place their sore limbs in a more relaxed position. They feel relieved at her very approach. One would say that she guesses everything which hurts them. This extremely delicate girl is rebuffed neither by the dirtiness nor the bad smell and knows how to make both disappear without ordering anyone about and without the sick being tormented. She who always seems so modest and sometimes so disdainful, she who would not for anything in the world have touched a man's bed with the tip of her finger, turns the injured man over and changes him without any scruple, and puts him in a position in which he can stay more comfortably for a long time. The zeal of charity outweighs modesty. What she does, she does so lightly and with so much skill that he feels relieved almost without having noticed that he has been touched. Wife and husband together bless the lovable girl who serves them, who pities them, who consoles them. It is an angel from heaven that God sends them. She has the appearance and the grace, as well as the gentleness and the goodness of an angel. Emile is moved and contemplates her in silence. Man, love your companion. God gives her to you to console you in your pains, to relieve you in your ills. This is woman.

The newborn child is baptized. The two lovers present it, yearning in the depths of their hearts to give others an occasion to perform the same task. They long for the desired moment. They believe they have reached it. All of Sophie's scruples have been removed, but mine are aroused. They are not yet where they think they are. Each must have his turn.

One morning, when they have not seen each other for two days, I enter Emile's room with a letter in my hand; staring fixedly at him, I say, "What would you do if you were informed that Sophie is dead?" He lets out a great cry, gets up, striking his hands together, and looks wild-eyed at me without saying a single word. "Respond then," I continue with the same tranquility. Then, irritated by my coolness, Emile approaches, his eyes inflamed with anger, and stops in an almost threatening posture: "What would I do . . . I don't know. But what I do know is that I would never again in my life see the man who had informed me." "Reassure yourself," I respond, smiling. "She is alive. She is well. She thinks of you, and we are expected this evening. But let us go and take a stroll, and we will chat."

The passion with which he is preoccupied no longer permits him to give himself to purely reasoned conversations as he had before. I have to interest him by this very passion to make him attentive to my lessons. This is what I have done by this terrible preamble. I am now quite sure that he will listen to me.

"You must be happy, dear Emile. That is the goal of every being which senses. That is the first desire which nature has impressed on us, and the only one which never leaves us. But where is happiness? Who knows it? All seek it, and none finds it. One man uses up life in pursuing it, and another dies without having attained it. . . .

"When you entered the age of reason, I protected you from men's opinions. When your heart became sensitive, I preserved you from the empire of the passions. If I had been able to prolong this inner calm to the end of your life, I would have secured my work, and you would always be as happy as man can be. But, dear Emile, it is in vain that I have dipped your soul in the Styx; I was not able to make it everywhere invulnerable. A new enemy is arising which you have not learned to conquer and from which I can no longer save you. This enemy is yourself. Nature and fortune had left you free. You could endure poverty; you could tolerate the pains of the body; those of the soul were unknown to you. You were bound to nothing other than the human condition, and now you are bound to all the attachments you have given to yourself. In learning to desire, you have made yourself the slave of your desires. Without anything changing in you, without anything offending you, without anything touching your being, how many pains can now attack your soul! How many ills you can feel without being sick! How many deaths you can suffer without dying! A lie, a mistake, or a doubt can put you in despair. . . .

"You know how to suffer and die. You know how to endure the law of necessity in physical ills, but you have not yet imposed laws on the appetites of your heart, and the disorder of our lives arises from our affections far more than from our needs. Our desires are extended; our strength is almost nil. By his wishes man depends on countless things, and by himself he depends on nothing, not even his own life. The more he increases his attachments, the more he multiplies his pains. Everything on earth is only transitory. All that we love will escape us sooner or later, and we hold on to it as if it were going to last eternally. What a fright you had at the mere suspicion of Sophie's death! Did you, then, count on her living forever? Does no one die at her age? She is going to die, my child, and perhaps before you. Who knows if she is living at this very instant? Nature had enslaved you only to a single death. You are enslaving yourself to a second. Now you are in the position of dying twice.

"How pitiable you are going to be, thus subjected to your unruly passions! There will always be privations, losses, and alarms. You will not even enjoy what is left to you. The fear of losing everything will prevent you from possessing anything. As a result of having wanted to follow only your passions, you will never be able to satisfy them. You will always seek repose, but it will always flee before you. You will be miserable, and you will become wicked. How could you not be, since you have only your unbridled desires as a law? If you cannot tolerate involuntary privations, how will you impose any on yourself voluntarily? How will you know how to sacrifice inclination to duty and to hold out against your heart in order to listen to your reason? You who already wish never again to see the man who will inform you of your mistress's death, how would you see the man who would want to take her from you while she is still living—the one who would dare to say to you, 'She is dead to you. Virtue separates you from her'? If you have to live with her no matter what, it makes no difference whether Sophie is married or not, whether you are free or not, whether she loves you or hates you, whether she is given you or refused you; you want her, and you have to possess her whatever the price. Inform me, then, at what crime a man stops when he has only the wishes of his heart for laws and knows how to resist nothing that he desires?

"My child, there is no happiness without courage nor virtue without struggle. The word *virtue* comes from *strength*. Strength is the foundation of all virtue. Virtue belongs only to a being that is weak by nature and strong by will. It is in this that the merit of the just man consists; and although we call God good, we do not call Him virtuous, because it requires no effort for Him to do good. I have waited for you to be in a position to understand me before explaining this much profaned word to you. So long as virtue costs nothing to practice, there is little need to know it. This need comes when the passions are awakened. It has already come for you. Raising you in all the simplicity of nature, I have not preached painful duties to you but instead have protected you from the vices that make these duties painful. I have made lying more useless than odious to you; I have taught you not so much to give unto each what belongs to him as to care only for what is yours. I have made you good rather than virtuous. But he who is only good remains so only as long as he takes pleasure in being so. Goodness is broken and perishes under the impact of the human passions. The man who is only good is good only for himself.

"Who, then, is the virtuous man? It is he who knows how to conquer his affections; for then he follows his reason and his conscience; he does his duty; he keeps himself in order, and nothing can make him deviate from it. Up to now you were only apparently free. You had only the precarious freedom of a slave to whom nothing has been commanded. Now be really free. Learn to become your own master. Command your heart, Emile, and you will be virtuous.

"Here, then, is another apprenticeship, and this apprenticeship is more painful than the first; for nature delivers us from the ills it imposes on us, or it teaches us to bear them. But nature says nothing to us about those which come from ourselves. It abandons us to ourselves. It lets us, as victims of our own passions, succumb to our vain sorrows and then glorify ourselves for the tears at which we should have blushed.

"You now have your first passion. It is perhaps the only one worthy of you. If you know how to rule it like a man, it will be the last. You will subject all the others, and you will obey only the passion for virtue.

"This passion is not criminal, as I well know. It is as pure as the souls which feel it. Decency formed it, and innocence nourished it. Happy lovers! For you the charms of virtue only add to those of love, and the gentle bond that awaits you is as much the reward of your moderation as it is of your attachment. But, tell me, sincere man, has this passion, which is so pure, any the less subjected you? Did you any the less make yourself its slave; and if tomorrow Sophie ceased being innocent, would you stifle it beginning tomorrow? Now is the moment to try your strength. There is no longer time to do so when that strength has to be employed. These dangerous trials ought to be made far from peril. A man does not exercise for battle in the face of the enemy but prepares himself for it before the war. He presents himself at the battle already fully prepared.

"It is an error to distinguish permitted passions from forbidden ones in order to yield to the former and deny oneself the latter. All passions are good when one remains their master; all are bad when one lets oneself be subjected to them. What is forbidden to us by nature is to extend our attachments further than our strength; what is forbidden to us by reason is to want what we cannot obtain; what is forbidden to us by conscience is not temptations but rather letting ourselves be conquered by temptations. It is not within our control to have or not to have passions. But it is within our control to reign over them. All the sentiments we dominate are legitimate; all those which dominate us are criminal. A man is not guilty for loving another's wife if he keep this unhappy passion enslaved to the law of duty. He is guilty for loving his own wife to the point of sacrificing everything to that love. . . .

"Do you want, then, to live happily and wisely? Attach your heart only to imperishable beauty. Let your condition limit your desires; let your duties come before your inclinations; extend the law of necessity to moral things. Learn to lose what can be taken from you; learn to abandon everything when virtue decrees it, to put yourself above events and to detach your heart lest it be lacerated by them; to be courageous in adversity, so as never to be miserable; to be firm in your duty, so as never to be criminal. Then you will be happy in spite of fortune and wise in spite of the passions. Then you will find in the possession even of fragile goods a voluptuousness that nothing will be able to disturb. You will possess them without their possessing you; and you will feel that man, who can keep nothing, enjoys only what he knows how to lose. You will not, it is true have the illusion of imaginary pleasures, but you will also not have the pains which are their fruit. You will gain much in this exchange, for these pains are frequent and real, and these pleasures are rare and vain. As the conqueror of so many deceptive opinions, you will also be the conqueror of the opinion that places so great a value on life. You will pass your life without disturbance and terminate it without fright. You will detach yourself from it as from all things. How many others are horror-stricken because they think that, in departing from life, they cease to be? Since you are informed about life's nothingness, you will believe that it is then that you begin to be. Death is the end of the wicked man's life and the beginning of the just man's." ...

"Do you believe, dear Emile, that a man, in whatever situation he finds himself, can be happier than you have been for these past three months? If you believe it, disabuse yourself. Before tasting the pleasures of life, you have exhausted its happiness. There is nothing beyond what you have felt. The felicity of the senses is fleeting. It always loses its flavor when it is the heart's habitual state. You have enjoyed more from hope than you will ever enjoy in reality. Imagination adorns what one desires but abandons it when it is in one's possession. Except for the single being existing by itself, there is nothing beautiful except that which is not. If your present state could have lasted forever, you would have found supreme happiness. But everything connected with man feels the effects of his transitoriness. Everything is finite and everything is fleeting in human life; and if the state which makes us happy lasted endlessly, the habit of enjoying it would take away our taste for it. If nothing changes from without, the heart changes. Happiness leaves us, or we leave it.

"Time, which you did not measure, was flowing during your delirium. The summer is ending; winter approaches. Even if we could continue our visits during so hard a season, they would never tolerate it. In spite of ourselves, we must change our way of life; this one can no longer last. I see in your impatient eyes that this difficulty does not bother you. Sophie's confession and your own desires suggest to you an easy means for avoiding the snow and no longer having to make a trip in order to go and see her. The expedient is doubtless convenient. But when spring has come, the snow melts, and the marriage remains. You must think about a marriage for all seasons.

"You want to marry Sophie, and yet you have known her for less than five months! You want to marry her not because she suits you but because she pleases you—as though love were never mistaken about what is suitable, and as though those who begin by loving each other never end by hating each other. She is virtuous, I know. But is that enough? Is being decent sufficient for people to be suitable for each other? It is not her virtue I am putting in doubt; it is her character. Does a woman's character reveal itself in a day? Do you know in how many situations you must have seen her in order to get a deep knowledge of her disposition? Do four months of attachment give you assurance for a whole life? Perhaps two months of absence will make her forget you. Perhaps someone else is only waiting for your withdrawal in order to efface you from her heart. Perhaps on your return you will find her as indifferent as up to now you have found her responsive. The sentiments do not depend on principles. She may remain very decent and yet cease to love you. She will be constant and faithful. I tend to believe it. But who is answerable to you for her, and who is answerable to her for you so long as you have not put one another to the test? Will you wait to make this test until it becomes useless for you? Will you wait to know each other until you can no longer separate?

"Sophie is not yet eighteen; you are just twenty-two. This is the age of love, but not that of marriage. What a father and mother of a family! To know how to raise children, at least wait until you cease being children! Do you know how many young persons there are who have had their constitutions weakened, their health ruined, and their lives shortened by enduring the fatigues of pregnancy before the proper age? Do you know how many children have remained sickly and weak for want of having been nourished in a body that was sufficiently formed? When mother and child grow at the same time and the substance necessary to the growth of each of them is divided, neither has what nature destined for it. How is it possible that both should not suffer from it? Either I have a very poor knowledge of Emile, or he would rather have a robust wife and robust children than satisfy his impatience at the expense of their life and their health.

"Let us speak about you. In aspiring to the status of husband and father, have you meditated enough upon its duties? When you become the head of a family, you are going to become a member of the state, and do you know what it is to be a member of the state? Do you know what government, laws, and fatherland are? Do you know what the price is of your being permitted to live and for whom you ought to die? You believe you have learned everything, and you still know nothing. Before taking a place in the civil order, learn to know it and to know what rank in it suits you.

"Emile, you must leave Sophie. I do not say abandon her. If you were capable of it, she would be only too fortunate not to have married you. You must leave in order to return worthy of her. Do not be so vain as to believe that you already merit her. Oh, how much there remains for you to do! Come and fulfill this noble task. Come and learn to bear her absence. Come and win the prize of fidelity, so that on your return you can lay claim to some honor from her and ask for her hand not as an act of grace but as a recompense." . . .

. . . Finally the sad day comes. They must separate.

Sophie's worthy father, with whom I have arranged everything, embraces me on receiving my farewell. Then, taking me aside, he says the following words to me in a grave tone and with a somewhat emphatic accent: "I have done everything to be obliging to you. I knew that I was dealing with a man of honor. There remains only one word to say to you. Remember that your pupil has signed his marriage contract on my daughter's lips."

What a difference there is in the bearing of the two lovers! Emile is impetuous, ardent, agitated, beside himself; he lets out cries, sheds torrents of tears on the hands of the father, the mother, the daughter; he sobs as he embraces all the domestics and repeats the same things a thousand times in a disorder that would cause laugher on any other occasion. Sophie is gloomy and pale, with expressionless eyes and a somber glance; she keeps quiet, says nothing, does not cry, and sees no one, not even Emile. It is in vain that he takes her hands and holds her in his arms; she remains immobile, insensitive to his tears, to his caresses, to everything he does. For her, he is already gone. How much more touching her behavior is than her lover's importunate complaints and noisy regrets! He sees it, he feels it, he is grieved by it. I drag him away with difficulty. If I leave him another moment, he will no longer be willing to part. I am charmed by the fact that he takes this sad image with him. If he is ever tempted to forget what he owes to Sophie, I shall recall her to him as he saw her at the moment of his departure. His heart would have to have changed very much for me not to be able to return it to her.

Tolstoy, *War and Peace:*
The Courtship of Pierre and Hélène

The background of the epic novel War and Peace *by Leo Tolstoy (1828–1910) is one of war and diplomacy; its foreground features men and women (who are not world-historical figures), the choices they make, and the obstacles they encounter. The novel begins in summer 1805, at a St. Petersburg soiree, and it is here that we first meet young Pierre, arguably Tolstoy's main protagonist. Though he is properly and fashionably dressed, broad, stout, bespectacled Pierre acts like a "child in a toy shop," exposing through his natural curiosity and frank enthusiasms the utter artificiality of all those around him. Twenty years old, fresh from his studies in France, armed with Rousseau's* Social Contract *and in love with Napoleon, Pierre seems ready for anything and everything life has to serve up. And for the moment he is. For though he has been reared with the privileges of young Russian aristocrats, his illegitimate birth has left him free to enjoy his naturally democratic rights—he is a man without responsibilities. By the end of 1805, three or four short months later, all this has changed. Thanks to the inheritance bequeathed to him in the interim by the death of his wealthy father, a former grandee in the court of Catherine the Great, Pierre acquires a fortune, a title, and the close attentions of the high priests and priestesses of social climbing. As we observe in the selection that follows, without ever seeming to act, to think, or to love, natural Pierre is transformed into social Pierre, which change is, in turn, consummated in his marriage to the beautiful (and also vain and fickle) Hélène.*

Tolstoy says Pierre here crossed a "significant boundary," an image he uses elsewhere to describe young men going into battle. The courtship of Pierre and Hélène resembles a military campaign, but Pierre is not in command. What makes him so vulnerable: lust, vanity, his new social position? What determines his "choice"? Could anything have helped him? Had he studied Emile *(rather than* The Social Contract*) or read the advice of Benjamin Franklin, could he have seen more clearly and acted more wisely? The selection is taken from Book 3, Chapter 1.*

Prince Vasíli was not a man who deliberately thought out his plans. Still less did he think of injuring anyone for his own advantage. He was merely a man of the world who had got on and to whom getting on had become a habit. Schemes and devices for which he never rightly accounted to himself, but which formed the whole interest of his life, were constantly shaping themselves in his mind, arising from the circumstances and persons he met. Of these plans he had not merely one or two in his head but dozens, some only beginning to form themselves, some approaching achievement, and some in course of disintegration. He did not, for instance, say to himself: "This man now has influence, I must gain his confidence and friendship and through him obtain a special grant." Nor did he say to himself: "Pierre is a rich man, I must entice him to marry my daughter and lend me the forty thousand rubles I need." But when he came across a man of position his instinct immediately told him that this man could be useful, and without any premeditation Prince Vasíli took the first opportunity to gain his confidence, flatter him, become intimate with him, and finally make his request.

He had Pierre at hand in Moscow and procured for him an appointment as Gentleman of the Bedchamber, which at that time conferred the status of Councilor of State, and insisted on the young man accompanying him to Petersburg and staying at his house. With apparent absent-mindedness, yet with unhesitating assurance that he was doing the right thing, Prince Vasíli did everything to get Pierre to marry his daughter. . . .

Pierre, on unexpectedly becoming Count Bezúkhov and a rich man, felt himself after his recent loneliness and freedom from cares so beset and preoccupied that only in bed was he able to be by himself. He had to sign papers, to present himself at government offices, the purpose of which was not clear to him, to question his chief steward, to visit his estate near Moscow, and to receive many people who formerly did not even wish to know of his existence but would now have been offended and grieved had he chosen not to see them. These different people—businessmen, relations, and acquaintances alike—were all disposed to treat the young heir in the most friendly and flattering manner: they were all evidently firmly convinced of Pierre's noble qualities. He was always hearing such words as: "With your remarkable kindness," or, "With your excellent heart," "You are yourself so honorable, Count," or, "Were he as clever as you," and so on, till he began sincerely to believe in his own exceptional kindness and extraordinary intelligence, the more so as in the depth of his heart it had always seemed to him that he really was very kind and intelligent. Even people who had formerly been spiteful toward him and evidently unfriendly now became gentle and affectionate. . . .

It seemed so natural to Pierre that everyone should like him, and it would have seemed so unnatural had anyone disliked him, that he could not but believe in the sincerity of those around him. Besides, he had no time to ask himself whether these people were sincere or not. He was always busy and always felt in a state of mild and cheerful intoxication. He felt as though he were the center of some important and general movement; that something was constantly expected of him, that if he did not do it he would grieve and disappoint many people, but if he did this and that, all would be well; and he did what was demanded of him, but still that happy result always remained in the future. . . .

In Petersburg, as in Moscow, Pierre found the same atmosphere of gentleness and affection. He could not refuse the post, or rather the rank (for he did nothing), that Prince Vasíli had procured for him, and acquaintances, invitations, and social occupations were so numerous that, even more than in Moscow, he felt a sense of bewilderment, bustle, and continual expectation of some good, always in front of him but never attained.

Of his former bachelor acquaintances many were no longer in Petersburg. The Guards had gone to the front; Dólokhov had been reduced to the ranks; Anatole was in the army somewhere in the provinces; Prince Andrew was abroad; so Pierre had not the opportunity to spend his nights as he used to like to spend them, or to open his mind by intimate talks with a friend older than himself and whom he respected. His whole time was taken up with dinners and balls and was spent chiefly at Prince Vasíli's house in the company of the stout princess, his wife, and his beautiful daughter Hélène.

Like the others, Anna Pávlovna Schérer showed Pierre the change of attitude toward him that had taken place in society.

Formerly in Anna Pávlovna's presence, Pierre had always felt that what he was saying was out of place, tactless and unsuitable, that remarks which seemed to him clever while they formed in his mind became foolish as soon as he uttered them, while on the contrary Hippolyte's stupidest remarks came out clever and apt. Now everything Pierre said was *charmant*. Even if Anna Pávlovna did not say so, he could see that she wished to and only refrained out of regard for his modesty.

In the beginning of the winter of 1805–6 Pierre received one of Anna Pávlovna's usual pink notes with an invitation to which was added: "You will find the beautiful Hélène here, whom it is always delightful to see."

When he read that sentence, Pierre felt for the first time that some link which other people recognized had grown up between himself and Hélène, and that thought both alarmed him, as if some obligation were being imposed on him which he could not fulfill, and pleased him as an entertaining supposition. . . .

. . . Anna Pávlovna received Pierre with a shade of melancholy, evidently relating to the young man's recent loss by the death of Count Bezúkhov (everyone constantly considered it a duty to assure Pierre that he was greatly afflicted by the death of the father he had hardly known), and her melancholy was just like the august melancholy she showed at the mention of her most august Majesty the Empress Márya Fëdorovna. Pierre felt flattered by this. Anna Pávlovna arranged the different groups in her drawing room with her habitual skill. The large group, in which were Prince Vasíli and the generals, had the benefit of the diplomat. Another group was at the tea table. Pierre wished to join the former, but Anna Pávlovna—who was in the excited condition of a commander on a battlefield to whom thousands of new and brilliant ideas occur which there is hardly time to put in action—seeing Pierre, touched his sleeve with her finger, saying:

"Wait a bit, I have something in view for you this evening." (She glanced at Hélène and smiled at her.) "My dear Hélène, be charitable to my poor aunt who adores you. Go and keep her company for ten minutes. And that it will not be too dull, here is the dear count who will not refuse to accompany you."

The beauty went to the aunt, but Anna Pávlovna detained Pierre, looking as if she had to give some final necessary instructions.

"Isn't she exquisite?" she said to Pierre, pointing to the stately beauty as she glided away. "And how she carries herself! For so young a girl, such tact, such masterly perfection of manner! It comes from her heart. Happy the man who wins her! With her the least worldly of men would occupy a most brilliant position in society. Don't you think so? I only wanted to know your opinion," and Anna Pávlovna let Pierre go.

Pierre, in reply, sincerely agreed with her as to Hélène's perfection of manner. If he ever thought of Hélène, it was just of her beauty and her remarkable skill in appearing silently dignified in society.

The old aunt received the two young people in her corner, but seemed desirous of hiding her adoration for Hélène and inclined rather to show her fear of Anna Pávlovna. She looked at her niece, as if inquiring what she was to do with these people. On leaving them, Anna Pávlovna again touched Pierre's sleeve, saying: "I hope you won't say that it is dull in my house again," and she glanced at Hélène.

Hélène smiled, with a look implying that she did not admit the possibility of anyone seeing her without being enchanted. The aunt coughed, swallowed, and said in French that she was very pleased to see Hélène, then she turned to Pierre with the same words of welcome and the same look. In the middle of a dull and halting conversation, Hélène turned to Pierre with the beautiful bright smile that she gave to everyone. Pierre was so used to that smile, and it had so little meaning for him, that he paid no attention to it. The aunt was just speaking of a collection of snuffboxes that had belonged to Pierre's father, Count Bezúkhov, and showed them her own box. Princess Hélène asked to see the portrait of the aunt's husband on the box lid.

"That is probably the work of Vinesse," said Pierre, mentioning a celebrated miniaturist, and he leaned over the table to take the snuffbox while trying to hear what was being said at the other table.

He half rose, meaning to go round, but the aunt handed him the snuffbox, passing it across Hélène's back. Hélène stooped forward to make room, and looked round with a smile. She was, as always at evening parties, wearing a dress such as was then fashionable, cut very low at front and back. Her bust, which had always seemed like marble to Pierre, was so close to him that his shortsighted eyes could not but perceive the living charm of her neck and shoulders, so near to his lips that he need only have bent his head a little to have touched them. He was conscious of the warmth of her body, the scent of perfume, and the creaking of her corset as she moved. He did not see her marble beauty forming a complete whole with her dress, but all the charm of her body only covered by her garments. And having once seen this he could not help being aware of it, just as we cannot renew an illusion we have once seen through.

"So you have never noticed before how beautiful I am?" Hélène seemed to say. "You had not noticed that I am a woman? Yes, I am a woman who may belong to anyone—to you too," said her glance. And at that moment Pierre felt that Hélène not only could, but must, be his wife, and that it could not be otherwise.

He knew this at that moment as surely as if he had been standing at the altar with her. How and when this would be he did not know, he did not even know if it would be a good thing (he even felt, he knew not why, that it would be a bad thing), but he knew it would happen.

Pierre dropped his eyes, lifted them again, and wished once more to see her as a distant beauty far removed from him, as he had seen her every day until then, but he could no longer do it. He could not, any more than a man who has been looking at a tuft of steppe grass through the mist and taking it for a tree can again take it for a tree after he has once recognized it to be a tuft of grass. She was terribly close to him. She already had power over him, and between them there was no longer any barrier except the barrier of his own will.

"Well, I will leave you in your little corner," came Anna Pávlovna's voice, "I see you are all right there."

And Pierre, anxiously trying to remember whether he had done any thing reprehensible, looked round with a blush. It seemed to him that everyone knew what had happened to him as he knew it himself.

A little later when he went up to the large circle, Anna Pávlovna said to him: "I hear you are refitting your Petersburg house?"

This was true. The architect had told him that it was necessary, and Pierre, without knowing why, was having his enormous Petersburg house done up.

"That's a good thing, but don't move from Prince Vasíli's. It is good to have a friend like the prince," she said, smiling at Prince Vasíli. "I know something about that. Don't I? And you are still so young. You need advice. Don't be angry with me for exercising an old woman's privilege."

She paused, as women always do, expecting something after they have mentioned their age. "If you marry it will be a different thing," she continued, uniting them both in one glance. Pierre did not look at Hélène nor she at him. But she was just as terribly close to him. He muttered something and colored.

When he got home he could not sleep for a long time for thinking of what had happened. What had happened? Nothing. He had merely understood that the woman he had known as a child, of whom when her beauty was mentioned he had said absent-mindedly: "Yes, she's goodlooking," he had understood that this woman might belong to him.

"But she's stupid. I have myself said she is stupid," he thought. "There is something nasty, something wrong, in the feeling she excites in me. I have been told that her brother Anatole was in love with her and she with him, that there was quite a scandal and that that's why he was sent away. Hippolyte is her brother . . . Prince Vasíli is her father . . . It's bad. . . . " he reflected, but while he was thinking this (the reflection was still incomplete), he caught himself smiling and was conscious that another line of thought had sprung up, and while thinking of her worthlessness he was also dreaming of how she would be his wife, how she would love him and become quite different, and how all he had thought and heard of her might be false. And he again saw her not as the daughter of Prince Vasíli, but visualized her whole body only veiled by its gray dress. "But no! Why did this thought never occur to me before?" and again he told himself that it was impossible, that there would be something unnatural, and as it seemed to him dishonorable, in this marriage. He recalled her former words and looks and the words and looks of those who had seen them together. He recalled Anna Pávlovna's words and looks when she spoke to him about his house, recalled thousands of such hints from Prince Vasíli and others, and was seized by terror lest he had already, in some way, bound himself to do something that was evidently wrong and that he ought not to do. But at the very time he was expressing this conviction to himself, in another part of his mind her image rose in all its womanly beauty.

In November, 1805, Prince Vasíli had to go on a tour of inspection in four different provinces. He had arranged this for himself so as to visit his neglected estates at the same time and pick up his son Anatole where his regiment was stationed, and take him to visit Prince Nicholas Bolkónski in order to arrange a match for him with the daughter of that rich old man. But before leaving home and undertaking these new affairs, Prince Vasíli had to settle matters with Pierre, who, it is true, had latterly spent whole days at home, that is, in Prince Vasíli's house where he was staying, and had been absurd, excited, and foolish in Hélène's presence (as a lover should be), but had not yet proposed to her.

"This is all very fine, but things must be settled," said Prince Vasíli to himself, with a sorrowful sigh, one morning, feeling that Pierre who was under such obligations to him ("But never mind that") was not behaving very well in this matter. "Youth, frivolity . . . well, God be with him," thought he, relishing his own goodness of heart, "but it must be brought to a head. The day after tomorrow will be Lëlya's* name day. I will invite two or three people, and if he does not understand what he ought to do then it will be my affair—yes, my affair. I am her father."

Six weeks after Anna Pávlovna's "At Home" and after the sleepless night when he had decided that to marry Hélène would be a calamity and that he ought to avoid her and go away, Pierre, despite that decision, had not left Prince Vasíli's and felt with terror that in people's eyes he was every day more and more connected with her, that it was impossible for him to return to his former conception of her, that he could not break away from her, and that though it would be a terrible thing he would have to unite his fate with hers. He might perhaps have been able to free himself but that Prince Vasíli (who had rarely before given receptions) now hardly let a day go by without having an evening party at which Pierre had to be present unless he wished to spoil the general pleasure and disappoint everyone's expectation. Prince Vasíli, in the rare moments when he was at home, would take Pierre's hand in passing and draw it downwards, or absent-mindedly hold out his wrinkled, clean-shaven cheek for Pierre to kiss and would say: "Till tomorrow," or, "Be in to dinner or I shall not see you," or, "I am staying in for your sake," and so on. And though Prince Vasíli, when he stayed in (as he said) for Pierre's sake, hardly exchanged a couple of words with him, Pierre felt unable to disappoint him. Every day he said to himself one and the same thing: "It is time I understood her and made up my mind what she really is. Was I mistaken before, or am I mistaken now? No, she is not stupid, she is an excellent girl," he sometimes said to himself, "she never makes a mistake, never says anything stupid. She says little, but what she does say is always clear and simple, so she is not stupid. She never was abashed and is not abashed now, so she cannot be a bad woman!" He had often begun to make reflections or think aloud in her company, and she had always answered him either by a brief but appropriate remark—showing that it did not interest her—or by a silent look and smile which more palpably than anything else showed Pierre her superiority. She was right in regarding all arguments as nonsense in comparison with that smile.

She always addressed him with a radiantly confiding smile meant for him alone, in which there was something more significant than in the general smile that usually brightened her face. Pierre knew that everyone was waiting for him to say a word and cross a certain line, and he knew that sooner or later he would step across it, but an incomprehensible terror seized him at the thought

*Lëlya, a pet name for Hélène.—A.M.

of that dreadful step. A thousand times during that month and a half while he felt himself drawn nearer and nearer to that dreadful abyss, Pierre said to himself: "What am I doing? I need resolution. Can it be that I have none?"

He wished to take a decision, but felt with dismay that in this matter he lacked that strength of will which he had known in himself and really possessed. Pierre was one of those who are only strong when they feel themselves quite innocent, and since that day when he was overpowered by a feeling of desire while stooping over the snuffbox at Anna Pávlovna's, an unacknowledged sense of the guilt of that desire paralyzed his will.

On Hélène's name day, a small party of just their own people—as his wife said—met for supper at Prince Vasíli's. All these friends and relations had been given to understand that the fate of the young girl would be decided that evening. The visitors were seated at supper. Princess Kuragina, a portly imposing woman who had once been handsome, was sitting at the head of the table. On either side of her sat the more important guests—an old general and his wife, and Anna Pávlovna Scherer. At the other end sat the younger and less important guests, and there too sat the members of the family, and Pierre and Hélène, side by side. Prince Vasíli was not having any supper: he went round the table in a merry mood, sitting down now by one, now by another, of the guests. To each of them he made some careless and agreeable remark except to Pierre and Hélène, whose presence he seemed not to notice. He enlivened the whole party. The wax candles burned brightly, the silver and crystal gleamed, so did the ladies' toilets and the gold and silver of the men's epaulets; servants in scarlet liveries moved round the table, and the clatter of plates, knives, and glasses mingled with the animated hum of several conversations. . . .

Everybody laughed a great deal. At the head of the table, where the honored guests sat, everyone seemed to be in high spirits and under the influence of a variety of exciting sensations. Only Pierre and Hélène sat silently side by side almost at the bottom of the table, a suppressed smile brightening both their faces . . . a smile of bashfulness at their own feelings. But much as all the rest laughed, talked, and joked, much as they enjoyed their Rhine wine, sauté, and ices, and however they avoided looking at the young couple, and heedless and unobservant as they seemed of them, one could feel by the occasional glances they gave that . . . the laughter and the food were all a pretense, and that the whole attention of that company was directed to—Pierre and Hélène. Prince Vasíli mimicked the sobbing of Sergéy Kuzmích and at the same time his eyes glanced toward his daughter, and while he laughed the expression on his face clearly said: "Yes . . . it's getting on, it will all be settled today." Anna Pávlovna threatened him on behalf of "our dear Vyazmítinov," and in her eyes, which, for an instant, glanced at Pierre, Prince Vasíli read a congratulation on his future son-in-law and on his daughter's happiness. The old princess sighed sadly as she offered some wine to the old lady next to her and glanced angrily at her daughter, and her sigh seemed to say: "Yes, there's nothing left for you and me but to sip sweet wine, my dear, now that the time has come for these young ones to be thus boldly, provocatively happy." "And what nonsense all this is that I am saying!" thought a diplomatist, glancing at the happy faces of the lovers. "That's happiness!"

Into the insignificant, trifling, and artificial interests uniting that society had entered the simple feeling of the attraction of a healthy and handsome young man and woman for one another. And this human feeling dominated everything else and soared above all their affected chatter. Jests fell flat, news was not interesting, and the animation was evidently forced. Not only the guests but even the footmen waiting at table seemed to feel this, and they forgot their duties as they looked at the beautiful Hélène with her radiant face and at the red, broad, and happy though uneasy face of Pierre. It seemed as if the very light of the candles was focused on those two happy faces alone.

Pierre felt that he was the center of it all, and this both pleased and embarrassed him. He was like a man entirely absorbed in some occupation. He did not see, hear, or understand anything clearly. Only now and then detached ideas and impressions from the world of reality shot unexpectedly through his mind.

"So it is all finished!" he thought. "And how has it all happened? How quickly! Now I know that not because of her alone, nor of myself alone, but because of everyone, it must inevitably come about. They are all expecting it, they are so sure that it will happen that I cannot, I cannot, disappoint them. But how will it be? I do not know, but it will certainly happen!" thought Pierre, glancing at those dazzling shoulders close to his eyes.

Or he would suddenly feel ashamed of he knew not what. He felt it awkward to attract everyone's attention and to be considered a lucky man and, with his plain face, to be looked on as a sort of Paris possessed of a Helen. "But no doubt it always is and must be so!" he consoled himself. "And besides, what have I done to bring it about? How did it begin? I traveled from Moscow with Prince Vasíli. Then there was nothing. So why should I not stay at his house? Then I played cards with her and picked up her reticule and drove out with her. How did it begin, when did it all come about?" And here he was sitting by her side as her betrothed, seeing, hearing, feeling her nearness, her breathing, her movements, her beauty. Then it would suddenly seem to him that it was not she but he who was so unusually beautiful, and that that was why they all looked so at him, and flattered by this general admiration he would expand his chest, raise his head, and rejoice at his good fortune. Suddenly he heard a familiar voice repeating something to him a second time. But Pierre was so absorbed that he did not understand what was said.

"I am asking you when you last heard from Bolkónski," repeated Prince Vasíli a third time. "How absent-minded you are, my dear fellow."

Prince Vasíli smiled, and Pierre noticed that everyone was smiling at him and Hélène. "Well, what of it, if you all know it?" thought Pierre. "What of it? It's the truth!" and he himself smiled his gentle childlike smile, and Hélène smiled too.

"When did you get the letter? Was it from Olmütz?" repeated Prince Vasíli, who pretended to want to know this in order to settle a dispute.

"How can one talk or think of such trifles?" thought Pierre.

"Yes, from Olmütz," he answered, with a sigh.

After supper Pierre with his partner followed the others into the drawing room. The guests began to disperse, some without taking leave of Hélène. Some, as if unwilling to distract her from an important occupation, came up to her for a moment and made haste to go away, refusing to let her see them off. The diplomatist preserved a mournful silence as he left the drawing room. He pictured the vanity of his diplomatic career in comparison with Pierre's happiness. The old general grumbled at his wife when she asked how his leg was. "Oh, the old fool," he thought. "That Princess Hélène will be beautiful still when she's fifty."

"I think I may congratulate you," whispered Anna Pávlovna to the old princess, kissing her soundly. "If I hadn't this headache I'd have stayed longer."

The old princess did not reply, she was tormented by jealousy of her daughter's happiness.

While the guests were taking their leave, Pierre remained for a long time alone with Hélène in the little drawing room where they were sitting. He had often before, during the last six weeks, remained alone with her, but had never spoken to her of love. Now he felt that it was inevitable, but he could not make up his mind to take the final step. He felt ashamed; he felt that he was occupying someone else's place here beside Hélène. "This happiness is not for you," some inner voice whispered to him. "This happiness is for those who have not in them what there is in you."

But, as he had to say something, he began by asking her whether she was satisfied with the party. She replied in her usual simple manner that this name day of hers had been one of the pleasantest she had ever had.

Some of the nearest relatives had not yet left. They were sitting in the large drawing room. Prince Vasíli came up to Pierre with languid foot steps. Pierre rose and said it was getting late. Prince Vasíli gave him a look of stern inquiry, as though what Pierre had just said was so strange that one could not take it in. But then the expression of severity changed and he drew Pierre's hand downwards, made him sit down, and smiled affectionately.

"Well, Lëlya?" he asked, turning instantly to his daughter and addressing her with the careless tone of habitual tenderness natural to parents who have petted their children from babyhood, but which Prince Vasíli had only acquired by imitating other parents.

And he again turned to Pierre.

"Sergéy Kuzmích—From all sides—" he said, unbuttoning the top button of his waistcoat.

Pierre smiled, but his smile showed that he knew it was not the story about Sergéy Kuzmích that interested Prince Vasíli just then, and Prince Vasíli saw that Pierre knew this. He suddenly muttered something and went away. It seemed to Pierre that even the prince was disconcerted. The sight of the discomposure of that old man of the world touched Pierre: he looked at Hélène and she too seemed disconcerted, and her look seemed to say: "Well, it is your own fault."

"The step must be taken but I cannot, I cannot!" thought Pierre, and he again began speaking about indifferent matters, about Sergéy Kuzmích, asking what the point of the story was as he had not heard it properly. Hélène answered with a smile that she too had missed it.

When Prince Vasíli returned to the drawing room, the princess, his wife, was talking in low tones to the elderly lady about Pierre.

"Of course, it is a very brilliant match, but happiness, my dear . . . "

"Marriages are made in heaven," replied the elderly lady.

Prince Vasíli passed by, seeming not to hear the ladies, and sat down on a sofa in a far corner of the room. He closed his eyes and seemed to be dozing. His head sank forward and then he roused himself.

"Aline," he said to his wife, "go and see what they are about."

The princess went up to the door, passed by it with a dignified and indifferent air, and glanced into the little drawing room. Pierre and Hélène still sat talking just as before.

"Still the same," she said to her husband.

Prince Vasíli frowned, twisting his mouth, his cheeks quivered and his face assumed the coarse, unpleasant expression peculiar to him. Shaking himself, he rose, threw back his head, and with resolute steps went past the ladies into the little drawing room. With quick steps he went joyfully up to Pierre. His face was so unusually triumphant that Pierre rose in alarm on seeing it.

"Thank God!" said Prince Vasíli. "My wife has told me everything!"—(He put one arm around Pierre and the other around his daughter.)—"My dear boy . . . Lëlya . . . I am very pleased." (His voice trembled.) "I loved your father . . . and she will make you a good wife . . . God bless you! . . . "

He embraced his daughter, and then again Pierre, and kissed him with his malodorous mouth. Tears actually moistened his cheeks.

"Princess, come here!" he shouted.

The old princess came in and also wept. The elderly lady was using her handkerchief too. Pierre was kissed, and he kissed the beautiful Hélène's hand several times. After a while they were left alone again.

"All this had to be and could not be otherwise," thought Pierre, "so it is useless to ask whether it is good or bad. It is good because it's definite and one is rid of the old tormenting doubt." Pierre held the hand of his betrothed in silence, looking at her beautiful bosom as it rose and fell.

"Hélène!" he said aloud and paused.

"Something special is always said in such cases," he thought, but could not remember what it was that people say. He looked at her face. She drew nearer to him. Her face flushed.

"Oh, take those off . . . those . . . " she said, pointing to his spectacles.

Pierre took them off, and his eyes, besides the strange look eyes have from which spectacles have just been removed, had also a frightened and inquiring look. He was about to stoop over her hand and kiss it, but with a rapid, almost brutal movement of her head, she intercepted his lips and met them with her own. Her face struck Pierre, by its altered, unpleasantly excited expression.

"It is too late now, it's done; besides I love her," thought Pierre.

"*Je vous aime!*" he said, remembering what has to be said at such moments: but his words sounded so weak that he felt ashamed of himself.

Six weeks later he was married, and settled in Count Bezúkhov's large, newly furnished Petersburg house, the happy possessor, as people said, of a wife who was a celebrated beauty and of millions of money.

Tolstoy, *Anna Karenina:*
Levin's Proposal to Kitty

Tolstoy's Anna Karenina *(1873–77) is primarily the story of Anna's adulterous love for Vronsky, a young officer, and her tragic fate. But intertwined with it, from the beginning, is the story of Constantin Levin, whose expectations from love are as great as Anna's. While Anna's story suggests a radical disjunction between passionate love and married family life, Levin's suggests that the two may be reconcilable. Early in the novel Levin proclaims his love to Kitty Shcherbatsky, but she rejects him, for she is at the time infatuated with Vronsky, the same dashing officer who seduces Anna. When Kitty later realizes that her love for Vronsky is unrequited, that Vronsky was in fact merely toying with her, Kitty, despite her basically practical nature, becomes depressed and despairing of her future. But Levin, in the meantime, loves Kitty all the more, perhaps because of her first refusal. Several years later, Levin and Kitty are guests at a dinner party at which, among other things, the status of women and marriage are spiritedly discussed. After dinner, they have an intimate "conversation," recounted in the selection below (Part IV, Chapter XIII), in which there is a true meeting of souls. How can this happen? Skeptical readers should know that the episode described here directly corresponds to an event in Tolstoy's own life.*

When everybody was leaving the table Levin wanted to follow Kitty into the drawing-room but he was afraid she would not like it because it would make his attentions to her too obvious. So he stopped with the group of men, taking part in their conversation. But without looking through the open door at Kitty he was conscious of her movements, her looks, the place in the drawing room where she sat.

He began at once, and without the slightest effort, to fulfil the promise he had made her, of thinking well of and always liking everybody. The conversation had turned to the question of village communes, in which Pestsov saw some principle which he called the 'choral principle.' Levin did not agree either with Pestsov or with his brother Sergius, who, in a way of his own, both admitted and did not admit the importance of the Russian Communal System. But he talked to them only with the idea of getting them to agree and softening their controversy. He was not at all interested in what he himself said, still less in what they were saying, and only desired one thing—that everybody should feel contented and pleased. He now knew the one thing that was important. And that one thing was at first there in the drawing-room, but afterwards began moving and paused in the doorway. Without looking round he felt a pair of eyes and a smile directed toward him, and he could not help turning. She stood in the doorway with Shcherbatsky and was looking at him.

'I thought you were going to the piano,' he said, moving toward her. 'That is what I miss in the country—music.'

'No, we were only coming to call you away. Thank you for coming,' she said, rewarding him with a smile as with a gift. 'What is the use of arguing? No one ever convinces another.'

'Yes, you are quite right,' said Levin, 'for the most part, people argue so warmly only because they cannot make out what it is that their opponent wants to prove.'

Levin had often noticed in arguments among the most intelligent people that after expending enormous efforts, and an immense number of logical subtleties and words, the disputants at last became conscious of the fact that the thing they had been at such pains to prove to one another had long ago, from the very beginning of the controversy, been known to them but that they liked different things and were disinclined to mention what they liked lest it should be attacked. He had experienced the fact that sometimes in the middle of a discussion one understands what it is that one's opponent likes, and suddenly likes it oneself, and immediately agrees with him, when all proofs become superfluous and unnecessary. Sometimes the reverse happens; one at last mentions the thing one likes, for the sake of which one has been devising arguments, and if this is said well and sincerely, one's opponent suddenly agrees and ceases to dispute. This was what he wanted to express.

She wrinkled her forehead, trying to understand. But as soon as he began to explain she understood.

'I see one must find out what one's opponent is contending for, what he likes, and then one can . . . '

She had completely grasped and found the right expression for his badly-expressed thought. Levin smiled joyfully: he was so struck by the change from the confused wordy dispute with his brother and Pestsov to this laconic, clear, and almost wordless communication of a very complex idea.

Shcherbatsky left them, and Kitty went up to a table prepared for cards, sat down, took a piece of chalk, and began drawing concentric circles on the new green cloth of the table.

They went back to the conversation at dinner about women's rights and occupations. Levin agreed with Dolly, that a girl who does not get married can find woman's work in the family. He supported this view by saying that no family can dispense with a help, and that in every family, rich or poor, there are and must be nurses, either paid or belonging to the family.

'No,' said Kitty, blushing, but looking all the more boldly at him with her truthful eyes: 'A girl may be so placed that she cannot enter into a family without humiliation, while she herself. . . . '

He understood the allusion.

'Oh yes!' he said, 'yes, yes, yes, you are right, you are right!'

And he understood all that Pestsov at dinner had been trying to prove about the freedom of women, simply because he saw in Kitty's heart fear of the humiliation of being an old maid, and, loving her, he too felt that fear and humiliation, and at once gave up his contention.

There was a pause. She still continued drawing on the table with the chalk. Her eyes shone with a soft light. Submitting to her mood, he felt in his whole being an ever-increasing stress of joy.

'Oh, I have scribbled over the whole table!' she said, and putting down the chalk moved as if to get up.

'How can I remain here alone, without her?' he thought horror-struck, and took up the chalk. 'Don't go,' he said, and sat down at the table.

'I have long wished to ask you something!'

He looked straight into her kind though frightened eyes.

'Please do.'

'There,' he said, and wrote the following letters,—W, y, a: i, c, n, b; d, y, m, t, o, n? These letters stood for: When you answered: it can not be; did you mean then, or never? It was quite unlikely that she would be able to make out this complicated sentence; but he looked at her with an expression as if his life depended on her understanding what those letters meant.

She glanced seriously at him and then, leaning her puckered forehead on her hand, began reading. Occasionally she looked up at him, her look asking him: 'Is it what I think?'

'I have understood,' she said with a blush.

'What word is this?' he asked pointing to the 'n' which stood for never.

'The word is never,' she said, 'but that's not true.'

He quickly rubbed out what he had written, handed her the chalk and rose. She wrote: T, I, c, n, a, o.

Dolly's sorrow, caused by her talk with Karenin, was quite dispelled when she saw those two figures: Kitty with the chalk in her hand, looking up at Levin with a timid, happy smile, and his fine figure bending over the table, with his burning eyes fixed now on the table, now on her. Suddenly his face beamed; he had understood. The letters meant 'Then I could not answer otherwise.'

He looked at her questioningly, and timidly.

'Only *then*?'

'Yes,' answered her smile.

'And n. . . . And now?' he said.

'Well, then, read this. I will tell you what I wish, what I very much wish!' and she wrote these initial letters: T, y, m, f, a, f, w, h. This meant, 'that you might forgive and forget what happened.'

He seized the chalk with nervous, trembling fingers, broke it, and wrote the initial letters of the following: 'I have nothing to forget or forgive, I never ceased to love you.'

She looked at him with an assured smile that did not waver.

'I understand,' she whispered.

He sat down and wrote out a long sentence. She understood it all and without asking if she was right, took the chalk, and wrote the answer at once.

For a long time he could not make out what she meant and he often looked up in her eyes. He was dazed with happiness. He could not find the words she meant at all; but in her beautiful eyes, radiant with joy, he saw all that he wanted to know. And he wrote down three letters. But before he had finished writing she read it under his hand, finished the sentence herself, and wrote the answer: 'Yes.'

'Playing "secretary"?' said the old Prince approaching them. 'Come now, we must be going, if you mean to come to the theatre.'

Levin rose and accompanied Kitty to the door.

Everything had been said in that conversation. She had said that she loved him, and would tell her father and mother, and he had said that he would call in the morning.

Austen, *Pride and Prejudice:*
The Courtship of Darcy and Elizabeth

However desperate Jane Austen's women may be to get married (see the earlier se-
lection in the section "Why Marry?" above), Austen nevertheless leaves little doubt
that women and men thrive only in good marriages and that good marriages are
never merely economically driven. Love, mutual respect, and esteem are of pri-
mary importance. Like Rousseau, Austen suggests the importance of tying sexual
attraction to the love of virtue, and the love of virtue to the love of the person
who will be one's husband or wife and one's best friend. The marriage of Elizabeth
Bennet and Fitzwilliam Darcy exemplifies the harmonious union Austen seems
most to esteem. Their courtship, which comprises the heart of the plot of Pride
and Prejudice, *is excerpted in seven selections.*

In following the course of the courtship, the following questions may be kept
in mind. How important are first impressions? (Compare with Rousseau's Emile.*)*
How do they get changed? How do pride and prejudice function in this courtship?
Should family connections and family character matter as much as they do here?
What finally moves Elizabeth to accept Darcy? What is the connection between
love and gratitude? between love and self-knowledge? What is the character of the
love between Elizabeth and Darcy? Should we be sanguine about their marriage?

I. *Charles Bingley, a rich young bachelor, has purchased Netherfield, a house*
near Longbourn, the home of the Bennet family. Shortly after assuming his ten-
ancy, Bingley attends a neighborhood ball, bringing with him his two sisters and
his friend Darcy. Bingley, as amiable and unreserved as his friend is the opposite,
is immediately smitten by the beauty and charm of the eldest Bennet sister, Jane.
Everyone is put off by Darcy's arrogance but especially Elizabeth. Being obliged,
by the scarcity of men, to sit out two dances, she was privy to the following ex-
change between Bingley and Darcy (from Volume I, Chapter 3).

"Come, Darcy," said he, "I must have you dance. I hate to see you standing
about by yourself in this stupid manner. You had much better dance."

"I certainly shall not. You know how I detest it, unless I am particularly
acquainted with my partner. At such an assembly as this, it would be insup-
portable. Your sisters are engaged, and there is not another woman in the room,
whom it would not be a punishment to me to stand up with."

"I would not be so fastidious as you are," cried Bingley, "for a kingdom!
Upon my honour, I never met with so many pleasant girls in my life, as I have
this evening; and there are several of them you see uncommonly pretty."

"*You* are dancing with the only handsome girl in the room," said Mr. Darcy, looking at the eldest Miss Bennet.

"Oh! she is the most beautiful creature I ever beheld! But there is one of her sisters sitting down just behind you, who is very pretty, and I dare say, very agreeable. Do let me ask my partner to introduce you."

"Which do you mean?" and turning round, he looked for a moment at Elizabeth, till catching her eye, he withdrew his own and coldly said, "She is tolerable; but not handsome enough to tempt *me;* and I am in no humour at present to give consequence to young ladies who are slighted by other men. You had better return to your partner and enjoy her smiles, for you are wasting your time with me."

Mr. Bingley followed his advice. Mr. Darcy walked off; and Elizabeth remained with no very cordial feelings towards him. She told the story however with great spirit among her friends; for she had a lively, playful disposition, which delighted in any thing ridiculous.

* * *

II. *Thanks to the machinations of Mrs. Bennet, who is bent upon marrying Jane to Bingley, in the weeks following the ball, Elizabeth and Darcy repeatedly find themselves in each other's company. Fueled by her own pride (wounded in the episode recounted above) and prejudice, as well as by the confessions and accusations of the unprincipled Mr. Wickham (son of the late steward of Darcy's estate), Elizabeth's aversion to Darcy grows with each new encounter. Not so Darcy's. For compared to the lifeless sycophants (Bingley's sisters) with whom he lives, Elizabeth's impertinence, wit, and liveliness, as well as the spontaneous and uncalculating affection she has for her sister, cannot help but impress him and he begins to fall in love. Still, because he is disgusted by the vulgarity of Mrs. Bennet and her two youngest daughters, he checks his own impulses. He also puts an end to the romance of Bingley and Jane by leaving Netherfield and persuading Bingley to go with him. Months later, Elizabeth visits her newly married friend, Charlotte Lucas, and again encounters Darcy. Still captivated by her in spite of himself, Darcy proposes to Elizabeth in terms which barely conceal his own wounded pride. The excerpt is from Volume II, Chapter 11.*

"In vain have I struggled. It will not do. My feelings will not be repressed. You must allow me to tell you how ardently I admire and love you."

Elizabeth's astonishment was beyond expression. She stared, coloured, doubted, and was silent. This he considered sufficient encouragement, and the avowal of all that he felt and had long felt for her, immediately followed. He spoke well, but there were feelings besides those of the heart to be detailed, and he was not more eloquent on the subject of tenderness than of pride. His sense of her inferiority—of its being a degradation—of the family obstacles which judgment had always opposed to inclination, were dwelt on with a warmth which seemed due to the consequence he was wounding, but was very unlikely to recommend his suit.

In spite of her deeply-rooted dislike, she could not be insensible to the compliment of such a man's affection, and though her intentions did not vary for an instant, she was at first sorry for the pain he was to receive; till, roused to resentment by his subsequent language, she lost all compassion in anger. She tried, however, to compose herself to answer him with patience, when he should have done. He concluded with representing to her the strength of that attachment which, in spite of all his endeavours, he had found impossible to conquer; and with expressing his hope that it would now be rewarded by her acceptance of his hand. As he said this, she could easily see that he had no doubt of a favourable answer. He *spoke* of apprehension and anxiety, but his countenance expressed real security. Such a circumstance could only exasperate farther, and when he ceased, the colour rose into her cheeks, and she said,

"In such cases as this, it is, I believe, the established mode to express a sense of obligation for the sentiments avowed, however unequally they may be returned. It is natural that obligation should be felt, and if I could *feel* gratitude, I would now thank you. But I cannot—I have never desired your good opinion, and you have certainly bestowed it most unwillingly. I am sorry to have occasioned pain to any one. It has been most unconsciously done, however, and I hope will be of short duration. The feelings which, you tell me, have long prevented the acknowledgment of your regard, can have little difficulty in overcoming it after this explanation."

Mr. Darcy, who was leaning against the mantle-piece with his eyes fixed on her face, seemed to catch her words with no less resentment than surprise. His complexion became pale with anger, and the disturbance of his mind was visible in every feature. He was struggling for the appearance of composure, and would not open his lips, till he believed himself to have attained it. The pause was to Elizabeth's feelings dreadful. At length, in a voice of forced calmness, he said,

"And this is all the reply which I am to have the honour of expecting! I might, perhaps, wish to be informed why, with so little *endeavour* at civility, I am thus rejected. But it is of small importance."

"I might as well enquire," replied she, "why with so evident a design of offending and insulting me, you chose to tell me that you liked me against your will, against your reason, and even against your character? Was not this some excuse for incivility, if I *was* uncivil? But I have other provocations. You know I have. Had not my own feelings decided against you, had they been indifferent, or had they even been favourable, do you think that any consideration would tempt me to accept the man, who has been the means of ruining, perhaps for ever, the happiness of a most beloved sister?"

As she pronounced these words, Mr. Darcy changed colour; but the emotion was short, and he listened without attempting to interrupt her while she continued.

"I have every reason in the world to think ill of you. No motive can excuse the unjust and ungenerous part you acted *there*. You dare not, you cannot deny that you have been the principal, if not the only means of dividing them from each other, of exposing one to the censure of the world for caprice and instability, the other to its derision for disappointed hopes, and involving them both in misery of the acutest kind."

She paused, and saw with no slight indignation that he was listening with an air which proved him wholly unmoved by any feeling of remorse. He even looked at her with a smile of affected incredulity.

"Can you deny that you have done it?" she repeated.

With assumed tranquillity he then replied, "I have no wish of denying that I did every thing in my power to separate my friend from your sister, or that I rejoice in my success. Towards *him* I have been kinder than towards myself."

Elizabeth disdained the appearance of noticing this civil reflection, but its meaning did not escape, nor was it likely to conciliate her.

"But it is not merely this affair," she continued, "on which my dislike is founded. Long before it had taken place, my opinion of you was decided. Your character was unfolded in the recital which I received many months ago from Mr. Wickham. On this subject, what can you have to say? In what imaginary act of friendship can you here defend yourself? or under what misrepresentation, can you here impose upon others?"

"You take an eager interest in that gentleman's concerns," said Darcy in a less tranquil tone, and with a heightened colour.

"Who that knows what his misfortunes have been, can help feeling an interest in him?"

"His misfortunes!" repeated Darcy contemptuously; "yes, his misfortunes have been great indeed."

"And of your infliction," cried Elizabeth with energy. "You have reduced him to his present state of poverty, comparative poverty. You have withheld the advantages, which you must know to have been designed for him. You have deprived the best years of his life, of that independence which was no less his due than his desert. You have done all this! and yet you can treat the mention of his misfortunes with contempt and ridicule."

"And this," cried Darcy, as he walked with quick steps across the room, "is your opinion of me! This is the estimation in which you hold me! I thank you for explaining it so fully. My faults, according to this calculation, are heavy indeed! But perhaps," added he, stopping in his walk, and turning towards her, "these offences might have been overlooked, had not your pride been hurt by my honest confession of the scruples that had long prevented my forming any serious design. These bitter accusations might have been suppressed, had I with greater policy concealed my struggles, and flattered you into the belief of my being impelled by unqualified, unalloyed inclination; by reason, by reflection, by every thing. But disguise of every sort is my abhorrence. Nor am I ashamed of the feelings I related. They were natural and just. Could you expect me to rejoice in the inferiority of your connections? To congratulate myself on the hope of relations, whose condition in life is so decidedly beneath my own?"

Elizabeth felt herself growing more angry every moment; yet she tried to the utmost to speak with composure when she said,

"You are mistaken, Mr. Darcy, if you suppose that the mode of your declaration affected me in any other way, than as it spared me the concern which I might have felt in refusing you, had you behaved in a more gentleman-like manner."

She saw him start at this, but he said nothing, and she continued,

"You could not have made me the offer of your hand in any possible way that would have tempted me to accept it."

Again his astonishment was obvious; and he looked at her with an expression of mingled incredulity and mortification. She went on.

"From the very beginning, from the first moment I may almost say, of my acquaintance with you, your manners impressing me with the fullest belief of your arrogance, your conceit, and your selfish disdain of the feelings of others, were such as to form that ground-work of disapprobation, on which succeeding events have built so immoveable a dislike; and I had not known you a month before I felt that you were the last man in the world whom I could ever be prevailed on to marry."

"You have said quite enough, madam. I perfectly comprehend your feelings, and have now only to be ashamed of what my own have been. Forgive me for having taken up so much of your time, and accept my best wishes for your health and happiness."

And with these words he hastily left the room, and Elizabeth heard him the next moment open the front door and quit the house.

The tumult of her mind was now painfully great. She knew not how to support herself, and from actual weakness sat down and cried for half an hour. Her astonishment, as she reflected on what had passed, was increased by every review of it. That she should receive an offer of marriage from Mr. Darcy! that he should have been in love with her for so many months! so much in love as to wish to marry her in spite of all the objections which had made him prevent his friend's marrying her sister, and which must appear at least with equal force in his own case, was almost incredible! it was gratifying to have inspired unconsciously so strong an affection. But his pride, his abominable pride, his shameless avowal of what he had done with respect to Jane, his unpardonable assurance in acknowledging, though he could not justify it, and the unfeeling manner in which he had mentioned Mr. Wickham, his cruelty towards whom he had not attempted to deny, soon overcame the pity which the consideration of his attachment had for a moment excited.

* * *

III. *The next morning Darcy gives Elizabeth a letter explaining his actions. Apparently, Elizabeth's indignant rejection of his proposal awakened his consciousness of his own pride and prejudice. His letter seems to affect Elizabeth similarly. The excerpt is from Chapters 12 and 13 of Volume II.*

Elizabeth awoke the next morning to the same thoughts and meditations which had at length closed her eyes. She could not yet recover from the surprise of what had happened; it was impossible to think of any thing else, and totally indisposed for employment, she resolved soon after breakfast to indulge herself in air and exercise. She was proceeding directly to her favourite walk, when the recollection of Mr. Darcy's sometimes coming there stopped her, and instead of entering the park, she turned up the lane which led her farther from the turnpike road. The park paling was still the boundary on one side, and she soon passed one of the gates into the ground.

After walking two or three times along that part of the lane, she was tempted, by the pleasantness of the morning, to stop at the gates and look into the park. The five weeks which she had now passed in Kent, had made a great difference in the country, and every day was adding to the verdure of the early trees. She was on the point of continuing her walk, when she caught a glimpse of a gentleman within the sort of grove which edged the park: he was moving that way; and fearful of its being Mr. Darcy, she was directly retreating. But the person who advanced, was now near enough to see her, and stepping forward with eagerness, pronounced her name. She had turned away, but on hearing herself called, though in a voice which proved it to be Mr. Darcy, she moved again towards the gate. He had by that time reached it also, and holding out a letter, which she instinctively took, said with a look of haughty composure, "I have been walking in the grove some time in the hope of meeting you. Will you do me the honour of reading that letter?"—And then, with a slight bow, turned again into the plantation,[1] and was soon out of sight.

With no expectation of pleasure, but with the strongest curiosity, Elizabeth

---

[1]Wood of planted trees.

opened the letter, and to her still increasing wonder, perceived an envelope containing two sheets of letter paper, written quite through, in a very close hand.—The envelope itself was likewise full.—Pursuing her way along the lane, she then began it. It was dated from Rosings, at eight o'clock in the morning, and was as follows:—

"Be not alarmed, Madam, on receiving this letter, by the apprehension of its containing any repetition of those sentiments, or renewal of those offers, which were last night so disgusting to you. I write without any intention of paining you, or humbling myself, by dwelling on wishes, which, for the happiness of both, cannot be too soon forgotten; and the effort which the formation, and the perusal of this letter must occasion, should have been spared, had not my character required it to be written and read. You must, therefore, pardon the freedom with which I demand your attention; your feelings, I know, will bestow it unwillingly, but I demand it of your justice.

"Two offences of a very different nature, and by no means of equal magnitude, you last night laid to my charge. The first mentioned was, that, regardless of the sentiments of either, I had detached Mr. Bingley from your sister,—and the other, that I had, in defiance of various claims, in defiance of honour and humanity, ruined the immediate prosperity, and blasted the prospects of Mr. Wickham.—Wilfully and wantonly to have thrown off the companion of my youth, the acknowledged favourite of my father, a young man who had scarcely any other dependence than on our patronage, and who had been brought up to expect its exertion, would be a depravity, to which the separation of two young persons, whose affection could be the growth of only a few weeks, could bear no comparison.—But from the severity of that blame which was last night so liberally bestowed, respecting each circumstance, I shall hope to be in future secured, when the following account of my actions and their motives has been read.—If, in the explanation of them which is due to myself, I am under the necessity of relating feelings which may be offensive to your's, I can only say that I am sorry.—The necessity must be obeyed—and farther apology would be absurd.—I had not been long in Hertfordshire, before I saw, in common with others, that Bingley preferred your eldest sister, to any other young woman in the country.—But it was not till the evening of the dance at Netherfield that I had any apprehension of his feeling a serious attachment.—I had often seen him in love before.—At that ball, while I had the honour of dancing with you, I was first made acquainted, by Sir William Lucas's accidental information, that Bingley's attentions to your sister had given rise to a general expectation of their marriage. He spoke of it as a certain event, of which the time alone could be undecided. From that moment I observed my friend's behaviour attentively; and I could then perceive that his partiality for Miss Bennet was beyond what I had ever witnessed in him. Your sister I also watched.—Her look and manners were open, cheerful and engaging as ever, but without any symptom of peculiar regard, and I remained convinced from the evening's scrutiny, that though she received his attentions with pleasure, she did not invite them by any participation of sentiment.—If *you* have not been mistaken here, *I* must have been in an error. Your superior knowledge of your sister must make the latter probable.—If it be so, if I have been misled by such error, to inflict pain on her, your resentment has not been unreasonable. But I shall not scruple to assert, that the serenity of your sister's countenance and air was such, as might have given the most acute observer, a conviction that, however amiable her temper, her heart was not likely to be easily touched.—That I was desirous of believing her indifferent is certain,—but I will venture to say that my investigations and decisions are not usually influenced by my hopes or fears.—I did not believe her to be indifferent because I wished it;—I believed it on impartial conviction, as truly as I wished it in reason.—My objections to the marriage were not merely those, which I last night acknowledged to have required the utmost force of passion to put aside, in my own case; the want of connection could not be so great an evil to my friend as to me.—But there were other causes of repugnance;—causes which, though still existing, and existing to an equal degree in both instances, I had myself endeavoured to forget, because they were not immediately before me.—These causes must be stated, though briefly.—The situation of your mother's family, though objectionable, was nothing in comparison of that total want of propriety so frequently, so almost uniformly betrayed by herself, by your three younger sisters, and occasionally even by your father.—Pardon me.—It pains me to offend you. But amidst your concern for the defects of your nearest relations, and your displeasure at this representation of them, let it give you consolation to consider that, to have conducted yourselves so as to avoid any share of the like censure, is praise no less generally bestowed on you and your eldest sister, than it is honourable to the sense and disposition of both.—I will only say farther, that from what passed that evening, my opinion of all parties was confirmed, and every inducement heightened, which could have led me before, to preserve my friend from what I esteemed a most unhappy connection.—He left Netherfield for London, on the day following, as you, I am certain, remember, with the design of soon returning.—The part which I acted, is now to be explained.—His sisters' uneasiness had been equally excited with my own; our coincidence of feeling was soon discovered; and, alike sensible that no time was to be lost in detaching their brother, we shortly resolved on joining him directly in London.—We accordingly went—and there I readily engaged in the office of pointing out to my friend, the certain evils of such a choice.—I described, and enforced them earnestly.—But, however this remonstrance might have staggered or delayed his determination, I do not suppose that it would ultimately have prevented the marriage, had it not been seconded by the assurance which I hesitated not in giving, of your sister's indifference. He had before believed her to return his affection with sincere, if not with equal regard.—But Bingley has great natural modesty, with a stronger dependence on my judgment than on his own.—To convince him, therefore, that he had deceived himself, was no very difficult point. To persuade him against returning into Hertfordshire, when that conviction had been given, was scarcely the work of a moment.—I cannot blame myself for having done thus much. There is but one part of my conduct in the whole affair, on which I do not reflect with satisfaction; it is that I condescended to adopt the measures of art so far as to conceal from him your sister's being in town. I knew it myself, as it was known to Miss Bingley, but her brother is even yet ignorant of it.—That they might have met without ill consequence, is perhaps probable;—but his regard did not appear to me enough extinguished for him to see her without some danger.—Perhaps this concealment, this disguise, was beneath me.—It is done, however, and it was done for the best.—On this subject I have nothing more to say, no other apology to offer. If I have wounded your sister's feelings, it was unknowingly done; and though the motives which governed me may to you very naturally appear insufficient, I have not yet learnt to condemn them.—With respect to that other, more weighty accusation, of having injured Mr. Wickham, I can only refute it by laying before you the whole of his connection with my family. Of what he has *particularly* accused me I am ignorant; but of the truth of what I shall relate, I can summon more than one witness of undoubted veracity. Mr. Wickham is the son of a very respectable man, who had for many years the management of all the Pemberley estates; and whose good conduct in the discharge of his trust, naturally inclined my father to be of service to him, and on George Wickham, who was his god-son, his kindness was therefore liberally bestowed. My father supported him at school, and afterwards at Cambridge;—most important assistance, as his own father, always poor from the extravagance of his wife, would have been unable to give him a gentleman's education. My father was not only fond of this young man's society, whose manners were always engaging; he had also the highest opinion of him, and hoping the church would be his profession, intended to provide for him in it. As for myself, it is many, many years since I first began to think of him in a very different manner. The vicious propensities—the want of principle which he was careful to guard from the knowledge of his best friend, could not escape the observation of a young man of nearly the same age with himself, and who had opportunities of seeing him in unguarded moments, which Mr. Darcy could not have. Here again I shall give you pain—to what degree you only can tell. But whatever may be the sentiments which Mr. Wickham has created, a suspicion of their nature shall not prevent me from unfolding his real character.

It adds even another motive. My excellent father died about five years ago; and his attachment to Mr. Wickham was to the last so steady, that in his will he particularly recommended it to me, to promote his advancement in the best manner that his profession might allow, and if he took orders, desired that a valuable family living might be his as soon as it became vacant. There was also a legacy of one thousand pounds. His own father did not long survive mine, and within half a year from these events, Mr. Wickham wrote to inform me that, having finally resolved against taking orders, he hoped I should not think it unreasonable for him to expect some more immediate pecuniary advantage, in lieu of the preferment, by which he could not be benefited. He had some intention, he added, of studying the law, and I must be aware that the interest of one thousand pounds would be a very insufficient support therein. I rather wished, than believed him to be sincere; but at any rate, was perfectly ready to accede to his proposal. I knew that Mr. Wickham ought not to be a clergyman. The business was therefore soon settled. He resigned all claim to assistance in the church, were it possible that he could ever be in a situation to receive it, and accepted in return three thousand pounds. All connection between us seemed now dissolved. I thought too ill of him, to invite him to Pemberley, or admit his society in town. In town I believe he chiefly lived, but his studying the law was a mere pretence, and being now free from all restraint, his life was a life of idleness and dissipation. For about three years I heard little of him; but on the decease of the incumbent of the living which had been designed for him, he applied to me again by letter for the presentation. His circumstances, he assured me, and I had no difficulty in believing it, were exceedingly bad. He had found the law a most unprofitable study, and was now absolutely resolved on being ordained, if I would present him to the living in question—of which he trusted there could be little doubt, as he was well assured that I had no other person to provide for, and I could not have forgotten my revered father's intentions. You will hardly blame me for refusing to comply with this entreaty, or for resisting every repetition of it. His resentment was in proportion to the distress of his circumstances—and he was doubtless as violent in his abuse of me to others, as in his reproaches to myself. After this period, every appearance of acquaintance was dropt. How he lived I know not. But last summer he was again most painfully obtruded on my notice. I must now mention a circumstance which I would wish to forget myself, and which no obligation less than the present should induce me to unfold to any human being. Having said thus much, I feel no doubt of your secrecy. My sister, who is more than ten years my junior, was left to the guardianship of my mother's nephew, Colonel Fitzwilliam, and myself. About a year ago, she was taken from school, and an establishment formed for her in London; and last summer she went with the lady who presided over it, to Ramsgate; and thither also went Mr. Wickham, undoubtedly by design; for there proved to have been a prior acquaintance between him and Mrs. Younge, in whose character we were most unhappily deceived; and by her connivance and aid, he so far recommended himself to Georgiana, whose affectionate heart retained a strong impression of his kindness to her as a child, that she was persuaded to believe herself in love, and to consent to an elopement. She was then but fifteen, which must be her excuse; and after stating her imprudence, I am happy to add, that I owed the knowledge of it to herself. I joined them unexpectedly a day or two before the intended elopement, and then Georgiana, unable to support the idea of grieving and offending a brother whom she almost looked up to as a father, acknowledged the whole to me. You may imagine what I felt and how I acted. Regard for my sister's credit and feelings prevented any public exposure, but I wrote to Mr. Wickham, who left the place immediately, and Mrs. Younge was of course removed from her charge. Mr. Wickham's chief object was unquestionably my sister's fortune, which is thirty thousand pounds; but I cannot help supposing that the hope of revenging himself on me, was a strong inducement. His revenge would have been complete indeed. This, madam, is a faithful narrative of every event in which we have been concerned together; and if you do not absolutely reject it as false, you will, I hope, acquit me henceforth of cruelty towards Mr. Wickham. I know not in what manner, under what form of falsehood he has imposed on you; but his success is not perhaps to be wondered at. Ignorant as you previously were of every thing concerning either, detection could not be in your power, and suspicion certainly not in your inclination. You may possibly wonder why all this was not told you last night. But I was not then master enough of myself to know what could or ought to be revealed. For the truth of every thing here related, I can appeal more particularly to the testimony of Colonel Fitzwilliam, who from our near relationship and constant intimacy, and still more as one of the executors of my father's will, has been unavoidably acquainted with every particular of these transactions. If your abhorrence of *me* should make *my* assertions valueless, you cannot be prevented by the same cause from confiding in my cousin; and that there may be the possibility of consulting him, I shall endeavour to find some opportunity of putting this letter in your hands in the course of the morning. I will only add, God bless you.

"FITZWILLIAM DARCY"

*

If Elizabeth, when Mr. Darcy gave her the letter, did not expect it to contain a renewal of his offers, she had formed no expectation at all of its contents. But such as they were, it may be well supposed how eagerly she went through them, and what a contrariety of emotion they excited. Her feelings as she read were scarcely to be defined. With amazement did she first understand that he believed any apology to be in his power; and stedfastly was she persuaded that he could have no explanation to give, which a just sense of shame would not conceal. With a strong prejudice against every thing he might say, she began his account of what had happened at Netherfield. She read, with an eagerness which hardly left her power of comprehension, and from impatience of knowing what the next sentence might bring, was incapable of attending to the sense of the one before her eyes. His belief of her sister's insensibility, she instantly resolved to be false, and his account of the real, the worst objections to the match, made her too angry to have any wish of doing him justice. He expressed no regret for what he had done which satisfied her; his style was not penitent, but haughty. It was all pride and insolence.

But when this subject was succeeded by his account of Mr. Wickham, when she read with somewhat clearer attention, a relation of events, which, if true, must overthrow every cherished opinion of his worth, and which bore so alarming an affinity to his own history of himself, her feelings were yet more acutely painful and more difficult of definition. Astonishment, apprehension, and even horror, oppressed her. She wished to discredit it entirely, repeatedly exclaiming, "This must be false! This cannot be! This must be the grossest falsehood!"—and when she had gone through the whole letter, though scarcely knowing any thing of the last page or two, put it hastily away, protesting that she would not regard it, that she would never look in it again.

In this perturbed state of mind, with thoughts that could rest on nothing, she walked on; but it would not do; in half a minute the letter was unfolded again, and collecting herself as well as she could, she again began the mortifying perusal of all that related to Wickham, and commanded herself so far as to examine the meaning of every sentence. The account of his connection with the Pemberley family, was exactly what he had related himself; and the kindness of the late Mr. Darcy, though she had not before known its extent, agreed equally well with his own words. So far each recital confirmed the other: but when she came to the will, the difference was great. What Wickham had said of the living was fresh in her memory, and as she recalled his very words, it was impossible not to feel that there was gross duplicity on one side or the other; and, for a few moments, she flattered herself that her wishes did not err. But when she read, and re-read with the closest attention, the particulars immediately following of Wickham's resigning all pretensions to the living, of his receiving in lieu, so considerable a sum as three thousand pounds, again was she forced to hesitate. She put down the letter, weighed every circumstance with what she meant to be impartiality—deliberated on the probability of each statement—but with little success. On both sides it was only assertion. Again she read on. But every line proved more clearly that the affair, which she had believed it impossible that any contrivance could so represent, as to render Mr. Darcy's conduct in it less than infamous, was capable of a turn which must make him entirely blameless throughout the whole.

The extravagance and general profligacy which he scrupled not to lay to Mr. Wickham's charge, exceedingly shocked her; the more so, as she could bring no proof of its injustice. She had never heard of him before his entrance into the _____ shire Militia, in which he had engaged at the persuasion of the young man, who, on meeting him accidentally in town, had there renewed a slight acquaintance. Of his former way of life, nothing had been known in Hertfordshire but what he told himself. As to his real character, had information been in her power, she had never felt a wish of enquiring. His countenance, voice, and manner, had established him at once in the possession of every virtue. She tried to recollect some instance of goodness, some distinguished trait of integrity or benevolence, that might rescue him from the attacks of Mr. Darcy; or at least, by the predominance of virtue, atone for those casual errors, under which she would endeavour to class, what Mr. Darcy had described as the idleness and vice of many years continuance. But no such recollection befriended her. She could see him instantly before her, in every charm of air and address; but she could remember no more substantial good than the general approbation of the neighbourhood, and the regard which his social powers had gained him in the mess. After pausing on this point a considerable while, she once more continued to read. But, alas! the story which followed of his designs on Miss Darcy, received some confirmation from what had passed between Colonel Fitzwilliam and herself only the morning before; and at last she was referred for the truth of every particular to Colonel Fitzwilliam himself—from whom she had previously received the information of his near concern in all his cousin's affairs, and whose character she had no reason to question. At one time she had almost resolved on applying to him, but the idea was checked by the awkwardness of the application, and at length wholly banished by the conviction that Mr. Darcy would never have hazarded such a proposal, if he had not been well assured of his cousin's corroboration.

She perfectly remembered every thing that had passed in conversation between Wickham and herself, in their first evening at Mr. Philips's. Many of his expressions were still fresh in her memory. She was *now* struck with the impropriety of such communications to a stranger, and wondered it had escaped her before. She saw the indelicacy of putting himself forward as he had done, and the inconsistency of his professions with his conduct. She remembered that he had boasted of having no fear of seeing Mr. Darcy—that Mr. Darcy might leave the country, but that *he* should stand his ground; yet he had avoided the Netherfield ball the very next week. She remembered also, that till the Netherfield family had quitted the country, he had told his story to no one but herself; but that after their removal, it had been every where discussed; that he had then no reserves, no scruples in sinking Mr. Darcy's character, though he had assured her that respect for the father, would always prevent his exposing the son.

How differently did every thing now appear in which he was concerned! His attentions to Miss King were now the consequence of views solely and hatefully mercenary; and the mediocrity of her fortune proved no longer the moderation of his wishes, but his eagerness to grasp at any thing. His behaviour to herself could now have had no tolerable motive; he had either been deceived with regard to her fortune, or had been gratifying his vanity by encouraging the preference which she believed she had most incautiously shewn. Every lingering struggle in his favour grew fainter and fainter, and in farther justification of Mr. Darcy, she could not but allow that Mr. Bingley, when questioned by Jane, had long ago asserted his blamelessness in the affair; that proud and repulsive as were his manners, she had never, in the whole course of their acquaintance, an acquaintance which had latterly brought them much together, and given her a sort of intimacy with his ways, seen any thing that betrayed him to be unprincipled or unjust—any thing that spoke him of irreligious or immoral habits. That among his own connections he was esteemed and valued—that even Wickham had allowed him merit as a brother, and that she had often heard him speak so affectionately of his sister as to prove him capable of *some* amiable feeling. That had his actions been what Wickham represented them, so gross a violation of every thing right could hardly have been concealed from the world; and that friendship between a person capable of it, and such an amiable man as Mr. Bingley, was incomprehensible.

She grew absolutely ashamed of herself.—Of neither Darcy nor Wickham could she think, without feeling that she had been blind, partial, prejudiced, absurd.

"How despicably have I acted!" she cried.—"I, who have prided myself on my discernment!—I, who have valued myself on my abilities! who have often disdained the generous candour of my sister, and gratified my vanity, in useless or blameable distrust.—How humiliating is this discovery!—Yet, how just a humiliation!—Had I been in love, I could not have been more wretchedly blind. But vanity, not love, has been my folly.—Pleased with the preference of one, and offended by the neglect of the other, on the very beginning of our acquaintance, I have courted prepossession and ignorance, and driven reason away, where either were concerned. Till this moment, I never knew myself."

From herself to Jane—from Jane to Bingley, her thoughts were in a line which soon brought to her recollection that Mr. Darcy's explanation *there*, had appeared very insufficient; and she read it again. Widely different was the effect of a second perusal.—How could she deny that credit to his assertions, in one instance, which she had been obliged to give in the other?—He declared himself to have been totally unsuspicious of her sister's attachment;—and she could not help remembering what Charlotte's opinion had always been.—Neither could she deny the justice of his description of Jane.—She felt that Jane's feelings, though fervent, were little displayed, and that there was a constant complacency in her air and manner, not often united with great sensibility.

When she came to that part of the letter in which her family were mentioned, in terms of such mortifying, yet merited reproach, her sense of shame was severe. The justice of the charge struck her too forcibly for denial, and the circumstances to which he particularly alluded, as having passed at the Netherfield ball, and as confirming all his first disapprobation, could not have made a stronger impression on his mind than on hers.

The compliment to herself and her sister, was not unfelt. It soothed, but it could not console her for the contempt which had been thus self-attracted by the rest of her family;—and as she considered that Jane's disappointment had in fact been the work of her nearest relations, and reflected how materially the credit of both must be hurt by such impropriety of conduct, she felt depressed beyond any thing she had ever known before.

* * *

IV. *Again, several months pass. It is summer. Elizabeth travels to the north of England with her uncle and aunt, Mr. and Mrs. Gardiner. Hitherto unaware of Elizabeth's relations to Darcy, the Gardiners propose a visit to Pemberley, Darcy's estate. Believing Darcy to be absent, Elizabeth very reluctantly agrees to join them. However, Darcy suddenly appears and welcomes the visitors. The selection is from Volume III, Chapter 1.*

Elizabeth, as they drove along, watched for the first appearance of Pemberley Woods with some perturbation; and when at length they turned in at the lodge, her spirits were in a high flutter.

The park was very large, and contained great variety of ground. They entered it in one of its lowest points, and drove for some time through a beautiful wood, stretching over a wide extent.

Elizabeth's mind was too full for conversation, but she saw and admired every remarkable spot and point of view. They gradually ascended for half a mile, and then found themselves at the top of a considerable eminence, where the wood ceased, and the eye was instantly caught by Pemberley House, situated on the opposite side of a valley, into which the road with some abruptness wound. It was a large, handsome, stone building, standing well on rising ground, and backed by a ridge of high woody hills;—and in front, a stream of some natural importance was swelled into greater, but without any artificial appearance. Its banks were neither formal, nor falsely adorned. Elizabeth was delighted. She had never seen a place for which nature had done more, or where natural beauty had been so little counteracted by an awkward taste. They were all of them warm in their admiration; and at that moment she felt, that to be mistress of Pemberley might be something!

They descended the hill, crossed the bridge, and drove to the door; and, while examining the nearer aspect of the house, all her apprehensions of meeting its owner returned. She dreaded lest the chambermaid had been mistaken. On applying to see the place, they were admitted into the hall; and Elizabeth, as they waited for the housekeeper, had leisure to wonder at her being where she was.

The housekeeper came; a respectable-looking, elderly woman, much less fine, and more civil, than she had any notion of finding her. They followed her into the dining-parlour. It was a large, well-proportioned room, handsomely fitted up. Elizabeth, after slightly surveying it, went to a window to enjoy its prospect. The hill, crowned with wood, from which they had descended, receiving increased abruptness from the distance, was a beautiful object. Every disposition of the ground was good; and she looked on all the whole scene, the river, the trees scattered on its banks, and the winding of the valley, as far as she could trace it, with delight. As they passed into other rooms, these objects were taking different positions; but from every window there were beauties to be seen. The rooms were lofty and handsome, and their furniture suitable to the fortune of their proprietor; but Elizabeth saw, with admiration of his taste, that it was neither gaudy nor uselessly fine; with less of splendor, and more real elegance, than the furniture of Rosings.

"And of this place," thought she, "I might have been mistress! With these rooms I might now have been familiarly acquainted! Instead of viewing them as a stranger, I might have rejoiced in them as my own, and welcomed to them as visitors my uncle and aunt.—But no,"—recollecting herself,—"that could never be: my uncle and aunt would have been lost to me: I should not have been allowed to invite them."

This was a lucky recollection—it saved her from something like regret.

She longed to enquire of the housekeeper, whether her master were really absent, but had not courage for it. At length, however, the question was asked by her uncle; and she turned away with alarm, while Mrs. Reynolds replied, that he was, adding, "but we expect him tomorrow, with a large party of friends." How rejoiced was Elizabeth that their own journey had not by any circumstance been delayed a day!

Her aunt now called her to look at a picture. She approached, and saw the likeness of Mr. Wickham suspended, amongst several other miniatures, over the mantlepiece. Her aunt asked her, smilingly, how she liked it. The house-keeper came forward, and told them it was the picture of a young gentleman, the son of her late master's steward, who had been brought up by him at his own expence.—"He is now gone into the army," she added, "but I am afraid he has turned out very wild."

Mrs. Gardiner looked at her niece with a smile, but Elizabeth could not return it.

"And that," said Mrs. Reynolds, pointing to another of the miniatures, "is my master—and very like him. It was drawn at the same time as the other—about eight years ago."

"I have heard much of your master's fine person," said Mrs. Gardiner, looking at the picture; "it is a handsome face. But, Lizzy, you can tell us whether it is like or not."

Mrs. Reynolds's respect for Elizabeth seemed to increase on this intimation of her knowing her master.

"Does that young lady know Mr. Darcy?"

Elizabeth coloured, and said—"A little."

"And do not you think him a very handsome gentleman, Ma'am?"

"Yes, very handsome."

"I am sure *I* know none so handsome; but in the gallery up stairs you will see a finer, larger picture of him than this. This room was my late master's favourite room, and these miniatures are just as they used to be then. He was very fond of them."

This accounted to Elizabeth for Mr. Wickham's being among them.

Mrs. Reynolds then directed their attention to one of Miss Darcy, drawn when she was only eight years old.

"And is Miss Darcy as handsome as her brother?" said Mr. Gardiner.

"Oh! yes—the handsomest young lady that ever was seen; and so accomplished!—She plays and sings all day long. In the next room is a new instrument just come down for her—a present from my master; she comes here to-morrow with him."

Mr. Gardiner, whose manners were easy and pleasant, encouraged her communicativeness by his questions and remarks; Mrs. Reynolds, either from pride or attachment, had evidently great pleasure in talking of her master and his sister.

"Is your master much at Pemberley in the course of the year?"

"Not so much as I could wish, Sir; but I dare say he may spend half his time here; and Miss Darcy is always down for the summer months."

"Except," thought Elizabeth, "when she goes to Ramsgate."

"If your master would marry, you might see more of him."

"Yes, Sir; but I do not know when *that* will be. I do not know who is good enough for him."

Mr. and Mrs. Gardiner smiled. Elizabeth could not help saying, "It is very much to his credit, I am sure, that you should think so."

"I say no more than the truth, and what every body will say that knows him," replied the other. Elizabeth thought this was going pretty far; and she listened with increasing astonishment as the housekeeper added, "I have never had a cross word from him in my life, and I have known him ever since he was four years old."

This was praise, of all others most extraordinary, most opposite to her ideas. That he was not a good-tempered man, had been her firmest opinion. Her keenest attention was awakened; she longed to hear more, and was grateful to her uncle for saying,

"There are very few people of whom so much can be said. You are lucky in having such a master."

"Yes, Sir, I know I am. If I was to go through the world, I could not meet with a better. But I have always observed, that they who are good-natured when children, are good-natured when they grow up; and he was always the sweetest-tempered, most generous-hearted, boy in the world."

Elizabeth almost stared at her.—"Can this be Mr. Darcy!" thought she.

"His father was an excellent man," said Mrs. Gardiner.

"Yes, Ma'am, that he was indeed; and his son will be just like him—just as affable to the poor."

Elizabeth listened, wondered, doubted, and was impatient for more. Mrs. Reynolds could interest her on no other point. She related the subject of the pictures, the dimensions of the rooms, and the price of the furniture, in vain. Mr. Gardiner, highly amused by the kind of family prejudice, to which he attributed her excessive commendation of her master, soon led again to the subject; and she dwelt with energy on his many merits, as they proceeded together up the great staircase.

"He is the best landlord, and the best master," said she, "that ever lived. Not like the wild young men now-a-days, who think of nothing but themselves. There is not one of his tenants or servants but what will give him a good name. Some people call him proud; but I am sure I never saw any thing of it. To my fancy, it is only because he does not rattle away like other young men."

"In what an amiable light does this place him!" thought Elizabeth.

"This fine account of him," whispered her aunt, as they walked, "is not quite consistent with his behaviour to our poor friend."

"Perhaps we might be deceived."

"That is not very likely, our authority was too good."

On reaching the spacious lobby above, they were shewn into a very pretty sitting-room, lately fitted up with greater elegance and lightness than the apartments below; and were informed that it was but just done, to give pleasure to Miss Darcy, who had taken a liking to the room, when last at Pemberley.

"He is certainly a good brother," said Elizabeth, as she walked towards one of the windows.

Mrs. Reynolds anticipated Miss Darcy's delight, when she should enter the room. "And this is always the way with him," she added.—"Whatever can give his sister any pleasure, is sure to be done in a moment. There is nothing he would not do for her."

The picture gallery, and two or three of the principal bed-rooms, were all that remained to be shewn. In the former were many good paintings; but Elizabeth knew nothing of the art; and from such as had been already visible below, she had willingly turned to look at some drawings of Miss Darcy's, in crayons, whose subjects were usually more interesting, and also more intelligible.

In the gallery there were many family portraits, but they could have little to fix the attention of a stranger. Elizabeth walked on in quest of the only face whose features would be known to her. At last it arrested her—and she beheld a striking resemblance of Mr. Darcy, with such a smile over the face, as she remembered to have sometimes seen, when he looked at her. She stood several minutes before the picture in earnest contemplation, and returned to it again before they quitted the gallery. Mrs. Reynolds informed them, that it had been taken in his father's life time.

There was certainly at this moment, in Elizabeth's mind, a more gentle sensation towards the original, than she had ever felt in the height of their acquaint. The commendation bestowed on him by Mrs. Reynolds was of no trifling nature. What praise is more valuable than the praise of an intelligent servant? As a brother, a landlord, a master, she considered how many people's happiness were in his guardianship!—How much of pleasure or pain it was in his power to bestow!—How much of good or evil must be done by him! Every idea that had been brought forward by the housekeeper was favourable to his character, and as she stood before the canvas, on which he was represented, and fixed his eyes upon herself, she thought of his regard with a deeper sentiment of gratitude than it had ever raised before; she remembered its warmth, and softened its impropriety of expression.

When all of the house that was open to general inspection had been seen, they returned down stairs, and taking leave of the housekeeper, were consigned over to the gardener, who met them at the hall door.

As they walked across the lawn towards the river, Elizabeth turned back to look again; her uncle and aunt stopped also, and while the former was conjecturing as to the date of the building, the owner of it himself suddenly came forward from the road, which led behind it to the stables.

They were within twenty yards of each other, and so abrupt was his appearance, that it was impossible to avoid his sight. Their eyes instantly met, and the cheeks of each were overspread with the deepest blush. He absolutely started, and for a moment seemed immovable from surprise; but shortly recovering himself, advanced towards the party, and spoke to Elizabeth, if not in terms of perfect composure, at least of perfect civility.

She had instinctively turned away, but, stopping on his approach, received his compliments with an embarrassment impossible to be overcome. Had his first appearance, or his resemblance to the picture they had just been examining, been insufficient to assure the other two that they now saw Mr. Darcy, the gardener's expression of surprise, on beholding his master, must immediately have told it. They stood a little aloof while he was talking to their niece, who, astonished and confused, scarcely dared lift her eyes to his face, and knew not what answer she returned to his civil enquiries after her family. Amazed at the alteration in his manner since they last parted, every sentence that he uttered was increasing her embarrassment; and every idea of the impropriety of her being found there, recurring to her mind, the few minutes in which they continued together, were some of the most uncomfortable of her life. Nor did he seem much more at ease; when he spoke, his accent had none of its usual sedateness; and he repeated his enquiries as to the time of her having left Longbourn, and of her stay in Derbyshire, so often, and in so hurried a way, as plainly spoke the distraction of his thoughts.

At length, every idea seemed to fail him; and, after standing a few moments without saying a word, he suddenly recollected himself, and took leave.

The others then joined her, and expressed their admiration of his figure; but Elizabeth heard not a word, and, wholly engrossed by her own feelings, followed them in silence. She was overpowered by shame and vexation. Her coming there was the most unfortunate, the most ill-judged thing in the world! How strange must it appear to him! In what a disgraceful light might it not strike so vain a man! It might seem as if she had purposely thrown herself in his way again! Oh! why did she come? or, why did he thus come a day before he was expected? Had they been only ten minutes sooner, they should have been beyond the reach of his discrimination, for it was plain that he was that moment arrived, that moment alighted from his horse or his carriage. She blushed again and again over the perverseness of the meeting. And his behaviour, so strikingly altered,—what could it mean? That he should even speak to her was amazing!—but to speak with such civility, to enquire after her family! Never in her life had she seen his manners so little dignified, never had he spoken with such gentleness as on this unexpected meeting. What a contrast did it offer to his last address in Rosing's Park, when he put his letter into her hand! She knew not what to think, nor how to account for it.

They had now entered a beautiful walk by the side of the water, and every step was bringing forward a nobler fall of ground, or a finer reach of the woods to which they were approaching; but it was some time before Elizabeth was sensible of any of it; and, though she answered mechanically to the repeated appeals of her uncle and aunt, and seemed to direct her eyes to such objects as they pointed out, she distinguished no part of the scene. Her thoughts were all fixed on that one spot of Pemberley House, whichever it might be, where Mr. Darcy then was. She longed to know what at that moment was passing in his mind; in what manner he thought of her, and whether, in defiance of every thing, she was still dear to him. Perhaps he had been civil, only because he felt himself at ease; yet there had been *that* in his voice, which was not like ease. Whether he had felt more of pain or of pleasure in seeing her, she could not tell, but he certainly had not seen her with composure.

At length, however, the remarks of her companions on her absence of mind roused her, and she felt the necessity of appearing more like herself.

They entered the woods, and bidding adieu to the river for a while, as-cended some of the higher grounds; . . . Whilst wandering on in this slow manner, they were again surprised, and Elizabeth's astonishment was quite equal to what it had been at first, by the sight of Mr. Darcy approaching them, and at no great distance. The walk being here less sheltered than on the other side, allowed them to see him before they met. Elizabeth, however astonished, was at least more prepared for an interview than before, and resolved to appear and to speak with calmness, if he really intended to meet them. For a few mo-ments, indeed, she felt that he would probably strike into some other path. This idea lasted while a turning in the walk concealed him from their view; the turn-ing past, he was immediately before them. With a glance she saw, that he had lost none of his recent civility; and, to imitate his politeness, she began, as they met, to admire the beauty of the place; but she had not got beyond the words "delightful," and "charming," when some unlucky recollections obtruded, and she fancied that praise of Pemberley from her, might be mischievously con-strued. Her colour changed, and she said no more.

Mrs. Gardiner was standing a little behind; and on her pausing, he asked her, if she would do him the honour of introducing him to her friends. This was a stroke of civility for which she was quite unprepared; and she could hardly suppress a smile, at his being now seeking the acquaintance of some of those very people, against whom his pride had revolted, in his offer to herself. "What will be his surprise," thought she, "when he knows who they are! He takes them now for people of fashion."

The introduction, however, was immediately made; and as she named their relationship to herself, she stole a sly look at him, to see how he bore it; and was not without the expectation of his decamping as fast as he could from such disgraceful companions. That he was *surprised* by the connexion was evident; he sustained it however with fortitude, and so far from going away, turned back with them, and entered into conversation with Mr. Gardiner. Elizabeth could not but be pleased, could not but triumph. It was consoling, that he should know she had some relations for whom there was no need to blush. She listened most attentively to all that passed between them, and gloried in every expression, every sentence of her uncle, which marked his intelligence, his taste, or his good manners.

The conversation soon turned upon fishing, and she heard Mr. Darcy invite him, with the greatest civility, to fish there as often as he chose, while he continued in the neighbourhood, offering at the same time to supply him with fishing tackle, and pointing out those parts of the stream where there was usually most sport. Mrs. Gardiner, who was walking arm in arm with Elizabeth, gave her a look expressive of her wonder. Elizabeth said nothing, but it gratified her exceedingly; the compliment must be all for herself. Her astonishment, however, was extreme; and continually was she repeating, "Why is he so altered? From what can it proceed? It cannot be for *me,* it cannot be for *my* sake that his manners are thus softened. My reproofs at Hunsford could not work such a change as this. It is impossible that he should still love me."

After walking some time in this way, the two ladies in front, the two gentlemen behind, on resuming their places, after descending to the brink of the river for the better inspection of some curious water-plant, there chanced to be a little alteration. It originated in Mrs. Gardiner, who, fatigued by the exercise of the morning, found Elizabeth's arm inadequate to her support, and consequently preferred her husband's. Mr. Darcy took her place by her niece, and they walked on together. After a short silence, the lady first spoke. She wished him to know that she had been assured of his absence before she came to the place, and accordingly began by observing, that his arrival had been very unexpected—"for your housekeeper," she added, "informed us that you would certainly not be here till to-morrow; and indeed, before we left Bakewell, we understood that you were not immediately expected in the country." He acknowledged the truth of it all; and said that business with his steward had occasioned his coming forward a few hours before the rest of the party with whom he had been travelling. "They will join me early to-morrow," he continued, "and among them are some who will claim an acquaintance with you,— Mr. Bingley and his sisters."

Elizabeth answered only by a slight bow. Her thoughts were instantly driven back to the time when Mr. Bingley's name had been last mentioned between them; and if she might judge from his complexion, *his* mind was not very differently engaged.

"There is also one other person in the party," he continued after a pause, "who more particularly wishes to be known to you,—Will you allow me, or do I ask too much, to introduce my sister to your acquaintance during your stay at Lambton?"

The surprise of such an application was great indeed; it was too great for her to know in what manner she acceded to it. She immediately felt that whatever desire Miss Darcy might have of being acquainted with her, must be the work of her brother, and without looking farther, it was satisfactory; it was gratifying to know that his resentment had not made him think really ill of her.

They now walked on in silence; each of them deep in thought. Elizabeth was not comfortable; that was impossible; but she was flattered and pleased. His wish of introducing his sister to her, was a compliment of the highest kind. They soon outstripped the others, and when they had reached the carriage, Mr. and Mrs. Gardiner were half a quarter of a mile behind.

* * *

V. *The next day, just as soon as his sister and Bingley arrive at Pemberley, Darcy insists that they visit Elizabeth. His manner is again as gentle and attentive as it had been the day before. That evening, Elizabeth lay awake, endeavoring to determine her feelings. The selection is from Volume III, Chapter 2.*

. . . She certainly did not hate him. No; hatred had vanished long ago, and she had almost as long been ashamed of ever feeling a dislike against him, that could be so called. The respect created by the conviction of his valuable qualities, though at first unwillingly admitted, had for some time ceased to be repugnant to her feelings; and it was now heightened into somewhat of a friendlier nature, by the testimony so highly in his favour, and bringing forward his disposition in so amiable a light, which yesterday had produced. But above all, above respect and esteem, there was a motive within her of good will which could not be overlooked. It was gratitude.—Gratitude, not merely for having once loved her, but for loving her still well enough, to forgive all the petulance and acrimony of her manner in rejecting him, and all the unjust accusations accompanying her rejection. He who, she had been persuaded, would avoid her as his greatest enemy, seemed, on this accidental meeting, most eager to preserve the acquaintance, and without any indelicate display of regard, or any peculiarity of manner, where their two selves only were concerned, was soliciting the good opinion of her friends, and bent on making her known to his sister. Such a change in a man of so much pride, excited not only astonishment but gratitude—for to love, ardent love, it must be attributed; and as such its impression on her was of a sort to be encouraged, as by no means unpleasing, though it could not be exactly defined. She respected, she esteemed, she was grateful to him, she felt a real interest in his welfare; and she only wanted to know how far she wished that welfare to depend upon herself, and how far it would be for the happiness of both that she should employ the power, which her fancy told her she still possessed, of bringing on the renewal of his addresses.

* * *

VI. *Shortly thereafter news reaches Elizabeth that her youngest sister, Lydia, has eloped with the ne'er-do-well Wickham. Horrified, she rushes off to find the Gardiners when Darcy suddenly appears. The excerpt is from Volume III, Chapters 4 and 8.*

"Good God! what is the matter?" cried he, with more feeling than politeness; then recollecting himself,

"I will not detain you a minute, but let me, or let the servant, go after Mr. and Mrs. Gardiner. You are not well enough;—you cannot go yourself."

Elizabeth hesitated, but her knees trembled under her, and she felt how little would be gained by her attempting to pursue them. Calling back the servant, therefore, she commissioned him, though in so breathless an accent as made her almost unintelligible, to fetch his master and mistress home, instantly.

On his quitting the room, she sat down, unable to support herself, and looking so miserably ill, that it was impossible for Darcy to leave her, or to refrain from saying, in a tone of gentleness and commiseration, "Let me call your maid. Is there nothing you could take, to give you present relief?—A glass of wine;—shall I get you one?—You are very ill."

"No, I thank you;" she replied, endeavouring to recover herself. "There is nothing the matter with me. I am quite well. I am only distressed by some dreadful news which I have just received from Longbourn."

She burst into tears as she alluded to it, and for a few minutes could not speak another word. Darcy, in wretched suspense, could only say something indistinctly of his concern, and observe her in compassionate silence. At length, she spoke again. "I have just had a letter from Jane, with such dreadful news. It cannot be concealed from any one. My youngest sister has left all her friends—has eloped;—has thrown herself into the power of—of Mr. Wickham. They are gone off together from Brighton. *You* know him too well to doubt the rest. She has no money, no connections, nothing that can tempt him to—she is lost for ever."

Darcy was fixed in astonishment. "When I consider," she added, in a yet more agitated voice, "that *I* might have prevented it!—*I* who knew what he was. Had I but explained some part of it only—some part of what I learnt, to my own family! Had his character been known, this could not have happened. But it is all, all too late now."

"I am grieved, indeed," cried Darcy; "grieved—shocked. But is it certain, absolutely certain?"

"Oh yes!—They left Brighton together on Sunday night, and were traced almost to London, but not beyond; they are certainly not gone to Scotland."

"And what has been done, what has been attempted, to recover her?"

"My father is gone to London, and Jane has written to beg my uncle's immediate assistance, and we shall be off, I hope, in half an hour. But nothing can be done; I know very well that nothing can be done. How is such a man to be worked on? How are they even to be discovered? I have not the smallest hope. It is every way horrible!"

Darcy shook his head in silent acquiescence.

"When *my* eyes were opened to his real character.—Oh! had I known what I ought, what I dared, to do! But I knew not—I was afraid of doing too much. Wretched, wretched, mistake!"

Darcy made no answer. He seemed scarcely to hear her, and was walking up and down the room in earnest meditation; his brow contracted, his air gloomy. Elizabeth soon observed, and instantly understood it. Her power was sinking; every thing *must* sink under such a proof of family weakness, such an assurance of the deepest disgrace. She could neither wonder nor condemn, but the belief of his self-conquest brought nothing consolatory to her bosom, afforded no palliation of her distress. It was, on the contrary, exactly calculated to make her understand her own wishes; and never had she so honestly felt that she could have loved him, as now, when all love must be vain.

But self, though it would intrude, could not engross her. Lydia—the humiliation, the misery, she was bringing on them all, soon swallowed up every private care; and covering her face with her handkerchief, Elizabeth was soon lost to every thing else; and, after a pause of several minutes, was only recalled to a sense of her situation by the voice of her companion, who, in a manner, which though it spoke compassion, spoke likewise restraint, said, "I am afraid you have been long desiring my absence, nor have I any thing to plead in excuse of my stay, but real, though unavailing, concern. Would to heaven that any thing could be either said or done on my part, that might offer consolation to such distress.—But I will not torment you with vain wishes, which may seem purposely to ask for your thanks. This unfortunate affair will, I fear, prevent my sister's having the pleasure of seeing you at Pemberley to day."

"Oh, yes. Be so kind as to apologize for us to Miss Darcy. Say that urgent business calls us home immediately. Conceal the unhappy truth as long as it is possible.—I know it cannot be long."

He readily assured her of his secrecy—again expressed his sorrow for her distress, wished it a happier conclusion than there was at present reason to hope, and leaving his compliments for her relations, with only one serious, parting, look, went away.

As he quitted the room, Elizabeth felt how improbable it was that they should ever see each other again on such terms of cordiality as had marked their several meetings in Derbyshire; and as she threw a retrospective glance over the whole of their acquaintance, so full of contradictions and varieties, sighed at the perverseness of those feelings which would now have promoted its continuance, and would formerly have rejoiced in its termination.

If gratitude and esteem are good foundations of affection, Elizabeth's change of sentiment will be neither improbable nor faulty. But if otherwise, if the regard springing from such sources is unreasonable or unnatural, in comparison of what is so often described as arising on a first interview with its object, and even before two words have been exchanged, nothing can be said in her defence, except that she had given somewhat of a trial to the latter method, in her partiality for Wickham, and that its ill-success might perhaps authorize her to seek the other less interesting mode of attachment. Be that as it may, she saw him go with regret; . . .

*

. . . She was humbled, she was grieved; she repented, though she hardly knew of what. She became jealous of his esteem, when she could no longer hope to be benefited by it. She wanted to hear of him, when there seemed the least chance of gaining intelligence. She was convinced that she could have been happy with him; when it was no longer likely they should meet.

* * *

VII. *Thanks to Darcy's efforts, all of which were unsolicited and meant to be kept secret, the fugitives are tracked down, their marriage is arranged, and they are duly provided for. Bingley and Jane are reunited and become engaged. And, finally, in spite of the insolent intervention of Darcy's imperious aunt, Lady Catherine de Bourgh, Darcy returns to Longbourn. We rejoin the narrative (Volume III, Chapter 16) as Elizabeth begins to execute her resolve to thank Darcy for his efforts on behalf of her renegade sister.*

"Mr. Darcy, I am a very selfish creature; and, for the sake of giving relief to my own feelings, care not how much I may be wounding your's. I can no longer help thanking you for your unexampled kindness to my poor sister. Ever since I have known it, I have been most anxious to acknowledge to you how gratefully I feel it. Were it known to the rest of my family, I should not have merely my own gratitude to express."

"I am sorry, exceedingly sorry," replied Darcy, in a tone of surprise and emotion, "that you have ever been informed of what may, in a mistaken light, have given you uneasiness. I did not think Mrs. Gardiner was so little to be trusted."

"You must not blame my aunt. Lydia's thoughtlessness first betrayed to me that you had been concerned in the matter; and, of course, I could not rest till I knew the particulars. Let me thank you again and again, in the name of all my family, for that generous compassion which induced you to take so much trouble, and bear so many mortifications, for the sake of discovering them."

"If you *will* thank me," he replied, "let it be for yourself alone. That the wish of giving happiness to you, might add force to the other inducements which led me on, I shall not attempt to deny. But your *family* owe me nothing. Much as I respect them, I believe, I thought only of *you*."

Elizabeth was too much embarrassed to say a word. After a short pause, her companion added, "You are too generous to trifle with me. If your feelings are still what they were last April, tell me so at once. *My* affections and wishes are unchanged, but one word from you will silence me on this subject for ever."

Elizabeth feeling all the more than common awkwardness and anxiety of his situation, now forced herself to speak; and immediately, though not very fluently, gave him to understand, that her sentiments had undergone so material a change, since the period to which he alluded, as to make her receive with gratitude and pleasure, his present assurances. The happiness which this reply produced, was such as he had probably never felt before; and he expressed himself on the occasion as sensibly and as warmly as a man violently in love can be supposed to do. Had Elizabeth been able to encounter his eye, she might have seen how well the expression of heart-felt delight, diffused over his face, became him; but, though she could not look, she could listen, and he told her of feelings, which, in proving of what importance she was to him, made his affection every moment more valuable.

They walked on, without knowing in what direction. There was too much to be thought, and felt, and said, for attention to any other objects. She soon learnt that they were indebted for their present good understanding to the efforts of his aunt, who *did* call on him in her return through London, and there relate her journey to Longbourn, its motive, and the substance of her conversation with Elizabeth; dwelling emphatically on every expression of the latter, which, in her ladyship's apprehension, peculiarly denoted her perverseness and assurance, in the belief that such a relation must assist her endeavours to obtain that promise from her nephew, which *she* had refused to give. But, unluckily for her ladyship, its effect had been exactly contrariwise.

"It taught me to hope," said he, "as I had scarcely ever allowed myself to hope before. I knew enough of your disposition to be certain, that, had you been absolutely, irrevocably decided against me, you would have acknowledged it to Lady Catherine, frankly and openly."

Elizabeth coloured and laughed as she replied, "Yes, you know enough of my *frankness* to believe me capable of *that.* After abusing you so abominably to your face, I could have no scruple in abusing you to all your relations."

"What did you say of me, that I did not deserve? For, though your accusations were ill-founded, formed on mistaken premises, my behaviour to you at the time, had merited the severest reproof. It was unpardonable. I cannot think of it without abhorrence."

"We will not quarrel for the greater share of blame annexed to that evening," said Elizabeth. "The conduct of neither, if strictly examined, will be irreproachable; but since then, we have both, I hope, improved in civility."

"I cannot be so easily reconciled to myself. The recollection of what I then said, of my conduct, my manners, my expressions during the whole of it, is now, and has been many months, inexpressibly painful to me. Your reproof, so well applied, I shall never forget: 'had you behaved in a more gentleman-like manner.' Those were your words. You know not, you can scarcely conceive, how they have tortured me;—though it was some time, I confess, before I was reasonable enough to allow their justice."

"I was certainly very far from expecting them to make so strong an impression. I had not the smallest idea of their being ever felt in such a way."

"I can easily believe it. You thought me then devoid of every proper feeling, I am sure you did. The turn of your countenance I shall never forget, as you said that I could not have addressed you in any possible way, that would induce you to accept me."

"Oh! do not repeat what I then said. These recollections will not do at all. I assure you, that I have long been most heartily ashamed of it."

Darcy mentioned his letter. "Did it," said he, "did it *soon* make you think better of me? Did you, on reading it, give any credit to its contents?"

She explained what its effect on her had been, and how gradually all her former prejudices had been removed.

"I knew," said he, "that what I wrote must give you pain, but it was necessary. I hope you have destroyed the letter. There was one part especially, the opening of it, which I should dread your having the power of reading again. I can remember some expressions which might justly make you hate me."

"The letter shall certainly be burnt, if you believe it essential to the preservation of my regard; but, though we have both reason to think my opinions not entirely unalterable, they are not, I hope, quite so easily changed as that implies."

"When I wrote that letter," replied Darcy, "I believed myself perfectly calm and cool, but I am since convinced that it was written in a dreadful bitterness of spirit."

"The letter, perhaps, began in bitterness, but it did not end so. The adieu is charity itself. But think no more of the letter. The feelings of the person who wrote, and the person who received it, are now so widely different from what they were then, that every unpleasant circumstance attending it, ought to be forgotten. You must learn some of my philosophy. Think only of the past as its remembrance gives you pleasure."

"I cannot give you credit for any philosophy of the kind. *Your* retrospections must be so totally void of reproach, that the contentment arising from them, is not of philosophy, but what is much better, of ignorance. But with *me*, it is not so. Painful recollections will intrude, which cannot, which ought not to be repelled. I have been a selfish being all my life, in practice, though not in principle. As a child I was taught what was *right*, but I was not taught to correct my temper. I was given good principles, but left to follow them in pride and conceit. Unfortunately an only son, (for many years an only *child*) I was spoilt by my parents, who though good themselves, (my father particularly, all that was benevolent and amiable,) allowed, encouraged, almost taught me to be selfish and overbearing, to care for none beyond my own family circle, to think meanly of all the rest of the world, to *wish* at least to think meanly of their sense and worth compared with my own. Such I was, from eight to eight and twenty; and such I might still have been but for you, dearest, loveliest Elizabeth! What do I not owe you! You taught me a lesson, hard indeed at first, but most advantageous. By you, I was properly humbled. I came to you without a doubt of my reception. You shewed me how insufficient were all my pretensions to please a woman worthy of being pleased."

"Had you then persuaded yourself that I should?"

"Indeed I had. What will you think of my vanity? I believed you to be wishing, expecting my addresses."

"My manners must have been in fault, but not intentionally I assure you. I never meant to deceive you, but my spirits might often lead me wrong. How you must have hated me after *that* evening?"

"Hate you! I was angry perhaps at first, but my anger soon began to take a proper direction."

"I am almost afraid of asking what you thought of me; when we met at Pemberley. You blamed me for coming?"

"No indeed; I felt nothing but surprise."

"Your surprise could not be greater than *mine* in being noticed by you. My conscience told me that I deserved no extraordinary politeness, and I confess that I did not expect to receive *more* than my due."

"My object *then*," replied Darcy, "was to shew you, by every civility in my power, that I was not so mean as to resent the past; and I hoped to obtain your forgiveness, to lessen your ill opinion, by letting you see that your reproofs had been attended to. How soon any other wishes introduced themselves I can hardly tell, but I believe in about half an hour after I had seen you."

He then told her of Georgiana's delight in her acquaintance, and of her disappointment at its sudden interruption; which naturally leading to the cause of that interruption, she soon learnt that his resolution of following her from Derbyshire in quest of her sister, had been formed before he quitted the inn, and that his gravity and thoughtfulness there, had arisen from no other struggles than what such a purpose must comprehend.

She expressed her gratitude again, but it was too painful a subject to each, to be dwelt on farther.

After walking several miles in a leisurely manner, and too busy to know any thing about it, they found at last, on examining their watches, that it was time to be at home.

"What could become of Mr. Bingley and Jane!" was a wonder which introduced the discussion of *their* affairs. Darcy was delighted with their engagement; his friend had given him the earliest information of it.

"I must ask whether you were surprised?" said Elizabeth.

"Not at all. When I went away, I felt that it would soon happen."

"That is to say, you had given your permission. I guessed as much." And though he exclaimed at the term, she found that it had been pretty much the case.

"On the evening before my going to London," said he "I made a confession to him, which I believe I ought to have made long ago. I told him of all that had occurred to make my former interference in his affairs, absurd and impertinent. His surprise was great. He had never had the slightest suspicion. I told him, moreover, that I believed myself mistaken in supposing, as I had done, that your sister was indifferent to him; and as I could easily perceive that his attachment to her was unabated, I felt no doubt of their happiness together."

Elizabeth could not help smiling at his easy manner of directing his friend.

"Did you speak from your own observation," said she, "when you told him that my sister loved him, or merely from my information last spring?"

"From the former. I had narrowly observed her during the two visits which I had lately made her here; and I was convinced of her affection."

"And your assurance of it, I suppose, carried immediate conviction to him."

"It did. Bingley is most unaffectedly modest. His diffidence had prevented his depending on his own judgment in so anxious a case, but his reliance on mine made every thing easy. I was obliged to confess one thing, which for a time, and not unjustly, offended him. I could not allow myself to conceal that your sister had been in town three months last winter, that I had known it, and purposely kept it from him. He was angry. But his anger, I am persuaded, lasted no longer than he remained in any doubt of your sister's sentiments. He has heartily forgiven me now." Elizabeth longed to observe that Mr. Bingley had been a most delightful friend; so easily guided that his worth was invaluable; but she checked herself. She remembered that he had yet to learn to be laught at, and it was rather too early to begin. In anticipating the happiness of Bingley, which of course was to be inferior only to his own, he continued the conversation till they reached the house. In the hall they parted.

F. WHY A WEDDING?
THE PROMISES OF MARRIAGE

The end of courtship—both its purpose and its final act—is the proposal of marriage. The entire courting drama and dance, having enabled the couple to discover that each has indeed found and won the right one, concludes with a decision to get married—not just to cohabit, but to enter into the recognized lawful estate of matrimony. Legally, getting married is easily done. In the United States, it can be accomplished simply, cheaply, and without any formal ceremony, merely by filing with the state for a marriage license. Why then have a wedding? Why get married "in public"? Why a religious ceremony? What does a formal wedding represent, symbolize, accomplish? The readings in this brief section speak to these questions.

Historically, the custom of having a wedding arose from the custom of wife-purchase: the *wed* was the security or purchase money (or its equivalent in horses, cattle, or other property) that the groom gave to the bride's father to seal the transaction. "Wedding"—the verb—was thus the *pledging of the troth* of the bride to the man who secured her by purchase. The practice of religious marriage, performed in the church or by a clergyman in the home, was not officially formalized in Christendom until the second half of the sixteenth century (the Council of Trent, 1563). Until that time the marriage ceremony was one which the couple themselves could perform; indeed, a clandestine and unconsecrated marriage was completely valid.

Although the customs of bride price and dowry have long disappeared, weddings in America are nonetheless big business. Notwithstanding that many couples live together, often for years, before marriage enters their minds, and notwithstanding their persisting ambivalence about marriage and all that it entails, couples continue to hold large celebratory weddings, wanting family and friends to rejoice with them over their decision to marry. True, such weddings are now usually planned and arranged by the couple themselves, not by their parents, and are more frequently held on the couple's, not their parents', turf—in many cases because the bride and groom are older and already have a home of their own, in some cases because their now divorced parents cannot be counted on to cooperate in making a wedding, and in other cases, because of familial frictions generated by a "mixed-faith" union. Nevertheless, weddings still tend to be as elaborate as budgets allow, sometimes even more so, and the gala parties are the product of protracted planning and fastidious, often fanatical, attention in pursuit of "the perfect wedding." This preoccupation is, in fact, the first subject addressed in the section on "Weddings" in *Miss Manners' Guide to Excruciatingly Correct Behavior:* "You, out there in Brideland, you sweet thing: Are you planning your wedding so that it will be perfect in every detail? Do you expect it to be the happiest day of your life?" Answering her own query, she proclaims: "Miss Manners sincerely hopes not. Few of those who prattle about that 'happiest day' seem to consider the dour expectations this suggests about the marriage from its second day on." Miss Manners' remarks are aimed especially at those who mistake the wedding reception for the wedding: "At any rate, someone whose idea of ultimate happiness is a day spent at a big party, even spent being the center of attention at a marvelous big party, is too young to get married." With emphasis placed mostly on the party, the serious purpose of the wedding can be, and often is, forgotten.

The marriage ceremony is the true heart of the matter. Where it is performed in accord with religious traditions, it is more sober than merry: the *solemnization* of matrimony is what the Book of Common Prayer used to call it. The meaning of the various traditional ceremonies reflects the meaning of marriage as each tradition understands it. The ceremony cannot be understood apart from the idea of what it is that people undertake when they undertake to marry. Yet despite differences between one culture or religion and another, marriage ceremonies generally symbolize and enact certain common truths about the meaning of marriage. The wedding is everywhere a rite of passage. Old family ties are loosened and reconfigured; new family linkages are established ("a man shall leave his father and mother and cleave to his wife"). Specially marked out familial, social, and religious places in the community are newly occupied, publicly witnessed by the congregation that receives the newly membered pair and joins in blessing their union. The very fact of ceremony testifies that marriage is more than a contract of mutual advantage or the sanctioned venue for the expression of mutual desire and erotic intimacy. And, especially significant, the bride and groom engage in acts of speech and symbolic deed that are meant to capture and determine the meaning of their new bond, now and for the future.

In many traditions, bride and groom take vows or make promises, pledging themselves one to the other. The vow is neither just an expression of present feelings nor a prediction or expressed hope for the future. It is, as the selection by May points out, a verbal commitment whose intent and whose function is to determine the future. The specific content of the vows may vary (see the selection of vows, below), but all have in common a pledge of faithfulness to one another (in some cases, also to God). As a result, marriage becomes defined as a covenanted life lived under a promise. Romance disciplined by courtship or "rational love" may have gotten the couple to the altar or *chuppah,* but from now on the foundation of the relationship will be fidelity to promises freely and deliberately made and to obligations freely accepted. Desiring and being desired, even giving and receiving, must be ruled by the "task of loving" pledged in the vow, by what De Rougemont (in the selection of this title) calls "Active Love, or Keeping Faith." This selection speaks for those (like C. S. Lewis in the selection "Eros," above) who insist that erotic love or Rousseauan romanticism is an insufficient basis for marriage, that the discipline of *eros* achieved through courtship cannot by itself enable love to fulfill its dream of permanence.

After the wedding, the couple stands in the world on a new foundation, ratified in custom and commemorated in ceremony. Traditionally, that new foundation is reflected, among other things, in the way in which the couple is thenceforth named and known in the community: for instance, Mr. and Mrs. John Smith. The last selection in this section (written by the editors) visits the question of the marriage name and, in the process, extends the discussion of the importance of custom in sustaining the meaning and strength of marriage, even—perhaps especially—today.

May, "The Covenant of Marriage"

In this very brief essay, written in 1993 for a meeting on the Ethics of Everyday Life, William F. May (see his essay "Four Mischievous Theories of Sex," in the section "What About Sex?" above) reflects on the meaning of the Christian marriage ceremony, including its publicity and its performative utterances, the vows and the blessings. May shows beautifully how the public promises of the wedding ceremony build a bridge between love and marriage and betoken the promise-based and promising nature of marital union.

First and most notably, two people enter into the marriage covenant quite publicly—"before God and these witnesses." Why this public event? Why not a private ceremony conducted by a member of the clergy or a justice of the peace? The custom of a public occasion, I suspect, helps to emphasize the difference between the opening movements of love and the marriage that follows.

Lovers, above all else, want to withdraw from the world. They can't get enough of each other. They try to give others the slip. As the saying goes: Two is company but three is a crowd. One of John Donne's poems captured beautifully this world-denying impulse of love. The poet compares his beloved to a nun and the place where they meet to a convent. The metaphor of chastity surprises the reader since no one can doubt the passionate, sensual embrace which was theirs. The image, however, expresses the lovers' need to shuck off the world. Love alone matters. But love that seeks to eliminate the world cannot last. That is the dark side of the cult of romantic love. Inevitably the world closes in and forces lovers apart. Too many obstacles block the way. Different families, different ties, different pasts, different agendas for the future make it impossible for such love to persist. So lovers poignantly part: their love can live on only in the moonbeams of nostalgia, the secret recesses of memory, or the aurora borealis of fantasy.

The wedding ceremony signals a very different kind of possibility. In marriage, lovers, still nourished and fortified by their own inner life together, now turn outward toward the world and learn how to function together in it and even how to serve it. The ceremony seeks to acknowledge and honor the inner and the outer aspects of love, a covenant undertaken between a couple but not just a private deal; rather, a promise undertaken before God and these witnesses. In a sense, we accommodate for this doubleness in marriage architecturally. A home has its private rooms that provide a haven for intimacy but also its public rooms—the living room and the dining room—in which the couple welcomes friends and strangers and offers hospitality.

The Christian faith recognizes in the doubleness of married life an image and parable for the relationship of Christ to the Church. The Church enjoys both its inner life of worship but also its outer work of service. In worship the church receives and celebrates the love of God in Christ which also impels it outward into the service of the world. The Church resembles a marriage partnership more than a love affair. Human marriage in full health requires both the systolic and the diastolic beat of love, both love's outward procession and its inner recovery and return, its habits of renewal and tenderheartedness with one another.

So understood, marriage reflects the very image of God in humankind. Traditionally, philosophers and theologians have associated the image of God with the godly faculty of reason or with the power of creativity or with the capacity to dominate creation. But as splendid as these powers may be, they go unmentioned in the decisive passage from Scripture on the *imago dei*, Genesis 1:27:

> "So God created man in His own image, in the image of God created He him; male and female created He them."

The passage suggests that the image of God in us points less to some power that we possess than to the relationship of a man and a woman to one another. Neither reason, creativity, nor sovereignty defines the human identity. Rather it spreads across a relationship, which, as we have reason to know from many other passages, depends for its life on the reciprocal dynamics of giving and receiving.

Human beings may exhaust themselves in the activities of acquiring and securing, controlling, anticipating, worrying, and humiliating, but the essence of human life displays itself in the transactions of giving and receiving. Male and female created he them. The later Church attempted to honor and celebrate this life in the God-head itself when it resorted to the three-fold name—Father-Giver, Son-Receiver, in the procession of the Spirit.

The vows in and through which the partners give and receive themselves are remarkably lean and spare. The ceremony is not a notably descriptive or expressive occasion. No one asks the bride and groom to describe or express their feelings for one another. No one obliges them to sing an aria with violins and trumpets in the background telling one another and the world how much they love one another. Rather, they exchange vows, vows which tersely comprehend the world which they are likely to know, including plenty and want, sickness and health, until death parts them.

The philosopher, J. L. Austin, drew the distinction, now famous, between two different kinds of utterances: descriptive and performative. Ordinary dec-

larative or descriptive sentences report a given item in the world. (It is raining. His kidneys are failing. The crisis is past.) Performative utterances, however, alter the world of those to whom they are extended. The marriage vow
quintessentially is such a performative utterance. (I, John, take thee Mary . . .
I, Mary, take thee John.) The partners alter one another's world through the
exchange of vows. This world altering character of their vows makes of it a
solemn occasion, not lightly to be entered into and freighted with pain for one
or both parties should it ever be withdrawn. This interpretation of marriage
does not altogether rule out the possibility of divorce. The dissolution of a
marriage may be called for under circumstances in which the partners harm
one another more together than they would apart. But harm one another apart,
for the most part, they surely do.

The wedding service also includes a second kind of performative utterance, one that J. L. Austin also cited in his original essay. That utterance is a
blessing. The modern world has trivialized the word, "blessing," reducing it to
the amiable invocation that an aunt or uncle offers after one sneezes. But the
word blessing, "berakha," originally referred to the power of God, and not just
any and all kinds of power, indeterminate and arbitrary, but the power of generative, reciprocating love.

> Bless, O Lord, this ring that he who gives it and she who wears it may abide in
> Thy peace, and continue in Thy favor, unto their life's end, through Jesus Christ,
> Our Lord. Amen.

Or again, at the end of the service,

> The Lord bless you and keep you; the Lord make His face to shine upon you, and
> be gracious unto you; the Lord lift up His countenance upon you, and give you
> peace. . . .

The performative opposite of a blessing is a curse. Only the shadow of
such a negative utterance lies across the ceremony, and that not explicitly in
the form of a curse, but in the threat of a blessing withheld should either of
the partners mock the occasion.

> I charge you both, before the Great God, the Searcher of all hearts, that if either
> of you know any reason why ye may not lawfully be joined together in marriage,
> ye do now confess it. For be ye well assured . . . their union is not blessed by Him.

Neither the promises binding the couple, nor the blessing upon them will
operate magically, dissolving the world of its difficulties, its stresses, and its

temptations. The vows bluntly recognize that the couple may well have to face both plenty and want, sickness and health; and death one day will surely part them. But the good news offered, the holy optimism of the occasion, signals to the couple and the community that love can span and persist and flourish even in the midst of these events. The community thus acknowledges no convent of love, no momentary respite of intimacy, but two ordinary people fortified by a promise and a blessing who can perdure in love to their life's end. To that degree, what they do takes place not simply before God but in God's image and reminds us of the image of God in us all.

Marriage Vows and Blessings

Many a contemporary wedding ceremony seems, at first glance, conspicuously traditional, in some ways oddly so. For the almost universally forgotten reasons behind some of the traditions clash deeply not only with modern sensibilities but even with the religious ceremonies in which they are imbedded. For example: brides still insist on being "given away," albeit not necessarily by their fathers—a symbolic survival of the practice of selling the bride; grooms are still accompanied by a "best man"—symbolically, the fellow warrior who, in days gone by, assisted the would-be bridegroom in carrying off the bride; and brides are still surrounded by their bridesmaids, all of whom are identically decked out—a practice originally intended to keep evil spirits away from the bride by confusing them.

Yet despite the evident regard for tradition in these more superficial appearances, the untraditional or novel nature of many contemporary wedding ceremonies becomes clear once one listens to what is said, and especially to the vows that are exchanged by the couple. As David Blankenhorn has pointed out (in the selection "I Do?" presented in the section "Where Are We Now?"), the vows and pledges in and through which the partners plight their troth are now very often entirely created by the couples, indeed sometimes even at their clergyman's urging. Understanding what this means, and what difference it might make, requires comparing the new creative and individualized vows with the older formal and formulaic vows, vows which have traditionally been exchanged in the context of religious marital services. To this end, we have selected several representative vows (or promises or pledges), some traditional, some contemporary, and invite readers to ponder their separate meanings and the significance of their differences.

For the traditional religious vows, we have taken examples from Christian, Jewish, Muslim, and Hindu ceremonies. Christian selections include Roman Catholic, (various) Protestant, and Russian Orthodox vows—in the latter case, from that sect of Orthodoxy that permits spoken vows. Because the vows, crucial though they be, are not said in isolation but within the context of a larger ceremony, we offer two examples—one from the Book of Common Prayer, the other from the Roman Catholic Rite for Celebrating Marriage During Mass—of the full ceremony.

No vows are spoken at a traditional Jewish wedding; instead, there is reading of the Ketubah, a legal document (reproduced below), signed by the groom and two witnesses, outlining the bride's rights and the groom's duties in marriage. Like the vows, it is not a declaration of love but a public declaration of life-long obli-

gation, here legally binding. The center of the ceremony is the recitation of the Seven Marriage Blessings, which locate the marriage in relation to Creation and all of time.

Blessings are, in fact, a crucial part of most wedding ceremonies. In some cases, they are pronounced or called down on the marrying couple; in others, God is blessed for the gift of marriage. A few examples are included to illustrate how the vows between the bride and groom are connected to the relation between the human and the divine. Why does the couple need or deserve a blessing? Why is marriage the occasion for offering up our blessings?

Choosing representative nontraditional vows and promises posed a more difficult task, given that, being individually designed, they are unlimited in number and variety, and being personal, they are rarely printed except, in some cases, for the sake of the wedding guests. The contemporary vows we present are taken from a book entitled Vows of Love and Marriage: 52 Promises, Pledges and Declarations *by Peg Kehret, written for couples who want help formulating and expressing their ideas and sentiments in order to make their ceremony "more than just another wedding." The reader will surely notice here the absence of formulae and of those blank spaces (or places marked "N." for proper names) where, in the traditional vows, the bride and groom, in their only unique "contribution" to the ceremony, insert their names.*

I. Traddional

A. The Book of Common Prayer *(Episcopal):*
The Form of Solemnization of Marriage (1952)

At the day and time appointed for Solemnization of Matrimony, the Persons to be married shall come into the body of the Church, or shall be ready in some proper house with their friends and neighbours; and there standing together, the Man on the right hand, and the Woman on the left, the Minister shall say,

Dearly beloved, we are gathered together here in the sight of God, and in the face of this company, to join together this Man and this Woman in holy Matrimony; which is an honourable estate, instituted of God, signifying unto us the mystical union that is betwixt Christ and his Church: which holy estate Christ adorned and beautified with his presence and first miracle that he wrought in Cana of Galilee, and is commended of Saint Paul to be honourable among all men: and therefore is not by any to be entered into unadvisedly or lightly; but reverently, discreetly, advisedly, soberly, and in the fear of God. Into this holy estate these two persons present come now to be joined. If any man can show just cause, why they may not lawfully be joined together, let him now speak, or else hereafter for ever hold his peace.

And also speaking unto the Persons who are to be married, he shall say,

I require and charge you both, as ye will answer at the dreadful day of judgment when the secrets of all hearts shall be disclosed, that if either of you know any impediment, why ye may not be lawfully joined together in Matrimony, ye do now confess it. For be ye well assured, that if any persons are joined together otherwise than as God's Word doth allow, their marriage is not lawful.

The Minister, if he shall have reason to doubt of the lawfulness of the proposed Marriage, may demand sufficient surety for his indemnification; but if no impediment shall be alleged, or suspected, the Minister shall say to the Man,

N. [*name*] wilt thou have this Woman to thy wedded wife, to live together after God's ordinance in the holy estate of Matrimony? Wilt thou love her, comfort her, honour, and keep her in sickness and in health; and, forsaking all others, keep thee only unto her, so long as ye both shall live?

The Man shall answer.

I will.

Then shall the Minister say unto the Woman,

N. wilt thou have this Man to thy wedded husband, to live together after God's ordinance in the holy estate of Matrimony? Wilt thou love him, comfort him, honour, and keep him in sickness and in health; and, forsaking all others, keep thee only unto him, so long as ye both shall live?

The Woman shall answer,

I will.

Then shall the Minister say,

Who giveth this Woman to be married to this Man?

Then shall they give their troth to each other in this manner. The Minister, receiving the Woman at her father's or friend's hands, shall cause the Man with his right hand to take the Woman by her right hand, and to say after him as followeth.

I *N*. take thee *N*. to my wedded Wife, to have and to hold from this day forward, for better for worse, for richer for poorer, in sickness and in health, to love and to cherish, till death us do part, according to God's holy ordinance; and thereto I plight thee my troth.

Then shall they loose their hands; and the Woman with her right hand taking the Man by his right hand, shall likewise say after the Minister,

I *N*. take thee *N*. to my wedded Husband, to have and to hold from this day forward, for better for worse, for richer for poorer, in sickness and in health, to love and to cherish, till death us do part, according to God's holy ordinance; and thereto I give thee my troth.

Then shall they again loose their hands; and the man shall give unto the Woman a Ring on this wise: the Minister taking the Ring shall deliver it unto the Man, to put it upon the fourth finger of the Woman's left hand. And the Man holding the Ring there, and taught by the Minister, shall say,

With this Ring I thee wed: In the Name of the Father, and of the Son, and of the Holy Ghost. Amen.

And, before delivering the Ring to the Man, the Minister may say as followeth,

Bless, O Lord, this Ring, that he who gives it and she who wears it may abide in thy peace, and continue in thy favour, unto their life's end; through Jesus Christ our Lord. Amen.

Then, the Man leaving the Ring upon the fourth finger of the Woman's left hand, the Minister shall say,

Let us pray.

Then shall the Minister and the People, still standing, say the Lord's Prayer.

Our Father, who art in heaven, Hallowed be thy Name. Thy kingdom come. Thy will be done, On earth as it is in heaven. Give us this day our daily bread. And forgive us our trespasses, As we forgive those who trespass against us. And lead us not into temptation, But deliver us from evil. For thine is the kingdom, and the power, and the glory, for ever and ever. Amen.

Then shall the Minister add,

O eternal God, Creator and Preserver of all mankind, Giver of all spiritual grace, the Author of everlasting life; Send thy blessing upon these thy servants, this man and this woman, whom we bless in thy Name; that they, living faithfully together, may surely perform and keep the vow and covenant betwixt them made, (whereof this Ring given and received is a token and pledge,) and may ever remain in perfect love and peace together, and live according to thy laws; through Jesus Christ our Lord. *Amen.*

The Minister may add one or both of the following prayers.

O almighty God, Creator of mankind, who only art the well-spring of life; Bestow upon these thy servants, if it be thy will, the gift and heritage of children; and grant that they may see their children brought up in thy faith and fear, to the honour and glory of thy Name; through Jesus Christ our Lord. *Amen.*

O God, who hast so consecrated the state of Matrimony that in it is represented the spiritual marriage and unity betwixt Christ and his Church; Look mercifully upon these thy servants, that they may love, honour, and cherish each other, and so live together in faithfulness and patience, in wisdom and true godliness, that their home may be a haven of blessing and of peace; through the same Jesus Christ our Lord, who liveth and reigneth with thee and the Holy Spirit ever, one God, world without end. *Amen.*

Then shall the Minister join their right hands together, and say,

Those whom God hath joined together let no man put asunder.

* * *

B. Rite for Celebrating Marriage During Mass (Roman Catholic)

INTRODUCTION   *All stand, including the bride and bridegroom, and the priest addresses them in these or similar words:*

My dear friends, you have come together in this church so that the Lord may seal and strengthen your love in the presence of the Church's minister and

this community. Christ abundantly blesses this love. He has already consecrated you in baptism and now he enriches and strengthens you by a special
sacrament so that you may assume the duties of marriage in mutual and lasting fidelity. And so, in the presence of the Church, I ask you to state your intentions.

QUESTIONS   *The priest then questions them about their freedom of*
                             choice, faithfulness to each other, and the acceptance and
                             upbringing of children:

    N. and N., have you come here freely and without reservation to give your-
selves to each other in marriage?

    Will you love and honor each other as man and wife for the rest of your
lives?

                The following question may be omitted if, for example,
                the couple is advanced in years.

    Will you accept children lovingly from God, and bring them up according
to the law of Christ and his Church?

                Each answers the questions separately.

CONSENT   *The priest invites the couple to declare their consent:*

    Since it is your intention to enter into marriage, join your right hands, and
declare your consent before God and his Church.

                They join hands.

                The bridegroom says:

    I, N., take you, N., to be my wife. I promise to be true to you in good times
and in bad, in sickness and in health. I will love you and honor you all the days
of my life.

                The bride says:

    I, N., take you, N., to be my husband. I promise to be true to you in good
times and in bad, in sickness and in health. I will love you and honor you all
the days of my life.

                If, however, it seems preferable for pastoral reasons, the
                priest may obtain consent from the couple through ques-
                tions.

                First he asks the bridegroom:

N., do you take N. to be your wife? Do you promise to be true to her in good times and in bad, in sickness and in health, to love her and honor her all the days of your life?
The bridegroom: I do.

Then he asks the bride:

N., do you take N. to be your husband? Do you promise to be true to him in good times and in bad, in sickness and in health, to love him and honor him all the days of your life?
The bride: I do.

In the dioceses of the United States, the following form may also be used:

I, N., take you, N., for my lawful wife, to have and to hold, from this day forward, for better, for worse, for richer, for poorer, in sickness and in health, until death do us part.

I, N., take you, N., for my lawful husband, to have and to hold, from this day forward, for better, for worse, for richer, for poorer, in sickness and in health, until death do us part.

If it seems preferable for pastoral reasons for the priest to obtain consent from the couple through questions, in the dioceses of the United States the following alternative form may be used:

N., do you take N. for your lawful wife (husband), to have and to hold, from this day forward, for better, for worse, for richer, for poorer, in sickness and in health, until death do you part?
The bride (bridegroom): I do.

Receiving their consent, the priest says:

You have declared your consent before the Church. May the Lord in his goodness strengthen your consent and fill you both with his blessings.
What God has joined, men must not divide.
Amen.

BLESSING OF RINGS   *Priest:*

May the Lord bless ✟ these rings which you give to each other as the sign of your love and fidelity.
Amen.

EXCHANGE OF RINGS *The bridegroom places his wife's ring on her ring finger. He may say:*

N., take this ring as a sign of my love and fidelity. In the name of the Father, and of the Son, and of the Holy Spirit.

The bride places her husband's ring on his ring finger. She may say:

N., take this ring as a sign of my love and fidelity. In the name of the Father, and of the Son, and of the Holy Spirit.

NUPTIAL BLESSING *After the Lord's Prayer, the priest faces the bride and the bridegroom and, with hands joined, says:*

My dear friends, let us turn to the Lord and pray that he will bless with his grace this woman (or N.) now married in Christ to this man (or N.) and that (through the sacrament of the body and blood of Christ,) he will unite in love the couple he has joined in this holy bond.

All pray silently for a short while. Then the priest extends his hands and continues:

Father, by your power you have made everything out of nothing. In the beginning you created the universe and made mankind in your own likeness. You gave man the constant help of woman so that man and woman should no longer be two, but one flesh, and you teach us that what you have united may never be divided.

Or:

Father, you have made the union of man and wife so holy a mystery that it symbolizes the marriage of Christ and his Church.

Or:

Father, by your plan man and woman are united, and married life has been established as the one blessing that was not forfeited by original sin or washed away in the flood.

Look with love upon this woman, your daughter, now joined to her husband in marriage. She asks your blessing. Give her the grace of love and peace. May she always follow the example of the holy women whose praises are sung in the scriptures.

May her husband put his trust in her and recognize that she is his equal and the heir with him to the life of grace. May he always honor her and love her as Christ loves his bride, the Church.

Father, keep them always true to your commandments. Keep them faithful in marriage and let them be living examples of Christian life.

Give them the strength which comes from the gospel so that they may be witnesses of Christ to others. (Bless them with children and help them to be good parents. May they live to see their children's children.) And, after a happy old age, grant them fullness of life with the saints in the kingdom of heaven.

We ask this through Christ our Lord.
Amen.

* * *

C. Other Christian Vows

1. Lutheran (from the *Lutheran Book of Worship*):

Assisting Minister: The Lord God in his goodness created us male and female, and by the gift of marriage founded human community in a joy that begins now and is brought to perfection in the life to come.

Because of sin, our age-old rebellion, the gladness of marriage can be overcast and the gift of the family can become a burden.

But because God, who established marriage, continues still to bless it with his abundant and ever-present support, we can be sustained in our weariness and have our joy restored.

Presiding Minister: _____name_____ and _____name_____, if it is your intention to share with each other your joys and sorrows and all that the years will bring, with your promises bind yourselves to each other as husband and wife.

> *Stand*
>
> *The bride and groom face each other and join hands. Each, in turn, promises faithfulness to the other in these or similar words:*

I take you, _____name_____, to be my *wife/husband* from this day forward, to join with you and share all that is to come, and I promise to be faithful to you until death parts us.

The bride and groom exchange rings with these words:

I give you this ring as a sign of my love and faithfulness.

The bride and groom join hands, and the minister announces their marriage by saying:

Presiding Minister: _____name_____ and _____name_____, by their promises before God and in the presence of this congregation, have bound themselves to one another as husband and wife.

Congregation: Blessed be the Father and the Son and the Holy Spirit now and forever.

Presiding Minister: Those whom God has joined together let no one put asunder.

Congregation: Amen.

Sit

The bride and groom kneel.

Presiding Minister: The Lord God, who created our first parents and established them in marriage, establish and sustain you, that you may find delight in each other and grow in holy love until your life's end.

Congregation: Amen.

2. Carpatho-Russian Orthodox (vow only):[1]

"I, _____, take you, _____, as my wedded wife/husband and I promise you love, honor and respect; to be faithful to you, and not to forsake you until death do us part. So help me God, one in the Holy Trinity, and all the Saints."

3. Presbyterian vow:

"I, _____, take you to be my wedded wife/husband, and I do promise and covenant, before God and these witnesses, to be your loving and faithful wife/husband, in plenty and in want, in joy and in sorrow, in sickness and in health, as long as we both shall live."

---

[1]This and the next two vows are taken from the *Complete Book of Wedding Vows,* ed. Diane Warren (Franklin Lakes, NJ: Career Press, 1996).

4. Quaker vow:

"In the presence of God and these our Friends I take thee to be my wife/husband, promising with Divine assistance to be unto thee a loving and faithful wife/husband so long as we both shall live."

* * *

D. Jewish: Marriage Proposal, Ketubah, and the Seven Marriage Blessings

[The Jewish wedding takes place under a *chuppah* or canopy, symbolizing the groom's house, the bride's new domain, and the home they will build together. Upon her entrance under the *chuppah*, the bride circles the groom seven times, a deed rich in symbolic meanings, much discussed by the Sages. The ceremony proper begins with a blessing over the wine and a betrothal blessing. An ancient formulaic marriage proposal immediately precedes the giving of the ring. The *Ketubah* is read aloud and then presented to the bride, to whom it belongs in perpetuity. The Nuptial ceremony comprises the Seven Blessings (*Sheva Berakhot*) and the breaking of a wine glass.]

Marriage Proposal: Before the groom places the ring on his bride's index finger, he recites the following marriage proposal in both Hebrew and English because it must be understood by bride and groom:

Harei at me'kudeshet li be'tabaat zo ke'dat mosheh ve'yisrael.
Behold, thou art consecrated unto me, with this ring, in accordance with the Law of Moses and Israel.

Ketubah

On the _____ day of the week, the _____ day of the month _____ in the year _____ since the creation of the world according to the reckoning which we are accustomed to use here in the city of _____ in _____, _____, son of _____ of the family _____ said to this maiden _____ daughter of _____ of the family _____
"Be thou my wife according to the law of Moses and Israel, and I will work for thee, honor, provide for, and support thee, in accordance with the practice of Jewish husbands, who work for their wives, honor, provide for and support them in truth. And I will set aside for thee 200 silver *zuz mohar* due thee for thy maidenhood which belong to thee (according to the law of the Torah) and thy food, clothing, and other necessary benefits which a husband is obligated to provide; and I will live with thee in accordance with the requirements prescribed for each husband." And _____ this maiden consented and became his wife. The dowry that she brought from her _____ house, in silver, gold, valuables, clothing, and household furnishings, all this _____

the said groom accepted in the sum of 100 silver *zuzim*, adding on his own another 100 silver *zuzim*, making a total of 200 silver *zuzim*. And thus said _____, the said groom: "I take upon myself, and my heirs after me, the surety of this *Ketubah*, of the dowry, and of the additional sum, so that all this shall be paid from the best part of my property, real and personal, that I now possess or may hereafter acquire. All my property, even the mantle on my shoulders, shall be mortgaged for the security of this *Ketubah* and of the dowry and of the addition made thereto, during my lifetime and after my life-time from this day forever." And the surety for all the obligations of this *Ketubah*, dowry and the additional sum has been assumed by _____ the said groom, with the full obligation dictated by all documents of *Ketubot* and additional sums due every daughter of Israel, executed in accordance with the enactment of our Sages, of blessed memory. It is not to be regarded as an indecisive contractual obligation nor as a stereotyped form. And we have completed the act of acquisition from _____ son of _____ of the family _____ the said bridegroom, for _____ daughter of _____ of the family _____ this maiden, for all that which is stated and explained above, by an instrument legally fit to establish a transaction. And everything is valid and established.

> Attested to by _____ witness
> Attested to by _____ witness

Seven Marriage Blessings

Blessed art Thou, O Lord our God, King of the universe, who has created the fruit of the vine.

Blessed art Thou, O Lord our God, King of the universe, who has created all things for His glory.

Blessed art Thou, O Lord our God, King of the universe, creator of man.

Blessed art Thou, O Lord our God, King of the universe, who hast made man in His image, after His likeness, and has prepared for him, out of his very self, a perpetual building [or 'fabric']. Blessed art Thou, O Lord, creator of man.

May she who was barren be exceedingly glad and rejoice when her children are united in her midst in joy. Blessed art Thou, O Lord, who makes Zion joyful through her children.

O make these beloved companions greatly rejoice even as thou didst rejoice Thy creation in the Garden of Eden as of old. Blessed art Thou, O Lord, who makes bridegroom and bride to rejoice.

Blessed art Thou, O Lord our God, King of the universe, who has created joy and gladness, bridegroom and bride, mirth and exultation, pleasure and delight, love, brotherhood, peace and fellowship. Soon may there be heard in the cities of Judah and in the streets of Jerusalem, the voice of joy and gladness, the voice of the bridegroom and the voice of the bride, the jubilant voices of the bridegrooms from their canopies, and of youths from their feasts of song. Blessed art Thou, O Lord, who makest the bridegroom to rejoice with the bride.

* * *

E. Muslim

[The Islamic marriage ceremony is very simple. It can be performed anywhere, though a mosque is preferred. It consists of an offer of marriage made by the bride or her agent to the groom or his agent, and of an expression of acceptance by the groom or by his agent. The offer and acceptance are made in the presence of witnesses, preferably many witnesses, in order to publicize the event. No other formalities are required. The bride and groom (or their agents) sit facing each other in such a way as to be seen and heard by the witnesses. The clergyman begins by addressing the assembled guests.]

Clergyman: (addressing the congregants):   Grateful praise is due to Allah, the Merciful, the Compassionate. He created man male and female, each in need of the other, and established the institution of marriage as a means of uniting the two souls in a blessed bond of love, leading to their pleasure and happiness in a way advantageous to mankind. In his Holy Book, our Lord says, "And He it is Who has created man from water; then He has made for him blood-relationship and marriage-relationship. And your Lord is ever Powerful."

And He reminds us of one of His great favors, saying, "And of His signs is this: that He has created mates for you from yourselves that you might enjoy blissful tranquility in their company. He promotes between you love and compassion. Surely there are signs in this for those who reflect."

And He commands: "Give away in marriage those among you who are single. . . . If they are needy, Allah will give them from His bounty. And Allah is the most Ample-giver, and Knowing."

And peace and blessings be upon His great and beloved Prophet and last Messenger, Muhammad, who emphatically urged Muslims to marry. He said: "O ye youth! Whoever of you can afford to marry, let him do so. For marriage is the best protection against lustful eyeing and a strong shield for your chastity."

Ladies and gentlemen, at this precious and auspicious moment we are uniting in the sacred bond of marriage, in obedience of the guidance of Allah and in adherence to the practice of His beloved Prophet, Miss _____ and Mr. _____, who have decided to live together as husband and wife, sheltered with the blessing of Allah and His divine Benevolence. May He fill their life with joy and may He grant them peace, health and prosperity! May they always live together in an atmosphere of tranquility and never-diminishing love and tender regard for each other.

After addressing separately the groom and the bride, reminding them of their distinctive marital duties, as these are prescribed in Islam, and of their mutual responsibility in caring for the children with which God may bless them, the clergyman again addresses the congregants as follows:

And now, ladies and gentlemen, we are about to listen to our bride and bridegroom giving themselves away to each other in a contractual sacred bond. We all are witnesses to this blissful event. So let us ourselves seek the pleasure and forgiveness of Allah. May He absolve our sins. May He accept our repentance. May he guide us in the right path and make us worthy of being witnesses of this marriage.

Our Lord! Bless this gathering. Bless us all. Bless our bride and our bridegroom. Grant them health, success, and prosperity. Amen!

The clergyman now asks the bride to offer herself to her groom in marriage, and helps her to say to the groom the following words:

I offer you myself in marriage in accordance with the guidance and the teaching of the Holy Koran and the Holy Prophet, peace and blessing be upon him.

He then asks the groom to address his bride as follows:

I accept your offer of marrying you in accordance with the teaching and the guidance of the Holy Koran and our Holy Prophet, peace and blessing be upon him.

The clergyman then asks the bride to address her husband again as follows:

I sincerely and honestly pledge myself to be a faithful and obedient wife to you.

And he then asks the bridegroom to say to his bride:

And I pledge myself honestly and sincerely to be a faithful and helpful husband to you.

* * *

F. Hindu

[There are many forms of Hindu marriage, eight types being listed in the Hindu scriptures. The Brahma type is one of the most laudable; it is still commonly observed in modern India. It is a very long and elaborate ritual, involving more than twenty separate ceremonies. We select here, in skeletal form, a few parts of the Brahma wedding rituals that resemble Western exchanges of promises and blessings.]

Pani-grahana:

> *The bridegroom steps up in front of the seated bride and with his left hand holds her right hand and with his right hand holds her right thumb. At this time, he repeats the following hymns. The bride repeats them after him, with appropriate gender changes.*

"O beautiful faced one! I accept you for prosperity and good progeny and may you acquire old age with me happily. This celestial and just Savita (the lord of creation) and the attending ones give you to me for household life from today we become husband and wife."

"O beloved! I as Bhaga hold you as Savita (with moral laws) hold your hand. You are my wife in accordance with *dharma* and in the same way I am your husband."

"O pure one! Brihaspati gave you for me. May I take care of you. May you, the one capable of progeny, live with me for one hundred autumns, happily."

"O auspicious-faced one! People become united on instructions from Brihaspati and the sages. May you get bright clothes and happiness. As the Savita decorates Surya, so shall I with this cloth, etc., and progeny adorn this woman."

"May Indra (war lord), Agni (fire lord), Dyava (sky), Prithvi (earth), Matarishvin (wind in the atmosphere), Mitra (the sun), Varuna (ocean lord), Bhaga (lord of prosperity), Ashvins (celestial physicians), Brihaspati (teacher of gods), Maruts (celestial sun god), Brahman, Soma (the moon) help the progeny of this woman grow."

"For the growth of my family and filled with love for you on account of your beauty, as I accept you so may you. As I shall not cheat you mentally or enjoy anything secretively and even though tired in later years I shall keep away from vices, so may you."

Pratijna-mantra [follows right after the Pani-grahana]:

Bridegroom (to bride): "I accept you with full knowledge and so may you accept me. I am the Sama and you are the Rik. I am like the rainbearing cloud and you are the earth. May we marry happily in unison to establish a family and have many sons. May they love long. May we carry out household responsibilities with interest and mutual happiness. May we see each other with love for one hundred autumns, and live blissfully for one hundred autumns, and hear pleasing words for one hundred autumns."

. . .

Sapta-padi (Seven steps):

The priest makes seven mandalas of rice. The bridegroom places his right hand upon the right shoulder of the bride and holds her right hand. Thereafter, they go towards the north of the sacrificial pit and stand together facing northward. The bridegroom asks the bride to take one step at a time with her right foot first and later join the left foot and thus they walk seven steps. He says "Please do not cross the right foot with the left foot."

"This is the first step. May you follow me favorably for joyous food. May I as Vishnu lead you. May we have many long-living sons."

"This is the second step for energy and strength. May I as Vishnu lead you. May we have many long-living sons."

"This is the third step for increase in wealth. May I as Vishnu lead you. May we have many long-living sons."

"This is the fourth step for happiness born out of proper knowledge. May I as Vishnu lead you. May we have many long-living sons."

"This is the fifth step for progeny. May I as Vishnu lead you. May we have many long-living sons."

"This is the sixth step for health in accordance with climate, etc. May I as Vishnu lead you. May we have many long-living sons."

"This is the seventh step for friendship. May I as Vishnu lead you. May we have many long-living sons."

Jala-abhishechana

After the sapta-padi, the bride and the bridegroom sit again at their respective seats, the bride to the right of the bridegroom and the water-bearer comes and sprinkles water on their foreheads.

Surya-avalokana:

> *The bridegroom says "Please look at the sun." She looks at the sun. Then they say:*

Bride and Groom: That sun is the eye of Brahman and helps the gods and is the first to appear and who goes high, may we see him for one hundred autumns, may we live one hundred autumns, may we speak one hundred autumns, may we hear one hundred autumns, may we never be down-trodden for one hundred autumns, may we have plenty for one hundred autumns by your grace.

. . .

Mangala-ashirvada:

> *The bride and the bridegroom approach the priest and he places his right hand on their forehead and says "O attending ones! Look at this auspicious bride and bless her for great fortunes and return to your homes."*

> *Then the bride and the bridegroom look at the guests and say "Bless us so that we may protect each other with love, enjoy life and prosperity, and strengthen each other with loving cooperation. May our studies brighten our households. May we never oppose each other."*

> *Then all the people say "May both of you use your energies for the common goal and have righteous love free from attachments and have all prosperity together."*

* * *

II. Contemporary Vows

A.   I want to tell you some of the reasons why I love you.

I love you because you are gentle. In a world full of violence, you dare to be tender. You are not ashamed to cry and you have great empathy for all living creatures.

I love you because you are optimistic. You see the good in every situation and you manage always to look for the positive and overlook the negative.

I love you because you like to have fun. You aren't afraid to act silly. You laugh and your laughter brings smiles to everyone around.

I love you because you are loyal. You refuse to gossip about your friends. I can trust you to keep my secrets. You believe in me and your belief makes it possible for me to achieve far more than I ever could otherwise.

I love you in more ways than I can ever hope to mention. Most of all, I love you because you are the one person with whom I can be totally myself. You have accepted me as I am.

I will try, in every way possible, to make you as happy as you have made me.

* * *

B.   I will try never to do anything which will embarrass you for I want you always to be proud of me and of our relationship.

I will care for my body so that my good health will be an asset to our relationship. I will strive for intellectual growth so that I may be an interesting and mentally stimulating companion.

I will try always to make you feel special for you are, indeed, special to me in a way that no one has ever been before. It is this uniqueness which I cherish above all else. It is what brings a smile to my lips when I think of you; it is what puts meaning in my life.

Having known your love, I would now be only a caricature of myself if I had to be without it. Your faith in me gives me faith in myself. Your pleasure in me gives me confidence. Your love for me gives me a joy far deeper than I ever imagined possible.

I promise that I will try in every way to be worthy of your love.

* * *

C.   Today is a new beginning. We are leaving behind our past lives and starting our new life together. I will leave behind as well any preconceived ideas of how you should act.

I want our marriage to be a partnership in every way. I promise to share with you the mundane household chores as well as the excitement of stimulating ideas.

I want for you that which brings you the greatest personal fulfillment. I promise to encourage and support you as you strive to attain the finest of which you are capable.

* * *

D. (in dialogue form)

      Bride: You came softly into my heart,
                 floating gently, as a fluff of dandelion
                 floats on the summer breeze. You
                 came softly into my heart and made me your own.

Groom: You crept slowly into my life,
moving imperceptibly, as the clouds
slide past the moon on a winter's eve.
You crept slowly into my life, and made me your own.

Bride: You came softly into my heart—and
changed my life forever. Because you
love me, I see with new eyes and hear
with new ears. I delight in the most everyday events.

Groom: You crept slowly into my life—and
changed my life forever. Because you
love me, I find joy in each awakening.
My senses are alive with the wonder of your love.

Bride: It is our wedding day and I promise now
to keep my heart ever open to you. I
will love you, comfort you and be
faithful to you in every way. I will be
the best person that I can be, so that
I will be worthy of sharing your life.

Groom: I promise now to keep my heart ever
open to you. I will love you, comfort
you and be faithful to you in every way.
I will be the best person that I can be,
so that I will be worthy of sharing your life.

Bride: You came softly into my heart and
made me your own. In so doing, you
have brought me happiness.

Groom: You crept slowly into my life and made
me your own. In so doing, you have
brought me joy.

* * *

E. (in dialogue form)

Together: We never meant to love so much.

Bride: I meant to be clear-headed, to keep my emotions under
control. I never meant to let myself care intensely because
I didn't want to become vulnerable.

Groom: I intended to be rational and calm. I never meant to let
your welfare become more important than my own.

Together: We never meant to love so much.

Bride: I thought I could care, but within boundaries.

Groom: I thought I could love, but with limitations.

Bride:	I meant to let you be a part of my life and instead you have become more important than life itself.
Groom:	I meant to keep our love in its own compartment and instead it has overflowed the boundaries into everything I say and do and feel.
Together:	We never meant to love so much.
Bride:	I meant to be cautious.
Groom:	I meant to stay uncommitted.
Bride:	Now I find that I do care intensely and I am, therefore, vulnerable. And I do not mind.
Groom:	Today I joyfully accept the commitments of marriage.
Together:	We never meant to love so much.
Bride:	But it has happened. And I am glad.
Groom:	It has happened. And I am glad.
Bride:	From this day forward, I promise to love you willingly and joyfully, withholding nothing.
Groom:	From this day forward, I promise to love you willingly and joyfully, withholding nothing.
Together:	We love too much to do otherwise.

* * *

De Rougemont, "Active Love, or Keeping Faith"

In the concluding section of his Love in the Western World *(see the earlier selection, "The Tristan Myth," in the section "Is This Love?" above), Denis De Rougemont develops his understanding of marital love, which he distinguishes sharply from romantic love. He insists that marriage can rest solidly only on a decision, rather than on either passionate love or rational calculation. He then argues that fidelity—keeping the marital promise that resulted from the decision— is the active force at the center of marriage, through which, by seeking the good of the other, each partner "rises into being a person." Finally, De Rougemont contends that only Agape, Christian love of the other, can rescue Eros from its usual tragic fate.*

How do promise-making and promise-keeping promote the growth both of each partner's "personhood" and of their binding love? What does it mean to promise to love? Is there no necessary connection between being in *love and being willing to make such a promise? Has De Rougemont succeeded in defending himself against the objection that his view of marriage makes marriage the grave of love?*

Marriage as a Decision

Once we ask ourselves what is involved in choosing a man or a woman *for the rest of one's life,* we see that to choose is to wager. Both in the lower and the middle classes the wiseacres urge young men 'to think it over' before taking the decisive step. They thus foster the delusion that the choice of a wife or husband may be governed by a certain number of accurately weighable pros and cons. This is a crude delusion on the part of common sense. You may try as hard as you like to put all the probabilities at the outset in your own favour—and I am assuming that life allows you the spare time for such nice calculations—but you will never be able to foresee how you are going to develop, still less how the wife or husband you choose is going to, and still less again how the two of you together are going to. The factors involved are too diverse. Suppose you could weigh them as they are now (assuming them to be finite in number) and you were so deeply versed in the conduct of human affairs as to know the values of every one of them and their order, you would still be unable to foresee how a union entered upon with all the *facts* duly weighed was going to shape. Nature is said to have required several hundreds of thousands of years for the selection of those species which now seem to us adapted to their surroundings. And yet we have the presumption to suppose that all of a sudden in the course of a single life we may solve the problem of the adaption to one another of two highly organized physical and moral beings! For this is what all unsatisfactorily married persons suppose whenever they grow convinced that a second or third trial is going to yield a closer approximation to 'happiness', notwithstanding that everything goes to show that even a hundred thousand trials would not provide the first inchoate and altogether empirical data upon which to build a science of 'happy marriage'. It needs to be recognized frankly that the problem with which we are confronted by the practical necessity of marriage becomes the more hopelessly insoluble the more we strive 'to solve' it in a rational way.

True, I have not stated the case quite fairly; for as a rule everything happens as if the happiness of a married pair actually did depend on a finite number of factors—character, beauty, fortune, social position, and so on. But as soon as individual demands are put forward, these external data lose importance, and it is imponderables that determine our decision. Thereupon it is common sense that turns out to have argued unfairly in recommending that our choice should result from a mature and reasonable submission of the data to impersonal criteria.

But after all the logical fallacy is negligible; what matters is the moral fallacy which the logical implies. When a young engaged couple are encouraged to calculate the probabilities in favour of their happiness, they are being distracted from the truly moral problem. The attempt to minimize or to conceal the fact that, when considered objectively, a choice of this kind is a wager fosters the belief that everything depends on wisdom or on a set of rules, when actually everything depends on a *decision*. And yet, inasmuch as no set of rules can be anything but imperfect and provisional, if we are to be guided by rules we also need some kind of guarantee. But the only possible guarantee would be one supplied by the strength of the decision whereby we commit ourselves during the rest of our lives 'for better, for worse'. And it is precisely to the extent that we persuade ourselves that the matter is above all one of calculation and of weighing up that the decision in itself is made to seem secondary or superfluous. I therefore feel that it would be more appropriate, both to the essential nature of marriage and to the facts for young people to be taught that their choice must always have an arbitrary element, of which they are undertaking to bear the consequences, whether the consequences turn out happy or unhappy. I do not seek to defend acting on 'rash impulse'; to the extent that probabilities can be weighed, it would be stupid not to weigh them. But I insist that the guarantee of a union in appearance sensible never lies in this appearance.

It must lie in that irrational event, a decision that we venture upon in spite of everything and that lays the foundation of a new life in being a consent to take new chances.

Let me forestall any misunderstanding. 'Irrational' in no way means 'sentimental'. To choose a woman for wife is not to say to Miss So-and-So: 'You are the ideal of my dreams, you more than gratify all my desires, you are the Iseult altogether lovely and desirable—and endowed with a suitable dowry—of whom I want to be the Tristan.' For this would be deceit, and nothing enduring can be founded on deceit. Nobody in the world can gratify me; no sooner were I gratified than I would change! To choose a woman for a wife is to say to Miss So-and-So: 'I want to live with you just as you are.' For this really means: 'It is you I choose *to share* my life with me, and that is the only *evidence* there can be that I love you.' If anybody says, 'Is that all?'—and this is no doubt what many young people will say, having been led by virtue of the myth to expect goodness knows what divine transports—he must have had little experience of solitariness and dread, little experience indeed of solitary dread.

Alone a decision of this kind, irrational but not sentimental, sober but in no way cynical, can serve as the basis for a real fidelity; and I do not say: 'A fidelity that will prove a recipe for "happiness"'; I only say: 'A feasible fidelity, because it is not being wrecked at birth by some necessarily inaccurate calculation.'

On Keeping Troth

The morals of marriage are distorted by the way the plighting of a troth is made into a problem when no problem ought to arise till *after* a troth has been plighted and is considered to be absolute. The problematical element in marriage belongs not to *cur* but to *quomodo,* to the 'how' and not to the 'why'. Kierkegaard says: 'Morality does not set out from an ignorance which needs to be changed into knowledge, but from a knowledge that requires to be put into practice.' It is not the nature of the pledge exchanged in marriage that is problematical, but the consequences involved by the pledge. (Likewise, theology is distorted by setting out from the 'problem of God'—exactly as though in unbelief—when the *real* problem is to know how to obey Him.) For a troth does not have to give its reasons, or then it is not a troth, any more than anything else potentially noble and great would be; any more than passion!

The moralists, and also some of the sociologists, have tried to maintain that monogamy is natural, and, moreover, beneficial. The theme is one open to interminable discussion. And it will become highly pertinent the day men behave rationally and in obedience to their own best interests, the day they no longer have passions and cease to prefer error as such, and no longer deserve the disturbing epithet of 'human' in the active sense. Meanwhile, I fancy that men and women as they are now must look upon fidelity as the least natural of virtues, the one most inimical to 'Happiness'. In their eyes and as they put it, faithful marriage can only exist as the result of an 'inhuman' effort. Their fundamental claim, their religion of Life, is diametrically opposed to it. They think fidelity is a discipline dictated (to our spontaneous impulses and desires) by an absurd and cruel prejudice, or else is a prudent abstinence. Or else again they regard it as the consequence of an inability to live to the full; of a spiritless liking for what is comfortable and conventional; of a lack of imagination; of a contemptible timidity; or of a sordid calculation. The habit of people today, their acquired nature, is to make the most of every situation for its own sake, without any longer referring their conduct to what 'judges' and 'measures' the enjoyment which they thereby obtain. Actually, an acquired respect for the social order is the only thing that still upholds the notion of fidelity. But this is not treated as a serious obstruction, and is circumvented in a hundred ways. Listen to the excuses of a husband who deceives his wife. He may say: 'It's of no importance, it doesn't alter our relations, it's merely a passing affair, a lapse without a sequel', or else: 'It's absolutely vital for me, and tremendously more important than all your petty morals and assurances of bourgeois happiness!' Between a cynical attitude and tragic romanticism there is no real contradiction . . . In each case it is a matter of *escaping* from some actual pledge, because a pledge is thought to be a hateful limitation.

Forgoing any rationalist or hedonist form of apology, I propose to speak only of a troth that is observed *by virtue of the absurd*—that is to say, simply because it has been pledged—and by virtue of being an absolute which will uphold husband and wife as persons. Fidelity, it must be admitted, stands emphatically athwart the stream of values nowadays admired by nearly every one. Fidelity is extremely *unconventional*. It contradicts the general belief in the revelatory value of both spontaneity and manifold experiences. It denies that in order to remain lovable a beloved must display the greatest possible *number* of qualities. It denies that its own goal is happiness. It offensively asserts first, that its aim is obedience to a Truth that is believed in, and secondly, that it is the expression of a wish to be constructive. For fidelity is not in the least a sort of conservatism, but rather a construction. An 'absurdity' quite as much as passion, it is to be distinguished from passion by its persistent refusal to submit to its own dream, by its persistent need of acting in behalf of the beloved, by its being persistently in contact with a reality which it seeks to control, not to flee.

I maintain that fidelity thus understood sets up the person. For the person is manifested like something made, in the widest sense of making. It is built up as a thing is made, thanks to a making, and in the same conditions as we make things, its first condition being a fidelity to something that before was not, but now is in process of being created. Person, made thing, fidelity—the three terms are neither separable nor separately intelligible. All three presuppose that a stand has been taken, and that we have adopted what is fundamentally the attitude of creators. Hence in the humblest lives the plighting of a troth introduces the opportunity of making and of rising to the plane of the person—on condition, of course, that the pledge has not been for 'reasons' in the giving of which there is a reservation which will allow those reasons to be repudiated some day when they have ceased to appear 'reasonable'! The pledge exchanged in marriage is the very type of a *serious* act, because it is a pledge given once and for all. The irrevocable alone is serious. Every life, even the most disinherited one, has some immediate potentiality of dignity, and it is in an 'absurd' fidelity that this dignity may be attained—in a readiness to say 'No' to dazzling passion, when there is every earthly reason for saying 'Yes'—to say 'No' by virtue of the absurd, by virtue of an old promise, of human unreason, of a reason of faith, of a pledge given to God and underwritten by God. And perhaps later on, afterwards, a man or woman may find that the folly of the accepted sacrifice was the greatest wisdom; and that the happiness he or she has forgone is being restored, even as Isaac was restored to Abraham. But this can only happen if he or she has not expected it. And it may also be that nothing rewards our loss: we are among dimensions where ordinary worldly measures no longer avail. But are we still capable of imagining a dignity and greatness in no way romantic and the opposite of excited ardour? The fidelity of which I am speaking is foolish, and yet our folly is then of the most sober and everyday kind. *A sober folly that rather closely simulates behaving sensibly;* that is neither heroic nor challenging, but a patient and fond application.

However, everything has still not been made plain. Tristan[1] also was faithful. And so is every true passion. (Not to mention the successive fidelities which we display in one after another of our 'affairs' nor the fidelity of all those Tristans who are really Don Juans in slow time.) It remains accordingly to show where the difference lies, and to ascertain why a faithful husband should not simply be the man who has identified his wife with Iseult.

When the lover in the Manichaean legend has undergone the great ordeals of initiation, he is met, you remember, by a 'dazzling maiden' who welcomes him with the words: 'I am thyself!' So with fidelity in the myth, and Tristan's. Fidelity is then a mystic narcissism—usually unconscious of course, and imagining itself to be true love for *the other*. In analysing the courtly legends, however, we saw that Tristan is not in love with Iseult, but with love itself, and be-

---

[1]See De Rougemont, "The Tristan Myth," an earlier selection in this anthology. [eds.]

yond love he is really in love with death—that is, with the only possible release there can be for a self guilty and enslaved. Tristan is true neither to a pledge nor to a symbolical being named Iseult. She is but a lovely pretext, and all the time he is being true to his most profound and secret passion. The myth seizes on 'the death instinct' inseparable from any form of created life, and transfigures it by bestowing upon it an essentially spiritual goal. To destroy oneself, to despise happiness is thereupon a way of salvation and of acceding to a higher life, to 'the highest bliss of being' sung of by the expiring Isolde. It is a fidelity destructive of life . . .

. . . But the troth of marriage is, on the contrary, a pledge given for *this* world. Inspired by an unreason 'mystical' (if you like) and, if not hostile, at least indifferent to happiness and the vital instinct, fidelity in marriage requires a re-entry into the real world, whereas courtesy meant only an escape from it. In marriage the loving husband or wife vows fidelity first of all to *the other* at the same time as to his or her true self. And whereas Tristan showed himself constant in a steadfast refusal, in a desire to exclude and deny creation in its diversity and to prevent the world from encroaching upon spirit, the fidelity of the married couple is acceptance of one's fellow-creature, a willingness to take the other as he or she is in his or her intimate particularity. Let me insist that fidelity in marriage cannot be merely that negative attitude so frequently imagined; it must be active. To be content not to deceive one's wife or husband would be an indication of indigence, not one of love. Fidelity demands far more: it wants the good of the beloved, and when it acts in behalf of that good it is creating in its own presence the neighbour. And it is by this roundabout way through the other that the self rises into being a person—beyond its own happiness. Thus as persons a married couple are a mutual creation, and to become persons is the double achievement of 'active love'. What denies both the individual and his natural egotism is what constructs a person. At this point faithfulness in marriage is discovered to be the law of a new life, though not of natural life (that would be polygamy) and not of life for the sake of death (that was Tristan's passion).

The love of Tristan and Iseult was the anguish of being *two;* and its culmination was a headlong fall into the limitless bosom of Night, there where individual shapes, faces, and destinies all vanish: 'Iseult is no more, Tristan no more, and no name can any longer part us!' The other has to cease to be the other, and therefore, to cease to be altogether, in order that he or she shall cease to make me suffer and that there may be only 'I myself am the world!' But married love is the end of anguish, the acceptance of a limited being whom I love because he or she is a summons to be created, and that in order to witness to our alliance this being turns with me towards day.

A life *allied* with mine, for the rest of our lives—that is the miracle of marriage. Another life that wills my good as much as its own, because it is united with mine: and were this not for the rest of our lives, it would be a menace, such as is ever present in the exchanged pleasures of an 'affair'! But few people now seem to be able to distinguish between an obsession which is undergone and a destiny that we shoulder.

Hence it must be shown with the help of a plain example.

To be in love is not necessarily *to love*. To be in love is a state; to love, an act. A state is suffered or undergone; but an act has to be decided upon. Now, the *promise* which marriage means cannot fairly be made to apply to the future of a state in which I am at the moment, but it can and should mortgage the future of conscious acts which I take on—to love, to remain faithful, to bring up my children. That shows how different are the meanings of the word 'to love' in the world of Eros and in the world of Agape. It is seen even better when it is noticed that the God of Scripture *orders us* to love. The first commandment of the Decalogue is: 'Thou shalt love the Lord thy God with all thy heart, with all thy soul, and with all thy mind'; it can only be concerned with acts. It would be altogether absurd to demand of a man a state of sentiment. The imperative, 'Love God and thy neighbour as thyself', creates structures of active relations. The imperative, 'Be in love!' would be devoid of meaning; or, if it could be obeyed, would deprive a man of his freedom.

Eros Rescued by Agape

Thereupon charitable love, Christian love—which is Agape—appears at last and risen to its full height. It is the expression of being in action. And it is Eros, passionate love, pagan love, that spread through the European world the poison of an idealistic *askesis*[2]—all that Nietzsche unjustly lays at the door of Christianity. And it is Eros, not Agape, that glorified our death instinct and sought 'to idealize' it. But Agape has got its own back by rescuing Eros. For Agape is incapable of destruction, and does not even wish to destroy what destroys.

'I desire not the death of a sinner, but that he may live.'

The god Eros is the slave of death because he wishes to elevate life above our finite and limited creature state. Hence the same impulse that leads us to *adore* life thrusts us into its negation. There lies the profound woe and despair characterizing Eros, his inexpressible bondage; and in making this bondage evident Agape has delivered Eros from it. Agape is aware that our terrestrial and temporal life is unworthy of adoration and even of being killed, but that it can be accepted in obedience to the Eternal. For, after all, it is here below that

---

[2]training or discipline

our fate is being decided. It is on earth that we must love. In the next world, we shall meet, not divinizing Night, but the forgiveness of our Creator and Judge. This prospect is one that natural man was unable to imagine. He was condemned to put his faith in Eros—to trust in his most powerful desire and to expect release through this desire. Yet Eros could lead him but to death. But a man who believes the revelation of Agape suddenly beholds the circle broken: faith delivers him from natural religion. Now he *may* hope for something; he is aware that there is some other release from sin. And thereupon Eros in turn has been relieved of his fatal office and delivered from his fate. *In ceasing to be a god, he ceases to be a demon.*[3] And he finds his proper place in the provisional economy of Creation and of what is human.

The Pagans could not do otherwise than make Eros into a god; Eros was the most powerful force within them, the most dangerous and the most mysterious, the most deeply bound up with the event of living. All pagan religions deify Desire. All seek to be upheld and saved by Desire, which is thus instantly transformed into the greatest enemy of life, the seduction of Nothingness. But once the Word was made flesh and had spoken to us in human language, we learned the tidings that it is not we who have to deliver ourselves but God Who will deliver us, *God Who loved man first* and came down to him. Salvation is no longer something beyond, and ever a little more out of reach during the interminable ascent of Desire, the consumer of life; it is here below and is attainable through obedience to the Word.

And hence what have we to fear from desire? It loses its absolute hold over us the moment we cease to deify it. This is attested by the display of fidelity in marriage. For the foundation of this fidelity is an initial refusal *on oath* 'to cultivate' the illusions of passion, to render them a secret worship, or to expect from them any mysterious intensification of life. I may also indicate how it is so by consideration of something well known. Christianity has asserted the complete equality of the sexes, and this as plainly as possible. Saint Paul says:

> 'The wife hath not power of her own body, but the husband; and likewise also the husband hath not power of his own body, but the wife.'

Once she is man's equal, woman cannot be 'man's goal'. Yet at the same time she is spared the bestial abasement that sooner or later must be the price of divinizing a creature. But her equality is not to be understood in the contemporary sense of giving rise to rights. It belongs to the mystery of love. It is but the sign and evidence of the victory of Agape over Eros. For a truly mutual love exacts and creates the equality of those loving one another. God showed

---

[3] Sin, it has been remarked by R. de Pury, is not Eros, but the sublimation of Eros.

His love for man by exacting that man should be holy even as God is holy. And a man gives evidence of his love for a woman by treating her as a completely human person, not as if she were the spirit of the legend—half-goddess, half bacchante, a compound of dreams and sex.

But from these premisses let us proceed to the concrete psychology of married equality. When a man is faithful to one woman, he looks on other women in quite another way, a way unknown to the world of Eros: other women turn into persons instead of being reflections or means. This 'spiritual exercise' develops new powers of judgement, self-possession, and respect.[4] The opposite in this of an erotic man, a steadfast man no longer strives to see a woman as merely an attractive or desirable body, as merely an unintended movement or a fascinating expression; he feels, as soon as tempted, the difficult and serious mystery of an independent, alien existence; he realizes that he has been desiring only an illusory or fleeting aspect of what is actually a complete life, and that perhaps this aspect has been but a projection of his own reverie. Thus temptation recedes disconcerted instead of *making* itself into an obsession; and fidelity is made secure by the clear-sightedness it induces. The sway of the myth is by so much weakened, and although this sway is unlikely ever to be entirely abolished without leaving traces in hearts drugged by images, hearts such as men harbour today, at least it loses its efficacy. The myth no longer determines a person.

In other words, it may be said that fidelity secures itself against unfaithfulness by becoming accustomed not to separate desire from love. For if desire travels swiftly and anywhere, love is slow and difficult; love actually does pledge one for the rest of one's life, and it exacts nothing less than this pledge in order to disclose its real nature. That is why a man who believes in marriage can no longer believe seriously in 'love at first sight', still less in the 'irresistible' nature of passion. 'Love at first sight' is no doubt a legend that was accredited by Don Juan, as the 'irresistible' nature of passion was earlier accredited by Tristan. Neither the excuse nor the alibi can deceive any one who does not wish to be deceived because he thinks deception will be to his advantage; they are tropes of a romantic rhetoric, and allowable in that form, but only becoming ridiculous if confused with psychological truth.

My analysis of the myth has made it plain why people like to *believe* in irresistibility, which is an alibi invoked by the guilty. 'I didn't do it, I wasn't there; it was an irresistible power that acted in the stead of my person.' That is the pious lie of a minister of Eros. But what a lot of self-encouragement resides in the word 'irresistible'! As for 'love at first sight', it is supposed to excuse Don

---

[4]'Respect', as I use the word here, means that we recognize in a being the fullness of a person. A person, according to Kant's famous definition, is what cannot be used by man as an instrument or thing.

Juan's lapses. All literature invites us to accept it as the sign of a very strongly sensual nature. Don Juan, the man of loves at first sight who led a 'tempestuous' life, passes for a kind of superman or supermale. This is a myth with an indeterminate power, hovering over moral contingencies; but we may be confident that it is a product of *compensatory dreams*—compensating either for an imposed and detested fidelity, or for a masochistic jealousy, or for the beginnings of impotence. Indeed, Don Juan's behaviour is typical enough of one kind of sexual weakness. It is in a state of general weariness, sexually localized, that the body is led to commit these sudden lapses, not unakin to the puns that obsess a weary mind. But when body and mind are normally vigorous the chances of love at first sight must be very slender. It would thus seem that monogamy, in making sexual relations normal, becomes the best assurance of pleasure—that is, of the entirely carnal eros, which is not in the least to be deified.

It may be objected that marriage must then be simply 'the grave of love'. But it is of course the myth once again that suggests this, thanks to its obsession of obstructed love. It would be more accurate to echo Croce and to say that 'marriage is the grave of savage love', and more often the grave of sentimentality. Savage and natural love is manifested in *rape*—the evidence of love among all savage tribes. But rape, like polygamy, is also an indication that men are not yet in a stage to apprehend the presence of an actual person in a woman. This is as much as to say that they do not know how to love. Rape and polygamy deprive a woman of her equality by reducing her to sex. Savage love empties human relations of personality. On the other hand, a man does not control himself owing to lack of 'passion' (meaning 'power of the libido'), but precisely because he loves and, in virtue of his love, will not inflict himself. He refuses to commit an act of violence which would be the denial and destruction of the person. He thus indicates that his dearest wish is for the other's good. His egotism goes round via the other. This, it will be granted, is a notable revolution.

And we may now pass beyond that altogether negative and privative statement of Croce's, and at last define marriage as *the institution in which passion is 'contained', not by morals, but by love.*

Kass and Kass, The Marriage Name

The marriage ceremony formally and publicly marks and celebrates the beginning of a new life. This new life, like newborn life, invites a distinctive name by which it can be identified. How should this new estate and new identity be reflected in the marriage name? When we marry, what surname or surnames should we adopt? What is the meaning of the marriage name? In this excerpt from their essay, "What's Your Name?" (1995), Amy A. Kass (born in 1940) and Leon R. Kass (born in 1939) explore these questions and provide arguments to support the traditional practice in which the couple shares the family name of the groom. What do you think of their defense of this matrimonial custom? Are they right about the wisdom of custom in general?

Whether we like it or not, choosing surnames at marriage is in today's America almost as much a matter of choice as the giving of first names at childbirth, a reflection (and perhaps also a cause) of novel conceptions of marriage, an institution the meaning of which is itself increasingly regarded as a matter of choice. The traditional bourgeois way—the husband gives and the wife accepts the husband's family name—customary for at least four hundred years in the English-speaking world, is no longer secure as customary; "because that's the way we've always done it" is, for young American ears, a losing reason. Besides, the true reasons for the old custom having been forgotten, the practitioners of the custom are impotent to defend it against charges of "patriarchy," "male hegemonism," "sexism," and the like. Thus, with no certain cultural guidance, the present generation (in fact, each couple independently) is being allowed—or should we say compelled, willy-nilly?—to think this through for itself.

We, the authors, accept the challenge, as a thought experiment, imagining ourselves as having to do it over again, but with the benefit of our now longer views of marriage and of life, and on the following additional condition: to think not on the basis of what *pleases us,* but on the basis of what we believe is appropriate to the meaning of marriage and hence, in principle, universalizable.

If marriage is, as we believe, a new estate, in fact changing the identities of both partners, there is good reason to have this changed identity reflected in some change of surname, one that reflects and announces this fact. If marriage, though entered into voluntarily, is in its inner meaning more than a contract between interested parties but rather a union made in expectation of permanence and a union open (as no simple contract of individuals can be) to the possibility of procreation, there is good reason to have the commitment to life long union reflected and announced in a common name that symbolizes and celebrates its special meaning. Whether they intend it or not, individuals who individualistically keep their original names when entering a marriage are symbolically holding themselves back from the full meaning of the union. Fearing "loss of identity" in change of name, they implicitly deny that to live now toward and for one's beloved, as soul mate, is rather to gain a new identity, a new meaning of living a life, one toward which eros itself has pointed us. Often failing to anticipate the future likelihood of having their own children, and, more generally, unable or unwilling to see the institution of marriage as directed toward or even connected with its central *generational* raison d'etre, they create in advance a confused identity for their unborn children.

The irony is that the clear personal identity to which they selfishly cling (in tacit denial of their new social identity) is in fact an identity they possess only because their parents were willing and able to create that singular family identity for them. We are, of course, aware that massive numbers of our youth stem from parents who divorce or remarry, and that the insecurity of identity already reflected in their having different names from their birth parents may lead them to cling tenaciously to their very own surnames, lest they lose the little, painfully acquired identity they have left; yet if they truly understood their plight, they would be eager to try to prevent such misfortunes from be-falling their own children, and would symbolically identify themselves in ad-vance as their (unborn) children's lifelong parents.

It is ironic that the same young people, who, in their social arrangements, live only on a first name basis, forgetful (at least symbolically) of where they come from, should at the time of forward-looking marriage turn backward to cling to the name of their family of origin. Faced with the "threat" of "losing themselves" in marriage, they reassert themselves as independent selves, now claiming and treating the original surname as if it were—just like their given *first* name—a chosen mark of their autonomy and individuality.

The human family, unlike some animal families, is exogamous, not inces-tuous; it is exogamous not by nature but by the wisest of customs. The near-universal taboo against incest embodies the insight that family means a for-ward-looking series of generations rather than an inward-turning merging and togetherness. It keeps lineage clear—in order, among other reasons, to distin-guish spouses from progeny in the service of tranquil relations, clear identity, and sound rearing—above all, to accomplish the family's primary human work of perpetuation and cultural transmission. The legal sanctification and support of marriage, a further expression of the insights embedded in the incest taboo, make sense only on this view of family; were sex not generative and families not generational, no one would much care with whom one wished to merge.

Thus, when entering a marriage, the partners are willy-nilly bravely stepping forward, unprotected by the family of origin, into the full meaning of human adulthood: they are saying good-bye to father and mother and cleaving to their spouse. They are, tacitly, accepting the death of their parents, and even more, their own mortality, as they embark on the road to the next generation. They express not only their love of one another but also their readiness to discover, by repeating the practice, how their own family identity and nurtured humanity was the product of deliberate human choice that affirmed and elevated the natural necessity of renewal. A common name deliberately taken at the time of marriage—like the family of perpetuation that the marriage anticipates and establishes—affirms the special union of natural necessity and human choice which the exogamous family itself embodies.

This is, perhaps, an appropriate place to observe that we are well aware that family or social identity is not the whole of our identity, that professional or "career" identity is both psychically and socially important (as are civic and religious identity). The loving-and-generative aspects of our nature are far from being the whole human story. Yet the familial is foundational, and it cannot without grave danger be subordinated or assimilated to the professional. Our arguments for a common social name for the married couple is, however, perfectly compatible with having one partner or the other—or both—keeping a distinct professional name. Some have argued that in today's world of rampant mobility and weakened family ties, and with both husband and wife in the workplace, much is lost and little is gained if professional identity is submerged in a common family name. But precisely to affirm and protect the precious realm of private life from the distorting intrusion of public or purely economic preoccupations, a common social name makes eminent sense—one might say *especially* under present conditions.

The argument advanced so far does not, of course, yet reach to the customary pattern of the bride taking the groom's name. If anything, it might even call into question the wisdom of allowing *either* partner to keep the surname of origin. To provide the same and new last name for the married couple, a name that proclaims their social unity and that will immediately confer social identity to their children, they could devise a hyphenated compound that both partners then adopt or they could jointly invent a totally new surname that leaves no trace of either family of origin. But these alternatives are both defective. The first is simply impractical beyond one or at most two generations; because of the exponential growth of life, one would have an exponential increase in names-to-be-hyphenated-in-new-marriages-and-in-newer-marriages-and-so-on-and-on-ad-infinitum. The structure of life itself makes impossible the universalizing of one's maxim to add-and-hyphenate.

The second alternative, in our view, too starkly severs the new social ties from the familial past (quite apart from what it means to the public individual identities of each of the partners) and to still living and remembered grand-parents. It would be to further accentuate the unraveling of intergenerational connections, symbolizing instead each little family's atomistic belief in its abil-ity to go it alone. In contrast, a family name that ties the new family of per-petuation to one old family of origin reflects more faithfully the truth about family as a series of generations and the moral and psychological meaning of lineage and attachment.

This leaves only the hard question: shall it be his family name or hers? A little reflection will show why, as a general rule, it should be his. Although we know from modern biology the equal contributions both parents make to the genetic identity of a child, it is still true to say that the mother is the "more natural" parent, that is, the parent *by birth*. A woman can give up a child for adoption or, thanks to modern reproductive technologies, can even bear a child not genetically her own. But there is no way to deny out of whose body the new life sprung, whose substance it fed on, who labored to produce it, who wondrously bore it forth. The father's role in all this is miniscule and invisible; in contrast to the mother, there is no *naturally* manifest way to demonstrate his responsibility.

The father is thus a parent more by choice and agreement than by na-ture (and not only because he cannot know with absolute certainty that the woman's child is indeed his own). One can thus explain the giving of the pa-ternal surname in the following way: the father symbolically announces "his choice" that the child is his, fully and freely accepting responsibility for its con-ception and, more importantly, for its protection and support, and answering in advance the question which only wise children are said to be able to answer correctly: Who's my Dad?

The husband who gives his name to his bride in marriage is thus not just keeping his own; he is owning up to what it means to have been given a family and a family name by his own father—he is living out his destiny to be a father by saying yes to it in advance. And the wife does not so much surrender her name as she accepts the gift of his, given and received as a pledge of (among other things) loyal and responsible fatherhood for her children. A woman who refuses this gift is, whether she knows it or not, tacitly refusing the promised devotion or, worse, expressing her suspicions about her groom's trustworthi-ness as a husband and prospective father.

Patrilineal surnames are, in truth, less a sign of paternal prerogative than of paternal duty and professed commitment, reinforced psychologically by gratifying the father's vanity in the perpetuation of his name and by offering this nominal incentive to do his duty both to mother and child. Such human speech and naming enables the father explicitly to choose to become the parent-by-choice that he, more than the mother, must necessarily be.

Fathers who will not own up to their paternity, who will not "legitimize" their offspring, and who will not name themselves responsible for child-rearing by giving their children their name are, paradoxically, not real fathers at all, and their wives and especially their children suffer. The former stigmatization of bastardy was, in fact, meant to protect women and children from such irresponsible behavior of self-indulgent men (behavior probably naturally rooted in mammalian male psychosexual tendencies), men who would take their sexual pleasures and walk away from their consequences. The removal of the stigma, prompted by a humane concern not to penalize innocent children by calling them "illegitimate," has, paradoxically but absolutely predictably, contributed mightily to an increase in such fatherless children.

The advantage a woman and her children gain from the commitment of the man to take responsibility and to stay the course—the commitment implied in his embracing the woman and her prospective children with his family name, now newly understood—is by itself sufficient reason why it is in a woman's interest as a married-woman-and-mother-to-be to readily take the bridegroom's name.

But there is a deeper reason why this makes sense. The change of the woman's name, from family of origin to family of perpetuation, is the perfect emblem for the desired exogamy of human sexuality and generation. The woman in marriage not only expresses her humanity in love (as does the man); she also embraces the meaning of marriage by accepting the meaning of her *womanly* nature as generative. In shedding the name of her family of origin, she tacitly affirms that children of her womb can be legitimated only exogamously. Her children will not bear the same name as—will not "belong to"—her father[1]; moreover, her new name allows also her father to recognize formally the mature woman his daughter has become. Whereas the man needs convention to make up—by expansion—for his natural deficiency, the woman needs convention to humanize—by restriction—the result of her natural prowess. By anticipating necessity and by thus choosing to accept the gift of her husband's name, the woman affirms the meaning of her own humanity by saying yes to customizing her given nature.

* * *

Almost none of what they now believe they understand about the meanings and uses of names did the authors know when, following custom, they

[1] See, in this connection, the selection, "Genesis 29–31: Jacob Finds a Wife," in which Jacob's father-in-law Laban claims ownership and possession of his married daughters and their children (31:43). [eds.]

first joined their lives together under the bridegroom's family name. They had, at best, only tacit and partial knowledge when they deliberately gave their children biblical names. Had they been left, in their youth, to invent their own practices of naming, it is doubtful that they would have gotten it right. In place of their own knowledge, they were guided by the blessed example of the strong, enduring, and admirable marriages and home-life of their parents, itself sustained by teachings silently conveyed through custom and ritual. Wisdom in these matters, for individual thinkers, comes slowly if at all. But custom, once wisely established, more than makes up for our deficiencies. It makes possible the full flourishing of our humanity.

William Butler Yeats said it best, in "A Prayer for My Daughter":

> And may her bridegroom bring her to a house
> Where all's accustomed, ceremonious;
> For arrogance and hatred are the wares
> Peddled in the thoroughfares.
> How but in custom and in ceremony
> Are innocence and beauty born?
> Ceremony's a name for the rich horn,
> And custom for the spreading laurel tree.

G. WHAT CAN MARRIED LIFE BE LIKE? THE BLESSINGS OF MARRIED LIFE

It may very well be true, to paraphrase Tolstoy's famous opening line of *Anna Karenina,* that "all happily married couples resemble one another, but each unhappily married couple is unhappy in its own way." Of course we want to know what befell Pamphilus and Maria, or Rachel and Israel Mittelman, or Miranda and Ferdinand, or Rosalind and Orlando, or Emile and Sophie, or Elizabeth and Darcy in their after-years. The short segment of their lives that was their courtship, however exciting in itself and however sanguine it made us regarding their prospects for the future, cannot be the whole story. Were their promises kept? Did latent problems, hidden vices, or, worse, willfully suppressed past faults and errors push them into decline, disappointment, disaffection, or just plain dullness? Or did they thrive, grow, and flourish as man and wife? Perhaps the fact that we don't know what happened to them is the best sign we can have of their success. No gapers line up at the doors of happily married couples; few poets and novelists are moved to tell the story of the dailiness, and seeming uneventfulness, of everyday married life.

Nevertheless, some writers and thinkers have managed to shed light on what married life is and could be like, both in its usual cases and at its best. The readings in this section speak rather directly to the subject, albeit in different tones and to different effect. Some are exuberant, others sober; some stress love between the couple, others the love of both for their children; some celebrate the simple delights of daily life or the sweetness of making a life together, others call attention to the internal and external threats to conjugal happiness. Each strikes us as persuasive in its own terms. Can they all be right? Are the various blessings of married life compatible, or are they in tension one with another?

Because each of the selected readings speaks clearly enough for itself, and because the richness of marital possibility is, we hope, known to many readers, there is little need for substantive introductory remarks. The following bird's-eye view of the selections and their groupings may nonetheless be helpful. We begin with three short ancient selections. The famous reunion scene from the

Odyssey, a book altogether about home and homecoming, speaks movingly about the longing for rootedness and the importance of shared bed and shared stories. In a dry-as-dust discussion of the friendship of husband and wife, Aristotle treats marriage as a community based on mutual pleasure, utility, and appreciation of character, held together especially by the common good of off-spring. Marital love in the absence of offspring is the theme of the short selection from the Jewish Midrash.

Next come three readings that look at the blessings of married life in relation to the larger community. Both Kipling's poem and Sullivan Ballou's letter to his wife treat the tension between family life and patriotic duty, the former lightheartedly, the latter most earnestly; home seems to mean different things to the two married soldiers. Tocqueville's famous nineteenth-century discussion of woman and the democratic family in America speaks about married life not in terms of private happiness, but in terms of noble if wearying service for both the children and the larger society, all under the banner of civilization. Without romanticizing, he makes vivid the spirit—and the costs as well as the blessings—of marriages built on shared dreams, common toil, and high moral purpose.

The final five selections return to marriage and family life seen from within. Rousseau aims for durable erotic satisfaction, a life still filled with the delights of courtship, now sustained by the joys of making love. Kierkegaard's "Married Man" also waxes enthusiastic over the treasure of his wife, less as erotic partner, more as loving companion and mother; it is his deep awareness of the meaning of time that especially enables him to love "the woman of years" and to escape from the shallow and fleeting passions of the aesthetic love of visible beauty. Configured time and space, in bed and at board, become the ground of a liturgical view of the dailiness of married life, in the seemingly humdrum selection by Capon. The penultimate reading comes from Tolstoy, the one novelist who, probably better than anyone, is perfectly willing and able to convey a full and winning picture of conjugal blessedness and family happiness, centered around the joys and cares of rearing one's children. The last word belongs to the poet Robert Frost; the last words of his poem—"wing to wing and oar to oar"—we have taken as the title of this anthology.

We take the liberty of ending this introduction, as we began the general Introduction to this book, on a personal note. Not the smallest blessing of married life is the friendship of a thoughtful and understanding soul mate with whom one can share endless hours trying to make sense of it all.

Homer, The Reunion of
Penelope and Odysseus

For ten years, the gods hound Odysseus as he struggles to make his way home after the Trojan War. Yet, here, at the end of the epic, after Odysseus finally reaches the shores of his native Ithaca, after he is reunited with his son, after he rids his palace of the besieging suitors, he is still detained, this time by his own wife, long-enduring and loyal Penelope. Not a god but Penelope administers his final test. Despite the clear sign that the man who has come to Ithaca is Odysseus—her trusted nurse told Penelope of the scar, Odysseus's most distinctive mark, which she spotted when washing his feet—Penelope is strangely silent as she sits at the hearth, staring into the face of the man she has longed for all these years. Penelope is wondering, it seems, not about the identity of the man before her, but about what he has become. As she well knows, twenty years of hardship can do strange things to the human spirit. Doubtless too, the slaughter of the 108 suitors, though necessary, even desirable, was cause for concern: Just who is it that has come home? Where is the heart of this wanderer? What does their marriage mean to him now? At last, she seems to hit on the perfect test: the test of the bed. Odysseus's response to her request to move their once sturdy marriage bed tells her all that she yearned to know. We are naturally invited to wonder why. Why is the bed of such great importance to her and Odysseus? What does the test show Odysseus about his wife? Why is his response so revelatory? How and to what extent does the fixed "rootedness" of one's marriage bed encapsulate the meaning and blessings of one's marriage? [See also Capon selection, below] Is there a connection between sharing a bed and sharing stories? The selection comes from Book XXIII *of the* Odyssey.

Up to the rooms the old nurse clambered, chuckling all the way,
to tell the queen her husband was here now, home at last.
Her knees bustling, feet shuffling over each other,
till hovering at her mistress' head she spoke:
"Penelope—child—wake up and see for yourself,
with your own eyes, all you dreamed of, all your days!
He's here—Odysseus—he's come home, at long last!
He's killed the suitors, swaggering young brutes
who plagued his house, wolfed his cattle down,
rode roughshod over his son!"

"Dear old nurse," wary Penelope replied,
"the gods have made you mad. They have that power,

putting lunacy into the clearest head around
or setting a half-wit on the path to sense.
They've unhinged you, and you were once so sane.
Why do you mock me?—haven't I wept enough?—
telling such wild stories, interrupting my sleep,
sweet sleep that held me, sealed my eyes just now.
Not once have I slept so soundly since the day
Odysseus sailed away to see that cursed city . . .
Destroy, I call it—I hate to say its name!
Now down you go. Back to your own quarters.
If any other woman of mine had come to me,
rousing me out of sleep with such a tale,
I'd have her bundled back to her room in pain.
It's only your old gray head that spares you that!"

    "Never"—the fond old nurse kept pressing on—
"dear child, I'd never mock you! No, it's all true,
he's here—Odysseus—he's come home, just as I tell you!
He's the stranger they all manhandled in the hall.
Telemachus knew he was here, for days and days,
but he knew enough to hide his father's plans
so *he* could pay those vipers back in kind!"

    Penelope's heart burst in joy, she leapt from bed,
her eyes streaming tears, she hugged the old nurse
and cried out with an eager, winging word,
"Please, dear one, give me the whole story.
If he's really home again, just as you tell me,
how did he get those shameless suitors in his clutches?—
single-handed, braving an army always camped inside."

    "I have no idea," the devoted nurse replied.
"I didn't see it, I didn't ask—all I heard
was the choking groans of men cut down in blood.
We crouched in terror—a dark nook of our quarters—
all of us locked tight behind those snug doors
till your boy Telemachus came and called me out—
his father rushed him there to do just that. Then
I found Odysseus in the thick of slaughtered corpses;
there he stood and all around him, over the beaten floor,

the bodies sprawled in heaps, lying one on another . . .
How it would have thrilled your heart to see him—
splattered with bloody filth, a lion with his kill!
And now they're all stacked at the courtyard gates—
he's lit a roaring fire,
he's purifying the house with cleansing fumes
and he's sent me here to bring you back to him.
Follow me down! So now, after all the years of grief,
you two can embark, loving hearts, along the road to joy.
Look, your dreams, put off so long, come true at last—
he's back alive, home at his hearth, and found you,
found his son still here. And all those suitors
who did him wrong, he's paid them back, he has,
right in his own house!"

                    "Hush, dear woman,"
guarded Penelope cautioned her at once.
"Don't laugh, don't cry in triumph not yet.
You know how welcome the sight of him would be
to all in the house, and to me most of all
and the son we bore together.
But the story can't be true, not as you tell it,
no, it must be a god who's killed our brazen friends—
up in arms at their outrage, heartbreaking crimes.
They'd no regard for any man on earth—
good or bad—who chanced to come their way. So,
thanks to their reckless work they die their deaths.
Odysseus? Far from Achaea now, he's lost all hope
of coming home . . . he's lost and gone himself."

    "Child," the devoted old nurse protested,
"what nonsense you let slip through your teeth.
Here's your husband, warming his hands at his own hearth,
here—and you, you say he'll never come home again,
always the soul of trust! All right, this too—
I'll give you a sign, a proof that's plain as day.
That scar, made years ago by a boar's white tusk—
I spotted the scar myself, when I washed his feet,
and I tried to tell you, ah, but he, the crafty rascal,
clamped his hand on my mouth—I couldn't say a word.

Follow me down now. I'll stake my life on it:
if I am lying to *you*—
kill me with a thousand knives of pain!"

    "Dear old nurse," composed Penelope responded,
"deep as you are, my friend, you'll find it hard
to plumb the plans of the everlasting gods.
All the same, let's go and join my son
so I can see the suitors lying dead
and see . . . the one who killed them."
                                    With that thought
Penelope started down from her lofty room, her heart
in turmoil, torn . . . should she keep her distance,
probe her husband? Or rush up to the man at once
and kiss his head and cling to both his hands?
As soon as she stepped across the stone threshold,
slipping in, she took a seat at the closest wall
and radiant in the firelight, faced Odysseus now.
There he sat, leaning against the great central column,
eyes fixed on the ground, waiting, poised for whatever words
his hardy wife might say when she caught sight of him.
A long while she sat in silence . . . numbing wonder
filled her heart as her eyes explored his face.
One moment he seemed . . . Odysseus, to the life—
the next, no, he was not the man she knew,
a huddled mass of rags was all she saw.

    "Oh mother," Telemachus reproached her,
"cruel mother, you with your hard heart!
Why do you spurn my father so—why don't you
sit beside him, engage him, ask him questions?
What other wife could have a spirit so unbending?
Holding back from her husband, home at last for *her*
after bearing twenty years of brutal struggle—
your heart was always harder than a rock!"
                                    "My child,"
Penelope, well-aware, explained, "I'm stunned with wonder,
powerless. Cannot speak to him, ask him questions,
look him in the eyes . . . But if he is truly
Odysseus, home at last, make no mistake:
we two will know each other, even better—

we two have secret signs,
known to us both but hidden from the world."

    Odysseus, long-enduring, broke into a smile
and turned to his son with pointed, winging words:
"Leave your mother here in the hall to test me
as she will. She soon will know me better.
Now because I am filthy, wear such grimy rags,
she spurns me—your mother still can't bring herself
to believe I am her husband.
                       But you and I,
put heads together. What's our best defense?
When someone kills a lone man in the realm
who leaves behind him no great band of avengers,
still the killer flees, goodbye to kin and country.
But *we* brought down the best of the island's princes,
the pillars of Ithaca. Weigh it well, I urge you."

    "Look to it all yourself now, father," his son
deferred at once. "You are the best on earth,
they say, when it comes to mapping tactics.
No one, no mortal man, can touch you there.
But we're behind you, hearts intent on battle,
nor do I think you'll find us short on courage,
long as our strength will last."
                       "Then here's our plan,"
the master of tactics said. "I think it's best.
First go and wash, and pull fresh tunics on,
and tell the maids in the hall to dress well too.
And let the inspired bard take up his ringing lyre
and lead off for us all a dance so full of heart
that whoever hears the strains outside the gates—
a passerby on the road, a neighbor round about—
will think it's a wedding-feast that's under way.
No news of the suitors' death must spread through town
till we have slipped away to our own estates,
our orchard green with trees. There we'll see
what winning strategy Zeus will hand us then."

    They hung on his words and moved to orders smartly.
First they washed and pulled fresh tunics on,

the women arrayed themselves—the inspired bard
struck up his resounding lyre and stirred in all
a desire for dance and song, the lovely lilting beat,
till the great house echoed round to the measured tread
of dancing men in motion, women sashed and lithe.
And whoever heard the strains outside would say,
"A miracle—someone's married the queen at last!"

  "One of her hundred suitors."
          "That callous woman,
too faithless to keep her lord and master's house
to the bitter end—"
      "Till he came sailing home."

   So they'd say, blind to what had happened:
the great-hearted Odysseus was home again at last.
The maid Eurynome bathed him, rubbed him down with oil
and drew around him a royal cape and choice tunic too.
And Athena crowned the man with beauty, head to foot,
made him taller to all eyes, his build more massive,
yes, and down from his brow the great goddess
ran his curls like thick hyacinth clusters
full of blooms. As a master craftsman washes
gold over beaten silver—a man the god of fire
and Queen Athena trained in every fine technique—
and finishes of his latest effort, handsome work . . .
so she lavished splendor over his head and shoulders now.
He stepped from his bath, glistening like a god,
and back he went to the seat that he had left
and facing his wife, declared,
"Strange woman! So hard—the gods of Olympus
made you harder than any other woman in the world!
What other wife could have a spirit so unbending?
Holding back from her husband, home at last for *her*
after bearing twenty years of brutal struggle.
Come, nurse, make me a bed, I'll sleep alone.
She has a heart of iron in her breast."
         "Strange *man*,"
wary Penelope said. "I'm not so proud, so scornful,
nor am I overwhelmed by your quick change . . .
You look—how well I know—the way he looked,

setting sail from Ithaca years ago
aboard the long-oared ship.

Come, Eurycleia,
move the sturdy bedstead out of our bridal chamber—
that room the master built with his own hands.
Take it out now, sturdy bed that it is,
and spread it deep with fleece,
blankets and lustrous throws to keep him warm."

Putting her husband to the proof—but Odysseus
blazed up in fury, lashing out at his loyal wife:
"Woman—your words, they cut me to the core!
Who could move my bed? Impossible task,
even for some skilled craftsman—unless a god
came down in person, quick to lend a hand,
lifted it out with ease and moved it elsewhere.
Not a man on earth, not even at peak strength,
would find it easy to prise it up and shift it, no,
a great sign, a hallmark lies in its construction.
I know, I built it myself—no one else . . .
There was a branching olive-tree inside our court,
grown to its full prime, the bole like a column, thickset.
Around it I built my bedroom, finished off the walls
with good tight stonework, roofed it over soundly
and added doors, hung well and snugly wedged.
Then I lopped the leafy crown of the olive,
clean-cutting the stump bare from roots up,
planing it round with a bronze smoothing-adze—
I had the skill—I shaped it plumb to the line to make
my bedpost, bored the holes it needed with an auger.
Working from there I built my bed, start to finish,
I gave it ivory inlays, gold and silver fittings,
wove the straps across it, oxhide gleaming red.
There's our secret sign, I tell you, our life story!
Does the bed, my lady, still stand planted firm?
I don't know—or has someone chopped away
that olive-trunk and hauled our bedstead off?"

Living proof—
Penelope felt her knees go slack, her heart surrender,
recognizing the strong clear signs Odysseus offered.
She dissolved in tears, rushed to Odysseus, flung her arms

around his neck and kissed his head and cried out,
"*Odysseus*—don't flare up at me now, not you,
always the most understanding man alive!
The gods, it was the gods who sent us sorrow—
they grudged us both a life in each other's arms
from the heady zest of youth to the stoop of old age.
But don't fault me, angry with me now because I failed,
at the first glimpse, to greet you, hold you, so . . .
In my heart of hearts I always cringed with fear
some fraud might come, beguile me with his talk;
the world is full of the sort,
cunning ones who plot their own dark ends.
Remember Helen of Argos, Zeus's daughter—
would *she* have sported so in a stranger's bed
if she had dreamed that Achaea's sons were doomed
to fight and die to bring her home again?
Some god spurred her to do her shameless work.
Not till then did her mind conceive that madness,
blinding madness that caused her anguish, ours as well.
But now, since you have revealed such overwhelming proof—
the secret sign of our bed, which no one's ever seen
but you and I and a single handmaid, Actoris,
the servant my father gave me when I came,
who kept the doors of our room you built so well . . .
you've conquered my heart, my hard heart, at last!"

The more she spoke, the more a deep desire for tears
welled up inside his breast—he wept as he held the wife
he loved, the soul of loyalty, in his arms at last.
Joy, warm as the joy that shipwrecked sailors feel
when they catch sight of land—Poseidon has struck
their well-rigged ship on the open sea with gale winds
and crushing walls of waves, and only a few escape, swimming,
struggling out of the frothing surf to reach the shore,
their bodies crusted with salt but buoyed up with joy
as they plant their feet on solid ground again,
spared a deadly fate. So joyous now to her
the sight of her husband, vivid in her gaze,
that her white arms, embracing his neck
would never for a moment let him go . . .
Dawn with her rose-red fingers might have shone

upon their tears, if with her glinting eyes
Athena had not thought of one more thing.
She held back the night, and night lingered long
at the western edge of the earth, while in the east
she reined in Dawn of the golden throne at Ocean's banks,
commanding her not to yoke the windswift team that brings men light,
Blaze and Aurora, the young colts that race the Morning on.
Yet now Odysseus, seasoned veteran, said to his wife,
"Dear woman . . . we have still not reached the end
of all our trials. One more labor lies in store—
boundless, laden with danger, great and long,
and I must brave it out from start to finish.
So the ghost of Tiresias prophesied to me,
the day that I went down to the House of Death
to learn our best route home, my comrades' and my own.
But come, let's go to bed, dear woman—at long last
delight in sleep, delight in each other, come!"

       "If it's bed you want," reserved Penelope replied,
"it's bed you'll have, whenever the spirit moves,
now that the gods have brought you home again
to native land, your grand and gracious house.
But since you've alluded to it,
since a god has put it in your mind,
please, tell me about this trial still to come.
I'm bound to learn of it later, I am sure—
what's the harm if I hear of it tonight?"
                                   "Still so strange,"
Odysseus, the old master of stories, answered.
"Why again, why force me to tell you all?
Well, tell I shall. I'll hide nothing now.
But little joy it will bring you, I'm afraid,
as little joy for me.
                        The prophet said
that I must rove through towns on towns of men,
that I must carry a well-planed oar until
I come to a people who know nothing of the sea,
whose food is never seasoned with salt, strangers all
to ships with their crimson prows and long slim oars,
wings that make' ships fly. And here is my sign,
he told me, clear, so clear I cannot miss it,

and I will share it with you now . . .
When another traveler falls in with me and calls
that weight across my shoulder a fan to winnow grain,
then, he told me, I must plant my oar in the earth
and sacrifice fine beasts to the lord god of the sea,
Poseidon—a ram, a bull and a ramping wild boar—
then journey home and render noble offerings up
to the deathless gods who rule the vaulting skies,
to all the gods in order.
And at last my own death will steal upon me . . .
a gentle, painless death, far from the sea it comes
to take me down, borne down with the years in ripe old age
with all my people here in blessed peace around me.
All this, the prophet said, will come to pass.”

        “And so,” Penelope said, in her great wisdom,
“if the gods will really grant a happier old age,
there’s hope that we’ll escape our trials at last.”

        So husband and wife confided in each other,
while nurse and Eurynome, under the flaring brands,
were making up the bed with coverings deep and soft.
And working briskly, soon as they’d made it snug,
back to her room the old nurse went to sleep
as Eurynome, their attendant, torch in hand,
lighted the royal couple’s way to bed and,
leading them to their chamber, slipped away.
Rejoicing in each other, they returned to their bed,
the old familiar place they loved so well.

        Now Telemachus, the cowherd and the swineherd
rested their dancing feet and had the women do the same,
and across the shadowed hall the men lay down to sleep.

        But the royal couple, once they’d reveled in all
the longed-for joys of love, reveled in each other’s stories,
the radiant woman telling of all she’d borne at home,
watching them there, the infernal crowd of suitors
slaughtering herds of cattle and good fat sheep—
while keen to win her hand—
draining the broached vats dry of vintage wine.

And great Odysseus told his wife of all the pains
he had dealt out to other men and all the hardships
he'd endured himself—his story first to last—
and she listened on, enchanted . . .
Sleep never sealed her eyes till all was told.

Aristotle, The Friendship
of Husband and Wife

Few if any philosophers have paid more attention to the importance of friendship than Aristotle (384–322 BC), who devoted fully one-fifth of his Nicomachean Ethics *to this subject. The highest friendship Aristotle locates in the friendship of "sharing speeches and thoughts," the so-called philosophic friendship ("the marriage of true minds"). But he also celebrates the friendships of the household: between parents and children, between siblings, and between husband and wife. The terms of his description will strike the modern ear (for good reason) as cool, abstract, passionless, and decidedly unerotic. Still, his short discussion (Book VIII, Chapter xii) reproduced here of the friendship of husband and wife (viewed apolitically, i.e., from inside the house, in terms of love, not rule) is remarkable for many things, each of which emphasizes the uniqueness of this friendship: the friendship is singularly natural; it can rest on all three grounds of friendly love— the pleasant, the useful, and the good (or the virtuous); the fact of commonality is emphasized throughout, by the repeated use not only of the term "common" (koinon) but also of the prefix "syn-" (or "sym-"), meaning "together with"; and most significantly, in what is the only use of this notion in the entire* Ethics, *children are uniquely called a "common good," good for both husband and wife. How are children "good," and in what ways "common"? Is there any other good of marriage that is able so truly to unite man and wife, body and soul? Is there any other human friendship that offers a comparable or superior common good?*

The friendship between husband and wife seems to be according to nature; for man is by nature coupling (*synduastikon*) more than political, inasmuch as the household is prior and more necessary than the *polis* [city], and making-offspring (*teknopoiia*) is more common (*koinoteron*) among animals. Now for the others [animals] the association (*koinônia*) is for such a thing (*teknopoiia*), but human beings house-together (*synoikousin*) not only for the sake of making-offspring but also for the things regarding life (*eis ton bion*); for straight-away the works are divided, and they are different for a man and woman; now they provide for one another, placing the private things into the common (*eis to koinon tithentes ta idia*). On account of this both the useful and the pleasant seem to be in this friendship. But it might be also on account of virtue, if they are decent (*epiekeis*); for there is the virtue of each, and they might rejoice in such. A bond (*syndesmos*) seems to be the children, therefore the childless ones are more swiftly dissolved; for children are a *common good* for both, and the common holds together (*synechei de to koinon*). How one ought to live together between husband and wife and generally between friend and friend, appears to be sought in nothing other than how justly; for it [the just] appears not [to be] the same from a friend toward his friend and a stranger (*othneion*) and his comrade and his schoolfellow (*symphoitêtên*).

Jewish Midrash, Childless Love

Children are in virtually all cultures reckoned among the blessings of married life.
But not every marriage is so blessed. What then? Placing an extremely high value
on procreation—"Be fruitful and multiply" is the first biblical commandment—
Jewish law permitted divorce in the case of barrenness. Nevertheless, as the fol-
lowing story reveals, the Jewish sages avoided applying the rabbinic injunc-
tions where they threatened a love-filled marriage. This version of the ancient
Midrashic tale is taken from Maurice Lamm, The Jewish Way in Love and Mar-
riage.

"A certain Israelite of Sidon, having been married more than ten years without
being blessed with children, determined to be divorced from his wife. With
this view he brought her before Rabbi Simeon, bar Yochai. The rabbi, who was
unfavorably disposed to divorces, tried to dissuade him from it. However, seeing that the man was not inclined to accept his advice, he said this to the couple: 'My children, when you were first joined in the holy bond of wedlock, did
you not rejoice? Did you not make a feast and entertain your friends? Now,
since ye are resolved to be divorced, let your separation be like your union. Go
home, make a feast, entertain your friends, and on the morrow come and I will
comply with your wishes.'

"So reasonable a request, coming from such an authority, could not, with
any degree of propriety, be rejected. Accordingly, they went home and prepared
a sumptuous party to which they invited their friends.

"During the entertainment the husband, elated with wine, said to his wife:
'My beloved, we have lived together happily these many, many years; it is only
the lack of children which makes me want a divorce. To convince you, however,
that I bear you no ill-will, I give you permission to take with you out of my
house anything you like best.'

"'Be it so,' rejoined the woman.

"The cup went round and the people were merry. Having drunk rather
freely, most of the guests fell asleep, among them the master of the feast. The
lady no sooner perceived it, than she ordered him to be carried to her father's
house, and to be put into a bed she prepared for just that purpose.

"As the fumes of the wine gradually evaporated, the man awakened. Finding himself in a strange place, he wondered and exclaimed, 'Where am I? How
did I come here? What does this all mean?'

"His wife, who had waited to see the result of her stratagem, stepped from behind a curtain. Begging him not to be alarmed, she told him that he was now in her father's house.

"'In your father's house!' exclaimed the still astonished husband. 'How did I come to be in your father's house?'

"'Be patient, my dear husband,' replied the prudent woman, 'and I will tell you all. Recollect, did you not tell me last night, I might take out of your house whatever I valued most? Now, believe me, my beloved, among all your treasures there is not one I value so much as I do you; no, there is not a treasure in this world I esteem so much as I do you.'"

(*Another version of the story adds the following conclusion:* "So they again went to R. Simeon ben Yochai, and he stood up and prayed for them, and they were remembered [by God and granted children].")

Kipling, "The Married Man: Reservist of the Line"

While many authors write of the blessings of marriage from the point of view of private family life, equally important, though ironically often less visible, are the blessings it bestows on public civic life. In his humorous verses on "The Married Man," Rudyard Kipling (1865–1936), widely known in his lifetime as England's poet laureate, captures the difference that marriage makes to men in battle. The married man, unlike the bachelor with whom he is here compared, never loses sight of the fact that war is for the sake of peace. Even on the battlefield, he never forgets his attachments to home—to "'Er an' It"— and its civilized ways—he wants to "get 'ome to 'is tea."

The bachelor 'e fights for one
    As joyful as can be;
But the married man don't call it fun,
    Because 'e fights for three—
For 'Im an' 'Er an' It
    (An' Two an' One make Three)
'E wants to finish 'is little bit,
    An' 'e wants to go 'ome to 'is tea!

The bachelor pokes up 'is 'ead
    To see if you are gone;
But the married man lies down instead,
    An' waits till the sights come on,
For 'Im an' 'Er an' a hit
    (Direct or ricochee)
'E wants to finish 'is little bit,
    An' 'e wants to go 'ome to 'is tea.

The bachelor will miss you clear
    To fight another day;
But the married man, 'e says, "No fear!"
    'E wants you out of the way
Of 'Im an' 'Er an' It
    (An' 'is road to 'is farm or the sea),
'E wants to finish 'is little bit,
    An' 'e wants to go 'ome to 'is tea.

The bachelor 'e fights 'is fight
    An stretches out an' snores
But the married man sits up all night—
    For 'e don't like out-o'-doors.
'E'll strain an' listen an' peer
    An' give the first alarm—
For the sake o' the breathin' 'e's used to 'ear,
    An' the 'ead on the thick of 'is arm.

The bachelor may risk 'is 'ide
    To 'elp you when you're downed;
But the married man will wait beside
    Till the ambulance comes round.
'E'll take your 'ome address
    An' all you've time to say,
Or if 'e sees there's 'ope, 'e'll press
    Your art'ry 'alf the day—

For 'Im an' 'Er an' It
    (An' One from Three leaves Two),
For 'e knows you wanted to finish your bit,
    An' 'e knows 'oo's wantin' you.
Yes, 'Im an' 'Er an' It
    (Our 'oly One in Three),
We're all of us anxious to finish our bit,
    An' we want to get 'ome to our tea!

Yes, It an' 'Er an' 'Im,
    Which often makes me think
The married man must sink or swim
    An'—'e can't afford to sink!
Oh, 'Im an' It an' 'Er
    Since Adam an' Eve began!
So I'd rather fight with the bacheler
    An' be nursed by the married man!

Ballou, Letter to Sarah

Like Kipling's poem "The Married Man," this letter to his wife by Major Sullivan Ballou of the 2nd Rhode Island regiment of the Union army addresses the relation between civic and private life. Written during the Civil War, a week before the battle of Manassas, the letter speaks of his two great loves, "love of Country" and love of Sarah, his wife. At first glance, the two loves appear to be strictly in conflict, the second willingly sacrificed to the first. However, closer reading makes one wonder whether it is not, in part, the blessings of private life, made secure by the American republic, that inspires Ballou's grateful commitment to defend "American Civilization." One wonders also whether it is not his steadfast, "deathless" love for Sarah, still binding him to her as he heads for battle, that inspirits him to face the threat of death on behalf of his love of country.

July 14, 1861
Camp Clark, Washington

My very dear Sarah:

The indications are very strong that we shall move in a few days—perhaps tomorrow. Lest I should not be able to write again I feel impelled to write a few lines that may fall under your eye when I shall be no more. . . .

Our movement may be one of a few days duration and full of pleasure—and it may be one of severe conflict and death to me. "Not my will, but Thine O God be done." If it is necessary that I should fall on the battlefield for my country, I am ready. I have no misgivings about, or lack of confidence in the cause in which I am engaged, and my courage does not halt or falter. I know how strongly American Civilization now leans on the triumph of the government, and how great a debt we owe to those who went before us through the blood and sufferings of the Revolution. And I am willing—perfectly willing—to lay down all my joys in this life, to help maintain this Government, and to pay that debt. . . .

But, my dear wife, when I know that with my own joys I lay down nearly all of yours, and replace them in this life with cares and sorrows—when, after having eaten for long years the bitter fruit of orphanage myself, I must offer it as their only sustenance to my dear little children—is it weak or dishonorable, while the banner of my purpose floats calmly and proudly in the breeze, that my unbounded love of you, my darling wife and children, should struggle in fierce, though useless, contest with my love of Country?

I cannot describe to you my feelings on this calm summer night, when two thousand men are sleeping around me, many of them enjoying the last, perhaps, before that of death—and I, suspicious that Death is creeping behind me with his fatal dart, am communing with God, my Country, and thee.

I have sought most closely and diligently, and often in my breast, for a wrong motive in thus hazarding the happiness of those I loved and could not find one. A pure love of my Country and the principles I have often advocated before the people, and "the name of honor that I love more than I fear death" have called upon me, and I have obeyed.

Sarah, my love for you is deathless, it seems to bind me with mighty cables that nothing but Omnipotence could break; and yet my love of Country comes over me like a strong wind and bears me unresistably on with all these chains to the battle field.

The memories of the blissful moments I have spent with you come creeping over me, and I feel most gratified to God and to you that I have enjoyed them so long. And hard it is for me to give them up and burn to ashes the hopes of future years, when, God willing, we might still have lived and loved together, and seen our sons grown up to honorable manhood around us. I have, I know, but few and small claims upon Divine Providence, but something whispers to me—perhaps it is the wafted prayer of my little Edgar—that I shall return to my loved ones unharmed. If I do not, my dear Sarah, never forget how much I love you, and when my last breath escapes me on the battlefield, it will whisper your name. Forgive my many faults, and the many pains I have caused you. How thoughtless and foolish I have often times been! How gladly would I wash out with my tears every little spot upon your happiness . . . and struggle with all the misfortunes of this world to shield you and my dear children from harm. But I cannot. I must watch you from the spirit land and hover near you, while you buffet the storms with your precious little freight, and wait with sad patience till we meet to part no more.

But, O Sarah! if the dead can come back to this earth and flit unseen around those they loved, I shall always be near you, in the gladdest days and in the darkest nights . . . always, always, and if there be a soft breeze upon your cheek, it shall be my breath, as the cool air fans your throbbing temple, it shall be my spirit passing by.

Sarah, do not mourn me dead; think I am gone and wait for thee, for we shall meet again. . . .

As for my little boys, they will grow up as I have done, and never know a father's love and care. Little Willie is too young to remember me long, and my blue-eyed Edgar will keep my frolics with him among the dimmest memories of his childhood. Sarah, I have unlimited confidence in your maternal care and your development of their characters and feel that God will bless you in your holy work.

Tell my two mothers I call God's blessing upon them.

O Sarah, I wait for you there. Come to me, and lead thither my children.

Sullivan Ballou was killed at the first battle of Bull Run.

Tocqueville, *Democracy in America:*
Marriage and Mores

In the early 1830s, the French aristocrat and social theorist, Alexis de Tocqueville (1805–1859), traveled to the United States, observing and interviewing citizens in the heart of American cities and at the western reaches of the frontier. He published his findings and reflections in his massive work, Democracy in America *(1835–40), still regarded by many—notwithstanding the lapse of time and our greatly changed socioeconomic conditions—as a most wise and prescient account of democracy in general and of American democracy in particular. Tocqueville traces the influence of the equality of conditions on the whole course of society, including the relations of man and woman and the institution of marriage. Struck by the turbulence of commercial, competitive, public life in America, Tocqueville saw the necessity of a protected domestic sphere, where less individualistic, more moderate, and more public-spirited habits of the heart could be cultivated; and he praised American women for anticipating and accepting the same necessity. He noted with appreciation the robust freedom in which girls, like boys, were reared and educated, but he noted with even greater appreciation the fact that, as wives, these same independent spirits freely chose to submit and to remain faithful to their husbands, to confine their interests to the home, and to accept their own social inferiority, all in the service of civilizing their children (and husbands). What he saw of American marriage and sexual mores led him to ascribe the extraordinary prosperity and growing power of this nation to the superiority of its women.*

In the first selection below (excerpted from Volume II, Part III, Chapters 9–12), Tocqueville shows how American girls are educated to independence and self-command, how the young woman as wife freely accepts the constraints of marriage, how the spirit of equality fosters sound marriages and good morals in America, and how Americans, while celebrating the equality of men and women, resist the move to social androgyny. In an additional selection (Appendix U), Tocqueville provides a haunting portrait of the pioneer woman at her hearth, whom he admires, as he admired American women in general, for her resolution. She followed and submitted to her husband for the sake of the next generation and by doing so helped tame, civilize, and elevate life, safeguarding genuine human possibility against the wild and lonely forest. Recent social changes in the role of women and in sexual mores make Tocqueville's description seem outdated, and few contemporary readers are likely to find the portraits of the virtuous wife and the pioneer woman attractive. Nevertheless, all of Tocqueville's reflections invite us to wonder whether the blessings such women provided are not, in fact, still blessings and still necessary. In our rush to conquer nature, have we really man-

aged permanently to subdue the forest, especially the wildness within? What will happen to the civilizing blessings of marriage and domestic life when women and men practice the same public social roles? Are the blessings of self-fulfillment through public achievement as important as the moral blessings of family life? Is the pioneer woman unfulfilled?

Chapter 9
Education of Girls in the United States

There never have been free societies without mores, and as I observed in the first part of this book, it is woman who shapes these mores. Therefore everything which has a bearing on the status of women, their habits, and their thoughts is, in my view, of great political importance. . . .

Long before the young American woman has reached marriageable age, the process of freeing her from her mother's care has started stage by stage. Before she has completely left childhood behind she already thinks for herself, speaks freely, and acts on her own. All the doings of the world are ever plain for her to see; far from trying to keep this from her sight, she is continually shown more and more of it and taught to look thereon with firm and quiet gaze. So the vices and dangers of society are soon plain to her, and seeing them clearly, she judges them without illusion and faces them without fear, for she is full of confidence in her own powers, and it seems that this feeling is shared by all around her.

Thus you can hardly expect an American girl to show that virgin innocence amid burgeoning desires and those naive and artless graces which in Europe generally go with the stage between childhood and youth. Seldom does an American girl, whatever her age, suffer from shyness or childish ignorance. She, like the European girl, wants to please, but she knows exactly what it costs. She may avoid evil, but at least knows what it is; her morals are pure rather than her mind chaste. . . .

It is easy to see that even in the freedom of early youth, an American girl never quite loses control of herself; she enjoys all permitted pleasures without losing her head about any of them, and her reason never lets the reins go, though it may often seem to let them flap. . . .

They [the Americans] realize that there must be a great deal of individual freedom in a democracy; youth will be impatient, tastes ill-restrained, customs fleeting, public opinion often unsettled or feeble, paternal authority weak, and a husband's power contested.

In such circumstances they have calculated that there was little chance of repressing in woman the most tyrannical passions of the human heart and that it was a safer policy to teach her to control them herself. Unable to prevent her chastity from being often in danger, they want her to know how to defend herself, and they count on the strength of her free determination more than on safeguards which have been shaken or overthrown. Instead, therefore, of teaching her to distrust herself, they seek to increase her confidence in her own powers. Unable and unwilling to keep a girl in perpetual and complete ignorance, they are in a hurry to give her precocious knowledge of everything. Far from hiding the world's corruption from her, they want her to see it at once and take her own steps to avoid it, and they are more anxious to ensure her good conduct than to guard her innocence too carefully.

Although the Americans are a very religious people, they have not relied on religion alone to defend feminine chastity; they have tried to give arms to her reasoning powers. In this they are using the same approach that they have employed in many other circumstances. In the first place, they make incredible efforts to provide that individual freedom shall be able to control itself, and it is only when they have reached the utmost limits of human strength that they call in the aid of religion.

I know that such an education has its dangers; I know too that it tends to develop judgment at the cost of imagination and to make women chaste and cold rather than tender and loving companions of men. Society may thus be more peaceful and better ordered, but the charms of private life are often less. But that is a secondary evil, which should be faced for the sake of the greater good. At the point we have now reached, we no longer have a choice to make; a democratic education is necessary to protect women against the dangers with which the institutions and mores of democracy surround them.

Chapter 10
The Young Woman as a Wife

In America a woman loses her independence forever in the bonds of matrimony. While there is less constraint on girls there than anywhere else, a wife submits to stricter obligations. For the former, her father's house is a home of freedom and pleasure; for the latter, her husband's is almost a cloister.

These two states are not perhaps as contradictory as one tends to think, and it is natural for Americans to pass through the one to reach the other.

Religious peoples and industrial nations take a particularly serious view of marriage. The former consider the regularity of a woman's life the best guarantee and surest sign of the purity of her morals. The latter see in it the surest safeguard of the order and prosperity of the house.

The Americans are both a Puritan and a trading nation. Therefore both their religious beliefs and their industrial habits lead them to demand much abnegation on the woman's part and a continual sacrifice of pleasure for the sake of business, which is seldom expected in Europe. Thus in America inexorable public opinion carefully keeps woman within the little sphere of domestic interests and duties and will not let her go beyond them.

When she is born into the world the young American girl finds these ideas firmly established; she sees the rules that spring therefrom; she is soon convinced that she cannot for a moment depart from the usages accepted by her contemporaries without immediately putting in danger her peace of mind, her reputation, and her very social existence, and she finds the strength required for such an act of submission in the firmness of her understanding and the manly habits inculcated by her education.

One may say that it is the very enjoyment of freedom that has given her the courage to sacrifice it without struggle or complaint when the time has come for that.

Moreover, the American woman never gets caught in the bonds of matrimony as in a snare set to catch her simplicity and ignorance. She knows beforehand what will be expected of her, and she herself has freely accepted the yoke. She suffers her new state bravely, for she has chosen it.

Because in America paternal discipline is very lax and the bonds of marriage very tight, a girl is cautious and wary in agreeing thereto. Precocious weddings hardly occur. So American women only marry when their minds are experienced and mature, whereas elsewhere women usually only begin to mature when they are married.

However, I am far from thinking that only the constraint of public opinion imposes this great change in the ways of women as soon as they are married. Often it is simply their own will which imposes this sacrifice on them.

When the time has come to choose a husband, her cold and austere powers of reasoning, which have been educated and strengthened by a free view of the world, teach the American woman that a light and free spirit within the bonds of marriage is an everlasting source of trouble, not of pleasure, that a girl's amusements cannot become the recreation of a wife, and that for a married woman the springs of happiness are inside the home. Seeing beforehand and clearly the only path that can lead to domestic felicity, from the first step she sets out in that direction and follows it to the end without seeking to turn back.

This same strength of will exhibited by the young married women of America in immediately submitting without complaint to the austere duties of their new state is no less manifest in all the great trials of their lives.

In no country of the world are private fortunes more unstable than in the United States. It is not exceptional for one man in his lifetime to work up through every stage from poverty to opulence and then come down again.

American women face such upheavals with quiet, indomitable energy. Their desires seem to contract with their fortune as easily as they expand.

Most of the adventurers who yearly go to people the empty spaces of the West belong . . . to the old Anglo-American stock of the North. Many of these who launch out so boldly in search of wealth have already gained a comfortable living in their own land. They take their wives with them and make them share the dangers and innumerable privations that always go with such undertakings. In the utmost confines of the wilderness I have often met young wives, brought up in all the refinement of life in the towns of New England, who have passed almost without transition from their parents' prosperous houses to leaky cabins in the depths of the forest. Fever, solitude, and boredom had not broken the resilience of their courage. Their features were changed and faded, but their looks were firm. They seemed both sad and resolute. (See Appendix U.)

I am sure that it was the education of their early years which built up that inner strength on which they were later to draw.

So, in America the wife is still the same person that she was as a girl; her part in life has changed, and her ways are different, but the spirit is the same. (See Appendix U.)

Chapter 11
How Equality Helps to Maintain Good Morals in America

. . . Although travelers who have visited North America differ on many points, they all agree that mores are infinitely stricter there than anywhere else. . . .

No doubt this great strictness of American mores is due partly to the country, the race, and the religion. But all those causes, which can be found elsewhere, are still not enough to account for the matter. To do so one must discover some particular reason.

I think that reason is equality and institutions deriving therefrom.

Equality of conditions does not by itself alone make mores strict, but there can be no doubt that it aids and increases such a tendency.

Among aristocratic peoples birth and fortune often make a man and a woman such different creatures that they would never be able to unite with one another. Their passions draw them together, but social conditions and the thoughts that spring from them prevent them from uniting in a permanent and open way. The necessary result of that is a great number of ephemeral and clandestine connections. Nature secretly gets her own back for the restraint imposed by laws.

Things do not happen in the same way when equality of conditions has swept down all the real or imaginary barriers separating man and woman. No girl then feels that she cannot become the wife of the man who likes her best, and that makes irregular morals before marriage very difficult. For however credulous passion may make us, there is hardly a way of persuading a girl that you love her when you are perfectly free to marry her but will not do so.

The same cause is at work, though in a more indirect way, after marriage.

Nothing does more to make illegitimate love seem legitimate in the eyes both of those who experience it and of the watching crowd than forced marriages or ones entered into by chance.

In a country where the woman can always choose freely and where education has taught her to choose well, public opinion is inexorable against her faults.

The severity of the Americans is in part due to this cause. They regard marriage as a contract which is often burdensome but every condition of which the parties are strictly bound to fulfill, because they knew them all beforehand and were at liberty not to bind themselves to anything at all.

The same cause which renders fidelity more obligatory also renders it easier.

The object of marriage in aristocratic lands is more to unite property than persons, so it can happen sometimes that the husband is chosen while at school and the wife at the breast. It is not surprising that the conjugal tie which unites the fortunes of the married couple leaves their hearts to rove at large. That is the natural result of the spirit of the contract.

But when each chooses his companion for himself without any external interference or even prompting, it is usually nothing but similar tastes and thoughts that bring a man and a woman together, and these similarities hold and keep them by each other's side. . . .

Almost all the men in a democracy either enter politics or practice some calling, whereas limited incomes oblige the wives to stay at home and watch in person very closely over the details of domestic economy.

All these separate and necessary occupations form as many natural barriers which, by keeping the sexes apart, make the solicitations of the one less frequent and less ardent and the resistance of the other easier.

Not that equality of conditions could ever make man chaste, but it gives the irregularity of his morals a less dangerous character. As no man any longer has leisure or opportunity to attack the virtue of those who wish to defend themselves, there are at the same time a great number of courtesans and a great many honest women.

Such a state of affairs leads to deplorable individual wretchedness, but it does not prevent the body social from being strong and alert; it does not break up families and does not weaken national morality. Society is endangered not by the great profligacy of a few but by the laxity of all. A lawgiver must fear prostitution much less than intrigues.

The disturbed and constantly harassed life which equality makes men lead not only diverts their attention from lovemaking by depriving them of leisure for its pursuit but also turns them away by a more secret but more certain path.

Everyone living in democratic times contracts, more or less, the mental habits of the industrial and trading classes; their thoughts take a serious turn, calculating and realistic; they gladly turn away from the ideal to pursue some visible and approachable aim which seems the natural and necessary object of their desires. Equality does not by this destroy the imagination, but clips its wings and only lets it fly touching the ground.

No men are less dreamers than the citizens of democracy; one hardly finds any who care to let themselves indulge in such leisurely and solitary moods of contemplation as generally precede and produce the great agitations of the heart.

They do, it is true, set great store on obtaining that type of deep, regular, and peaceful affection which makes life happy and secure. But they would not willingly chase violent and capricious emotions which disturb life and cut it short. . . .

Chapter 12
How the American Views the Equality of the Sexes

I have shown how democracy destroys or modifies those various inequalities which are in origin social. But is that the end of the matter? May it not ultimately come to change the great inequality between man and woman which has up till now seemed based on the eternal foundations of nature?

I think that the same social impetus which brings nearer to the same level father and son, master and servant, and generally every inferior to every superior does raise the status of women and should make them more and more nearly equal to men.

But in this I need more than ever to make myself clearly understood. For there is no subject on which the crude, disorderly fancy of our age has given itself freer rein.

In Europe there are people who, confusing the divergent attributes of the sexes, claim to make of man and woman creatures who are, not equal only, but actually similar. They would attribute the same functions to both, impose the same duties, and grant the same rights; they would have them share everything—work, pleasure, public affairs. It is easy to see that the sort of equality forced on both sexes degrades them both, and that so coarse a jumble of nature's works could produce nothing but feeble men and unseemly women.

That is far from being the American view of the sort of democratic equality which can be brought about between man and woman. They think that nature, which created such great differences between the physical and moral constitution of men and women, clearly intended to give their diverse faculties a diverse employment; and they consider that progress consists not in making dissimilar creatures do roughly the same things but in giving both a chance to do their job as well as possible. The Americans have applied to the sexes the great principle of political economy which now dominates industry. They have carefully separated the functions of man and of woman so that the great work of society may be better performed.

In America, more than anywhere else in the world, care has been taken constantly to trace clearly distinct spheres of action for the two sexes, and both are required to keep in step, but along paths that are never the same. You will never find American women in charge of the external relations of the family, managing a business, or interfering in politics; but they are also never obliged to undertake rough laborer's work or any task requiring hard physical exertion. No family is so poor that it makes an exception to this rule.

If the American woman is never allowed to leave the quiet sphere of domestic duties, she is also never forced to do so.

As a result, American women, who are often manly in their intelligence and in their energy, usually preserve great delicacy of personal appearance and always have the manners of women, though they sometimes show the minds and hearts of men.

Nor have the Americans ever supposed that democratic principles should undermine the husband's authority and make it doubtful who is in charge of the family. In their view, every association, to be effective, must have a head, and the natural head of the conjugal association is the husband. They therefore never deny him the right to direct his spouse. They think that in the little society composed of man and wife, just as in the great society of politics, the aim of democracy is to regulate and legitimatize necessary powers and not to destroy all power.

That is by no means an opinion maintained by one sex and opposed by the other.

I have never found American women regarding conjugal authority as a blessed usurpation of their rights or feeling that they degraded themselves by submitting to it. On the contrary, they seem to take pride in the free relinquishment of their will, and it is their boast to bear the yoke themselves rather than to escape from it. That, at least, is the feeling expressed by the best of them; the others keep quiet, and in the United States one never hears an adulterous wife noisily proclaiming the rights of women while stamping the most hallowed duties under foot.

In Europe one has often noted that a certain contempt lurks in the flattery men lavish on women; although a European may often make himself a woman's slave, one feels that he never sincerely thinks her his equal.

In the United States men seldom compliment women, but they daily show how much they esteem them.

Americans constantly display complete confidence in their spouses' judgment and deep respect for their freedom. They hold that woman's mind is just as capable as man's of discovering the naked truth, and her heart as firm to face it. They have never sought to place her virtue, any more than his, under the protection of prejudice, ignorance, or fear.

It would seem that in Europe, where men so easily submit to the despotic sway of women, they are nevertheless denied some of the greatest attributes of humanity, and they are regarded as seductive but incomplete beings. The most astonishing thing of all is that women themselves end by looking at themselves in the same light and that they almost think it a privilege to be able to appear futile, weak, and timid. The women of America never lay claim to rights of that sort.

It may, moreover, be said that our moral standards accord a strange immunity to man, so that virtue is one thing in his case and quite another for his spouse, and that the same act can be seen by public opinion as a crime in the one but only a fault in the other.

The Americans know nothing of this unfair division of duties and rights. With them the seducer is as much dishonored as his victim.

It is true that the Americans seldom lavish upon women the eager attentions which are often paid to them in Europe, but their conduct always shows that they assume them to be virtuous and refined; and they have such respect for their moral freedom that in their presence every man is careful to keep a watch on his tongue for fear that they should be forced to listen to language which offends them. In America a young woman can set out on a long journey alone and without fear.

American legislators, who have made almost every article in the criminal code less harsh, punish rape by death; and no other crime is judged with the same inexorable severity by public opinion. There is reason for this: as the Americans think nothing more precious than a woman's honor and nothing deserving more respect than her freedom, they think no punishment could be too severe for those who take both from her against her will.

In France, where the same crime is subject to much milder penalties, it is difficult to find a jury that will convict. Is the reason scorn of chastity or scorn of woman? I cannot rid myself of the feeling that it is both.

To sum up, the Americans do not think that man and woman have the duty or the right to do the same things, but they show an equal regard for the part played by both and think of them as beings of equal worth, though their fates are different. They do not expect courage of the same sort or for the same purposes from woman as from man, but they never question her courage. They do not think that a man and his wife should always use their intelligence and understanding in the same way, but they do at least consider that the one has as firm an understanding as the other and a mind as clear.

Thus, then, while they have allowed the social inferiority of woman to continue, they have done everything to raise her morally and intellectually to the level of man. In this I think they have wonderfully understood the true conception of democratic progress.

For my part, I have no hesitation in saying that although the American woman never leaves her domestic sphere and is in some respects very dependent within it, nowhere does she enjoy a higher station. And now that I come near the end of this book in which I have recorded so many considerable achievements of the Americans, if anyone asks me what I think the chief cause of the extraordinary prosperity and growing power of this nation, I should answer that it is due to the superiority of their women.

* * *

Appendix U

I find the following passage in my travel diary and it will serve to show what trials are faced by those American women who follow their husbands into the wilds. The description has nothing but its complete accuracy to recommend it.

" . . . From time to time we came to new clearings. As all these settlements are exactly like one another, I will describe the place at which we stopped tonight. It will provide a picture of all the others.

"The bells which the pioneer is careful to hang round his beasts' necks, so as to find them again in the forest, warned us from afar that we were getting near a clearing. Soon we heard the sound of an ax cutting down the forest trees. The closer we got, the more signs of destruction indicated the presence of civilized man. Our path was covered with severed branches; and tree trunks, scorched by fire or cut about by an ax, stood in our way. We went on farther and came to a part of the wood where all the trees seemed to have been suddenly struck dead. In full summer their withered branches seemed the image of winter. Looking at them close up, we saw that a deep circle had been cut through the bark, which by preventing the circulation of the sap had soon killed the trees. We were informed that this is commonly the first thing a pioneer does. As he cannot, in the first year, cut down all the trees that adorn his new property, he sows corn under their branches, and by striking them to death, prevents them from shading his crop. Beyond this field, itself an unfinished sketch, or first step toward civilization in the wilds, we suddenly saw the owner's cabin. It is generally placed in the middle of some land more carefully cultivated than the rest, but where man is yet sustaining an unequal fight against the forest. There the trees have been cut, but not grubbed up, and their trunks still cover and block the land they used to shade. Around these dry stumps wheat and oak seedlings and plants and weeds of all kinds are scattered pell-mell and grow together on rough and still half-wild ground. It is in the midst of this vigorous and variegated growth of vegetation that the planter's dwelling, or as it is called in this country, his log house, stands. Just like the field around it, this rustic dwelling shows every sign of recent and hasty work. It is seldom more than thirty feet long and fifteen high; the walls as well as the roof are fashioned from rough tree trunks, between which moss and earth have been rammed to keep out the cold and rain from the inside of the house.

"As the night was coming on, we decided to go and ask the owner of the log house to put us up.

"At the sound of our steps the children playing among the scattered branches got up and ran to the house, as if frightened at the sight of a man, while two large, half-wild dogs, with ears prickled up and outstretched muzzles, came growling out of the hut to cover the retreat of their young masters. Then the pioneer himself appeared at the door of his dwelling; he looked at us with a rapid, inquisitive glance, made a sign to the dogs to go indoors, and set them the example himself, without showing that our arrival aroused either his curiosity or apprehension.

"We went into the log house; the inside was quite unlike that of the cottages of European peasants; there was more that was superfluous and fewer necessities; a single window with a muslin curtain; on the hearth of beaten earth a great fire which illuminated the whole interior; above the hearth a good rifle, a deerskin, and plumes of eagles' feathers; to the right of the chimney a map of the United States, raised and fluttering in the draft from the crannies in the wall; near it, on a shelf formed from a roughly hewn plank, a few books; a Bible, the first six cantos of Milton, and two plays of Shakespeare; there were trunks instead of cupboards along the wall; in the center of the room, a rough table with legs of green wood with the bark still on them, looking as if they grew out of the ground on which they stood; on the table was a teapot of English china, some silver spoons, a few cracked teacups, and newspapers.

"The master of this dwelling had the angular features and lank limbs characteristic of the inhabitants of New England. He was clearly not born in the solitude in which we found him. His physical constitution by itself showed that his earlier years were spent in a society that used its brains and that he belonged to that restless, calculating, and adventurous race of men who do with the utmost coolness things which can only be accounted for by the ardor of passion, and who endure for a time the life of a savage in order to conquer and civilize the backwoods.

"When the pioneer saw that we were crossing his threshold, he came to meet us and shake hands, as is their custom; but his face was quite unmoved. He opened the conversation by asking us what was going on in the world, and when his curiosity was satisfied, he held his peace, as if he was tired of the importunities and noise of the world. When we questioned him in our turn, he gave us all the information we asked and then turned, with no eagerness, but methodically, to see to our requirements. Why was it that, while he was thus kindly bent on aiding us, in spite of ourselves we felt our sense of gratitude frozen? It was because he himself, in showing his hospitality, seemed to be submitting to a tiresome necessity of his lot and saw in it a duty imposed by his position, and not a pleasure.

"A woman was sitting on the other side of the hearth, rocking a small child on her knees. She nodded to us without disturbing herself. Like the pioneer, this woman was in the prime of life; her appearance seemed superior to her condition, and her apparel even betrayed a lingering taste for dress; but her delicate limbs were wasted, her features worn, and her eyes gentle and serious; her whole physiognomy bore marks of religious resignation, a deep peace free from passions, and some sort of natural, quiet determination which would face all the ills of life without fear and without defiance.

"Her children cluster around her, full of health, high spirits, and energy; they are true children of the wilds; their mother looks at them from time to time with mingled melancholy and joy; seeing their strength and her weariness, one might think that the life she has given them exhausted her own, and yet she does not regret what they have cost her.

"The dwelling in which these immigrants live had no internal division and no loft; its single room shelters the whole family in the evening. It is a little world of its own, an ark of civilization lost in a sea of leaves. A hundred paces away the everlasting forest spreads its shade, and solitude begins again."

Rousseau, *Emile:* Married Lovers

Rousseau's Emile *ends with the marriage of Emile and Sophie. (An excerpt recounting their courtship appeared in the section "How Can I Find and Win the Right One?") In this selection from the very end of the book (Book V), the tutor gives obtrusive and not altogether welcome advice to the newlyweds on their wedding day, about how they can sustain their present bliss. The secret is to continue being lovers throughout one's marriage, and Rousseau, needless to say, has some very explicit suggestions—radical for his time—for how this might be done. Is the goal realizable? Is it the chief blessing of marriage?*

The end of the selection also makes clear that the blessings of married life include not only the happiness of the lovers, but also the supreme happiness of the tutor and the parents, who have reared Emile and Sophie precisely for this end. Might not providing for this renewal of life's bounty be the chief blessing of married life for the parents? A greater blessing than being lovers?

Why am I not permitted to paint Emile's return to Sophie and the conclusion of their love or rather the beginning of the conjugal love which unites them— love founded on esteem which lasts as long as life, on virtues which do not fade with beauty, on suitability of character which makes association pleasant and prolongs the charm of the first union into old age? But all these details might be pleasing without being useful, and up to now I have permitted myself only those agreeable details which I believed were of some utility. Shall I abandon this rule at the end of my task? No; I also feel that my pen is weary. I am too weak for works requiring so much endurance and would abandon this one if it were less advanced. In order not to leave it imperfect, it is time for me to finish.

Finally I see dawning the most charming of Emile's days and the happiest of mine. I see my attentions consummated, and I begin to taste their fruit. An indissoluble chain unites the worthy couple. Their mouths pronounce and their hearts confirm vows which will not be vain. They are wed. In returning from the temple, they let themselves be led. They do not know where they are, where they are going, or what is done around them. They do not hear; they respond only with confused words; their clouded eyes no longer see anything. O delirium! O human weakness! The sentiment of happiness crushes man. He is not strong enough to bear it.

There are very few people who know how to adopt a suitable tone with newly-weds on their wedding day. The gloomy propriety of some and the light remarks of others seem equally out of place to me. I would prefer to let these young hearts turn in on themselves and yield to an agitation that is not without charm rather than to cruelly distract them in order to make them gloomy by a false seemliness or embarrass them by tasteless jokes. For even if such jokes were to please at all other times, they would very surely be importunate on such a day.

In the sweet languor which excites them, my two young people seem to hear none of the speeches made to them. Would I, who want every day of life to be enjoyed, let them lose such a precious one? No, I want them to taste it, to savor it, and to enjoy its delight by themselves. I tear them away from the tactless crowd harassing them and take them for a walk. I bring them back to themselves by speaking to them about themselves. I wish to speak not only to their ears but to their hearts. I am not ignorant of the sole subject which can occupy them on this day.

Taking them both by the hand, I say to them, "My children, three years ago I saw the birth of this lively and pure flame which causes your happiness today. It has grown constantly. I see in your eyes that it is at its highest degree of intensity. It can only become weaker." Readers, do you not see Emile's transports, his fury, his vows; do you not see the disdainful air with which Sophie disengages her hand from mine and the tender protestations they make to each other with their eyes that they will adore each other until their last breath? I let them go on, and then I continue.

"I have often thought that if one could prolong the happiness of love in marriage, one would have paradise on earth. Up to now, that has never been seen. But if the thing is not utterly impossible, you both are quite worthy of setting an example that you will not have been given by anyone and that few couples will know how to imitate. Do you want me to tell you, my children, a means which I imagine can achieve that, a means which I believe to be the only possible one?"

They look at each other, smiling and making fun of my simplicity. Emile thanks me curtly for my recipe, saying he believes Sophie has a better one, and that so far as he is concerned, that one is enough for him. Sophie approves his response and appears just as confident. However, beneath her mocking manner I believe I detect a bit of curiosity. I examine Emile. His ardent eyes devour the charms of his wife. This is the only thing he is curious about, and all my remarks do not upset him at all. I smile in turn, saying to myself, "I shall soon be able to make you attentive."

The almost imperceptible difference between these secret emotions is the sign of a most characteristic difference between the two sexes, one quite contrary to the received prejudices. It is that men generally are less constant than women and grow weary of happy love sooner than they do. The woman has a presentiment of the man's inconstancy and is uneasy about it. This is also what makes her more jealous. When he begins to become lukewarm, she is forced, in order to keep him, to give him all the attentions he formerly gave to her; she cries and she humiliates herself in her turn, but rarely with the same success. Attachment and attentions win hearts, but they rarely regain them. I return to my recipe against the cooling off of love in marriage.

"The means is simple and easy," I continue. "It is to go on being lovers when one is married." "Quite so," Emile says, laughing secretly. "It won't be hard for us."

"It will be harder for you who are doing the talking than you may think. I beg you, give me the time to explain myself.

"Knots that one wants to tighten too much will burst. This is what happens to the marriage knot when one wants to give it more strength than it ought to have. The fidelity it imposes on the two spouses is the holiest of all rights, but the power it gives to each of the two over the other is too great. Constraint and love go ill together, and pleasure is not to be commanded. Do not blush, Sophie, and do not think of fleeing. God forbid that I should want to offend your modesty. But the destiny of your life is at issue. For so great a matter, tolerate speech between a husband and a father that you would not tolerate elsewhere.

"It is not so much possession as subjection which satiates, and a man stays attached to a kept woman far longer than to a wife. How could a duty be made of the tenderest caresses and a right be made of the sweetest proofs of love? It is mutual desire which constitutes the right. Nature knows no other. Law can restrict this right, but it cannot extend it. Voluptuousness is so sweet in itself! Should it receive from painful constraint the strength it could not draw from its own attractions? No, my children, hearts are bound in marriage, but bodies are not enslaved. You owe each other fidelity, not compliance. Each of you ought to belong only to the other. But neither of you ought to be the other's more than he pleases.

"If it is true, then, dear Emile, that you want to be your wife's lover, let her always be your mistress and her own. Be a fulfilled but respectful lover. Obtain everything from love without demanding anything from duty, and always regard Sophie's least favors not as your right but as acts of grace. I know that modesty flees formal confessions and asks to be conquered. But does the lover who has delicacy and true love make mistakes about his beloved's secret will? Is he unaware when her heart and her eyes accord what her mouth feigns to refuse? Let each of you always remain master of his own person and his caresses and have the right to dispense them to the other only at his own will. Always remember that even in marriage pleasure is legitimate only when desire is shared. Do not fear, my children, that this law will keep you at a distance. On the contrary, it will make both of you more attentive to pleasing each other, and it will prevent satiety. Since you are limited solely to each other, nature and love will bring you sufficiently close together."

Upon hearing these remarks and others of the kind, Emile becomes irritated and protests. Sophie is ashamed; she holds her fan over her eyes and says nothing. The most discontented of the two is perhaps not the one who complains the most. I insist pitilessly. I make Emile blush at his lack of delicacy. I stand as guarantor for Sophie's accepting the treaty on her side. I provoke her to speak. One can easily guess that she does not dare to give me the lie. Emile uneasily consults the eyes of his young wife. He sees that beneath their embarrassment they are full of a voluptuous agitation which reassures him about the risk he takes in trusting her. He throws himself at her feet, ecstatically kisses the hand she extends to him, and swears that, with the exception of the promised fidelity, he renounces every other right over her. "Dear wife," he says to her, "be the arbiter of my pleasures as you are of my life and my destiny. Were your cruelty to cost me my life, I would nonetheless give to you my dearest rights. I want to owe nothing to your compliance. I want to get everything from your heart."

Good Emile, reassure yourself: Sophie is too generous herself to let you die a victim of your generosity.

That evening, when I am ready to leave them, I say to them in the gravest tone possible for me, "Remember, both of you, that you are free, and that the question here is not one of marital duties. Believe me, let there be no false deference. Emile, do you want to come with me? Sophie gives you permission." Emile is in a fury and would like to hit me. "And you, Sophie, what do you say about it? Should I take him away?" The liar, blushing, says yes. How charming and sweet a lie, worth more than the truth!

The next day . . . The image of felicity no longer attracts men. The corruption of vice has depraved their taste as much as it has depraved their hearts. They no longer know how to sense what is touching nor how to see what is lovable. You who wish to paint voluptuousness and can only imagine satisfied lovers swimming in the bosom of delights, how imperfect your paintings still are! You have captured only the coarsest half of it. The sweetest attractions of voluptuousness are not there. O who among you has never seen a young couple, united under happy auspices, leaving the nuptial bed? Their languid and chaste glances express all at once the intoxication of the sweet pleasures they have just tasted, the lovable assurance of innocence, and the certitude—then so charming—of spending the rest of their days together. This is the most ravishing object which can be presented to man's heart. This is the true painting of voluptuousness! You have seen it a hundred times without recognizing it. Your hardened hearts are no longer capable of loving it. Sophie is happy and peaceful, and she passes the day in the arms of her tender mother. This is a very sweet rest to take after having passed the night in the arms of a husband.

On the day after that, I already perceive some change of scene. Emile wants to appear a bit discontented. But beneath this affectation I note such tender eagerness and even such submissiveness that I augur nothing very distressing. As for Sophie, she is gayer than the day before. I see satisfaction gleaming in her eyes. She is charming with Emile. She is almost flirtatious with him, which only vexes him more.

These changes are hardly noticeable, but they do not escape me. I am uneasy about them. I question Emile in private. I learn that, to his great regret and in spite of all his appeals, he had had to sleep in a separate bed the previous night. The imperious girl had hastened to make use of her right. Explanations are given. Emile complains bitterly, and Sophie responds with jests. But finally, seeing him about to get really angry, she gives him a glance full of sweetness and love; and, squeezing my hand, she utters only these two words, but in a tone which goes straight to the soul: "The ingrate!" Emile is so dumb that he understands none of this. I understand it. I send Emile away, and now I speak to Sophie in private.

"I see the reason for this caprice," I say to her. "One could not have greater delicacy nor make a more inappropriate use of it. Dear Sophie, reassure yourself. I have given you a man. Do not fear to take him for a man. You have had the first fruits of his youth. He has not squandered it on anyone. He will preserve it for you for a long time.

"My dear child, I must explain to you what my intentions were in the conversation all three of us had the day before yesterday. You perhaps perceived in my advice only an art of managing your pleasures in order to make them durable. O Sophie, it had another object more worthy of my efforts. In becoming your husband, Emile has become the head of the house. It is for you to obey, just as nature wanted it. However, when the woman resembles Sophie, it is good that the man be guided by her. This is yet another law of nature. And it is in order to give you as much authority over his heart as his sex gives him over your person that I have made you the arbiter of his pleasures. It will cost you some painful privations, but you will reign over him if you know how to reign over yourself; what has happened already shows me that this difficult art is not beyond your courage. You will reign by means of love for a long time if you make your favors rare and precious, if you know how to make them valued. Do you want to see your husband constantly at your feet? Then keep him always at some distance from your person. But put modesty, and not capriciousness, in your severity. Let him view you as reserved, not whimsical. Take care that in managing his love you do not make him doubt your own. Make yourself cherished by your favors and respected by your refusals. Let him honor his wife's chastity without having to complain of her coldness.

"It is by this means, my child, that he will give you his confidence, listen to your opinions, consult you about his business, and decide nothing without deliberating with you about it. It is by this means that you can bring him back to wisdom when he goes astray; lead him by a gentle persuasion; make yourself lovable in order to make yourself useful; and use coquetry in the interests of virtue and love to the benefit of reason.

"Nevertheless, do not believe that even this art can serve you forever. Whatever precautions anyone may take, enjoyment wears out pleasures, and love is worn out before all others. But when love has lasted a long time, a sweet habit fills the void it leaves behind, and the attraction of mutual confidence succeeds the transports of passion. Children form a relationship between those who have given them life that is no less sweet and is often stronger than love itself. When you stop being Emile's beloved, you will be his wife and his friend. You will be the mother of his children. Then, in place of your former reserve, establish between yourselves the greatest intimacy. No more separate beds, no more refusals, no more caprices. Become his other half to such an extent that he can no longer do without you, and that as soon as he leaves you, he feels he is far from himself. You were so good at making the charms of domestic life reign in your paternal household; now make them reign in your own. Every man who is pleased in his home loves his wife. Remember that if your husband lives happily at home, you will be a happy woman.

"As for the present, do not be so severe with your lover. He has merited more obligingness. He would be offended by your fears. No longer be so careful about his health at the expense of his happiness, and enjoy your own happiness. You must not expect disgust, nor rebuff desire. You must refuse not for refusing's sake but to give value to what is granted."

Then I reunite them, and I say to her young husband in her presence: "It is necessary to bear the yoke which you have imposed on yourself. Try to merit having it made light for you. Above all, sacrifice to the graces, and do not imagine that you make yourself more lovable by pouting." It is not difficult to make peace between them, and everyone can easily figure out the terms. The treaty is signed with a kiss. Then I say to my pupil, "Dear Emile, a man needs advice and guidance throughout his life. Up to now I have done my best to fulfill this duty toward you. Here my long task ends, and another's begins. Today I abdicate the authority you confided to me, and Sophie is your governor from now on."

Little by little the first delirium subsides and allows them to taste the charms of their new condition in peace. Happy lovers! Worthy couple! To honor their virtues and to paint their felicity, one would have to tell the history of their lives. How many times, as I contemplate my work in them, I feel myself seized by a rapture that makes my heart palpitate! How many times I join their hands in mine while blessing providence and sighing ardently! How many kisses I give to these two hands which clasp each other! How many times have these hands felt the tears I shed on them! The young couple share my raptures, and they too are moved. Their respectable parents once again enjoy their youth in that of their children. They begin, so to speak, to live again in them—or rather they come to know the value of life for the first time. They curse their former wealth which prevented them from tasting so charming a fate at the same age. If there is happiness on earth, it must be sought in the abode where we live.

Kierkegaard, Lasting Love

In "Some Reflections on Marriage in Answer to Objections" (from Stages on Life's *Way; see earlier selection in the section "Why Marry?"), Kierkegaard (under the pseudonym "A Married Man") explores the nature and blessings of married life, seeking to vindicate it against its detractors. A major question concerns the apparent tension between the immediacy of falling in love and the spiritual demands of faith. Marriage, he claims, is threatened from both sides: in the absence of religious faith, the dangers of eros's penchant for seduction (instead of marriage) and of its wandering eye and unstable attachments (after marriage); in the presence of overspiritualization, a forgetfulness of the concreteness both of the beloved and of falling and being in love. The solution (offered in a difficult but rich argument not presented here) lies in the idea and fact of resolution, the decision to marry, which for Kierkegaard must itself come as an immediacy, coincident with falling in love, rather than as an afterthought. Only if falling in love is joined with resolving to marry can erotic love be lifted up into permanence and reach its highest expression. Other writers (De Rougemont, for example) distinguish between erotic love and the love that informs marriage. Is Kierkegaard right in unifying them?*

The present selection is an encomium to marriage and to the woman as wife and mother. At one point he calls marriage an "epic" and an "idyll" and at another, "divine . . . civic . . . poetic." What do these claims mean, concretely? What does Kierkegaard mean by calling marriage "the fullness of time"? Finally, what do we make of his claims for the superior beauty of "the woman of years" and of his account of mother love? Has Kierkegaard made a case sufficient to silence the critics of marriage?

There is an old saying that perhaps has fallen somewhat into discredit, but never mind; the saying goes like this: What does one not do for the sake of wife and children? *Antwort* [Answer]: One does everything, everything. . . . — From a purely external point of view, there certainly are hundreds and hundreds more who have risked more than a married man, risked kingdoms and countries, millions and millions of millions have lost thrones and principalities, fortunes and prosperity, and yet the married man risks more. For the person who loves risks more than all these things, and the person who loves in as many ways as it is possible for a man to love risks most of all. Suppose that the married man is a king, a millionaire—there is no need for that, there is no need for that; all those other things merely confuse the clarity of the arithmetical problem—suppose that he is a beggar, he risks the most. Suppose that the brave one dares to do the hero-dance on the battlefield, or dance upon the heaving sea, or leap across the abyss—there is no need for that, there is no need for that, for everyday use there is no need for that. In a theater it might be needed, but mankind would be in a bad way if life and our Lord did not have a few reserve battalions of heroes who are not applauded even though they risk more. A married man risks every day, and every day the sword of duty hangs over his head, and the journal is kept up as long as the marriage keeps on, and the ledger of responsibility is never closed, and the responsibility is even more inspiring than the most glorious epic poet who must testify for the hero. Well, it is true that he does not take the risk for nothing—no, like for like; he risks everything for everything, and if because of its responsibility marriage is an epic, then because of its happiness it certainly is also an idyll.

Thus marriage is the beautiful focal point of life and existence, a center that reflects just as deeply as that which it manifests is high: a disclosure that in its concealment manifests the heavenly. And every marriage does this, just as not only the ocean but the quiet lake does, provided the water is not turbid. To be a married man is the most beautiful and meaningful task; the person who did not become married is an unfortunate whose life either did not permit him that or who never fell in love, or he is a suspicious character whom we eventually ought to take into custody. Marriage is the fullness of time. He who did not become a married man is always regarded as unhappy by others or he is that also to himself; in his eccentricity he wants to feel time as a burden. This is what marriage is like. It is divine, for falling in love is the wonder; it is earthly, for falling in love is nature's most profound myth. Love is the unfathomable ground that is hidden in darkness, but the resolution is the triumphant victor who, like Orpheus, fetches the infatuation of falling in love to the light of day, for the resolution is the true form of love, the true explanation and transfiguration; therefore marriage is sacred and blessed by God. It is civic, for by marriage the lovers belong to the state and the fatherland and the common concerns of their fellow citizens. It is poetic, inexpressibly so, just as is falling in love, but the resolution is the conscientious translator that translates the enthusiasm into actuality, and this translator is so scrupulous, oh, so scrupulous! The voice of falling in love "sounds like the fairies' from the grottoes on a summer night," but the resolution has the earnestness of perseverance that sounds through the fleeting and the transitory. The movement of falling in love is light, like dancing in the meadow, but the resolution catches hold of the weary one until the dance begins again. This is what marriage is like. It is happy like a child, and yet solemn, for it continually has the wonder before its eyes. It is modest and concealed, yet festivity lives within, but just as the storekeeper's door to the street is locked during a divine service, so is marriage's door always shut, because a divine service is going on continually. It is concerned, but this concern is not unbeautiful, since it rests in understanding of and feeling for the deep pain of all life. Whoever does not know this pain is unbeautiful: it is solemn and yet mitigated in jest, for not to will to do everything is a poor jest, but to do one's utmost and then to understand that it is little, so little, nothing at all compared with love's desire and with resolution's demand—that is a blessed jest. It is humble and yet courageous; indeed, courage such as this is found only in marriage, because it is formed from the strength of the man and the frailty of the woman and is rejuvenated by the child's freedom from care. It is faithful; truly, if marriage were not faithful, where then would there be faithfulness! It is secure, at peace, enfranchised in life; no danger is a real danger, but only a spiritual conflict. It is content with little, it also knows how to use much; but it knows how to be beautiful in scarcity and knows how to be no less beautiful in abundance! It is satisfied and yet full of expectancy; the lovers are sufficient unto themselves and yet exist only for the sake of others. It is plain and everyday—indeed, what is as plain and everyday as marriage; it is totally temporal, and yet the recollection of eternity listens and forgets nothing. . . .

As a critic of marriage, I am a *tiro* [novice]; I have no shallow introductory studies from a man-about-town period, which at times is more poisonous than one thinks. My love story is in a certain sense short. I have minded my own business and tended to my studies; I have not inspected the girls at parties and on the promenades, at theaters and concerts. I have not entered into it recklessly, nor have I done it with the idiotic seriousness in which a marriageable male is pleased to think that a girl must be extraordinary to be good enough for him. Thus without any experience I became acquainted with her who now is mine. I have never been in love before, and my prayer is that I may not fall in love later on, but if for a moment I were to think what for me is indeed unthinkable—that death took her from me, that my life underwent a change such that I would be dedicated to being a husband a second time, I am convinced that my marriage has not spoiled me or made me more competent to criticize, select, and inspect. No wonder one hears so much silly talk about love, since to hear so much talk is already an indication that reflection is universally forcing its way in to disturb the quiet, more modest life where love prefers to reside because in its modesty it is so close to piety.

Thus I am well aware that Messrs. Esthetes will promptly declare me incompetent for discussion, and all the more so when I do not conceal that despite being married for eight years I still do not definitely know in a critical sense what my wife looks like. To love is not to criticize, and marital faithfulness does not consist of detailed criticism. Yet this ignorance of mine is not entirely due to my being uncultured; I, too, am able to observe the beautiful, but

I observe a portrait, a statue, in that way, not a wife. I thank her in part for that, for if she had found any vain delight whatsoever in being the object of a philanderer's critical adoration, who knows whether I, too, might not have become a philanderer and as usual ended up becoming a grumpy critic and husband. Neither do I see myself able to move easily and routinely in some of the *termini* [technical terms] the connoisseurs sling about; I do not ask for that and do not go to banquets with connoisseurs. To put it as mildly as possible, to me such connoisseurs seem like those who sit and change money in the forecourt of the sanctuary; and just as it must be nauseating for someone entering the temple in an exalted frame of mind to hear the jingling of coins, so is it nauseating to me to hear the noise of words such as "slim," "shapely," "svelte," etc. When I read these words in a primitive poet, flowing out of originality of mood and of the mother tongue, I am delighted, but I do not profane them, and, as far as my wife is concerned, I am not sure to this day whether she is slim. My joy and my being in love are not that of a horse dealer or the irascible unwholesomeness of a cunning seducer. If I were to express myself about her in that way, I am sure I would talk nonsense. Having refrained from it up to now, I am very likely saved from it for the rest of my life, for just the mere presence of an infant makes being in love even more bashful than it is intrinsically. I have often pondered this, and for that reason I have always found it unbecoming for an older man with children to marry a very young girl.

Precisely because my love is everything to me, all critical output is in my opinion sheer nonsense. If I were to praise the female sex in the esthetic way people speak about praising, I would do it only humorously, for all this slimness and svelteness and the eyebrows and flashing eyes do not constitute falling in love, still less a marriage, and only in marriage does being in love have its true expression; outside marriage it is seduction or flirtation. . . .

. . . It is precisely marriage's sense of security that sustains the humorous; based upon experience, it does not have the restlessness of erotic love's first bliss, even if marriage's bliss is far from being minor. And when I as a married man, a married man of eight years, rest my head on her shoulder, I am not a critic, who admires or sees the lack of some earthly beauty; nor am I an infatuated youth who celebrates her bosom, but nevertheless I am as deeply moved as the first time. For I know what I knew and what I am repeatedly convinced of—that there within my wife's breast beats a heart, quietly and humbly, but steadily and smoothly; I know that it beats for me and my welfare and for what is mutually ours; I know that its calm, tender movement is uninterrupted—ah, while I am busy about my affairs, while I am distracted by so many different things, I know that at whatever time, in whatever situation I turn to her, it has not stopped beating for me. And I am a believer: just as the lover believes that the beloved is his life, so I spiritually believe that this tenderness—like mother's milk, which, as also stated in that little book, natural scientists maintain is lifesaving for someone who is sick unto death—I believe that this tenderness that unfailingly struggles for an ever more intimate expression, I believe that this tenderness that was her rich bridal dowry, I believe that it returns rich dividends; I believe that it will double itself if I do not squander her resources. I believe that if I were ill, sick unto death, and this tender gaze rested upon me—ah, as if she herself and not I were the dying gladiator—I believe that it would summon me back to life if God in heaven did not himself use his power, and if God does use his power, then I believe that this tenderness once again binds me to life as a vision that visits her, as one deceased whom death cannot really persuade, until we are again united. But until then, until God uses his power in this way, I believe that through her I absorb peace and contentment into my life and many times am rescued from the death of despondency and evil torment of vexation of spirit.

This is the way every husband talks—better, provided he is a better husband, better, provided he is talented. He is not an amorous youth, his expressions do not have the passion of the moment, and what an insult to want to give thanks for a love like that in the emotional blaze of the moment. He is like that honest bookkeeper who once almost became the object of suspicion, because, when the stern auditors, in a case of fraud, came to his door and demanded to see his account books, he replied: I have none; I keep all my accounts in my head. How suspicious! But all honor to the old man's head, his accounts were absolutely correct! A husband may even be talking a bit humorously when he speaks of this to his wife, but this humor, this carefree giving of thanks, this receipt—not on paper but in the ledger of recollection—demonstrates precisely that his accounting is trustworthy and that his marriage has an abundant supply of the daily bread of demonstration.

With this I have already suggested in what direction I seek woman's beauty. Alas, even upright people have contributed to the deplorable mistaken notion at which, all the worse, a rash young woman snatches all too eagerly, without considering that it is despair—the mistaken notion that a girl's only beauty is the first beauty of youth, that she blossoms for only a moment, that this is the time of falling in love, and that one loves only once.

Quite true, one does love only once, but with the years woman increases particularly in beauty and is so far from diminishing that the first beauty is somewhat questionable when compared with the later. Indeed, who, unless he is desperately in love, has not looked at a young girl without sensing a certain sadness because the fragility of mortal life shows itself here in its most extreme contrasts: vanity as swift as a dream, beauty as fair as a dream. But however fair that first beauty is, it is still not the truth; it is an envelope, a garment, from which only with the years does the true beauty extricate itself before the husband's grateful eyes.

On the other hand, look at the woman of years. You do not instinctively snatch at her beauty, for it is not the fleeting kind that hurries away like a dream. No, sit down beside her and observe her more closely. With her motherly solicitude, whose busy time, however, is now over, she belongs entirely to the world, and only the solicitude itself remains, and inside it she hovers like an angel over the ark of the covenant. Truly, if you do not here feel what reality a woman has, then you are and remain a critic, a reviewer, a connoisseur perhaps—that is, a person in despair who rushes along in the fury of despair, shouting: Let us love today, for tomorrow it is all over—not with us, that would be sad, but with erotic love—and that is abominable. Take some time now; sit down beside her. This is not the delightful fruit of desire; beware of any presumptuous thoughts or of wanting to use the connoisseurs' *termini;* if you foam within, then sit here so that you may calm down. This is not the froth of the moment; do you dare to surrender something like that in her presence, or would you dare to offer her your hand in a waltz! Then perhaps you prefer to avoid her company. Oh, even if the young generation milling around her are discourteous (so presumably thinks the fashionable gentleman who feels that she needs his conversation), no, are delinquent enough to let her sit all alone, she does not miss the pleasure of their company, she feels no sting of insult. She is reconciled with life, and if you once again feel the urge for a reconciling word, if you should feel the urge to forget the dissonances of life, then go to her, sit worthily with this worthy one—and which one, then, is more beautiful, the young mother who nourishes with the power of nature or the mother full of years who nourishes you again with her solicitude! Or if you are not so badly taken up with the troubles of the world, just sit worthily with this worthy one. Her life, too, is not devoid of melody; this age also is *non sine cithara* [not without its lyre], and nothing of what has been experienced is forgotten—when this voice touches the strings of memory, all the sounds from life's various ages sweetly harmonize. You see, she has arrived at life's solution; indeed she herself is the solution to life, audible and visible. A man never finishes his life in this way, ordinarily his accounts are more complicated; but a housewife has only elementary events, the everyday distresses and the everyday joys, but therefore also this happiness, for if a young girl is happy, then the woman of years is even happier. Tell me, then, what is more beautiful—the young girl with her happiness or the woman full of years who accomplishes a work of God, who provides the solution to the worried person and for the cheerful person is the best eulogy on existence by being life's beautiful solution!

Now I leave the woman of years, whose company I am not, however, really avoiding; I go back in time, happy that with the help of God I still have a beautiful part of my life left, but also without knowing any of that cowardliness that fears growing old, or fears it on his wife's behalf, for I do indeed assume that woman becomes more beautiful with the years. To my eyes, as a mother she is already far more beautiful than a young girl. A young girl, after all, is a phantasm; one scarcely knows whether she belongs to actuality or is a vision. And is that supposed to be the highest? Well, let the fantasts believe it. As a mother, however, she belongs totally to actuality, and mother love itself is not like the longings and presentiments of youth but is an inexhaustible source of inwardness. Neither is it so that all this was present as a possibility in the young girl. Even if it were so, a possibility is still less than an actuality, but it is not so. Inwardness is no more present in a young girl's breast than mother's milk. This is a metamorphosis that has no analogy in the man. If one can jokingly say that the man is not completely finished until he has his wisdom teeth, then one in all seriousness can say that a woman's development is not complete until she is a mother; only then does she exist in all her beauty—and in her beautiful actuality. So let that nimble, light, flirtatious, happy girl skip over the meadow, duping anyone who wants to catch her—ah, yes, I also delight in looking at it, but now, now she has been caught, imprisoned. I certainly did not catch her (to that end how futile and vainly foolish). I certainly do not imprison her (how weak a prison!). No, no, she has trapped herself and sits imprisoned beside the cradle; imprisoned, and yet she has complete freedom, a boundless freedom in which she binds herself to the child; I am sure that she is willing to die in her nest. . . .

To what a multiplicity of collisions mother love is exposed, and how beautiful the mother is every time her self-renouncing, self-sacrificing love comes out victorious! I am not speaking here of what certainly is well known and is a given, that the mother sacrifices her life for the child. That sounds so exalted, so sentimental, and does not have the proper marital stamp. It is just as discernible, just as great, and just as endearing in small things. . . .

Mother love is just as beautiful in the routine of everyday life as it is on the most crucial occasion, and it is actually essentially beautiful in the routine of everyday life, for there it is in its element, because there, without receiving any impulse or any increment of force through external catastrophes, it is motivated solely within itself, is nourished by itself, quickens itself through its own original drive, is unpretentious and yet always up and doing its beloved work. Poor man, who must go out in the world to seek a daisy such as that and yet does not find it; poor man, who at most has a notion that his neighbor grows it; happy the married man who really knows how to rejoice in his thousandfold joy. If he finds this flower somewhere else than in his own yard, this flower that—just as that century plant is remarkable for blossoming only once every hundred years—has the even more seldom rarity that it blossoms every day, and does not even close at night—then he has the joy of telling at home what he has seen out in the world. . . .

As a bride, woman is more beautiful than as a maiden; as a mother she is more beautiful than as a bride; as a wife and mother she is a good word in season, and with the years she becomes more beautiful. The young girl's beauty is obvious to many; it is more abstract, more extensive. This is why they flock about her, the fantasts, the pure and the impure. Then the god brings the one who is her lover. He really sees her beauty, for one loves the beautiful, and this must be understood as being synonymous with: to love is to see the beautiful. Thus reflection inevitably misses the beautiful. From now on her beauty becomes more intensive and concrete. The housewife does not have a flock of adorers; she is not even beautiful, she is beautiful only in the eyes of her husband. To the same degree this beauty becomes more and more concrete, she becomes less and less subject to evaluation by ordinary appraising and selecting. Is she therefore less beautiful? Is an author less rich in ideas because ordinary observation finds nothing, while the reader who has made him his sole study nevertheless discovers an ever-greater wealth? Is it a perfection in human works of art that they look best at a distance? Is it an imperfection in the meadow flower, as in all the works of God, that under microscopic scrutiny it becomes lovelier and lovelier, more and more exquisite, more and more delicate? . . .

Capon, *Bed and Board:* Liturgies of Home

Not everyone celebrates the blessings of marriage in exciting or lofty terms. On the contrary, some locate them rather in the homely routines of everyday life. In his book, Bed and Board: Plain Talk About Marriage *(1965), Robert Farrar Capon (born in 1925), an Episcopal priest, presents a most prosaic (yet religious) account of married life. At the same time, Capon makes clear how marital love and marital life, rightly regarded, are vehicles for sanctification, as the loving couple "communicates the glory to each other" and establishes around the family table a liturgy that brings unity and meaning into lives otherwise lonely and empty. Especially in our time, when the family meal is in many homes honored more in the breach than in the observance, Capon's account shows not only why indifference to board may breed indifference to marriage, but also reminds us of the blessings we thereby forego. These excerpts are taken from the chapters on "Bed" and "Board," the two centerpieces of married life. (Capon's account of the bed is usefully compared with the selection from the* Odyssey.) *Young people, in our experience, do not find this account of married life attractive. Should they? Why does Capon regard our marital condition as "absurd"? How can it be both absurd and glorious? To what extent does Capon's account tell the truth?*

Bed

A geography of matrimony; with two maps and a careful but inconclusive discussion of one of the principal quagmires.

But the functions are not the whole story. *Things* enter into marriage as well as persons. The Holy Estate of Matrimony is a highly material proposition. It takes *place*, at *times*, and is thoroughly tied down to the particularities of a bodily world. It's all very well to talk about the roles of the dancers and the need to know them better, but the dancers' movements are defined as much by the shape of the stage as by their parts. Life is not a series of abstract designs, of elegant plans and outlines, but a headlong stumbling through real valleys full of historic potholes. Therefore it's not enough simply to know the goal of the journey, nor even the nature of the travelers: Knowledge of the terrain is essential. Hardware and geography enter into the essence of marriage.

In premarital instructions, as part of the effort to focus attention on what really matters, I usually say that you need only two things, two pieces of matter, to make a home: a bed and a table. It's an oversimplification, but it's a good one—it comes close to being a diagram. For Bed and Board are the fundamental geographical divisions of the family; they are the chief places, and it is in them, at them and around them that we dance the parts we are given. More, they are boundaries that mark the areas of our freedom in marriage. It is precisely the confines of the stage that render the dancers' freedom effective: The ballet is saved from enslavement to limitless idea by the lights in front and the drops in back. The graceful flight up the curving staircase, the pursuit, the capture, the embrace, are delivered from being mere concepts, delivered into the real world—delivered as a child is delivered—by the very solidity of the stairs, by the precise height of the risers and the depth of the treads. Geography snatches them from the edge of the boundless void and defines them into freedom. And so marriage is delivered by the bed. The untamability of romance, the endlessness of the vision of the beloved, threaten constantly to send us off in successive limitless expeditions after something that grows successively harder to define. The movie star on her fifth marriage seems always to be less clear about what she wants and less free to make her wanting serve her well. For under it all lies the endlessly expansive pride of a being who cannot add a cubit to her stature or a minute to her life. That is our dilemma: desire is endless; we are not. Listen.

And the Lord God said, Behold, the man is become as one of us, to know good and evil; the unexpansible is expanding. *And now, lest he put forth his hand, and take also of the tree of life, and eat, and live forever;* lest he use grace and freedom only to confirm his breach with nature; *therefore the Lord God sent him forth from the garden of Eden . . . and he placed . . . Cherubims, and a flaming sword which turned every way, to keep the way of the tree of life.* And so Adam goes out to his land of thorns and thistles, and Eve to her bed of conception and birth, precisely to be saved by geography, to be restored by the tilling of the ground, to become more than dust by returning to dust, to be defined by being confined.

All this the marriage rite knows. Marriage was instituted in the time of man's innocency, but it has operated ever since under the shadow of the fall. Therefore its materialities, along with all our other materialities, become the means of our cure. He who perished by a tree is saved by a tree. He who died by an apple is restored by eating the flesh of his Saviour. Our lust is to be healed by being brought down to one bed, our savagery tamed by the exchanges around a lifelong table. Bed, Board, rooftree and doorway become the choice places of our healing, the delimitations of our freedom. By setting us boundaries, they hold us in; but they trammel the void as well. By confining, they keep track of us—they leave us free to be found, and to find ourselves. The vow of lifelong fidelity to one bed, one woman, becomes the wall at the edge of the cliff that leaves the children free to play a little, rather than be lost at large. Marriage gives us somewhere to *be. . . .*

I shall get to the Board and its adjuncts by and by. Table and rooftree, nursery and kitchen, even patio and rumpus room, will all have their turn. But the first must come first, and that is the Bed: the couple's initial piece of real estate. The things that come later in a marriage are, one way or another, extensions of this—added parcels, adjacent lots, buffer strips and subdivisions. The bed itself is their first soil, the uncrossed plain waiting for boundary and marker, for plough and seed. If this is well laid and planted, the rest will have order and comeliness; if not, they will be senseless bits of gerrymandering, spreading far and wide for reasons that have nothing to do with the good of the people of the land. The bed is the heart of home, the arena of love, the seedbed of life, and the one constant point of meeting. It is the place where, night by night, forgiveness and fair speech return that the sun go not down upon our wrath; where the perfunctory kiss and the entirely ceremonial pat on the backside become unction and grace. It is the oldest, friendliest thing in anybody's marriage, the first used and the last left, and no one can praise it enough.

But there is mystery in it too. It is a strange piece of terrain, and finding ourselves in it is as unlikely as it is marvelous. We marry on attack or rebound. We come at each other for an assortment of pretty thin and transitory reasons. We ask, and are taken in matrimony; and in the haste of charge or retreat, we find ourselves thrown down into a very small piece of ground indeed. The marriage bed is a trench; adversity has made us bedfellows. I turn over at night. I try to see where I am and who is with me. It is not what I imagined at all. Where are the two triumphant giants of love I expected, where the conqueror smiling at conqueror? There are only the two of us, crouched down here under a barrage of years, bills and petty grievances, waiting for a signal which shows no sign of coming. Most likely we shall die in this trench. There is really no place else to go, so in the meantime we talk to each other. The sum and substance of what we manage to say, however, is "Well, here we are."

We have come to a calamitous involvement. What are we doing here, in position ridiculous, at pleasure transitory, with results disastrous? What will we not cause? What consequences to self and others? Indeed, what others will we not cause? Children! Independent beings to go forth to their own births, involvements and deaths; to love, to skin their knees, to have their hearts broken, and to lie in other trenches, distant but not different from this. I am Abraham. I pick up the knife and fire when I beget. This bed, this trench, is cut *across* my line of march. I can crawl along it, but not past it. It is a lateral passage, a byroad to Mount Moriah, a side trip into terror. All the rosy marriage books about the joys of procreation, all the neat, even true, theological niceties about its being my share in the creative process, leave me literally cold—with fear and trembling. The only comfort is my first comfort—that it is absurd and therefore sane. In terms of its actual results—in the real and logical framework in which all such treatments try to put it—it remains insoluble, a surd, the square root of −1. It is only when taken as insoluble, and when put into another framework, that it begins to give answers. I am not being obscure; let me say at once, in plain English, what that framework is. It is the Cross of Christ, where God Incarnate works to reconcile the broken and dishonored fragments of the City by being himself broken and dishonored. If I were not invited into that mystery, I do not think I could afford to be honest about what a calamity we are all in. Only Christian marriage has a real chance to save nature. Not that mine is very natural—it can't be, because it isn't very Christian; but the truth remains. The disciple is not above his master; the Cross is foolishness, and the marriage bed is absurd. That much rings true. So far, so good. . . .

The bed, then, is both light and dark, fertile upland and beleaguered trench. Now anything that big is going to be hard to grasp in one piece, and it is precisely the inadequacy of their grasp that makes most of the comments on it unreal. But there are a couple of them that are worth the time of any-body's day, and as you might suspect, they are in the old places. The first is the traditional list of the three ends of marriage found now in the rite of the Church of England and also in the Latin originals. Marriage, the priest tells the company present, was instituted for the procreation of children, for a rem-edy against sin, and for mutual society, help and comfort. The second is the priceless sentence with which, in the same rite, the groom gives the ring to his bride: With this ring I thee wed, with my body I thee worship, with all my worldly goods I thee endow, in the name of the Father and of the Son and of the Holy Ghost. (Once again the bowdlerizers have put their sticky fingers into the pie. Every smitch of this, with the exception of "With this ring I thee wed" and the invocation of the name of God has been chopped out of the Ameri-can Prayer Book. I don't know how they missed what they left. Oh, such dread-ful, well-meaning revisers—committees composed of equal numbers of liberal higher critics and Victorian spinsters. Between the two of them they managed to remove a good many of the heights and most of the depths of the rite. The critics took care of Significance: Adam and Eve, Isaac and Rebekah, Abraham and Sarah all went down under the same hatchet; the spinsters finished off Spice: The body's worship was just too much for their nasty-nice sensibilities. Someday we will put it all back, to serve them, and us, right. The Church is a peasant with her feet on solid earth where they belong. She will never look right up on a lecture platform trying to hide her old hat just because it isn't stylish.)

Taken together anyway, these two old formularies lay hold of the full width of even the widest bed. What a marvelous set of measurements they are. They begin with an accurate statement of the most calamitous of all the bed's results—children. Procreation comes first on the list. Next, they take seriously the idea of marriage as a remedy against sin, and isn't that a strange one now? We don't talk much any more about lust as a disease. We don't see ourselves as imperiled by fornication; instead we name it Sex and praise it to the skies; but a disease it is nonetheless, and marrying remains its cure. Sex teaches me to desire all women above a very low passing grade. Marriage gives me only one. If it's Sex I'm after, the conjugal bed is not much of an improvement over celibacy. The result of it all is that we enjoy our beds for a while, and after that, we grumble. The one thing we don't do is take the treatment full force. Don't think we do. We would be a lot healthier than we are if we did. Our bodies may be in it, but our minds and eyes are too often elsewhere to let us be cured. And then there is the last of the three purposes: mutual society, help and comfort. It is the most palatable of the old ideas: Everybody agrees with it, takes it for granted, and promptly loses sight of it, sometimes for years on end. We were meant to meet, to sustain and to ease each other, and in the marriage bed we lie down to do just that. It is an island in a sea of troubles, where there is nothing else to do but rest and refresh. Yet how resourceful we are, with our turned backs and stubborn silences, or with our interminable pouts and dreadful debates about What's Wrong With Us.

And then take the main item in the ring bestowal: With my body I thee worship. A man can give his wife so little besides trouble. He makes a life of hard labor for her, preempts most of her available time by begetting children upon her, and then leaves her alone with the whole business for the greater part of every working day. It is precisely the worship of his body for her that she so badly needs and so seldom gets. And from an occasionally aroused husband she will never have it, though she wait a hundred years. That can come only from a worshipful spouse who works at his devotions with discipline and perseverance. People admit it's hard to pray. Yet they think it's easy to make love. What nonsense. Neither is worth much when it is only the outcropping of intermittent enthusiasm. Both need to be done without ceasing; and that puts a premium on the minor manifestations. Obviously the sexual act itself is central. But the circle that is drawn around it consists of a thousand small passes and light touches. What they lack in moment they more than make up for by sheer weight of numbers, and it is a poor bed that sees only the grand piece of business that really arrives. It is precisely the unconsummated nonsense that makes the main absurdity fruitful. Sexual intercourse is indeed *society* (though often not too mutual), and it is certainly a *comfort*, when it goes well; but it is seldom much *help* unless its disastrousness is softened by a vast amount of incidental tenderness.

That will do, I think, for the list. Perhaps our biggest trouble is thinking we know it all. Even when we don't disagree with the ends of marriage and the old form of the vow, we have a way of expecting the whole thing to be obvious, and to be quite capable of taking care of itself. The truth is, though, that it isn't, and doesn't; and it needs, in consequence, a lot more thought than it gets. I have a little to say about some of it in a while, but before that there are a couple of things that can make a big difference. We think in terms of images. That was true a while back on the subject of roles in marriage. It is true in bed, too. The conjugal act is performed in the presence of the remembered and unremembered pictures of sexuality that the partners have in their heads. The images are, so to speak, carved upon the posts of the marriage bed. They dominate the scene. And, as always, they may be good or they may be bad. Usually they are somewhat less than adequate, to say the least. Therefore, if there are any gilt-edged images around, we ought to be quite diligent about making as much of them as possible. I think there are such, and I am willing to name two of them. One is from the Bible, the other from literature; the Bridegroom and the Bride from the Song of Solomon, and the figure of Beatrice from Dante.

Beatrice first.

She takes us straight to the connection between the marriage bed and romantic love. Think of a crowd of people. If you are a man, imagine the women among them dressed alike and with simplicity—as peasants, for instance, or nuns. Then imagine yourself there watching, beholding. You know what will happen. For every man there will be, somewhere in that crowd, a woman who even under those conditions of concealment and plainness cannot be hid from him—who goes home hard to him. There may even be several. Without speaking, they speak easily; motionless perhaps themselves, they move him mightily. He is drawn; and drawn by a force the fair equal of any in this world. Now take the comparison out of the imagination and into history. The thing has happened, once or oftener, to every one of us. Even a picture will do it. I remember an illustration in a book I once read. It was only a line drawing of a rather thin girl standing on a hilltop with the wind in her black hair. The book has long since been forgotten, and I cannot even remember how old I was. Eight? Twelve? Not more than that. But I have been looking for that girl ever since. I suppose I have found her, too, not as such, but in hints and guesses in others.

Now why? I am not about to make much of the picture. As a matter of fact, I think I remember seeing it again years later, and being disappointed. The point is that the picture did not *cause* my wonder; rather, it spoke *to* it. I was already looking for wonder before I opened that book. What is it all about?

The cheap answer is that it's about biology—the itch. But that just won't do. First, because I have itched in lots of circumstances where I never came within a hundred miles of wonder. And second, because when I have really struck the note of wonder, I have never failed to notice that the itch was fundamentally separate from it. Sometimes it was just plain irrelevant; often, actually inimical. On the other hand, the easy, up-to-date answer is just as useless. That says that it's about conditioning—about the way my history has trained me to delight in certain key features, like dark hair or high cheekbones. But that's no answer to *why* it happens. Even if it's true, it only says *how* it works. It never even begins to answer the real question: Why is man the kind of being who responds to high cheekbones, or whatever?

To find that answer you have to get away from the biological boosters of explanations that just won't work, and the psychological knockers of things they don't understand. You have to go back to somebody who really loved and could really write: Dante. . . . Dante says that romantic love is about the Mystical Body—the City—the mystery of membership in each other. Which, of course, is what I have been getting at all along. The general idea is that this astonishing thing of being lifted out of one's self by the mere sight of the beloved, this ability of the beloved to seem so much more than flesh and blood, her aptness to communicate, to come across hard, is a hint that the whole business of love was designed to be a communication. Not, mind you, the girl's communication of something *in her,* but God's communication *through her* of the mystery of the Coinherence. She is an image, a diagram, of the glory of the City—of that collection of created pieces made to tend ceaselessly toward the oneness of the Body. Admittedly that's a big order for one small girl with little more than dark hair and high cheekbones, but it happens every day, nonetheless. Not that it's often recognized as such; but it is felt to be something pretty nearly as big as that with remarkable regularity.

Of course, we usually miss the point of it all. We like to think that Beatrice is saying something about herself, and we begin, after the first wonder, to aim at her rather than the glory behind her. After the chivalry wears off, people in love usually act as if the whole process meant that they were supposed to find their fulfillment in each other—as if they were, respectively, each other's final goal. "You're the only girl in the world for me." "We were meant for each other." That, of course, is nonsense if you believe Dante. They were not meant *for* each other; they were meant to communicate the glory *to* each other. They are not gods, but ministers. Beatrice is precisely a priestly figure. She is not my destiny, but the agent, the delightful sacrament, of it. If I treat her as an end, delight is about all I can bargain for, and not even that for long. If I take her as a sacrament, I receive, along with the delight, the joy that lies behind her.

But Dante never went to bed with Beatrice. In our book, we would have to say he hardly even knew her. What, then, has Beatrice got to do with Bed?

Just this. For better or worse, we have made romance the basis for marriage. Falling in love is supposed to be the reason why people end up in matrimony. (The Church, you will recall, doesn't commit herself on the subject. Romance or family arrangement, it's all the same to her, provided they know what they're doing and are willing to stick with it till they die.) Romance as the justification for marriage is pretty much a folk invention of less than eight hundred years' standing. On the whole, it's not a bad one at all. It's mostly better than worse. For if marriage itself is the mystery written small—if it is indeed the earthly image of the union of Christ and his Church—then it would be hard to find a better starting point than the glimpsing of that same mystery in the Beloved. Dante never married Beatrice, but we feel obliged to; all in all, it is rather a good idea. As a matter of fact, the only thing wrong with it is the lies about it.

One of them I've already mentioned. It's the "You are my destiny" bit. Only God can be that, and any attempt to put so large a demand on a mere creature always comes a cropper. Besides, in marriage it's hard to keep up the appearance of being somebody's destiny; it's even hard to look like a halfway decent agent of destiny. Beatrice burning the toast, or leaving the socks unmended, is practically unrecognizable.

The other lie is just as palpable but a little trickier. "You're the only girl in the world for me" is not very often the truth. Precisely because Beatrice is only an agent of the glory, it usually turns out that the glory can be glimpsed through other agents as well. Dante spends quite a bit of time looking at other girls. There was Giovanna and there was the Lady of the Window. And for Sam Smith, there is the girl in the office or the lady next door. If he marries with the idea that the thing that has clicked with Beatrice is the one and only click he will ever have, he is usually going to be in for a surprise. Marriage is monogamous; the romantic intimation of the glory is not. It will take a bit of learning the hard way, if he is not prepared for the distinction. And if he never learns it—if he goes on believing the lies—he will do exactly what so many do: spend his life going from one absolutely final, true and glorious love affair to the next, and believing every time that it is just as final, true and glorious. We will all most likely have a succession of Beatrices. That can be handled, and profitably. What is unmanageable is a succession of beds.

All the lies to one side, however, Beatrice does pretty well as a wife. Romantic love is about as close to the real point of marriage as anything can be: It is a mystery leading to a mystery, an absurdity inviting a further absurdity. We were meant for greatness, for glory, for the vast coinherence of the City. Our romantic notions fit that. If our marriages do not, it is not because marriage is contrary to romance, but because we have violated romance itself, have made the fatal mistake of stopping at Beatrice instead of the glory. My wife is not my destiny, and she cannot stand being treated as if she were. Romance in marriage is not the artificial prolongation of the initial wonders of courtship. I cannot be her swain ever again. But I can enter with her into the fellowship of the mystery, and that is romance indeed. Beatrice, then, lies in my bed, and grows old and worn along with me. She is the minister of more than herself; that is exactly why I need not fear for her inevitable growing less. We must decrease, but the Glory will increase. The bed is one more of the exchanges of the City.

The other image—or, better said, collection of images—is the Song of Solomon. God has, of course, taken pains with all the books of the Bible, but he was apparently extra solicitous for this one. Here the image of the coinherence, of the union of Christ and his Church, is deliberately and expressly stated in terms of marriage. The book is not only an inspired composition; the Holy Ghost has seen to it that it had the benefit of genius all the way along. First there was the author. I am utterly unable to subscribe to the view that he wrote "only a marriage poem," and that all the mystery is the work of later interpreters. Chiefly, because a great marriage poem cannot be only a marriage poem. Marriage is the sacrament of the mystery. A good description, even of "mere marriage," will perforce be itself mysterious. Besides, I think anyone capable of writing that well is quite up to deliberate and monumental *double entendre*. The second instance of genius was just as great. Somebody actually talked some kind of group into including it in the canon of Scripture. It is one of the few instances in history of a committee's getting something right. And the genius doesn't stop there. There were the geniuses who translated it into Latin and English. I would hate to have to choose between St. Jerome and the King James Bible. Both are quite beyond mere praise. And so are the geniuses among the Fathers who saw clearly the mystery in the book and wrote priceless commentaries and more poems—St. John of the Cross, for one. And last but not least, there was the modest genius who wrote the running page headings in the Authorized Version. Of course, the hatchet men have removed them from subsequent translations, but they remain in their old places, and most people still get to see them. (Just to give you an idea of the caliber of this kind of critic: In seminary, I bought a paperback series of commentaries on the Bible. They were designed for popular consumption, and written in the question-and-answer style. The section on the Song of Solomon began as follows: Q. *What book of the Bible is of even less religious value than Ecclesiastes? A. The Song of Solomon.* The rest was just as bad.)

The wonderful thing about the book, however, is that its appeal is not limited to geniuses. The peasants read it with delight. Dante is forbidding, and the commentaries on him are almost as bad as the theological obscurities I come up with. The Song of Songs is a joy. It comes across on all levels at once, and if you're not in the mood for mystery you can read it in bed and still find more than you can possibly handle. I say no more about it. Only read, mark, learn and inwardly digest it. Pray by it, or make love by it. You can't go wrong. . . .

One last item. . . . The exaltation of the sexual act, especially by the marriage manuals, has not been terribly helpful. As I said, they get very solemn about the raptures of it all (again, don't misunderstand—I am not against raptures, only solemnity), and they work up a real mystique of intercourse, in which one of the principal magic phrases is *simultaneous orgasm*. I think it's fair to say that that's a subject most people have heard about. I even think that a lot of people have gotten the idea that it's the One Best Way of All. I think it's very odd. Admittedly, as a piece of advice to a man—namely: Be sure you try to give your wife pleasure before you take it yourself—it is excellent. Good manners are essential. There is no place where it is more fitting to be a gentleman than in bed. But. As a piece of advice to *two* people—namely: Make sure you *come* together—I find it utterly irrelevant, and dangerous too. What does one orgasm add to another? As a matter of fact what does all this thinking about orgasms add to the stature of anybody's marriage? All I think it does is to make the idea of sexual intercourse indistinguishable from the concept of mutual masturbation. And that is hardly a welcome addition. The two are in fact as different as night and day. The one is self-giving, the other self-regarding; the one natural, the other perverse. Perhaps I am wrong about how common this is. Maybe I have read the wrong books. All I know is that this business of synchronized desire was a big irrelevancy to me. It kept me from seeing *love* for a good long while.

I am afraid, however, that bed is not really my subject. I can see what it's about, I can criticize what's wrong, and I can more or less keep myself afloat. But that's about it. If you want something solid to hang on to, keep looking; my raft isn't going to support much weight beside my own. I think the bed matters. I am sure that if I could ever hack my way through the jungle of Sex, back to the hills of naturalness, it would matter marvelously. But even then I don't think it would be life's greatest matter. The meeting in bed is not the end. Its greatness lies in the ends that it serves. And the greatest of them all is not the meeting of lover and beloved, of Dante and Beatrice, but the meeting of the whole Body of the Coinherence, the entrance of man into the City of God.

So the main theme returns. In bed as elsewhere, absurdity is the touchstone of our calling. The bed cannot be made foolproof, because only fools are available to occupy it, but it can be made sane. The calling is absurd, but if we will lie down with the foolishness of Christ, we can rise up with the wisdom of God. The Christian marriage Bed is strictly for sports, plungers, and heavy spenders. Double-entry bookkeepers, and sewing circle treasurers need not apply. The vow of fidelity is an absurd commitment, but it is the heart of marriage. If we will only sit still and eat our own bread till we die, we will get well. My own cure is slow in coming, but after fifteen years I think I see a few signs of strength. And that is not to be sneezed at. In this department, even to be a little better is a monumental achievement.

Board

The geography of marriage continued; the Table analyzed and exalted; fair speech, television, canned soup, and the Liturgy of St. John Chrysostom examined and properly oriented.

The bed may be the first of the great pieces of matter in marriage, but it is by no means the only one. It is not even the most obvious: We put doors on our bedrooms, and we retire from the rest of the house when we go to them. The dining room is something else again. Whether it is a room in its own right, or a kitchen used to make shift, it is invariably central in the house. In fact, with the current fashion of open and contiguous living areas, it has, more often than not, no door at all. It is not only visible, it is unmistakable, as the sanctuary of a church is unmistakable. And in its center is the family's other great piece of matter, the Table. Duncan Phyfe or early Grand Rapids, Danish modern or discount-house chromium, the Table defines both the room it occupies and the household that gathers around it. It is the other first investment, and as long as the household lasts, it remains the one thing that everybody uses most—the one and often the only place where the family meets in fact.

Think of it first as a *thing*. To begin with, it is matter, not thought; it is not with us as the living-room furniture is with us—because we think it's a good idea; but with us as the bed is with us—because we cannot function without it. The poorest house has a table, and is by that very thing not so poor after all. But because it is a thing, because it is true to itself, it comes to us as things always come: raw, intractable and unfinished. Planks on packing crates, or polished mahogany on delicate turnings, it is only itself. It will not turn from table into Board on its own motion any more than box spring and mattress will become marriage Bed without considerable care. It is there, and it is suitable, but the household that gathers around it must work to bring it into the dance. The table enters the exchanges of the family exactly as the stage enters into the ballet: as a thing, as itself, by being faithful to its own mute and stubborn materiality. It is the floor that makes possible the marvelous leap of grace; it is also the floor that punishes the less than marvelous one with disgrace. The table can make us or break us. It has its own laws and will not change. Food and litter will lie upon it; fair speech and venom will pour across it; it will be the scene of manners or meanness, the place of charity or the wall of division, depending. Depending on what is done with it, at it and about it. But whatever is done, however it enters, it will allow only the possible, not the ideal. No one has ever created the Board by fiat. God himself spread his table, but Judas sat down at it. There is no use thinking that all we have to do is wish for a certain style of family life, and wait for it to happen. The Board is a union of thing and persons; what it becomes depends on how the thing is dealt with by the persons.

There is one result, however, which will be produced automatically: The Board will always give birth to *liturgy.* I don't mean specifically religious liturgy here. I mean liturgy in the old sense that the word had before Christians picked it up. In that sense, liturgy is not simply a function of religion but an inevitable feature of the life of the city. The Greeks were, I think, the first to define it. In the small city-state of antiquity, each citizen was assigned a portion of the material work of the city as his personal responsibility: the repair of so many feet of wall, for example, or the construction of so many yards of drainage facility. The word they used for this assignment was *leitourgia.* They saw that community of life meant community in *things,* and that unless the citizens joined in the doing of the things, the city could not thrive. Each was to have his peculiar *liturgy;* but it was to be his as a member of the body politic, not on the basis of his private tastes. It was a brilliant notion. As cities became larger and more complex, of course, it became unwieldy. But it is precisely the absence of visible liturgy that nowadays makes the common life less obvious to common men. Twenty feet of stone wall erected at my own charges speaks clearly to me of my involvement in the city; a lever on a voting machine turned down over the name of a mayoralty candidate who will by and by appoint a commissioner of public works is a little vague. It really is the same thing, but it is not drawn as sharply—it is not so elegant a diagram. In societies that have remained small, however, in bodies which have kept their materialities simple, it still applies in its old form. The Church needs only priest, people, table, bread and wine; the union of those remains the taproot of all its liturgy. So also with the family. Parents and children, table and food are the fundamental pieces. Given these, there will develop, with absolute inevitability, a way of doing business native to that Board and its distinctive materialities. "At our house, we always have icebox cake on Daddy's birthday." That is genuine liturgy. The key to its true rationale is the phrase "We always do. . . . " The test of its germaneness is not its conformity to some abstract standard of perfection, but simply whether it constitutes an honest doing of the work of the city with the materials at hand. Liturgy is a local matter: The Church has had almost as many liturgies as she has had altars. The massive attempts at enforced conformity to what somebody considers an ideal norm—the great master service books and universal rites— have had only middling success. And since the family is so utterly local a proposition, its truest liturgies will be home-grown—and very often peculiar, in both senses of the word. They will be wordy or brief, elaborate or plain, high or low, according to the tastes and the talents of the families that make them. But their constant feature is that they will never fail to be made. The Table is simply the kind of thing that brings them forth.

And that brings up the second point about the materiality of the table. It is not only a thing, it is a *place*. The Board is geography even more obviously than the Bed is. It is the principal territory of the family as a whole. And it is the guarantee that the household is a real society and not a legal fiction; all true societies are defined geographically. They are unities of place, not of interest; they are *bodies*, not *clubs*. The parish, the village, the city, the nation are precisely territorial entities. Principles and ideals shape them, but they do not make them. America is democratic, Russia is communistic; but they are truer to their geographical roots than to their ideal ones most of the time. America finds the Panama Canal handy for reasons that lie closer to the earth than political principle; Russia, Czarist or Communist, always looks longingly on warm-water ports. The American standard of living is due at least as much to the land and its people as to democratic ideals; the Battle of Stalingrad was a Russian victory before it was a Communist one. So too with the family. I do not associate with my wife and children because of my principles. I do it because I have to—we inhabit the same small plot of land. The soil may be rich or thin, the land peaceful or shaken by earthquakes; we stay on because it is this or nothing. Love and fear entirely to one side, it is our land, and we are not about to move. Our roots go down around this board; all our sowing was in one bed, and all but myself have grown from the soil that is my wife. From Bed and Womb to Breast and Board, we are one by origin and by place; geography is our first unity.

The Board, then, stands as the published map of the family. The bed was our *place* of being for only minutes; the womb and the breast for no more than months; but the table is our territory literally for years. It is the great clue to the mystery of being. We have sprung from local and common roots, but we have grown into discreteness and separateness and now we sit around this table. We do not huddle together only to keep warm or to take advantage of one another; economics and pride explain only *how* we do it, not *why*. We are no club; we meet for no purpose of our own forming. We began as pieces of a piece, common matter fragmented, but we are here because we have been invited to dance our discreteness into the mutuality of God himself. From a body we came into bodies; it is the table that now draws us into the Body that shall be. From a mother, we were born into isolation; it is the table that begins now to lift us into Jerusalem the mother of us all.

In the eighteenth chapter of the Book of Genesis, it is reported that God the Father, God the Son and God the Holy Ghost sat down once and had lunch with Abraham in the plains of Mamre. The table has been the hallmark of the Trinity ever since. The world is about the mystery by which the created order of pieces and parts is to become the image of the coinherence of the three divine Persons; about the forming of the Body of Christ, the building of the City of God. And the Board is the first of the places at which it happens. If that sounds a little fancy for your own table full of upset glasses and brawling children, remember Abraham: He set God the best table he could, but his wife embarrassed him by being rude. From his point of view, the occasion was hardly a success. As it turned out, however, it didn't matter; he became the father of the people of the coinherence anyway. The City of God began with a meal that didn't go right; your spilled milk isn't going to hold up the building of it too much.

*

It won't hold it up, that is, if it is only spilled milk. The table has its natural intractabilities as well as its native virtues, and we can learn to work with them all. But there are other things that can come to the table that are not natural to it. There are foreign accretions and imported difficulties, and it is to those that we need to pay attention. Some of them are helpful, some not; they need sorting.

I said before that the 1950's were, matrimonially speaking, not a bad period. We did quite a bit of thinking about the family, and specifically about the table, and we brought a welter of things to it, mostly with the idea of making it work better. We rediscovered the dining room. We revived the big family. We reinstituted the groaning board. The homemaking consultants and the food editors had a field day. They conjured up a vision of the household as a populous and bustling city, and they published reams of practical advice about how to give it flesh. In short, they trained our sights on the very thing the table was about: the movement of nature into membership. Not bad, indeed.

As usual, however, the forces of the opposition were not ideal. The imports and additions to the household—the liturgies suggested to us in such profusion—did not always strengthen the table's natural aptness for building the City. The innate motion toward membership was often countered by a resident and demonic drive back in he direction of fragmentation and discreteness. For example. We discovered cooking again, and with a vengeance. The plainest house could bring off a pizza or a *coq au vin* simply by following the directions in the local supermarket family magazine. Newlyweds served Beef Stroganoff and *babas au rhum*. It was marvelous. There was a richness, an interest, on the table that had not been seen for years, if ever. Unfortunately, it was not generally followed up. No sustained effort was made to bring these liturgies of food home and make them local by adaptation. They tended to remain larks, splendid irrelevancies that found no permanent resting place. And so we missed the boat. After the novelty of the *haute cuisine* had worn off, food itself—one of the table's greatest bonds of unity—was either left pretty much as it had been, or turned into an occasion of eclectic dilettantism. Neither was any use to the family.

Again, we rediscovered wine. I firmly believe that, along with real bread, it is one of the pieces without which the Board can hardly be itself. What was even better, we put it back on the table; we drank it with our meals. But here again, the drive toward the real restoration was countered and stopped short of its goal. For most people, wine too was only a sometime thing; it never had a chance to speak its real piece in its steady and ancient voice. And for those who did put it back, the devil was ready with that most banal of all perversions, wine snobbery. What might have become a true liturgy rooted in earth and history was, with alarming frequency, reduced to a lot of high church popery-jiggery. And its advocates were, with equal frequency, crashing bores.

And then there was the dining room—and the living room and the family room which were its extensions. In some resourceful designs (I am not over-fond of them personally, but they were honestly liturgical) all of these areas were in sight of each other. The Board positively defined the whole; it was the true lord of the things of the household. It was in many ways the best thing we did—or, better said, the best thing we almost did, for we missed the boat there, too. We built those areas, but we made no liturgy to go on in them. As often as not, the fireplace was taken to be the center of attraction. We built conversation pits around it, and spacious living and family rooms to house it. But we produced no true liturgy by it because in this age of central heating, even a real fireplace is fake. No one really needs it; you have to go out of your way to use it. Only the real things of life can enter into liturgy. The sad part about our brilliant near miss in home design was that the great real thing—the table itself—was bypassed. As often as not, the best and truest table in the house was used only for the occasional liturgy of parties; the daily liturgies of the family had to make shift for themselves around a depressing kitchen set or at (abomination of desolation) one of those lunch-counter arrangements, fittingly called islands. We almost had the whole thing in the palm of our hand; the mainland of the table was almost conquered. But the advantage was not pressed and the initiative was lost. We continued in far too many homes to live offshore from our own territory and to wonder why we still felt homesick.

That's about where we stand now. We sit at our tables, still looking for the relevant liturgies that will restore us to our real functions and our rightful places. We are still trying to build the City, but the competition has become fierce. We are continuously being invaded by other cities: TV during dinner (let alone at other times) is precisely the overwhelming of the village by the metropolis. So is recorded music. So are frozen spinach soufflé, commercial bread and canned soup. And so are the PTA, the Rifle Club, the Boy Scouts, the Bowling League and the thousand other plausible intrusions which so disrupt the pattern of home life that no native liturgy ever forms. Don't misunderstand, however. I would not suggest for a minute that we make any attempt to turn back the clock and live without all these.

First of all, we shouldn't. They are by no means all evil. They are only other liturgies, other ways of dealing with the host of things which an abundant society showers upon us. Many, many of them are superb. The damage they cause is due chiefly to their number, to their diversity, and to their polish. There are far too many of them for anyone to use. Choice is essential; no house can possibly take everything that comes over the TV or off the supermarket shelves. More, they are far too varied: There are good programs and bad, helpful products and useless, liberating diversions and stifling ones; not only choice, but discerning choice is needed. Last, they are done with more slickness than the average home can ever manage: The music around my table does not measure up to the music in my record collection; if I use my records at the wrong time, I will smother the local liturgy of singing. And the list can go on indefinitely. The home cannot stand constant comparison with the metropolis. I know women who will not learn to cook proper rice, because precooked rice has made them ashamed of their own efforts with the genuine article. Worse, I know women who will not explore the endless and utterly local liturgy of soup, because opening cans is the only ceremony they know on the subject. What we need is discernment. Canned soups, for instance, are a brilliant device. For emergencies they are invaluable, and as an ingredient for stretching a local and peculiar masterpiece they are priceless. We just have to keep them contributory to us, to make them serve rather than dominate. We have to fight for the rights of the small town a little more zealously, and work at its liturgies a lot harder. Every man's table should develop a proud and somewhat stubborn provincialism. We don't need purblindness and mere insularity, but we are, after all, country bumpkins, and we should keep the city slickers at a respectful distance.

In the second place, we simply cannot live without the distraction and competition of the greater liturgies. We have built ourselves a way of life that makes them necessary to our existence. For example, consider our large-scale migration to the suburbs. The reasoning behind it is sound: People feel that their families will be better off as families out in the country. It is precisely in order to build the local city among themselves that they move away from the metropolis. But the move itself creates pressures and distractions. More often than not, the time spent in commutation is so great that the Board itself is bro-

ken: The father does not eat with his children. Again, the suburb is less compact than the metropolis. Most children have to go to school on buses. When
they sit down to their noon meal, it is in a cafeteria; the table of their own
home sees them at midday only on weekends. As a matter of fact, between dis-
jointed breakfast schedules and fatherless suppers, the suburban household
hardly meets at all on five days out of seven.

I suppose there is no immediate way around this. The system does not
seem to be about to change, and we do not seem to have any practical way to
get out of cooperating with it. We have to make a living. The rosy dream of
packing up dolls and dishes and heading for Vermont—of settling down far
out in the country—is no solution for most of us. It is, literally and figuratively,
just too far out. The real solution will have to face the fact that most of us are
both bound and determined to live in the kind of community we now inhabit.
Monochrome though it may be, and overspecialized and distracted, too, it is
the only one that will provide us with the place in which we can get the kind
of money we need to pay our way, and the kind of schooling we would like to
see our children have. That leaves us holding a thoroughly mixed bag.

It also defines our work. What we have to do is sort the contents of that
bag, and distinguish carefully between the real items and the fake ones. The
sorting will have to be precisely a sorting of *things* and, above all, of liturgies
and their attendant ceremonies. As elsewhere, I have a few ideas about principles, plus a few highly local and probably untransferable adaptations to offer.
They will come out by and by. Right here I want only to say something rather
general.

To begin with, the job isn't easy. Partly because of all the competition I
have been talking about, but partly because of the very nature of the work
itself. The gluing together of a clutch of human beings into some semblance
of a city has never been more than remotely possible. We are all sinners, and
it's the people closest to us that see us at our worst. The family gets the lion's
share of life's provocations, aggravations and enervations. Nowhere is there so
much fur quite so ready to be rubbed the wrong way.

But beyond that, there is the question of the sorting itself. What precisely
do I want to see around my table? There is so much, new and old, that I hardly
know where to begin. I have a couple of ideas, though, and the first one is my
usual pet: Try on the old hats first. Take manners, for instance. Things like sons
helping their mother into her chair at dinner, like thanking her afterward, like
asking to be excused from the table, like kissing people goodbye. Carry it a
little farther from the table. Take not interrupting, take the rule that one person talks at a time, take knocking on doors before bursting into a room, take
"How do you do," and "Please," and "Thank you." They are all very old-hat,
but who will say they're not becoming? No advances in technology preclude

them, no alterations in manner of life have made them fake; they are rooted in the nature of man and the exchanges of the city. But if you take them, remember one thing. They are not ideas, they are liturgies; they are only good when they become simply *the way we do things,* when they acquire the naturalness of an old priest making the sign of the cross. That puts a very large burden on parents. First, they will have to have enough sensible manners of their own to make the drive convincing; and second, they will need perseverance. It is, very, very hard. It takes years. And maybe 80 per cent of it will inevitably be waste motion. Decent liturgies don't come easily; even if they are not driven out by positively demonic ones, a lot of perfectly good ritual simply falls by the wayside because nobody was quite prepared for the heroic labor of keeping it going.

Manners are only an example. There are dozens of other old hats. There are parties—the liturgical celebrations of the city's history. There are vacations: the city's forays into other lands for conquest and plunder, and for memories of derring-do to be recounted down the years over coffee and dessert. There are hobbies: the city's exaltation of the peculiar talents of its singers, its painters, and its whittlers. All of these liturgies are as old as man; they will never cease to be contemporary. On the Day of Judgment someone will be taken in the act of rigging a ship model; another will be left while blowing out the candles on his birthday cake. We are not quite as far at sea as we think we are. The ancient rites of the home are as good as new, if we work at them.

What about the new hats, though? Well, here is where the sorting comes in full force. Think of television. I think I was one of the last holdouts against it. I still think it is a dangerous monster. But the assassination of the President convinced me that it was a monster whose cage I had to enter. I may tame it, or it may eat me, but I must face it. The great city has become so great that television is a necessity. It is precisely our marketplace, the one center where we can all meet and talk and look. All of us watched the caisson move down Pennsylvania Avenue; we all saw our own faces file past his coffin in the Rotunda. For a society of such unintelligible complexity, it was a fabulous achievement. Of course, as a true marketplace, TV is also filled with trash, hucksters, and shoddy merchandise. My small city needs only enough of that to teach it to be healthily suspicious of strangers, and of Greeks bearing gifts. Therefore, the liturgy of watching television needs constant revision and refinement. But note that it is precisely a liturgy. If my children watch *Huckleberry Hound* for three weeks running, no one can talk them out of the fourth: "We *always* watch *Huckleberry Hound* on Thursdays." *We do,* you see; the liturgy of St. John Chrysostom had neither more nor less justification than that. But with anything that powerful, the work of taming it isn't going to be easy. My television, for example, may not be turned on during dinner; the great city will overwhelm my little village. I have few local liturgies capable of winning out over Huntley, Brinkley and *The Three Stooges*. Even *The Mickey Mouse Club* is frequently too much for us. Again it should not be allowed so to monopolize time that hobbies, reading and schoolwork have to operate on its leavings. This is all obvious, but it all happens. It needs endless and forceful watching.

And television is only one example. There are records—the liturgy of listening: I must watch that it doesn't destroy the local liturgy of singing, playing, and telling my own stories. When I go to a man's house, I should hear *his* children, not the Kingston Trio; *his* jokes, not Shelley Berman's. And there are outside activities—the broadening liturgies by which the family becomes the beneficiary of its members' involvement in Power Squadron or Integration Movement: Watch that they don't so disrupt the domestic liturgy that there is not time to share the benefits.

But enough. We need good liturgies, and we need natural ones; we need a life neither patternless nor over-patterned, if the city is to be built. And I think the root of it all is *caring*. Not that that will turn the trick all by itself, but that we can produce nothing good without it. True liturgies take things for what they really are, and offer them up in loving delight. Adam naming the animals is instituting the first of all the liturgies: speech, by which man the priest of creation picks up each of the world's pieces and by his wonder bears it into the dance. "By George," he says, "there's an *elephant* in my garden; isn't that *something!*" Adam has been at work a long time; civilization is the fruit of his priestly labors. Culture is the liturgy of nature as it is offered up by man. But culture can come only from caring enough about things to want them really to be themselves—to want the poem to scan perfectly, the song to be genuinely melodic, the basketball actually to drop through the middle of the hoop, the edge of the board to be utterly straight, the pastry to be really flaky. Few of us have very many great things to care about, but we all have plenty of small ones; and that's enough for the dance. It is precisely through the things we put on the table, and the liturgies we form around it, that the city is built; *caring* is more than half the work.

Tolstoy: *War and Peace*, First Epilogue: Parents and Children

By the very end of Tolstoy's War and Peace, *all the wars are over: Russia has endured and stayed the Napoleonic advance; so too have Tolstoy's main protagonists endured the tumultuous self-doubts and self-reproaches of youthful romance, illusion, disappointment, longing, and adventure. Peace reigns. Life's burning questions—What should I do? Where should I go? Why? Wherefore?—seem to be settled. Domestic life blossoms. Tolstoy's young women become exemplary wives and mothers, settling down to pregnancies, births, and child-rearing; his young men become exemplary husbands and fathers, settling into lives of farming, thinking, protecting, and appreciating. The once beautiful young enchantress Natásha Rostóv marries the ever-searching Pierre Bezúkhov; the sad but soulful Mary Bolkónski marries the once-dashing young hussar Nicholas Rostóv. Both unions, which would have seemed most unlikely at the outset of the novel, are thriving at the end. Though their marriages are strikingly different from each other, in Tolstoy's view both couples are supremely happy precisely because they now live in the everyday stream of real life, far away from the unreal world of political and social ambition. Tolstoy allows us to glimpse their married lives in his First Epilogue, several years and many children after their vows were taken. Both families are gathered at Bald Hills, the former country seat of old Prince Bolkónski, Mary's father, which was rebuilt after the war by Nicholas Rostóv. The selections are in three parts, taken, respectively, from Chapters 2, 3 and 4.*

I. Nicholas' and Mary's family life. Tolstoy's portrayal of the family happiness of Nicholas and Mary includes moments of fear and anxiety on the part of Mary with respect to her children and to her husband, as well as favoritism on the part of papa Nicholas with respect to their young daughter Natásha. How can this be? On what understanding of happiness can their lives be regarded as happy or blessed?

It was the eve of St. Nicholas, the fifth of December, 1820. Natásha had been staying at her brother's with her husband and children since early autumn. Pierre had gone to Petersburg on business of his own for three weeks as he said, but had remained there nearly seven weeks and was expected back every minute.

Besides the Bezúkhov family, Nicholas' old friend the retired General Vasili Dmítrich Denísov was staying with the Rostóvs this fifth of December.

On the sixth, which was his name day when the house would be full of visitors, Nicholas knew he would have to exchange his Tartar tunic for a tail coat, and put on narrow boots with pointed toes, and drive to the new church he had built, and then receive visitors who would come to congratulate him, offer them refreshments, and talk about the elections of the nobility; but he considered himself entitled to spend the eve of that day in his usual way. He examined the bailiff's accounts of the village in Ryazan which belonged to his wife's nephew, wrote two business letters, and walked over to the granaries, cattle yards and stables before dinner. Having taken precautions against the general drunkenness to be expected on the morrow because it was a great saint's day, he returned to dinner, and without having time for a private talk with his wife sat down at the long table laid for twenty persons, at which the whole household had assembled. At that table were his mother, his mother's old lady companion Bélova, his wife, their three children with their governess and tutor, his wife's nephew with his tutor, Sónya,[1] Denísov, Natásha, her three children, their governess, and old Michael Ivanovich, the late prince's architect, who was living on in retirement at Bald Hills.

Countess Mary sat at the other end of the table. When her husband took his place she concluded, from the rapid manner in which after taking up his table napkin he pushed back the tumbler and wineglass standing before him, that he was out of humor, as was sometimes the case when he came in to dinner straight from the farm—especially before the soup. Countess Mary well knew that mood of his, and when she herself was in a good frame of mind quietly waited till he had had his soup and then began to talk to him and make him admit that there was no cause for his ill humor. But today she quite forgot that and was hurt that he should be angry with her without any reason, and she felt unhappy. She asked him where he had been. He replied. She again inquired whether everything was going well on the farm. Her unnatural tone made him wince unpleasantly and he replied hastily.

"Then I'm not mistaken," thought Countess Mary. "Why is he cross with me?" She concluded from his tone that he was vexed with her and wished to end the conversation. She knew her remarks sounded unnatural, but could not refrain from asking some more questions.

Thanks to Denísov the conversation at table soon became general and lively, and she did not talk to her husband. When they left the table and went as usual to thank the old countess, Countess Mary held out her hand and kissed her husband, and asked him why he was angry with her.

"You always have such strange fancies! I didn't even think of being angry," he replied.

---

[1]Sónya, an orphaned niece to old Count Rostóv, had been the childhood sweetheart of Nicholas Rostóv. She grew up in her uncle's home and now lives at Bald Hills in the home of Nicholas and Mary.

But the word *always* seemed to her to imply: "Yes, I am angry but I won't tell you why."

Nicholas and his wife lived together so happily that even Sónya and the old countess, who felt jealous and would have liked them to disagree, could find nothing to reproach them with; but even they had their moments of antagonism. Occasionally, and it was always just after they had been happiest together, they suddenly had a feeling of estrangement and hostility, which occurred most frequently during countess Mary's pregnancies, and this was such a time.

"Well, *messieurs et mesdames,*" said Nicholas loudly and with apparent cheerfulness (it seemed to Countess Mary that he did it on purpose to vex her), "I have been on my feet since six this morning. Tomorrow I shall have to suffer, so today I'll go and rest."

And without a word to his wife he went to the little sitting room and lay down on the sofa.

"That's always the way," thought Countess Mary. "He talks to everyone except me. I see . . . I see that I am repulsive to him, especially when I am in this condition." She looked down at her expanded figure and in the glass at her pale, sallow, emaciated face in which her eyes now looked larger than ever.

And everything annoyed her—Denísov's shouting and laughter, Natásha's talk, and especially a quick glance Sónya gave her.

Sónya was always the first excuse Countess Mary found for feeling irritated.

Having sat awhile with her visitors without understanding anything of what they were saying, she softly left the room and went to the nursery.

The children were playing at "going to Moscow" in a carriage made of chairs and invited her to go with them. She sat down and played with them a little, but the thought of her husband and his unreasonable crossness worried her. She got up and, walking on tiptoe with difficulty, went to the small sitting room.

"Perhaps he is not asleep; I'll have an explanation with him," she said to herself. Little Andrew, her eldest boy, imitating his mother, followed her on tiptoe. She did not notice him.

"Mary, dear, I think he is asleep—he was so tired," said Sónya, meeting her in the large sitting room (it seemed to Countess Mary that she crossed her path everywhere). "Andrew may wake him."

Countess Mary looked round, saw little Andrew following her, felt that Sónya was right, and for that very reason flushed and with evident difficulty refrained from saying something harsh. She made no reply, but to avoid obeying Sónya beckoned to Andrew to follow her quietly and went to the door. Sónya went away by another door. From the room in which Nicholas was sleeping came the sound of his even breathing, every slightest tone of which was familiar to his wife. As she listened to it she saw before her his smooth handsome forehead, his mustache, and his whole face, as she had so often seen it in the stillness of the night when he slept. Nicholas suddenly moved and cleared his throat. And at that moment little Andrew shouted from outside the door: "Papa! Mamma's standing, here!" Countess Mary turned pale with fright and made signs to the boy. He grew silent, and quiet ensued for a moment, terrible to Countess Mary. She knew how Nicholas disliked being waked. Then through the door she heard Nicholas clearing his throat again and stirring, and his voice said crossly:

"I can't get a moment's peace . . . Mary, is that you? Why did you bring him here?"

"I only came in to look and did not notice . . . forgive me. . . . "

Nicholas coughed and said no more. Countess Mary moved away from the door and took the boy back to the nursery. Five minutes later little black-eyed three-year-old Natásha, her father's pet, having learned from her brother that Papa was asleep and Mamma was in the sitting room, ran to her father unobserved by her mother. The dark-eyed little girl boldly opened the creaking door, went up to the sofa with energetic steps of her sturdy little legs, and having examined the position of her father, who was asleep with his back to her, rose on tiptoe and kissed the hand which lay under his head. Nicholas turned with a tender smile on his face.

"Natásha, Natásha," came Countess Mary's frightened whisper from the door. "Papa wants to sleep."

"No, Mamma, he doesn't want to sleep," said little Natásha with conviction. "He's laughing."

Nicholas lowered his legs, rose, and took his daughter in his arms.

"Come in, Mary," he said to his wife.

She went in and sat down by her husband.

"I did not notice him following me," she said timidly. "I just looked in."

Holding his little girl with one arm, Nicholas glanced at his wife and, seeing her guilty expression, put his other arm around her and kissed her hair.

"May I kiss Mamma?" he asked Natásha.

Natásha smiled bashfully.

"Again!" she commanded, pointing with a peremptory gesture to the spot where Nicholas had placed the kiss.

"I don't know why you think I am cross," said Nicholas, replying to the question he knew was in his wife's mind.

"You have no idea how unhappy, how lonely, I feel when you are like that. It always seems to me . . . "

"Mary, don't talk nonsense. You ought to be ashamed of yourself!" he said gaily.

"It seems to me that you can't love me, that I am so plain . . . always . . . and now . . . in this cond . . . "

"Oh, how absurd you are! It is not beauty that endears, it's love that makes us see beauty. It is only Malvinas and women of that kind who are loved for their beauty. But do I love my wife? I don't love her, but . . . I don't know how to put it. Without you, or when something comes between us like this, I seem lost and can't do anything. Now do I love my finger? I don't love it, but just try to cut it off!"

"I'm not like that myself, but I understand. So you're not angry with me?"

"Awfully angry!" he said, smiling and getting up. And smoothing his hair he began to pace the room.

"Do you know, Mary, what I've been thinking?" he began, immediately thinking aloud in his wife's presence now that they had made it up.

He did not ask if she was ready to listen to him. He did not care. A thought had occurred to him and so it belonged to her also. And he told her of his intention to persuade Pierre to stay with them till spring.

Countess Mary listened till he had finished, made some remark, and in her turn began thinking aloud. Her thoughts were about the children.

"You can see the woman in her already," she said in French, pointing to little Natásha. "You reproach us women with being illogical. Here is our logic. I say: 'Papa wants to sleep!' but she says, 'No, he's laughing.' And she was right," said Countess Mary with a happy smile.

"Yes, yes." And Nicholas, taking his little daughter in his strong hand, lifted her high, placed her on his shoulder, held her by the legs, and paced the room with her. There was an expression of carefree happiness on the faces of both father and daughter.

"But you know you may be unfair. You are too fond of this one," his wife whispered in French.

"Yes, but what am I to do? . . . I try not to show . . . "

At that moment they heard the sound of the door pulley and footsteps in the hall and anteroom, as if someone had arrived.

"Somebody has come."

"I am sure it is Pierre. I will go and see," said Countess Mary and left the room.

In her absence Nicholas allowed himself to give his little daughter a gallop round the room. Out of breath, he took the laughing child quickly from his shoulder and pressed her to his heart. His capers reminded him of dancing, and looking at the child's round happy little face he thought of what she would be like when he was an old man, taking her into society and dancing the mazurka with her as his old father had danced Daniel Cooper with his daughter.

"It is he, it is he, Nicholas!" said Countess Mary, re-entering the room a few minutes later. "Now our Natásha has come to life. You should have seen her ecstasy, and how he caught it for having stayed away so long. Well, come along now, quick, quick! It's time you two were parted," she added, looking smilingly at the little girl who clung to her father.

Nicholas went out holding the child by the hand.

Countess Mary remained in the sitting room.

"I should never, never have believed that one could be so happy," she whispered to herself. A smile lit up her face but at the same time she sighed, and her deep eyes expressed a quiet sadness as though she felt, through her happiness, that there is another sort of happiness unattainable in this life and of which she involuntarily thought at that instant.

II. Natásha's and Pierre's family life. The family happiness of the Bezúkhovs appears to require the absolute devotion of Natásha to her children, the neglect of everything else once so important to her (for example, her looks, her words, her music), and the complete subjection of her husband to her whims. Pierre was allowed to be away from home but only for the sake of business and, when abroad, so powerful was Natásha's jealousy, he was expressly forbidden from speaking smilingly to any other woman. Though Pierre, in turn, we are told, had the right to regulate the household as he chose, one wonders what it means for him to rule. How can such arrangements be conducive to family happiness? Can true happiness be compatible with jealousy? Does it necessarily require such single-minded devotion?

Natásha had married in the early spring of 1813, and in 1820 already had three daughters besides a son for whom she had longed and whom she was now nursing. She had grown stouter and broader, so that it was difficult to recognize in this robust, motherly woman the slim, lively Natásha of former days. Her features were more defined and had a calm, soft, and serene expression. In her face there was none of the ever-glowing animation that had formerly burned there and constituted its charm. Now her face and body were often all that one saw, and her soul was not visible at all. All that struck the eye was a strong, handsome, and fertile woman. The old fire very rarely kindled in her face now. That happened only when, as was the case that day, her husband returned home, or a sick child was convalescent, or when she and Countess Mary spoke of Prince Andrew (she never mentioned him to her husband, who she imagined was jealous of Prince Andrew's memory),[2] or on the rare occasions when something happened to induce her to sing, a practice she had quite abandoned since her marriage. At the rare moments when the old fire did kindle in her handsome, fully developed body she was even more attractive than in former days.

Since their marriage Natásha and her husband had lived in Moscow, in Petersburg, on their estate near Moscow, or with her mother, that is to say, in Nicholas' house. The young Countess Bezúkhova was not often seen in society, and those who met her there were not pleased with her and found her neither attractive nor amiable. Not that Natásha liked solitude—she did not know whether she liked it or not, she even thought that she did not—but with her pregnancies, her confinements, the nursing of her children, and sharing every moment of her husband's life, she had demands on her time which could be satisfied only by renouncing society. All who had known Natásha before her marriage wondered at the change in her as at something extraordinary. Only the old countess with her maternal instinct had realized that all Natásha's outbursts had been due to her need of children and a husband—as she herself had once exclaimed at Otrádnoe not so much in fun as in earnest—and her mother was now surprised at the surprise expressed by those who had never understood Natásha, and she kept saying that she had always known that Natásha would make an exemplary wife and mother.

"Only she lets her love of her husband and children overflow all bounds," said the countess, "so that it even becomes absurd."

Natásha did not follow the golden rule advocated by clever folk, especially by the French, which says that a girl should not let herself go when she marries, should not neglect her accomplishments, should be even more careful of her appearance than when she was unmarried, and should fascinate her husband as much as she did before he became her husband. Natásha on the contrary had at once abandoned all her witchery, of which her singing had been an unusually powerful part. She gave it up just because it was so powerfully seductive. She took no pains with her manners or with delicacy of speech, or with her toilet, or to show herself to her husband in her most becoming attitudes, or to avoid inconveniencing him by being too exacting. She acted in contradiction to all those rules She felt that the allurements instinct had formerly taught her to use would now be merely ridiculous in the eyes of her husband, to whom she had from the first moment given herself up entirely—that is, with her whole soul, leaving no corner of it hidden from him. She felt that her unity with her husband was not maintained by the poetic feelings that had attracted

[2]Prince Andrew was Natásha's first love. He died of a wound incurred on the battlefield before they were married.

him to her, but by something else—indefinite but firm as the bond between her own body and soul.

To fluff out her curls, put on fashionable dresses, and sing romantic songs to fascinate her husband would have seemed as strange as to adorn herself to attract herself. To adorn herself for others might perhaps have been agreeable—she did not know—but she had no time at all for it. The chief reason for devoting no time either to singing, to dress, or to choosing her words was that she really had no time to spare for these things.

We know that man has the faculty of becoming completely absorbed in a subject however trivial it may be, and that there is no subject so trivial that it will not grow to infinite proportions if one's entire attention is devoted to it.

The subject which wholly engrossed Natásha's attention was her family: that is, her husband whom she had to keep so that he should belong entirely to her and to the home, and the children whom she had to bear, bring into the world, nurse, and bring up.

And the deeper she penetrated, not with her mind only but with her whole soul, her whole being, into the subject that absorbed her, the larger did that subject grow and the weaker and more inadequate did her own powers appear, so that she concentrated them wholly on that one thing and yet was unable to accomplish all that she considered necessary.

There were then as now conversations and discussions about women's rights, the relations of husband and wife and their freedom and rights, though these themes were not yet termed questions as they are now; but these topics were not merely uninteresting to Natásha, she positively did not understand them.

These questions, then as now, existed only for those who see nothing in marriage but the pleasure married people get from one another, that is, only the beginnings of marriage and not its whole significance, which lies in the family.

Discussions and questions of that kind, which are like the question of how to get the greatest gratification from one's dinner, did not then and do not now exist for those for whom the purpose of a dinner is the nourishment it affords; and the purpose of marriage is the family.

If the purpose of dinner is to nourish the body, a man who eats two dinners at once may perhaps get more enjoyment but will not attain his purpose, for his stomach will not digest the two dinners.

If the purpose of marriage is the family, the person who wishes to have many wives or husbands may perhaps obtain much pleasure, but in that case will not have a family.

If the purpose of food is nourishment and the purpose of marriage is the family, the whole question resolves itself into not eating more than one can digest, and not having more wives or husbands than are needed for the family—that is, one wife or one husband. Natásha needed a husband. A husband was given her and he gave her a family. And she not only saw no need of any other or better husband, but as all the powers of her soul were intent on serving that husband and family, she could not imagine and saw no interest in imagining how it would be if things were different.

Natásha did not care for society in general, but prized the more the society of her relatives—Countess Mary, and her brother, her mother, and Sónya. She valued the company of those to whom she could come striding disheveled from the nursery in her dressing gown, and with joyful face show a yellow instead of a green stain on baby's napkin, and from whom she could hear reassuring words to the effect that baby was much better.

To such an extent had Natásha let herself go that the way she dressed and did her hair, her ill-chosen words, and her jealousy—she was jealous of Sónya, of the governess, and of every woman, pretty or plain—were habitual subjects of jest to those about her. The general opinion was that Pierre was under his wife's thumb, which was really true. From the very first days of their married life Natásha had announced her demands. Pierre was greatly surprised by his wife's view, to him a perfectly novel one, that every moment of his life belonged to her and to the family. His wife's demands astonished him, but they also flattered him, and he submitted to them.

Pierre's subjection consisted in the fact that he not only dared not flirt with, but dared not even speak smilingly to, any other woman; did not dare dine at the Club as a pastime, did not dare spend money on a whim, and did not dare absent himself for any length of time, except on business—in which his wife included his intellectual pursuits, which she did not in the least understand but to which she attributed great importance. To make up for this, at home Pierre had the right to regulate his life and that of the whole family exactly as he chose. At home Natásha placed herself in the position of a slave to her husband, and the whole household went on tiptoe when he was occupied—that is, was reading or writing in his study. Pierre had but to show a partiality for anything to get just what he liked done always. He had only to express a wish and Natásha would jump up and run to fulfill it.

The entire household was governed according to Pierre's supposed orders, that is, by his wishes which Natásha tried to guess. Their way of life and place of residence, their acquaintances and ties, Natásha's occupations, the children's upbringing, were all selected not merely with regard to Pierre's expressed wishes, but to what Natásha from the thoughts he expressed in conversation supposed his wishes to be. And she deduced the essentials of his wishes quite correctly, and having once arrived at them clung to them tenaciously. When Pierre himself wanted to change his mind she would fight him with his own weapons.

Thus in a time of trouble ever memorable to him after the birth of their first child who was delicate, when they had to change the wet nurse three times and Natásha fell ill from despair, Pierre one day told her of Rousseau's view, with which he quite agreed, that to have a wet nurse is unnatural and harmful. When her next baby was born, despite the opposition of her mother, the doctors, and even of her husband himself—who were all vigorously opposed to her nursing her baby herself, a thing then unheard of and considered injurious—she insisted on having her own way, and after that nursed all her babies herself.

It very often happened that in a moment of irritation husband and wife would have a dispute, but long afterwards Pierre to his surprise and delight would find in his wife's ideas and actions the very thought against which she had argued, but divested of everything superfluous that in the excitement of the dispute he had added when expressing his opinion.

After seven years of marriage Pierre had the joyous and firm consciousness that he was not a bad man, and he felt this because he saw himself reflected in his wife. He felt the good and bad within himself inextricably mingled and overlapping. But only what was really good in him was reflected in his wife, all that was not quite good was rejected. And this was not the result of logical reasoning but was a direct and mysterious reflection. . . .

III. *The two married couples and their mutual relations. After the business of the day is over, the children tucked away, each of the couples is left alone. They converse with great mutual regard and affection but their conversations seem neither logical nor coherent. To an outsider, they even seem to be speaking right past each other. How can the intimacy revealed here be regarded as blessed?*

. . . After supper Nicholas, having undressed in his study and given instructions to the steward who had been waiting for him, went to the bedroom in his dressing gown, where he found his wife still at her table, writing.

"What are you writing, Mary?" Nicholas asked.

Countess Mary blushed. She was afraid that what she was writing would not be understood or approved by her husband.

She had wanted to conceal what she was writing from him, but at the same time was glad he had surprised her at it and that she would now have to tell him.

"A diary, Nicholas," she replied, handing him a blue exercise book filled with her firm, bold writing.

"A diary?" Nicholas repeated with a shade of irony, and he took up the book.

It was in French.

"December 4. Today when Andrúsha" (her eldest boy) "woke up he did not wish to dress and Mademoiselle Louise sent for me. He was naughty and obstinate. I tried threats, but he only grew angrier. Then l took the matter in hand: I left him alone and began with nurse's help to get the other children up, telling him that I did not love him. For a long time he was silent, as if astonished, then he jumped out of bed, ran to me in his shirt, and sobbed so that I could not calm him for a long time. It was plain that what troubled him most was that he had grieved me. Afterwards in the evening when I gave him his ticket, he again began crying piteously and kissing me. One can do anything with him by tenderness."

"What is a 'ticket'?" Nicholas inquired.

"I have begun giving the elder ones marks every evening, showing how they have behaved."

Nicholas looked into the radiant eyes that were gazing at him, and continued to turn over the pages and read. In the diary was set down everything in the children's lives that seemed noteworthy to their mother as showing their characters or suggesting general reflections on educational methods. They were for the most part quite insignificant trifles, but did not seem so to the mother or to the father either, now that he read this diary about his children for the first time.

Under the date "5" was entered:

"Mítya was naughty at table. Papa said he was to have no pudding. He had none, but looked so unhappily and greedily at the others while they were eating! I think that punishment by depriving children of sweets only develops their greediness. Must tell Nicholas this."

Nicholas put down the book and looked at his wife. The radiant eyes gazed at him questioningly: would he approve or disapprove of her diary? There could be no doubt not only of his approval but also of his admiration for his wife.

Perhaps it need not be done so pedantically, thought Nicholas, or even done at all, but this untiring, continual spiritual effort of which the sole aim was the children's moral welfare delighted him. Had Nicholas been able to analyze his feelings he would have found that his steady, tender, and proud love of his wife rested on his feeling of wonder at her spirituality and at the lofty moral world, almost beyond his reach, in which she had her being.

He was proud of her intelligence and goodness, recognized his own insignificance beside her in the spiritual world, and rejoiced all the more that she with such a soul not only belonged to him but was part of himself.

"I quite, quite approve, my dearest!" said he with a significant look, and after a short pause he added: "And I behaved badly today. You weren't in the study. We began disputing—Pierre and I—and I lost my temper. But he is impossible: such a child! I don't know what would become of him if Natásha didn't keep him in hand. . . . Have you any idea why he went to Petersburg? They have formed . . . "

"Yes, I know," said Countess Mary. "Natásha told me."

"Well, then, you know," Nicholas went on, growing hot at the mere recollection of their discussion, "he wanted to convince me that it is every honest man's duty to go against the government, and that the oath of allegiance and duty . . . I am sorry you weren't there. They all fell on me—Denísov and Natásha . . . Natásha is absurd. How she rules over him! And yet there need only be a discussion and she has no words of her own but only repeats his sayings . . . " added Nicholas, yielding to that irresistible inclination which tempts us to judge those nearest and dearest to us. He forgot that what he was saying about Natásha could have been applied word for word to himself in relation to his wife.

"Yes, I have noticed that," said Countess Mary.

"When I told him that duty and the oath were above everything, he started proving goodness knows what! A pity you were not there—what would you have said?"

"As I see it you were quite right, and I told Natásha so. Pierre says everybody is suffering, tortured, and being corrupted, and that it is our duty to help our neighbor. Of course he is right there," said Countess Mary, "but he forgets that we have other duties nearer to us, duties indicated to us by God Himself, and that though we might expose ourselves to risks we must not risk our children."

"Yes, that's it! That's just what I said to him," put in Nicholas, who fancied he really had said it. "But they insisted on their own view: love of one's neighbor and Christianity—and all this in the presence of young Nicholas, who had gone into my study and broke all my things."

"Ah, Nicholas, do you know I am often troubled about little Nicholas,"[3] said Countess Mary. "He is such an exceptional boy. I am afraid I neglect him in favor of my own: we all have children and relations while he has no one. He is constantly alone with his thoughts."

"Well, I don't think you need reproach yourself on his account. All that the fondest mother could do for her son you have done and are doing for him, and of course I am glad of it. He is a fine lad, a fine lad! This evening he lis-

---

[3]Young Nicholas Bolkónski, Countess Mary's nephew, is the son of Mary's brother, the late Prince Andrew Bolkónski, by his first wife, who died in childbirth.

tened to Pierre in a sort of trance, and fancy—as we were going in to supper I looked and he had broken everything on my table to bits, and he told me of it himself at once! I never knew him to tell an untruth. A fine lad, a fine lad!" repeated Nicholas, who at heart was not fond of Nicholas Bolkónski but was always anxious to recognize that he was a fine lad.

"Still, I am not the same as his own mother," said Countess Mary. "I feel I am not the same and it troubles me. A wonderful boy, but I am dreadfully afraid for him. It would be good for him to have companions."

"Well it won't be for long. Next summer I'll take him to Petersburg," said Nicholas. "Yes, Pierre always was a dreamer and always will be," he continued, returning to the talk in the study which had evidently disturbed him. "Well, what business is it of mine what goes on there—whether Arakcheev is bad, and all that? What business was it of mine when I married and was so deep in debt that I was threatened with prison, and had a mother who could not see or understand it? And then there are you and the children and our affairs. Is it for my own pleasure that I am at the farm or in the office from morning to night? No, but I know I must work to comfort my mother, to repay you, and not to leave the children such beggars as I was."

Countess Mary wanted to tell him that man does not live by bread alone and that he attached too much importance to these matters. But she knew she must not say this and that it would be useless to do so. She only took his hand and kissed it. He took this as a sign of approval and a confirmation of his thoughts, and after a few minutes' reflection continued to think aloud.

"You know, Mary, today Elias Mitrofánych" (this was his overseer) "came back from the Tambov estate and told me they are already offering eighty thousand rubles for the forest."

And with an eager face Nicholas began to speak of the possibility of repurchasing Otrádnoe before long, and added: "Another ten years of life and I shall leave the children . . . in an excellent position."

Countess Mary listened to her husband and understood all that he told her. She knew that when he thought aloud in this way he would sometimes ask her what he had been saying, and be vexed if he noticed that she had been thinking about something else. But she had to force herself to attend, for what he was saying did not interest her at all. She looked at him and did not think, but felt, about something different. She felt a submissive tender love for this man who would never understand all that she understood, and this seemed to make her love for him still stronger and added a touch of passionate tenderness. Besides this feeling which absorbed her altogether and hindered her from following the details of her husband's plans, thoughts that had no connection with what he was saying flitted through her mind. She thought of her nephew. Her husband's account of the boy's agitation while Pierre was speaking struck her forcibly, and various traits of his gentle, sensitive character recurred to her mind; and while thinking of her nephew she thought also of her own children. She did not compare them with him, but compared her feeling for them with her feeling for him, and felt with regret that there was something lacking in her feeling for young Nicholas.

Sometimes it seemed to her that this difference arose from the difference in their ages, but she felt herself to blame toward him and promised in her heart to do better and to accomplish the impossible—in this life to love her husband, her children, little Nicholas, and all her neighbors, as Christ loved mankind. Countess Mary's soul always strove toward the infinite, the eternal, and the absolute, and could therefore never be at peace. A stern expression of the lofty, secret suffering of a soul burdened by the body appeared on her face. Nicholas gazed at her. "O God! What will become of us if she dies, as I always fear when her face is like that?" thought he, and placing himself before the icon he began to say his evening prayers.

Natásha and Pierre, left alone, also began to talk as only a husband and wife can talk, that is, with extraordinary clearness and rapidity, understanding and expressing each other's thoughts in ways contrary to all rules of logic, without premises, deductions, or conclusions, and in a quite peculiar way. Natásha was so used to this kind of talk with her husband that for her it was the surest sign of something being wrong between them if Pierre followed a line of logical reasoning. When he began proving anything, or talking argumentatively and calmly and she, led on by his example, began to do the same, she knew that they were on the verge of a quarrel.

From the moment they were alone and Natásha came up to him with wide-open happy eyes, and quickly seizing his head pressed it to her bosom, saying: "Now you are all mine, mine! You won't escape!"—from that moment this conversation began, contrary to all the laws of logic and contrary to them because quite different subjects were talked about at one and the same time. This simultaneous discussion of many topics did not prevent a clear understanding but on the contrary was the surest sign that they fully understood one another.

Just as in a dream when all is uncertain, unreasoning, and contradictory, except the feeling that guides the dream, so in this intercourse contrary to all laws of reason, the words themselves were not consecutive and clear but only the feeling that prompted them.

Natásha spoke to Pierre about her brother's life and doings, of how she had suffered and lacked life during his own absence, and of how she was fonder than ever of Mary, and how Mary was in every way better than herself. In saying this Natásha was sincere in acknowledging Mary's superiority, but at the same time by saying it she made a demand on Pierre that he should, all the same, prefer her to Mary and to all other women, and that now, especially after having seen many women in Petersburg, he should tell her so afresh.

Pierre, answering Natásha's words, told her how intolerable it had been for him to meet ladies at dinners and balls in Petersburg.

"I have quite lost the knack of talking to ladies," he said. "It was simply dull. Besides, I was very busy."

Natásha looked intently at him and went on:

"Mary is so splendid," she said. "How she understands children! It is as if she saw straight into their souls. Yesterday, for instance, Mítya was naughty . . . "

"How like his father he is," Pierre interjected.

Natásha knew why he mentioned Mítya's likeness to Nicholas: the recollection of his dispute with his brother-in-law was unpleasant and he wanted to know what Natásha thought of it.

"Nicholas has the weakness of never agreeing with anything not generally accepted. But I understand that you value what opens up a fresh line," said she, repeating words Pierre had once uttered.

"No, the chief point is that to Nicholas ideas and discussions are an amusement—almost a pastime," said Pierre. "For instance, he is collecting a library and has made it a rule not to buy a new book till he has read what he had already bought—Sismondi and Rousseau and Montesquieu," he added with a smile. "You know how much I . . . " he began to soften down what he had said; but Natásha interrupted him to show that this was unnecessary.

"So you say ideas are an amusement to him. . . . "

"Yes, and for me nothing else is serious. All the time in Petersburg I saw everyone as in a dream. When I am taken up by a thought, all else is mere amusement."

"Ah, I'm so sorry I wasn't there when you met the children," said Natásha. "Which was most delighted? Lisa, I'm sure."

"Yes," Pierre replied, and went on with what was in his mind. "Nicholas says we ought not to think. But I can't help it. Besides, when I was in Petersburg I felt (I can say this to you) that the whole affair would go to pieces without me—everyone was pulling his own way. But I succeeded in uniting them all; and then my idea is so clear and simple. You see, l don't say that we ought to oppose this and that. We may be mistaken. What I say is: 'Join hands, you who love the right, and let there be but one banner—that of active virtue.' Prince Sergey is a fine fellow and clever."

Natásha would have had no doubt as to the greatness of Pierre's ideal, but one thing disconcerted her. "Can a man so important and necessary to society be also my husband? How did this happen?" She wished to express this doubt to him. "Now who could decide whether he is really cleverer than all the others?" she asked herself, and passed in review all those whom Pierre most respected. Judging by what he had said there was no one he had respected so highly as Pláton Karatáev.[4]

"Do you know what I am thinking about?" she asked. "About Pláton Karatáev. Would he have approved of you now, do you think?"

Pierre was not at all surprised at this question. He understood his wife's line of thought.

"Pláton Karatáev?" he repeated, and pondered, evidently sincerely trying to imagine Karataev's opinion on the subject. "He would not have understood . . . yet perhaps he would."

"I love you awfully!" Natásha suddenly said. "Awfully, awfully!"

"No, he would not have approved," said Pierre, after reflection. "What he would have approved of is our family life. He was always so anxious to find seemliness, happiness, and peace in everything, and I should have been proud to let him see us. There now—you talk of my absence, but you wouldn't believe what a special feeling I have for you after a separation. . . . "

"Yes, I should think . . . " Natásha began.

"No, it's not that. I never leave off loving you. And one couldn't love more, but this is something special. . . . Yes, of course—" he did not finish because their eyes meeting said the rest.

"What nonsense it is," Natásha suddenly exclaimed, "about honeymoons, and that the greatest happiness is at first! On the contrary, now is the best of all. If only you did not go away! Do you remember how we quarreled? And it was always my fault. Always mine. And what we quarreled about—I don't even remember!"

"Always about the same thing," said Pierre with a smile. "Jealo . . . "

"Don't say it! I can't bear it!" Natásha cried, and her eyes glittered coldly and vindictively. "Did you see her?" she added, after a pause.

"No, and if I had I shouldn't have recognized her."

They were silent for a while.

"Oh, do you know? While you were talking in the study I was looking at you," Natásha began, evidently anxious to disperse the cloud that had come over them. "You are as like him as two peas—like the boy." (She meant her little son.) "Oh, it's time to go to him. . . . The milk's come. . . . But I'm sorry to leave you."

They were silent for a few seconds. Then suddenly turning to one another at the same time they both began to speak. Pierre began with self-satisfaction

---

[4]Pláton Karatáev was a peasant whom Pierre met when they were prisoners of war. Platon's ability to live joyfully and immediately, even under the most terrible circumstances, as well as his many stories, impressed Pierre profoundly.

and enthusiasm, Natásha with a quiet, happy smile. Having interrupted one another they both stopped to let the other continue.

"No. What did you say? Go on, go on."

"No, you go on, I was talking nonsense," said Natásha.

Pierre finished what he had begun. It was the sequel to his complacent reflections on his success in Petersburg. At that moment it seemed to him that he was chosen to give a new direction to the whole of Russian society and to the whole world.

"I only wished to say that ideas that have great results are always simple ones. My whole idea is that if vicious people are united and constitute a power, then honest folk must do the same. Now that's simple enough."

"Yes."

"And what were you going to say?"

"I? Only nonsense."

"But all the same?"

"Oh nothing, only a trifle," said Natásha, smiling still more brightly. "I only wanted to tell you about Pétya: today nurse was coming to take him from me, and he laughed, shut his eyes, and clung to me. I'm sure he thought he was hiding. Awfully sweet! There, now he's crying. Well, good-by!" and she left the room. . . .

Frost, "The Master Speed"

This sonnet, written by Robert Frost (1874–1963) on the occasion of his daughter's wedding, concludes with an exquisitely simple pair of images, "wing to wing" and "oar to oar," that capture the togetherness of the married couple, empowered to resist the flux of wind and water. Frost is not the first to use the language of speed or quickness to show how love may quicken the life of a couple into a vitality that far exceeds what each partner might attain alone. But Frost also plays on the archaic meaning of "speed," "prosperity or success in an undertaking," as well as on its Latin root, spes, meaning "hope," to point to the possibility of rest within motion, permanence within change, the eternal within the perishable. What then, precisely, is "the master speed"? Does it reside with each, or only with the couple, with "two such as you"? Do the partners discover, and therefore agree, to the truth that "life is only life forevermore . . . ", or do they make such a truth by their performative utterance, by their act of agreement or vow? How do the different ways of interpreting the last couplet, and the sonnet as a whole, point to different answers to the question, What can married life be like?

No speed of wind or water rushing by
But you have speed far greater. You can climb
Back up a stream of radiance to the sky,
And back through history up the stream of time.
And you were given this swiftness, not for haste,
Nor chiefly that you may go where you will,
But in the rush of everything to waste,
That you may have the power of standing still—
Off any still or moving thing you say.
Two such as you with such a master speed
Cannot be parted nor be swept away
From one another once you are agreed
That life is only life forevermore
Together wing to wing and oar to oar.

ACKNOWLEDGMENTS

We wish to acknowledge, with deep gratitude, the help of several individuals who contributed to the preparation of this volume. Jan Harbaugh did extensive bibliographic research, offered invaluable suggestions for inclusion, found and scanned the selections, typed, proof-read, and corrected the manuscript, and prepared the entire document in a form suitable for the publisher. Anna Dannhauser Marks helped with some of the scanning. Ellis Whitman provided able assistance securing permissions to reprint the various selections. Rebecca DeBoer at the University of Notre Dame Press rendered excellent help in copyediting and shepherding the volume through production. We are also grateful to: Craig Dykstra and the Lilly Foundation for their generous support of the Ethics of Everyday Life project; Christopher DeMuth and the American Enterprise Institute for a fellowship year for Leon R. Kass, during which this volume was brought to completion; Elizabeth Lurie and the William H. Brady, Jr. Foundation for their generous support in defraying the costs of permissions to reprint; Jeffrey L. Gainey, associate director of the University of Notre Dame Press, for his unflagging enthusiasm for our project; Irwin and Cita Stelzer for suggesting and lending us their Millais engraving ("Yes") for the cover; our colleagues in the Ethics of Everyday Life project, Tim Fuller, Gil Meilaender, Richard John Neuhaus, and Mark Schwehn, and our special consultants Inger Thomsen Brodey, Barbara Dafoe Whitehead, and Lee Yearley for their excellent suggestions regarding selections and organization and their critical comments on our own introductory materials; and, finally, our students at the University of Chicago, for helping us understand their dilemmas and for their thoughful discussions of many of these readings.

SOURCES AND CREDITS

The editors and the publisher thank the owners of copyright for their permission to include selections within this anthology.

Abraham, Pearl. "The Engagement," from *The Romance Reader* by Pearl Abraham. © 1995 by Pearl Abraham. Used by permission of Putnam Berkley, a division of Penguin Putnam, Inc. Reprinted from *Commentary* 100 (July 1995), pp. 36–44, by permission; all rights reserved.

Aquinas, St. Thomas. *Summa Theologica*, translated by the Fathers of the English Dominican Province. New York: Benziger Brothers, Inc., 1948. © 1948 by Benziger Brothers, Inc. Reprinted 1981 by Christian Classics.

Aristotle. *Nicomachean Ethics*, Book VIII, Chapter xii, translated by Leon R. Kass.

Austen, Jane. *Pride and Prejudice*, edited by D. J. Gray. New York: W. W. Norton & Company, 1966, pp. 6–7, 73–79, 85–88, 130–34, 134–44, 166–72, 173–75, 181, 188–91, 213, 252–56.

Bacon, Sir Francis. *The Essays*, in *Selected Writings of Francis Bacon*, introduction and notes by H. G. Dick. New York: Modern Library, 1955, pp. 22–23.

Bailey, Beth L. *From Front Porch to Back Seat: Courtship in Twentieth-Century America*. Baltimore: The Johns Hopkins University Press, 1988, pp. 13–24. © 1988 by The Johns Hopkins University Press. Used by permission of The Johns Hopkins University Press.

Ballou, Sullivan. "Letter to Sarah," in Ballou, Adin, *An Elaborate History and Genealogy of the Ballous in America*. Providence, R.I.: A. and L. W. Ballou, 1888.

Blankenhorn, David. "I Do?" *First Things* 77 (November 1997), pp. 14–15. Reprinted by permission of *First Things* and the author.

Bloom, Allan. *The Closing of the American Mind*. New York: Simon & Schuster, 1987, pp. 82–83, 84, 86–87, 97–108, 109–10, 112–18, 118–19, 120–21, 122–32, 132–37. © 1987 by Allan Bloom. Reprinted with permission of Simon & Schuster, Inc.

Borowitz, Eugene B. "Speaking Personally," from *Choosing a Sex Ethic: A Jewish Inquiry*. New York: Schocken Books, 1969, pp. 112–13. © 1969 by Eugene B. Borowitz. Reprinted by permission of Schocken Books, distributed by Pantheon Books, a division of Random House, Inc.

Capon, Robert Farrar. *Bed and Board: Plain Talk about Marriage*. New York:

Simon & Schuster, 1965, pp. 67–84, 89–109. © 1965 by Robert Farrar Capon. Reprinted by permission of the author.

Darwin, Charles. *The Autobiography of Charles Darwin*, edited by Nora Barlow. New York: Norton Library, 1958, pp. 231–34.

de Rougemont, Denis. *Love in the Western World*, translated by Montgomery Belgion. Princeton, N.J.: Princeton University Press, 1983, pp. 26–30, 38–46, 303–15. © 1940, 1956 by Pantheon Books. English translation of preface and postscript © 1983 by Princeton University Press. Reprinted by permission of Princeton University Press.

de Tocqueville, Alexis. *Democracy in America*, edited by J. P. Mayer and Max Lerner, translated by George Lawrence. Garden City, N.Y.: Anchor Books, 1969, pp. 590–96, 598, 600–603, 731–33. English translation © 1965 by Harper and Row Publishers, Inc., copyright renewed. Reprinted by permission of HarperCollins Publishers, Inc.

Divakaruni, Chitra Banerjee. "The Word Love," from *Arranged Marriage* by Chitra Divakaruni. New York: Anchor Books, 1995, pp. 57–71. © 1995 by Chitra Divakaruni. Used by permission of Doubleday, a division of Random House, Inc.

Erasmus, Desiderius. "Letter on Marriage," from *The Collected Works of Erasmus*, vol. 25, edited by J. K. Sowards. Toronto: University of Toronto Press, 1985, pp. 129–45. © 1985 by University of Toronto Press. Reprinted with permission of the publisher.

———. "Courtship," from *The Collected Works of Erasmus*, vol. 39, translated by Craig R. Thompson. Toronto: University of Toronto Press, 1997, pp. 257–68. © 1997 by University of Toronto Press. Reprinted with permission of the publisher.

Franklin, Benjamin. *A Benjamin Franklin Reader*, edited by N. G. Goodman. New York: Crowell, 1971, pp. 690–706.

———. *Benjamin Franklin: Writings*, edited by J. A. Leo Lemay. New York: Library of America, 1987, p. 924.

Frost, Robert. "The Master Speed," from *The Poetry of Robert Frost*, edited by Edward Connery Lathem. © 1936 by Robert Frost. © 1964 by Lesley Frost Ballantine. © 1969 by Henry Holt and Company, LLC. Reprinted by permission of Henry Holt and Company, LLC.

Herodotus. "The Story of Candaules and Gyges," *Histories*, I, 8–12, translated by Leon R. Kass.

Homer. *The Odyssey*, translated by R. Fagles. New York: Viking Penguin, 1996. "The Coupling of Ares and Aphrodite," pp. 200–203; "The Reunion of Penelope and Odysseus," pp. 455–65. Translation © 1996 by Robert Fagles. Used by permission of Viking Penguin, a division of Penguin Putnam, Inc.

Kant, Immanuel. "Conjectural Beginning of Human History," translated by

Emil L. Fackenheim in *Kant on History,* edited by Lewis White Beck. Indianapolis: Bobbs Merrill Co., 1963, pp. 56–57.

Kass, Amy A., and Leon R. Kass. "What's Your Name?" *First Things* 57 (November 1995), pp. 22–25.

Kehret, Peg. *Vows of Love and Marriage: 52 Promises, Pledges and Declarations.* Colorado Springs, Colo.: Arthur Meriwether, 1979. © 1979 by Arthur Meriwether Publishing Ltd., Colorado Springs, Colo. 80907.

Kierkegaard, Søren. *Stages on Life's Way,* Kierkegaard's Writings 11, edited and translated by H. V. Hong and E. H. Hong. Princeton, N.J.: Princeton University Press, 1988, pp. 89–95, 116–18, 124–26, 129–35, 136, 138, 140–41. © 1989 by Princeton University Press. Reprinted by permission of Princeton University Press.

Kipling, Rudyard. "The Married Man," *Rudyard Kipling's Verse: Definitive Edition.* New York: Doubleday, Doran and Co., 1940, pp. 472–73.

Lamm, Maurice. *The Jewish Way in Love and Marriage.* Middle Village, N.Y.: Jonathan David Publishers, 1991, p. 17.

Lewis, C. S. "Eros," from *The Four Loves.* New York: Harcourt Brace Jovanovich, Inc., 1960, pp. 131–60. © 1960 by Helen Joy Lewis, renewed 1988 by Arthur Owen Barfield. Reprinted by permission of Harcourt, Inc.

Martin, Judith. *Miss Manners' Guide to Excruciatingly Correct Behavior.* New York: Warner Books, 1982, pp. 276–82, 286–87. © 1982 by Judith Martin. Reprinted by permission of the author.

May, William F. "The Covenant of Marriage," 1993. Printed by permission of the author.

May, William F. "Four Mischievous Theories of Sex: Demonic, Divine, Casual, and Nuisance," from *Passionate Attachments: Thinking About Love,* edited by Willard Gaylin, M.D., and Ethel Person, M.D. New York: Free Press, 1988, pp. 27–40. Reprinted with permission of The Free Press, a division of Simon & Schuster, Inc. © 1988 by the Friends of Columbia Psychoanalytic Center, Inc.

Meilaender, Gilbert. "Men and Women—Can We Be Friends?" *First Things* 34 (June-July 1993), pp. 9–14. Reprinted with permission of *First Things* and the author.

Muir, Edwin. "Annunciation," *Collected Poems.* Oxford: Oxford University Press, 1960. © 1960 by Willa Muir. Reprinted by permission of Oxford University Press.

Pitt-Rivers, J. A. *The People of the Sierra.* Chicago: University of Chicago Press, 1961, pp. 89–97, 109–18. © 1961 by the University of Chicago Press. Reprinted by permission of the University of Chicago Press.

Plato. *Symposium,* from *The Dialogues of Plato,* edited by Erich Segal, translated by Seth Benardete. New York: Bantam Books, 1986, pp. 250–54, 263–

74. Introduction © 1986 by Erich Segal, translation © 1986 by Seth Bernadete. Used by permission of Bantam Books, a division of Random House, Inc.

Riezler, Kurt. "Comment on the Social Psychology of Shame," *American Journal of Sociology* 48 (January 1943), pp. 457–65. Reprinted by permission of the University of Chicago Press.

Rilke, Rainer-Marie. *Rilke on Love and Other Difficulties,* translated by John J. L. Moud. New York: W. W. Norton & Company, 1975, pp. 23–24, 27–33. © 1975 by W. W. Norton & Company, Inc. Reprinted by permission of W. W. Norton & Company, Inc.

Rousseau, Jean-Jacques. *Emile: or, On Education,* introduction, translation, and notes by Allan Bloom. New York: Basic Books, Inc., 1979, pp. 357–62, 363–65, 412–29, 433–42, 443, 443–45, 446, 447–48, 450, 475–80. © 1979 by Basic Books, Inc. Reprinted by permission of Basic Books, a member of Perseus Books, LLC.

Shakespeare, William. *As You Like It,* edited by David Bevington. New York: Bantam Books, 1988, pp. 12–18, 43–44, 46–51, 53–56, 68–74, 76–80, 83–85. Glossary footnotes by David Bevington, © 1988 by David Bevington. Used by permission of Bantam Books, a division of Random House, Inc.

——. *Romeo and Juliet,* edited by John E. Hankins. Baltimore, Md.: Penguin Books, 1960, pp. 53–58, 60–68, 138–39.

——. Sonnets #18, #115, #116.

——. *The Tempest,* edited by Northrup Frye. Baltimore, Md.: Penguin Books, 1959, pp. 48–53, 73–77.

Stone, Lawrence. "Passionate Attachments in the West in Historical Perspective," in *Passionate Attachments: Thinking About Love,* edited by Willard Gaylin, M.D., and Ethel Person, M.D. New York: Free Press, 1988, pp. 15–22, 25–26. Reprinted with permission of The Free Press, a division of Simon & Schuster, Inc. © 1988 by the Friends of Columbia Psychoanalytic Center, Inc.

The Tanakh: The New JPS Translation according to the Traditional Hebrew Text. © 1985 by The Jewish Publication Society. Excerpts used by permission.

Tolstoy, Leo. *Anna Karenina,* translated by Louise and Aylmer Maude. Oxford: Oxford University Press, 1918, revised 1939. Reprinted by permission of Oxford University Press.

——. *War and Peace,* translated by Louise and Aylmer Maude. Oxford: Oxford University Press, 1933. Reprinted by permission of Oxford University Press.

Tucker, William. "Monogamy and Its Discontents," *National Review,* October 4, 1993, pp. 28–38. © 1993 by National Review, Inc., 215 Lexington Avenue, New York, N.Y. 10016. Reprinted by permission.